ROBERTS
NESTS & EGGS
of southern African birds

ROBERTS
NESTS & EGGS
of southern African birds

A comprehensive guide to the nesting habits
of over 720 bird species in southern Africa

Warwick Tarboton

published by the trustees of the John Voelcker Bird Book Fund

for Michèle, *bkly*

Published by the Trustees of the John Voelcker Bird Book Fund,
9 Church Square, Cape Town, 8001.

First published 2011
Second impression 2014

Copyright © in text: Warwick Tarboton
Copyright © in photographs: as specified on each image
Copyright © in published edition: John Voelcker Bird Book Fund
Design & layout: Warwick & Michèle Tarboton

Distributed by Jacana Media
www.jacana.co.za

Printed and bound by Craft Print International Ltd

All rights reserved. No part of this publication may be reproduced, stored in a retrieval system, or transmitted, in any form or by any means, electronic, mechanical, photocopying, recording or otherwise, without the prior written permission of the copyright owner/s.

ISBN 978-0-620-50629-8
Job No. 002229

ABOVE: Greater Flamingos breeding on Makgadikgadi Saltpan, Feb 2005 (Hayden Oake)
FRONT COVER: African Jacana, male settling on its eggs (Guy Upfold)
TITLE PAGE: A Lizard Buzzard nest, characteristically lined with *Usnea* lichen (Fin O'Donoghue)

Contents

John Voelcker Bird Book Fund	4
Acknowledgements	5
Introduction	7
Glossary	18
Species accounts	20
Egg plates	352
Species index	400

The John Voelcker Bird Book Fund

This fund has been responsible for publishing successive revisions of 'Roberts' since the book's inception in 1940. A brief account of the fund is given below on the left, while below on the right, using the African Jacana as an example, the changing artwork and progressively more detailed information given in the text in the successive revisions is shown.

In December 1935, the South African Bird Book Fund was formed to fund a complete and up-to-date new bird book for southern Africa under the authorship of Austin Roberts and illustrated by Norman C. K. Lighton. The successful and popular first edition, titled *The Birds of South Africa*, was published in June 1940. The affairs of the fund were handled by the secretary, John Voelcker, who became the chairman after the untimely death of Austin Roberts in 1948. He, together with the other trustees of the Fund, became the driving force that ensured that the original edition was revised and updated. In 1957, seventeen years after the release of the first edition, the Trustees published the second edition under the authorship of G. R. McLachlan and R. Liversidge. They also revised the third (1970) and fourth (1978) editions, titled *Roberts' Birds of South Africa*. The Trust had by now become known as the John Voelcker Bird Book Fund, a non-profit organisation with limited funding derived from subscriptions and minimal profit from the sale of books. The fifth and sixth editions (1985 and 1993), now titled *Roberts' Birds of Southern Africa*, were revised by Gordon L. Maclean. The seventh edition (2005), entrusted to the Percy FitzPatrick Institute of African Ornithology, was completely rewritten under the editorship of P. A. R. Hockey, W. R. J. Dean and P. G. Ryan. With well over 300 000 copies of Roberts books sold to date, the John Voelcker Bird Book Fund is committed to remaining the forerunner in the publication of up-to-date bird information in the region, and to making publications as affordable as possible to the southern African birding community.

Roberts 1 (1940)

" .... It breeds in Natal and northwards, the clutch consisting of four eggs, which are long ovals, rather pointed at both ends, tan-yellow in ground-colour, almost hidden by numerous black lines and blots, and measures 32 x 24, very highly glossed."

Roberts 2 (1957), Roberts 3 (1970), Roberts 4 (1978)

" ...Eggs 3-4, normally 4, are extremely beautiful pyriform objects, tan-yellow in ground colour almost hidden by long lines, dots and scrolls of black, the whole egg having a very high gloss as if varnished. Average (100) 33.0 x 33.2 (30.5-37.4 x 21.5-24.8). Incubation 21-24 days."

Roberts 5 (1985), Roberts 6 (1993)

" ... *Clutch*: (28) 2-3.6-4 eggs (usually 4, rarely 5). *Eggs*: Pointed at narrow end; deep tan yellow to brown, heavily streaked, scrolled and dotted with black; measure (200) 32.9 x 23.2 (29.9-37.4 x 21-24.8)."

Roberts 7 (2005)

"... Eggs: 4 (determinate), rarely 3 or 5 (3.93, n=155). Laid at 1 d intervals, between 06h00-08h00 (n=14). Pyriform, thick-shelled, smooth and highly glossed as a result of distinctive plugged pore structure. Ground colour tan, variably marked with thick, wavy, evenly spread, scroll-like black and dark brown lines; occasional clutches streaked or blotched; rarely unmarked. Although egg coloration varies between ♀ ♀, 1 ♀ lays a consistent egg-type through her life. Size (361) 28.2-36.0 x 19.7-25.1 mm (32.6 x 23.1 mm). Mass (n=64, fresh) 7.9-10.5 g (8.9 g) ♀ lays up to 10 clutches/season, at intervals of 4-28 d (12 d, n=24) between clutches. When rate of clutch loss is high, most replacement clutches laid for 1 dominant ♂. When clutch survival high, successive clutches laid for other ♂ ♂, up to 7 in 1 season."

Acknowledgements

I am indebted to a great many people for providing much of the material that has been used to compile this book – published and unpublished records and innumerable snippets of information made available through the medium of one or other journal or bird club magazine. In addition, I gratefully acknowledge the willing assistance and support given to me by friends and colleagues, listed alphabetically below, who have assisted in large or small ways in the project; I am sure that each will recognise the particular contribution he or she has made when they browse through the book.

For their varied and valued inputs I thank:

David Allan, Mark Anderson, Colin Baker, Adri Barkhuysen, the late Bill Barnes, Janet Bartlet, Garth Batchelor, Lawrence Baxter, Keith Begg, Martin Benadie, Marita Beneke, Sheila Blane, Bob Bloomfield, Andre Botha, Henk Bouwman, Meyrick & Kerin Bowker, Helen Boyer, the late Gerry Broekhuyzen, Bulawayo National Museum, Duncan Butchart, Cape Bird Club, Patrick & Marie-Louise Cardwell, John Carlyon, Tamar Cassidy, Peter Castell, the late Charles Clinning, Deon Coetzee, Brian Colahan, Hugh Chittenden, Murray Christian, Niel Cillié, Jeffory Coburn, Callan Cohen, Derek Coley, Alvin & Flik Cope, Adrian Craig, Rob Crawford, Greg Darling, Greg Davies, Richard Dean, Dawie de Swardt, Colleen Downs, Dennis & Greet Driver, Ditsong National Museum of Natural History (Pretoria), Dup du Plessis, Andre du Toit, Durban Natural Science Museum, Paul Dutton, Bruce Dyer, Derek Engelbrecht, Doug Galpin, Rudy & Zeta Erasmus, Marietjie Froneman, Guy Gibbon, Peter Ginn, Jan & Riëtte Griesel, Johann & Lizet Grobbelaar, Martin & Fimmie Grond, Pierre Hofmeyr, Pete Hancock, Trevor & Margaret Hardaker, Pierre Hofmeyr, Clem Haagner, James Haslam & Judith Hawarden, Phil Hockey, the late G. Hopkinson, Emlyn & Liz Horne, Kit Hustler, Isiko South African Museum (Cape Town), Tim Jackson, Rob Jeffery, Andrew Jenkins, David & Sally Johnson, John Jones, Dusty Joubert, Rick & Linda Kleyn, Alan Kemp, Johan Kloppers, Joris Komen, Sonja Krueger, Scotty & Diane Kyle, Tasso Leventis, Johan Lotter, Ian Little, Rob Little, Derek Longrigg, Gerard Malan, Chris Marais, Johannes & Christine Maree, Etienne Marais, Flip Mare, Rob Martin, André Marx, Alex Masterson, Geoff McIleron, Alistair McInnes, John Mendelsohn, Johan Moolman, David Moore, Pete Morgan, Muchai Muchane, Mark Muller, Peter Mundy, Clemence Muzenda, the late Nico Myburgh, National Museum of Namibia, Chris & Judy New, the late Bill Nichol, Rick Nuttall, Hayden Oake, Ken Oake, the late Fin O'Donoghue, Jane O'Donoghue, Duncan Parkes, Mark Paxton, Richard Peek, Mike Perrin, Kobus Pienaar, Darrel Plowes, Chris Pohl, Robin Pope, Jenny Preston, Matt Pretorius, Mike & Jean Prinsloo, Glenn Ramke, Hamish Robertson, Pieter & Christine Roussouw, Peter Ryan, Colin Saunders, Otto Schmidt, Rob Simmons, Ian Sinclair, Leon Snyders, Derek Solomon, Mike Soroczynski, Peter Steyn, Craig Symes, Michèle Tarboton, Philip Tarboton, Tony Tree, Les Underhill, Guy Upfold, the late C. J. Uys, Brian Vanderwalt, Johann van Niekerk, Petrus van Rensburg, Mich & Saarkie Veldman, Albie Venter, Carl Vernon, Alan Weaving, Phil Whittington, Gavin Whyte, Ian Whyte.

Among these names are the 87 photographers who have allowed me to include their images of birds nests. In this respect, I particularly thank Peter Steyn, Hugh Chittenden, Jane O'Donoghue (who gave me access to her late husband's amazing collection of birds of prey nest photographs), Peter Ginn, Richard Peek, Ken Oake, Guy Upfold, Johann Grobbelaar, Rudy Erasmus, Garth Batchelor and Derek Engelbrecht for going out of their way to accommodate my requests. It will be seen on the plates that the photographer involved is credited alongside each picture.

Hugh Chittenden encouraged me to produce the book under the 'Roberts' umbrella and opened the door for me to do so, and I sincerely thank him for this, as I do the other Trustees of the John Voelcker Bird Book Fund for financing the book's publication. It is an honour to be part of the 'Roberts' stable and I've used the page alongside to provide a brief history of this remarkable institution and, using the African Jacana as an example, to show how the artwork and text has evolved through the various editions of 'Roberts' since 1940 when the Fund published the first edition of this unrivalled book.

For access to egg collections I am indebted to a number of people, but especially to the collection managers at the various museums (in Pretoria, Durban, Bulawayo, Windhoek) where I spent days photographing the eggs that appear in the book. The oldest of these (the egg of an Egyptian Vulture, collected in 1869 near Malmesbury) was photographed for me at the South African Museum in Cape Town by Hamish Robertson. Marita Beneke is thanked for putting colour onto some of the old black-and-white nest photographs that I've used – I wonder if anyone can identify the ones thus transformed! Peter Steyn took kindly to the project, checked the plates and offered many useful and incisive comments along the way. Staff at Jacana, especially Jenny Prangley, were very supportive and helped in many ways and I thank them too for this.

But my greatest thanks goes to Michèle without whose energy, creative ideas, technical skills, vast amount of help, enthusiasm and encouragement the book would never have reached completion. She should have been co-author, but wouldn't hear of it. Those who know her will appreciate how large her contribution has been and how little I would have achieved without her.

The world's largest bird's nest - up to 500 Sociable Weavers build and maintain a nest of this size

Introduction

About 730 bird species breed in southern Africa and this book is about their nesting habits. It is partly a revision of my previous 'A guide to the nests and eggs of southern African birds' published in 2001 and long out of print, and partly a new production, illustrating the nests of many more species than before and laid out here in a fieldguide format, with pages of text facing pages of colour images of birds and their nests, with their eggs shown separately, at life-size, in a separate section at at the back (pages 352-399).

Deciding how many species actually breed in the region is confounded by several things. One is the unresolved status of a number of closely related species-pairs, where the two are treated as species by some authorities and as subspecies by others. Examples are the Cinnamon-breasted and Rufous-bellied Tits, the two saw-wings, and the Short-toed Rock Thrush and so-called 'Pretoria' Rock Thrush. Sooner or later these issues do get ironed out but, until they do, putting a precise total to the nesting species-count is not possible.

Then, for quite a number of birds on the southern African list, there has not yet been confirmation that they breed in the region. Souza's Shrike, for example, was, until recently, considered a non-breeding vagrant, but it is now known to be a breeding resident. Several others (Shelley's Sunbird, Yellow-breasted Hyliota, Böhm's Bee-eater are examples) will probably turn out this way too, but at the moment there is no evidence of their nesting here. And, for a couple of our more northerly species (they include Barred Long-tailed Cuckoo, Scarce Swift and Pallid Honeyguide), absolutely nothing is known of their nesting habits, here or anywhere else.

Gaps like these provide great opportunities for birders to make a significant contribution to the bird knowledge pool. All it takes is to spend time with the bird in question, get to know it intimately, carefully record every aspect of its life, and place this on record. Much of what is known about our birds, and particularly about their nesting habits, is based on the findings made by non-scientists who have set about unravelling and methodically recording the secrets of a previously little-known bird.

Finding nests is fun and, provided one is circumspect, it can be entirely non-impacting. It is an activity that takes one beyond simply identifying a bird, to examining its behaviour closely and interpreting what the observed behaviour means: is the bird nesting, and if so, where is the nest? Of course, many species nest so obviously that there is no skill involved in this, but others are masters at concealing their nests and at covering their tracks. Try, for example, to find the nest of a Barratt's or Victorin's Warbler, or even the nest of a pair of White-fronted Plovers that are frequenting the same stretch of beach every day. These often become a battle of wits between man and bird, a test of patience, and more often than not, a 1-0 victory to the birds.

Not yet known to breed in southern Africa, a Böhm's Bee-eater at the entrance to its nest-hole, photographed in Malawi

Taking an undue interest in nests is often subtly or overtly discouraged in birding circles, and the reasons for this are often valid. During their breeding period birds are particularly sensitive to disturbance and at their most vulnerable. Finding nests may be fun for us, but for the birds involved it can be a life-and-death situation; not only are eggs or young at risk if the nest is exposed to predators or extreme temperatures, but the parents too, in their drive to incubate their eggs or attend their nestlings, place themselves at greater risk. Therefore nesting, like any other pursuit, should be played according to rules and our desire to find a nest should always be tempered by an awareness that our interference may place the birds in question, or their nests, in jeopardy. Just as it is irresponsible to hound or disrupt the life of a rare or endangered bird for the sake of adding it to one's life list, so it is irresponsible to put the desire to find a bird's nest above the welfare of the bird. Colonial nesting birds are particularly susceptible, and any disturbance at colonies is likely to increase the risk to nests being successful.

There have been a couple of other books published on the nests and eggs of the birds in this region before. Captain Cecil Priest's 1948 book *Eggs of Birds Breeding in Southern Africa*, was the first and it illustrated the eggs of 398 species in 20 finely painted plates. It also provided brief information on each species' nesting habits. In 1996 Peter Steyn's beautifully illustrated book *Nesting Birds* was published, and it included photographs of the nests of about 400 species and it summarised the information then available on the breeding biology of each bird family. This book extends the coverage of nest photographs to about 680 species, and the nests of many species are illustrated here for the first time.

The southern African region is that part of Africa lying south of the line formed by the Zambezi and Kunene rivers and it thus includes Namibia, Botswana, Zimbabwe, South Africa, Lesotho, Swaziland, and southern and central Mozambique. Its considerable bird diversity (960 or so species) is a product of the great diversity of environments represented, from a 5 000 km-long coastline fringed largely by sandy beaches, but also in places by extensive stretches of rocky shoreline; offshore islands contribute to the mix, especially in the west, providing breeding sites for large concentrations of seabirds. The topographically diverse interior extends across relief-free plains to rolling hills to towering mountain chains.

Superimposed on these rich landscapes are seven major vegetation types (biomes) which include the desert zone along the west coast, the fynbos in the southern winter rainfall region, the arid and semi-arid karoo (a dwarf shrubland, divided into winter and summer rainfall components), the interior grassland plateau (the 'highveld') and the most extensive of these, the savanna that covers more than half the region. Each of these has a distinctive bird community.

As the accompanying map shows, the savanna belt is 'semi-arid' in the low-rainfall west (the pale green area on the map, where it is dominated by acacias, commiphoras and other drought-resistant tree types) and is 'mesic' in the east (these are the dark green areas) where a taller, often denser woodland is developed. It includes, in the north-east, extensive tracts of so-called miombo woodland which supports a particularly distinctive bird community.

Forests of several types occur widely but thinly, everywhere associated with areas of highest rainfall.

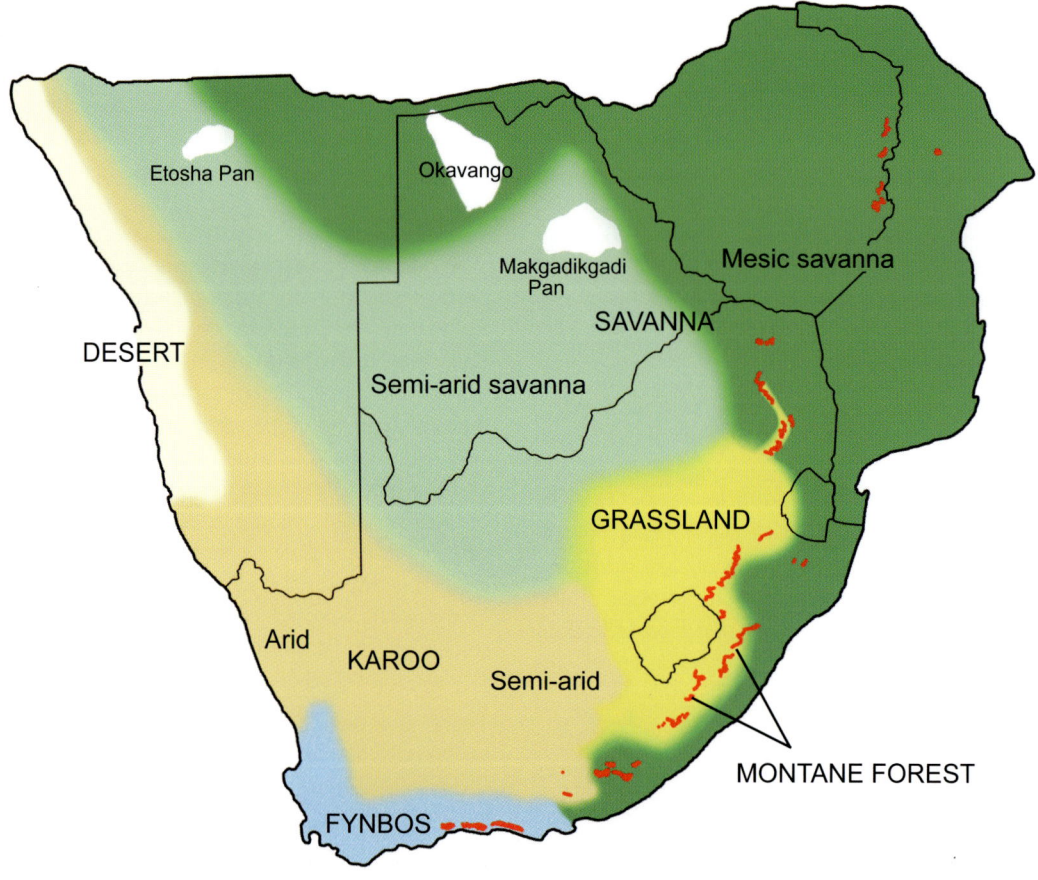

One type, 'montane forest' (red areas on the map), extends in isolated pockets from the southern Cape up the eastern side of the subcontinent along mountainous scarps that catch the precipitation. These, too, support a distinctive bird community. Along the eastern coastal plain (not demarcated on the map) lowland forest of various types occurs, in places extending far inland along rivers and providing narrow ribbons of 'riparian forest' in otherwise non-forested country.

Lastly, there is a great diversity of wetlands in the region. These include the spectrum of large and small rivers draining the subcontinent and their associated floodplains, estuaries, lagoons and man-made dams, the ephemeral and permanent lakes and pans, and the myriad of seeps, vleis, marshes and lesser swamps. The jewel in the region's wetland crown is almost certainly Botswana's 1.2 million hectare Okavango delta; a host of others vie for second place.

Family order & species' names

What family order should be followed, and what bird name should be used in a guide of this type are two hotly debated subjects. Recent molecular studies have shown that the familiar 'Roberts' order of old (and its associated 'Roberts bird number') no longer reflects current understanding of familial relationships in birds. Francolins and guineafowl, for example, are now viewed as very primitive families and their correct systematic placing follows closely after the ostrich; the region's warblers, once lumped together in a single family, are now dispersed between seven families, with the unpleasant result that you meet up with 'warblers' again and again in different places in the sequence. Some of the 'old' flycatchers are now warblers (Livingstone's Flycatcher, for example) and the 'flycatcher' family (Muscicapidae) now includes thrushes, chats, robin-chats and others. The Bush Blackcap, once a bulbul, then a babbler, is now a warbler!

Does one arrange the families in a book of this type with the familiar, but flawed phylogenic arrangement of the past, or adopt the not-yet-stable new arrangement of families that reflects the current state of knowledge? For better or worse, what has been adopted here is the most recent arrangement of the families which, in the space of six years, already differs significantly from the state-of-play family arrangement adopted in 2005 by 'Roberts 7' and the 'Roberts' fieldguide. Because this sequence differs from that used in other bird fieldguides for the region, quick indexes to the families have been included on the inside covers, an English one in the front and an Afrikaans one at the back.

The choice of which bird name to use is an even more vexing issue. Southern African birders have been faced with successive waves of changes in the English name used for our birds, and what name a person uses or prefers much depends on one's vintage as a birder.

The many new names introduced in 'Roberts 7' were the result of an internationalisation process (some call it a macdonaldisation process) aimed at having a single globally-used name for each and every bird species. But since then the process has continued and many 'Roberts 7' names have changed. In the process we have lost a number of culturally familiar regional names (like dikkop and lourie), and many of the new 'international' names are long-winded, burdened with qualifiers that attempt to do what the scientific name is supposed to do. Does anyone actually use a name like 'Black-and-white Shrike-Flycatcher' (its 'international name') for the Vanga Flycatcher out in the field?

Another change, but less of an issue, is a new policy on when to, and when not to, hyphenate bird names (e.g. snake-eagle is now snake eagle); also, a number of bird names, following the international approach, are run together (e.g. helmetshrike, bushshrike). The approach I have taken in this book is a bridging one. I have used the new hyphenation approach to all bird names and I have included all the new (post-Roberts 7) names that have been introduced. Some, though, I have given as an alternate name, with the more familiar regional name retained as the primary name: few local birders, for example, will recognise the Green-backed Heron under its 'international' name of Striated Heron, so a name like this has been listed here as an alternate name.

What is almost inevitable is that we have not seen the end to bird names changing and, despite what names become used in books and magazines, birds will be called different things by different people. The scientific names used here are those currently listed by the International Ornithological Congress's bird name committee (see their website www.worldbirdnames.org) and the Afrikaans names are those that have been adopted by BirdLife South Africa.

Open cup nest of Cape Batis; the open cup is most common type of nest

The well-hidden ball-shaped nest of the Green-backed Camaroptera, its outer shell comprising leaves stitched togther using cobweb

The mud nest of a White-throated Swallow, built from hundreds of pellets collected and added one by one

Birds' nests

The diversity of nests built by birds is one of the more remarkable features of the animal kingdom: there are huge nests and tiny nests, skilfully woven nests and nests that barely hold together; some nests are amazingly well concealed while others are seemingly placed in the most conspicuous position possible.

In most species the nest is built by a pair of birds that work together to gather the material and to undertake construction. There are, however, many variations to this arrangement: in some, one sex gathers the material, while its mate constructs the nest (e.g. herons and doves), in others only one sex builds (canaries), or one sex builds a portion of the nest and the other completes it (e.g. in many of the weavers); in a few species all the members of a cooperative group participate in building the nest (e.g. babblers), while in rare cases a whole flock of birds participates to build a communally-used nest (e.g. Sociable Weaver).

It is a common misperception that birds build nests primarily to sleep in at night; a few species do (Sociable Weavers, for instance, use their nests all year round as sleeping quarters), but this is the exception. Most species build a nest, use it for a single breeding attempt and thereafter show no further interest in it. Again, there are exceptions: many birds of prey, for example, reuse the same nest annually, adding to it in each successive nesting cycle. A number of birds, too, make use of nests that were originally built by some other species.

For most species, the nests' primary function is to provide a receptacle for their eggs and, in species that have altricial young, the nest continues to serve this purpose until the chicks fledge. Eggs need to be maintained at a temperature of around 35-38°C for the embryo to develop, and in most species this is achieved by the parent bird incubating the eggs by applying its body heat to the eggs from an area of bare skin on the abdomen known as a 'brood patch'. In some species, especially those living in cold climates, the nest is designed to assist in this process by being built or lined with well-insulated material, thereby reducing heat loss from the eggs when the parent is off the nest. Nest architecture is often driven by other environmental conditions; for example, weaver nests are specially constructed so that the eggs don't spill out during strong winds, and grebe nests are built to float and so can survive rises and falls in water level. And some species include stems of strongly aromatic plants, thought to act as parasite repellants, in the construction of their nests.

An overriding theme in many nests is the need for concealment. Predator avoidance is often critical to the success of the breeding attempt and many species go to extraordinary lengths to hide their nests or make them blend with their surroundings. In some species this involves cladding the nest with lichen to match the branch that supports it, or the nest may be built to resemble debris caught up on a branch. Several species place their nests alongside those of wasps (e.g. some sunbirds and waxbills do this) to gain protection from these; some weaver species commonly place their colonies in the branches of a tree containing an active eagle's nest, presumably for the same reason and, where humans are non-threatening to nesting birds (such as in the rest camps of game parks) birds often nest right alongside human habitations. Many ground-nesting birds make no nest at all but lay eggs that closely match their surroundings, or the parent bird, which rarely leaves the eggs uncovered, is cryptically marked and selects a nest site on a substrate on which it blends into the surroundings. It is nests such as these that add so much to the challenge and stimulation of 'nesting'.

With the exception of those species that do not construct nests, birds' nests have two components – a supporting framework, and an egg-receptacle in the form of a cup or depression, which is usually built (or 'lined') using finer or softer material than is used in the framework. In some species the entire nest is in the shape of an open cup, with coarser material used to build the foundation and finer material to line the inner cup. This type of structure (an 'open cup') is used by more bird species in southern Africa – nearly 200 – than any other, and it is characteristic of the nests of batises, larks, crows, bulbuls, thrushes, many warblers, flycatchers, pipits, shrikes, canaries and many others.

The next most frequent nest design (used by about 130 species) is an enclosed ball-shaped nest that has an entrance that leads into the nest-cup from one side or from underneath: sunbirds, cisticolas, weavers and bishops, estrildid finches, coucals and many warblers are typical examples of families that build such nests.

Another common nest type, built by about 100 species in the region, is a saucer-shaped platform that can be built with branches (in large birds) or sticks and twigs (in smaller species). Most birds of prey build such structures; so do herons, storks, cormorants,

doves, turacos and others. Many ground- and marsh-nesting birds (about 100 species) build nests that are a variation on this: their nests are pads or mounds of plant material with a depression on top in which the eggs are laid. Such nests are typical of ducks, crakes and rails, gulls, francolin, guineafowl and grebes. Some ground-nesting birds (for example, nightjars, korhaans, dikkops and several coursers) lay their eggs on bare ground where no nest-scrape is made and no nest-lining material is brought to the site.

Masters of camouflage, nightjars such as this Fiery-necked Nightjar (brooding its chick), select a spot on the ground to lay their eggs where their plumage blends with the leaf litter.

Over a hundred species nest in holes. Cavities in trees attract the greatest range of such hole-nesters (about 90 species), but some (about 20 species) use holes in the ground instead, these being mostly located in the walls of vertical banks. In the case of tree-hole nesters, many species simply occupy natural cavities caused by stem rot (called here 'rot-holes'), but two families (woodpeckers and barbets) have developed the ability to excavate nest cavities inside tree stems. These holes are very commonly occupied by a succession of other hole-nesters that would otherwise be reliant on rot-holes for nest sites. Parrots, owls, kingfishers, rollers, hoopoes, hornbills, tits, starlings and sparrows are typical examples of such birds. Some of these (tits and starlings, for instance) build a nest for themselves inside the cavity (using grass, feathers, and so on), whereas others (rollers, for instance) simply lay their eggs on the floor of the chamber.

The species that nest in holes in the ground mostly excavate these for themselves; bee-eaters, kingfishers and martins, for instance, excavate tunnels into the sides of earth banks, as do Horus Swift, Ant-eating Chat, Pied Starling and a number of other unrelated birds. Some of the ground hole-nesters, though, do not excavate their own cavities but are reliant

Olive Woodpecker peering out from its nest-hole, a cavity that takes 2-3 weeks to excavate

on existing holes, and Grey-rumped Swallow and Capped Wheatear are unusual in selecting rodent burrows in open, flat ground for their nest site.

Swifts and swallows are among the most specialised nest-builders using saliva and mud, respectively, to construct their nests. Swifts collect feathers, grass and other air-borne debris in flight and glue these together, using their saliva which dries to a rock-hard paste, to form a cup or bowl-shaped structure. The African Palm Swift goes further by also gluing its eggs to the nest. Swallows collect pellets of mud from the edges of pools and place these, one upon the other, to form the walls of what becomes a solid mud shell in the form of an inverted bowl.

Finally, there are three unrelated bird families in the region that do not build nests of their own but instead lay their eggs in the nests of selected host species. The best known of these parasites are the cuckoos of which there are 11 in the region; six are honeyguides and the remaining nine are the Vidua finches. The deceptive ploys used by these species and the counter-strategies used by their respective hosts, are intriguing (see pages 134-138 for how this works in the cuckoos, 178 for the honeyguides and 342-343 for the Viduas).

The nest dimensions given in the species accounts are largely self-explanatory. The measurements of open-cupped nests comprise the outside diameter, the inside (or cup) diameter and the inside and outside depth of the nest (termed here cup depth and nest height or thickness respectively). Roughly finished nests with pieces of material protruding untidily beyond the body of the nest (those of doves, for instance) are not as precisely measurable as those that have a compact, finely finished structure. The measurement given for these usually refers to the main nest body only, ignoring odd stems projecting beyond the main nest. The measurements given for ball-shaped nests (which in most species are oval-shaped, long axis vertical), usually include outside nest height, outside nest width (across the front entrance and from front-to-back) and the diameter of the entrance hole. In some species that have appendages to this basic structure (e.g. the hoods and tails of some sunbird nests), these are also given. The measurements given for weaver nests differ from those given for other nests because of their particular structure: their height (measured outside, from the roof to base of nest chamber), width (both front-to-back, and across the nest chamber), and length and diameter of the entrance funnel are given.

Birds' eggs

Anyone who has looked into a bird's nest cannot but have marvelled at what has been referred to as 'nature's miracle of packaging'. This description of a bird's egg comes from the title of Robert Burton's book on eggs (*Egg, Nature's Miracle of Packaging* published in 1987 by Collins, London) which provides a comprehensive reference to the various facets of egg biology that won't be repeated here. Suffice to say that the great variety to be found in the shapes, colours and markings of birds' eggs is fertile ground for research and much has been written on the relationships between egg size, clutch size, egg colour, egg shape, shell structure, shell thickness, and the life histories and ecologies of the birds producing these miracle packages.

The shell of a bird's egg comprises two or more layers of calcium carbonate (as well as other calcium salts) that are deposited around the yoke and albumen during the developing egg's passage through the oviduct in the lead-up to egg-laying. The colour of this shell is usually white, but in some species it is pale blue, and many species lay eggs that have no further pigmentation added (the turaco and babbler eggs alongside are examples). In others, however, a yellow pigment is added secondarily and how far below the surface of the shell this is deposited determines to what extent this pigment's colour is muted. White-shelled eggs enriched by this pigment take on a shade of buff, and blue-shelled eggs take on a shade of green: look at the robin-chat and guineafowl eggs alongside for examples of this.

The eggs of many species have a third and final layer of pigment secreted onto the outer surface of the shell in the final stages of the egg's passage through the oviduct. This pigmentation takes the form of speckles, spots, blotches, streaks or scrolls and it is deposited in shades of red, brown and/or black. How intense these colours are depends on how deep they lie within the shell and to what extent they have been masked by further calcium carbonate layers above them. How they are distributed on the shell (evenly or in a zone) is likely a result of where the egg was positioned during deposition, and whether it was stationary or in motion while pigment was being secreted. In a few species, the ground-colour is entirely obscured by this final pigment layer and the resulting egg is uniformly dark red or dark brown (as in one of the Red-capped Robin-Chat eggs shown alongside). Occasionally this final pigmentation fails, and such birds, instead of laying their normal well-marked eggs, lay instead plain white or blue eggs where the carbonate shell is all that colours the egg.

As a rule, most bird species lay eggs that are very consistent in pigmentation, size and shape, and eggs can thus very often be identified to species. In birds that lay richly pigmented eggs (jacanas, for example) it is even possible to recognise individual females by their egg colour/marking 'finger-print' – some individuals lay eggs pigmented with dark, heavy scolls, others have thin wiry markings or very pale substrates. Some groups of birds, including weavers, cisticolas and the prinias (shown alongside) lay exceptionally variably coloured and marked eggs (the term 'polychromatic' describes this). Within the polychromatism, though, the egg laid by each female in the population remains consistent through her lifetime, and the great variability in, say, Southern Masked or Village weaver eggs (see page 397) is the result of egg colour differences between different females.

Egg of Helmeted Guineafowl, exceptionally tough-shelled, and pigmented with yellow

Pyriform, heavily pigmented egg of African Jacana (left) and spherical, unpigmented egg of Purple-crested Turaco (right)

Close-matching egg of Levaillant's Cuckoo (left) alongside eggs of its host, the Arrow-marked Babbler (right)

Variably pigmented eggs of Red-capped Robin-Chat

Polychromatic eggs of Tawny-flanked Prinia

Egg coloration is commonly (but not invariably) related to a species' nesting habits and/or the type of nest it uses. Hole-nesters, such as kingfishers, woodpeckers, owls, rollers and parrots, typically lay unmarked white eggs. Two hole-nesting chats, Ant-eating Chat and Capped Wheatear, also lay unmarked white eggs, whereas other chats that don't nest in holes mostly lay well-marked eggs. It has been suggested that white eggs have better survival value in dark nest sites because they are more easily seen by the parent arriving at the nest and are thus less likely to be inadvertently damaged when it enters the hole.

Most ground-nesting birds (plovers, gulls, bustards and many others) lay heavily pigmented eggs with dark backgrounds and streaks and blotches of shades of darker brown which serve to match the eggs with the substrate on which they are laid. There are especially good examples of these among coursers: Temminck's Courser and Bronze-winged Courser, for example, both nest on fire-blackened ground and their eggs are particularly darkly coloured, whereas those of the Double-banded Courser, which lays on light-coloured substrates (typically on calcrete soils), are similarly light-coloured, being off-white with fine scribbled markings of grey.

Egg of Temminck's Courser (left) usually laid on fire-blackened substrates and egg of Double-banded Courser (right) usually laid on pale, calcareous substrates

Most species that make open-cupped nests lay speckled eggs and this perhaps provides the best concealment for the dappled lighting of their situations. Among thrushes it has been noted that species breeding inside forests tend to lay relatively unmarked deep blue eggs, whereas the thrush species that nest in savanna lay paler blue-green eggs, well marked with brown speckles.

The shape of most birds' eggs is so characteristic that the term 'egg-shaped' is commonly used to describe things other than eggs. Eggs that taper to a point at one end (the 'acute' end) and are blunt at the other end are usually termed 'oval' or 'ovate' (e.g. the babbler and robin-chat eggs shown on page 13). Eggs that have a particularly sharply-pointed acute end (as in the African Jacana egg) are termed 'pyriform', while eggs that lack obvious acute and blunt ends (e.g. the eggs of grebes) are termed 'elliptical'. The commonest bird egg-shape is probably 'sub-elliptical', which lies between oval and elliptical. In each of these four categories there are long and short versions of the shape (e.g. 'long elliptical' or 'short ovate', see further on page 416) and these terms accurately define the range of variation in birds' eggs. A few species (e.g. turacos) lay remarkably rounded eggs and these are either described as being 'short elliptical' in shape or, more simply, as 'spherical' or 'spheroidal'.

Eggs that have been collected and had their contents removed (this is referred to as their being 'blown') often fade. The eggs of sandgrouse and nightjars are particularly prone to this, and eggs of these species seen in collections seldom match their eggs when seen in the wild. The pink tint found in freshly laid eggs of many species is often caused by the yolk showing through the shell and, once this is removed by blowing, these eggs become dull white. Colours also change as the incubation proceeds and the developing embryo draws increasingly on the calcium from the shell. The eggs of many waterbird species, which are a clean white when laid, quickly become discoloured as they are stained by the parent's wet feet or the nest material (see, for example, on page 356, the difference between freshly laid and well-incubated eggs of the Hamerkop and two of the grebe species.

It is not surprising, given their delicateness, infinite variety, often beauty, and the fact that once they are blown they can be stored indefinitely, that eggs have over a long period of time been much prized as collectable natural history items. Fifty years ago collecting eggs ('oology') was one of the more common activities associated with an interest in birds and the large collections of birds' eggs held in such natural history museums as those in Pretoria, Durban and Bulawayo owe their existence to this interest in the subject. Today that phase of natural history interest has all but disappeared and permits are required by the respective nature conservation authorities in each country to collect eggs. These permits are only issued to bona fide museum collectors or university researchers.

The species' accounts

The species' texts in this book follow a standard format and the amount written per species is a broad measure of how much is known about the bird. Firstly, the type of habitat in which the bird breeds is sketched in broad terms; space constraints have meant that little detail is given. Nor, for the same reason, is a map showing the bird's distribution included.

Whether the bird is a solitary or colonial breeder is covered next, and then, where known, its breeding density, or the typical spacing between adacent pairs in ideal habitat is given. The nest is then described – its position, height above the ground, its structure, what materials it is made of, its dimensions, how well it is hidden, and so on. If information on nest-building is known (who builds, how long it takes, are nests reused, etc.) this comes last.

This general nesting description is followed by a synopsis of the main breeding parameters for the species, under the following headings.

Laying months: The single most definitive point in the breeding cycle of a species is the stage when it lays its eggs. Before egg-laying, many species spend indeterminate amounts of time repairing or building their nests; some even continue nest-building year-round. Once incubation is underway, different species are involved in breeding for different amounts of time depending on how long their incubation and nestling periods last (e.g. Cape Vultures, although having a brief egg-laying period are involved in breeding for most of the year because of their prolonged incubation and nestling periods). So it is usual to define a species' breeding season in terms of the month/s in which it lays its eggs. In most species, these months are well defined, although there may be regional variation (e.g. populations living in summer- versus winter-rainfall areas lay in different months), or between-year variability (e.g. if the rains are late, the birds lay late). In the species texts 'mainly Sep-Oct (Aug-Jan)' means that at least half of all egg-laying occurs between September and October, the rest occurring in the other months between August and January; if all that is given is 'Aug-Jan' it means that the sample is too small to indicate any peak months but that all reported records fall within these months. Where it has been recorded that a species lays a second clutch, either after the first fails, or after successfully raising a first brood, it is stated under this heading.

Clutch size: Most birds lay a discrete and fairly consistent number of eggs at a time, these being known as a 'clutch'. Clutch size is given thus '3 (2-5)' meaning that three eggs are most usually laid with a range between 2-5; where just a '1' or '2' is given means this bird is only known to lay one or two eggs. Occasionally nests contain more eggs than the range given and this is usually the result of two females laying in the nest. Where the interval between the laying of each egg in a clutch is known, it is given as, e.g. 'laid at

Cape Cormorant, a colonial breeder

This and the other uncredited photographs in the introduction were taken by Warwick Tarboton.

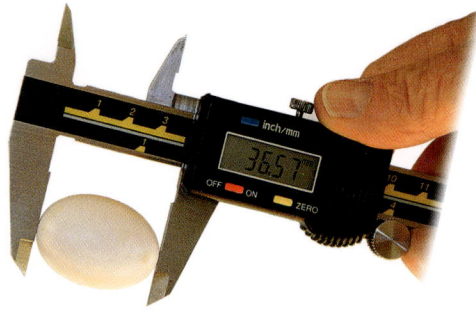

Digital calipers being used to measure a bird's egg

Crimson-breasted Shrike incubating; in this species both sexes share incubation, rotating at hourly intervals

Southern Hyliota: male feeding female while she incubates

1-day intervals' (i.e. this species lays its clutch at a rate of one egg a day).

Eggs: Measurements of eggs, length and breadth, are given in millimetres in the format minimum-average-maximum. Egg measurements came largely from Roberts 7 (and these in turn came mostly from Roberts 5 & 6). In the absence of an egg photograph, the egg is described here and if the species is an occasional or regular host of a cuckoo or honeyguide, this information is also given here.

Incubation period: This is the time it takes an egg to hatch, starting when incubation begins and ending when the nestling emerges. In birds that lay more than one egg per clutch, the eggs are laid at intervals of at least one day, and because some species begin incubation before completing their clutch, measuring the incubation period is not as simple as it may seem. It can be measured most accurately by marking the last-laid egg in the clutch and measuring the time between when it was laid and when it hatches. As a next-best approximation, it can be measured as the time taken between the laying of the last egg in the clutch to the hatching of the last egg, irrespective of whether or not this last-hatched was also the last-laid one. In some species the incubation period shows little variation (say 1-2 days), whereas in others it is much affected by ambient conditions (e.g. cold conditions retard embryo development and lengthen the incubation period) or by the level of attentiveness of the parent birds.

Incubation periods of many birds are not known and those measured are seldom more accurate than to the nearest day. When given as '15 days (14-16)' it means that the eggs take, on average, 15 days to hatch, with a range between 14-16 days. Where the measurements are from aviary-nesting birds – which may differ from wild-nesting birds – this is stated as being obtained 'in captivity'. If known, it is noted whether both sexes, or just one member of the pair incubates and how long their respective shifts last. If known, it is also noted whether the incubation starts before or once the clutch is completed.

Nestling/fledging period: This refers to the time it takes from hatching to first flight. In bird species with altricial young (for which the term 'nestling period' is used), first flight is taken as being when a nestling flies from the nest for the first time. In species with precocial young (for which the term 'fledging period' is used), the chicks move away from the nest on foot when they hatch, and as a result first flight is difficult to determine since they have long left the nest before they fly. Many precocial gamebirds 'flutter-fly' from just a few days old and this flight does not mark the point at which they actually 'fledge'. When it is stated that this period is '22-25 days', it means that it has not been measured more accurately than this; '24 days' means that it has been accurately measured as this at least once; '15 days (14-16)' means that it has been accurately measured as being 14, 15 and 16 days, averaging 15 days. Where information is available, it is noted whether both sexes, or just one member of the pair broods the nestlings and/or feeds them.

Useful 'nesting' equipment

Notebook, camera, GPS, tape measure and calipers are all useful tools to have when documenting a nest. In addition, I have a portable 'mirror stick' which allows one to inspect the contents of nests above eye-level height with minimal impact. It is home-made, using an extendable golfball-retrieving stick, with a round mirror, 70 mm in diameter, fixed to the retrieving end, set (with Pratley putty) at a 30° angle. Shorter versions of this can be made the same way from car radio antennae, and much longer versions, capable of reaching up into the treetops 20-30 m from the ground (useful for examining the contents of birds of prey nests) can be made using a series of 2-m long sturdy aluminium tubes which slot into each other with a (larger) mirror affixed to the end pole.

Another useful home-made device is a dentist-type mirror and a light bulb connected to a battery via a length of flex. By lowering the light bulb into a nest cavity, lighting up the interior, and angling the mirror into the correct position, you can see what the cavity contains. If you use it to look into closed mud nests of striped swallows, it is called a 'hirundiscope'; for looking into tunnel nests in banks is becomes a 'riparioscope'.

Keeping nest records and submitting these to one or other regional nest record scheme adds purpose to nesting and the information one submits may have many uses. It is especially valuable if nests are visited systematically and at sufficiently frequent intervals to determine when the last egg was laid, when it hatched and when the young fledged. Even when nests fail before the cycle is completed, the information gathered provides useful material for making overall assessments of the nesting success in a species.

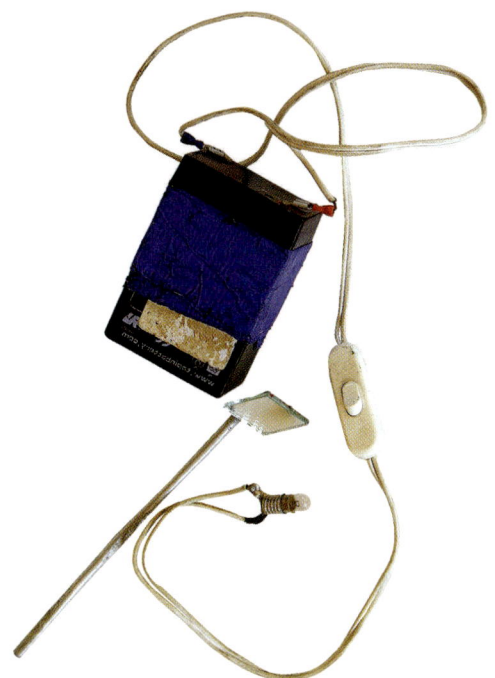

A rechargeable battery connected to a light bulb and a dentist-type mirror (above) for looking into enclosed nest-holes, and a mirror-stick (below), being used here to examine the contents of a Fork-tailed Drongo nest

Glossary

♂, ♀ – abbreviations used for male, female, respectively

s, e, n, w, ne, nnw, etc – abbreviations used for south, east, etc.

Afrotropical – term applied to that part of the African continent lying south of the Sahara Desert.

altricial – a young bird that is born with its eyes closed and little or no down cover; it is incapable of locomotion when it hatches and is fed by the parents (such young born with a covering of down are referred to as semi-altricial).

arid – refers to regions where average annual rainfall is low (<300 mm).

asynchronous (hatching) – refers to a clutch of eggs in which there is an interval between the hatching of each egg (the converse of synchronous hatching).

Baikiaea woodland – a broad-leaved woodland type, usually tall and with a closed canopy, restricted to Kalahari sands and dominated by *Baikiaea plurijuga*.

belly-wetting (or belly-soaking) – behaviour found in a few ground-nesting birds which cool their eggs (plovers, pratincoles, skimmers), or carry water to their chicks (sandgrouse), by soaking their belly-feathers in water before returning to the nest or young.

bracken – a robust fern (*Pteridium* sp.) that forms dense thickets in montane grasslands and on forest verges.

brancher/branching – refers to a stage in the development of young birds of some species (especially birds of prey), which, before they make their first flight, walk onto the surrounding branches and wait there for food.

brood patch – a bare area of skin on a bird's belly used to maintain its eggs at the bird's body temperature during incubation; hormonal activity at the onset of breeding causes the feathers in this area to be shed and the skin to become vascularised.

cainism – sibling aggression (the 'Cain & Abel' struggle) often found in broods of raptors in which the second-hatched young usually dies from the injuries inflicted by its older sibling.

chitinous – the hard, undigestable shells of beetles and other insects that pass intact through a bird's digestive system.

clutch – a set of eggs laid by a female in one nesting attempt.

'cock's nest' – refers to nests or structures added to nests (e.g. on the roofs of nests of some waxbill species) that are not used for breeding purposes; their function may be to decoy predators from the true nest or provide the male with a roost.

colony – nests clumped together constitute a colony; they may be nests built by different pairs (e.g. gannets) or the nests built by a single polygynous male (e.g. some weaver species).

cooperative breeding – refers to those breeding systems in which a breeding pair is assisted during the nesting cycle by one or more 'helpers'; it occurs invariably in some birds (e.g. babblers, helmetshrikes) and occasionally in others.

covey – collective term for a flock of francolin or partridge.

cryptic – has protective colouration.

dambo – seasonally wet grassland found along drainage lines in savanna, especially miombo.

disruptive background – many ground-nesting birds (e.g. plovers, coursers) lay their eggs alongside objects such as stones or dung which serve to 'disrupt' the outline of the eggs.

diurnal – active during the day (as opposed to during the night).

double-brooded – refers to the laying of a second clutch in a single breeding season after rearing a first brood successfully (multiple-brooded refers to more than two broods per season).

down – feathers that lack a central vane, have a soft fluffy texture and good insulation properties.

'egg-dumping' – refers to the behaviour of female birds that lay occasional eggs in nests other than their own or, in the case of cuckoos, in nests other than those of regularly used hosts.

elliptical – describes a particular egg shape that does not have one end broader than the other.

endemic – refers to the geographic range of a species (e.g. a species that is 'endemic' to the grassland region is only found in that region); 'near-endemic' implies that >90% of the population is restricted to the region.

ephemeral – refers to wetlands which often remain dry for much of the time, only filling during periods of high rainfall.

erythrism – aberrant colouration, usually reflected in plumage (but also in egg markings) which results from the deposition of excess of red-brown (erythromelanin) pigment.

exfoliation – refers to a weathering pattern found on granite hills in which surface layers of rock peel away from the core rock; these often provide protected nest sites for swifts and other birds.

false-brooding – a behaviour used by ground-nesting birds threatened by a predator: the bird squats low, pretending to be incubating thus luring the predator away from the real nest.

felted – the texture attained in the nests of some species (e.g. penduline tits) by knitting the nest material finely together.

feral – the term describes a population of birds derived from captive stock that has become free-living on a sustainable basis.

forb – a low herbaceous plant, neither a grass nor grass-like.

forest – refers here specifically to woodland types that are dominated by evergreen tree species, usually >10 m tall, usually forming a closed canopy; a variety of florisitically distinguishable types (montane, coastal, lowland, riparian) are recognised.

'forest fibre' – dark-coloured fibrous material (usually strands of fern root or *Marasmius* fungus) used by many forest-living birds (sunbirds, robin-chats, etc.) for building nests.

fynbos – shrubland vegetation dominated by proteas, ericas and restios and characteristic of s Cape.

gens/gentes – refers specifically to cuckoos in which 'clans' (or gentes) of the population have particular hosts and have evolved eggs that match the eggs of these hosts in colouration.

'gomoti' – local name used for the flooded thickets of the tree *Ficus verruculosa* that are found in the Okavango swamps and provide favoured breeding sites for colonial waterbirds.

grassland – refers here specifically to southern Africa's grassland biome: a grassy, mainly treeless plain that extends across the interior of South Africa and Lesotho where winters are cold and the average annual rainfall is >400 mm.

ground-colour – the colour of an egg beneath any speckling or other markings it may have.

helpers – the non-breeding assistants that form part of the group in cooperative-breeding birds.

heronry – a colony of breeding herons; is also applied to mixed-species colonies where cormorants, ibises, spoonbills and others breed in association with herons.

incubation period – the time that elapses between the laying and hatching of an egg; in the context of a clutch of eggs, it is usually taken as the time that elapses from when the last egg is laid to when the last egg hatches.

karoo – in the context of this book the Karoo refers to the arid shrublands comprising the 'Nama-Karoo' and 'Succulent Karoo' biomes; these extend from s Cape through Namibia into s Angola.

katbos – low, thorny shrub; an *Asparagus* sp.

koppie – a hill, often with a rocky summit.

lek – a display area used by males in some species of polygynous breeding birds to which females are attracted for mating.

mesic – the converse of 'arid'; refers to regions where average annual rainfall is >700 mm (e.g. mesic grassland, mesic savanna).

miombo – a broad-leaved savanna dominated by *Brachystegia* and *Julbernardia* spp. and restricted, in southern Africa, to Zimbabwe and Mozambique.

mixed-species heronry – a heronry in which several species breed together.

monogamous – a mating system in which a single male and single female form a pair to breed.

monospecific – refers here to a breeding colony occupied by a single species.

mopane – woodland dominated by the tree *Colophospermum mopane* and usually found on poorly drained soils.

mouth spots – spots that form a characteristic pattern inside the mouths of the nestlings of warblers and waxbills.

multiple-brooded – refers to the laying of more than two clutches in a single breeding season after successfully rearing earlier broods.

nesting failure – refers to a nesting attempt that is not successful in raising young, either because the eggs fail to hatch (clutch failure), or because the young fail to reach maturity (brood failure); the causes of such failure are very variable.

nest-stained – refers to eggs, especially of waterbirds, that become stained by damp plant material used in building the nest.

nidicolous – describes a young bird that remains in the nest after hatching.

nidifugous – describes a young bird that leaves the nest immediately after hatching (semi-nidifugous refers to those that leave within a few days).

noduled – refers to the bumpy texture on the shell of some birds' eggs (e.g. Southern Pied Babbler).

ossuary – the accumulation of bones and fur that may surround the nest of certain ground-nesting owls.

parental care – care of eggs and/or young for the duration of the breeding cycle.

petiole – the short, usually pliable stalk that attaches a leaf to the twig of a tree; these are widely used by birds for lining nests.

polychromatism – a variety of colours (either in plumage or in eggs) found within a single species.

polyandry/polyandrous – a form of polygamy in which a breeding female has more than one male partner; in these systems males usually undertake all parental care.

polygamy/polygamous – a mating system in which a breeding bird has more than one partner.

polygyny/polygynous – a form of polygamy in which a breeding male has more than one female partner; in these systems females usually undertake all parental care.

post-fledging – the period in a young bird's life after it has left the nest but is still dependent on its parents for food.

precocial – a young bird that hatches with its eyes open, has a covering of downy plumage and has the ability to walk from the time of hatching ('semi-precocial' refers to young in which such development is less complete).

pyriform – describes the shape of an egg that is sharp-pointed at one end and nearly flat at the other (i.e. top-shaped).

renosterveld – fynbos shrubland, usually dominated by the renosterbos *Elytropappus rhinocerotis*.

replacement clutch – a clutch laid to replace an earlier one that failed.

restio – refers to grasslike plants in the families Cyperaceae and Restionaceae which are characteristic components of fynbos.

rot-hole – a cavity in a tree stem that has formed where decay has set in, usually at a point where a branch has broken off.

savanna – one of Africa's major biomes: a mainly tropical vegetation type comprising deciduous trees with an understorey of grass; thornveld and miombo are two widespread savanna types; the term 'woodland' is applied when the tree canopy becomes continuous (>80% cover); mesic-savanna, semi-arid savanna and arid-savanna are progressively drier savanna types.

scree – rock- or boulder-strewn hillslope.

shrubland – vegetation dominated by woody shrubs <2 m tall.

solitary-breeding – opposite of colonial-breeding, i.e. nesting pairs are spaced well apart from one another.

strandveld – fynbos and/or karoo shrubland restricted to the coastline along the s and w Cape.

synchronous (hatching) – refers to egg clutches in which all the eggs hatch simultaneously (converse of asynchronous hatching).

taxon/taxa – a general term used for any group of related species.

thornveld – a savanna dominated by thorn-bearing trees, especially *Acacia* spp.

Usnea – generic name of a soft, pale green, strand-like lichen ('old man's beard') that drapes trees in high rainfall areas and is much-used by birds as nesting material.

'yard egg' – single eggs that are occasionally laid and abandoned by pelicans and flamingos in roosting or loafing areas.

OSTRICHES Family Struthionidae Worldwide 2 species; both endemic to Afrotropics; 1 breeds in southern Africa. With few exceptions, the ostriches found across most of South Africa are introduced hybrids that originate from the Somali Ostrich, originally bred commercially for meat and feathers. Non-hybrid Common Ostriches occur widely across Botswana, Namibia and ne Zimbabwe; also in Kruger Park in South Africa. Mainly polygynous; nests on the ground; lays the largest egg in the world; young precocial and nidifugous, leave nest permanently when they hatch.

Common Ostrich *Struthio camelus* Volstruis  page 352

Breeds in arid savanna and semi-desert, nesting in open country with good visibility. **Nest:** a scrape in the ground, 2-3 m in diameter; may be reused for successive clutches. Breeds in pairs or in polygynous groups of one ♂ and 2-5 ♀s, all of which lay eggs in a single communal nest. The ranking of the ♀ dictates which eggs receive the best chance of hatching: those laid by the dominant hen lie at the centre of the clutch, where they are most effectively incubated and are least exposed to predation. She prevents subordinate ♀s from sharing the incubation and, while incubating, keeps her own eggs in the central position. Despite her great size, the incubating female is easily overlooked as she keeps her head and neck close to the ground when sensing danger and from a distance appears to be merely a dark mound on the ground.

Laying months: opportunistic, dependent on rain, laying in any month; peaks in Jul-Sep in Zimbabwe, and Aug-Dec in Botswana; single-brooded. **Clutch size:** eggs/nest variable, dependent on number of ♀s laying; 2-5 ♀s usually lay/nest; each lays 3-8 eggs, resulting in 16-23 eggs/nest; max. of 43 recorded in one nest. Each ♀ lays at 2-3 day intervals. **Eggs:** 122-145-158 x 110-121-130 mm; mass 1.2-1.35-1.7 kg. **Incubation period:** 42-46 (39-53) days; starts about 16 days after first-laid egg; shared by ♂ (during night) and dominant ♀ (during day); she sidelines eggs laid by subordinates to edge of nest. **Nestling/fledging period:** young leave nest at about 3 days, reach half-adult height at 4-5 mo, full height at 12 mo; adult mass at 18 mo.

GUINEAFOWL Family Numididae Worldwide 6 species; all endemic to Afrotropics, 2 breed in southern Africa. Monogamous, but >1 ♀ may lay in same nest. Nest is a well-hidden scrape in the ground, eggs buff-coloured, thick-shelled and deeply pored, Clutch size large; incubation by ♀ without ♂ assistance; young precocial and nidifugous, leaving nest permanently when they hatch; 'flutter-fly' from a very young age (6-14 days).

Crested Guineafowl *Guttera pucherani* Kuifkoptarentaal  page 352

Breeds on the fringes of lowland, riparian and sand forest; usually nests in open glades and forest edges where grass cover provides concealment for the nest. **Nest:** well hidden in rank grass, a shallow scrape in the ground lined with blades and stems of grass and weeds. ♀ sits tight if the nest is approached, blends well into the surroundings and only flushes if closely approached.

Laying months: mainly Nov (Oct-Feb). **Clutch size:** 4-7 (2-12); clutches >7 eggs probably laid by more than one ♀. **Eggs:** 47.0-52.0-55.8 x 39.2-41.0-43.2 mm. **Incubation period:** 23 days; by ♀ only. **Nestling/fledging period:** young flutter-fly at 2 weeks; fly well at 5-6 weeks; young cared for by both sexes; they remain as a family group through winter.

Helmeted Guineafowl *Numida meleagris* Gewone Tarentaal  page 352

Breeds widely, especially in the savanna and grassland regions; an abundant bird in many grain-growing areas. The large flocks of this species that form in winter, divide up in early summer into pairs that nest solitarily, but often within a few hundred metres of each other. Areas of rank grass are sought out for nesting; these may be grass patches that have remained unburnt for a few years, or ungrazed, or along the edges of marshy ground. **Nest:** a shallow scrape in the ground, 200-320 mm in diameter and 50-80 mm deep, lined with blades and stems of grass and weeds; invariably in dense cover in grass, weeds, or under a bush. ♀ selects the site and adds nest lining through the incubation. She leaves the nest unattended at intervals to feed, sits tight if the nest is approached, blends well into the surroundings and only flushes if closely approached.

Laying months: a summer breeder, laying earliest in sw Cape (mainly Sep-Nov), latest in Namibia (mainly Feb-Mar) and mainly Nov-Jan elsewhere in the region. **Clutch size:** 6-18 (2-41); clutches >12 probably laid by more than one ♀; laid at 1-day intervals. **Eggs:** 46.4-52.6-57.6 x 34.7-40.2-42.5 mm; mass 40 g. **Incubation period:** 26 days (24-27); by ♀ only, leaving the nest unattended for short periods during the day to feed; begins when clutch is completed. **Nestling/fledging period:** young flutter-fly at 14 days; cared for by both sexes; they remain as a family group through winter.

PEAFOWL Family Phasianidae A large family (see further on page 22) that includes turkeys, grouse, ptarmigans and other well-known Palearctic and North American species; it also includes well-known Asian species such as the junglefowl, pheasants and peafowl. Indian Peafowl are included in the southern African list because of the small feral populations established from introduced birds.

Indian Peafowl *Pavo cristatus* Makpou page 352

Small feral populations of this Asian species exist on Robben Island (where it was introduced in 1968) and at a few other sites in s Cape. Polygynous (Asia). Its nesting habits in southern Africa are poorly known. A nest at Robben Island was a shallow, unlined scrape in sand.

Laying months: Feb (Robben Is). **Clutch size:** 4 (Robben Is); 3-6 (Asia). **Eggs:** 65.2-66.1-67.2 x 49.3-49.9-50.9 mm; mass 63 g (Robben Is). **Incubation period:** 28-30 days; by ♀ only, leaving nest 2x/day to feed (Asia). **Nestling/fledging period:** not recorded.

Common Ostrich

Crested Guineafowl

Common Ostrich (TWO ABOVE)

Helmeted Guineafowl

Indian Peafowl

FRANCOLINS, PARTRIDGES, SPURFOWL, QUAIL, PEAFOWL Family Phasianidae Worldwide 181 species; 43 breed in Afrotropics, 19 in southern Africa, of which 2 (Indian Peafowl, Chukar Partridge) are introduced and have small feral populations on Robben Island. Most species are probably monogamous; Swainson's Francolin is probably polygynous. Eggs are laid in a scrape in the ground, usually well concealed in thick vegetation; they are thick-shelled and plain-coloured in francolins, partridges, spurfowl; thinner-shelled and cryptically marked in quail. Where known, incubation is by the ♀ without ♂ assistance; she sits tight if approached only leaving nest when almost trodden on; 4-8/clutch; young are precocial and nidifugous, leaving the nest when they hatch; they can 'flutter-fly' from a very young age (6-14 days).

Red-winged Francolin *Scleroptila levaillantii* Rooivlerkpatrys  page 353

Breeds in mesic grasslands, and patchily in mountain fynbos; favours hilly, rocky country with dense, rank grass; occurs alongside Grey-winged Francolin in places, but prefers a denser grass cover than that species, and so more commonly found in grasslands that are subject to relatively light grazing and are infrequently burnt (2-3 year-old grass); often nests on vlei margins. **Nest:** a shallow scrape in the ground about 150 mm in diameter, well lined with strands of green and dry grass, and hidden between grass tufts. The incubating bird sits tight and is not easily flushed.

Laying months: mainly Nov-Dec (Aug-Mar,) but later in winter-rainfall areas (Mar-Jul). **Clutch size:** 4-5 (4-10). **Eggs:** 38.3-40.1-43.5 x 31.3-32.3-33.3 mm. **Incubation period:** 22 days, by ♀ only. **Nestling/fledging period:** not recorded; cared for by both sexes.

Grey-winged Francolin *Scleroptila africana* Bergpatrys  page 353

Breeds in mesic, upland grasslands, also in low shrubby fynbos and along the fringes of the karoo; favours open, treeless country where the grass cover is short and subject to periodic grazing and burning. **Nest:** a shallow scrape in the ground, sparsely lined with blades of dry grass, well hidden between grass tufts; measures 165-169-175 mm in diameter, 36-48-65 mm in depth. The incubating bird sits tight, blending well with the surroundings and she is not easily flushed. She leaves the nest at intervals during the day to feed; single birds (as opposed to coveys of birds) seen repeatedly in the same area during the breeding season are probably ♀s temporarily off their nests.

Laying months: mainly Nov-Dec (Aug-Mar), except in winter-rainfall areas where it peaks in Aug-Oct; single-brooded. **Clutch size:** 5-6 (4-15); clutches of >8 eggs probably laid by two ♀s. **Eggs:** 37.2-39.9-44.6 x 28.3-30.1-32.1 mm. **Incubation period:** 22 days (21-23); by ♀ only. **Nestling/fledging period:** 5-6 weeks; young flutter-fly from 14 days old (they lie still, if threatened, before this); cared for by both sexes; they remain as family group through winter.

Orange River Francolin *Scleroptila levaillantoides* Kalaharipatrys  page 353

Breeds in semi-arid grasslands and savanna; in flat or undulating country, either in open grassland or among scattered trees and shrubs. **Nest:** a scrape in the ground placed between or against grass tufts and sparsely lined with blades of dry grass. It measures 135-160-180 mm in diameter and 25-40-55 mm in depth. It is built by the ♀ and she does all the incubation, sitting tight if the nest is approached; ♂s call more during the breeding season than at other times and the nest is usually located within the general area from where he calls.

Laying months: mainly Aug-Nov, but recorded in all months; usually lays a replacement clutch after an earlier failure. **Clutch size:** 4-5 (3-8). **Eggs:** 34.3-36.6-40.7 x 26.2-28.8-32.0 mm. **Incubation period:** 20-21 days; by ♀ only, starts when the clutch is complete; she usually leaves the nest once a day, in the morning, to feed. **Nestling/fledging period:** 5-6 weeks; young flutter-fly from 12-14 days old; cared for by both sexes, or by family group.

Shelley's Francolin *Scleroptila shelleyi* Laeveldpatrys page 353

Breeds in mesic savanna, usually in hilly country, often on rocky hillsides and where there is a dense grass cover. **Nest:** a deep, well-lined scrape in the ground concealed beneath or between grass tufts or under a small bushy shrub. The incubating bird sits tight and blends well with the nest's surroundings.

Laying months: all months recorded, but mainly Sep-Dec (Aug-Apr). **Clutch size:** 4-5 (3-8). **Eggs:** 26.9-38.7-43.8 x 29.2-31.2-35.4 mm. **Incubation period:** 20-22 days; by ♀ only. **Nestling/fledging period:** about 5 weeks; young flutter-fly from 12 days old; cared for by both sexes.

Chukar Partridge *Alectoris chukar* Asiatiese Patrys page 352

Introduced (from Eastern Europe) onto Robben Island in 1964 where a small population survives. Little is known of its nesting habits here and the information below refers mostly to its occurrence in its natural range. A nest containing 10 eggs, found on Robben Island in September 1994 was a sparsely lined scrape, hidden under a *Tetragonia* sp. shrub. The incubating bird sat tight, flying off the nest when it was nearly trodden on (B Dyer).

Laying months: Sep (Robben Is). **Clutch size:** 10 (Robben Is); usually 8-15 (6-20, Israel) where laid at 1-2 day intervals. **Eggs:** about 37-39-41 x 29-30-31 mm; mass 19 g. **Incubation period:** 22-24 days; begins when clutch is completed; by ♀ only (Palearctic). **Nestling/fledging period:** young flutter-fly at 7-10 days; ad size at 50 days; cared for by ♀, sometimes by both sexes (Palearctic).

female incubating

Red-winged Francolin

female incubating, well concealed

Grey-winged Francolin

Orange River Francolin

Shelley's Francolin

Chukar Partridge

Spurfowl

Red-billed Spurfowl *Pternistis adspersus* **Rooibekfisant** page 353

Breeds in semi-arid and arid savanna, most common in riparian thickets and along the margins of floodplains, especially in acacia-dominated habitats. **Nest:** more exposed than those of other spurfowl; it is a shallow, unlined (or sparsely lined) scrape in the ground, placed where there is some form of cover, either among tufts of grass or beneath a shrub; the eggs are easily visible when the nest is unattended.

Laying months: mainly Mar-May; but all months recorded. **Clutch size:** 5 (3-10). **Eggs:** 38.9-42.2-46.5 × 31.9-33.4-35.2 mm. **Incubation period:** 22 days (in captivity); by ♀ only; starts when clutch completed. **Nestling/fledging period:** not recorded.

Natal Spurfowl *Pternistis natalensis* **Natalse Fisant**  page 353

Breeds in mesic savanna, extending locally into grasslands where wooded thickets provide habitat; commonly along watercourses, at the base of rocky hills, or along the margins of forest; nests in short, rank grass or in some other low, dense plant cover. **Nest:** a shallow, well-concealed scrape in the ground, thinly lined with grass stems and (sometimes) a few feathers. The incubating ♀ sits tight if approached, only flushing off the nest when almost trodden on.

Laying months: mainly Mar-May (Feb-Sep, occasionally in other months). **Clutch size:** 5-6 (4-10); larger clutches probably laid by >1 ♀. **Eggs:** 36.1-41.9-46.8 × 28.4-34.2-37.8 mm. **Incubation period:** 20-22 days (in captivity); by ♀ only; starts when clutch completed; she leaves the nest unattended for short periods a few times a day to feed when usually joined by the ♂. **Nestling/fledging period:** young flutter-fly from 10-14 days; fly well 7-8 weeks; young cared for by both sexes.

Cape Spurfowl *Pternistis capensis* **Kaapse Fisant**  page 353

Restricted to s and w Cape where it breeds in coastal fynbos and strandveld, extending along watercourses into the karoo; also in unmanaged land in suburban areas, where it favours a dense cover of heath, rooikrans thicket or other shrubby habitat. **Nest:** a shallow scrape in the ground, sparsely lined with grass or weed stems; usually well concealed under shrubs, among sedges or in cut brush; occasionally placed conspicuously in the open.

Laying months: mainly Sep-Oct (Aug-Feb). **Clutch size:** 6-8; occasionally up to 14 eggs, when probably laid by >1 ♀. **Eggs:** 42.0-47.0-55.7 × 35.2-37.0-38.8 mm. **Incubation period:** 23 days (22-26); by ♀ only; starts when clutch is completed. **Nestling/fledging period:** young flutter-fly from 12 days old; brooded by both sexes.

Swainson's Spurfowl *Pternistis swainsonii* **Bosveldfisant**  page 353

Breeds across the savanna belt from the semi-arid west to the mesic east; its range has extended widely into agricultural areas in the grassland region in the past century and, where once absent, it is now a common breeding bird in the highveld's maize-farming areas. ♂s are probably polygynous, with all parental care performed by ♀s; nests in thick grass, among weeds and forbs, under a thorny sapling, or in shrubby vegetation such as *Stoebe vulgaris*; also commonly nests in lands under crops (especially maize), either in the weedy growth between rows of crops, or in the rough grass verges, or in old lands that are regenerating back to grass or bush. Probably polygynous. **Nest:** built by the ♀, a shallow scrape in the ground, sparsely lined with grass and/or a few feathers; it measures 150 mm in diameter and 50 mm in depth. Nests are usually, but not invariably, well concealed by plant cover. The ♀ sits tight on the eggs when approached, only flying off when almost trodden on.

Laying months: mainly in Dec-Apr (Nov-Jun, occasionally in other months). **Clutch size:** 4-6 (3-12); larger clutches probably laid by >1 ♀. **Eggs:** 40.3-45.0-49.0 × 30.2-35.9-38.0 mm. **Incubation period:** 23 days (in captivity); by ♀ only; starts when clutch completed; she leaves the nest unattended for short periods a few times a day to feed. **Nestling/fledging period:** young flutter-fly at 10-14 days; full grown at 3 months; cared for by ♀ only; young remain with ♀ for at least 6 months.

Red-necked Spurfowl *Pternistis afer* **Rooikeelfisant**  page 353

Confined to the mesic east, from s Cape northwards; breeds on forest verges and in lowland savanna in rank grass, in bracken or in other low undergrowth. **Nest:** built by ♀, a shallow, sparsely lined scrape in the ground, well concealed by surrounding vegetation; sometimes positioned against a sapling.

Laying months: mainly Nov-Apr; peaks earlier (Nov-Jan) in the south of its range than in the north (Dec-Apr). **Clutch size:** 4-7 (3-9). **Eggs:** 40.3-45.0-49.0 × 30.2-35.9-38.0 mm. **Incubation period:** 23 days (in captivity); by ♀ only, starting when clutch is complete. **Nestling/fledging period:** young flutter-fly at 10 days; full grown at 3-4 months; cared for by ♂ and ♀.

Red-billed Spurfowl

Natal Spurfowl

Cape Spurfowl

Swainson's Spurfowl   Red-necked Spurfowl

Francolin, Spurfowl, Quail

Coqui Francolin *Peliperdix coqui* **Swempie** page 352

Breeds in mesic savanna, extending patchily into the semi-arid west, and into grassland where scattered trees, or copses of trees (including aliens such as eucalypts and wattles) are present. **Nest:** a shallow scrape in the ground, 150 mm in diameter and 30 mm deep, thinly lined with dry blades of grass. It is placed beneath or between short grass tufts and, when a bird is not in attendance, the eggs are usually clearly visible; they are, however, seldom left uncovered once incubation commences, and the cryptically marked plumage of sitting ♀, blends well with the cover. She sits tight when she incubates, only flying up if nearly trodden on.
Laying months: mainly Nov-Feb (Sep-Mar, occasionally other months) in South Africa, later (May in Botswana and n Namibia). **Clutch size:** 4-6 (3-8). **Eggs:** 30.3-32.5-34.6 × 25.5-27.3-28.6 mm; mass 16 g. **Incubation period:** unknown; by ♀ only, begins when clutch is complete. **Nestling/fledging period:** unknown; young cared for by both sexes; young flutter-fly at 7-10 days.

Crested Francolin *Dendroperdix sephaena* **Bospatrys** page 352

Breeds widely across the savanna belt, from the semi-arid west to the mesic east; nests in woodlands with sufficient grass cover to conceal nests. Pairs nest solitarily, are territorial year-round, and are widely spaced. **Nest:** a scrape in the ground, 100-170 mm in diameter and 60-100 mm deep, often placed against the trunk of a sapling, or else between aloe plants, against a stone, or between grass tufts; the eggs are usually easily visible when not attended. The incubating bird blends well with its surroundings, sitting tight if approached. She leaves the eggs a few times a day to feed, when she is joined by the ♂.
Laying months: mainly Oct-Nov (Oct-May), in South Africa and a few months later (Dec-Mar) further north. **Clutch size:** 5-6 (3-9, rarely more). **Eggs:** 36.3-39.7-43.7 × 26.7-30.4-32.2 mm; exceptionally thick-shelled. **Incubation period:** 19-22 days; by ♀ only, starts when clutch is complete. **Nestling/fledging period:** unknown; young flutter-fly when <¼-grown; young cared for by both sexes; they remain as a family group through winter.

Hartlaub's Spurfowl *Pternistis hartlaubi* **Klipfisant** page 353

Breeds in c and n Namibia, especially along the escarpment; on rocky, boulder-strewn hills and koppies in semi-arid or arid, acacia-dominated savanna; pairs are territorial year-round, spaced at about a pair/12 ha, each territory extending over one or more clusters of rocky koppie habitat, often separated from other similar habitat by open plains. **Nest:** on the ground part way up a rocky slope; it is a shallow, sparsely lined scrape between or under rocks. Few nests have been recorded and nesting habits are poorly known.
Laying months: mainly Jun-Aug (Apr-Sep, rarely other months). **Clutch size:** 3 (2-4). **Eggs:** 40.0-41.6-43.5 × 29.0-30.2-32.1 mm. **Incubation period:** 23 days; by ♀ only. **Nestling/fledging period:** young flutter-fly from 3 days; fledge at 12 days; young cared for by both sexes.

Blue Quail *Excalfactoria adansonii* **Bloukwartel** page 353

An erratic visitor to the north-east parts of southern Africa in years of high rainfall, breeding in moist grasslands, often on the margins of seasonally waterlogged ground. Nesting habits are poorly known. **Nest:** placed on the ground, hidden in rank grass or sedge; a thickly padded bowl of dry grass stems, measuring about 90-100 mm in diameter.
Laying months: Jan-Apr. **Clutch size:** 3-9. **Eggs:** 23.6-24.9-28.4 × 18.2-19.5-21.0 mm; mass 4.5 g. **Incubation period:** 16 days; by ♀ only. **Nestling/fledging period:** not recorded.

Common Quail *Coturnix coturnix* **Afrikaanse Kwartel** page 353

A breeding visitor arriving in Sep-Oct; occurs widely, but mainly in the grassland region, favours open, primary grassland <300 mm in height; also in fallow lands, in pastures, and in weeds between rows of growing crops; ♂s utter a repetitive call-note throughout the breeding period. Monogamous, but a few instances of polygyny recorded. Pairs nest solitarily, sometimes <100 m apart. **Nest:** a shallow scrape in the ground placed between or beneath grass tufts; it measures 110-140 mm in diameter and 15 mm deep; it is lined with a pad of dry grass stems, with coarser material used at the base and finer grass ends lining the shallow cup. It is usually well concealed, especially when the cryptically marked ♀ is incubating; she sits tight if approached, only leaving when almost trodden on.
Laying months: Sep-Apr, peaking earlier (Sep-Nov) in winter-rainfall areas than elsewhere in its range (Dec-Apr); relays after early nest failure (Europe). **Clutch size:** 5-7 (2-14); laid at 1-day intervals; larger clutches probably laid by >1♀. **Eggs:** 23.4-30.3-33.1 × 19.3-23.4-25.1 mm; mass 6.5-7.0-8.1 g. **Incubation period:** 17-20 days (Europe); by ♀ only; begins when clutch is completed; ♀ leaves eggs to feed several times/day for 7-20 min. **Nestling/fledging period:** young flutter-fly at 11 days; fly at 19-21 days (Europe); cared for by ♀ only.

Harlequin Quail *Coturnix delegorguei* **Bontkwartel** page 353

A sporadic, but sometimes abundant breeding visitor to the savanna belt arriving in Nov-Dec; in occurs in open or sparsely wooded semi-arid to mesic savanna; often in old agricultural lands; the birds' presence is given away by ♂s uttering a repetitive call-note throughout the breeding period. **Nest:** a shallow scrape in the ground, well concealed between or beneath grass tufts and thinly lined with dry grass stems. The ♀ builds the nest and incubates without ♂ assistance; she sits tight if the nest is approached, only flying up when almost trodden on.
Laying months: linked to heavy rains; mainly Jan-Feb (Nov-May, occasionally in other months). **Clutch size:** 4-8; larger clutches (e.g. 22 recorded) probably laid by >1♀. **Eggs:** 27.4-29.2-30.9 × 21.7-22.4-23.5 mm. **Incubation period:** 14-18 days; by ♀ only. **Nestling/fledging period:** young flutter-fly at about 5 days old.

Ducks, Geese

DUCKS, GEESE Family Anatidae Worldwide 165 species; 20 breed in Afrotropics, 16 in southern Africa. Nesting habits of these 16 are very variable, some nesting in holes in trees, another using a mammal burrow in the ground, others nesting on dry ground away from water, and others making a floating nest over deep water. Most are monogamous breeders, a few are polygynous; pair bonds in many species do not persist through the breeding cycle, and in 13 species ♀s undertake the incubation and parental care without ♂ assistance. These species add a thick down layer to the nest to maintain egg temperature when the ♀ leaves to feed. In 3 species where the incubation is shared, no down is used in the nest. Clutch size is large (6-10 eggs/clutch); eggs are unmarked, white or ivory-coloured, often discoloured over time; chicks are precocial and nidifugous.

White-backed Duck *Thalassornis leuconotus* Witrugeend  page 354

Breeds widely but patchily on seasonal pans and floodplains and in the vegetated upper-reaches of dams; in emergent vegetation over deep water (>0,7 m). Several pairs may nest close to one another (<10 m apart). **Nest:** always over water and usually well concealed in grass or sedges, a substantial bowl anchored to the stems of emergent plants which are bent over to form the walls of the nest; it measures 300-340 mm in diameter and 110-250 mm high, usually with an access ramp up one side; the cup measures 150-200 mm in diameter and is 50-100 mm deep. Being anchored, nests are prone to being flooded by rising water. Both sexes build (in captivity) and material is added through the incubation; down is not added to the nest lining. Under ideal conditions breeding at a site may persist uninterrupted for as long as 17 successive months. Pairs call briefly at incubation change-overs and usually approach and leave the nest under water.
Laying months: mainly Feb-May, but commonly lays in all months. **Clutch size:** 6 (4-10); laid at 1-day intervals. **Eggs:** 55.0-61.8-68.8 x 44.9-48.5-51.7 mm; 77-81-94 g. The eggs are coffee-coloured, which distinguishes them from the eggs of all other ducks in the region. **Incubation period:** 32 days (29-33) (in captivity); by both sexes, ♀ at night, ♂ for most of the day; starts when clutch is completed. **Nestling/fledging period:** 55 days; young cared for by both sexes.

White-faced Duck (White-faced Whistling Duck) *Dendrocygna viduata* Nonnetjie-eend  page 354

Breeds widely in mesic savanna and grassland, mostly on the fringes of seasonal, shallow-water wetlands, the nest usually placed in a raised position above the water level (on an island or embankment); sometimes far from the nearest water (1-3 km away) in open bushveld. **Nest:** a scrape in the ground, 160-180 mm in diameter, lined with dry grass to form a bowl about 140 mm across and 50 mm deep; it is well hidden by vegetation. No down is added to the nest lining. The incubating bird sits tight, only flying up off the nest if it is closely approached. In prime breeding habitat (grassy islands surrounded by shallow water) there may be several nests of this and other duck species close to one another.
Laying months: mainly Dec-Feb (Sep-May); single-brooded. **Clutch size:** 9-11 (7-13, rarely up to 16); laid at 1-day intervals. **Eggs:** 48.5-49.0-50.2 x 38.4-37.4-39.8 mm; mass 27.5-35.0-52.3 g. **Incubation period:** 26-30 days; by both sexes; usually change over twice a day, morning and evening; nest rarely left unattended. **Nestling/fledging period:** 63 days; young tended by both sexes.

Fulvous Duck (Fulvous Whistling Duck) *Dendrocygna bicolor* Fluiteend  page 354

Breeds widely but sparsely in rank grass, sedges or reeds close to, or over water. **Nest:** either a shallow scrape in the ground, 190-260 mm in diameter, lined with dry grass or sedge stems; or a more substantial bowl built into a sedge or grass clump over water. No down is added to the nest lining; it is built by both sexes (in captivity). In ideal breeding conditions several pairs may nest within 50 m of each other. The incubating bird sits tight, only flying up off the nest if it is closely approached.
Laying months: mainly Dec-Feb (Nov-Apr), two months earlier in winter-rainfall region, but all months recorded. **Clutch size:** 6-11; laid at 1-day intervals. **Eggs:** 48.0-51.5-55.0 x 37.0-39.8-41.6 mm; mass 41.5-50.0-59.0 g. **Incubation period:** 27 days (25-31); by both sexes; change-over twice a day, ♀ sitting at night. **Nestling/fledging period:** 52 days; young tended by both sexes.

Spur-winged Goose *Plectropterus gambensis* Wildemakou page 354

Breeds widely on both seasonal and permanent wetlands where there is extensive grass or sedge cover. May be monogamous or polygynous. **Nest:** site chosen varies; it is usually a large, shallow scrape, 420-500 mm in diameter and 70-100 mm deep, hidden in dense cover on the ground, either on a raised embankment or low island that is surrounded by, or close to, water. Above-ground sites range from being in large tree cavities, in raptor nests (Martial and African Fish Eagle nests recorded), or on top of a Hamerkop or Sociable Weaver nest; these can be up to 16 m above the ground, and 1 km from the nearest water. The nest, built by the ♀, is a bowl of grass, 150-240 mm across and 70 mm thick, and nest material and white-coloured down is added throughout the incubation. The eggs are covered with down when the ♀ leaves the nest to feed.
Laying months: mainly Dec-Mar in most of its range, Aug-Sep in the winter-rainfall region, but virtually all months have been recorded. **Clutch size:** 9-12 (6-27); clutches >12 eggs are probably laid by two ♀s; laid at 1-day intervals. **Eggs:** 68.0-75.2-86.2 x 49.2-55.4-59.2 mm; mass 122-127 g. **Incubation period:** 30-33 days; by ♀ only; begins when clutch is completed. **Nestling/fledging period:** 85 days; young cared for by ♀ only.

White-backed Duck

White-faced Duck

Fulvous Duck

nesting on the ground (the more usual site)   Spur-winged Goose   using an African Fish Eagle nest

Ducks, Geese

Egyptian Goose *Alopochen aegyptiaca* Kolgans page 354

Breeds widely in the region, absent only from waterless areas. Pairs nest solitarily, defending territories along wide, shallow rivers (at ½-2 km intervals) or along the edges of lakes, pans and dams; well adapted to urban environments and a familiar bird in parks, on golf courses, etc. **Nest:** site used is very variable: most are on the ground close to or over water, usually well hidden in grass or sedges on an island; also commonly nests on old stick nests of crows, birds of prey, herons or cormorants, these either in trees or on telephone/electricity poles 1-25 m above the ground; where available, Hamerkop nests are much favoured, the geese either nesting on top or inside, enlarging the entrance to gain access (Hamerkops in occupation can be evicted when taking possession of the nest); other sites include the top of Sociable Weaver nests, cliff ledges, especially where they overlook water (as shown opposite), large cavities in tree trunks, window boxes and shelves on buildings (60 m up from the ground) and offshore shipwrecks. The nest is a warmly lined bowl, built by the ♀, 230-500 mm in diameter and 70-100 mm thick; down and grass form the lining and this is used to cover the eggs when the ♀ is not in attendance. Sites may be reused in successive years. Young leave high nests by leaping to the ground and they are walked to the nearest water by the parents.
Laying months: all months, but mainly Jul-Oct; relays after an early clutch loss; single-brooded. **Clutch size:** 7-8 (4-14, rarely up to 22); laid at 1-day intervals. **Eggs:** 57.9-68.5-76.7 × 46.0-51.2-57.9 mm; mass 78.5-98.0-110.0 g. **Incubation period:** 28-30 days; by ♀ only; begins when clutch is completed; she leaves the nest once a day for about ½ hr to feed. **Nestling/fledging period:** young make a flapping run at 10 weeks; fly at 11 weeks; are tended by both sexes.

South African Shelduck *Tadorna cana* Kopereend  page 354

Breeds in the karoo and grassland regions, most common in semi-arid and arid areas. Pairs nest solitarily in open country near a farm dam or natural pan, the nest usually located 0.1-2 km away from water. **Nest:** a bowl of grass and down placed at the end of a deep hole in the ground, mostly (80% of records) dug by an aardvark, in which the nest can be as far as 9 m in from the entrance. Less often, the hole of a porcupine or springhare is used, or a hole in rocks or in a haystack. The ♀ leaves the nest once or twice a day to join the ♂ to feed on the dam, and the chicks are walked to the dam when they've hatched and they are reared there by both parents. The nest site is selected by the ♀ and she lines the scrape with grass and a thick layer of down. Sites are regularly reused in successive years.
Laying months: mainly Jul-Aug (May-Sep); may relay after an early loss; single-brooded. **Clutch size:** 7-11 (4-15). **Eggs:** 64.5-68.7-72.0 × 48.0-50.3-52.0 mm; mass 74.5-89.0-99.5 g. **Incubation period:** unknown; by ♀ only; leaves nest in the late afternoon to feed. **Nestling/fledging period:** 10 weeks; young tended by both sexes.

Knob-billed Duck *Sarkidiornis melanotos* Knobbeleend  page 354

Breeds widely across the savanna belt in wetland/woodland mosaics where large trees provide nest holes and seasonal freshwater wetlands provide habitat for rearing ducklings. ♂s usually polygynous, one paired with 1-4 ♀s. **Nest:** a cavity in a tree with a floor space >20 cm diameter is used, 1-12 m up from the ground, either a natural hole in the main trunk of a large tree or in the top of a rotten palm stump; also recorded using the chamber of an old Hamerkop nest and an African Barn Owl nest box; occasionally nests on the ground. The nest site can be in dry woodland as far as 2 km away from the nearest water; sites are regularly reused in successive years. The nest is lined with dry grass and the ♀'s grey-coloured down feathers, and these are used to cover the eggs when, once or twice a day, she leaves the eggs unattended to feed. When incubating, she sits tight, giving no indication of her presence. ♀ selects the nest site and incubates and raises the brood without ♂ assistance; once incubation begins, ♂s do not visit the nest.
Laying months: mainly Dec-Mar (Nov-Apr). **Clutch size:** 8-11 (6-20); large clutches are probably laid by two ♀s. **Eggs:** 53.0-58.6-71.0 × 38.6-43.0-46.5 mm; 55.2-56.6-58 g. **Incubation period:** 28-30 days; by ♀ only; begins when clutch is completed. **Nestling/fledging period:** 9-10 weeks; young cared for by ♀ only.

African Pygmy Goose *Nettapus auritus* Dwerggans  page 354

Breeds in tropical and subtropical woodland/wetland mosaics, usually at a site <½ km from a lily-covered freshwater pan or dam and often overhanging water. **Nest:** typically 4-6 m up (2-20) in a cavity in a tree; holes used are 150-380-600 mm deep with an entrance 70 mm or more in diameter; hollow trunks that have been chopped open by honey gatherers are commonly used. Artificial logs are used when available, and occasionally cavities other than those in trees, e.g. in a rock face, a termitarium, or the chamber of a Hamerkop nest. The nest is lined with dry grass and the ♀'s white down feathers, and these are used to cover the eggs when she leaves the eggs unattended and joins the ♂ to feed; she does this a few times a day.
Laying months: mainly Nov-Feb (Sep-May); relays after an early clutch loss. **Clutch size:** 7-9 (6-13); laid at 1-2 day intervals. **Eggs:** 40.8-43.5-46.5 × 30.6-32.8-35.8 mm; 24.6-26.1-27.1 g. **Incubation period:** 24 days (24-28); by ♀ only. **Nestling/fledging period:** chicks leave nest hole within a day of hatching; fly at 42 days; young cared for by both sexes.

female incubating on cliff ledge   Egyptian Goose

Egyptian Goose

nesting in an aardvark tunnel in foreground   South African Shelduck

another active hole

Knob-billed Duck

African Pygmy Goose

Yellow-billed Duck *Anas undulata* Geelbekeend page 355

Breeds widely across South Africa, patchily elsewhere; it nests on the fringes of dams, pans, vleis and seasonal floodplains. **Nest:** typically placed in thick grass near, but not over the water; usually <20 m, and seldom >100 m from water's edge. It is often situated in the centre of a tuft (rather than under it) and, where available, under a low thorny bush. It is built by the ♀, a shallow bowl 180-200-210 mm in diameter and 90-100-110 mm deep, made with grass or other plant stems, and it is thickly lined with down which is added (together with the grass lining) during egg-laying. The down lining may be 40-50 mm thick and a flap of it is used to cover the eggs when the parent bird is not in attendance. In ideal breeding habitat, nests of adjacent ♀s may be within 10 m of each other, and a similar distance from nests of other duck species. The ♀ incubates without ♂ assistance and she leaves the nest in the mornings and evenings to feed, usually joining her mate on a nearby water-body. Otherwise, she continually remains on the nest, sitting tight if approached, and only flying off at the last moment.

Laying months: commonly lays in all months; but peaks in Jul-Sep in winter-rainfall region and in Dec-Mar elsewhere. **Clutch size:** 6-9 (4-12, rarely up to 17) laid at 1-day intervals. **Eggs:** 51.0-54.7-60.6 x 37.0-41.5-46.0 mm; 44-55-62 g. **Incubation period:** 26-29 days; by ♀ only; begins before clutch is complete. **Nestling/fledging period:** 68 days; young cared for by ♀ only and they remain with her for a further 6 weeks.

Mallard *Anas platyrhynchos* Groenkopeend   no nest or egg photo

Feral populations of this Holarctic duck occur in Gauteng and the w Cape where the birds are present on numerous artificial and natural wetlands. Its nesting habits are poorly known in southern Africa, but they probably do not differ greatly from those of the Yellow-billed Duck. **Nest:** built by ♀ only, a shallow bowl of grass, and other soft plant stems, well lined with down, placed on the ground in dense grass or sedges or, less frequently, in a low tree cavity or nesting box (Europe).

Laying months: no data available for southern Africa. **Clutch size:** 4-18 (Europe); laid at 1-day intervals. **Eggs:** 50-57-65 x 37-41-46 mm; mass 42-51-59 g (Europe). **Incubation period:** 24-28-32 days; by ♀ only (Europe). **Nestling/fledging period:** 50-60 days; young cared for by ♀ only (Europe).

African Black Duck *Anas sparsa* Swarteend page 355

Breeds along streams and rivers, pairs defending a stretch of 0.5-2 km of river from which other pairs are excluded; their nests are consequently never close to each other as often occurs in other anatids. **Nest:** placed close to water (<5 m away) and well hidden, either in dense grass or other ground cover on the bank, or in caught-up flood debris, in tangled roots, or in a hollow stump; occasionally in an old, collapsed Hamerkop nest or on a low cliff ledge. It is a bowl 194-219-265 mm in diameter and 78-87-100 mm deep, built by the ♀ with grass and thickly lined with downy feathers (500-3500) which are used to cover the eggs when she is not in attendance. The ♀ incubates without ♂ assistance, sitting for long, uninterrupted stretches, leaving the nest (for 22-69-165 min) 2x/day to feed; when she does, she flies to join her mate in a 'waiting area' within a few hundred metres upstream or downstream. When incubating, she sits tight if approached, only flying off the nest at the last moment; she may perform injury-feigning distraction display when doing so.

Laying months: recorded in most months but mainly during Jun-Oct (peaking in Aug); single-brooded, but may relay if first clutch is lost. **Clutch size:** 6 (4-11); laid at 1-day intervals. **Eggs:** 57.0-59.3-66.0 x 43.6-44.9-46.5 mm; mass 63-68-73 g. **Incubation period:** 28-32 days; by ♀ only; starts when clutch completed. **Nestling/fledging period:** 77 days; young cared for mainly by ♀, sometimes joined by ♂; eggshells remain in the nest after hatching.

Cape Teal *Anas capensis* Teeleend page 355

Breeds on open pans, dams, vleis, especially in nutrient-rich, brackish or saline waters, and characteristically on ephemeral wetlands in semi-arid areas. **Nest:** almost always on dry ground (and not over water), within 50 m of the water's edge; low, grass-covered islands, where they occur, are favoured sites and several pairs may nest on such islands within a few metres of each other. The nest, built by the ♀ in 2-10 days before laying, is well hidden, either in thick grass or below some woody shrubbery; it is a scrape in the ground (about 230 mm wide and 75 mm deep), lined with a basal layer of dry grass or other plant material, and a thick upper lining (30-40 mm) of downy feathers (1500-2000) which are added during the egg-laying period. The nest bowl is 100-160 mm in diameter and 60-65 mm deep. The ♀ incubates without ♂ assistance, although he remains in the vicinity through the Incubation period. She leaves the nest 2x/day to feed, covering the eggs with a flap of down before departing. While incubating, she sits tight if approached, only flying off the nest at the last moment, sometimes performing an injury-feigning display.

Laying months: opportunistic in response to rainfall and all months recorded but most records for May-Nov. **Clutch size:** 7-9 (4-13, rarely more); laid at 1-day intervals. **Eggs:** 43.0-49.6-56.8 x 31.0-36.1-45.5 mm; mass 25.5-30.5-39 g. **Incubation period:** 28 days (26-30); by ♀ only; begins when clutch is complete. **Nestling/fledging period:** 7 weeks; young cared for by both sexes.

eggs uncovered   Yellow-billed Duck   eggs covered during female's absence

eggs covered (above), uncovered (below)   African Black Duck

Cape Teal

Cape Shoveler *Anas smithii* Kaapse Slopeend  page 355

Breeds mainly in the highveld grasslands and in the w Cape, patchily elsewhere; nests in grass, weeds, scrub, sedges or other vegetation on the edges of open water on vleis, pans and shallow, temporarily flooded areas; low islands are especially favoured where several pairs may nest close together (e.g. 31 nests on a 170 m² island), or close to other nesting anatids; nests on dry ground but almost always <50 m from water's edge. **Nest:** a warmly lined bowl of dry grass and down placed in a shallow (75-155 mm) scrape in the ground, usually well concealed by overhanging and surrounding vegetation; the nest is 150-170-200 mm in diameter and 75-100-150 mm thick; it is built by the ♀ in 2-10 days before laying when 300-2100 down feathers are added; these are used to cover the eggs when she leaves the nest unattended; she usually does this 2x/day (in morning and late afternoon), joining her mate then to feed. She sits tight when incubating.
Laying months: mainly Jul-Oct, but recorded in all months. **Clutch size:** 9-10 (5-13); laid at 1-day intervals. **Eggs:** 48.4-53.4-59.5 x 34.5-38.8-43.4 mm; mass 34-38-43.5 g. **Incubation period:** 28 days (27-31); by ♀ only; begins when clutch is completed. **Nestling/fledging period:** 8 weeks; young cared for by ♀ only.

Hottentot Teal *Anas hottentota* Gevlekte Eend  page 355

Breeds widely but patchily on shallow, freshwater wetlands that have clumps of emergent bulrushes (*Typha*), reeds (*Phragmites*) or sedges; several pairs may nest 5-20 m apart. **Nest:** placed over water and usually inside a dense reed or sedge tuft, or in a flooded tree or shrub that has been overgrown with rank grass. It is typically ½ m above the water (0.15-0.75 m up), is well concealed, with a single access hole leading into the nest. Old nests of African Moorhen and African Swamphen are occasionally used; nest sites are sometimes reused. The nest is a 150-180 mm wide bowl made with dry plant stems and it is thickly lined with charcoal-coloured down, added during egg-laying. The ♀ leaves the nest 1x/day in the morning, for about an hour, to feed; eggs are then covered with down. While off, she joins the ♂ who remains near the nest throughout the incubation.
Laying months: all months recorded, with a peak between Jan-May. **Clutch size:** 6-7 (5-12); laid at 1-day intervals. **Eggs:** 41.0-44.0-48.0 x 31.0-32.7-34.0 mm. **Incubation period:** 25-27 days; by ♀ only; begins when clutch is complete. **Nestling/fledging period:** 60-65 days; young cared for mainly by ♀, sometimes with ♂ assistance.

Red-billed Teal *Anas erythrorhyncha* Rooibekeend  page 355

Breeds widely, from the semi-arid west to the mesic east; nests on the edges of, and on islands in pans, dams, seasonal vleis and floodplains; adjacent nests may be <10 m apart, and alongside nests of other ducks. **Nest:** always on dry ground but close to water (usually <100 m) and typically on a raised area that is surrounded by water; usually well hidden in thick grass, or under a small, shrubby plant. The nest is a shallow scrape into which is set a bowl of dry grass-blades and feather-down, 150-160-180 mm in diameter and 65-90-100 mm thick. The ♀ selects the site and places a large number (700-2000-3200) of down feathers in the nest during egg-laying; a flap of these is used to cover the eggs when she leaves the nest unattended. She does this 2x/day (early morning, late afternoon) to feed, being off for about 1½ hr each time. While incubating she sits tight and, if approached, only flies up at the last moment, often performing an injury-feigning display when doing so.
Laying months: mainly Dec-Apr, but earlier in the winter-rainfall region (Jul-May). **Clutch size:** 9-10 (5-15); laid at 1-day intervals. **Eggs:** 43.4-49.8-54.1 x 34.5-37.7-41.0 mm; mass 36-37.7-40 g. **Incubation period:** 25-27 days; by ♀ only; begins when clutch is completed. **Nestling/fledging period:** 8 weeks; young cared for by ♀, occasionally assisted by ♂;

Southern Pochard *Netta erythrophthalma* Bruineend  page 354

Breeds widely on freshwater wetlands, especially in temporarily inundated areas (seasonal pans, vleis, floodplains, etc). **Nest:** usually built over shallow water in flooded grass; a broad, deep bowl made of stems of green and dry grass and aquatic plants, often having stems pulled over the top to form a canopy and an access ramp on one side; usually well hidden in rank vegetation, with a tunnel that leads to the nest; occasional nests are placed on dry ground on islands or embankments, hidden in thick grass or beneath a shrub. The nest measures 300-400 mm in diameter and is 100-300 mm high (from water to lip of cup), the cup (160-180 mm diameter, 80 mm deep) lined with 500-850-1100 down feathers, apparently more used in winter nests than summer nests. When off feeding, the ♀ covers the eggs with down flap.
Laying months: all months recorded, peaking in Jan-Apr; earlier in winter-rainfall region (Aug-Nov). **Clutch size:** 8-9 (6-15); laid at 1-day intervals. **Eggs:** 53.2-56.5-62.4 x 41.0-43.8-45.9 mm; mass 59 g. **Incubation period:** 25-26 days (20-28); by ♀ only; begins when clutch is completed. **Nestling/fledging period:** 7-8 weeks; young cared for by ♀, occasionally assisted by ♂.

Maccoa Duck *Oxyura maccoa* Bloubekeend  page 355

Breeds on deep ponds, lakes and pans with emergent vegetation, usually bulrushes (*Typha*) or sedges; mainly on the highveld and in the w Cape. ♂s are polygynous (1♂ with 1-8 mates) and territorial, excluding other ♂s from his territory; his ♀s may nest <3 m apart. **Nest:** a bulky basket made by pulling plant stems down from their standing position, and criss-crossing and weaving these into a bowl about 200 mm in diameter; open cup, 80 mm deep, 100-230 mm above the water; some nests have an access ramp; nests would be conspicuous were they not screened by vegetation. Because they are anchored, nests are prone to flooding if water-levels rise. Old nests of Red-knobbed Coot and Great Crested Grebe are used occasionally. No down lining is added to the nest.
Laying months: most months recorded, but mainly Jan-Apr, earlier in winter-rainfall region (Oct-Dec). **Clutch size:** 5-6 (2-16, >8 probably laid by 2 ♀s); laid at 1-2 day intervals; frequently lays single eggs in nests of other ducks and Red-knobbed Coot – either a case of 'egg-dumping' or incipient parasitism. **Eggs:** 63.0-66.9-72.8 x 45.8-50.5-52.7 mm; mass 73-87.9-98 g; large for the size of the bird; pale blue colour is distinctive. **Incubation period:** 25-27 days; by ♀ only; begins when clutch is completed; she leaves the nest unattended at intervals to feed, away for 11-34-71 min at a time. **Nestling/fledging period:** unknown; young cared for by ♀ only.

Cape Shoveler

Hottentot Teal

Red-billed Teal

Southern Pochard

Maccoa Duck

PENGUINS Family Spheniscidae Worldwide 19 species; 1 (endemic to southern Africa) breeds in Afrotropics. Colonial breeders; monogamous; incubation and parental care is shared by the sexes; eggs white, unmarked, 2/clutch; young are semi-altricial and nidicolous.

African Penguin *Spheniscus demersus* Brilpikkewyn   page 355

Breeds in large colonies, mainly on offshore islands along w coast; numbers are declining and the main breeding concentrations are shifting: in 2006 there were 25 active island colonies, the largest being on St Croix Is in Algoa Bay (17000 pairs), and 3 mainland colonies, the largest at Boulders Beach (established in 1985, now 1000 pairs); Dassen Is, once supporting a million breeding birds, had 21400 pairs in 2001 and only 5000 pairs in 2009. In the larger colonies nesting pairs are spaced at densities of 1-16 nests/100 m². **Nest:** where there is a sufficiently deep substrate of clay or guano, an inclined burrow (about ½ m deep, 18 cm high and 32 cm wide) is excavated by both sexes and the eggs are laid at the end of this on the bare soil or on a sparse lining of plant debris. In the absence of guano, the penguins burrow under plants, rocks, concrete blocks, etc, or they build a rough bowl in the open of whatever loose material is available; these exposed nests are subject to much higher depredation by Kelp Gulls than nests in burrows.

Laying months: all months recorded, but mainly Jan-Sep in South Africa, peaking 1-2 months later in Namibia. **Clutch size:** 2 (1-3); laid at a 3-day interval. **Eggs:** 54.1-68.6-76.0 x 47.2-52.1-55.9 mm; mass 75-106-131 g. **Incubation period:** 37 days (38-41); starts with first-laid egg, shared equally by both sexes, alternating in 1-2 day shifts. **Nestling/fledging period:** 64-73-86 days; cared for by both sexes; young left unguarded from 26-30 days old.

STORM PETRELS Family Hydrobatidae Worldwide 23 species; 1 of these breeds in southern Africa. Monogamous; egg white, unmarked or faintly marked with red; lays a single-egg clutch; young are semi-altricial and nidicolous.

Leach's Storm Petrel *Oceanodroma leucorhoa* Swaelstertstormswael   page 355

Breeding in the region is known from a single site, an offshore island in w Cape. A bird with a brood patch was discovered here for the first time in 1995, and in 1996 and 1997 1-6 active nests were recorded. There has been no subsequent information on the species from the island since this time. **Nest:** a cavity in an old stone wall, 50-60 cm into the wall, accessed by a narrow tunnel entering the wall 25 cm up from the ground; cavity sparsely lined with pieces of woody vegetation. Elsewhere known to excavate a nest burrow in the ground and to reuse the site in successive seasons.

Laying months: Oct-Jan (Dyer Is, South Africa); may relay after early failure (Europe). **Clutch size:** 1. **Eggs:** 32.9 x 23.7 mm; dull white, faintly marked with pale red speckles (South Africa). **Incubation period:** 38-42 days; shared equally by both sexes in 1-3-5 day shifts (Europe). **Nestling/fledging period:** 61-70 days; fed by both sexes (Europe).

GANNETS, BOOBIES Family Sulidae Worldwide 10 species; 1 (endemic to southern Africa) breeds in Afrotropics. A colonial breeder, the world breeding population of Cape Gannet confined to 6 coastal islands, monogamous; egg a long oval, unmarked, chalky white, 1/clutch; nestling altricial and nidicolous.

Cape Gannet *Morus capensis* Witmalgas   page 355

Breeds in large, densely packed colonies ('gannetries') on six offshore islands (Mercury, Ichaboe, Possession, Lambert's Bay, Malgas and Bird) in the region; the largest colony (>60000 pairs) is on Bird Is in Algoa Bay, e Cape; small numbers have occasionally nested on other islands (Robben, Dyer); pairs show strong colony- and nest site fidelity. Breeding birds have been impacted by invasions of Cape Fur Seals onto some islands. **Nest:** a mound of guano, twigs, feathers and other material, scraped together by both sexes; 8-106-300 mm high with a shallow depression on top on which the egg is laid; nesting density 2.8-3.5-6.3/m²; nests spaced 0.4-0.6 m apart. On islands where guano is absent or has been recently collected, nest mounds are rudimentary or non-existent (<3 cm high). Most gannetries are subject to guano collection outside the breeding season (Mar-Jun).

Laying months: mainly Oct-Dec; breeding is over by Mar; may relay 2-4 weeks after egg-loss. **Clutch size:** 1, rarely 2. **Eggs:** 73,0-82.5-84.0 x 45.6-47.6-49.0 mm; mass 98 g. **Incubation period:** 43-44 days; by both sexes, in shifts of 1-2 days; incubated by holding egg under webbed feet. **Nestling/fledging period:** 90-97-105 days; cared for by both sexes; left largely unattended after 40 days.

African Penguin   nesting in excavated burrows

Leach's Storm Petrel   nest hole indicated

African Penguin   an open nest

Cape Gannet   portion of the breeding colony at Lambert's Bay

Grebes

GREBES Family Podicipedidae Worldwide 21 species; 3 breed in Afrotropics (plus 2 more in Madagascar); all 3 breed in southern Africa. Monogamous; pairs nest solitarily or in dispersed colonies. Grebes build a floating nest from aquatic plants which is added to throughout the incubation; eggs are biconical, initially unmarked white, but soon becoming stained brown by the nest; 3-5/clutch. Two unusual grebe behaviours are: the incubating parent covers the eggs with nesting material before leaving the nest unattended; and young chicks are carried on the parents' backs. Young leave the nest within hours of hatching and they are precocial and semi-nidifugous.

Great Crested Grebe *Podiceps cristatus* Kuifkopdobbertjie   page 356

Largely confined to South Africa, it breeds on larger (>5 ha) freshwater lakes, dams and pans, and especially on waterbodies that have a fringe of emergent vegetation (grass or sedges) in which the nest can be concealed. Smaller waterbodies likely to support only single nesting pairs whereas very large pans may support up to 50 pairs, and here pairs may nest semi-gregariously with adjacent nests 2-25 m apart. **Nest:** a floating heap of sodden plant material measuring 40-60 cm in diameter (of which 28-45 cm is exposed above the water); cup 40-70 mm above the water. Nests are usually situated in water >2 m deep and >5 m from the shore; they are hidden in emergent plants where available but some nests are on open water; old platforms of Red-knobbed Coots are sometimes used. Both sexes build the nest in about 8 days, dragging aquatic plants to the site in their bills and adding further material during the incubation. The incubating bird covers the eggs with nest material if disturbed off the nest.
Laying months: mainly Nov-Feb in winter-rainfall region but Apr-Aug elsewhere; all months recorded. **Clutch size:** 3-4 (2-7); laid at 2-day intervals. **Eggs:** 47.0-52.9-57.0 x 33.0-35.5-37.8 m; mass 35-38-43 g. **Incubation period:** 27-29-30 days; by both sexes; begins before clutch complete. **Nestling/fledging period:** 71-79 days (Europe); young cared for by both sexes; they leave the nest on hatching and are carried on parent's back up to 21 days; forage for themselves from 56 days.

Black-necked Grebe *Podiceps nigricollis* Swartnekdobbertjie   page 356

A nomadic species, seldom present in one area for long; breeds mainly in the w Cape, karoo and grassland regions, nesting mostly on recently filled freshwater and saline pans, especially those where some emergent vegetation (grass or sedges) provides cover for nests. Breeds in colonies; usually 5-10 pairs/colony, up to 65 recorded; sometimes nests in association with Whiskered Terns. **Nest:** a floating heap of sodden plant material 40-50 cm across with a shallow cup on top raised 50-100 mm above the water; nests are usually anchored to a plant; usually in deep water (>1 m) and >5 m from the shore. Both sexes build, completing a nest in a week, dragging aquatic weeds to the site in their bills. The incubating bird covers the eggs with nest material if disturbed off the nest.
Laying months: mainly Jan-Apr, earlier in winter-rainfall areas (Sep-Oct); but most months recorded. **Clutch size:** 3-4 (2-7); laid at 1-2 day intervals. **Eggs:** 33.5-42.3-49.2 x 22.0-28.4-33.3 mm. **Incubation period:** 20-21-22 days; by both sexes; begins before clutch complete. **Nestling/fledging period:** not recorded; young cared for by both sexes.

Little Grebe *Tachybaptus ruficollis* Kleindobbertjie   page 356

Breeds commonly and widely in the region and found on most freshwater wetlands, favouring recently rain-filled waterbodies for breeding. Pairs nest solitarily but as many as 22 pairs are recorded nesting simultaneously on a 30-ha pan; adjacent nests usually >100 m apart, occasionally as close as 13 m apart. **Nest:** a floating heap of sodden plant material 30-40 cm across, with a shallow cup on top, raised 50-150 mm above the water; nests are usually placed over deep water (>1 m), and mostly screened from view by emergent plants, to which the nest is also sometimes anchored. Both sexes build, dragging aquatic weeds to the site in their bills and adding further material to the nest throughout the incubation. The pair is especially vocal in the early stages of the nesting cycle but become silent once incubation commences. The incubating bird covers the eggs with nest material if disturbed off the nest.
Laying months: mainly Dec-Mar, earlier in winter-rainfall areas (Oct-Nov); but all months recorded. **Clutch size:** 3-5 (2-9); laid at 1 day intervals. **Eggs:** 32.0-37.8-39.5 x 23.8-25.6-28.8 mm. **Incubation period:** 20 days (18-25); by both sexes; begins with first-laid egg. **Nestling/fledging period:** young cared for by both sexes; they leave the nest on hatching; are carried on parent's back when small; full grown at 50 days and can flutter across the water then.

Great Crested Grebe

Black-necked Grebe

Black-necked Grebe   part of a larger breeding colony shared with Whiskered Terns

eggs covered during parent's absence   Little Grebe

Flamingos, Storks

FLAMINGOS Family Phoenicopteridae Worldwide 6 species; 2 breed in Afrotropics, both breed in southern Africa. Both species breed erratically in large colonies at remote, inhospitable sites, sometimes in spectacular numbers, nests packed close together. Monogamous; sexes share nest-building, incubation and nestling care; egg an elongate oval, white, unmarked, chalky-textured, 1/clutch; chicks are precocial and semi-nidifugous; young form crèches from 1-2 weeks old.

Greater Flamingo *Phoenicopterus roseus* Grootflamink   page 356
Breeds regularly in southern Africa at only two sites (Sua Pan in Botswana and Etosha Pan in Namibia); elsewhere it has attempted to breed at <10 other sites, nowhere more than once or twice. Breeds colonially, nesting in huge, densely packed colonies numbering up to 40000 pairs at Sua and 27000 pairs at Etosha; breeding attempted in 17/40 years at the latter site; elsewhere colonies have numbered 120-800 pairs. At Sua and Etosha it nests alongside Lesser Flamingos, usually arriving and initiating breeding 1-2 months before them. Both sites depend on above-average rainfall to fill the pans and create favourable breeding conditions, and nesting success is dependent on how long these conditions persist. These colonies are located far into the pans on low islands surrounded by temporary water. **Nest:** a turret-shaped mound of mud, generally broader and squatter than that of Lesser Flamingo, 38-54 cm basal diameter, 30-40 diameter at the top, 7-14 cm in height, with a shallow depression (20-50 mm) on top; in the absence of mud, the egg is laid on bare ground. Nest density 1½/m²; nests spaced 35 cm apart. Both sexes build the nest.
Laying months: dependent on rainfall – earliest laying occurs in Nov, more usually in Jan-Mar, continuing through to Aug if suitable conditions persist. **Clutch size:** 1, rarely 2. **Eggs:** 79.0-88.8-103.0 x 48.3-54.0-54.1 mm. **Incubation period:** 28-31 days; shared equally by both sexes. **Nestling/fledging period:** young crèches from 3 weeks old; they fly at 75-90 days; brooded and fed by both sexes.

Lesser Flamingo *Phoeniconaias minor* Kleinflamink   page 356
Breeds in southern Africa at two natural sites (Sua Pan in Botswana and Etosha Pan in Namibia) and, since 2007, on a man-made island at Kimberley. Breeds colonially, nesting in huge, densely packed colonies numbering up to 150000 pairs at Sua, 1000 pairs at Kimberley. At Sua and Etosha its nests alongside Greater Flamingos, usually arriving and initiating breeding 1-2 months after them. Both sites depend on above-average rainfall to fill the pans and create favourable breeding conditions, and nesting success is dependent on how long these conditions persist; a series of low islands in the centre of Sua Pan is used for each breeding attempt with 4000-28000 nest/ha built here. **Nest:** a conical turret of mud 5-21-39 cm tall, 35-43-56 cm wide at its base, with a shallow depression on top (35 mm deep, 160 mm wide) in which the egg is laid. Nests are closely packed (up to 5, usually 1,4 nests/m²) and usually dispersed in several sub-colonies, each consisting of hundreds or thousands of nests. Small groups of Lesser Flamingos (usually immature birds) occasionally build clusters of nests at sites other than these mentioned (e.g. on sewage works and commercial saltpans) but they rarely lay eggs here and never rear young.
Laying months: at Sua and Etosha laying dependent on rainfall – mostly initiated in Jan-Feb, peaking in Apr and persisting through to Aug if conditions remain suitable; at Kimberley, peak in May-Jun. **Clutch size:** 1, very rarely 2. **Eggs:** 72.0-82.3-94.0 x 44.0-49.9-56.0 mm; mass 61-97-118 g. **Incubation period:** 28 days (East Africa); by both sexes; change-over 1x/day. **Nestling/fledging period:** young join crèches at 6 days; fly weakly at 70-75 days (East Africa); young brooded and fed by both sexes.

STORKS Family Ciconiidae Worldwide 19 species; 8 breed in Afrotropics, 7 breed in southern Africa; 4 are solitary breeders, 3 are colonial; monogamous, the sexes sharing incubation and nestling care; nest a large stick platform; eggs white, unmarked, chalky textured; 2-5/clutch, depending on species. Chicks are semi-altricial and nidicolous.

African Openbill *Anastomus lamelligerus* Oopbekooievaar   page 356
Breeds erratically and opportunistically in savanna areas where extensive shallow-water habitat has resulted from above-average rains. A colonial nester, up to 180 pairs/colony; sometimes nests in association with Yellow-billed Storks, cormorants, darters, spoonbills or herons. **Nest:** a loosely constructed platform of sticks placed in a fork of a temporarily flooded tree, 4-10 nests/tree; occasionally nests in reedbeds, when reed stems are used. Nests measure 40-60 cm in diameter, 60-200 mm high; cup 20 cm wide and 50 mm deep, lined with grasses or aquatic plants. Nest height variable: 0,3-10 m up from the water. The nest is built by both sexes over a period of a week.
Laying months: mainly Jan-Mar, also Aug-Oct in Okavango. **Clutch size:** 3-4 (2-5); laid at 2-day intervals. **Eggs:** 51.0-55.4-61.4 x 36.7-40.0-43.2 mm; mass 35-50 g. **Incubation period:** 25 days (21-30); by both sexes; begins with first-laid egg. **Nestling/fledging period:** about 50-55 days; brooded and fed by both sexes.

Yellow-billed Stork *Mycteria ibis* Nimmersat   page 356
Breeds on large, seasonally inundated wetlands, most regularly in the Okavango (Botswana), and in n KwaZulu-Natal where 10-100 pairs nest annually; breeds erratically and seldom >20 pairs at a few other sites in the Kruger National Park and elsewhere. A colonial nester, usually breeding in association with herons, ibises, pelicans, darters, spoonbills and/or cormorants. **Nest:** a saucer-shaped platform of sticks 0.6-1.0 m in diameter and 15-30 cm high, the shallow cup lined with dry grass or leaves. Nests are placed in trees over water, 4-10 m up, adjacent nests sometimes touching; in the Okavango, 'gomoti' thickets (*Ficus verruculosa*) are favoured; in Mkuze and elsewhere tall acacias; the same trees are regularly reused in successive seasons. Both sexes build the nest in 7-10 days and they continue adding material through the breeding cycle.
Laying months: mainly Feb-Jul in KwaZulu-Natal, Jun-Sep (Mar-Oct) in the Okavango. **Clutch size:** 3 (1-4); laid at 2-day intervals. **Eggs:** 59.0-66.2-72.3 x 42.0-44.4-47.6 mm; mass 77 g. **Incubation period:** 30 days; by both sexes. **Nestling/fledging period:** 55 days; young brooded and fed by both sexes.

Greater Flamingo   part of breeding colony on Makgadikgadi Pan

part of breeding colony on Makgadikgadi Pan   Lesser Flamingo

African Openbill

Yellow-billed Stork

Storks

White Stork *Ciconia ciconia* **Witooievaar** page 357

Mainly a non-breeding Palearctic migrant to the region, with a small (<10 pairs), isolated, breeding population in s Cape; first known to breed here between 1933-1941 (Oudtshoorn); since 1961 several more have nested regularly in open, agricultural landscapes in the Bredasdorp district. **Nest:** a large stick platform 80-150 cm in diameter and 1-2 m high, built in a large, lone-standing tree, 2½-13 m up from the ground; melkbos, rooikrans, blackwood and eucalypt have been used, one was on top of a tree-aloe, another on a platform erected for the birds. Nests are reused in successive years and they increase in size as material is added each season. Pairs reoccupy their nests in Aug, and both sexes refurbish the nest in the month before they lay and building continues through the nesting cycle.

Laying months: Sep-Nov (southern Africa). **Clutch size:** 4-5 (2-5) (southern Africa); laid at 1-4 day intervals (southern Africa). **Eggs:** 79.3 x 52.0 mm (southern Africa); mass 96-111-119 g (Europe). **Incubation period:** 30 days; by both sexes. **Nestling/fledging period:** 45-70 days; young brooded and fed by both sexes.

Woolly-necked Stork *Ciconia episcopus* **Wolnekooievaar** page 357

Breeds sparsely in the region, mostly close to low-lying wetlands, rivers, estuaries, etc.; increasingly adapted to suburban environments in KwaZulu-Natal (Durban-Pietermaritzburg). Pairs nest solitarily, rarely in loose aggregations of <5 pairs. **Nest:** a flat platform of sticks placed high up (usually >10 m) in a fork of a lateral branch inside a well-foliaged tree, often overhanging water, along a river or in swamp forest; it measures 0,6-1,0 m in diameter and is 30-40 cm high; cup, 34 cm wide, is lined with dry grass and a few leaves. Both sexes build the nest and continue adding material during the nesting cycle. Nests are sometimes reused in successive seasons (one for 4 years); if a new one is built, it is usually placed close to the previous year's nest.

Laying months: Aug-Dec. **Clutch size:** 3 (2-4); laid at 2-3 day intervals. **Eggs:** 59.3-62.0-67.0 x 43.0-44.4-45.4 mm; 53-59.3-70 g. **Incubation period:** 30-35 days; shared by both sexes, changing over at intervals of 2-4 hrs; starts with first-laid egg. **Nestling/fledging period:** 55-65 days; start 'branching' from 40 days; brooded and fed by both sexes.

Black Stork *Ciconia nigra* **Grootswartooievaar** page 357

Breeds on cliffs, sites varying from high escarpment cliffs to rock faces on isolated koppies, along ravines and in gorges. Pairs nest solitarily and are widely spaced, adjacent nests seldom <2 km apart. **Nest:** a platform of dry sticks placed on a flat ledge or in a pothole, often overhung by rock above and sheer below; along rivers overhanging water, sometimes <10 m up from cliff-base but mostly higher (some >100 m up); is typically about 1 m in diameter and 20 cm high with a cup that is thickly lined with dry grass; very large nests (2 m across and 2 m high) are exceptional and were probably built originally by Verreaux's Eagles. Nest is often reused in successive years, some sites occupied for decades; smaller nests often disintegrate as nestlings mature, only a few sticks remaining by the time they fledge. Both sexes build or refurbish the nest in early winter; in some years they do this, but do not lay.

Laying months: mainly Jun (Apr-Sep); laying does not occur every year. **Clutch size:** 2-5; laid at 2-day intervals. **Eggs:** 60.0-68.4-74.0 x 45.0-48.7-56.0 mm; mass 86 g. **Incubation period:** 35-36 days; by both sexes; starts before clutch complete. **Nestling/fledging period:** 63-71 days (Europe); young brooded and fed by both sexes.

Saddle-billed Stork *Ephippiorhynchus senegalensis* **Saalbekooievaar** page 357

Breeds very sparsely in the savanna region, always associated with larger rivers (1 pair/13 km on Zambezi), freshwater lakes, pans and floodplains (1 pair/100 km^2 in Okavango). Pairs occupy year-round territories and nest solitarily. **Nest:** built on the top of a large tree, 4-30 m up, <500 m from water; in appearance similar to nest of a large eagle or vulture; old nests of Secretarybird may be used. It is a substantial platform of sticks, 1-2 m in diameter and 0,3-1,5 m high, with a wide, deep central cup that is thickly lined with dry grass. Nest, or same nest site, is reused in successive years; it is built or refurbished by both sexes. Pairs do not breed annually, laying most frequently in years of good rainfall, least frequently during droughts.

Laying months: mainly Feb-Jun (Jan-Aug). **Clutch size:** 3 (1-4). **Eggs:** 75.5-80.1-86.3 x 55.3-57.6-61.0 mm. **Incubation period:** about 30-35 days; shared equally by both sexes, alternating in long (1-6 hr) shifts. **Nestling/fledging period:** about 70-100 days; young brooded and fed by both sexes.

Marabou Stork *Leptoptilos crumeniferus* **Maraboe** page 357

Breeds annually in the Okavango (50-200 pairs); sporadically and in small numbers elsewhere in n savanna areas; none in South Africa, one colony in Swaziland. Nests colonially, using flooded 'gomoti' (*Ficus verruculosa*) thickets in the Okavango, but mostly in large, isolated trees (acacias, baobabs) elsewhere; beyond southern Africa colonies are also on cliffs and in trees in towns and villages. **Nest:** a large, flat platform of sticks, about 1 m across and 20-30 cm high with a shallow cup, 36 cm wide, lined with grass and other plant material. In Okavango breeds alongside other colonial waterbirds, usually in the highest positions, 2-8 m up from the water, nests <1 m apart; in Swaziland 1-3-5 nests/tree, all 5-6 m up in *Acacia tortilis*; elsewhere, nests much higher, 10-40 m from the ground. Both sexes build nest in 7-10 days and they continue adding material during incubation.

Laying months: mainly Jun-Sep but most months recorded. **Clutch size:** 2-3 (1-4); laid at 1-3 day intervals. **Eggs:** 71.0-76.1-86.2 x 50.0-55.9-62.0 mm; mass 138 g. **Incubation period:** 29-31 days; by both sexes; starts with first-laid egg. **Nestling/fledging period:** 95-115 days; young cared for by both sexes.

White Stork

Woolly-necked Stork

Black Stork

Saddle-billed Stork

Marabou Stork

Ibises, Spoonbill

IBISES, SPOONBILLS Family Threskiornithidae Worldwide 34 species (28 ibises, 6 spoonbills); 11 breed in Afrotropics, 5 in southern Africa; 4 are colonial breeders, 1 nests solitarily; monogamous, the sexes sharing incubation and nestling care; all build a saucer-shaped nest platform; eggs, 2-3/clutch, colour variable between species; chicks are nidicolous and semi-altricial.

African Sacred Ibis *Threskiornis aethiopicus* Skoorsteenveër   page 357

Breeds widely and commonly across the region. Nests colonially, usually associated with other waterbirds in mixed-species heronries; typically 10-50 pairs/colony, occasionally 100s and up to 1500 pairs, when a large part of the heronry is monopolised by this species. Breeding sites vary, usually in reedbeds or trees over water, but on protected islands may nest on the bare ground. **Nest:** a saucer-shaped bowl of twigs or reed-stems, 28-34-43 cm in diameter and 20 cm high; in large colonies, nests often merge to form rafts of abutting nests (as shown opposite); the nest is built by both sexes, ♂ gathering material and ♀ building. In mass-breeding attempts laying and hatching is well synchronised and chicks gather and remain in crèches.
Laying months: mainly Aug-Nov; but all months recorded. **Clutch size:** 2-3 (2-5). **Eggs:** 59.0-66.2-73.8 × 39.7-43.6-51.2 mm; mass 62 g. **Incubation period:** 21-25 days; by both sexes; begins when clutch is completed. **Nestling/fledging period:** fly weakly 35-40 days (Ethiopia); brooded and fed by both sexes; young join crèches at 2-3 weeks.

African Spoonbill *Platalea alba* Lepelaar   page 357

Breeds widely but sparsely in the region, mostly in years of above-average rainfall. It nests colonially, 5-20 pairs/colony, rarely as many as 200 pairs; usually, but not invariably alongside other colonial-breeding species, especially African Sacred Ibis. Nesting sites vary from reedbeds or trees over water (½-6 m up), to nesting on bare ground on protected islands. **Nest:** a platform made of reed or sedge stems, or twigs if in a tree; it measures 37-48 cm in diameter and is 20 cm high; cup, 6-11 cm wide, lined with dry grass. The nest is built by both sexes, ♂ gathering material and ♀ building; it is added to through the incubation.
Laying months: Feb-Dec, but mainly Aug-Oct (sw Cape) and Mar-Aug (elsewhere). **Clutch size:** 2-3, rarely 4; laid at 2-day intervals. **Eggs:** 57.0-68.0-82.0 × 39.7-45.0-48.0 mm; mass 69 g. **Incubation period:** 25-26-29 days; by both sexes; begins before clutch complete. **Nestling/fledging period:** young flee nest if disturbed at 2 weeks, join crèches at 3 weeks, fly weakly at 4 weeks; young brooded and fed by both sexes.

Glossy Ibis *Plegadis falcinellus* Glansibis   page 358

First known to breed in southern Africa (in Gauteng) in 1950; prior to that assumed to be a non-breeding summer visitor from the Palearctic. It now breeds widely across the region, especially in above-average rainfall years, nesting colonially in mixed-species heronries, up to 200 pairs/colony, its nests dispersed, rather than clustered, in such colonies. Most sites are in large, undisturbed reedbeds over water, less often in flooded trees, and in 'gomoti' (*Ficus verruculosa*) fig thickets in the Okavango. **Nest:** a platform of reed or sedge-stems, 23-30-33 cm in diameter and 10-15 cm high; cup 5-8 cm deep, lined with finer plant stems. The nest is built by both sexes in 2 days (n America); ♂ collects material and ♀ builds.
Laying months: mainly Oct-Feb (Jul-Mar); 2 months earlier in winter-rainfall region (Sep-Nov). **Clutch size:** 3 (2-4); laid at 1-day intervals (n America). **Eggs:** 49.3-51.1-54.7 × 34.8-35.5-37.1 mm; mass 31-39 g. **Incubation period:** 20-23 days (n America); by both sexes. **Nestling/fledging period:** young gather in crèches from 2 weeks; fly at 6 weeks; brooded and fed by both sexes.

Southern Bald Ibis *Geronticus calvus* Kalkoenibis   page 358

Breeds on cliffs in hilly and mountainous mesic grasslands of e South Africa. A colonial nester, with single pairs occasionally nesting solitarily; colonies number 5-20 pairs, a few reach as many as 120 pairs in some years; most sites have been in regular use for decades, some for >100 years. Most larger colonies are on sheltered cliffs overhanging a ravine, and many of these are located alongside waterfalls; exposed scarp cliffs are used in places, as are rock faces in abandoned quarries; a few small tree-nesting colonies are known (in pines, eucalypts). **Nest:** a flimsy bowl of twigs, weed-stems, feathers, dry grass; 35 cm in diameter and 10 cm high; it rapidly becomes encrusted with the birds' faeces and disintegrates as the nestlings grow. It is built by both sexes, ♂ gathering material and ♀ building. Numbers breeding annually varies according to previous year's rainfall, fewer nesting in dry years.
Laying months: mainly Aug-Sep (Jul-Nov); single-brooded; relays after an early failure. **Clutch size:** 2 (1-5); laid at a 1-day interval. **Eggs:** 57.0-64.2-71.0 × 38.0-42.8-49.0 mm; mass 68 g. **Incubation period:** 27-31 days; shared equally by both sexes; change-overs 1-4/day; begins with first-laid egg. **Nestling/fledging period:** young leave nest at 5 weeks; fly 6-7 weeks; brooded and fed by both sexes.

Hadeda Ibis *Bostrychia hagedash* Hadeda   page 358

Breeds widely and commonly everywhere except in arid areas. Pairs nest solitarily, though nests of adjacent pairs occasionally <10 m apart. **Nest:** a thin platform of sticks, some so transparent that the eggs can be see though them from below; it is built on a lateral forked branch of a tree (typically well away from main trunk), often overhanging a river or dam, usually 4-5 m up (1-25 m); nests increasingly frequently in suburban parks, gardens, timber plantations and on man-made structures (telephone poles, pylons, pergolas, dam walls). Nest measures 20-45 cm in diameter and 10-15 cm high; built by both sexes in 10 days. Same nest occasionally reused in successive years (one for 4 years); more usually a new nest built on same site, or close by. In contrast to their normal noisy behaviour at other times, nesting birds are relatively silent.
Laying months: mainly Sep-Nov (Jun-Feb). **Clutch size:** 3 (1-6); laid at 2-day intervals. **Eggs:** 54.0-60.3-62.0 × 38.0-42.0-48.0 mm; mass 84 g. **Incubation period:** 25-28 days; by both sexes in shifts up to 3 hrs; begins with first-laid egg. **Nestling/fledging period:** 34 days (32-37); young brooded and fed by both sexes.

African Sacred Ibis

African Spoonbill & African Sacred Ibis

African Spoonbill

Glossy Ibis

Southern Bald Ibis

Hadeda Ibis

HERONS, EGRETS, BITTERNS Family Ardeidae Worldwide 66 species; 22 breed in Afrotropics, 17 in southern Africa. Many members of this family are gregarious birds that forage, roost and breed together. Breeding colonies can range in size from a few pairs to 10s of 1000s of birds of mixed species, and the latter often provide remarkable bird spectacles. Large breeding colonies are known as 'heronries' and, when several species are involved, as 'mixed-species heronries'; it is not unusual at highly favoured sites to have 5-10 species of herons, as well as cormorants, darters, ibises, spoonbills, storks and others nesting alongside one another. Heronries are typically located where they are protected from predators, often sited in trees over water, in reedbeds, or on islands. All ardeids build simple, saucer-shaped nest platforms made of twigs, reeds or other plant stems, their size varying according to size of bird; eggs are oval-shaped, unmarked, in most cases, pale blue or white, 3-5/clutch. In many ardeids, hormonal changes at the start of the nesting cycle result in bill, cere and eye-colour changing briefly and/or elongated plumes ('aigrettes') growing from crown, chest or back. Breeding is much influenced by rainfall and is erratic in many of the aquatic herons, with minimal nesting during droughts and large-scale breeding during high-rainfall periods. All but a few ardeids are monogamous; chicks are semi-altricial and nidicolous.

Goliath Heron *Ardea goliath* Reusereier
page 358

Breeds widely but very sparsely throughout the region on large permanent wetlands, dams, estuaries and rivers. Pairs either nest solitarily or in monospecific aggregations of 2-7 pairs, or they may join other species in mixed-species heronries. Nest sites are varied; most are placed in flooded trees or bushes, 1-10 m up from the water; reedbeds are used in places, occasionally bushes growing out of cliff faces; on protected islands, the nest may be built on bare ground. **Nest:** a large, saucer-shaped platform built with sticks and/or reed-stems, lined with grass and finer plant material; it measures 1-1½ m in diameter and is 30-75 cm high. It is built by both sexes. **Laying months:** mainly Aug-Nov; but all months commonly recorded. **Clutch size:** 3 (2-5). **Eggs:** 64.8-72.0-76.0 x 51.4-53.1-55.5 m; mass 92-108-117 g. **Incubation period:** 24-30 days; by both sexes; begins with first-laid egg. **Nestling/fledging period:** 40 days; young brooded and fed by both sexes.

Grey Heron *Ardea cinerea* Bloureier
page 358

Breeds widely throughout the region, associated everywhere with rivers, lakes, floodplains or other large waterbodies. Nests colonially, usually in small numbers (usually 2-3 pairs and seldom >20), and often alongside other breeding herons, egrets, cormorants, ibises, etc. in mixed-species heronries. Sites used range from tall trees, usually over water, reedbeds, bushes growing out of cliff faces, or on bare ground on a protected island. As with the next species, this heron commands the most central and highest sites for its nests, above those of the smaller species. **Nest:** a large, saucer-shaped platform of sticks and/or reed-stems, 44-73 cm in diameter and 19-23 cm high. It is built by both sexes, ♂ collecting material and ♀ constructing the nest.

Laying months: mainly Jul-Nov, but all months recorded. **Clutch size:** 3 (2-4); laid at 2-3 day intervals. **Eggs:** 53.0-60.4-72.0 x 34.0-43.2-48.8 mm; mass 61 g. **Incubation period:** 23-25-27 days; by both sexes; begins with first-laid egg. **Nestling/fledging period:** young 'branch' from 20 days, fly at about 52 days; young brooded and fed by both sexes.

Black-headed Heron *Ardea melanocephala* Swartkopreier
page 358

Breeds widely in all but the most arid areas; a colonial nester, sometimes nesting in monospecific groups of 5-30 pairs, these often far from water, frequently situated in tall trees alongside farm homesteads; more usually, pairs (up to 160) nest alongside other species in mixed-species heronries and these are usually in large reedbeds over water, less often in trees. In such heronries this species commands the most central and highest sites for its nests, above those of smaller species. Sites are reused annually or intermittently, dependent on rainfall, and some are known to have been in use for 50+ years. **Nest:** a large, saucer-shaped platform of sticks and/or stems of reeds or weeds, 44-60-73 cm in diameter and 19-20-23 cm high. Both sexes build, the ♂ bringing material, ♀ constructing the nest.

Laying months: all months, but more frequent in the rainy season. **Clutch size:** 3 (2-4); laid at 2-day intervals. **Eggs:** 52.0-61.3-73.0 x 39.0-43.7-46.1 mm; mass 60 g. **Incubation period:** 25 days (23-27); shared equally by both sexes, in shifts of 3-3½ hr; begins with first-laid egg. **Nestling/fledging period:** 52 days (40-55); young brooded and fed by both sexes.

Purple Heron *Ardea purpurea* Rooireier
page 358

Breeds widely but sparsely, and largely absent from the semi-arid and arid areas. Pairs nest solitarily in places, but are more usually colonial breeders, typically 2-25 pairs (occasionally up to 100 pairs), either nesting in a monospecific colony or alongside other species in a mixed-species heronry. Tall, dense reedbeds of *Phragmites* or *Typha*, or sedges, over water are the favoured nesting site for this species; in the Okavango, flooded 'gomoti' fig thickets are also used. **Nest:** a saucer-shaped, loosely made platform of reed-stems and sticks, placed 2-3 m up from the water; it measures 20-36-76 cm in diameter and is 10-18-46 cm high, those in *Typha* apparently less substantial than those in *Phragmites*. The ♂ chooses the nest site, both sexes build.

Laying months: all months recorded; peaks in Aug-Oct in permanent wetlands, later in the summer (Jan-Jun) in seasonally flooded wetlands. **Clutch size:** 3-4 (2-5); laid at 1-3 day intervals. **Eggs:** 49.7-55.8-67.5 x 37.0-40.1-45.0 mm; mass 39-47-59 g. **Incubation period:** 25-26-27 days; by both sexes in long, irregular shifts; begins with first-laid egg. **Nestling/fledging period:** young 'branch' from 20 days; fly at 40-50 days; brooded and fed by both sexes.

Grey Heron & Goliath Heron

Goliath Heron

Grey Heron

Black-headed Heron (TWO ABOVE)

Purple Heron

Egrets

Great Egret *Ardea alba* Grootwitreier
page 358

Breeds sparsely and erratically in southern Africa, mostly in years of above-average rainfall. Colonial, invariably nesting alongside other species in mixed-species heronries, from 2-3 pairs/colony up to 200; little breeding synchrony is shown in large colonies, some pairs starting to nest when others have large young. Most large nesting colonies are in *Phragmites* reedbeds, but trees over water are also used; nests in mixed-species colonies are typically placed as high and as central as possible. **Nest:** a saucer-shaped platform, untidy and loosely made from reed-stems (or sticks if nesting in trees); 2-3 m above the water in reedbeds, up to 8 m in trees; it measures 29-34-46 cm in diameter and is 9-12-15 cm high, distinctly smaller than the nests of Grey and Black-headed Heron. Both sexes build, the ♂ collecting the material and the ♀ constructing the nest, and material continues to be added during incubation.

Laying months: mainly Dec-Feb (May-Mar), rarely in other months. **Clutch size:** 3-4 (2-5); laid at 2-day intervals. **Eggs:** 51.1-56.0-65.6 x 30.9-39.8-45.5 mm; mass 61 g. **Incubation period:** 24-26-27 days; shared equally by both sexes with change-overs 3x/day; begins with first-laid egg. **Nestling/fledging period:** young fly weakly at 40 days, strongly at 45-50 days; brooded and fed by both sexes.

Yellow-billed Egret (Intermediate Egret) *Egretta intermedia* Geelbekwitreier
page 358

Breeds widely but sparsely throughout the region. Nests colonially, and almost invariably nesting alongside other species in large, mixed-species heronries; from 2-70 pairs/colony; nests are dispersed (not clustered) within these colonies. Breeding sites are usually over water and mostly in reedbeds (1-2 m above the water), less often in trees (up to 6 m); sites are commonly re-used annually. **Nest:** a saucer-shaped platform, made from sticks and/or reed-stems, measuring 20-26-80 cm in diameter and is 15-40 cm high; built by both sexes, ♀ collecting material and ♀ building.

Laying months: all months recorded, but peaks in Sep-Feb in summer-rainfall areas, Aug-Oct in winter-rainfall areas. **Clutch size:** 2-3 (2-5). **Eggs:** 43.8-48.7-53.5 x 33.2-35.5-39.1 mm; mass 35-38-42 g. **Incubation period:** 24-27 days; by both sexes. **Nestling/fledging period:** young leave nest at 21 days; fly at 35 days; brooded and fed by both sexes.

Western Cattle Egret *Bulbulcus ibis* Veereier
page 358

Breeds widely and commonly, and the most abundant ardeid in the region. Nests colonially, either in monospecific colonies, or in large mixed-species heronries where they often outnumber all the other nesting birds combined; numbers/colony variable, from <50 to >10 000 pairs. Most breeding occurs in years of above-average rainfall. Colonies are often over water, either in *Phragmites* reedbeds or in trees; it also nests, in agricultural areas, in trees far from water. Some sites are reused in successive seasons, others used once and not again. **Nest:** a loosely made, saucer-shaped platforms of dry twigs, weed- or reed-stems; nests are often close together, some touching; in mixed heronries this species usually nests well below the nests of larger herons. The nest measures 17-30-44 cm in diameter and is 6-12-25 cm high, with a central depression about 50 mm deep. Both sexes build, taking 5-10 days to complete nest and material continues to be added to it during incubation. Collectively, the nests in a large colony comprise an estimated 12 million sticks and they have a mass of 2 tons. Breeding colonies are very conspicuous, noisy, smelly places and they are not easily overlooked.

Laying months: a summer nester, between Sep-Mar; earlier in the winter-rainfall region (Sep-Oct) than elsewhere (Oct-Jan). **Clutch size:** 3 (2-7); laid at 1-2 day intervals. **Eggs:** 40.0-44.9-52.1 x 29.8-33.8-35.5 mm; mass 25-27-30 g. **Incubation period:** 22-24-26 days; shared equally by both sexes with change-overs 1-4x/day; begins with first-laid egg. **Nestling/fledging period:** 25-30-35 days, but young clamber off nest if alarmed from 9-15 days; young brooded and fed by both sexes.

Little Egret *Egretta garzetta* Kleinwitreier
page 358

A colonial breeder, mostly nesting alongside other species in large, mixed-species heronries; from 2-120 pairs/colony; nests are dispersed (not clustered) within mixed-species colonies and locating and distinguishing Little Egret nests from those of Cattle Egrets and other egrets in the colony is impossible unless parent birds are seen in attendance. Nesting sites are usually over water, either in trees or in reedbeds; also nests at a few sites in bushes growing on cliff-faces. **Nest:** a saucer-shaped platform, made from sticks and/or reed-stems, measuring 17-26-35 cm in diameter and 12 cm high; it is built by both sexes, the ♂ collecting material and the ♀ building.

Laying months: mainly Nov-Mar in summer-rainfall areas, Aug-Dec in winter-rainfall areas. **Clutch size:** 2-3 (2-5); laid at 1-2 day intervals. **Eggs:** 41.0-46.5-58.1 x 31.0-34.2-43.4 mm; mass 25-28-30 g. **Incubation period:** 21-25 days; by both sexes; begins with first egg. **Nestling/fledging period:** young leave nest at 30 days; fly at 40-50 days; brooded and fed by both sexes.

Great Egret

Yellow-billed Egret

Western Cattle Egret

Little Egret

Egrets, Herons

Slaty Egret *Egretta vinaceigula* Rooikeelreier
Breeds in the Okavango and Chobe floodplains, and in the panveld around Tsumbwe (ne Namibia); twice in South Africa (Nylsvley, Blesbokspruit). Nests colonially in large mixed-species heronries, 3-60 pairs/colony, with one 1990 Okavango record of 500 pairs; commonly breeds in association with Rufous-bellied Heron and Little Egret in the Okavango; nests in the Okavango over water in dense, undisturbed reedbeds, in flooded 'gomoti' fig thickets, in flooded *Phoenix* palms, or in low, flooded acacia trees (Tsumkwe); its nests are usually clumped in mixed-species colonies. Breeds erratically, usually during years of exceptionally high floods. **Nest:** a saucer-shaped platform made of twigs, or reed- and creeper-stems, sparsely lined with reed-blades or dry grass; 1-2 m above the water; it measures 19-41 cm in diameter and is 10-22 cm high. Unless attending parent is seen, nest and eggs are indistinguishable from those of other small herons; nestlings have blackish down.
Laying months: Feb-May. **Clutch size:** 3 (2-4); laid at 1-day intervals. **Eggs:** 39.0-41.7-45.9 × 29.5-31.2-32.6 mm; mass 21-23-25 g. **Incubation period:** 23 days; starts with first-laid egg. **Nestling/fledging period:** young temporarily flee nest from 7 days; fledge before 40 days.

Black Heron *Egretta ardesiaca* Swartreier page 359
A scarce and sporadic breeding species in southern Africa, first recorded doing so in the region (in Durban bayhead) in 1962. Nests colonially (1-20 pairs) alongside other species in large, mixed-species heronries; usually in reedbeds over water, occasionally in trees, including mangroves; usually only in years of high rainfall. **Nest:** a saucer-shaped platform of reed-stems or twigs, measuring 26-35 cm in diameter; 1-2 m above water in reedbeds, <6 m up in trees. Nest and eggs are only distinguishable from those of other small herons in the colony by seeing the parent birds; nestlings have black down.
Laying months: mainly Dec-Mar; rarely in other months. **Clutch size:** 3 (2-4). **Eggs:** 41.9-44.8-48.0 × 30.2-32.4-33.5 mm; mass 28 g. **Incubation period:** not recorded. **Nestling/fledging period:** not recorded.

Squacco Heron *Ardeola ralloides* Ralreier page 359
Breeds sporadically and sparsely in southern Africa. Nests colonially (2-20 pairs, occasionally 100s) alongside other species in large mixed-species heronries, sometimes in smaller (<10 pairs) monospecific colonies; mainly in years of high rainfall. Mostly nests in reedbed colonies, their nests positioned well below the nests of the larger herons, 1-2 m above the water; less often in the branches of temporarily flooded trees. **Nest:** a saucer-shaped platform made of reed-stems and/or twigs and lined with grass; it measures 160-200-240 mm in diameter and is 120 mm high; it is built by the ♂ in 1-3 days (Europe).
Laying months: mainly Dec-May, later in the Okavango (Jul-Aug). **Clutch size:** 3 (2-4). **Eggs:** 35.8-38.2-42.6 × 27.0-28.9-31.1 mm. **Incubation period:** 18 days (Madagascar); 22-24 days (Europe); by both sexes. **Nestling/fledging period:** young temporarily flee nest at 14 days; leave nest permanently at 35 days; fly at 45 days (Madagascar); brooded and fed by both sexes.

Rufous-bellied Heron *Ardeola rufiventris* Rooipensreier page 359
Breeds mainly in the extensive seasonal floodplains of the Okavango, Chobe and Linyanti wetlands; occasionally in Zimbabwe and on the Nylsvley wetland in South Africa. Nests in small colonies (2-80 pairs), often alongside other colonial-breeding herons, storks and cormorants; sites used range from temporarily flooded acacia trees to flooded 'gomoti' fig thickets and dense, undisturbed *Phragmites* reedbeds. **Nest:** a small saucer-shaped platform made of reed-stems or twigs, sometimes lined with some dry grass, 1½-4 m above the water; it measures 20-30-38 cm in diameter and is 5-12 cm high. The nest and eggs are indistinguishable from those of other small herons; the nestlings are covered with purplish-grey down from the time of hatching.
Laying months: linked to subsidence of flooding, mainly Mar-Aug in n Botswana, Dec-May elsewhere. **Clutch size:** 3 (2-4); laid at 2-day intervals. **Eggs:** 29.0-37.7-42.6 × 25.0-28.6-30.7 mm. **Incubation period:** 21-22 days; starts with first-laid egg; by both sexes. **Nestling/fledging period:** young flee temporarily from nest from 5 days; fly weakly at 24 days, strongly at 32 days; brooded and fed by both sexes.

Green-backed Heron (Striated Heron) *Butorides striata* Groenrugreier page 359
Breeds along wooded margins of slow-flowing rivers, along edges of pans, dams and estuaries, and on flooded islands in floodplains. Pairs nest solitarily or in loose aggregations of 3-4 pairs, max 15 pairs; does not nest in mixed-species heronries. Breeding triggered by flooding following high rainfall. **Nest:** a saucer-shaped platform of twigs placed in the branches of a tree overhanging water, or standing in water; usually <3 m up (up to 7 m), concealed in foliage; it measures 23-33 cm in diameter and is 12 cm high; built by both sexes in 3-4 days, the ♂ gathering material and the ♀ building. Given their similarity, care is needed in distinguishing the nests of this species and Dwarf Bittern.
Laying months: mainly Sep-Mar; but all months recorded. **Clutch size:** 3 (2-5); laid at 2-day intervals. **Eggs:** 33.0-37.6-41.5 × 26.1-28.3-30.0 m; mass 17 g. **Incubation period:** 21-27 days; shared equally by both sexes, change-overs at 3-hr intervals. **Nestling/fledging period:** young may temporarily flee nest from 7-8 days; fly weakly at 21 days, strongly at 34-35 days; brooded and fed by both sexes.

Slaty Egret

Black Heron

Squacco Heron

Green-backed Heron

Rufous-bellied Heron

Green-backed Heron

White-backed Night Heron *Gorsachius leuconotus* Witrugnagreier page 359

Breeds along well-wooded margins of dams and slow-flowing rivers with trees and bushes overhanging the water, also on islands in dams and rivers. Pairs nest solitarily and are widely spaced. **Nest:** a saucer-shaped platform of twigs, usually hidden inside a densely foliaged tree or shrub over water; usually <1 m up, occasionally up to 8 m; some are not built over water – especially on small islands – built here in a tree or shrub, in reeds or among rocks; the nest is rarely in an exposed position (e.g. in a dead tree standing in open water). Nests are seldom reused in successive years, but they are frequently built close to a previously used site. Nest size variable, 25-60 cm in diameter and 20-45 cm high; cup 20-30 cm wide, 8-9 cm deep. Nesting birds are secretive and are easily overlooked; if disturbed, the incubating bird slowly withdraws from the nest and creeps away deeper into the nest tree; its mate is usually perched close by.

Laying months: most months recorded, but mainly Aug-Nov, except in Okavango where peaks in Mar-May; relays after an early failure. **Clutch size:** 2-3 (2-4); laid at 2-day intervals. **Eggs:** 43.3-45.9-49.0 x 33.3-34.9-37.0 mm; mass 28 g. **Incubation period:** 23-26 days; by both sexes. **Nestling/fledging period:** 7-8 weeks; brooded and fed by both sexes.

Black-crowned Night Heron *Nycticorax nycticorax* Gewone Nagreier page 359

Breeds widely but sparsely in the region. Nests colonially, usually alongside other herons and egrets; occasionally in monospecific colonies; numbers nesting at a site 10-500 pairs, rarely 1000s. Nest sites almost always over water, usually in reedbeds, less often in trees; occasionally on bushed cliff-faces overhanging a river. Their nests are usually dispersed through the colony rather than being clumped. **Nest:** a small saucer-shaped platform of reed-stems or twigs, not distinguishable from those of other smaller egrets and herons unless bird is seen in attendance. It measures 25-35 cm in diameter and is 10 cm high. Built by ♀ from material collected by ♂.

Laying months: all months recorded, but mainly Oct-Feb, peaking earlier in winter-rainfall region (Sep-Oct), later in the Okavango and associated floodplains (Mar-May). **Clutch size:** 2-3 (2-4); laid at 2-day intervals. **Eggs:** 43.3-45.5-48.1 x 33.0-34.9-37.2 mm; mass 28-34 g. **Incubation period:** 22-26 days; by both sexes. **Nestling/fledging period:** young leave nest at 20-25 days; fly at 40-45 days; brooded and fed by both sexes.

Dwarf Bittern *Ixobrychus sturmii* Dwergrietreier page 359

Breeds on seasonal or ephemeral floodplains and pans in n savanna. Pairs mostly nest solitarily, some in loose aggregations where adjacent nests can be <15 m apart. **Nest:** a flimsy, saucer-shaped platform of twigs and/or coarse grass, placed 0.3-1.0-3.7 m above water in a tree and bush temporarily flooded by rising water; occasionally in flooded reed- or sedge-clumps; the nest measures 23-38 cm in diameter and is 7-12 cm high. Both sexes build the nest in 1-2 days and continue adding to it during the incubation. Birds arrive in nesting areas within days of flooding occurring and begin nesting immediately, ♂s uttering a barking call from potential nest trees to attract ♀s.

Laying months: Nov-Apr, usually peaking in the month after flooding. **Clutch size:** 4-5 (2-6); laid at 1-day intervals. **Eggs:** 33.2-37.1-40.0 x 25.8-27.8-31.0 mm; 19.0-19.5-20.2 g. **Incubation period:** 18-20-26 days; by both sexes; begins when first egg is laid. **Nestling/fledging period:** young temporarily flee nest (if disturbed) from 7 days; leave permanently at 12-13 days.

Little Bittern *Ixobrychus minutus* Kleinrietreier page 359

Breeds widely but sparsely, in both permanent reedbeds, and in seasonally flooded sedge and grass. Pairs mostly nest solitarily, some semi-gregariously (2-10 adjacent nests, closest about 5 m apart). **Nest:** a small, saucer-shaped platform, variable in size, 12-28-35 cm in diameter and 10-20-25 cm high; invariably placed over water, either in reeds (*Phragmites*), bulrushes (*Typha*), sedges or flooded grass (*Oryza*), 0,2-1,4 m up; usually well hidden, set deep into the vegetation and well below the canopy. Built by both sexes, mainly ♂, in 4-5 days, with additional material added during the incubation. At the onset of breeding ♂s call frequently, uttering a repeated, sharp bark, to attract mates.

Laying months: mainly Oct-Feb, but most months recorded; peaks earlier (Sep-Nov) in winter-rainfall region; relays after an early failure; sometimes double-brooded. **Clutch size:** 3-4 (2-5); laid at 1-2 day intervals. **Eggs:** 32.0-34.5-37.8 x 24.4-26.3-27.9 mm. **Incubation period:** 18-19-20 days; starts before clutch complete; shared equally by both sexes, in shifts of 1-2-9 hrs each. **Nestling/fledging period:** young temporarily flee nest (if disturbed) from 8 days; leave permanently at 15 days; fly weakly at 23 days.

Eurasian Bittern *Botaurus stellaris* Grootrietreier page 359

Once widely recorded in South Africa, now known from very few localities in the region. Nesting habits poorly known in southern Africa, with <10 nests recorded from the region. Palearctic race (*B. s. stellaris*) is polygynous, a ♂ having 2-5 mates; local race (*capensis*) is apparently also polygynous. Breeds in permanent sedge- and reed-marshes and in seasonal grass floodplains, its presence detected by ♂s booming during the breeding period from hidden sites in such habitat. Nests solitarily, with one record of two nests 20 m apart. **Nest:** a shallow, saucer-shaped platform, made of stems of reeds, sedges or grass, measuring 25-30-38 cm in diameter and 150 mm high; small for the size of the bird, inconspicuous, and easily overlooked; it is placed over water (6-30 cm up) in dense reeds, sedges or grass, usually close to a site where a ♂ is booming.

Laying months: Oct-Jan; perhaps continues to Jun, as ♂s have been recorded booming through to Jun. **Clutch size:** 3 (2-4). **Eggs:** 49.6-50.2-51.0 x 37.9-38.8-40.0 mm; mass 42 g. **Incubation period:** 25-26 days (Europe); begins with first-laid egg (Europe); by ♀ only. **Nestling/fledging period:** young flee nest temporarily from 15 days, fly at 50-55 days; young brooded and fed by ♀ only (Europe).

White-backed Night Heron

Black-crowned Night Heron

Dwarf Bittern

Little Bittern

Eurasian Bittern

Hamerkop, Darter, Pelicans

HAMERKOP Family Scopidae Worldwide 1 species, endemic to Afrotropics, breeds in southern Africa. Most breeding information comes from W African race *Scopus umbretta minor*; nesting habits of hamerkops and storks show many similarities.

Hamerkop *Scopus umbretta* Hamerkop   page 356

Monogamous, but some pairs have helpers. Breeds widely across southern Africa, but absent from areas lacking surface water. Pairs nest solitarily, usually widely spaced. **Nest:** A unique nest, remarkable for its large size; dome-shaped, up to 2 m wide and high, enclosing a mud-plastered chamber, 45-60 cm wide and 30-40 cm high; this is accessed from one side by a 80-cm long, down-sloping tunnel that leads in from a side entrance hole 13 x 15 cm in diameter. Nest has a mass of 25-50 kg, may comprise up to 8000 nest-material items ranging from sticks, grass-tufts and leaves to almost any movable debris available – cardboard, bones, tins, plastic, etc. Nests are mostly built in trees, in a stout fork in the main trunk, 3-15 m from the ground; 2 or more nests, built in successive years, are occasionally found in the same tree. May also place nests on rock ledges, on a boulder in a dam or, occasionally, on the roof of a building. Nest built by both sexes, shared equally, occasionally assisted by helpers; nest building is most intense – and noisy – in the early mornings; takes 4-6 weeks to complete, sometimes longer; usually used only once, but up to 4 times recorded. Many nests are usurped by other hole-nesting birds especially Western Barn Owl and Egyptian Goose, also snakes, monitor lizards, genets and bees; one pair built 18 successive nests in 4 years because of nest piracy.
Laying months: mainly Aug-Sep (Jul-Jan), but all months recorded. **Clutch size:** 4-5 (3-9); laid at 1-2 day intervals. **Eggs:** 41.3-45.7-52.5 x 32.0-34.8-36.8 mm; mass 25-28-31 g. **Incubation period:** 30 days (26-32); by both sexes, but mostly by the ♀; begins before clutch is completed. **Nestling/fledging period:** 45-50 days; brooded and fed by both sexes.

DARTERS Family Anhingidae Wordwide 4 species; 1 breeds in Afrotropics, including southern Africa. The family shares many breeding characteristics with cormorants; colonial, commonly nesting with other colonial waterbirds. Nest, a shallow-cupped platform of sticks over water; egg sub-elliptical, unmarked, white, chalky-textured, 4/clutch; nestlings are altricial and nidicolous, swim long before they can fly; down of nestlings is white in contrast to cormorants, which have black down.

African Darter *Anhinga rufa* Slanghalsvoël   page 359

Breeds widely, but erratically on freshwater wetlands, especially on recently filled dams or recently inundated pans. Colonial, typically 10-50 pairs (occasionally 100s), usually alongside other colonial-nesting waterbirds (cormorants, sponnbills, herons). **Nest:** usually built in an upper forked branch in a tree standing in water, often in a dead tree standing in a large dam, or in trees growing on islands in rivers, or on floodplains; rarely in reedbeds; a platform of sticks, reeds, grass 400-450 mm in diameter, lined with finer material; built by both sexes, the ♂ gathering material and the ♀ constructing the nest; can be completed in a day; further material is added during the incubation. Colonies tend to be occupied for one or a few waves of breeding and then abandoned.
Laying months: year-round, usually determined by rainfall; Aug-Oct peak in winter-rainfall region, late summer elsewhere. **Clutch size:** 3-4 (2-7); laid at irregular intervals. **Eggs:** 48.5-54.4-60.0 x 30.2-35.5-39.8 mm; mass 37 g. **Incubation period:** 22 days (21-27); by both sexes, several change-overs/day; begins with first-laid egg. **Nestling/fledging period:** young leave nest temporarily at 3 weeks, permanently at 5-6 weeks; fly at 7 weeks; brooded and fed by both sexes.

PELICANS Family Pelecanidae Worldwide 8 species; 2 breed in Afrotropics, both of these breed in southern Africa. Monogamous; colonial breeders, nesting at very few sites; nest a platform of sticks; clutch 2; eggs greatly elongated, unmarked white, chalky textured. Nestlings are altricial and nidicolous; in both species sibling aggression usually results in the death of the second-hatched chick.

Pink-backed Pelican *Pelecanus rufescens* Kleinpelikaan   page 359

Colonial (15-140 nesting pairs), breeding in two areas in the region: in n KwaZulu-Natal and in the Okavango-Linyanti-Chobe wetland complex. **Nest:** in the top branches of trees, usually over water and often alongside nesting herons, storks, cormorants and spoonbills; a platform of sticks, 500-700 mm in diameter and 200-400 mm high; built by both sexes, the ♂ gathering material and the ♀ building; takes 6-8 days, with further material added during incubation. Some sites are reused seasonally; others sporadically.
Laying months: mainly Dec-Feb (KwaZulu-Natal) and Jun-Aug (n Botswana). **Clutch size:** 2 (1-4); laid at a 2-3 day interval. **Eggs:** 88.1-93.2-105.6 x 56.2-60.1-66.7 mm. **Incubation period:** 30-35 days, shared equally by both sexes, alternating in 1-day shifts; begins with first-laid egg. **Nestling/fledging period:** 70-75 days (E Africa); young cared for by both sexes.

Great White Pelican *Pelecanus onocrotalus* Witpelikaan   page 359

Colonial (20-3000 nesting pairs/colony), breeding regularly (at 1-5 year intervals) at a few localities in the region (Lake St Lucia, Dassen Is, Walvis Bay bird platform, Sua Pan), occasionally elsewhere (Etosha Pan, Lake Ngami, Hardap Dam). **Nest:** on the ground in tightly packed colonies, adjacent nests often almost touching; a flimsy platform of grass, sticks, feathers and other debris gleaned from nearby, 350-600 mm in diameter, built by both sexes, the ♂ bringing material to the ♀; material continues to be added through the incubation. Colonies may be abandoned where they are excessively disturbed. In the month preceding breeding, single eggs ('yard eggs') are often laid away from the colony in areas where the birds loaf.
Laying months: all months, and breeding may continue year-round; peak Jun-Aug (Walvis Bay), Mar-Oct (Sua Pan), Mar-Jun (St Lucia), Sep-Feb (Dassen Is). **Clutch size:** 2 (1-3, rare 4-5 eggs laid by >1 ♀; laid at a 1-2 day interval. **Eggs:** 84.4-94.8-107.5 x 52.7-60.3-67.9 mm; mass 140-188-250 g. **Incubation period:** 37-41 days; shared equally by both sexes, alternating in 1-3 day shifts; begins with first-laid egg. **Nestling/fledging period:** gather in pods at 20-25 days, fledge at 65-70 days; young cared for by both sexes; sibling aggression usually results in death of one chick in the brood.

in a tree   Hamerkop   on a cliff ledge

African Darter

African Darter

Pink-backed Pelican    Great White Pelican (TWO ABOVE)

CORMORANTS Family Phalacrocoracidae Worldwide 36 species; 5 breed in Afrotropics, 5 in southern Africa; 3 are marine-living and endemic to the west coast; 1 is an inland species, and 1 (White-breasted Cormorant found on four continents) occurs both inland and along the coast. All are monogamous, breed colonially, numbers ranging from a few pairs to 1000s; commonly nest in association with other colonial waterbirds. Nests are shallow-cupped platforms; egg elliptical to elongate-oval, white, unmarked, chalky textured, 2-3/clutch for coastal species, 3-4/clutch for inland species; nestlings are altricial and nidicolous.

White-breasted Cormorant *Phalacrocorax lucidus* Witborsduiker — page 360

Breeds widely along the coast and inland, the coastal population using offshore islands, rock stacks, cliffs or artificial nest platforms; inland birds nest in flooded trees standing in water, on cliffs overhanging water, or on the ground on protected islands; tall, dead trees standing in large, recently filled dams are especially favoured. Colonial, most colonies <50 pairs, rarely up to 700. Sites often shared with darters, herons, spoonbills, etc. and reused annually. **Nest:** a solid platform of sticks, reeds, grass and, on offshore sites, of whatever material can be gleaned in the vicinity; it measures 35-40-50 cm in diameter and is 6-20-30 cm high; built by both sexes in 7 days, the ♂ gathering material and the ♀ building. Material continues to be added during the incubation.
Laying months: all month, but mainly Mar-Jul in the interior, Sep-Dec on the coast. **Clutch size:** 3-4 (2-5); laid at 1-2 day intervals. **Eggs:** 52.0-63.0-70.7 x 32.4-39.9-42.2 mm; mass 36-54-64 g. **Incubation period:** 27-28 days; by both sexes, change-over 2x/day; begins with first-laid egg. **Nestling/fledging period:** 49-53-56 days; young cared for by both sexes.

Bank Cormorant *Phalacrocorax neglectus* Bankduiker — page 360

Breeds colonially, usually with other cormorants, on west coast (s of Swakopmund and w of Agulhas) on offshore islands, man-made guano platforms, breakwaters, and on inshore rock stacks and rounded granite islets; about 50 breeding sites known; numbers declining (about 3000 pairs in 2001), most on two Namibian islands (Ichaboe Is, 1600 pairs in 2004, and Mercury Is); 20-100 pairs at other sites. **Nest:** a bulky platform 47 cm diameter and 15 cm high, made largely or entirely of seaweed, which is collected wet (by the ♂, underwater) and plastered onto the site; built by both sexes in 5 weeks; nests are often on sloping rock where stick nests of other cormorants would not remain intact; they are particularly susceptible to being washed away during high seas.
Laying months: all months, but mainly May-Oct in Cape, Nov-Apr in Namibia; double-brooded, next clutch laid 40 days after first chicks fledge. **Clutch size:** 2 (1-3); laid at a 3-day interval. **Eggs:** 50.0-59.0-67.1 mm x 31.3-38.4-42.1 mm, last-laid eggs smaller than first-laid; mass 44-50-69 g. **Incubation period:** 28-30-32 days; equally by both sexes, starting with first egg; incubated on top of webbed feet. **Nestling/fledging period:** 55-70 days; young cared for by both sexes.

Crowned Cormorant *Microcarbo coronatus* Kuifkopduiker — page 360

The smallest and least numerous of the marine cormorants, it breeds from Tsitsikamma (s Cape), west to Cape Town, and up the west coast to Möwe Bay in Namibia; breeds colonially at 48 sites, most on offshore islands, on artificial guano platforms, on ship-wrecks and on inshore rock stacks; a few on mainland sites (e.g. pier blocks in protected harbours); occasionally in trees (Robben Is). Nests in clusters of 5-30 nests (max 157 nests), often in association with breeding penguins, gannets, gulls or other cormorants; shows little site fidelity between years. **Nest:** a shallow-bowled platform 12-15 cm in diameter, 10-30 cm high, built mostly by ♀, from seaweed, sticks, plastic, ropes, feathers and other debris collected by ♂.
Laying months: year-round, peaking in Sep-Mar in w Cape, Oct-Mar in Namibia. **Clutch size:** 2-3 (1-5); laid at 2-3 day intervals. **Eggs:** 42.0-46.8-52.0 x 27.6-30.5-32.9 mm; mass 19-24-29 g. **Incubation period:** 21-23-25 days; by both sexes, begins with first-laid egg. **Nestling/fledging period:** young join crèches at 22 days; fledge at 35 days.

Reed Cormorant *Microcarbo africanus* Rietduiker — page 360

Breeds widely throughout the interior; not on the coast. Colonial, almost invariably associated with other colonial-breeders, especially Cattle Egrets and other herons; usually 10-50 pairs per colony, rarely up to 350 pairs; nests are dispersed through the colony (not clumped). **Nest:** a small platform of sticks and/or reed-stems, 25-27-30 cm in diameter with a deep, grass-lined cup; always over water, either in a reed-bed (nests 2-2½ m above the water) or in the branches of a flooded tree; built by both sexes in 7 days, ♂ collecting material and ♀ building; further material added through the incubation.
Laying months: all months recorded, peaking in Nov-Mar; earlier (Aug-Oct) in winter-rainfall region; relays after early failure. **Clutch size:** 3-4 (2-6); laid at 1-2 day intervals. **Eggs:** 40.2-44.2-47.5 x 26.9-29.4-34.1 mm; mass 17-21-25 g. **Incubation period:** 23-24 days; by both sexes; begins with first-laid egg; several change-overs/day. **Nestling/fledging period:** 5 weeks; young cared for by both sexes.

Cape Cormorant *Phalacrocorax capensis* Trekduiker — page 360

The most common (72000 pairs in 1996) marine cormorant in the region, breeding from s Angola to Algoa Bay; declining; colonial, nesting at 70 sites in large, densely packed colonies (3 nests/m^2), many numbering 1000s of nests. Most are on off-shore islands or guano platforms, fewer on islands in estuaries or at protected sites on the mainland. Numbers breeding vary yearly in response to varying abundance of fish stocks. **Nest:** a loose pile of sticks, feathers, bones, dry seaweed and beach debris, built on flat ground, on concrete jetties and piers, on abandoned buildings and boats, on platforms, cliffs and inshore rock stacks. It measures 30 cm in diameter, height variable; nests of late breeders sometimes made mostly of feathers as access to other material diminishes.
Laying months: year-round, peaking Sep-Feb. **Clutch size:** 2-3 (1-7), clutches >5 probably laid by >1 ♀; laid at 1-3 day intervals. **Eggs:** 47.3-54.6-61.2 x 32.7-35.5-37.9 mm; mass 35-38-45 g. **Incubation period:** 22-23 days (22-28); shared equally by the sexes, in shifts of 1-3½ hrs. **Nestling/fledging period:** young cared for by both sexes; join crèches at 5 weeks; fledge at 7-9 weeks.

White-breasted Cormorant

Bank Cormorant (highest nests, draped with seaweed) and Crowned Cormorant (lower stick nests)

Reed Cormorant

Cape Cormorant (TWO ABOVE)

BIRDS OF PREY Four families (Sagittariidae, Accipitridae, Pandionidae, Falconidae) make up the world's 318 species, of which 83 breed in the Afrotropics, 53 of these in southern Africa. They are a very diverse group that include Secretarybird, vultures, eagles, kites, buzzards, sparrowhawks, goshawks, harriers, falcons and kestrels. Most species are monogamous breeders; a few are sometimes polygynous or polyandrous; most nest solitarily, a few are colonial; most build a platform nest from sticks; falcons and kestrels are exceptional in not building a nest but use other birds' nests or lay on a bare rock ledge. Clutch size varies between 1-6; egg colour variable, from unmarked white in some species to richly pigmented red-brown eggs in others; 'cainism' (where the first-hatched chick kills its younger sibling) occurs in some species but not others; chicks are semi-altricial and nidicolous; parental-care systems variable, shared in some species, mainly by the ♀ in others.

African Cuckoo-Hawk *Aviceda cuculoides* Koekoekvalk   page 360

Breeds in tall woodland, in riparian forest and in forest-agriculture mosaics. Pairs nest solitarily and are widely spaced. **Nest:** a flimsy, saucer-shaped platform of twigs placed in the upper branches of a tall, leafy tree, 10-15 m up (7-30), usually well hidden by foliage; it measures 250-400 mm in diameter and is 120-200 mm high; cup diameter 100-150 mm. It is made mostly from live branchlets that have foliage attached to them; this, its height above the ground, and its small size means it is easily overlooked. Green leaves are used to line the cup and these continue to be added during the incubation. Nests are not normally re-used. Both sexes build and they share parental duties, briefly exchanging calls during nest change-overs.
Laying months: mainly Oct (Sep-Mar); sometimes double-brooded. **Clutch size:** 2, rarely 3, laid at a 3-day interval. **Eggs:** 41.0-43.7-48.3 x 33.4-35.6-37.8 mm; mass 28 g; the eggs of this species and Lizard Buzzard are commonly misidentified. **Incubation period:** 32 days (28-36); by both sexes. **Nestling/fledging period:** 35 days (30-42); young brooded and fed by both sexes.

Bat Hawk *Macheiramphus alcinus* Vlermuisvalk   page 360

Breeds widely but very sparsely in tropical and subtropical savanna, also, in South Africa, in stands of tall eucalypts on e escarpment. Pairs nest solitarily and are very widely spaced. **Nest:** a platform of sticks placed high up (10-30 m) in a large tree, characteristically on a horizontal forked branch away from the centre of the tree. Preferred nest trees are typically pale-barked (e.g. baobabs, *Sterculia africana*, *Brachystegia glaucescens*, *Khaya nyasica*, eucalypts); they are often on hillsides, the nest on a branch on the downslope side of the tree. It measures 560-660 mm in diameter and is 380 mm high; it has a deep cup, 140-180 mm across. Nests are commonly reused in successive years; pair remains close to the nest year-round, using the nest-tree as a daytime roost and when one parent is incubating, the other is usually perched close by. Both sexes build or refurbish the nest doing this at dawn and dusk, from 30-50 days before the egg is laid. Green foliage is added to the nest through the incubation.
Laying months: mainly Sep-Oct (Aug-Feb, rarely in other months); usually lays a replacement clutch after an early failure; occasionally breeds twice in a year. **Clutch size:** 1, rarely 2. **Eggs:** 56.2-61.2-67.2 x 43.0-46.2-49.3 mm; mass 73.5 g. **Incubation period:** 51-53 days; by both sexes, but mainly by ♀. **Nestling/fledging period:** 67 days; young brooded and fed by ♀; provisioned by the ♂.

Black-shouldered Kite (Black-winged Kite) *Elanus caeruleus* Blouvalk   page 360

Breeds widely and commonly across southern Africa; thornveld, open savanna and agricultural landscapes are much favoured. May nest prolifically in one year and sparsely in the next in response to rodent abundance; pairs, and occasionally polyandrous trios, nest solitarily; in rodent plague years adjacent nests may be <200 m apart. **Nest:** a saucer-shaped platform of dry twigs and weed-stems placed in the upper branches of a tree, usually just below the canopy; height above ground variable – in thornveld, typically about 4 m up (1.7-8), in grasslands and cultivated areas where the only available sites are usually stands of alien trees (eucalypts, pines, poplars) often much higher (12-22 m), placed in the highest available fork; occasionally on electricity pylons and telephone poles. The nest measures 250-300-450 mm in diameter and is 50-100 mm high. Its cup is lined with dry grass which continues to be added during the incubation; the nest later becomes a bed of rodent hair from castings by the nestlings. Nests are rarely reused for successive clutches. Both sexes build, taking 7-13 days; they are especially vocal then (♂ whistling, ♀ food-begging), and often perform a fluttering display flight then. Incubating ♀ is not easily flushed from the nest and is fed by ♂, who brings her prey a few times a day.
Laying months: all months recorded, but peaks at end of rainy season, i.e. in Aug-Oct (sw Cape) and Feb-Apr (elsewhere); sometimes double-brooded; usually lays a replacement clutch after an early failure. **Clutch size:** 3-4 (2-6); laid at 1-2 day intervals. **Eggs:** 36.8-40.1-44.3 x 28.6-31.7-32.8 mm; mass 21 g; very variably marked, even within a clutch. **Incubation period:** 31 days (30-33); by ♀, starting with first-laid egg; the ♂ sometimes incubates if the ♀ is inattentive (<20% of the time); ♀ fed by ♂. **Nestling/fledging period:** 35 days (32-38); young brooded and fed by ♀; prey brought by ♂.

Yellow-billed Kite *Milvus parasitus* Geelbekwou (or Black Kite *Milvus migrans parasitus*)   page 360

A breeding summer migrant, pairs taking up territories in Aug-Sep, nesting, and departing in Mar. Nests widely in woodland, savanna, and in alien vegetation, often around rural settlements. Pairs nest solitarily, adjacent nests usually >500 m apart (rarely <100 m). **Nest:** a platform of dry sticks placed inside a tree on a forked branch, 5-25 m up, occasionally higher if a tall eucalypt is used. Often concealed in foliage and easily overlooked; it measures 450-800 mm in diameter, is 300-500 mm high, cup 200-250 mm wide. The nest's lining is distinctive - rags, dung, paper, hair, pieces of plastic, and tufts of grass with soil attached and other debris is used. It is built by both sexes; nests are routinely reused in successive years; a new nest is usually located near a previously used site.
Laying months: mainly Sep-Oct (Aug-Dec). **Clutch size:** 2 (1-3); laid at a 1-day interval. **Eggs:** 49.8-53.5-58.5 x 38.0-40.1-45.0 mm; mass 39.5-48.9-59.5 g; very variably marked, even within the same clutch. **Incubation period:** 37 days (34-38); mainly by ♀, fed by ♂; starts with first-laid egg. **Nestling/fledging period:** 42-45 days; young brooded mainly/entirely by ♀; fed by both sexes.

African Cuckoo-Hawk

Bat Hawk

Black-shouldered Kite

Yellow-billed Kite

Western Osprey *Pandion haliaetus* Visvalk   no nest photo   page 368

A summer visitor from the Palearctic which may occasionally breed in southern Africa. The egg illustrated on pg 368 was taken from a bird that was shot near the Limpopo River in December 1933 or January 1934, and a possible nest with two large young was reported from Ndumo, n KwaZulu-Natal in October 1963. Claimed Osprey eggs, collected from nests in the early 1900s (from the Berg River, s Cape, and from north of Pretoria) have been disproved. Birds have been reported from various parts of South Africa as carrying fish away after catching them with the suggestion that these birds may have been feeding nestlings in undiscovered nests.

Secretarybird *Sagittarius serpentarius* Sekretarisvoël   page 361

Breeds widely in open country. Pairs nest solitarily, nests of adjacent pairs spaced at intervals of 9-13 km in suitable habitat. **Nest**: a large, saucer-shaped stick platform built on top of a tree, typically on a lone-standing, thorny, flat-topped tree (especially an acacia); it often covers the entire tree-top. Choice of tree is largely dependent on local availability, and exotics such as wattle, pine and *Pyracantha* are used where acacias are absent; height above the ground usually 4-5 m (2-12). It measures 100-250 cm in diameter and is 20-50 cm high, the base built of dry sticks and/or thick, long stems of weedy plants, and the cup thickly lined with dry grass. Nests are not usually reused except where suitable sites are limited; new nest is often in a tree in the vicinity of one or more old nests; both sexes build and continue adding dry grass to the lining through the breeding cycle. Nest building sometimes continues indefinitely without culminating in laying, and unoccupied nests are often used as night-time roosts.
Laying months: year-round, with no consistent seasonality. **Clutch size**: 2 (1-3, rarely 4); laid at a 2-3 day interval. **Eggs**: 68.0-77.5-92.0 x 51.2-56.4-65.0 mm; mass 130 g. **Incubation period**: >42 days; begins with first-laid egg; mostly by ♀, fed by ♂. **Nestling/fledging period**: 85 days (64-106); young brooded and fed by both sexes.

Palm-nut Vulture *Gypohierax angolensis* Witaasvoël   page 361

Breeds in small numbers (5-10 pairs) in areas with *Raphia* palms in n KwaZulu-Natal; first recorded breeding here in 1953. **Nest**: a large platform of dry sticks, mostly placed 15-20 m up in a *Raphia* palm, built either beneath the fruit crown against the main stem or a short distance out from the trunk on a leaf frond; one in a tall eucalypt. Elsewhere in Africa routinely nests high up in non-palm trees, especially baobabs. Nests measure 60-90 cm in diameter and 30-60 cm high; the cup is lined with dry grass, sisal fibre and other items, including dung. Both sexes build or refurbish the nest, and it is commonly reused in successive years.
Laying months: Aug-Sep (n KwaZulu-Natal), but May-Jul in Angola. **Clutch size**: 1. **Eggs**: 66.1-70.5-78.3 x 50.2-53.6-55.4 mm (Angola). **Incubation period**: 42-47 days; by both sexes, but mainly the ♀. **Nestling/fledging period**: 89-91 days; young cared for by both sexes.

Bearded Vulture *Gypaetus barbatus* Baardaasvoël   page 361

Breeds in Maluti and Drakensberg mountains (<200 pairs). Pairs nest solitarily, adjacent nests spaced closer together (6 km apart) along the escarpment than in the interior of Lesotho (15 km apart). **Nest**: a large, untidy platform of twigs and branches, placed in a pothole or small cave, high up on a tall vertical cliff; nesting cliffs 24-212-732 m in height, nest site usually ¾ up; occasionally on an open ledge; most sites receive no direct sunlight and face e or s away from prevailing winter wind. Nests measure 1-2 m across and 50-60 cm high, with a cup 40 cm in diameter that is thickly lined with wool, hair, skin and other debris. Despite their large size, nests are not obvious, usually hidden from view in a pothole and not made conspicuous by whitewash. Both sexes build, and during Apr-May when nests are refurbished, the birds carrying material often give away the nest position. Nests are reused seasonally; some nests have been known for more than a century. Most pairs have >1 nest (2-5) and usage is rotated annually between these. One young is reared per breeding attempt.
Laying months: mainly Jun (May-Aug). **Clutch size**: 2 (1-3); laid at a 3-5 day interval. **Eggs**: 86.3-86.9-95.5 x 62.8-65.4-68.5 mm; freshly laid eggs are white with faint grey markings, but they rapidly discolour to dark rusty-brown as a result of rub-off of the pigmentation on the adults' breast feathers. **Incubation period**: 56-58 days; shared equally by both sexes during the day, ♀ at night; change-overs at 2-2½ hr intervals. **Nestling/fledging period**: 124-128 days; young brooded and fed by both parents.

Egyptian Vulture *Neophron percnopterus* Egiptiese Aasvoël   page 361

Once widespread, now a rare vagrant in southern Africa. Last confirmed breeding in the region was in 1923 in a nest used for at least 4 years (e Cape); it may still nest here and in nw Namibia (a probable 'active nest' was reported from here in the 1990s). Breeding populations occur in East and West Africa and elsewhere in the world, and most information on its nesting habits is from these areas. **Nest**: placed on a cliff, typically in a pothole or on a sheltered ledge; it resembles that of a Bearded Vulture but is smaller, being a bulky platform of sticks, hair, wool, dung, bones and other debris, with a deep central cup. Nest sites are usually reused annually and, although not a colonial breeder, adjacent pairs may breed within 200 m of each other. (Nest photographs opposite are from Europe/Middle East).
Laying months: Aug-Nov (e Cape). **Clutch size**: 2; laid at a 3-5 day interval (Europe). **Eggs**: 67.0-67.6-68.6 x 51.9-53.5-54.4 mm (South Africa). **Incubation period**: 42 days (39-45); by both sexes (Europe). **Nestling/fledging period**: 75 days (71-85) (Europe); cared for by both sexes; one young is reared per breeding attempt (Europe).

Secretarybird

Palm-nut Vulture

Bearded Vulture

Egyptian Vulture

White-backed Vulture *Gyps africanus* **Witrugaasvoël** page 362

Breeds widely across the savanna belt from the arid west to the mesic east; favours plains where scattered tall trees provide nest sites. Pairs (in lifetime partnerships) nest in loosely aggregated clusters (mostly <20 pairs), adjacent nests (1 or occasionally 2/tree) are built within sight of each other. **Nest:** a platform of sticks placed high up (7-25 m) in a tall tree usually, if it has a flat canopy, on top. Trees along drainage lines are commonly selected and *Acacia* sp. are much favoured; it may occasionally nest on the top crossbars of electricity transmission towers. Nests measure 34-83-100 cm in diameter and 10-21-90 cm high, larger nests are the result of annual refurbishment; the cup, 200 mm across, is lined with dry grass. Nests of eagles (Martial, African Hawk-Eagle), buffalo weavers, storks or Secretarybird are occasionally taken over. Some colonies are used for many successive years or decades, others are active for only 1-2 years during temporary food abundance (from disease, hunting or culling), then abandoned.
Laying months: mainly May (Apr-Jun); usually relays after an early failure. **Clutch size:** 1, rarely 2. **Eggs:** 79.5-88.1-97.9 x 59.2-66.3-71.5 mm; mass 220 g. **Incubation period:** 56-58 days; by both sexes, change-over 1x/day. **Nestling/fledging period:** 130 days (108-140); young brooded and fed by both sexes.

Cape Vulture *Gyps coprotheres* **Kransaasvoël** page 362

Breeds in colonies, numbering from a few pairs to >700, on large cliffs; about 85 sites are currently active (in the 2000s), the majority in South Africa; range and numbers are much reduced from 100 years ago. Pairs (in lifetime partnerships) return to the same colonies and often to the same ledges to breed annually. Colonies are located on high, inaccessible, vertical cliffs, most s or e facing; quartzite or sandstone formations that provide layers of ledges are favoured; nests are spaced on extensive ledges 1.5-2.3-3 m apart; colonies are visible from kilometres away as a result of extensive whitewashing. **Nest:** a rudimentary platform of sticks and feathers, about 45-70-100 cm wide, 2-11-30 cm high, with a shallow bowl, lined with dry grass, 250-350-500 mm wide. Nest built by both sexes, starting 2-3 months before laying. Breeding cycle lasts >200 days and pairs are tied to the nest site for most of the year.
Laying months: mainly May (Apr-Jul); occasionally relays after early failure. **Clutch size:** 1, rarely 2. **Eggs:** 83.2-91.6-103.0 x 62.5-68.3-73.8 mm; mass 255 g. **Incubation period:** 57 days (56-59); shared equally by both sexes, with change-overs at 1-2 day intervals. **Nestling/fledging period:** 140-145 days (125-171); young brooded and fed by both sexes.

Hooded Vulture *Necrosyrtes monachus* **Monnikaasvoël** page 363

Breeds sparsely across the savanna belt; in South Africa virtually absent outside of protected areas. Pairs nest solitarily, usually widely spaced (>1 km apart). **Nest:** a platform of sticks built in a main fork of a large, well-foliaged tree (often *Diospyros mespiliformis* or *Xanthocercis zambesiaca*), usually well-concealed, often along a wooded watercourse; 13-15 m up from the ground (7-18). It measures 500-620-760 mm in diameter, 250-400-610 mm high, with a central cup, lined with green leaves (unusual in vultures), 230-290-320 mm across. Much like the nest of a Wahlberg's Eagle, and these, and other eagles' nests are sometimes taken over. Nests are frequently reused in successive seasons (one for >10 years); Both sexes share in building or refurbishing the nest.
Laying months: mainly Jun-Jul (May-Oct); relays a replacement clutch after early failure. **Clutch size:** 1. **Eggs:** 68.6-76.2-85.5 x 53.2-56.4-58.9 mm; mass 74-108-157 g. **Incubation period:** 50-51 days (48-54); by both sexes, ♀ at night. **Nestling/fledging period:** 100-120 days (90-130); young brooded and fed by both sexes.

Lappet-faced Vulture *Torgos tracheliotus* **Swartaasvoël** page 362

Breeds sparsely in semi-arid savannas. Pairs (in lifetime partnerships) nest solitarily or in loose clusters, adjacent nests sometimes within 700 m of each other. **Nest:** a large platform of sticks built on top of an isolated tree with a flat canopy; some nests occupy the entire tree-top; height above ground variable according to tree, from 3-23 m up; acacias, *Boscia* sp. and *Terminalia pruinoides* often used. The nest measures 1.2-1.8-2.2 m in diameter and 30-50-70 cm high, with a wide, shallow cup 70 cm across and 18 cm deep, lined with dry grass, hair and skin. Both sexes build. Nests are usually reused in successive years, but some pairs alternate between 2-3 nests, located 70 m to 10 km apart.
Laying months: Feb-Oct, peaking in Jun-Jul in South Africa, Sept in Namibia; relays after an early failure. **Clutch size:** 1, rarely 2. **Eggs:** 82.8-92.6-104.0 x 65.7-70.6-78.6 mm; mass 235-318 g. **Incubation period:** 55 days; by both sexes. **Nestling/fledging period:** 125 days (120-128); young brooded and fed by both sexes; 1-2 feeding visits/day.

White-headed Vulture *Trigonoceps occipitalis* **Witkopaasvoël** page 363

Breeds across the savanna belt from Zululand northwards; in South Africa confined to conservation areas. Pairs (in lifetime partnerships) nest solitarily and are widely spaced (11-29 km apart). **Nest:** a large, conspicuous platform of sticks built on the top of a tall tree that stands above its surroundings and commands a wide view; baobabs are much favoured, but tall acacias are commonly used, also *Terminalia pruinoides*; usually >12 m up from the ground (11-15-21 m). The nest measures 82-118-122 cm in diameter and is 22-36-61 cm high; cup, lined with dry grass, is 30-34-47 cm wide. Both sexes build and refurbish the nest and most pairs routinely use the same nest in successive seasons; some alternate annually between 2 nests located <2 km apart.
Laying months: mainly Jun-Jul (May-Oct); sometimes relays after an early failure. **Clutch size:** 1. **Eggs:** 78.7-85.5-94.5 x 60.5-65.5-71.6 mm; 170-195-208 g. **Incubation period:** 55-56 days; by both sexes. **Nestling/fledging period:** 115 days; young brooded and fed by both sexes.

Rüppell's Vulture *Gyps rueppellii* **Rüppellaasvoël**

A vagrant in the region, known from single birds seen in 1990s and 2000s at two northern Cape Vulture colonies; one of these birds was attending a nest, apparently paired with a Cape Vulture.

White-backed Vulture

Hooded Vulture

Cape Vulture

Lappet-faced Vulture

White-headed Vulture

Black-chested Snake Eagle *Circaetus pectoralis* Swartborsslangarend   page 364

Breeds widely from semi-desert to mesic savanna. Pairs nest solitarily; in some areas breeding birds are permanently territorial, in others, their occurrence is more sporadic. Adjacent pairs are usually widely spaced, but occasionally can be as close as 1.6 km between nests. **Nest:** a shallow, saucer-shaped platform of small sticks, built on top of a tree, often on a flat-topped acacia, sometimes on a euphorbia; rarely placed on an electricity pylon or utility pole. Nests are commonly built in smallish trees and they are typically 3½-7½ m up from the ground – low compared with other similar-sized raptors – an exception was one placed 24 m up in a pine tree. The nest measures 60-70 cm in diameter and is 20-25 cm high, with a shallow cup, well lined with green leaves; it is easily overlooked, given its small size and that it is frequently concealed by foliage or hidden in a cluster of mistletoe. Nests may be reused in successive seasons, but more usually a new site is chosen each year close to a previously used nest. It is built by both sexes, and green foliage is added to the cup through the breeding cycle.
Laying months: mainly Jun-Sep (Mar-Oct); does not relay after a nesting failure. **Clutch size:** 1, very rarely 2. **Eggs:** 69.6-72.5-78.7 x 52.0-57.0-62.1 mm. **Incubation period:** 51-52 days; by the ♀ with short sessions by ♂ while she feeds. **Nestling/fledging period:** 89-113 days; young brooded by ♀; fed by both sexes.

Brown Snake Eagle *Circaetus cinereus* Bruinslangarend   page 364

Breeds in semi-arid and mesic savannas in flat, hilly or mountainous country. Pairs nest solitarily and are widely spaced. **Nest:** much like that of Black-chested Snake Eagle, a shallow, saucer-shaped platform of small sticks, built on the top of a tree, often on a flat-topped acacia, *Faurea saligna*, *Diplorrhynchus condylocarpon* or euphorbia, and ranging in height above the ground between 3½-12 m. It is small for the size of the bird, measuring 60-70 cm in diameter and 15-25 cm high, with a cup, 25 cm wide, thickly lined with green leaves. Given the nest's small size, it usually being concealed by foliage, and seldom used more than once, it is easily overlooked. Occasionally, the nest of another raptor (Wahlberg's, Tawny and African Hawk-Eagle, African Harrier-Hawk) is taken over. Both sexes build, completing the nest in a month; green foliage continues to be added during the breeding cycle.
Laying months: mainly Dec-Feb (Dec-Mar, rarely in other months); sometimes relays after an early failure. **Clutch size:** 1. **Eggs:** 69.5-75.5-78.6 x 58.2-60.9-66.0 mm; mass 170 g (unusually large for a medium-sized raptor). **Incubation period:** 49-50 days; by ♀ only. **Nestling/fledging period:** 109 days (97-113); young brooded and fed by ♀; provisioned by ♂.

Southern Banded Snake Eagle *Circaetus fasciolatus* Dubbelbandslangarend

Breeds sparsely in coastal and riparian forest along the coastal plain from n KwaZulu-Natal through Mozambique. Nesting habits are poorly known. Pairs nest solitarily. **Nest:** a shallow platform of sticks built by both sexes and placed in a fork in a tree, usually one entwined with creeper, 6-12 m off the ground; the nest measures 50-70 cm in diameter and 17 cm high with a shallow (40 mm) cup, lined with green leaves. One nest was reused in two successive seasons. Both sexes build the nest and during the nest-building period the pair often call and perform aerial displays near the nest, especially in the mornings.
Laying months: Aug-Oct. **Clutch size:** 1. **Eggs:** about 70 x 50 mm; (not illustrated) unmarked white but becomes nest-stained during the incubation. **Incubation period:** 49-51 days; mainly by ♀, ♂ taking short shifts. **Nestling/fledging period:** not recorded; young fed by both sexes.

Western Banded Snake Eagle *Circaetus cinerascens* Enkelbandslangarend   page 364

Breeds in riparian forest and associated woodland on floodplains of n Zimbabwe, Botswana and Caprivi. Nesting habits are poorly known. Pairs nest solitarily and are widely spaced. **Nest:** a shallow platform of small sticks placed in the upper branches of a riparian tree that is thickly entwined with creeper such as *Capparis*, *Jasminum* or *Bauhinia*; usually 9-11 m above the ground. The nest may be supported by the stems of the creepers rather than by the tree itself and it is well hidden. It measures 40-60 cm in diameter and is 15-25 cm high, with a nest cup 20-23 cm across and 50-90 mm deep, lined with green leaves. Nests are not reused in successive breeding seasons. Both sexes call frequently in the vicinity of the nest while breeding, and the nestling utters a loud food-begging call from the nest.
Laying months: Dec-Feb. **Clutch size:** 1. **Eggs:** 66.0-67.5-70.6 x 52.0-53.9-55.0 mm; mass 97 g; egg differs from those of other snake eagles by being faintly marked with lilac-grey and red-brown scrawls, spots and small blotches. **Incubation period:** about 36-42 days. **Nestling/fledging period:** not recorded.

Black-chested Snake Eagle

Brown Snake Eagle

Southern Banded Snake Eagle

Western Banded Snake Eagle (TWO ABOVE)

Eagles

Bateleur *Terathopius ecaudatus* Berghaan page 364

Breeds across the savanna belt from the semi-arid west to the mesic east; its breeding range is much diminished in stock-farming areas as a result of poisoning. Pairs nest solitarily and defend permanent territories; in the Kruger Park pairs are spaced at 5-km intervals. **Nest:** similar to that of a Wahlberg's Eagle, a smallish platform of sticks built in a multiple fork, usually about ¾ up a leafy tree, often one growing along a watercourse; where they occur, knobthorn, jackalberry and sycamore fig are commonly used. The nest is about 12 m up from the ground (8-26) and measures 45-77-100 cm in diameter and is 25-41-100 cm high; the nest-cup, thickly lined with green leaves, is about 44 cm across and 10 cm deep. Newly built nests are less substantial than those in use for several years. Nests are reused seasonally, with a new one built about every 3-5 years. It is built mainly or entirely by the ♂ in 5-6 weeks. Nests of Wahlberg's Eagle are occasionally usurped.

Laying months: mainly Jan-Mar (Dec-Jun, occasionally other months); infrequently relays after an early failure. **Clutch size:** 1. **Eggs:** 74.2-79.1-87.0 x 57.0-62.7-68.1 mm. **Incubation period:** 55 days; shared equally by both sexes. **Nestling/fledging period:** 113 days (95-125); young brooded and fed by both sexes.

African Fish Eagle *Haliaeetus vocifer* Visarend page 363

Breeds widely on larger rivers, estuaries, floodplains, lakes and dams. Pairs occupy permanent territories and nest solitarily; the nests of adjacent pairs are very variably spaced, much dependent on habitat: they occur at a high density (0.4-0.5 km apart) on the Boro River in the Okavango but are 5-15 km apart on Vaal and Orange rivers. Dams and lakes <100 ha in size are unlikely to support breeding pairs. **Nest:** a large stick platform, almost always built in a tree, usually in the largest in the area, and usually, but not always, close to water (up to 2 km from water recorded); dead trees, especially those standing in water, are often used; the nest is usually built in an upper forked branch, sometimes on the crown; eucalypts, willows and poplars are commonly used in otherwise treeless areas. It is typically high up (12-15 m), but occasional nests are found just a few metres (2-4 m) off the ground, usually on a bush on a steep slope. Rarely, nests are built on rock pinnacles, on cliff ledges, or on bushes growing out of a cliff face. Nests measure 1.1-1.3-1.9 m in diameter, their height varying according to age, from 0.4 m (newly built) to 2.2 m (in use for 10-20 years). The nest cup is thickly lined with dry plant material (unlike other eagles where green tree foliage is used). Both sexes build or refurbish the nest, the ♂ taking the larger share in this, and a new nest takes 2 months to complete. Nests are commonly reused in successive seasons, and some are known to have been in use for decades; in some instances pairs use 2 or more nests in rotation. During the nesting cycle the pair often duet at dusk and dawn from the nest tree.

Laying months: mainly May-Jun (Mar-Aug, occasionally in other months); seldom relays after an early failure. **Clutch size:** 2 (1-3, rarely 4); laid at a 2-3 day interval. **Eggs:** 61.1-71.1-84.5 x 52.4-54.1-67.9 mm; mass 94-96-98 g. **Incubation period:** 42-45 days; by both sexes, but mainly by ♀; begins when first egg is laid. **Nestling/fledging period:** 70-75 days; young brooded and fed by both sexes; cainism is infrequent.

Tawny Eagle *Aquila rapax* Roofarend page 364

Breeds in semi-arid and mesic savanna, extending into the karoo where electricity-transmission towers and alien trees provide nest sites; its breeding range is much fragmented in stock-farming areas as a result of poisoning. Pairs nest solitarily and defend permanent territories; nest spacing variable, from 4-6 km between nests of adjacent pairs in areas alongside the Kruger Park to 22-24 km in semi-arid country. **Nest:** a large, flat platform of sticks placed about 12 m up from the ground (5-30) on the top of a prominent tree; acacias, especially knobthorn and camelthorn, are commonly used; where available, the top crossbars of pylons are used in relatively treeless areas. The nest is about 1 m in diameter and 30-50 cm high; the cup, 20-45 cm wide, is usually lined with dry grass, rather than green leaves as is usual in other eagles. Nests are reused in successive years, some for decades; new nests are usually built close to a previous nest. Both sexes build or refurbish the nest.

Laying months: mainly Apr-Jun (Mar-Sep, rarely other months); sometimes relays after an early failure. **Clutch size:** 2, rarely 1 or 3; laid 2-days apart. **Eggs:** 64.0-69.6-75.7 x 48.9-54.8-59.5 mm. **Incubation period:** 42 days (39-44); begins with first-laid egg; mostly by ♀ with brief spells by ♂. **Nestling/fledging period:** 11-12 weeks; young brooded and fed mostly by ♀, provisioned by ♂; second-hatched chick usually dies as result of cainism.

Long-crested Eagle *Lophaetus occipitalis* Langkuifarend page 363

Breeds in tall woodland in mesic savanna and in forest/grassland mosaics. Pairs nest solitarily, adjacent pairs spaced 6-7 km apart at a site in Mpumalanga; an exceptional density of 4 pairs in 16 ha once recorded near Harare. **Nest:** a smallish platform of sticks, usually built high up (13-26 m, one was 45 m up) in an upper fork of a tall foliaged tree; eucalypts are commonly used. It measures 50-60 cm in diameter and 15-30 cm high; the cup, 25-30 cm wide, is thickly lined with green foliage which continues being added during the breeding cycle. Pairs follow an erratic breeding cycle, in some years not nesting, in other years doing so twice. A new nest is usually built for each breeding attempt, but some pairs reuse the same nest in successive seasons (one for 5 years), or alternate between 2 or more nests. Disused nests of Black Sparrowhawk, African Harrier-Hawk and Lizard Buzzard are occasionally taken over.

Laying months: mainly Aug-Oct (Jul-Nov, rarely in other months); sometimes relays after an early failure; occasionally double-brooded. **Clutch size:** 2, rarely 1. **Eggs:** 54.1-59.4-67.0 x 45.0-48.4-51.1 mm; mass 75 g. **Incubation period:** 42 days; mostly by ♀, ♂ sitting briefly and infrequently; begins with first-laid egg. **Nestling/fledging period:** 55 days (53-58); young brooded and fed mostly by ♀; provisioned by ♂; cainism is unusual and two chicks are frequently reared.

Bateleur

African Fish Eagle

Tawny Eagle

Long-crested Eagle

Eagles

Verreaux's Eagle *Aquila verreauxii* **Witkruisarend** page 365

Breeds widely in mountainous country where cliffs provide nest sites and rock hyrax provide prey; most common in semi-arid areas and absent from most of the Kalahari basin and the coastal plains of Mozambique and n KwaZulu-Natal. Pairs nest solitarily and defend year-round territories that usually centre on one or more regularly used nest sites. Highest known breeding density is at Matopos, se Zimbabwe (1 pair/10 km^2) where nests of adjacent pairs are typically 1-2 km apart; elsewhere, nesting pairs are mostly more widely spaced, up to 15 km apart. **Nest:** a large platform of sticks, placed on a ledge on a vertical cliff face, occasionally in a large tree, on a microwave-transmission tower, an electricity-transmission tower or on some other man-made structure. Cliff nests are typically on a shelf backed by a vertical wall, on a rock face 15-300 m high and they are often beneath an overhang. With annual refurbishment the nest's size increases with age; most are about 1½-2½ m in diameter and ½-1 m high but old nests may be built up to 4 m high. The nest cup, 30-40 cm in diameter, is thickly lined with green leaves which are continuously added during the breeding cycle. Nests are reused in successive seasons (some known to have been in regular use for 40+ years), but most pairs rotate usage between 2-5 alternate nests. The nest is built or refurbished by both sexes, this starting 1-4 months before laying. Pairs do not breed annually but fail to lay, on average, 1 year in 3.

Laying months: mainly May (Apr-Jul, rarely other months); seldom relays after an early failure. **Clutch size:** 2, less often 1, rarely 3; laid at a 3-4 day interval. **Eggs:** 66.7-75.0-86.0 × 52.0-58.3-62.0 mm. **Incubation period:** 45 days (44-48); mostly or entirely by the ♀. **Nestling/fledging period:** 94 days (90-98); young brooded and fed mostly or entirely by ♀; provisioned by ♂; second-hatched chick almost invariably dies as a result of cainism.

Crowned Eagle *Stephanoaetus coronatus* **Kroonarend** page 365

Breeds in montane, lowland and riparian forest and associated woodland. Pairs defend permanent territories and nest solitarily; spacing between the nests of adjacent pairs is very variable, much dependent on habitat; in continuous forest adjacent nests may be <2 km apart. **Nest:** a large stick platform built high up in the fork of a tree; dead trees are sometimes selected and in these the nest is very conspicuous, but more usually a large, thickly foliaged tree in the forest interior or at the head of a valley is used; *Podocarpus*, *Celtis* and *Cussonia* sp. are commonly used in montane forests; in the lowland riparian areas, baobabs are commonly used and in timber-growing areas many are placed in large eucalypts. The nest is typically 15-20 m up from the ground (8-54), usually in the first fork of a smooth-trunked tree, often at the base of a cliff, or in a ravine; nests are very rarely built on cliff ledges; there is one record of a Verreaux's Eagle nest being taken over. Nests measure 1½-2½ m in diameter and are 2-3 m high, increasing in size with years of reuse. Both sexes build and they continue adding green foliage to the nest lining through the breeding cycle; they are especially vocal at the onset of breeding, frequently performing pendulum displays over the nesting area and returning to the nest on termination. Large chicks call loudly and persistently from the nest. Most pairs reuse a single nest repeatedly (one for 50+ years), building a new nest only if the old one falls down. Pairs lay annually in some areas, biannually in others.

Laying months: mainly Sep (Jul-Oct, seldom in other months); rarely relays after an early failure. **Clutch size:** 2, rarely 1; laid at a 4-day interval. **Eggs:** 56.4-68.8-74.8 × 49.6-55.3-60.0 mm; mass 87-100 g. **Incubation period:** 49-51 days; by ♀; begins when first egg is laid. **Nestling/fledging period:** 110 days (103-116); young brooded and fed by ♀; provisioned by ♂; second-hatched chick invariably dies as a result of cainism.

Martial Eagle *Polemaetus bellicosus* **Breëkoparend** page 365

Breeds widely but very sparsely across southern Africa. Pairs nest solitarily and defend permanent territories. Direct and indirect persecution has diminished populations in many areas; in prime habitat where populations have not been persecuted the nests of adjacent pairs are spaced 10-20 km apart. **Nest:** a substantial platform of dry branches built in a fork in a large tree, typically 10-12 m up from the ground (5-19); dead or partly dead trees are frequently used, as are transmission line towers, especially in arid areas; occasionally nests are placed on cliff ledges or on top of a very large boulder. Nests increase in size with years of use and they measure 1.2-1.4-1.9 m in diameter and are 0.3-0.5-2.2 m high; the cup, 40-50 cm wide, is thickly lined with green foliage which is continuously added throughout the breeding cycle. Both sexes build or refurbish the nest in 2-6 weeks before laying. Most pairs reuse a single nest in successive seasons (one for 23 years), some (38%) rotate usage between 2-4 alternate nests. Pairs do not breed every year, and years when a chick was successfully reared are often followed by a year of no breeding.

Laying months: mainly Apr-Jun (Mar-Aug); rarely relays after an early failure. **Clutch size:** 1, very rarely 2. **Eggs:** 72.0-79.9-87.5 × 60.0-63.4-69.0 mm. **Incubation period:** 48 days (47-53); by ♀, provisioned by ♂. **Nestling/fledging period:** 98 days (90-109); young brooded and fed by ♀; provisioned by ♂.

Verreaux's Eagle

Crowned Eagle

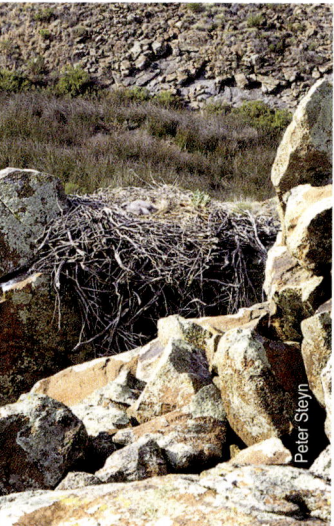

Martial Eagle

Eagles

African Hawk-Eagle *Aquila spilogaster* Grootjagarend   page 366

Breeds widely across the savanna belt, from the semi-arid west to the mesic east, favouring areas with tall trees. Pairs nest solitarily and defend permanent territories that centre on the nest site; in suitable habitat adjacent pairs are spaced at intervals of 3-10 km. **Nest:** a large platform of dry branches; it is exceptionally large for the size of the bird, built in a main fork of a large tree, usually 10-12 m up from the ground (6-19); nests in hillside trees are lower (6-8 m) than average. Rarely, the nest is placed on a cliff ledge or in a bush growing out of a cliff. The nest tree is usually the largest available: knobthorns and baobabs are much favoured in areas where they occur; occasional nests are built on transmission line pylons. The nest measures 0.8-1.1-1.8 m in diameter and is 0.5-0.8-1.4 m high; the cup, 30-50 cm wide and 60-80 mm deep, is thickly lined with green leaves which continue being added during incubation; nests increase in size with annual refurbishment. Pairs mostly reuse the same nest in successive seasons, but some rotate use between >1 alternate nests. Both sexes build or refurbish the nest, beginning a month before laying. Pairs do not breed annually, missing, on average, 1 year in 3.
Laying months: mainly Jun-Jul (Apr-Aug, rarely in other months); seldom lays a replacement clutch after an early failure. **Clutch size:** 2, less often 1; laid at a 3-4 day interval. **Eggs:** 59.5-64.5-75.2 x 46.0-51.3-55.7 mm; mass 70-87-100 g. **Incubation period:** 43 days (42-44); begins with first-laid egg; mostly by ♀, ♂ sitting briefly while she feeds. **Nestling/fledging period:** 67 days (62-70); young brooded and fed mostly by ♀; provisioned by ♂; second-hatched chick usually dies as result of cainism.

Ayres' Eagle *Hieraaetus ayresii* Kleinjagarend   page 365

Nesting habits are poorly known in southern Africa. Breeds in Zimbabwe (not yet recorded doing so in South Africa) in mesic woodland and forest-woodland mosaics, especially in hilly country. **Nest:** a large platform of sticks built in the fork of a large, well-foliaged tree, 8-20 m up from the ground; it measures 70-130 cm in diameter and is 30-100 cm high; the cup, 21-37 cm wide, is thickly lined with green foliage which continues to be added through the breeding cycle. The nest is reused in successive seasons; both sexes refurbish the nest, starting a month before laying.
Laying months: mainly Apr-May (Apr-Sep). **Clutch size:** 1. **Eggs:** 59.0-60.9-62.7 x 47.0-49.7-51.3 mm; mass 64.2-69.4-74.0 g. **Incubation period:** 43-45 days (Kenya); mainly by ♀, ♂ taking brief shifts when she leaves nest to feed. **Nestling/fledging period:** 75 days (Kenya); young brooded and fed by ♀, provisioned by ♂ (Kenya).

Wahlberg's Eagle *Hieraaetus wahlbergi* Bruinarend   page 365

A breeding migrant to the savanna belt, nesting in open woodland. Pairs arrive and settle in their nesting territories in Aug, breed, and depart in March; they nest solitarily and, in optimum habitat, are spaced at intervals of 0.8-3 km. **Nest:** a smallish platform of dry sticks is built in an upper fork below the crown of a large foliaged tree, typically 10-11 m up from the ground (5-22); often along a drainage line. It measures 38-60-71 cm in diameter and is 16-41-60 cm high; cup 20-24-27 cm wide, thickly lined with green foliage which continues being added during the breeding cycle; nests in long use are much thicker than newly built ones. Both sexes build or refurbish the nest and a new nest can be completed in <2 weeks. Some pairs reuse a single nest over many successive years (one for at least 28 years) while others rotate usage between 2-5 alternate nests.
Laying months: mainly Sep-Oct (Aug-Dec); some pairs relay after early egg failure; not if a chick is lost. **Clutch size:** 1, very rarely 2. **Eggs:** 57.0-61.5-66.0 x 44.0-49.0-52.9 mm. **Incubation period:** 44 days (43-46); mostly by ♀, ♂ sitting briefly while she feeds. **Nestling/fledging period:** 70-77 days; young brooded and fed mostly by ♀; provisioned mainly by ♂.

Booted Eagle *Hieraaetus pennatus* Dwergarend   page 366

A breeding migrant to the s, w and e Cape where an estimated 700 pairs nest in hilly and mountainous country, mostly in semi-arid areas and especially in deep, cliff-lined ravines; a few isolated pairs also nest in n Namibia. Pairs arrive in their nesting territories in the Cape in Aug, breed, and leave Jan-Feb; they nest solitarily, but adjacent nests may occasionally be within 200 m of each other. **Nest:** a platform of dry sticks, mostly built on a cliff ledge, occasionally in a tree (several are in eucalypts in nw Cape); it is well hidden, usually placed at the base of a bush growing out of a rock face, less often on an exposed ledge and often invisible from below. It measures 45-65 cm in diameter and is 30-50 cm high; the cup is 28-30 cm wide and 70 mm deep; it is thickly lined with green leaves, which continue to be added during the breeding cycle. Nests are reused in successive seasons (one known to be in use for 36 years). Some pairs rotate usage between 2-3 alternate nests, these usually located near each other. Both sexes build and refurbish the nest and are then demonstrative and vocal, displaying over the nesting area, but they become largely silent and are easily overlooked once incubation commences.
Laying months: mainly Sep (Aug-Nov) in the Cape; in Jun in Namibia (2 records). **Clutch size:** 2; laid at a 3-4 day interval. **Eggs:** 51.5-54.6-58.0 x 42.2-44.0-45.8 mm; mass 54-60 g. **Incubation period:** 40 days; mostly by ♀, ♂ may incubate briefly while she feeds; begins with first-laid egg. **Nestling/fledging period:** 50-54 days; young brooded and fed mostly by ♀; provisioned mainly by ♂; cainism is rare – both young normally reared.

African Hawk-Eagle

Ayres' Eagle

Wahlberg's Eagle

Booted Eagle

African Marsh Harrier *Circus ranivorus* Afrikaanse Vleivalk page 367

Breeds widely but sparsely in marshy areas, typically in *Phragmites* or *Typha* reedbeds, also in sedges and, occasionally, in temporarily flooded grass. Pairs nest solitarily, needing a wetland of about 100 ha in extent; density in s Cape about 1 pr/120 ha, with nests of adjacent pairs, on occasion, as close as 80 m apart. **Nest:** a saucer-shaped platform of dry weeds, reeds, sedges, usually placed over shallow water in marshy vegetation, supported on a base of emergent plant stems, ½-2½ m above the water. Rarely, nests are built on dry ground (such as in fynbos or in a wheatland); one recorded in a low bush. The nest measures 45-50-90 cm in diameter and is 10-30 cm high; the cup, 20-23 cm across, is thickly lined with dry grass. Both sexes build, the ♂ laying the base and the ♀ lining it; material continues to be added during incubation. The pair call frequently and perform aerial displays while nest-building and often terminate these flights by landing on the nest. Once incubation commences the ♀ sits tight and is not easily flushed. She is fed by the ♂ which brings prey that she takes from him in a characteristic aerial food-pass performed above the nest.

Laying months: mainly Aug-Nov, but recorded year-round. **Clutch size:** 3-4 (2-6); laid at 2-3 day intervals. **Eggs:** 41.0-46.6-54.5 x 32.4-37.1-40.3 mm; mass 29-30 g. **Incubation period:** 32 days (31-33); by ♀ only; fed by ♂. **Nestling/fledging period:** 38-45 days; brooded and fed mainly by ♀; provisioned by ♂.

Black Harrier *Circus maurus* Witkruisvleivalk page 367

Breeding range extends across coastal lowlands and mountains of w Cape into grasslands in the east, and riverbeds in n Cape, nesting mainly in fynbos, less so in restios, sedges, marshy grassland and karoo scrub. Pairs nest solitarily or, in w Cape strandveld, semi-colonially, where adjacent nests may be as close as 30 m apart. In the highly fragmented renosterveld, breeding is restricted to fragments >100 ha in extent. Breeds erratically in some areas (n Cape, Free State), regularly in others (w Cape). Mainly monogamous with instances of polygyny recorded in 8% of nests in mountain fynbos. **Nest:** a flimsy platform, with a base of sticks, weed-stems, sedges, reeds, or grass tussocks that supports a grass-lined nest cup; it is placed on, or just above the ground, where usually dry or damp underfoot, not over water, and it is well concealed by surrounding rank vegetation. It measures 35-45 cm in diameter and is 10-15 cm high. Pairs frequently nest in the same area in successive years, one nest site used for 26 years. Both sexes build, the ♂ laying the foundation and the ♀ adding the lining. Once incubation commences the ♀ sits tight and is not easily flushed unless the nest is closely approached. She is fed by the ♂ during this time, and he brings prey to her a few times a day which she takes from him in a characteristic aerial food-pass performed above the nest.

Laying months: mainly Aug-Sep (Jul-Nov); relays after early failure. **Clutch size:** 3-4 (1-5); laid at 1-2 day intervals. **Eggs:** 41.9-45.5-50.2 x 34.2-36.6-38.5 mm; mass 27.5-32.3-39.5 g. **Incubation period:** 31-34 days; by ♀ only; fed by ♂; starts with first-laid egg. **Nestling/fledging period:** 35-40 days; brooded and fed mainly by ♀; provisioned by ♂.

African Harrier-Hawk (Gymnogene) *Polyboroides typus* Kaalwangvalk page 369

Breeds widely in any wooded habitat, most common in hilly, dissected landscapes, with wooded, steep-sided valleys and cliff-lined ravines. Pairs nest solitarily, and adjacent nests in such terrain are spaced at about 5-km intervals. **Nest:** a platform of sticks, thickly lined with green leaves; in mountainous areas the nest is typically built in a recess on a cliff face, or at the base of an aloe, a fig or some other tree growing out of the cliff, or in the crown of a tree growing out of the side of the valley, especially one overhanging a pool of water. In flat country the nest is built in a tall tree, often one along a river, or in a baobab where these occur. It measures 45-75 cm in diameter and is 20-30 cm high, the cup 20-30 cm across. Nests are reused in successive years, some known to have been in use for decades. Nests of other raptors (Black Sparrowhawk, Long-crested Eagle and others) are sometimes taken over. Both sexes refurbish or build the nest, taking a month to do the latter.

Laying months: mainly Sep-Nov (Aug-Dec). **Clutch size:** 2 (1-3); laid at a 3-day interval. **Eggs:** 50.0-55.7-63.0 x 40.4-43.9-48.8 mm; mass 49.4-59.6-64 g. **Incubation period:** 35-36 days; mainly by ♀; the ♂ takes short turns while ♀ feeds; starts with first-laid egg. **Nestling/fledging period:** 45-55 days; brooded and fed mainly by ♀; provisioned by ♂; second-hatched chick sometimes dies as result of cainism.

Lizard Buzzard *Kaupifalco monogrammicus* Akkedisvalk page 366

Breeds in mesic savannas and is especially common in miombo. Pairs nest solitarily. **Nest:** a smallish, saucer-shaped platform of sticks, in the mid- to upper-branches of a well-foliaged tree, placed either in a multiple vertical fork or on a forked lateral branch. The nest is distinguished from those of other small hawks by being built with branched, stout twigs (10-20 mm in diameter), and by often having the nest cup lined with *Usnea* or some other lichen. Nests are typically 10-12 m (3-25) up from the ground; they measure 30-40 cm in diameter and are 15 cm thick; the cup is 15 cm wide and 45 mm deep. Both sexes build the nest and it is not reused in successive years.

Laying months: mainly Oct (Aug-Jan). **Clutch size:** 2 (1-3); laid at a 2-day interval. **Eggs:** 39.9-44.0-48.5 x 32.0-35.2-38.0 mm; mass 29.3 g. Eggs are very variable in coloration, even in same clutch, from white, unmarked eggs to eggs that are heavily blotched with red-brown. **Incubation period:** 32-34 days; mostly or entirely by ♀; begins with first-laid egg. **Nestling/fledging period:** 32-40 days; brooded by ♀, fed by both sexes.

African Marsh Harrier

Black Harrier

Black Harrier

African Harrier-Hawk

Lizard Buzzard

Goshawks

African Goshawk *Accipiter tachiro* Afrikaanse Sperwer page 367

Breeds in Afromontane, lowland, coastal and riparian forests, wooded kloofs and dense thickets along rivers; sometimes in plantations of exotic trees. Pairs nest solitarily and, along densely wooded rivers, are spaced at intervals of 0.7-5 km. **Nest:** a substantial platform (for the size of the bird) of dry sticks, thickly lined with green leaves or lichen, built in a tree, usually one that is densely foliaged and draped in creepers; nests are often relatively low down, 4-9-20 m off the ground; other nest site differences between this and other accipiters are that the nest is often built on a side branch away from the main trunk, or in creeper-stems rather than in the tree itself. It measures 45-64-100 cm in diameter, and 20-45 cm thick, with a 20 cm wide cup; green lining continues to be added during the incubation; an old Hadeda nest once used. Nest sometimes reused in successive years, but more often not; when a new nest is built it is usually in the vicinity of, or even in the same tree as a previously used nest. Both sexes build, mostly in the morning, taking about 3 weeks, and the ♀ remains in its vicinity during this time, feeding on prey brought by the ♂.
Laying months: mainly Oct (Jul-Dec, rarely in other months). **Clutch size:** 2 (1-3, once 4), laid at a 3-day interval. **Eggs:** 39.5-44.5-48.7 x 33.1-36.0-38.7 mm; mass 24.3-29.4-35.0 g. **Incubation period:** 35-37 days; by ♀, provisioned by ♂; ♂ rarely incubates. **Nestling/fledging period:** 30-35 days; brooded and fed by ♀; provisioned by ♂; fledged young remain in nest area for about 6 weeks.

Gabar Goshawk *Micronisus gabar* Witkruissperwer page 367

Breeds in savanna, and especially in thornveld and along watercourses in semi-arid areas. Pairs nest solitarily, spaced in arid areas at 4-6 km intervals. **Nest:** a platform of twigs placed in a multiple fork in the upper branches of a tree, usually a thorny acacia. Height above ground variable (2-7.7-25 m) according to tree availability: in arid areas generally lower (<5 m) than elsewhere (>10 m). The nest measures 23-25-30 cm in diameter and 10-16-25 cm thick, with a cup, 10-13-15 cm across and 25-47-70 mm deep. It is lined with dry material (grass, leaves, wool, fur, rags, old nests of penduline tits), and active nests of social spider (*Stegodyphus* sp.) are usually added to the edges of the nest; these, as the breeding cycle progresses, envelop the nest with a mass of spider web, a feature making Gabar Goshawk nests easily recognisable. Nests are rarely reused in successive years, but pairs commonly nest in successive years in the same area; it is built by the ♀ in 2-6 weeks.
Laying months: mainly Oct (Aug-Nov, rarely in other months). **Clutch size:** 3 (2-4); laid at 2-3 day intervals. **Eggs:** 37.0-39.8-43.7 x 29.4-31.1-35.0 mm; mass 18.5-20.2-21.5 g. **Incubation period:** 33-35 days; shared by sexes, ♀ taking the larger share. **Nestling/fledging period:** 35-36 days, the young 'branching' from 26 days; brooded and fed mainly by ♀; provisioned by ♂.

Pale Chanting Goshawk *Melierax canorus* Bleeksingvalk page 367

Breeds widely in the semi-arid and arid regions. Pairs, and sometimes polyandrous trios (20% of the breeding groups), live in permanently defended territories 2-10 km² in extent; they nest solitarily and, in arid areas, erratically in response to varying rainfall. **Nest:** a platform of sticks built in a tree or bush, often along a watercourse; typically in an acacia (49% of nests) or *Boscia*. It is placed among branches below the canopy and is often concealed by foliage. Tall trees around farmsteads (pines, casaurinas) are sometimes used and, occasionally, the cross-bars of telephone poles, pylons or survey beacons. Nest height above ground 2-4.2-12 m, dependent on tree availability, one nest in the Namib Desert was in a shrub only 16 cm off the ground. Nests measure: 47-58-80 cm in diameter, 25-50 cm high, the cup 20-22 cm across and 10 cm deep, typically lined with pieces of dry animal dung; sometimes hair, sheep's wool, spider nests and man-made debris (rags, paper, etc). Some nests are reused in successive years (up to 5 years), but more usually a new nest is built each season, within a few hundred metres of a previous nest. Both sexes (and helpers where polyandrous) build the nest over a period of a month.
Laying months: mainly Aug-Sep in South Africa, a month later in Namibia; (Jul-Dec, rarely in other months); relays after an early failure; occasionally double-brooded. **Clutch size:** 2 (1-1.9-2); reported instances of 3 and 4 eggs in nests are probably the result of unhatched eggs remaining in the nest from previous clutches; laid at a 2-day interval. **Eggs:** 48.7-55.8-61.9 x 38.7-43.0-46.6 mm; mass 43-53-65 g. **Incubation period:** 35 days; mainly by ♀ in 1-2 hr shifts; ♂ participation varies, usually small. **Nestling/fledging period:** 44-51 days; brooded and fed mainly by ♀; provisioned by ♂s.

Dark Chanting Goshawk *Melierax metabates* Donkersingvalk page 367

Breeds in tall woodland. **Nest:** a platform of sticks built in a multiple fork in the main stem of a large tree (including knobthorn, miombo, mopane, marula), about half or two-thirds up the tree, and 3.1-6.3-9 m up from the ground. It measures 35-60 cm in diameter, the cup 20-25 cm wide, and 60 mm deep, lined with an assortment of animal dung, pieces of raw cotton, rags, hair, seedpods, spider nests and cobweb-based birds' nests (sunbirds, penduline tits). Nests sometimes become festooned with spiderweb as a result of live spider nests being brought to line the cup, which then spread. Both sexes build the nest. Old nests are occasionally reused in successive years, but typically a new nest is built each year.
Laying months: mainly Sep (Jul-Nov). **Clutch size:** 1-2, rarely 3; laid at a 3-day interval. **Eggs:** 49.4-54.3-60.6 x 40.1-42.5-45.5 mm; mass 43.5-49-54 g. **Incubation period:** 36-38 days, begins with first-laid egg; mainly by ♀ provisioned by ♂. **Nestling/fledging period:** 50 days; young 'branch' at 35-43 days.

African Goshawk

Gabar Goshawk

Pale Chanting Goshawk

Dark Chanting Goshawk

Shikra *Accipiter badius* Gebande Sperwer page 367

Breeds widely across the savanna belt, from the semi-arid west to the mesic east; has also adapted to nesting in copses and plantations of eucalypts and other exotic trees, here sometimes nesting in close proximity to Ovambo and/or Little Sparrowhawks. Pairs nest solitarily, adjacent nests typically 4-5 km apart. **Nest:** a small, saucer-shaped platform of dry twigs, 8-12 m up (5-16), in a central multiple fork in the upper branches of a tall tree. It measures 20-25-30 cm in diameter and is 8-15 cm high; the cup is 10 cm wide and is characteristically lined with bark-flakes which are added by the ♀ during the egg-laying period; these distinguish the nest of this species from those of other small accipiters. Previous year's nests may be refurbished and reused (if they haven't fallen down, as commonly happens) or a new nest is built close to the previous year's site. Nest-building shared equally by the sexes; ♀ remains close to nest during this time when she is provisioned by ♂.
Laying months: mainly Oct (Aug-Feb, once Apr); relays in a new nest after early failure. **Clutch size:** 2-3 (1-4); laid at 2-3 day intervals. **Eggs:** 33.2-36.9-43.2 x 27.3-29.6-34.2 mm; mass 14.2-16.6-18.0 g. **Incubation period:** 28-29 days; mostly by ♀ in shifts of 2-40-161 min, ♂ incubates briefly when she leaves nest to feed. **Nestling/fledging period:** 32 days, young 'branch' at 22 days; brooded and fed mainly by ♀; provisioned by ♂.

Little Sparrowhawk *Accipiter minullus* Kleinsperwer page 367

Breeds widely across the savanna belt from the semi-arid west to the mesic east; also in riparian and coastal forest; has adapted to nesting in copses and plantations of eucalypts and poplars where it sometimes breeds alongside Shikra and other accipiters. Pairs nest solitarily, mostly >1 km apart. **Nest:** a small, saucer-shaped platform of dry twigs about 13 m up (5-23) in a multiple fork in the upper branches of a tall tree; it measures 15-35 cm in diameter and is 10-20 cm high; the cup, 7-9 cm across, is unlined. Nests are sometimes reused in successive seasons; new nests, when built, are usually close to a previous nest. The nest is built mainly by the ♀ and she remains close to it during this time, provisioned by the ♂.
Laying months: mainly Oct (Sep-Dec); occasionally relays after an early failure. **Clutch size:** 2, rarely 1 or 3; laid at a 2-day interval. **Eggs:** 32.6-35.0-37.9 x 26.7-28.2-31.6 mm; 13.7-14.5-15.7 g; distinguished from those of other small accipiters by being plain white. **Incubation period:** 31-32 days; shared, but mainly by ♀; begins with first-laid egg. **Nestling/fledging period:** 26 days (25-27); brooded and fed mainly by ♀; provisioned by ♂.

Rufous-breasted Sparrowhawk *Accipiter rufiventris* Rooiborssperwer page 367

Breeds in Afromontane forest/open country mosaics and has adapted to nesting in copses and plantations of exotics trees (eucalypts, pine, poplars, wattles), its range now extending more widely into grassland and karoo areas as a result; an established nesting bird in suburban Cape Town. Pairs nest solitarily, spaced at ½-5 km intervals (adjacent nests only 200 m apart in one instance). **Nest:** a saucer-shaped platform built with 500-1200 long slender twigs, placed in the upper branches of a tall tree, usually in a multiple fork, or against the trunk, 6-14-30 m up from the ground. It measures 19-50 cm in diameter, is 6-50 cm high; the cup is 19 cm wide and 6 cm deep and is usually lined with fine twigs, bark flakes, moss or grass. A new nest is built each year, usually close to, or on the previous year's site; it is built by both sexes, the ♀ taking the larger share, in 22-29 days.
Laying months: mainly Sep-Oct (Aug-Dec). **Clutch size:** 3 (2-4); laid at 1-day intervals. **Eggs:** 36.7-40.8-43.4 x 29.0-32.3-35.1 mm; mass 19.3-21.7-23.7 g. **Incubation period:** 34-35 days; by ♀ only, fed by ♂. **Nestling/fledging period:** 29-40 days; brooded by ♀, fed by both sexes.

Ovambo Sparrowhawk *Accipiter ovampensis* Ovambosperwer page 367

Breeds widely but sparsely across the savanna belt, its range having extended marginally into grasslands through its use here of copses of mature eucalypts and poplars for nesting sites. Pairs nest solitarily, adjacent nests 5-6 km (1½-8) apart. **Nest:** a saucer-shaped platform built with long, thin twigs, placed high up in in a multiple fork in the upper branches of a tall tree (12-17-26 m up in eucalypts and poplars). It measures 30-50 cm in diameter and is 20-25 cm high; the cup is 15 cm wide and 7 cm deep, lined with fine twigs and/or bark. A new nest is usually built each year, close to the previous year's nest; occasionally a nest is reused in successive years, or the old nest of another accipiter is refurbished. It is built mainly by the ♀ in 20-40 days; she stays close to the nest then, when she is provisioned by the ♂.
Laying months: mainly Sep-Oct (Aug-Nov); relays after an early failure. **Clutch size:** 3 (1-5); laid at 2-day intervals. **Eggs:** 38.6-41.9-46.2 x 28.7-32.8-35.2 mm; mass 20.0-23.5-26.7 g. **Incubation period:** 35-36 days; by ♀ only, fed by ♂. **Nestling/fledging period:** 33-35 days; brooded and fed by ♀; provisioned by ♂.

Shikra — nest invariably has bark flakes in lining

Little Sparrowhawk — no bark lining, eggs white, unmarked

Rufous-breasted Sparrowhawk

Ovambo Sparrowhawk

Sparrowhawk, Buzzards

Black Sparrowhawk *Accipiter melanoleucus* Swartsperwer   page 367

Breeds in tall woodland, in forest, along forested rivers and in mature copses and plantations of eucalypts, poplars or pines growing in otherwise open or agricultural country; its range has expanded as exotic timber has extended its breeding habitat. Pairs nest solitarily, spaced, where habitat is suitable, at 2-10 km intervals. **Nest:** a large stick platform, reused annually, sometimes for decades (once for 22 years); placed high in an upper, multiple fork in the largest tree available; typically 12-15 m up from the ground, lower in more arid areas, as high as 37 m in tall forest. Many nests are in plantations of exotics, especially mature eucalypts. The nest measures 50-60-90 cm in diameter, 30-75 cm in height, its size dependent on its age; cup 20-25 cm wide, thickly lined with green foliage which continues being added through the incubation. Nests of other raptors are sometimes taken over (and its own nests, in turn, are sometimes usurped by Egyptian Goose, Verreaux's Eagle-Owl, and others). The nest is refurbished by both sexes, starting 50-145 days before laying; the ♀ remains in its vicinity during this time when she is provisioned by the ♂. Breeding birds are unobtrusive until the nestlings become feathered whereafter the ♀ and chicks, when they fledge, become very vocal.
Laying months: mainly Jul-Sep (Mar-Nov); relays after early failure; rarely double-brooded. **Clutch size:** 3 (1-4); laid at 3-day intervals. **Eggs:** 49.2-55.8-61.3 × 38.1-43.3-47.2 mm; mass 49.5-56.6-61.5 g. **Incubation period:** 37-45 days; mainly by ♀, ♂ taking short shifts when she feeds; begins with first-laid egg. **Nestling/fledging period:** 37-45 days; brooded and fed mainly by ♀; provisioned by ♂.

Forest Buzzard *Buteo trizonatus* Bosjakkalsvoël   page 366

Breeds in forests and plantations in s and w Cape. Pairs nest solitarily, spaced ½-3½ km apart. **Nest:** a substantial platform of dry sticks placed high up in a large tree; it is commonly in an exotic tree (especially in *Pinus radiata* or *P. pinaster*) in a commercial timber plantation, otherwise in a large tree in natural forest. The nest is usually built against the main trunk where side branches provide support, 14-18 m up from the ground (9-30); it measures 56-70 cm in diameter and 30-35 mm high; cup 14-20 cm wide and 80 mm deep; it is lined with green leaves, *Usnea* and/or pine needles. Nests are commonly reused in successive years and they are built or refurbished by both sexes. During the nest-building period pairs are noisy and conspicuous, circling the nesting area and uttering their mewing call, but they become silent once incubation commences. A dozen or more nesting pairs of a dark form of this species (or perhaps they constitute a recently established breeding population of Steppe Buzzard *Buteo buteo*) has been found in w Cape; all known nests have been in alien trees (*Pinus* sp.); their nests, eggs and nesting habits are similar to that of Forest Buzzard.
Laying months: mainly Sep-Oct (Aug-Nov). **Clutch size:** 2 (1-3). **Eggs:** 52.5-54.9-58.2 × 41.0-42.5-45.0 mm; mass 49.0-50.8-52.5 g. **Incubation period:** not recorded. **Nestling/fledging period:** 47 days; role of sexes not recorded.

Augur Buzzard *Buteo augur* Witborsjakkalsvoël   page 366

Breeds in hilly and mountainous country, especially in areas of scattered rocky koppies. Pairs, and occasional polyandrous trios, nest solitarily and defend year-round territories; adjacent nests are spaced about 1½-3½ km apart (in Matopos). **Nest:** mostly placed on a cliff, usually facing e, at the base of a vertical crack, on a horizontal ledge, in a pothole, or at the base of a tree growing out from the cliff; it is often invisible from below. Much less frequently, nests are built in trees, about 10 m up and placed either in a main fork or on a side branch, rarely built on the crown of the tree. It is a substantial platform of dry sticks, measuring 45-64 cm in diameter and 15-19 cm high; the cup is thickly lined with green leaves which continue to be added during incubation. Nests are usually reused in successive seasons but some pairs rotate between 2 or more alternate nests. Both sexes share in the building or refurbishing of the nest.
Laying months: mainly Aug-Sep (Jul-Nov); may relay after early failure. **Clutch size:** 2, rarely 1 or 3; laid at a 2-4 day interval. **Eggs:** 55.1-57.6-63.9 × 43.5-46.3-50.8 mm; mass 53.8-63.1-74.6 g. **Incubation period:** 39-40 days; by both sexes; begins with first-laid egg. **Nestling/fledging period:** 48-53 days; brooded by both sexes but ♀ takes larger share (66%); young fed mostly by ♀, provisioned by ♂; second-hatched chick in most instances dies as result of cainism.

Jackal Buzzard *Buteo rufofuscus* Rooiborsjakkalsvoël   page 366

Breeds in hilly and mountainous country. Most pairs are monogamous, but some breeding by polyandrous trios has been recorded. Pairs nest solitarily and defend year-round territories; in prime habitat adjacent nests are spaced 0.7-1.7-3.4 km apart (Lesotho). **Nest:** a substantial platform of sticks usually built on a sheltered ledge on a smallish cliff (9-25-162 m high), more than halfway up. It also nests, less often, in trees and occasionally on windmill stands; tree nests are placed in a main fork 6-10.4-15 m up from the ground, and exotic trees, especially eucalypts, poplars and pines are commonly used for this purpose. The nest varies in size according to its age and measures 38-91-205 cm in diameter, 12-30-100 cm high, with a cup 20-28-38 cm wide and 60-90-120 mm deep, lined with grass and/or green leaves. Nests are reused in successive years and some are known to have been used for decades; some pairs rotate usage between 2-3 alternate nests. Both sexes build or refurbish the nest.
Laying months: mainly Jul-Sep (May-Nov); late clutches are probably replacements for early failures. **Clutch size:** 2, rarely 1 or 3. **Eggs:** 56.1-60.6-70.6 × 43.2-47.5-50.7 mm; mass 55.0-69.5-87.2 g. **Incubation period:** 39-40 days; by both sexes, mainly ♀. **Nestling/fledging period:** 50-53 days; young fed mostly by ♀, provisioned by ♂; second-hatched chick in most instances dies as result of cainism.

Black Sparrowhawk

Forest Buzzard

Augur Buzzard   nest in tree   nest on cliff

Jackal Buzzard

Falcons

Peregrine Falcon *Falco peregrinus* Swerfvalk   page 368

Breeds widely but sparsely, mainly in hilly and mountainous country where high, sheer cliffs along escarpments, in ravines or on high inselbergs provide nest sites. Pairs nest solitarily, about 3½ km apart in optimum habitat. **Nest:** typically breeds on the highest cliff available to it, and on an inaccessible ledge that is protected from above by an overhang, or in a pothole. Nest cliffs may vary between 30-300 m in height and the site used is usually at least half-way up the face. The eggs are laid in a shallow scrape; occasionally an old nest of a Verreaux's Eagle, White-necked Raven or Black Stork is used. Since the 1990s one or more pairs have bred in boxes erected for their use on high buildings in sw Cape, and a few pairs also nest here on the walls of quarries; unlike the Lanner Falcon, it is not known in southern Africa to breed in trees in raptor or crow nests. Pairs remain at their nest cliffs year-round, but may range widely during the day outside the breeding period. Many sites are known to have been occupied by breeding Peregrines for decades, these birds using either the same ledge annually or alternating between 2 or more nest sites. In places, Lanners and Peregrines may nest within a few hundred metres of one another and the two species can be easily mistaken for one another. At the start of the breeding cycle the birds are vocal and demonstrative around their nesting cliff but they become quiet once incubation commences and then are easily overlooked.

Laying months: mainly Aug-Oct (Jul-Nov); peak laying varies by about a month between the north (where earliest) and the south of its range. **Clutch size:** 3 (1-4); laid at 2-3 day intervals. **Eggs:** 45.8-51.3-56.1 × 37.3-41.1-46.6 mm; mass 45-50 g. **Incubation period:** 32-36 days; by both sexes, but mostly by ♀; begins when second-last egg is laid. **Nestling/fledging period:** 42-46 days; young fed mostly by ♀, provisioned by ♂.

Taita Falcon *Falco fasciinucha* Taitavalk   page 368

A rare, localised breeding bird in southern Africa, pairs nesting solitarily and in small numbers at a few favourable sites in Zimbabwe and northern South Africa. **Nest:** uses a deep (300-400 mm), wind-eroded pothole or a deeply recessed slit or ledge located in the upper half of a large cliff, usually >120 m high (15-290). Such cliffs may form the walls of deep gorges (as below Victoria Falls, Zimbabwe), be placed on isolated inselbergs, or form the edge of steep escarpments (as above the Blyde River in Mpumalanga); White-necked Raven nests on such cliffs are occasionally used, but the eggs are typically laid in a shallow unlined scrape on the ledge. Sites are reused in successive years, except where interference by Peregrine Falcons (which lay 2-3 weeks before the Taitas) displaces them and they are forced to move. The birds are secretive and easily overlooked while breeding.

Laying months: mainly in Sep (Aug-Oct). **Clutch size:** 3-4; laid at 3-4 day intervals. **Eggs:** 42.3-44.0-46.1 × 32.3-33.4-34.3 mm; mass 25.2-26.2-28.3 g. **Incubation period:** 34 days; by both sexes but mostly by ♀; starts with 2nd or last-laid egg. **Nestling/fledging period:** 42 days; fed by ♀, provisioned by ♂.

Lanner Falcon *Falco biarmicus* Edelvalk   page 368

Breeds widely in open country in both arid and mesic areas, and in mountainous and flat country. Pairs nest solitarily, their spacing much dependent on nest site availability; along continuous cliffs, adjacent nests may be 2-5 km apart (rarely as close as 200 m); on transmission towers, where crow nests are used, they are typically at intervals of about 7 km. **Nest:** mainly a cliff-nester, laying its clutch in a scrape on an inaccessible ledge, usually in a pothole or beneath a protective overhang; is not as restricted as the Peregrine to nesting on high cliffs in mountainous country, and some pairs nest on relatively insignificant cliffs in ravines, on isolated koppies, or in disused quarries; old nests on cliffs of White-necked Raven, Jackal Buzzard, Verreaux's Eagle and Black Stork are often used. In the absence of cliffs, Lanners routinely use stick-nests of crows or other raptors (including those of African Fish Eagle, Martial Eagle, Wahlberg's Eagle and Bateleur); the old nests of Pied and Black Crows on transmission-line towers are favoured sites. In some cities (Pretoria, Durban, Harare and probably elsewhere) pairs are known to have nested on ledges of high-rise buildings. Pairs frequently breed in the same general area in successive years and some cliff sites have long histories of occupation. At the start of the breeding cycle the pair is often vocal and demonstrative but once incubation commences, they become quiet and are then easily overlooked.

Laying months: mainly Jul (Jun-Sep, rarely other months); peak laying varies by about a month between the north (earliest) and the south of its range. **Clutch size:** 3-4 (1-5); laid at 2-3 day intervals. **Eggs:** 47.7-52.2-58.3 × 39.6-40.8-44.6 mm; mass 45 g; more variably coloured than the range illustrated; eggs are consistently lighter than those of Peregrine Falcon. **Incubation period:** 32 days; by both sexes, but mostly by ♀. **Nestling/fledging period:** 42-45 days (37-45); young fed mostly by ♀, provisioned by ♂.

Peregrine Falcon

Taita Falcon   nest ledge (lower arrow), perched bird (upper)

Peregrine Falcon (TWO ABOVE)

Lanner Falcon

African Hobby *Falco cuvierii* Afrikaanse Boomvalk page 368

Rare and localised in southern Africa with very few records of it breeding in the region (Zimbabwe 2x, s Mozambique 1x); much more common in central and West Africa where up to 17 pairs/27 km² recorded. **Nest:** old stick-nests of Wahlberg's Eagle and Yellow-billed Kite were used in Zimbabwe; in Maputo it bred in a disused White-breasted Cormorant nest. In central Africa, crow nests are commonly used, especially those built high up (20-30 m) in eucalypts (as shown opposite) or in tall palm trees. No lining is added to these sites, the eggs being laid in a depression in the centre. Sites may be reused in successive years.

Laying months: Sep-Nov (Zimbabwe). **Clutch size:** 3 (2-4). **Eggs:** 38.2-39.2-40.3 x 30.7-31.1-32.0 mm (Uganda). **Incubation period:** 30 days (West Africa), mostly by ♀. **Nestling/fledging period:** 30 days (West Africa).

Red-necked Falcon *Falco chiquera* Rooinekvalk page 368

Breeds widely but sparsely in semi-arid savanna and shrubland in the west, with a second population in central Mozambique; adjacent nests about 7 km apart along Nossob River in Kgalagadi Transfrontier Park, 3-8-10 km apart along sparsely wooded drainage lines in the central Namib. **Nest:** in the Kalahari and Namib deserts, this falcon uses the stick-nests of crows (and less often of birds of prey) for breeding purposes, these nests typically being in acacia trees, 4-5 m up (2-9) from the ground. In *Borassus* or *Hyphaene* palm savannas (usually associated with floodplains and open grasslands in the north) it nests high up (10-30 m) in the crown of a palm tree, either laying in a depression at the base of a palm frond or in a crow nest if available. No additional material is added to the site. Sites, if they remain intact, are commonly reused in successive years.

Laying months: mainly Aug-Sep (Jul-Oct, rarely other months). **Clutch size:** 3 (2-4); laid at 1-3 day intervals. **Eggs:** 41.4-44.0-47.0 mm x 30.8-32.7-34.5 mm; mass 21.2-23.3-25.3 g; eggs of w race *horsbrughi* (these measurements) are marginally larger than eggs of e race *ruficollis*. **Incubation period:** 34 days (32-35); mostly or entirely by ♀ (>80%); begins when clutch is completed. **Nestling/fledging period:** 36 days (34-37); fed by ♀, provisioned by ♂.

Greater Kestrel *Falco rupicoloides* Grootrooivalk page 368

Breeds in open, relief-free country, most common in semi-arid areas. Pairs nest solitarily, adjacent pairs spaced 3-6 km apart. **Nest:** old nests of Pied and Cape Crows are most commonly used; these may be placed in trees, on transmission-line towers, or in the top crossbars of telephone poles. Less often, the disused stick-nests of raptors (Tawny Eagle, Black-chested Snake Eagle, Lappet-faced Vulture, Secretarybird) are used, and occasionally a platform on a water-tank or windmill; it is not known to nest on cliff ledges. No material is added to the site and the eggs are laid in a shallow depression. Sites are often reused in successive years for as long as they remain intact. Pairs perch prominently in the vicinity of their chosen nests in the months preceding breeding.

Laying months: mainly Sep-Oct (Jul-Dec, occasionally other months), peaks a month later (Oct) in Namibia than elsewhere (Sep); relays after an early failure; occasionally double-brooded. **Clutch size:** 3-4 (2-5, rarely 7); laid at 1-2 day intervals. **Eggs:** 38.4-41.9-45.0 x 31.0-33.6-36.5 mm; mass 25 g; very variably marked, even within the same clutch. **Incubation period:** 32-33 days; mostly by ♀, ♂ taking brief shifts when she feeds; begins before clutch is completed. **Nestling/fledging period:** 33 days (32-35); young brooded and fed mostly by ♀, provisioned by ♂.

Rock Kestrel *Falco rupicolus* Kransvalk page 368

Breeds widely in hilly or mountainous open country, especially in alpine grasslands, karoo and fynbos. Pairs nest solitarily, adjacent pairs typically about 2 km apart; rare instances of semi-colonial breeding are known (e.g. 12 pairs in a single quarry, adjacent nests <30 m apart). **Nest:** uses a pothole or deeply recessed crack in a rock face, typically on a cliff 20-50 m high; no nest is made, the eggs being laid in a shallow scrape; also lays in disused nests of White-necked Raven and Pied Crow, in cavities in walls of quarries, deep dongas, high road embankments, ledges under high road or rail bridges, and occasionally on ledges and window boxes of city buildings. Tree nests of crows and other raptors may also be used where cliffs are absent. Sites are commonly reused in successive years. Pairs are noisy and demonstrative around their nest site at the start of the breeding cycle, and during incubation the ♂ brings prey to the incubating ♀, uttering a distinctive trilling call on his approach to the nest to call the ♀ off to feed.

Laying months: mainly Sep-Nov (Aug-Jan); relays after early failure; occasionally double-brooded. **Clutch size:** 3-4 (2-5); laid at 1-3 day intervals. **Eggs:** 33.1-39.1-44.2 x 29.7-32.4-35.6 mm; mass 22 g. **Incubation period:** 28-29 days (26-32); mostly or entirely by ♀; begins when third or fourth egg is laid. **Nestling/fledging period:** 33 days (30-36); young brooded and fed mostly by ♀, provisioned by ♂.

using old nest of Pied Crow | African Hobby

using old nest of Cape Crow | Red-necked Falcon | using old nest of crow

using old nest of Cape Crow | Greater Kestrel | using old nest of Pied Crow

Rock Kestrel | using old nest of Cape Crow

Falcon, Kestrels

Pygmy Falcon *Polihierax semitorquatus* Dwergvalk   page 369

Breeds in semi-arid to arid scrub and savanna, its range largely coinciding (in southern Africa) with that of the Sociable Weaver. Mainly monogamous, with a few instances of polyandrous nesting trios recorded. **Nest:** uses the Sociable Weaver nests for breeding and roosting. Pairs and trios nest solitarily, usually >1 km apart, rarely <200 m. On average, one in four Sociable Weaver colonies have resident Pygmy Falcons, but occasional colonies are shared by more than one Pygmy Falcon pair; rarely breeds in old nests of White-browed Sparrow-Weaver and Wattled Starling. The falcons make use of both active and abandoned Sociable Weaver colonies, favouring larger colonies rather than smaller ones. They occupy the site year-round, roosting in one or more of the nest chambers outside the breeding season and nesting in one in summer. If the birds are absent, the presence of the falcons at a colony can be ascertained by looking for entrance holes to nest chambers that are ringed with whitewash: these chambers (usually numbering 2-4 in a colony) are the ones being used by the falcons, either as roosts or nests. Holes that are roosted in during winter are frequently used to nest in during summer; no additional material is added and the eggs are laid on the bare floor of the chamber. During the incubation, done largely by the ♀, the ♂ brings prey to her at intervals during the day, calling her off the nest with a twittering note as he arrives at the colony.

Laying months: mainly Oct-Nov (Aug-Mar); occasionally double-brooded. **Clutch size:** 3 (1-4); laid at 1-3 day intervals. **Eggs:** 26.1-28.1-29.8 x 21.3-22.7-23.8 mm. **Incubation period:** 28-30 days (27-31); begins when first or second egg is laid; mostly by ♀, ♂ taking brief shifts when she is off feeding. **Nestling/fledging period:** 30 days (27-40); young brooded and fed by ♀ when small; later fed by both sexes.

Dickinson's Kestrel *Falco dickinsoni* Dickinsonse Grysvalk   page 368

Breeds in tropical woodland and savanna, especially in areas where baobabs or tall palms are common. Pairs nest solitarily and are widely spaced (mostly >10 km apart, although in Zambia, nests of adjacent pairs may be <300 m apart). **Nest:** a hole in a tree is used, high up (10-15 m) in a deep hollow at the top of a dead *Hyphaene* palm trunk, in a main stem of a large baobab, or in some other dead tree; the nest cavity typically measures 250-300 mm in diameter and is 200-400 mm deep. Less often, the inside chamber of a disused Hamerkop nest is used; also, once, an inspection hole in a steel suspension bridge (Birchenough Bridge, Zimbabwe). No material is added to the site and the eggs are laid in a shallow depression. Sites are frequently reused in successive years.

Laying months: mainly Sep-Oct (Sep-Nov). **Clutch size:** 3-4 (1-5). **Eggs:** 35.8-39.8-42.8 x 28.4-31.5-33.8 mm. **Incubation period:** 30-32 days; mostly or entirely by ♀, fed at the nest by the ♂ every 3 hrs. **Nestling/fledging period:** 33-35 days; young brooded and fed by ♀ when small; later fed by both sexes.

Grey Kestrel *Falco ardosiaceus* Donkergrysvalk

In southern Africa the breeding range of this species is restricted to northern Namibia, centering on the Cuvelai drainage system that links Etosha Pan to southern Angola; a small population, estimated to number about 40 pairs. There is only one confirmed record of it breeding in the region, in 1993, of an active nest 11 m up in a hole near the top of a lone-standing, dead *Hyphaene* palm trunk adjacent to a rural settlement, a site typical of that used by Dickinson's Kestrel. Elsewhere in its range it commonly breeds inside Hamerkop nests.

Laying months: Aug-Sep (Namibia). **Clutch size:** 4 (Namibia). **Eggs:** 40.4-41.0-43.0 x 31.6-33.3-34.0 mm (West Africa). **Incubation period:** 27-30 days; mainly by ♀, the ♂ taking brief shifts when she leaves nest to feed; begins when clutch is completed (Kenya). **Nestling/fledging period:** >1 month (Tanzania).

Pygmy Falcon (LEFT & THREE ABOVE, using chamber in Sociable Weaver nest)

Dickinson's Kestrel

using old nest of Hamerkop   Grey Kestrel

Bustards

BUSTARDS, KORHAANS Family Otidae Worldwide 27 species; 20 breed in Afrotropics, 11 in southern Africa. Large, terrestrial, ground-living birds; 7 species are polygynous; in these, ♂s display from regularly used sites to attract ♀s which visit displaying ♂s, select one, mate, then lay, incubate and care for the young without ♂ assistance; 4 species are monogamous; these live in pairs or extended family groups, and incubation is shared in some, and by the ♀ in others. Eggs laid on bare ground; elliptical to spherical in shape; cryptically coloured; the eggs in a clutch often dissimilar; 1-2/clutch; young are precocial and nidifugous.

Kori Bustard *Ardeotis kori* Gompou page 369

Breeds mainly in semi-arid regions of the savanna and karoo, favouring flat rather than hilly country. ♂s are polygynous and display during summer in dispersed leks; most displaying occurs in the early morning and late afternoon, ♂s inflating their neck, drooping wings, cocking and fanning the tail and uttering a deep booming call. ♀s mate at leks and thereafter lay, hatch and raise young without ♂ assistance. **Nest:** eggs are laid on the ground in a shallow, unlined scrape, 30-45 cm in diameter, 10 mm deep, usually within a few metres of a tree, shrub, anthill or rocky outcrop. ♀ sometimes relays in same area in successive seasons. If approached the incubating bird either slips away from the nest unobtrusively or sits tight only flying up at the last moment.
Laying months: mainly Oct-Nov in the east, Jan-Feb in the west (Jul-Apr). **Clutch size:** 2, occasionally 1; laid 2+ days apart. **Eggs:** 75.0-82.6-90.2 x 54.5-59.7-64.6 mm; mass 140-146-152 g. **Incubation period:** 23-25 days; by ♀ only; incubation sessions last 4-71-147 min; eggs covered 51-98% of day. **Nestling/fledging period:** flies weakly at 4-5 weeks, strongly at 3-4 months; young cared for by ♀ only, remaining with her for >12 months.

Denham's Bustard *Neotis denhami* Veldpou page 369

The race *N. d. stanleyi*, breeding from the w Cape to Limpopo, is virtually endemic to South Africa; it nests in open country, especially in open grassland or low fynbos, often in hilly country with scattered rocky outcrops. ♂s are polygynous and display conspicuously (but silently) during Sep-Nov at regularly used sites ('dispersed leks'), between 0.7-2 km apart and visible from >2 km away when its white chest is inflated during the 'balloon' display; they display mostly in early morning and late afternoon. ♀s mate with such ♂s and undertake all parental care without ♂ assistance. **Nest:** eggs are laid on the ground in an open space 20-30 cm wide between low vegetation: may be among rocks, grass tufts, or some other ground cover sufficiently tall to conceal the incubating bird; usually no nest scrape, nor any material (pebbles, etc) brought to the site; nest may be up to 4 km from nearest displaying ♂. ♀ leaves the eggs unattended a few times a day to feed. Incubating bird creeps unobtrusively from the nest if approached.
Laying months: mainly Oct-Nov (Sep-Dec); peaks a month earlier in winter-rainfall region. **Clutch size:** 2 (1-2). **Eggs:** 74.9-77.6-82.4 x 51.3-55.7-58.5 mm; egg markings within clutch often very different. **Incubation period:** 23-25 days; by ♀ only; she leaves the eggs unattended to feed at about hourly intervals (32-166 mins) and the eggs are covered for about 80% of day. **Nestling/fledging period:** flies weakly at 7 weeks; young cared for by ♀ only.

Ludwig's Bustard *Neotis ludwigii* Ludwigse Pou page 369

Breeds in semi-arid and arid, sparsely vegetated plains broken by inselbergs and rocky hills. ♂s are polygynous and display for about 6 weeks during the rainy season at regularly used sites, often on hillsides, in a dispersed lek system; adjacent ♂s are mostly >300 m apart and visible from 2-3 km away; they display from first light for 2-3 hrs, then again towards sunset; unlike Denham's Bustard, ♂s utter a booming call while displaying. ♀s mate at the lek then lay, incubate and rear young without ♂ assistance; their chosen nest site is in the general area where ♂s display. **Nest:** eggs are laid on the ground among rocks or shrubs, sometimes on a level spot on a hillside, or alongside a jackal-proof fence-line, apparently as a defence against predators. The eggs lie in a wide, shallow scrape 30 m in diameter, 30-50 mm deep, some scrapes being rimmed with a ring of pebbles. The incubating bird usually sits tight if approached, only flying up at the last moment.
Laying months: probably rainfall driven; mainly Jul-Sep in winter-rainfall regions and Feb-May in arid west. **Clutch size:** 2, less often 1, rarely 3. **Eggs:** 68.6-74.5-83.0 x 49.5-55.0-62.1 mm; mass 103-114.5-125 g. **Incubation period:** not recorded; by ♀ only. **Nestling/fledging period:** young cared for by ♀ only.

Black-bellied Bustard *Lissotis melanogaster* Langbeenkorhaan page 370

Breeds in areas of tall (>1 m) grass, either among trees, or in open grassland, and found in both flat and hilly country. ♂s are polygynous and display (by calling and making visually striking flights) at regularly used sites during the breeding season; ♀s, after mating, undertake all parental care without ♂ assistance. **Nest:** a shallow scrape on the ground among tufts of long grass, sometimes at the base of a sapling or termite mound.
Laying months: mainly Oct-Jan (Sep-Mar), peaking a month or two later in west. **Clutch size:** 1-2. **Eggs:** 50.1-58.5-65.0 x 46.4-51.9-54.6 mm; mass 73-77 g; eggs virtually spherical in shape. **Incubation period:** 23 days (in captivity); by ♀ only. **Nestling/fledging period:** young cared for by ♀ only.

Kori Bustard

Denham's Bustard

Ludwig's Bustard

Ludwig's Bustard

Black-bellied Bustard

Karoo Korhaan *Eupodotis vigorsii* Vaalkorhaan page 370

Endemic to the karoo, breeding widely across the Nama and succulent karoos, in flat to undulating, sparsely vegetated dwarf shrublands, especially in gravelly and stony terrain; also in fallow wheatlands of the s Cape. Pairs and family groups are territorial, these ranging in size between 45-500 ha, their size linked to aridity (largest in the most arid areas). Monogamous, nesting in pairs or trios, the latter assumed to be a pair plus young of a previous brood. **Nest:** eggs are laid in a shallow scrape on the ground, the site sometimes ringed by pebbles. In the karoo the nest site is usually among scattered rocks or small shrubs, whereas in wheatlands and cultivated pastures it is often in crop stubble, or at a site devoid of cover. The ♀ incubates, leaving the egg unattended at intervals when she joins the ♂ or family group to feed.
Laying months: mainly Oct-Nov (Jun-Feb). **Clutch size:** 1. **Eggs:** 63.7-65.7-67.8 × 43.1-43.6-44.3 mm; mass 70 g. **Incubation period:** not recorded; by ♀ only. **Nestling/fledging period:** not recorded.

Rüppell's Korhaan *Eupodotis rueppellii* Woestynkorhaan page 370

Breeds in the arid gravel- and sandy-plains of the Namib Desert where rainfall is both low (<200 mm/a) and unpredictable; found in places where the plains are virtually devoid of vegetation, but more usually occurs where there is some sparse, low-scrub cover. Monogamous, but frequently breeds in extended family groups of 3 or more birds, these assumed to be a pair plus young of a previous brood, which may assist with parental care. **Nest:** eggs are laid in a shallow scrape on the ground, situated among scattered rocks and stones.
Laying months: irregular and recorded in most months, dependent on rainfall; most records between Feb-May. **Clutch size:** usually 1, less often 2, rarely 3. **Eggs:** 55.1-58.3-61.3 × 38.6-42.0-45.0 mm. **Incubation period:** not recorded; by ♀ only. **Nestling/fledging period:** not recorded; young attended by family group.

Blue Korhaan *Eupodotis caerulescens* Bloukorhaan page 370

Endemic to the grasslands and grassy karoo regions of South Africa, this species breeds in flat to undulating, treeless grassland and dwarf shrubland where ground cover <250 mm high; avoids hilly areas, cultivated lands and pastures for breeding. Monogamous, living in pairs or family groups (pair plus 1-3 offspring from previous years) which occupy permanent territories 200-250 ha in size; adjacent nests may be 350-400 m apart. **Nest:** eggs laid in a shallow, unlined scrape 15-20-23 cm in diameter, placed between grass tufts, usually in sufficient cover to screen the incubating bird. Incubating ♀ is sometimes fed by ♂ when she leaves nest to feed.
Laying months: mainly Oct-Nov (Sep-Feb, once May); relays after an early failure. **Clutch size:** 2, less often 1, rarely 3.
Eggs: 49.6-57.8-64.1 × 39.6-42.8-46.0 mm; mass 58-60 g; the eggs in a clutch usually differ greatly in colour and markings. **Incubation period:** 24-28 days; by ♀s only; where >1 ♀, in shifts of 16-80-135 min; where single ♀, eggs unattended about 40% of the day. **Nestling/fledging period:** about 5 weeks; cared for by both sexes or family group.

Karoo Korhaan

Rüppell's Korhaan

Blue Korhaan

Korhaans

Red-crested Korhaan *Lophotis ruficrista* Boskorhaan page 370
A largely woodland-dependent species, breeding widely across the savanna belt, extending into semi-arid shrublands in the west. Polygynous; ♂s call and display through the summer at regularly used sites, their whistling call often culminating in a brief vertical flight above the tree canopy followed by a closed-wing descent to the ground; ♀s mate at these sites but may lay some distance away, undertaking the incubation and chick-rearing without ♂ assistance. **Nest:** eggs are laid in a shallow, unlined scrape on the ground, usually under a sapling or shrub, often in areas where there is a thick layer of leaf litter. The ♀ incubates without ♂ assistance, leaving the eggs unattended for periods during the day to feed.
Laying months: mainly Oct-Feb (Sep-Apr), peaking 1-2 months later in semi-arid west. **Clutch size:** 1-2. **Eggs:** 46.2-50.4-53.4 x 40.4-42.9-44.7 mm. **Incubation period:** 19-21 days (in captivity); by ♀ only. **Nestling/fledging period:** young fly poorly at 6 weeks; cared for by ♀ only.

Northern Black Korhaan *Afrotis afraoides* Witvlerkkorhaan page 370
Breeds in open, semi-arid to arid savanna and grassland; open, treeless plains are favoured, or areas of flat, open ground among scattered trees and shrubs; often in heavily grazed areas. Polygynous; ♂s display at dispersed leks, calling raucously from the ground, mostly during summer, and performing a noisy circular flight during which they may pursue other ♂s; ♀s are inconspicuous and, while breeding, unobtrusive and secretive. ♀s undertake all parental care and lay their clutch 0.1-3 km from a ♂'s display area. **Nest:** eggs are laid on bare ground, sometimes in rudimentary scrape 15 cm wide, among scattered grass-tufts or shrubs, sometimes under a small thorn tree; also in old lands. When incubating, ♀ usually sits tight if approached rather than leaving the nest; eggs are left unattended several times a day when she leaves to feed.
Laying months: mainly Sep-Mar, but all months recorded, rainfall-driven in arid areas. **Clutch size:** 1-2, rarely 3. **Eggs:** 46.0-49.7-54.1 x 38.3-39.9-44.0 mm; mass 43 g. **Incubation period:** 21-23 days (in captivity); by ♀ only. **Nestling/fledging period:** not recorded; young cared for by ♀; fly when only half-grown.

Southern Black Korhaan *Afrotis afra* Swartvlerkkorhaan page 370
Breeds in lowland fynbos and along the southern margins of the karoo, favouring open, flat shrubland with areas of bare ground; occasionally in wheatlands. Polygynous; ♂ behaviour similar to that of Northern Black Korhaan, calling raucously from regularly used sites and performing noisy aerial displays; after mating ♀ lays nearby and undertakes all parental care without ♂ assistance. **Nest:** eggs are laid on bare ground in a small open clearing between low shrubs.
Laying months: mainly Aug-Nov in winter-rainfall region (Aug-Jan), Oct-Dec in e Cape. **Clutch size:** 1, occasionally 2. **Eggs:** 47.7-52.3-57.7 x 38,9-41.4-45.0 mm. **Incubation period:** not recorded; by ♀ only. **Nestling/fledging period:** not recorded; cared for by ♀ only.

White-bellied Korhaan (White-bellied Bustard) *Eupodotis senegalensis* Witpenskorhaan page 370
Breeds in hilly or undulating open grassland, or in sparsely wooded savanna, favouring areas with a good grass cover >30 cm high. Probably monogamous, as it occurs year-round in pairs or, less often, in trios thought to comprise a pair plus offspring from the previous year; territorial and, in prime habitat, a pair/100 ha. Nesting habits are poorly known. **Nest:** eggs are laid on the ground in a small clearing between grass-tufts, sometimes in a shallow, unlined scrape. The ♂ does not incubate but he does remain in the vicinity of the nest and accompanies the ♀ when she leaves the eggs to feed.
Laying months: mainly Nov (Oct-Jan). **Clutch size:** 2, less often 1, rarely 3. **Eggs:** 49.5-52.0-56.6 x 39.6-41.6-42.8 mm. **Incubation period:** 23 days (in captivity); by ♀ only. **Nestling/fledging period:** unknown; young cared for by both sexes.

female approaching nest Red-crested Korhaan

female incubating, panting in the heat Northern Black Korhaan (LEFT & TWO ABOVE)

White-bellied Korhaan Southern Black Korhaan

Flufftails

FLUFFTAILS Family Sarothruridae Worldwide 9 species; all endemic to Afrotropics, 4 breed in southern Africa (perhaps 5, but White-winged Flufftail not yet proved to breed in the region). Small, secretive, ground-nesting rail-like birds; their presence is given away by their hooting calls; monogamous breeders, eggs oval-shaped, plain white, 3-5/clutch; incubation and parental care shared by the sexes; young are initially covered with black down; they are precocial and nidifugous.

Buff-spotted Flufftail *Sarothrura elegans* Gevlekte Vleikuiken
page 371

Breeds in forests, sometimes in well-wooded gardens, nesting on the ground among ground creepers, grass (*Oplismenus hirtellus*), fallen twigs or plant leaves, sometimes against a fallen log or tree trunk. Pairs nest solitarily but adjacent pairs may nest <100 m apart. **Nest:** placed on the ground, the nest is a small, well-hidden, ball- or retort-shaped structure with a domed roof and an entrance hole on one side, sometimes extending to a spout; it is made of dead or skeletonised leaves, moss, grass-stems, twigs, bark, even pine needles; the walls are 3-6 cm thick, the nest cup 8 cm wide; it is lined with fine plant material. The nest measures: external length 13-23 cm; external width 16-21 cm; height 9.5-15 cm; the entrance is 6-10 cm wide, 6-7 cm high; the nest chamber is 8.5-10.5 cm wide, 6-7.5 cm high. The ♂ builds the nest in 2-3 days. ♂s hoot frequently at the onset of breeding, but become silent during the incubation.

Laying months: mainly Nov (Sep-Apr); earlier on the coast than inland; double- or multiple-brooded, interval between clutches 30-36-40 days. **Clutch size:** 3-5, laid at 1-day intervals. **Eggs:** 26.0-28.5-31.3 × 20.6-21.5-22.8 mm. **Incubation period:** 15-16 days, by both sexes, ♂ in day, ♀ at night. **Nestling/fledging period:** young leave nest after 1-2 days, fly at 19-21 days; young cared for by both sexes.

Red-chested Flufftail *Sarothrura rufa* Rooiborsvleikuiken
page 371

Breeds in marshy vegetation, wet or damp underfoot, often where the grass and/or sedge is rank and tangled. Pairs nest solitarily, but adjacent pairs can be within 50 m of each other. **Nest:** a small, shallow, rootlet- and grass-lined cup, 13 cm outside diameter, 8-10 cm cup diameter with a 3-4 cm deep cup; well hidden in a grass tuft, up to 30 cm above the water, and concealed from above by the canopy formed by plant-stems above the nest. Reports of it building a domed nest result from misidentification of Buff-spotted Flufftail nest. Where it occurs alongside the Streaky-breasted Flufftail, the nests of the two species can be confused (see comment in that species).

Laying months: Sep-Mar, peaking earlier in winter-rainfall region (Aug-Jan) than elsewhere; double-brooded. **Clutch size:** 2-3 (2-5); laid at 1-day intervals. **Eggs:** 24.0-27.6-29.4 × 17.6-19.8-22.2 mm. **Incubation period:** 16-18 days; by both sexes, ♂ during day, ♀ at night. **Nestling/fledging period:** young leave nest at 2-3 days, independent at 3-4 weeks.

Striped Flufftail *Sarothrura affinis* Gestreepte Vleikuiken
page 371

Breeds in grassland or fynbos, usually where dry underfoot (not marshy) and where ground-cover is dense and >35 cm in high. Nesting habits are poorly known. Pairs nest solitarily in territories 1.1-1.6-2.3 ha in extent. **Nest:** placed on the ground between grass- or sedge-tufts, it is a small bowl of dry grass-stems and -blades, 9 cm in diameter, the cup 2.5 cm deep; living grass-stems are drawn over to form a loosely tangled canopy above the nest. It is much like the nest of Red-chested Flufftail but is always placed in a drier situation; incubating bird often sits tight and is not easily flushed, and it may hiss like a snake if approached closely.

Laying months: Sep-Mar. **Clutch size:** 4 (4-5). **Eggs:** 25.0-26.3-27.5 × 18.0-19.6-20.5 mm. **Incubation period:** >15 days, by both sexes. **Nestling/fledging period:** young leave nest within a day of hatching.

Streaky-breasted Flufftail *Sarothrura boehmi* Streepborsvleikuiken
page 371

A breeding migrant to n mesic savanna in wet summers (Nov-Apr), nesting in seasonally flooded grasslands, favouring areas where grass cover is rather sparse and 20-35 cm in height over mud or shallow water. **Nest:** a shallow saucer is made of grass-stems and -blades, 9-12 cm in diameter, placed in a grass-tuft, with living stems pulled over to form a dome above the nest; the nest is built up further during the incubation. It is usually on squelchy wet ground rather than over water, and is either built at ground level or is slightly raised (30-80 mm up); where it and the similar Red-chested Flufftail occur together, their nests can be distinguished by the latter placing its nest higher up and in denser, more rank vegetation. ♂s call on arrival, but become silent once nesting starts. The nest is built by the ♂ (in captivity).

Laying months: Nov-Mar; peaking in Jan. **Clutch size:** 4 (2-5), laid at 1-2 day intervals (in captivity). **Eggs:** 24.9-27.0-29.0 × 18.4-19.5-20.8 mm; white, usually unmarked, occasional eggs have some fine speckling. **Incubation period:** 14-18 days (in captivity); by both sexes; ♂ during day, ♀ at night. **Nestling/fledging period:** young leave nest at 1-3 days, fledge at about 35 days (in captivity).

White-winged Flufftail *Sarothrura ayresi* Witvlerkvleikuiken
page 371

Breeding unrecorded in southern Africa but it possibly does so as it is found in summer in suitable breeding habitat. Nesting habits are poorly known. In Ethiopia it nests in short grass (30-45 cm tall) over damp or wet ground in upland wetlands that dry out and reflood seasonally. **Nest:** a domed nest built in a tuft of *Eliocharis* sedge or grass, its base about 10 mm above the ground; it is built with stems and blades of grass and sedges, with live plant-stems drawn over to form the roof. It measures 150 mm outside diameter; 95 mm cup diameter, 48 mm entrance diameter.

Laying months: Aug (Ethiopia). **Clutch size:** 5 (Ethiopia). **Eggs:** 28.0 × 20.2 mm. **Incubation period:** not recorded. **Nestling/fledging period:** not recorded

Buff-spotted Flufftail

Red-chested Flufftail

Striped Flufftail

Streaky-breasted Flufftail

White-winged Flufftail

Crakes, Rail

CRAKES, RAILS, MOORHENS, GALLINULES, COOTS Family Rallidae Worldwide 130 species; 13 breed in Afrotropics, 10 in southern Africa. A diverse family of wetland-living birds, some species extremely secretive, others quite the opposite. With one exception they are monogamous, both sexes sharing nest-building, incubation and chick-rearing (Striped Crake, below, is polyandrous and ♂s in this species undertake all parental care); eggs oval-shaped buff- or brown-coloured, variably marked with shades of darker brown; 4-8/clutch; young are precocial and nidifugous.

Black Crake *Amaurornis flavirostris* Swartriethaan — page 371

Breeds widely in any marshy ground, including sedges, bulrushes and *Phragmites* reedbeds. Pairs or cooperatively breeding family groups nest solitarily, at densities ranging between 1 pair/0.2 -7.5 ha; young from previous broods assist in rearing subsequent broods. **Nest:** invariably placed over water in grass, sedges or reeds; a deep cup made of blades and stems of aquatic plants, some nests with a canopy of plant-stems drawn over the top; usually well-hidden, variable in height above water, between 1 cm and 3 m up. Nests are often built where rank grass has grown thickly into a flooded tree, shrub or fence line. The nest measures 100-200 mm in diameter and is 50-90 mm thick. Change-overs at the nest are often accompanied by raucous duetting.

Laying months: mainly Nov-Mar; but may lay in any month; double-brooded. **Clutch size:** 5-7 (3-9); laid at 1-day intervals. **Eggs:** 29.5-32.6-37.6 × 22.0-24.0-26.1 mm. **Incubation period:** 13-19 days; by both sexes, sometimes shared with helpers. **Nestling/fledging period:** young leave nest within a day of hatching; fledge at 5 weeks.

African Rail *Rallus caerulescens* Grootriethaan — page 371

Breeds in rank, marshy vegetation where it is wet underfoot; *Phragmites* reedbeds and rank vegetation in permanent swamps is favoured over seasonal or ephemeral wetlands. Pairs nest solitarily; 1-4 pairs/ha in prime habitat. **Nest:** a small, saucer-shaped pad, usually placed 10-40 cm above the water, well hidden inside or between grass- or sedge-tufts. It is 15-20 cm in diameter and 5-10 cm thick, made of blades and stems of dry and green grass, and deepening in the centre to form a cup about 20 mm deep. Stems of surrounding plants are drawn over the top of nest, concealing it from above. During nest change-overs one or both birds often call close to the nest.

Laying months: mainly Sep-Feb (Jul-May); relays after early failure. **Clutch size:** usually 4-5 (2-6), laid at 1-day intervals. **Eggs:** 36.2-37.9-40.3 × 25.4-27.6-30.3 mm. **Incubation period:** 20 days; by both sexes. **Nestling/fledging period:** young leave nest soon after hatching; are well feathered by 6-7 weeks.

Baillon's Crake *Porzana pusilla* Kleinriethaan — page 371

Breeds erratically and opportunistically in the region, usually appearing at a suitable breeding site, nesting and disappearing. Typical nesting habitat is shallow, temporarily flooded grass/sedge, often along the margins of a permanent wetland. **Nest:** a small, saucer-shaped pad of dry stems of sedge or grass placed within or between grass-tussocks on squelchy ground or in shallow water (<25 cm deep). It measures 70-190 mm in diameter, the cup 10-30 mm deep and is placed close to the water, usually <20 cm up (4-60). Surrounding grass is drawn over the top of the nest to form a canopy. The incubating bird sometimes sits tight, only flushing when closely approached; at other times it leaves unobtrusively.

Laying months: mainly Dec-Feb (Sep-May). **Clutch size:** 4 (2-7); laid at 1-day intervals. **Eggs:** 26.1-28.5-31.0 × 19.4-20.7-24.9 mm; mass 5-6-9 g (Europe). **Incubation period:** 17-20 days; by both sexes. **Nestling/fledging period:** 7-8 weeks; young cared for by both sexes.

African Crake *Crex egregia* Afrikaanse Riethaan — page 371

A breeding summer visitor, arriving in Nov and breeding widely but sparsely in moist grassland, often along the margins of vleis where damp underfoot. Pairs nest solitarily, 1 pair/ha in high-quality habitat. **Nest:** a saucer-shaped pad of plant-stems well hidden in grass 40-70 cm high. It is placed inside or between sedge- or grass-tufts and measures 140-150 mm in diameter, the cup about 40 mm deep, between 10 mm and 15 cm off the ground (higher over water). Material is added to the nest during incubation and the living grass is increasingly drawn over the top of the nest to form a canopy. ♂s are very vocal in the weeks before egg-laying. The incubating bird usually sits tight if approached, only flushing when almost trodden on.

Laying months: mainly Dec-Feb (Nov-Mar). **Clutch size:** 6-8 (3-9); laid at 1-day intervals. **Eggs:** 31.5-34.8-36.8 × 24.0-25.5-27.3 mm; mass 10.4-11.9-13.1 g. **Incubation period:** unknown; by both sexes; starts before clutch is complete. **Nestling/fledging period:** young leave nest soon after hatching; fledge at 4-5 weeks old.

Striped Crake *Aenigmatolimnas marginalis* Gestreepte Riethaan — page 371

An erratic seasonal visitor to savanna wetlands, mainly in the north, arriving in Dec-Jan in summers of above-average rainfall and breeding in recently flooded, grass/sedge wetlands; a density of 8 nests/24 ha recorded near Harare. Sequentially polyandrous in captivity where ♂s undertook all parental care. **Nest:** a small saucer-shaped pad of dry grass, about 80 mm in diameter, well concealed by having surrounding grass drawn over the top of the nest to form a canopy. It is typically placed 100-150 mm above the water in a grass-tuft, often in a tuft of older (previous summer's) grass rather than recent emergent growth; it is built up further as the incubation progresses. The general nesting area is given away by the ♀s calling early in the breeding season (mostly at night); once eggs are laid the birds become quiet. The incubating bird sits tight, only flushing when closely approached.

Laying months: mainly Jan (Dec-Mar); relays after early failure. **Clutch size:** 4-5, laid at 1-2 day intervals. **Eggs:** 27.0-29.0-33.0 × 19.2-21.1-22.2 mm. **Incubation period:** 17-18 days (in captivity); by ♂ only. **Nestling/fledging period:** 46-53 days (in captivity).

Black Crake

African Rail

Baillon's Crake

African Crake

Striped Crake

Common Moorhen *Gallinula chloropus* **Grootwaterhoender** page 371

Breeds on ponds, dams, pans, rivers with fringing bulrushes or *Phragmites* reeds; also in sedge-marshes and on seasonally inundated floodplains. Pairs nest solitarily but nests of adjacent pairs can be <30 m apart; some pairs assisted by young of previous brood in rearing subsequent brood. **Nest:** a shallow bowl, made of plant stems, typically of broad-bladed leaves (bulrushes etc.), always over water and 15-25 cm above it; usually, but not invariably well concealed, built in or between sedges, bulrushes or *Phragmites*. or in the lower branches of a flooded tree overgrown with rank grass. It measures 180-230 mm in diameter, is 80-120 mm thick, with a cup 120-170 mm wide. Built by both sexes assisted, if present, by helpers. Unlike Lesser Moorhen, does not usually weave a roof canopy of plant-stems over the nest.
Laying months: all months, with slight summer peak; multi-brooded. **Clutch size:** 5-7 (4-12); large clutches perhaps laid by >1 ♀; laid at 1-day intervals. **Eggs:** 38.0-42.3-46.3 x 28.3-30.5-35.0 mm. **Incubation period:** 21-22 days; by both sexes, ♂>♀. **Nestling/fledging period:** young remain in the nest 1-2 days after hatching; fledge at 40-50 days; cared for by both sexes.

Lesser Moorhen *Gallinula angulata* **Kleinwaterhoender** page 371

A seasonal visitor, arriving in Dec and breeding erratically, but sometimes prolifically, in grassy pans and floodplains that become briefly inundated during summers of high rainfall; the birds arrive within days of flooding, call through the day and night after their arrival and quickly commence nesting. Pairs (and perhaps occasional trios as nests occur in which 2 females have laid) nest solitarily, sometimes as close as 20 m apart. **Nest:** a small bowl made from live grass-stems drawn together and pulled over to form a canopy; it is a skimpy structure when egg-laying commences but is substantially built up as incubation progresses. Nests are invariably built over water (usually >½ m deep), the nest placed about 15 cm above the water; nests measure 130-180 mm in diameter with a cup diameter of 90-120 mm.
Laying months: mainly Jan-Feb (Dec-Mar). **Clutch size:** 5-9 (4-10); laid at 1-day intervals; large clutches probably laid by >1 ♀. **Eggs:** 29.9-34.2-38.3 x 22.7-24.8-27.0 mm. **Incubation period:** 19-20 days; by both sexes; starts before clutch complete. **Nestling/fledging period:** 35-38 days; young leave nest within a day of hatching.

African Swamphen *Porphyrio madagascariensis* **Grootkoningriethaan** page 372

Breeds widely and commonly in the region in most marshy habitats. Pairs nest solitarily, some are assisted by young of previous broods. **Nest:** a bulky, bowl-shaped nest, invariably placed over water, usually well hidden in emergent vegetation. It is about the same size as the nest of a Red-knobbed Coot – 300 mm diameter and 200 mm thick – differing mainly in being placed well above the water (15-60 cm up) and hidden in dense grass, sedges, bulrushes or reeds, with plant-stems drawn over the top to form a canopy; occasional nests are poorly concealed; some have an access ramp up one side. It is built by both sexes, with helpers assisting (if present) and material is added through the incubation.
Laying months: all months, but mainly Oct-Mar. **Clutch size:** 4-5 (2-6), laid at 1-day intervals. **Eggs:** 45.3-53.9-59.9 x 32.3-36.6-40.0 mm. **Incubation period:** 23-25 days, by both sexes, mostly the ♀; starts with last-laid egg. **Nestling/fledging period:** 8 weeks; young leave nest soon after hatching, but return to it to roost and feed; cared for by both sexes.

Allen's Gallinule *Porphyrio alleni* **Kleinkoningriethaan** page 371

A summer visitor to n mesic savanna, arriving in Dec and breeding erratically, but sometimes prolifically, in ephemeral wetlands during summers of high rainfall. Preferred habitat is tall emergent grasses and sedge over fairly deep water (½-1½ m) interspersed with lily-covered ponds. **Nest:** a small bowl built with blades of grass and sedge, well hidden in emergent vegetation, placed 0,3-1,0 m above the water; it measures 130-180 mm in diameter, 60-100 mm thick; cup 50 mm deep; could easily be mistaken for the nest of a Black Crake but eggs are significantly larger. Nest-building continues during the incubation, and at change-overs the relieving bird may come flying in carrying nest material.
Laying months: mainly Jan-Feb (Dec-Apr). **Clutch size:** 4-5 (3-8), laid at 1-day intervals. **Eggs:** 31.8-36.6-39.8 x 23.6-26.2-27.5 mm. **Incubation period:** >18 days, by both sexes; starts before clutch complete. **Nestling/fledging period:** young leave nest soon after hatching; cared for by both sexes.

Red-knobbed Coot *Fulica cristata* **Bleshoender** page 372

Breeds widely and commonly in the region on most open waterbodies, even those devoid of emergent vegetation. Small ponds or dams usually support single breeding pairs, whereas large pans can support dozens and even hundreds of nesting birds, their nests conspicuously spaced evenly across the water with no attempt at concealment. Pairs nest solitarily, some assisted by young of previous broods; nests of adjacent pairs can be within 30 m of each other. **Nest:** an untidy mound of whatever plant material is available nearby (stems of sedges, bulrushes, reeds, grass, submerged aquatic plants, etc.), with a large deep cup on top. It measures 300-400 mm in diameter, is 150-250 mm high; the cup, usually lined with finer plant material, is 120 mm in diameter and 50 mm deep. There is often an extended ramp down one side of the nest. Nests may be anchored to reeds, sedges or branches of submerged trees, or they float; nest-building continues through the incubation.
Laying months: all months; no peak except in winter-rainfall region (Jul-Oct). **Clutch size:** 5-7 (3-11); laid at 1-day intervals. **Eggs:** 49.0-53.6-61.1 x 32.8-37.7-42.0 mm; mass 45-45.3-46 g. **Incubation period:** 18-25 days; by both sexes with frequent change-overs. **Nestling/fledging period:** 8 weeks; young hatch asynchronously and leave nest within a day of hatching; both parents, and sometimes older siblings, care for the young.

Common Moorhen

Lesser Moorhen

African Swamphen

Allen's Gallinule (TWO ABOVE)

Red-knobbed Coot

CRANES Family Gruidae Worldwide 15 species; 4 breed in Afrotropics, 3 in southern Africa. Large, stately, ground-living birds of open country, most associated with wetlands. Monogamous; incubation and parental care is shared by the sexes. Some species build a substantial nest over water; others make no nest and lay their eggs on bare ground; eggs oval-shaped, colour variable between species, from unmarked white to cryptically marked with shades of brown; 1-3/clutch; young are precocial and nidifugous.

Wattled Crane *Bugeranus carunculatus* Lelkraanvoël   page 372

Breeds in several small, fragmented populations across the region, with the largest concentration found in the Okavango (estimated 200 pairs). Pairs nest solitarily in extensive, shallow wetlands; in the Okavango it nests in widely scattered pairs on seasonally inundated floodplains; in South Africa and Zimbabwe it nests in relatively permanent upland marshes where adjacent nests can be within 300 m of each other. **Nest:** a large, flat heap of plant-stems, 0,75-1,0-1,5 m in diameter, with the egg lying on top, 12-20-50 cm above the water. It is built from material drawn together from the vicinity of the nest, a process that creates a surrounding moat of shallow water. Sites are frequently reoccupied in successive seasons; some nests are built in shallow ponds of open water, sometimes alongside old nest mounds from previous years. In open marshes the incubating bird is conspicuous, often visible from > 1 km away; less often the nest site is screened from view by emergent vegetation. It is built by both sexes.

Laying months: mainly in winter (May-Aug); but all months recorded; relays after early failure. **Clutch size:** 1-2; single-egg clutches, more common in South Africa than Zimbabwe and Botswana; laid at a 2-4 day interval. **Eggs:** 91.0-104.1-117.0 × 58.7-64.1-71.5 mm; mass 186-338 g. **Incubation period:** 33-36 days (31-40); starts with first-laid egg; by both sexes, in shifts of 151-157-163 min (by ♂) and 69-238-439 min (by ♀); the second egg is abandoned when the first egg hatches. **Nestling/fledging period:** 90-130 days; young cared for by both sexes, remains with parents 7-12 months.

Blue Crane *Anthropoides paradiseus* Bloukraanvoël   page 372

Breeds in open grassland, dwarf, semi-arid shrubland and, especially in w Cape, in planted pastures or harvested/fallow lands. In flocks during winter, with pairs separating off in spring to nest solitarily; most nesting pairs are spaced > ½ km apart. Most clutches are laid on dry ground, fewer on damp ground, and occasionally a nest platform is built over shallow water; occasionally nests on an island in a dam from which the nestlings have to swim to leave. The nest site is always positioned to command a wide view of the surroundings. **Nest:** usually no nest is made, the eggs being laid in a small clearing, 40-50 cm across, on bare ground; in some cases, they are encircled by a ring of pebbles, by grass stubble or sheep droppings. Grassland nest sites are often on open hillsides or near the headwaters of a stream where there is some damp ground. and in these cases a pad of plant material may be brought to the site to keep the eggs dry. In captivity the ♂ selects the site a week before egg-laying. Pairs frequently nest in the vicinity of a previous year's nest.

Laying months: mainly Oct-Dec (Aug-Apr), later in n Namibia (Dec-Mar); relays after early failure; single-brooded. **Clutch size:** 2, rarely 1; laid at a 2-3 day interval. **Eggs:** 82.4-93.3-101.0 × 56.2-60.3-65.0 mm; mass 168-185-202 g. **Incubation period:** 29-30 days; starts with first-laid egg; by both sexes, in shifts of 29-64-89 min (by ♂) and 57-94-190 min (by ♀). **Nestling/fledging period:** 12 weeks; young cared for by both sexes; in contrast to the Wattled Crane, 2 young are commonly reared from 2-egg clutches.

Grey Crowned Crane *Balearica regulorum* Mahem   page 373

Breeds mainly in mesic grasslands and savanna, in tall grass-, sedge- or reed-marshes over shallow (<0,4 m deep) water. Pairs nest solitarily, but in suitable habitat they may nest in close proximity to one another, e.g. at one site 13 pairs in a 100 ha wetland, neighbouring nests here <50 m apart. **Nest:** well screened by tall sedge or grass, the nest is a substantial pile of plant material obtained by trampling down the vegetation in 5-9 m diameter area and heaping these together to form the nest; it measures 0,6-1.2-2 m in diameter and stands 20-30 cm above the water; the eggs are laid in a shallow cup, 25 cm wide, on top of this. In Zimbabwe it occasionally nests in trees, using the large treetop platform nest of a Secretarybird or Tawny Eagle, 5-8 m up from the ground; in marshes old nests of Wattled Crane are occasionally taken over, or nest is built on a dry island surrounded by water. Pairs frequently nest at, or close to, the position of a previous year's nest. The nest is built by both sexes.

Laying months: mainly Dec-Jan (Nov-Mar, rarely Apr-May); relays after an early failure; single-brooded. **Clutch size:** 3 (2-4); laid at 2-4 day intervals. **Eggs:** 75.9-85.3-93.9 × 52.0-57.4-69.3 mm; mass 182 g; eggs plain white or pale blue, unmarked (unusual for a crane). **Incubation period:** 29-31 days; starts with first-laid egg (in captivity); by both sexes, ♂ shifts 100-152 min, ♀ shifts 102-116 min; 6-7 change-overs/day; eggs unattended about 9% of the day. **Nestling/fledging period:** 56-100 days; young leave nest within hours of hatching; cared for by both sexes; remain with parents on breeding territory 4+ months, before joining winter flock.

Wattled Crane

Wattled Crane

Blue Crane

Grey Crowned Crane (LEFT & TWO ABOVE)

BUTTONQUAILS Family Turnicidae Worldwide 17 species; 4 breed in Afrotropics, 3 in southern Africa. A family of small, secretive, terrestrial gamebird-like birds of uncertain affinities. The Hottentot and Black-rumped Buttonquails, given species status here, are treated as races (*nanus* and *hottentotus*) by some authorities as the differences between them are slight (eye colour and minor plumage differences; *hottentotus* resident, *nanus* apparently migratory). They are sexually dichromatic (♀s brighter) and ♀s utter a far-carrying booming call when breeding to attract ♂s. Captive-breeding studies have shown that the Kurrichane Buttonquail is sequentially polyandrous and it is assumed that *nanus* and *hottentotus* are as well. The nest is a shallow scrape in the ground; eggs, oval-pyriform, cryptically marked; 3-4/clutch; the young are precocial and nidifugous.

Kurrichane Buttonquail *Turnix sylvaticus* Bosveldkwarteltjie page 373

Nomadic and irruptive in savanna and semi-arid regions; present and breeding widely in some years but not others; favours short, sparse grassland, often among trees, or in fallow lands. ♀s make their presence known by uttering a far-carrying, low-pitched hooting call, often after dark. A solitary nester. **Nest:** a small, shallow scrape in the ground, 60-75 mm in diameter, 10 mm deep, sparsely lined with pieces of dry grass. It is placed against a grass-tuft, or between tufts that conceal the eggs to some extent, although they are often easily seen from above. The ♂, which undertakes all parental care without ♀ assistance, sits tight on eggs if approached, flying off at the last moment.
Laying months: mainly Dec-Mar (Sep-May, rarely in other months). **Clutch size:** 3-4 (rarely 2 or 5), laid at 1-day intervals. **Eggs:** 20.8-23.8-26.2 x 17.0-18.4-20.0 mm; markings on eggs are usually browner in this species than in Black-rumped Buttonquail. **Incubation period:** 14 days (12-15, in captivity), by ♂ only; he leaves nest about 8x/day to feed (in captivity). **Nestling/fledging period:** fly at 7-9 days, full grown at 35 days (in captivity); young cared for by the ♂.

Black-rumped Buttonquail *Turnix nanus* Swartrugkwarteltjie page 373

A nomadic or perhaps migratory species that breeds in summer in mesic grasslands and wetland edges, commonly present in one year and absent in another, its occurrence perhaps related to seasons of good rainfall. At the start of breeding, ♀s call to attract ♂s, uttering a distinctive, frequently repeated, low-pitched hoot; probably polyandrous. A solitary nester. **Nest:** a shallow scrape in the ground, 50-75 mm in diameter, 20 mm deep, often in damp ground, concealed in grass about 250-500 mm tall, away from trees; it is placed against a grass-tuft, or between tufts and is sparsely lined with dry grass and loosely screened from above by having live grass-stems drawn over to form a thin canopy above the eggs.
Laying months: mainly Dec-Mar (Sep-Mar). **Clutch size:** 3 (2-4). **Eggs:** 21.3-23.0-24.5 x 17.3-18.5-20.0 mm. **Incubation period:** 12-14 days; by ♂ only. **Nestling/fledging period:** not recorded.

Hottentot Buttonquail *Turnix hottentottus* Kaapse Kwarteltjie

Restricted to winter-rainfall region of s Cape; favours lowish (20-40 cm) shrubland of fynbos or restios; also fallow lands; probably moves about locally in response to changing conditions. A solitary nester. Nesting habits poorly known; probably polyandrous. **Nest:** a scrape in the ground 100 mm in diameter, between or beneath plant-tufts.
Laying months: mainly Oct (Sep-Dec). **Clutch size:** 3-4 (2-5). **Eggs:** 23.5-24.1-24.8 x 19.0-20.1-20.2 mm. **Incubation period:** not recorded. **Nestling/fledging period:** not recorded.

Kurrichane Buttonquail (THREE ABOVE)

Black-rumped Buttonquail

Hottentot Buttonquail

DIKKOPS (THICK-KNEES) Family Burhinidae Worldwide 10 species; 3 breed in Afrotropics, 2 in southern Africa. Nocturnal, terrestrial birds; monogamous; sexes share incubation and parental care; pairs nest solitarily; eggs, oval-shaped, cryptically marked, 2/clutch; laid on bare ground or in a shallow scrape; young are precocial and nidifugous.

Spotted Dikkop (Spotted Thick-knee) *Burhinus capensis* Gewone Dikkop — page 373

Breeds widely in the region, typically in flat, open or lightly wooded landscapes where there are areas of bare ground and the grass or forb cover is short; also commonly nests in open land in cities and towns (in parks, golf courses, playing fields, vacant land, large gardens, etc). Pairs nest solitarily but occasionally in some urban environments, adjacent pairs are recorded nesting within a few metres of each other. **Nest:** eggs are laid on the ground with little or no scrape being made, and no pebbles or other nest-lining material is usually brought to the site. Typically, the site commands a view in all directions, and the pairs often lie among old branches, between stones or tufts of vegetation, these serving to disrupt the background and conceal the eggs; the site chosen is frequently near, or under a tree or bush, if available and is often close to a previous season's nest. Birds nesting in rural areas are cautious and unobtrusive at the nest and, if approached, the incubating bird slips off the eggs long before one is aware of it; urban-nesting birds, however, are often bold, sitting tight when approached by humans or animals, or they stand their ground over the nest, adopting a threatening, stiff-wing-spreading display.

Laying months: mainly Sep-Oct (Aug-Apr), peaks 2 months later in arid west; relays after earlier failure; sometimes double-brooded. **Clutch size:** 2, rarely 1 or 3; laid at a 2-day interval. **Eggs:** 46.9-52.0-58.7 × 34.6-38.1-41.8 mm. **Incubation period:** 24-27 days; by both sexes; mostly by ♀ during day. **Nestling/fledging period:** 8 weeks (in captivity); young cared for by both sexes.

Water Dikkop (Water Thick-knee) *Burhinus vermiculatus* Waterdikkop — page 373

Breeds close to water, usually <20 m from the water's edge along sandy margins of rivers, lakes and dams, and on islands; also on sandy beaches at estuaries and, infrequently, along the coast. Pairs nest solitarily and are widely spaced. **Nest:** eggs are laid in an unlined, or sparsely lined shallow scrape in the sand, typically alongside some disruptive feature like driftwood, beach debris, leaf litter, animal dung, stones and rocks, or some vegetation. In the absence of seeing the parent bird, the eggs of this species can be distinguished from those of the Spotted Dikkop by having larger, but more sparse blotches so that more of the ground-colour of the egg shows through. A coastal nest could, at a glance, be mistaken for that of an African Oystercatcher.

Laying months: mainly Sep-Nov (Jul-Jan); sometimes double-brooded. **Clutch size:** 2, rarely 1. **Eggs:** 44.0-49.2-54.0 × 32.7-35.7-39.0 mm. **Incubation period:** 22-25 days; by both sexes. **Nestling/fledging period:** 61-63 days; young cared for by both sexes.

STILTS, AVOCETS Family Recurvirostridae Worldwide 10 species; 2 breed in Afrotropics and in southern Africa. Aquatic wading birds; monogamous; sexes share incubation and parental care; pairs nest solitarily or, more usually, colonially, from a few pairs to hundreds; eggs, pyriform in shape, cryptically marked, 4/clutch; young are precocial and nidifugous.

Black-winged Stilt *Himantopus himantopus* Rooipootelsie — page 373

Breeds in shallow-water wetlands (pans, lakes, floodplains), especially those recently flooded or drying out: seldom nests regularly at any one place. Pairs occasionally nest solitarily, but more often colonially, usually 5-10 pairs (rarely >50 pairs) spaced at 20-50 m intervals. **Nest:** a raised pad of water-weed and other aquatic plant-stems, built in shallow water (typically 50-300 mm deep), or on a muddy islet surrounded by water, on short tufts of grass or sedge, or on some other feature that supports the nest (including skeletons of drowned animals!). It is 150 mm in diameter and 50-250 mm high; some are conspicuous (e.g. if placed on open mud), but most blend well with their surroundings. Receding water-levels may leave the nest high and dry; if water-levels rise, the birds usually build up the nest. Stilts call excitedly and frequently when nesting and fly up together to mob any potential predator that approaches.

Laying months: all months recorded, but mainly Aug-Nov, peaking later in Namibia (Feb-Apr). **Clutch size:** 4 (2-5; 6-7 eggs probably laid by >1 ♀); laid at 1-day intervals. **Eggs:** 40.7-43.3-46.3 × 27.6-31.5-33.4 mm. **Incubation period:** 24-26-27 days; by both sexes, but mostly the ♀; starts when clutch complete. **Nestling/fledging period:** 28-32 days (Europe); young cared for by both sexes.

Pied Avocet *Recurvirostra avosetta* Bontelsie — page 373

Breeds mainly on seasonal wetlands, especially in open, semi-arid areas; it typically nests when water-levels are receding, exposing bare, muddy shorelines and low, flat islands; also nests, less regularly, in marshes with emergent vegetation, sites that are more typical of Black-winged Stilt; the two species occasionally nest alongside one another in these situations. Pairs nest solitarily or, more usually, in small colonies of 2-10 pairs (rarely >50), adjacent nests sometimes within 5 m of each other. **Nest:** a scrape in the ground, usually in an exposed position providing good visibility, on an island or along a bare shoreline; in hard substrates an animal footprint, or some other indentation in the ground, is used; nest scrape either unlined or, more usually, a pad of grass, twigs or other material is made, 220-300 mm in diameter and 30-50 mm high, built by both sexes. During incubation, the bird sitting on the nest is conspicuous but it quickly leaves if approached.

Laying months: all months recorded, but mainly Aug-Nov. **Clutch size:** 4 (2-5); laid at 1-2 day intervals. **Eggs:** 48.0-51.3-53.9 × 34.2-35.3-37.0 mm; mass 28-32-40 g (Europe). **Incubation period:** 22-24-27 days; shared equally by both sexes. **Nestling/fledging period:** 26-27-28 days; young cared for by both sexes.

Spotted Dikkop

Water Dikkop

Black-winged Stilt

Pied Avocet

Oystercatcher, Lapwings

OYSTERCATCHERS Family Haematopodidae Worldwide 11 species; 1 breeds in Afrotropics, and it is endemic to southern Africa. Monogamous, both sexes preparing the nest, incubating and rearing the young. Eggs oval to pyriform; 2/clutch, cryptically marked; young are precocial and nidifugous.

African Oystercatcher *Haematopus moquini* Swarttobie   page 373

Breeds along the southern and west coasts (from s KwaZulu-Natal to the Hoanib River in Namibia). Pairs nest solitarily and are spaced at intervals of 100-600 m in suitable habitat along mainland beaches; on offshore islands, however, adjacent pairs often nest <20 m apart (and rarely within 1½ m). Pairs remain together year-round and breed in the same territories annually. **Nest:** a shallow scrape, 210 mm in diameter and 40 mm deep, usually on a rise or in some other position giving a commanding view; often among washed-up kelp, among stones, or low shrubby vegetation which provide some concealment for the eggs and the sitting bird. Occasional clutches are laid on bare rock, or on ledges of rock stacks. Both sexes prepare the nest site and the same positions are sometimes reused in successive seasons. Nests on offshore islands are typically well lined with shell fragments (apparently to conceal them from Kelp Gulls); in contrast, mainland beach nests are seldom lined. Beach nests are usually about 50 m back from the tidal slope.
Laying months: mainly Nov-Jan (Sep-Apr), peaking a month later in Namibia; single-brooded, lays up to three replacement clutches after earlier failures. **Clutch size:** 2 (1-2, rarely 3); laid at a 2-day interval. **Eggs:** 49.1-60.7-65.2 × 37.9-41.0-43.7 mm; mass 45-55.8-65 g. **Incubation period:** 27-30-39 days; by both sexes; begins (intermittently) with first-laid egg. **Nestling/fledging period:** 35-40 days; young cared for by both sexes.

LAPWINGS, PLOVERS Family Charadriidae Worldwide 67 species; 16 breed in Afrotropics, 11 in southern Africa. The smaller species in the family are known as plovers and the larger species as lapwings; monogamous; sexes share incubation and chick-rearing; nest on the ground in a shallow scrape; eggs oval to pyriform, cryptically marked, 2/clutch in plovers, 3-4/clutch in lapwings; some bury their eggs when left unattended; some control high egg temperatures by bringing water to the nest in belly feathers ('belly-wetting'); young are precocial and nidifugous.

Crowned Lapwing *Vanellus coronatus* Kroonkiewiet   page 374

Breeds widely wherever open ground with short grass (<6 cm tall) is to be found; favours recently burnt or heavily grazed grasslands, but also nests on airfields, sports grounds, golf courses, old lands and, locally, on mowed road-verges. Pairs nest solitarily, occasionally semi-gregariously (e.g. 9 pairs in 4 ha); ♂s occasionally polygynous (♂ with 2 mates, nesting 3 m part). **Nest:** a shallow scrape in the ground, 150 mm in diameter and 30-40 mm deep, sometimes positioned alongside a mound of dry cow-dung, among pebbles/stones or where some object disrupts the background. It is lined with grass-stubble, flakes of dry dung, or pebbles, and these continue to be added to the nest during the incubation; the amount of such lining is indicative of how far the incubation has advanced; in thickly lined nests, the eggs often lie partly buried in the lining.
Laying months: all months recorded, mainly Aug-Oct; in man-modified habitats (golf courses, etc.) often a second laying peak in Feb-Apr; relays after early failures; sometimes double-brooded. **Clutch size:** 3 (2-4, once 5, probably laid by 2 ♀s); laid at 1-day intervals. **Eggs:** 32.0-40.0-45.9 × 26.0-28.9-31.5 mm. **Incubation period:** 29-30-31days; by both sexes, but mostly by ♀; begins before clutch is completed. **Nestling/fledging period:** 29-31 days; young cared for by both sexes.

Black-winged Lapwing *Vanellus melanopterus* Grootswartvlerkkiewiet   page 374

Breeds on high-lying ground in mesic grasslands in the interior and in coastal areas in s Cape; favours areas where grass cover is short as a result of recent burning or heavy grazing; occasionally in ploughed land. Pairs nest solitarily or semi-gregariously, 3-6 pairs nesting within 50-100 m of each other; it sometimes also nests in loose association with nesting Crowned Lapwings. **Nest:** a shallow scrape, 125-200 mm in diameter, often placed alongside a mound of dry cow-dung. It is well lined with grass-stubble and flakes of dry dung, and these materials continue to be added during the incubation. When unattended, the eggs often lie half-buried in the lining.
Laying months: mainly Aug-Oct (May-Nov). **Clutch size:** 3 (2-4). **Eggs:** 36.5-41.8-46.5 × 26.7-29.4-31.3 mm. **Incubation period:** 30-31 days; by both sexes, taking shifts of about 90 min each; begins when clutch is complete. **Nestling/fledging period:** 29-31 days; young cared for by both sexes; remain with adults until following breeding season.

Senegal Lapwing *Vanellus lugubris* Kleinswartvlerkkiewiet   page 374

Breeds in hot, low-lying savanna in e southern Africa, in open, bare, short-grass (<50 mm tall) areas within acacia or other woodland, especially where recently burnt or heavily grazed; typically on flat, hard, dry, clayey ground; sometimes in old lands. Pairs nest solitarily or in loose colonies (e.g. 5 pairs in 2 ha) when adjacent nests can be <50 m apart. **Nest:** a shallow scrape in the ground, 70-120 mm in diameter and 35-40 mm deep, lined with grass-stubble, flakes of dung, antelope droppings or pebbles; this material continues to be added to the nest during the incubation, and the eggs are often partly buried in the lining when they are left unattended.
Laying months: mainly Aug-Sep; less often Jun-Nov, once in Jan. **Clutch size:** 3 (2-4, rarely 5). **Eggs:** 33.0-36.1-38.3 × 25.3-26.7-28.0 mm. **Incubation period:** 27-28 days; by both sexes, change-overs at 40-min intervals; begins with first-laid egg. **Nestling/fledging period:** 29-32 days; young cared for by both sexes; young remain with adults until following breeding season.

African Oystercatcher nest on rocky beach (left) and sandy beach (centre & right)

Crowned Lapwing

Black-winged Lapwing

Senegal Lapwing

Lapwings

Blacksmith Lapwing *Vanellus armatus* Bontkiewiet page 374
Breeds throughout the region, nesting on the margins of virtually all waterbodies that have bare, muddy edges or shortly cropped fringing vegetation; most nest sites are on damp or wet ground within a few metres of the water's edge, occasional nests are located away from water. Pairs nest solitarily, and adjacent pairs along the margins of a large pan or dam are usually spaced about 100 m apart; rare instances of polygyny are known. **Nest:** eggs are often laid in the hoof-print of an animal, or in some other indentation; otherwise in a shallow scrape in the ground is prepared by both sexes; it is usually within a few metres of the water's edge, especially where the water is receding. The scrape is lined with grass-stubble, fragments of dung, or mud flakes, in which the eggs often lie half-buried; this material continues to be added during the incubation. Rarely, a more substantial nest is built over shallow water similar to that built by Black-winged Stilt (see page 103).
Laying months: all months, but mainly Jul-Oct; relays after early failure; sometimes double-brooded. **Clutch size:** 3-4, less often 2; rare clutches of 5-6 eggs probably laid by >1 ♀; laid at 1-2 day intervals. **Eggs:** 35.0-39.6-42.5 x 27.0-29.0-31.3 mm. **Incubation period:** 26-29-33 days; begins with first-laid egg; by both sexes, change-overs at 40-80 min intervals. **Nestling/fledging period:** 40 days; young cared for by both sexes.

African Wattled Lapwing *Vanellus senegallus* Lelkiewiet page 374
Breeds widely in mesic grasslands and savanna in close proximity to vleis or streams, favouring recently burnt or shortly grazed grassland; the nest is typically within 100 m of the nearest water and is positioned where it commands a wide view. Pairs nest solitarily, adjacent pairs seldom <1 km apart. **Nest:** a shallow scrape in the ground, 140-150 mm in diameter and 25 mm deep, thickly lined with root-stubble and fragments of grass-stems, dung and other debris; this continues to be added during the incubation; when the eggs are left unattended they usually lie half-buried. Belly-wetting to maintain egg temperature has been recorded in Zambia, but not in southern Africa.
Laying months: mainly Sep-Oct (Jul-Dec); single-brooded; rarely relays after an earlier failure. **Clutch size:** 4 (2-4); laid at a 1-2 day intervals. **Eggs:** 43.6-48.8-53.8 x 31.0-34.3-36.0 mm. **Incubation period:** 28-30-32 days; by both sexes; change-overs at 40-45 min intervals. **Nestling/fledging period:** 40 days; young cared for by both sexes.

Long-toed Lapwing *Vanellus crassirostris* Witvlerkkiewiet page 374
Breeds in tropical savanna in the north on seasonally inundated wetlands; the timing of its breeding coincides with the drying out of these systems after flooding. Pairs are highly territorial and nest solitarily, a pair/0.1-0.3-0.7 ha (Kenya). **Nest:** usually placed over water on a raft of floating vegetation, otherwise on the muddy water-verges, or on a freshly exposed islet surrounded by boggy ground; often over water >1 m deep and rarely on dry ground; it is a substantial nest for a lapwing, a pad of plant material 50-100 mm thick and the incubating bird is often screened from view by surrounding sedges and grass.
Laying months: mainly Jul-Sep (Apr-Oct); sometimes relays after early failure. **Clutch size:** 3-4 (2-4); laid at 1-4 day intervals. **Eggs:** 40.5-43.3-47.8 x 29.0-30.6-33.5 mm. **Incubation period:** 27 days; by both sexes. **Nestling/fledging period:** 8 weeks; young cared for by both sexes.

White-crowned Lapwing *Vanellus albiceps* Witkopkiewiet page 374
Breeds along larger, low-lying, meandering rivers with extensive sandbank in n and ne southern Africa. Pairs nest solitarily, and vigorously defend a territory that extends ½-1 km in length, along a stretch of river. Breeds at the end of winter when sandbanks and islands reach maximum exposure as a result of low-water flow. **Nest:** a shallow scrape in the sand, 12-15-18 cm in diameter, and 1-20 m from the water's edge; some are placed alongside a tuft of grass, drift, or some other distracting object, others are in open, bare sand. Several scrapes are prepared before the eggs are laid in one, and the scrape is left unlined. While nesting, the birds are extremely vigilant, the incubating bird leaving the nest at the first sign of a threat; if cattle, buffalo or ungulates approach the nest too closely when they come to drink, they are driven away from the nest by the birds. In the heat of the day egg temperature is maintained by belly-wetting.
Laying months: mainly Aug-Oct (Jul-Nov); coincides with lowest flow in rivers. **Clutch size:** 3-4 (2-4, one record of 6 probably laid by >1 ♀). **Eggs:** 39.7-43.0-47.6 x 28.0-31.2-34.3 mm. **Incubation period:** at least 26 days; by both sexes. **Nestling/fledging period:** not recorded; young cared for by both sexes.

Blacksmith Lapwing

African Wattled Lapwing

Long-toed Lapwing

White-crowned Lapwing

Kittlitz's Plover *Charadrius pecuarius* **Geelborsstrandkiewiet**   page 374

Breeds widely in the region on bare, flat, open shores of pans and dams where the water is receding. Pairs nest solitarily, and on suitable stretches of shoreline may be spaced at 50-100 m intervals, occasionally within 10 m of each other. **Nest:** a scrape in dry ground (i.e. not on moist or wet ground), typically in hard, dry mud, occasionally in sand; mostly within 150 m of the water's edge. The scrape is 80-110-140 mm wide and 20-30-45 mm deep and it is thickly lined with fragments of grass, mud flakes, dung or small pebbles; this material is collected in the vicinity of the nest and brought to the site while the eggs are being laid and more is added during the incubation. Several scrapes are prepared before one is selected. Whenever the nest is left unattended, the eggs are completely covered with the nest lining, and the departing bird invariably does this (with a characteristic kick-and-rotate action), even when under pressure and anxious to flee. As shown opposite, the covered eggs are virtually undetectable. Eggs may be left buried like this unattended for long periods (5-7 hrs) in the day.

Laying months: mainly Aug-Sep (summer-rainfall areas) and Oct-Jan (winter-rainfall); but all months recorded. **Clutch size:** 2, less often 1 (very rarely 3); laid at a 1-2 day interval. **Eggs:** 27.9-31.2-34.5 x 20.0-22.1-23.4 mm. **Incubation period:** 22-25-28 days; by both sexes; begins with last-laid egg. **Nestling/fledging period:** 22-30-32 days; young cared for by both sexes.

Chestnut-banded Plover *Charadrius pallidus* **Rooibandstrandkiewiet**   page 374

Breeding range is closely associated with saline watebodies, both along west coast at large, shallow-water bays (Walvis Bay and others) and inland at large and small saltpans and commercial saltworks; the bulk of the region's breeding birds are on Makgadikgadi Pan (Botswana) and Etosha Pan (Namibia). Pairs nest solitarily or in loose aggregations, usually spaced at 20-100 m intervals. **Nest:** a shallow scrape in the ground, usually in a pebbly substrate, otherwise on dry mud; usually <50 m from the nearest water. The nest scrape is 60 mm in diameter and 13 mm deep, sparsely or well lined with pebbles or, occasionally, with other beach debris (including flamingo feathers); several scrapes are made before one is selected. Eggs are often left unattended for long periods, and when they are, they are not covered with nest material or sand; belly-wetting to cool eggs has been recorded in hot weather.

Laying months: all months recorded, but peak laying months varies regionally: Apr-May (Namibia), Aug-Sep (Botswana), Nov-Dec (w Cape). **Clutch size:** 2, less often 1; laid at a 1-2 day interval. **Eggs:** 28.6-30.6-33.2 x 20.7-22.6-24.4 mm. **Incubation period:** not recorded; by both sexes. **Nestling/fledging period:** not recorded; young cared for by both sexes.

White-fronted Plover *Charadrius marginatus* **Vaalstrandkiewiet**   page 374

Breeds widely and commonly along the coast (the subspecies *arenaceus*) and inland along larger, east-flowing rivers (the subspecies *mechowi*). Pairs nest solitarily; coastal birds are typically spaced >100 m apart, but occasionally adjacent nests may be within 15 m of one another. Coastal birds remain paired and territorial year-round. **Nest:** a shallow scrape in sand or gravel 100-150 mm in diameter and 25 mm deep, some lined with shell fragments or pebbles, others unlined; several scrapes are made before one is used; it is typically placed where the sitting bird has a good view, and usually close to driftwood, a plant, rock or shells that provide a disruptive background. Eggs usually lie partly buried in sand when the nest is left unattended. Pairs nesting on popular recreational beaches become used to people, and the incubating bird often allows a close (<25 m) approach. Belly-wetting to cool the eggs has been recorded by incubating birds on the Zambezi River.

Laying months: year-round on the coast, peaking in Dec-Jan (Namibia), Sep-Nov (w Cape); Jul-Sep (east coast); inland population peaks in Jul-Oct; relays after early failure; sometimes double-brooded. **Clutch size:** 2 (1-3, rarely 4); laid at a 2-7 day interval. **Eggs:** 24.5-32.1-35.9 x 20.0-22.8-25.0 mm (race *arenaceus*); eggs of inland race are smaller and darker, about 28 x 21 mm. **Incubation period:** 27-28-29 days; begins with last-laid egg; by both sexes. **Nestling/fledging period:** 35-38 days; young cared for by both sexes.

Three-banded Plover *Charadrius tricollaris* **Driebandstrandkiewiet**   page 374

Breeds widely in the region; always close to water, either along a stream or river, or on the shores of a pan, dam, or other freshwater wetland. Pairs nest solitarily and are widely spaced (usually >1 km apart). The nest is typically <100 m from water's edge, usually on a raised position that provides good visibility, and usually among pebbles or rocks; less often, it may nest up to ½ km from water, and on dry mud, not among pebbles. **Nest:** a shallow scrape 80-150 mm in diameter and 25 mm deep, well lined with small pebbles or, where a dry mud surface is used, flakes of mud or dung; some nests are placed alongside cattle dung or between similar-coloured pellets of antelope dung (as shown in the photograph opposite); several scrapes may be prepared before one is used; nests are frequently located in the same general area in successive years. Behaviour at incubation change-overs differs from other plovers in that they usually arrive and depart from the nest by flying, and the pair frequently call briefly to each other while doing so.

Laying months: mainly Jul-Oct, but all months recorded; relays after an early failure; sometimes double-brooded. **Clutch size:** 2, occasionally 1 (3 or 4 eggs very rarely recorded); laid at a 1-2 day interval. **Eggs:** 27.0-30.0-32.7 x 20.0-22.0-24.1 mm. **Incubation period:** 28 days (26-31); begins with last-laid egg. **Nestling/fledging period:** fly weakly at 3 weeks, fledge at 30-32 days; young cared for by both sexes.

Kittlitz's Plover

Kittlitz's Plover   eggs uncovered (left), covered (right)

Chestnut-banded Plover

White-fronted Plover

Three-banded Plover

Jacanas, Painted Snipe, Finfoot

JACANAS Family Jacanidae Worldwide 8 species; 2 breed in Afrotropics, both in southern Africa. One is polyandrous (African Jacana) and the ♂ performs all parental duties, the other (Lesser Jacana) is monogamous and both sexes share incubation and chick rearing; both nest on floating vegetation on freshwater wetlands; eggs pyriform, highly glossed, cryptically coloured, 3-4/clutch; the young are precocial and nidifugous.

African Jacana *Actophilornis africanus* Grootlangtoon page 374

Breeds on pans, dams, lagoons, floodplains and other freshwater wetlands where there is a cover of floating aquatic vegetation, especially *Nymphaea* sp., *Potamogeton* sp. or *Ludwigia stolonifera*. ♂s defend breeding territories 0,2-0,6 ha in size; adjacent nests >50 m apart; polyandrous ♀s exclude other ♀s from larger territories that encompass 1-3 (max of 7) ♂ territories, and they lay successive clutches (up to 10/season), many as replacements, for the ♂s in their territory. **Nest:** a small, sodden heap of plant stems (typically *Ceratophyllum* sp.), placed on floating vegetation; 95-200-330 mm wide and 20 mm high; it is built by the ♂ by pulling stems of these plants to the site, continuing this through the incubation. Nests are usually very exposed, but some are hidden in vegetation (especially in *Ludwigia*, if present). If water levels rise dramatically, eggs may be moved (by floating them) from a sinking nest to a new position. All parental care is by the ♂, and on warm days the eggs are left unattended for most of the daytime.

Laying months: all months recorded, but mainly Nov-Mar; the season is progressively extended towards the equator; relays after early nest failures; occasionally double-brooded. **Clutch size:** 4, less often 3 (rarely 5); laid at 1-day intervals. **Eggs:** 28.2-32.6-36.0 x 19.7-23.1-25.1 mm; mass 7.9-8.9-10.5 g. **Incubation period:** 23-24-26 days; by ♂ only; starts with third-laid egg; ♂ attentiveness varies according to ambient temperature, 71% on cool days, 44% on hot days; incubating shifts 1-11-39 min; 'off' shifts 1-10-54 min. **Nestling/fledging period:** 39-44 days; young cared for by ♂; carried under wings for first 14 days.

Lesser Jacana *Microparra capensis* Dwerglangtoon page 374

In the region, breeds most abundantly and regularly in the Okavango; elsewhere its occurrence as a breeding species is sporadic and unpredictable. Pairs nest solitarily, sometimes within 100 m of each other. **Nest:** a skimpy platform of aquatic plant-stems placed on floating vegetation over deep water, usually where there is some grass or sedge cover and usually placed alongside an emergent plant; it measures 100-200 mm in diameter and is 5-10 mm thick. Both sexes build the nest and continue adding material during the incubation. If water levels rise dramatically, eggs may be moved (by floating them) from a sinking nest to a new position.

Laying months: Mar-Apr (Feb-Nov). **Clutch size:** 3 (2-5); laid at 1-day intervals. **Eggs:** 23.0-24.9-26.9 x 16.9-18.0-18.8 mm. **Incubation period:** 21 days (once 34 days); by both sexes, shared equally, in alternating shifts of 5-41-77 min; nest attendance high (82%); belly-wetting occurs on hot days; starts when clutch complete. **Nestling/fledging period:** 32-40 days; young cared for by both sexes; young are carried under the wing when young.

PAINTED SNIPES Family Rostratulidae Worldwide 3 species, 1 breeds in Afrotropics and in southern Africa. Polyandrous; ♂ incubates and rears young; ground nester; eggs oval-shaped, cryptically marked, 4/clutch; young are precocial and nidifugous.

Greater Painted Snipe *Rostratula benghalensis* Goudsnip page 374

Breeds widely but sparsely and unpredictably in the region, attracted to temporarily flooded areas to nest, and moving away when they dry out. ♀s are sequentially polandrous, laying successive clutches for 2-4 ♂s which incubate and rear the young without ♀ assistance. ♂s nest solitarily, but may be locally concentrated (2-20 nests) where habitat – a mosaic of sedges/grass and shallow water/mud – provides ideal nesting conditions. **Nest:** a saucer-shaped pad of dry plant-stems, usually hidden in short marshy vegetation (sedges or grass), some with a canopy of live plant-stems drawn over the top; it measures 100 mm in diameter and is 30-40 mm thick; also recorded laying on dry mud away from vegetation, the nest similar to that of a plover.

Laying months: most months recorded, but mainly Jan-Apr in summer-rainfall region, Aug-Oct in winter-rainfall region. **Clutch size:** 4 (2-5); laid at 1-day intervals. **Eggs:** 31.0-35.5-37.3 x 23.6-25.0-26.5 mm. **Incubation period:** 19 days; by ♂ only; begins when clutch is complete; incubation shifts during day 24-40-110 min; at night 78-93-111 min (Japan). **Nestling/fledging period:** 30-35 days; young cared for by ♂.

FINFOOTS Family Heliornithidae Worldwide 3 species, 1 breeds in Afrotropics and in southern Africa. Monogamous, incubation by ♀; nests over water; eggs short-oval shaped; glossy brown, 2/clutch; young are precocial and nidifugous.

African Finfoot *Podica senegalensis* Watertrappe page 372

Breeds widely but sparsely in the e half of southern Africa, on well-wooded, slow-flowing rivers and their inlets into dams, favouring braided stretches overhung with vegetation or fringed with trapped flood debris. Pairs are territorial year-round and nest solitarily spaced at intervals of >½ km on prime habitat. **Nest:** a substantial, untidy bowl made of coarse dry grass, placed on a branch, in driftwood or overhanging reeds, 1-2½ m (1-4) up from the water; it is easily overlooked for caught-up flood debris; it measures 24-34 cm in diameter and is 8-14 cm thick; the cup, 15-16 cm wide and 6 cm deep, is lined with dry leaves. Nest sites are sometimes reused in successive years. The incubating ♀ sits tight; if disturbed, she drops quietly into the water and swims away.

Laying months: mainly Sep-Jan (Jul-May). **Clutch size:** 2 (1-3); laid at a 1-day interval. **Eggs:** 48.0-54.4-59.0 x 34.0-39.7-42.1 mm. **Incubation period:** not recorded; by ♀ only. **Nestling/fledging period:** not recorded; young cared for mainly by ♀.

African Jacana

Lesser Jacana

Greater Painted Snipe

African Finfoot

SNIPE Family Scolopacidae Worldwide 93 species (these include sandpipers, phalaropes and other 'scolopacids'), 1 breeds in Afrotropics and in southern Africa; it is a marsh-nesting bird; monogamous but probably also promiscuous; birds display by making a mechanical drumming sound in a swooping flight; incubation probably by the ♀ (this is the case in the closely related European species); eggs are oval, cryptically marked, 2/clutch (in southern Africa); young are precocial and nidifugous.

African Snipe *Gallinago nigripennis* Afrikaanse Snip   page 374

Breeds widely in marshy ground, typically in areas of shallow water (<50 mm deep) where there is soft mud and a dense cover of shortly cropped grass/sedge (<300 mm tall), conditions usually created along wetland margins that are subject to heavy grazing. Where such habitat is extensive, hundreds of birds may be attracted to nest, and their drumming aerial displays render them very conspicuous. Drumming occurs throughout the breeding cycle, but its function and the roles of the sexes in this behaviour are not adequately understood. Adjacent nests can be within 30 m of each other. **Nest:** a flimsy, saucer-shaped pad of dry grass, 100 mm in diameter, hidden in or between grass-tufts just above the water- or mud-level (<100 mm up). Nests are usually concealed by having grass-stems pulled over to form a canopy above them. When approached, the incubating bird sits tight, only flying up at the last moment, making a sucking sound and often defecating as it leaves. The roles of the sexes in the nesting cycle are not known.
Laying months: mainly Jun-Sep, but may breed in any month if conditions are favourable. **Clutch size:** 2 (rarely 1 or 3). **Eggs:** 36.9-41.2-44.8 x 27.0-29.6-32.0 mm. **Incubation period:** not recorded. **Nestling/fledging period:** not recorded; young leave the nest within hours of hatching.

COURSERS, PRATINCOLES Family Glareolidae Worldwide 17 species; 10 breed in Afrotropics, 7 in southern Africa. Ground-nesting birds, some colonial, others solitary nesters; monogamous, sexes share incubation and parental care; eggs laid on the ground; short-oval to oval, cryptically marked, 1-3/clutch; some species maintain egg temperature by belly-wetting; young are precocial and nidifugous.

Burchell's Courser *Cursorius rufus* Bloukopdrawwertjie   page 375

Breeds in semi-arid and arid regions on open, stony or gravelly plains, or in sparsely vegetated, heavily grazed, semi-arid grasslands. Nomadic over much of its range, its movements and timing of breeding probably dictated by rainfall. Pairs nest solitarily, but adjacent nests may occasionally be as close as 50 m apart. **Nest:** eggs are laid on bare ground without any attempt at making a nest or nest-scrape; they are usually laid among antelope or sheep droppings, or among scattered, egg-sized stones. At the least hint of danger the incubating bird runs rapidly from the nest.
Laying months: all months recorded, but mostly between Aug-Dec. **Clutch size:** 2, rarely 1. **Eggs:** 27.8-30.4-32.9 x 22.8-24.0-26.2 mm. **Incubation period:** not recorded; by both sexes. **Nestling/fledging period:** not recorded; young cared for by both sexes; they leave the nest site within hours of hatching.

Temminck's Courser *Cursorius temminckii* Trekdrawwertjie   page 375

Breeds widely in grassland, savanna and semi-arid regions favouring open, flat, short-grass areas, especially recently burnt grassland where the birds often arrive within hours of a fire and commence nesting within days; it is nomadic and nowhere permanently resident. It also nests in heavily grazed grasslands, in fallow lands, on pans, airfields and on shortly cropped road verges. Pairs nest solitarily and at widely spaced intervals. **Nest:** eggs are laid on bare ground without any attempt at making a nest or nest-scrape; they are commonly laid among antelope or sheep droppings (as shown in the photograph opposite) and their dark colour blends well when laid on burnt ground. At the least hint of danger the incubating bird runs rapidly from the nest.
Laying months: Jul-Nov, rarely in other months. **Clutch size:** 2, rarely 1. **Eggs:** 25.0-27.8-30.6 x 21.3-22.8-24.8 mm. **Incubation period:** 19-22 days; by both sexes, change-overs at 75-120 min. **Nestling/fledging period:** young fly strongly at 34 days; cared for by both sexes; they leave the nest within hours of hatching.

Double-banded Courser *Rhinoptilus africanus* Dubbelbanddrawwertjie   page 375

Breeds in arid and semi-arid areas, favouring flat, open, treeless plains that are sparsely grassed, or have low, scattered shrubs and forbs, interspersed with stretches of gravel or bare ground. Pairs nest solitarily and at widely spaced intervals. **Nest:** a single egg is laid on bare ground at a site where visibility is good and, usually, where the substrate matches the pale colour of the egg; no nest or nest-scrape is made; the egg is commonly laid alongside antelope or sheep droppings. The non-incubating bird remains near the nest while its mate incubates.
Laying months: all months recorded with slight peak between Oct-Feb; double- or multiple-brooded when suitable conditions persist. **Clutch size:** 1. **Eggs:** 28.5-31.6-35.6 x 23.0-25.3-28.8 mm. **Incubation period:** 25-27 days; by both sexes, change-overs occurring at 1½-2 hr (74-218 min) intervals; egg may be left unattended for long periods when ambient temperature is between 20-30°C. **Nestling/fledging period:** 5-6 weeks; young cared for by both sexes; it leaves nest site within 24 hrs of hatching.

African Snipe

Burchell's Courser

Temminck's Courser

Double-banded Courser

Coursers, Pratincoles

Three-banded Courser *Rhinoptilus cinctus* Driebanddrawwertjie page 375

Breeds in the northern savanna areas, mainly in hot, low-lying country, favouring open, bare, hard-clay areas between woodland. Pairs nest solitarily and are widely spaced. **Nest:** this species is unique among coursers in laying its eggs in a scrape in the ground which is filled with particles of dry soil. The eggs initially lie loosely in this material, just a small part of the shells exposed, but if the soil is moistened, the eggs may become firmly embedded in the soil so that they cannot be turned or rolled. When the eggs hatch, the chicks break out from whichever side of the egg is exposed (and not from top end as is more usual in birds). The mate of the incubating bird is usually found standing in shade in the vicinity of the nest.
Laying months: mainly Aug-Oct (Mar-Nov). **Clutch size:** 2 (3 recorded in e Africa). **Eggs:** 36.4-38.2-41.2 x 25.5-26.1-27.0 mm. **Incubation period:** 25-27 days; by both sexes, change-overs every 90-120 min; starts when clutch complete. **Nestling/fledging period:** not recorded; young cared for by both sexes; they leave the nest site within 24 hrs of hatching.

Bronze-winged Courser *Rhinoptilus chalcopterus* Bronsvlerkdrawwertjie page 375

Breeds in the savanna belt, especially in mopane and miombo woodlands; resident in parts of its range and a seasonal visitor in others; it typically nests in recently burnt areas with very short, sparse grass cover. Pairs nest solitarily, usually > 100 m apart. **Nest:** the eggs are laid in a shallow scrape, indentation or animal footprint on bare ground; little or no lining is added to the hollow and the site has good all-round visibility. The mate of the incubating bird is usually found standing in shade in the vicinity of the nest.
Laying months: breeds during the dry season, laying mainly Sep-Oct (Jul-Dec). **Clutch size:** 2-3. **Eggs:** 32.6-37.4-41.4 x 25.2-27.2-28.5 mm; eggs are unusually marked for a courser and more closely resemble those of a plover. **Incubation period:** 25-27 days; by both sexes, change-overs every 1-2 hrs. **Nestling/fledging period:** not recorded; young cared for by both sexes.

Collared Pratincole *Glareola pratincola* Rooivlerksprinkaanvoël page 375

Breeds sparsely but sometimes abundantly on subtropical and tropical wetlands from Zululand northwards, on the bare, shortly cropped margins of floodplains, lakes, large rivers and estuaries, occasionally in ploughed lands. Breeds colonially, from a few nesting pairs to hundreds; nests in these colonies are well spread out (mostly > 10 m apart, some occasionally within 1 m of each other). **Nest:** eggs are laid on dry ground in a shallow depression, often an animal footprint, 65-75 mm wide; flakes of mud or grass stubble is occasionally added as a nest lining, and the eggs are often laid alongside a disruptive feature such as some animal dung; sites selected usually provide good all-round visibility. Breeding colonies are made conspicuous by the noisy mobbing behaviour of the birds towards any intruder that approaches the nesting area.
Laying months: mainly Sep-Nov (Jun-Dec). **Clutch size:** 2, rarely 1; laid at a 1-day interval. **Eggs:** 29.0-31.6-34.3 x 22.2-24.0-25.6 mm. **Incubation period:** 17-18 days; by both sexes; uses belly-wetting to cool eggs in the heat. **Nestling/fledging period:** 25-30 days (Europe); young cared for by both sexes.

Rock Pratincole *Glareola nuchalis* Withalssprinkaanvoël page 375

A breeding summer visitor to areas of rapids on the Zambezi, Chobe and Okavango rivers, arriving in August when receding water-levels expose rocky islands on which the birds nest; at the end of the breeding cycle, in December, when river water-levels begin rising, the birds leave the area. Pairs nest solitarily, or in loose aggregations of up to 26 pairs, smaller rock islands supporting single nesting pairs and larger islands up to 5 pairs; adjacent nests may be within 9 m of each other. **Nest:** none made, the eggs are laid in a depression, crack, small pothole, or on a flat surface where some sand or gravel has gathered. Eggs are laid 0,1-5 m from the water's edge and 2-4 m above the water-level.
Laying months: mainly Oct (Aug-Nov); relays after early nest failure. **Clutch size:** 2, less often 1. **Eggs:** 27.2-29.4-32.4 x 20.2-21.7-22.8 mm. **Incubation period:** 20 days; by both sexes, with frequent change-overs and frequent belly-wetting to maintain egg temperature; starts with second-laid egg. **Nestling/fledging period:** 20-30 days; young cared for by both sexes; young leave nest site within 24 hrs, swim well at 2-3 days; fledge at 20-30 days.

Three-banded Courser   eggs buried

Bronze-winged Courser

Collared Pratincole

Rock Pratincole

Gulls, Skimmer

GULLS, TERNS, SKIMMERS Family Laridae Worldwide 102 species; 10 breed in Afrotropics, 9 in southern Africa, of which 3 are gulls, 5 are terns and 1 a skimmer. All are monogamous breeders; incubation and parental care is shared by the sexes; most breed colonially (only Damara Tern, African Skimmer not invariably so); 6 are primarily marine birds, 3 breed on inland wetlands; all nest on the ground or over water; eggs variable in shape (sub-elliptical, oval, semi-pyriform), cryptically marked, 1-3/clutch; young are precocial and semi-nidifugous.

African Skimmer *Rynchops flavirostris* Waterploeër   page 376

A breeding visitor to slow-flowing sections of the Okavango, Chobe and Zambezi rivers, and occasionally to other rivers in the region where sandbars free of vegetation become exposed during low-flow periods (Aug-Nov). The birds take occupation of nesting sites during June and nest as solitary pairs or, more usually, in small, dispersed colonies, usually numbering <10 pairs (but up to 28 recorded); the nests of adjacent pairs may be within 10-20 m of each other. Sites are commonly reused in successive seasons, provided they remain undisturbed and free of vegetation. **Nest:** a deep, unlined scape in dry sand, usually <20 m from the water's edge, <½ m above the waterline and mostly, but not invariably, on an island; the nest scrape measures 150-188-250 mm in diameter and is 50-100 mm deep. Several scrapes may be made before laying in one. While nesting, the birds are conspicuous and demonstrative, flying and alarm-calling over their colonies if disturbed; they are aggressive to potential nest predators and engage in distraction displays and false brooding.
Laying months: Aug-Sep (Jul-Nov); relays after early nest failure. **Clutch size:** 2-3 (1-4); laid at 1-5 day intervals. **Eggs:** 37.3-39.3-44.2 x 26.3-28.4-30.4 mm; mass 10.0-16.1-19.0 g. **Incubation period:** 21 days; by both sexes with frequent nest change-overs (at 5-10 min intervals in the heat of the day) and frequent belly-wetting; starts with first-laid egg. **Nestling/fledging period:** 5-6 weeks; brooded and fed by both sexes; young leave nest scrape at 1-2 days; if threatened, they bury themselves in the sand to avoid detection.

Grey-headed Gull (Grey-hooded Gull) *Choicocephalus cirrocephalus* Gryskopmeeu   page 375

A colonial breeder, nesting in widely scattered colonies, these mainly located on larger inland lakes and pans, especially where islands provide safe sites; some sites are reoccupied annually, whereas others are used intermittently or occasionally. Colonies range in size from a few pairs to >100 (rarely up to 300 pairs); sometimes breeds alongside other gulls and terns, or flamingos, African Spoonbills or African Sacred Ibis. In large colonies adjacent nests can be 1-4 m apart, but they are usually more widely scattered than this. **Nest:** a shallow bowl, built with twigs, grass and weed-stems and lined with finer material; it measures 170-200 mm in diameter and is about 80 mm deep; it can be placed on bare ground, among rocks or in emergent vegetation over water; old nests of Red-knobbed Coots may be used. Breeding colonies are made conspicuous by the birds' behaviour of rising in a cloud above the nesting area if approached and screaming noisily and swooping on the intruder.
Laying months: a winter breeder, mainly Jun-Sep (Feb-Nov); single-brooded. **Clutch size:** 2-3; laid at 1-5 day intervals. **Eggs:** 50.2-53.5-57.8 x 34.4-37.5-38.5 mm; mass 40-40.5-42 g. **Incubation period:** not recorded; by both sexes; starts with first-laid egg. **Nestling/fledging period:** not recorded.

Hartlaub's Gull *Chroicocephalus hartlaubii* Hartlaubse Meeu   page 375

A colonial-nesting marine species that breeds along the s and w coast from the Swartkops Estuary at Algoa Bay westwards to the Cape Peninsula and then as far north up the w coast as Swakopmund. Most colonies are located on offshore islands or guano platforms; currently, the largest colony is on Robben Is (>4000 pairs); often nests alongside Swift Terns; pairs/colony range from a few to thousands; known to breed at >50 sites in the region; in recent years a few colonies have become established at inland sites, the furtherest of these at Paarl, 48 km from the sea. **Nest:** a roughly made bowl, 19-26-38 cm in diameter with a cup 10-14-18 cm wide, built of dry grass, weeds, roots, twigs and other debris and placed on the ground among rocks or low vegetation; in places it may nest on harbour buildings, roofs and other man-made structures.
Laying months: all months recorded, but mostly in winter, (Mar-Jun in Namibia, Feb-Apr and Aug-Sep in s and w Cape). **Clutch size:** 2 (1-3); laid at a 1-4 day interval. **Eggs:** 46.9-53.7-60.3 x 27.1-36.6-49.7 mm; mass 28-39-46 g; thick-shelled relative to other gulls; egg colour very variable, even within the same clutch (see nest photograph opposite). **Incubation period:** 25 days; by both sexes; begins with first-laid egg. **Nestling/fledging period:** 40 days; young cared for by both sexes.

Kelp Gull *Larus dominicanus* Swartrugmeeu   page 375

A marine species that breeds widely along w and s coasts, from e Cape westwards. Primarily a colonial breeder, with single pairs nesting in places on beaches; colonies number from a few pairs to thousands, and two islands (Dassen, Schaapen) each support >6000 nesting pairs; most colonies are on off-shore islands like these, and colonies on the mainland are smaller, located either on sea-facing cliffs or on sandbanks and islands in estuaries, lagoons, sewage ponds and saltpans; also recorded nesting on guano platforms, shipwrecks, roofs of buildings; some breeding sites are shared with Swift Terns. In very large colonies, adjacent nests are spaced 20-100 cm apart, 4 nests/m². **Nest:** a rough bowl, built with whatever plant material is available (seaweed, kelp, shells, feathers or other beach debris), about 30 cm in diameter. Breeding colonies are rendered conspicuous by the birds' behaviour of mobbing potential predators approaching the nesting area, hovering and circling above, screaming incessantly.
Laying months: Sep-Jan, peaking in s and w Cape (Oct) earlier than in Namibia (Dec). **Clutch size:** 2 (1-3, rarely 4, perhaps laid by >1 ♀); laid at a 1-3 day interval. **Eggs:** 64.4-72.0-80.7 x 43.1-48.6-58.3 mm; 74-89.5-109 g; egg colour very variable, even within the same clutch. **Incubation period:** 26-27 days; by both sexes; starts with first-laid egg. **Nestling/fledging period:** 46-61-73 days; young brooded and fed by both sexes.

African Skimmer

Grey-headed Gull

Hartlaub's Gull

Kelp Gull

Terns

Caspian Tern *Hydroprogne caspia* Reusesterretjie   page 375
A bird of coastal estuaries and lagoons and, increasingly, of large inland lakes and pans; currently breeds regularly at about 10 sites in the region, mostly along the coast, a few on large inland dams and pans. Colonial, from a few pairs to about 150/colony, usually alongside other colonial-breeders (Kelp Gulls at the coast, Grey-headed Gulls inland). Most colonies are on flat, exposed islands or protected sandbars in lagoons, estuaries, open lakes and commercial saltpans; the colonies on islands in Lake St Lucia, Gariep Dam, at commercial saltworks in Port Elizabeth and Swakopmund, and at the Berg River estuary support most of the region's breeding population; some sites have been in regular use for many decades. **Nest:** shallow, unlined scrape in dry mud or sand; measures 22-25-29 cm in diameter and 25-40-50 mm deep. In large colonies adjacent nests may be as close as 0.7 m apart.
Laying months: all months recorded, the periods of peak laying varying regionally; Namibia mainly March; Lake St Lucia mainly May-July; Algoa Bay mainly Feb-Jun; w Cape mainly Oct-Jan. **Clutch size:** 2 (1-3); laid at a 1-2 day interval. **Eggs:** 56.8-63.8-69.2 x 40.4-44.0-47.4 mm; mass 52-63-72 g. **Incubation period:** 22-24 days; by both sexes, but mostly the ♀. **Nestling/fledging period:** 30-35 days; young cared for by both sexes; leave nest at 3 days.

Swift Tern *Thalasseus bergii* Geelbeksterretjie   page 376
A marine species that breeds along the s and w coast between Algoa Bay and Swakopmund, nesting in tightly packed colonies of 100s to 1000s of pairs, often alongside Hartlaub's Gulls. It breeds annually at about 6-7 sites, but the sites selected change from year to year, some used once and not again; depredation by pelicans is partially to blame for this on w Coast. Most breeding, involving colonies of 200-6000 pairs (rarely >10000), takes place on offshore islands (main ones currently used being Robben, Dyer, Bird and Possession); mainland sites used include islands in commercial saltpans and in protected areas inside harbours. Colony size is related to abundance of pelagic fish prey. **Nest:** a shallow unlined scrape, 14-21 cm wide, in open, bare, flat ground, sometimes among rocks or in short vegetation; adjacent nests in large colonies 30-40 cm apart; occasional pairs recorded nesting on the roofs of buildings. The birds are sensitive to human disturbance and prone to abandon a colony if subjected to this.
Laying months: Jan-Sep, peak laying varying regionally, earliest in w Cape (Feb-Mar), later in Namibia and Algoa Bay (Mar-Jul); relays after early nest failure. **Clutch size:** 1, rarely 2. **Eggs:** 55.4-61.8-66.8 x 39.3-42.9-45.3 mm. **Incubation period:** 21-30 days (Australia); by both sexes, in average shifts of 41-213 min. **Nestling/fledging period:** 38-40 days; young leave nest at 1-2 days; cared for by both sexes.

Roseate Tern *Sterna dougallii* Rooiborssterretjie   page 376
A marine species with small numbers (100-300 pairs) breeding annually at 2, sometimes 3, sites on offshore islands along the s Cape coast; the vast majority of these nest in colonies on Bird Is in Algoa Bay (part of this colony is shown in the upper photograph opposite). The birds annually reoccupy their nesting sites on the islands between May and Oct and, once breeding is over, they disperse widely along the coast. Breeding on Bird Is takes place in several sub-colonies, and nests are located in low vegetation or on stone- and rock-strewn slopes, adjacent nests averaging 0,6 m apart (0,2-7 m). **Nest:** a shallow scrape in sand, usually unlined, but some having a few pebbles added to the scrape; several scrapes may be prepared (by both sexes) before one is used.
Laying months: mainly Jun-Jul (Jun-Sep); relays after early failure. **Clutch size:** 1-2, rarely 3, these probably laid by >1 ♀; laid at a 2-3 day interval. **Eggs:** 39.8-42.1-44.5 x 28.6-30.1-31.5 mm. **Incubation period:** 25 days; by both sexes, change-overs at ½-1½ h interval. **Nestling/fledging period:** 23-28 days; remain in nest for 7 days; cared for by both sexes.

Damara Tern *Sternula balaenarum* Damarasterretjie   page 376
A summer-visiting marine species that breeds along the s and w coasts from east of Algoa Bay to s Angola, moving to w Africa in winter; the vast majority of birds nest along the Namibian coast (98% of about 7000 pairs), with small, isolated nesting populations at De Mond and Alexandra. Pairs nest on the mainland, either solitarily or in dispersed colonies, adjacent nests 20-200 m apart and well back from the sea, typically 100-600 m inland (up to 11 km in Namibia), in flat, unvegetated gravel plains which often form the slacks between dunes; or on hardened salt pans or in stony areas. A slightly elevated position is favoured, and the egg is usually laid close to a feature that disrupts the otherwise uniform background (a stone, piece of driftwood, a tyre track or footprint). **Nest:** the single egg is laid on bare ground, some in a shallow, sparsely lined scrape; often close to the site used the previous year.
Laying months: Oct-Jun; peaking in Nov-Jan in Namibia, earlier in s and w Cape (Oct-Jan). **Clutch size:** 1, very rarely 2. **Eggs:** 29.6-32.2-36.2 x 22.1-23.8-25.3 mm; mass 9.3 g. **Incubation period:** 18-22 days, by both sexes, but mainly ♀, fed by ♂; ave incubating shift 69 min. **Nestling/fledging period:** 20-21 days; young leaves nest at 2 days and moves towards the sea; brooded and fed by both sexes.

Whiskered Tern *Chlidonias hybrida* Witbaardsterretjie   page 376
A summer breeding visitor to inland wetlands where it nests widely but rather erratically, favouring seasonal or ephemeral pans and floodplains that fill with water during summers of high rainfall. Colonial, nesting in colonies of 5-30 pairs (rarely up to 80, and then in scattered sub-colonies); adjacent nests 2-20 m apart. **Nest:** a mound of grass/sedge/*Polygonum* stems, variable in size, but typically 50 cm across at water-level, built up 70-150 mm above the water with a shallow cup 10-12 cm wide; it is built on floating aquatic vegetation or is attached to emergent tufts of grass or sedge; usually in water >1 m deep and well away from the shore. Both sexes build and continue adding material and enlarging the nest during the incubation.
Laying months: mainly Jan-Mar (Oct-Apr), but peaking earlier in s Cape (Oct-Nov). **Clutch size:** 3 (2-3). **Eggs:** 35.3-39.1-42.1 x 26.5-28.6-30.8 mm; egg colour very variable, even within the same clutch. **Incubation period:** 20-21 days (18-22); by both sexes; starts when clutch complete. **Nestling/fledging period:** 23 days (Europe); young cared for by both sexes.

Caspian Tern

Swift Tern

Roseate Tern (TWO ABOVE)

Damara Tern

Damara Tern

Whiskered Tern

Sandgrouse

SANDGROUSE Family Pteroclididae Worldwide 16 species; 7 breed in Afrotropics, 4 in southern Africa. Ground-living, pigeon-like birds; all are monogamous breeders that nest solitarily (one, Namaqua Sandgrouse, sometimes may nest in loose aggregations), incubation is shared by the sexes (♂s in the day, ♀s at night); nests on the ground; eggs elliptical, cryptically marked, 3/clutch; water is carried daily to non-flying young by the parent (mainly ♂), in its breast feathers; young are precocial and nidifugous, and can fly before fully grown.

Namaqua Sandgrouse *Pterocles namaqua* Kelkiewyn   page 376

Breeds widely in semi-arid and arid regions, favouring flat, open ground, mostly on calcrete, sand or on shingle/gravel plains. Pairs nest solitarily or in scattered aggregations, adjacent nests sometimes within 20 m of each other. **Nest:** a shallow scrape in the ground, 100-110 mm in diameter and 20-30 mm deep; placed among, or close to scattered stones, low shrubs or tufts of grass (but not usually set right against a stone or bush); scrape initially unlined, but a sparse bed of grit and rim of small pebbles gets added during the incubation. Incubating bird crouches on nest if approached, flushing at 3-5 m; may perform injury-feigning distraction display.
Laying months: mainly winter months (Apr-Aug) across most of its range, but Sep-Oct in winter-rainfall areas; a few records for all months. **Clutch size:** 3, less often 2; laid at 2-day intervals. **Eggs:** 31.0-36.1-41.6 x 22.5-25.2-27.1 mm; mass 11-12.5 g. **Incubation period:** 21 days; starts when clutch complete; by both sexes, ♂s at night, ♀s during day; change-overs occur, on average, 151 min after sunrise and 105 min before sunset. **Nestling/fledging period:** chicks leave nest when last-hatched is <12 hrs old; fly weakly at 30 days, strongly at 42 days; young cared for by both sexes; water is carried daily to the chicks by ♂ for 2 months.

Burchell's Sandgrouse *Pterocles burchelli* Gevlekte Sandpatrys   page 376

Breeds in semi-arid savanna, favouring grass-covered, sandy soils among trees or shrubs ('sandveld'). Pairs nest solitarily. Nesting habits are poorly known. **Nest:** a shallow scrape in the soil, about 150 mm wide, lined sparingly with dry grass; usually more concealed than the nests of other sandgrouse species, often under cover of a fallen branch or concealed by shrubs or grass.
Laying months: a winter nester, mainly May-Jun (Apr-Oct). **Clutch size:** 3, rarely 2. **Eggs:** 34.5-36.7-38.8 x 23.4-25.7-27.3 mm. **Incubation period:** not recorded. **Nestling/fledging period:** young fly weakly at 15 days, well at 28 days; are cared for by both sexes; water is carried to the young by the ♂.

Yellow-throated Sandgrouse *Pterocles gutturalis* Geelkeelsandpatrys   page 376

Breeds in open, flat, treeless areas where there is limited grass cover but an abundance of weedy plants; areas with heavy clay soils are favoured and the birds commonly nest in abandoned agricultural lands. Pairs nest solitarily, usually >100 m apart (occasionally <45 m apart). **Nest:** a shallow, circular scrape, 110-130-155 mm in diameter and 15-25-30 mm deep, lined to a variable degree with pieces of dry grass or stems of weeds. Where grass is present, the nest is usually concealed between tufts, otherwise it is concealed among weeds or forbs; it is rarely placed in a completely exposed position. The incubating bird usually sits tight if approached, flushing when one is within a few metres.
Laying months: a winter nester, mainly Jun-Jul (Apr-Oct); late-laid clutches are probably replacements following earlier failures. **Clutch size:** 3, less often 2; laid at 2-day intervals. **Eggs:** 43.4-45.8-49.7 x 31.2-33.9-37.0 mm. **Incubation period:** 26 days; by both sexes, ♂ at night, ♀ during day, changing over in the morning (08h30-10h00) and evening (16h00-16h30). **Nestling/fledging period:** not recorded; young fly when half the size of adults; cared for by both sexes; water is carried to young daily by the ♂.

Double-banded Sandgrouse *Pterocles bicinctus* Dubbelbandsandpatrys   page 376

Breeds in woodland and savanna, in both flat and hilly country and on a variety of substrates, from stony to sandy soils; mopane woodland is much favoured. Pairs nest solitarily. **Nest:** a shallow scrape in the ground, sparsely lined with pieces of dry grass and twigs, often among leaf litter, and usually against a shrub or under a fallen branch. If approached, the incubating bird sits tight, only flying up when one is within a few metes.
Laying months: a winter nester, mainly May-Sep (Feb-Oct). **Clutch size:** 3, less often 2; laid at 1-2 day intervals. **Eggs:** 34.6-37.1-40.4 x 24.5-26.6-28.5 mm. **Incubation period:** 23-24 days (in captivity); by both sexes, ♂ at night and early morning, ♀ late-morning and afternoon; starts when clutch is complete. **Nestling/fledging period:** 4 weeks; young cared for by both sexes; young fly well before adult size; water is carried to the young by the ♂.

Namaqua Sandgrouse   female with just-hatched young

Namaqua Sandgrouse

Burchell's Sandgrouse

Yellow-throated Sandgrouse

Double-banded Sandgrouse

Pigeons

PIGEONS, DOVES Family Columbidae Worldwide 321 species; 32 breed in Afrotropics, 14 in southern Africa; monogamous; pairs nest solitarily; nest a flimsy open saucer of twigs, built by both sexes in trees or on cliffs (Speckled Pigeon, Common Pigeon); eggs oval to sub-elliptical, white or cream, unmarked; 1-2/clutch; sexes share incubation and chick-rearing; young are altricial and nidicolous; their faeces are not removed and accumulate around the nest rim.

Speckled Pigeon *Columba guinea* Kransduif   page 377

Breeds widely throughout South Africa, especially in villages, towns and cities; occurrence more patchy in neighbouring countries. Ancestrally restricted to nesting on sheltered ledges on cliffs, but in South Africa now nests widely on buildings and other man-made structures – under house eaves, on ledges, on roof girders, in gutters, in holes in walls, under bridges, in windmill- and tank-stands, in grain silos, in discarded machinery, in mine shafts and elsewhere; also nests, occasionally, in trees, especially in large, craggy old trees. Pairs nest solitarily but sometimes in close proximity to one another (<10 m apart). **Nest:** a saucer-shaped platform of dry twigs and/or stems of grass and weed, with finer stems used at the top and coarser stems at the base. Occasional nests incorporate other material (nails, pieces of wire, etc); rarely, the eggs are laid on a bare surface without a nest being built. The nest measures 300-370 mm wide and is 40-65 mm thick, with a central depression 30-40 mm deep. It is built by both sexes in 5-7 days, one collecting and delivering twigs, the other constructing the nest. Nests or nest sites are often reused for successive clutches.
Laying months: all months; some seasonality (mainly Sep-Jan) in winter-rainfall areas; multiple-brooded, lay up to 6 clutches/year. **Clutch size:** 2 (1-3); laid at a 1-day interval. **Eggs:** 33.8-36.5-42.7 × 25.0-27.5-31.2 mm; mass 20 g. **Incubation period:** 15 days (14-16); starts with second-laid egg; by both sexes, alternating in long (about 6 hr) shifts. **Nestling/fledging period:** 24-25 days (20-26, rarely longer); young brooded and fed by both sexes.

African Olive Pigeon *Columba arquatrix* Geelbekbosduif   page 377

Breeds mostly in forested areas, also, increasingly, in wooded suburbs of Gauteng. Nesting habits are poorly known. Pairs nest solitarily. **Nest:** a frail saucer-shaped platform, 130-300 mm in diameter; made of twigs, with coarser stems used for the base of the nest, and finer stems, including leaf petioles and tendrils as a lining; built either in a fork or on a lateral branch of a leafy tree, typically 6-9 m up from the ground (1-15); frequently nests in pines or in some other exotic tree; nest built by both sexes, ♂ collecting twigs and ♀ constructing the nest.
Laying months: all months recorded. **Clutch size:** 1, rarely 2. **Eggs:** 36.2-39.0-42.2 × 26.3-29.3-31.5 mm. **Incubation period:** 20 days; by both sexes, with change-overs in early morning and late afternoon. **Nestling/fledging period:** 19-20 days; young fed by both sexes.

Common Pigeon (Feral Pigeon) *Columba livia* Tuinduif   page 377

Feral populations are widely established in larger cities in the region, nesting in covered recesses or on sheltered ledges on buildings, bridges, dam walls, grain silos and on other man-made structures; also nests in holes in coastal and other cliffs, offshore islands and in large ornamental palms and other trees. Nesting habits well known in Europe but little known in southern Africa. **Nest:** a loosely built, saucer-shaped pad of twigs, dry plant-stems, roots and other material, indistinguishable from that of a Speckled Pigeon; where the situation permits, several pairs may nest in close proximity to each other. Both sexes, but mainly the ♀, builds the nest.
Laying months: all months (southern Africa); multiple-brooded. **Clutch size:** 2; laid at a 2-day interval (Europe). **Eggs:** 36-39-43 × 27-29-32 mm; mass 10.2 g (S Africa). **Incubation period:** 16-19 days; by both sexes; begins when first egg is laid (Europe). **Nestling/fledging period:** 24-25 days (23-28, rarely longer); young brooded and fed by both sexes (Europe).

Eastern Bronze-naped Pigeon (Delegorgue's Pigeon) *Columba delegorguei* Withalsbosduif   page 377

Rare and localised in southern Africa, breeding in lowland, coastal and mid-altitude evergreen forest. Nesting habits are poorly known. **Nest:** a flimsy saucer-shaped platform of dry twigs, 220 mm in diameter, placed in the canopy of a well-foliaged forest tree, 5-20 m above the ground; it is built by the ♀ with twigs collected by the ♂. At Dlinza Forest, Eshowe, the birds breeding apparently coincides with the fruiting season (Mar-Apr) of *Cassipourea gerrardii*; at this locality the birds are most vocal during the summer months.
Laying months: one Dec record; probably Nov-Apr. **Clutch size:** 2. **Eggs:** 31.5-33.1-34.5 × 26.9-26.9-27.0 mm. **Incubation period:** not recorded; by both sexes (Kenya). **Nestling/fledging period:** not recorded; by both sexes (Kenya).

African Green Pigeon *Treron calvus* Papegaaiduif   page 377

Breeds widely in well-wooded savanna and forest verges. Pairs nest solitarily and are usually widely spaced, but sometimes concentrated around human habitations, where adjacent nests can be 20-30 m apart. **Nest:** a flimsy, saucer-shaped platform, usually distinguishable from nests of other doves by being built mainly with thickish twigs that are zigzagged or branched, and which interlock to give the nest a relatively tight-knitted structure; leaf petioles are also used, mainly as a lining; placed in mid- to upper-branches of a well-foliaged tree in a multiple fork, typically 5-7 m up from the ground (2½-21). It measures 130-150 mm in diameter and is 30-40 mm thick; one nest consisted of 52 twigs. Nests or nest sites are sometimes reused in successive seasons. The bird attending the nest blends well with its surroundings and it tends to sit tight if approached, rather than fly off. Both sexes build, the ♂ collecting and delivering material to the site, while the ♀ constructs the nest; twigs are not collected from the ground (as in most other doves) but are broken off tree branches.
Laying months: mainly Sep-Dec, rarely in other months. **Clutch size:** 2, rarely 1 or 3; laid at a 1-2 day interval. **Eggs:** 28.3-30.5-34.3 × 21.6-23.7-25.7 mm. **Incubation period:** 13-14 days; by both sexes. **Nestling/fledging period:** 12-13 days; young brooded and fed by both sexes.

Speckled Pigeon

African Olive Pigeon

Common Pigeon

Eastern Bronze-naped Pigeon

African Green Pigeon

Doves

Lemon Dove (Cinnamon Dove) *Columba larvata* **Kaneelduifie** — page 377

Breeds in coastal and montane forests and in forested parks and gardens. Pairs nest solitarily and are widely spaced. **Nest:** a dove-type platform, built with thin dry twigs and/or leaf-petioles, with a sparse lining of rootlets or finer twigs; it is placed in deep shade, usually close to the ground, typically 2½ m up (1-9), usually on one or more criss-crossing horizontal branches of a smallish, large-leafed subcanopy tree (such as *Rawsonia*), sometimes on creepers, or on a bed of caught-up leaves. It is larger than the nests of Laughing or Cape Turtle Doves, measuring 170-180 mm in diameter and 30 mm thick. Nests are sometimes reused in successive seasons (one for 3 years), or a new nest is built <50 m from a previous site. It is built by both sexes in 7-8 days; is not easily seen and the incubating bird leaves late if approached, flying off noisily. The chicks are left unattended for long periods and they remain very still on the nest while the parent is away. The parent birds seldom call in the vicinity of the nest.
Laying months: mainly Nov-Dec (Oct-Apr, rarely in other months). **Clutch size:** 2, rarely 1 or 3; laid at a 1-day interval. **Eggs:** 25.8-28.6-30.5 x 20.8-22.0-23.6 mm. **Incubation period:** 14-18 days; by ♀ only (Kenya). **Nestling/fledging period:** 20 days; young fed by both sexes.

Red-eyed Dove *Streptopelia semitorquata* **Grootringduif** — page 377

Breeds widely in well-wooded country, in both natural woodlands and in plantations and copses of alien trees, and other man-transformed habitats where tall trees are available. Pairs nest solitarily and are usually spaced; occasionally, e.g. on a small island, several pairs may nest in close proximity. **Nest:** a typical dove-type platform made of dry twigs, or stalks of grass and weed, with finer material including rootlets lining the cup; usually placed in a tree in a central fork or on a lateral branch where concealed to some degree by foliage or mistletoe; often nests over water and may then be also placed in a clump of reeds or in a thick grass tuft surrounded by water; such sites are low down (½-2 m up) whereas away from water the nest is usually >5 m up (and up to 18 m). Nests are sometimes built on top of an old nest of another dove, or some other bird (waxbill, crow, egret, thrush) and some are reused for two or more successive broods. The nest is larger than that of a Cape Turtle or Laughing Dove, measuring 130-200 mm in diameter and 35-50 mm thick (up to 100 mm thick if an old nest is refurbished). It is built by both sexes, ♂s mainly collecting and delivering material to the site and ♀s constructing the nest. When collecting twigs, the ♂ breaks these off branches rather than picking them up off the ground. During change-overs one or both of the pair often call at the nest.
Laying months: all months recorded, with a poorly defined peak between Aug-Jan; relays after early nest failure; multiple-brooded. **Clutch size:** 2, rarely 1; laid at a 1-day interval. **Eggs:** 27.2-31.1-34.5 x 21.9-23.7-25.6 mm; mass 9.7 g. **Incubation period:** 16 days (14-17); by both sexes, changing over about 2x/day (at about 08h00 and 15h00); begins when first egg is laid. **Nestling/fledging period:** 16 days (15-20); young brooded and fed by both sexes.

Cape Turtle Dove (Ring-necked Dove) *Streptopelia capicola* **Gewone Tortelduif** — page 377

Breeds widely and commonly throughout the region, absent only from arid, waterless areas and montane forest; likely to nest wherever there are trees in both urban and rural environments. Pairs nest solitarily, usually widely spaced (>100 m apart, but occasionally within 25-30 m). **Nest:** a typical dove-type platform of dry twigs, stalks of grass and weed, or leaf petioles, usually unlined; it is typically 3-4 m up (½-15), placed in a tree or bush, either in a vertical multiple-forked branch or on a horizontal side branch; it is seldom well hidden but easily overlooked, given its flimsy construction. Occasional nests are built on top of old nests, either of doves or some other bird; they are seldom built on man-made structures (in roof-eaves, lamp posts, etc) in contrast to Laughing Dove. Nests and nest sites are occasionally reused for more than one brood (once used 5x). The nest measures 100-150 mm in diameter and is 25-35 mm thick; reused nests up to 150 mm thick. Both sexes build the nest in 3-8 days, ♂s mainly collecting and delivering material to the site and ♀s constructing the nest; building activity lasts for a few hours in the mornings. The sexes share the incubation; at nest change-overs, the relieving bird calls when approaching the nest, usually answered by its partner from the nest.
Laying months: all months, with weak Aug-Oct peak in summer-rainfall areas and strong Sep-Dec peak in winter-rainfall areas; peaks in Jan-Mar in n Namibia; double- or multiple-brooded. **Clutch size:** 2, rarely 1; rare clutches of 3-4 probably laid by >1 ♀; laid at a 1-day interval. **Eggs:** 24.2-28.1-32.0 x 18.7-21.6-23.4 mm; smaller in Zimbabwe (27.0 x 21.1). **Incubation period:** 14 days (13-16); by both sexes, ♂ during the day, ♀ at night, changing over about 2x/day (10h00 and 16h30); begins when first egg is laid. **Nestling/fledging period:** 16-17 days; young brooded and fed by both sexes.

African Mourning Dove (Mourning Collared Dove) *Streptopelia decipiens* **Rooioogtortelduif** — page 377

Breeds in lowland savanna, most commonly in tall riparian woodland along the margins of rivers and wetlands. Pairs nest solitarily, but several may nest near each other in flooded trees. Nesting habits are poorly known. **Nest:** a flimsy dove-type platform built with twigs or grass- and weed-stems and sparsely lined with rootlets; placed on a vertical or horizontal fork in a tree or bush, sometimes one that is standing in water, 1½-15 m up from the ground. The nest measures about 150 mm in diameter, and it may be reused for two or more successive clutches. Both sexes build, ♂s collecting and delivering material to the site and ♀s constructing the nest.
Laying months: all months recorded, with most records for Nov-Dec. **Clutch size:** 2, less often 1. **Eggs:** 29.6-29.9-30.3 x 22.0-22.4-22.7 mm; mass 8.5 g. **Incubation period:** 13-14 days (in captivity). **Nestling/fledging period:** 15-18 days.

Lemon Dove

Red-eyed Dove

Lemon Dove (TWO ABOVE)

Red-eyed Dove

Cape Turtle Dove

African Mourning Dove

Doves

Laughing Dove *Spilopelia senegalensis* Rooiborsduifie   page 377

A very common and widespread breeding species, absent from only the most arid regions (Namib, central Kalahari) and from montane forest. Outside of these environments it nests wherever there are trees, and is especially common in man-transformed landscapes. Pairs mostly nest solitarily, but occasionally >1 nest/tree (up to 4 recorded). **Nest:** a typical flimsy dove-type platform is made of dry twigs, stalks of grass and weed, sparsely lined with rootlets; very variably placed – most usually in a tree or bush, typically 2-4 m up (0,3-15), in the mid-stratum, either in a vertical multiple-forked branch or on a horizontal side branch; seldom hidden but often easily overlooked, given its flimsy construction; leafless trees are as likely to be used as those with foliage; in suburbia often nests in eaves of buildings, flower pots, window ledges, etc. Nests and nest sites are frequently reused for successive clutches and they are regularly built on top of other birds' nests. Nest measures 80-140 mm in diameter and when new are 30-40 mm thick; reused nests may, however, reach 170 mm thick; one nest record being reused 12x. Where Cape Turtle and Laughing Doves nest alongside each other, the latter consistently nests closer to the ground but to distinguish the nests of the two species with certainty requires the parent attending the nest to be seen. Both sexes build the nest over a period of 2-4 days, ♂'s collecting and delivering material to the site and ♀s constructing the nest. During incubation, the bird attending the nest often calls from it, especially during nest change-overs.
Laying months: all months, peaking weakly in w Cape in Sep-Oct; in summer-rainfall areas in Mar-Sep; in n Namibia in Feb-Mar; usually double- or multiple-brooded. **Clutch size:** 2, rarely 1; occasional clutches of 3-4 probably laid by two ♀s; laid at a 1-day interval. **Eggs:** 24.5-26.2-29.5 x 18.0-20.1-22.8 mm. **Incubation period:** 13 days (12-14); by both sexes, changing over about 2x/day (in the morning and evening, ♂ sitting during the day, ♀ at night); begins when first egg is laid. **Nestling/fledging period:** 14 days (11-18); young brooded and fed by both sexes.

Emerald-spotted Wood Dove *Turtur chalcospilos* Groenvlekduifie   page 377

Breeds widely in deciduous woodland and savanna. Pairs nest solitarily and are widely spaced. **Nest:** a small dove-type platform loosely constructed from a few dry twigs or grass/weed-stems forming the base, a lining of rootlets forming the cup; placed in a smallish live or dead tree, usually about midway up on an outer, horizontal branch, or where two branches cross; sometimes in a coppicing stump, a tree-aloe or tall euphorbia; it is typically 2-3 m up from the ground (½-6 m) and measures 75-100 mm in diameter and is 25-35 mm thick. It is not hidden but is easily overlooked, given its small size and frail structure. Nests or nest sites are sometimes reused in successive clutches.
Laying months: all months, with weak summer peak. **Clutch size:** 2, rarely 1. **Eggs:** 21.8-23.2-24.9 x 16.8-17.6-19.1 mm. **Incubation period:** 17 days; by both sexes, but mainly the ♀. **Nestling/fledging period:** 16 days; young brooded and fed by both sexes.

Blue-spotted Wood Dove *Turtur afer* Blouvlekduifie   page 377

Breeds in and on the margins of lowland and riparian evergreen forests. Pairs nest solitarily. Nesting habits are poorly known. **Nest:** a small, frail, loosely constructed, dove-type structure, about 75 mm in diameter, made of rootlets, dry twigs and other thin plant stems; it is placed low down (1-3 m from the ground) in a horizontal fork of a sapling or small shrubby tree which may stand apart from others in a clearing; twice reported to nest on an old thrush nest.
Laying months: few data from the region – Apr, June, Aug, Dec. **Clutch size:** 2. **Eggs:** 22.0-23.0-24.6 x 16.9-17.2-17.5 mm. **Incubation period:** 15-17 days (in captivity). **Nestling/fledging period:** 15-18 days (in captivity).

Tambourine Dove *Turtur tympanistria* Witborsduifie   page 377

Breeds in and on the margins of evergreen forest. Pairs nest solitarily and are widely spaced. **Nest:** a flimsily made, dove-type structure, distinctive for being made largely or entirely from fine forest tendrils, with a few dry twigs forming the base of the nest; placed in a tree or bush, usually a sapling on an outer horizontal branch or in a vertical multiple fork 2-3 m up from the ground (1-10), often in a tree entwined with creepers, bracken fronds, reeds or other tangle. It measures 90-130 mm in diameter (with stray wisps of tendril extending well beyond this) and 25-40 mm thick; an old Laughing Dove nest once used as a base. Both sexes build, the ♂ collecting and delivering material and the ♀ constructing the nest, completing it in 7 days.
Laying months: all months recorded, mainly Sep-Nov. **Clutch size:** 2, rarely 1. **Eggs:** 22.9-24.5-26.0 x 16.6-18.0-19.0 mm. **Incubation period:** 17-20 days; by both sexes, mainly the ♀. **Nestling/fledging period:** 19-22 days; young brooded and fed by both sexes.

Namaqua Dove *Oena capensis* Namakwaduifie   page 377

Breeds in semi-arid areas, especially in thornveld; nomadic in more mesic habitats but does occasionally breed there. Pairs nest solitarily and they are usually widely spaced. **Nest:** a typical dove-type structure, but smaller than those of most doves, made of twigs, stalks of grass or weed and/or rootlets; it is placed close to the ground, even on the ground on occasion, typically about 1 m up and rarely >3 m up; usually on a horizontal branch of a small, broken-down thorny tree or bush, on a heap of dead branches, on cut brushwood, cut maize stalks or reeds, even in rank grass; no attempt is made to conceal it. It measures 55-100 mm in diameter and 20-40 mm thick; nests are rarely reused. Both sexes build the nest.
Laying months: all months, peaking (weakly) in dry-season months across its range. **Clutch size:** 2, rarely 1 or 3; laid at a 1-2 day interval. **Eggs:** 18.5-21.3-24.5 x 14.2-15.7-17.8 mm; mass 3.2 g; eggs cream- or buff-coloured (unlike eggs of most other doves). **Incubation period:** 13-16 days; by both sexes, changing over about 2x/day (in the morning and evening, ♂ incubating during day, ♀ at night); begins when first egg is laid. **Nestling/fledging period:** 16 days; young brooded and fed by both sexes.

Laughing Dove

Emerald-spotted Wood Dove

Tambourine Dove

Blue-spotted Wood Dove

Namaqua Dove

Parrots, Lovebirds

PARROTS, LOVEBIRDS Family Psittacidae Worldwide 349 species; 20 breed in Afrotropics, 7 in southern Africa; hole-nesters, 6 using tree cavities, one (Rosy-faced Lovebird) using holes in rocks, weaver nests, man-made structures; monogamous; ♀ incubates, both sexes rear young; eggs white, unmarked, spherical or nearly so; 3-5/clutch; young are altricial and nidicolous.

Cape Parrot *Poicephalus robustus* Woudpapegaai   page 377
Breeds in a small, fragmented range in montane evergreen forest. **Nest:** uses a natural cavity (often a rot-hole) in an upper dead branch of a tall forest tree, usually a large yellowwood, 6-12 m up from the ground; birds may widen and deepen it before laying: cavities measure 650-660 mm deep, 200-300 mm wide at the nest floor, with an entrance about 90 mm wide. Nests boxes placed in forest trees have been used successfully. Eggs are laid on a bed of wood chips. Cavities are reused in successive years. **Laying months:** Aug-Dec. **Clutch size:** 3-4 (2-5), laid at 1-2 day intervals (captivity). **Eggs:** 31.5-33.0-35.5 × 25.0-28.0-29.0 mm. **Incubation period:** 28-30 days (wild); by ♀ only (captivity). **Nestling/fledging period:** 55-79 days (captivity); fed by both sexes.

Grey-headed Parrot (Brown-necked Parrot) *Poicephalus fuscicollis* Savannepapegaai   page 377
Breeds in mesic woodlands in n savannas. Pairs nest solitarily and are widely spaced. **Nest:** a natural cavity, 300-900 mm deep, 150-180 mm wide with an entrance 65-75-85 mm in diameter, in a tree trunk, typically a hole facing n or ne, in the main trunk of a large tree, especially a baobab, 7-12 m up from the ground; cavities are commonly reused in successive years. **Laying months:** mainly Apr-May (Mar-Nov). **Clutch size:** 3-4, occasionally 2, laid at 1-3 day intervals (in captivity). **Eggs:** 30.4-33.3-36.0 × 26.0-27.3-29.2 mm. **Incubation period:** 28-30 days; by ♀ only; fed at nest by ♂. **Nestling/fledging period:** 68-83 days; fed by both sexes.

Brown-headed Parrot *Poicephalus cryptoxanthus* Bruinkoppapegaai   page 377
Breeds in lowland savanna. Pairs nest solitarily and are widely spaced; 7 pairs/200 ha in one study. **Nest:** uses a natural cavity or woodpecker hole in the stem of a large tree, 4-10 m up from the ground; entrance about 100-120 mm in diameter, cavity 500-900 mm deep, 120 mm wide; eggs are laid on a bed of wood chips. Holes are commonly reused in successive years (one for 20 years). **Laying months:** Mar-Apr. **Clutch size:** 3; laid at 1-2 day intervals. **Eggs:** 27.2-28.9-30.8 × 22.8-23.6-24.6 mm. **Incubation period:** 28 days; by ♀ only (in captivity); fed on nest by ♂. **Nestling/fledging period:** 50-54 days; fed by both sexes.

Rose-ringed Parakeet *Psittacula krameri* Ringnekparkiet
Feral populations, derived from escaped aviary birds, breed in Gauteng and in coastal KwaZulu-Natal. Nesting habits poorly known in the region. In Johannesburg nests in cavities (300-500 mm deep, 150 mm wide inside, entrance 70 mm wide) in dead branches and trunks of willow and other trees, 6-10 m up from the ground; sites used probably include barbet holes widened by the parakeets. **Laying months:** Sep (Johannesburg). **Clutch size:** 2 (Johannesburg); 3-4, rarely 5 or 6. **Eggs:** 29.0-30.7-33.0 × 23.0-23.8-25.0 mm. **Incubation period:** 28 days; by ♀ only. **Nestling/fledging period:** 6-7 weeks; fed by both sexes.

Meyer's Parrot *Poicephalus meyeri* Bosveldpapegaai   page 377
Breeds in mesic and semi-arid savannas, favouring tall, open woodland. Pairs nest solitarily and are widely spaced. **Nest:** a cavity in the stem of a large dead or living tree is used; either a natural hole or one made by a woodpecker; usually in main vertical stems, 3-10 m up from the ground; entrance hole may be widened by the parrots to 50-55 mm diameter; cavity 400-450 mm deep; eggs are laid on a floor of wood chips. Cavities are frequently reused in successive years. **Laying months:** mainly Apr-May (Mar-Aug). **Clutch size:** 3-4; laid at 1-3 day intervals (captivity). **Eggs:** 23.6-26.0-28.5 × 18.5-20.7-23.2 mm. **Incubation period:** 29-31 days (captivity), by ♀. **Nestling/fledging period:** 60-84 days (captivity); fed by both sexes.

Rüppell's Parrot *Poicephalus rueppellii* Bloupenspapegaai   page 377
Breeds in semi-arid woodlands in n Namibia. Pairs nest solitarily, occasionally <20 m apart. **Nest:** a natural cavity or woodpecker hole is used, 4-5 m (3.1-17.6) up from the ground in the main trunk of a tall tree; entrance-hole 51-56 mm wide (max 85 mm); eggs are laid on a bed of wood chips. Holes are regularly reused in successive years and roosted in at night when not breeding. **Laying months:** mainly Jan-Mar (Jan-Jun). **Clutch size:** 3-5. **Eggs:** 27.3 × 24.0 mm; mass 8.4 g. **Incubation period:** 24-30 days (in captivity); by ♀ only. **Nestling/fledging period:** 51 days (50-63) (in captivity); young fed by both sexes.

Rosy-faced Lovebird *Agapornis roseicollis* Rooiwangparkiet   no nest photo   page 377
Breeds widely in the semi-arid west, in rocky and mountainous country or in arid woodlands away from mountains. Pairs nest solitarily or 2 or more pairs may share a Sociable Weaver nest colony. **Nest:** a cavity is used, either in a rock face, a chamber in the nest of a Sociable Weaver, Red-billed Buffalo Weaver, or White-browed Sparrow-Weaver, or a hole in a man-made structure (in house eaves, nest boxes, cavities under bridges, etc). The cavity is lined with strips and shreds of soft, pliable bark and/or grass and leaves carried to the site tucked into the bird's rump feathers. **Laying months:** Feb-Apr. **Clutch size:** 4-5 (3-8), laid at 2-day intervals. **Eggs:** 21.0-23.8-26.3 × 16.8-17.6-19.0 mm. **Incubation period:** 23 days; by ♀ only; begins with first-laid egg. **Nestling/fledging period:** 43 days; fed by both sexes.

Lilian's Lovebird *Agapornis lilianae* Njassaparkiet   no nest photo   page 377
Breeds in mopane and acacia woodland in the Zambezi river valley. Nesting habits are poorly known in the wild, most information is from captive birds. Pairs nest solitarily. **Nest:** a tree cavity is used, especially one in a mopane tree; it is lined with bark-strips, grass-stalks and other material; unlike the Rosy-faced Lovebird, nest material is transported to the site in the bird's bill. **Laying months:** probably Jan-Apr. **Clutch size:** 4-5. **Eggs:** 19.7-21.3-22.8 × 15.6-16.4-17.0 mm. **Incubation period:** 22 days (in captivity); by ♀ only. **Nestling/fledging period:** 44 days (in captivity); fed by both sexes.

Cape Parrot

Grey-headed Parrot

Brown-headed Parrot

Rose-ringed Parakeet

Meyer's Parrot

Rüppell's Parrot

Turacos

TURACOS Family Musophagidae Worldwide 23 species; all are endemic to the Afrotropics, 5 breed in southern Africa. Monogamous; pairs nest solitarily; nest a flimsy saucer-shaped platform of twigs; both sexes build the nest, share incubation and nestling care; eggs spherical or nearly so, white, unmarked, 2-3/clutch; young are altricial and nidicolous; they leave the nest on foot before they can fly; their faeces are eaten by the parents.

Purple-crested Turaco *Tauraco porphyreolophus* Bloukuifloerie   page 377

Breeds widely in mesic woodland and in coastal and lowland forests, also in wooded gardens and parks. Although in flocks for much of the year, pairs disperse to breed and they nest solitarily. **Nest:** a flimsy, unlined, saucer-shaped platform of dry twigs, similar to a dove nest but larger (300-350 mm in diameter); it is placed in the mid- to upper-canopy of a densely branched, well-foliaged tree, commonly one entwined with creepers, and it is well hidden in the foliage; typically 4-5 m up from the ground (3-9). Both sexes build the nest, one collecting and delivering twigs to the site, the other constructing the nest; twigs are collected from trees, not from the ground.
Laying months: mainly Oct-Jan (Aug-Feb). **Clutch size:** 2-3, rarely 4; laid at 1-2 day intervals. **Eggs:** 35.7-37.6-39.5 x 32.8-34.5-36.3 mm; mass 23-25.3-27 g. **Incubation period:** 22 days (22-24, in captivity); by both sexes. **Nestling/fledging period:** young leave nest before they can fly at about 3 weeks; fly when about 38 days old (in captivity); young brooded and fed by both sexes.

Knysna Turaco *Tauraco corythaix* Knysnaloerie   no nest photo   page 377

Breeds in and on the fringes of evergreen forest and in forested parks and gardens. Pairs nest solitarily. **Nest:** a thin, saucer-shaped platform of dry twigs, measuring 200-300 mm in diameter and 100-120 mm thick; placed inside a creeper-festooned forest tree, or in a thickly foliaged tree on the edge of a clearing, also in a bougainvillea and in the crown of a tree fern; 3-9 m up from the ground, usually well concealed by foliage. Both sexes build the nest in about 5 days, working mainly in the morning; one of the pair collects and delivers twigs to the site while the other constructs the nest; twigs are broken off branches in trees, not collected from the ground. While building, the pair frequently call to each other at the nest with soft purring and clucking notes; once incubation commences, however, they become silent and secretive in the vicinity of the nest.
Laying months: mainly Sep-Nov (May-Feb). **Clutch size:** 2, less often 1; laid at a 1-day interval. **Eggs:** 35.5-38.2-40.9 x 31.6-33.6-35.8 mm; mass 25.5-26.5-27 g (in captivity). **Incubation period:** 23 days (20-24); by both sexes; begins with first-laid egg; eggs rarely left unattended. **Nestling/fledging period:** young leave nest at about 3 weeks (in captivity); first fly at about 28 days (in captivity); young brooded and fed by both sexes.

Livingstone's Turaco *Tauraco livingstonii* Mozambiekloerie   page 377

Breeds in and on the fringes of Afromontane, riparian or coastal forest. Pairs nest solitarily; average density 1 pair/4 ha (Malawi). **Nest:** a thin, saucer-shaped platform of dry twigs, placed inside a thickly foliaged forest tree, either among the stems of a creeper festooning a tree, or in the dense latticework of cross-branches in the mid- to upper-canopy of the tree; 3½-13 m up from the ground. Both sexes build the nest. The birds are secretive while breeding and nest change-overs are done in silence; if approached, the incubating bird usually sits until the last moment.
Laying months: mainly Oct-Jan (Sep-Feb). **Clutch size:** 2. **Eggs:** 35.8-37.9-40.9 x 31.6-32.9-35.0 mm. **Incubation period:** not recorded; by both sexes. **Nestling/fledging period:** not recorded; young brooded and fed by both sexes.

Schalow's Turaco *Tauraco schalowi* Langkuifloerie   no nest or egg photo

Breeds in riparian forest. Nesting habits are poorly known. **Nest:** not described but likely to be a thin, saucer-shaped platform of dry twigs similar to those built by other turacos; placed 4-8 m up from the ground (Zambia, Malawi).
Laying months: Oct-Feb (Zambia, Malawi). **Clutch size:** 2, less often 1. **Eggs:** 35.7-39.5-43.2 x 32.0-32.5-34.0 mm. **Incubation period:** 20-22 days (in captivity); by both sexes. **Nestling/fledging period:** 25-28 days (in captivity).

Grey Lourie (Grey Go-away-bird) *Corythaixoides concolor* Kwêvoël   page 377

Breeds in savanna, from semi-arid thornveld to broad-leafed woodland; also, since its arrival there in the early 1980s, in wooded suburban parks and gardens in Gauteng. Pairs nest solitarily, but adjacent nests may be within 100 m of one another; some nests attended by >2 birds, the additional birds presumed young from previous broods. **Nest:** a flimsy, unlined saucer made of dry twigs, 200-300 mm in diameter and 30-40 mm thick; the eggs are often visible from below through the floor of the nest. It is built in the upper, central branches of a tree, mostly 4-6 m up (1½-20 m) and commonly in a tree that stands apart from others. In rural areas nests are mostly in thorny trees (especially *Acacia tortilis*), or in a non-thorny tree that is in full leaf, or in a mistletoe (*Loranthus*, *Viscum*) cluster growing on an upper branch. In these cases the nest is well concealed, but in some, no effort is made to conceal it. Despite its flimsy appearance, nests often remain intact for a year or more and they may be reused by the louries and, frequently, by Southern White-faced Owls. Grey Louries tend to be silent in the vicinity of their nests and, if a nest is approached, the parent attending it flies off silently – in contrast to this bird's noisy response when disturbed in other situations.
Laying months: commonly in all months, with weak Sep-Oct peak. **Clutch size:** 3, less often 2, rarely 4; laid at 2-day intervals. **Eggs:** 37.6-40.8-45.1 x 31.0-33.0-34.8 mm. **Incubation period:** 26-29 days; by both sexes; begins with first-laid egg (in captivity). **Nestling/fledging period:** young leave nest at 18-21 days before they can fly; fly at about 35 days; young brooded and fed by both sexes and helpers.

Purple-crested Turaco (LEFT & TWO ABOVE)

Livingstone's Turaco

Grey Lourie

COUCALS, MALKOHAS form part of the cuckoo family, **Cuculidae**. Worldwide 42 coucal species; 6 breed in southern Africa; 5 are monogamous, 1 is poylandrous. Coucals build large oval-shaped nests with a side entrance, malkoha nest is an open saucer; eggs oval; white, unmarked, 4/clutch in coucals, 2-3/clutch in malkohas; chicks are altricial and leave the nest before they can fly.

Senegal Coucal *Centropus senegalensis* Senegalvleiloerie   page 378

Breeds in n mesic savanna where there are bushy thickets and/or tall, tangled grass; often along drainage lines; also in wooded suburban gardens. **Nest:** similar to those built by other coucals, a bulky, oval-shaped structure with a wide side entrance, built with coarse, dry grass, thin twigs, leaves and other plant material, the cup sparsely lined with green leaves; usually <2 m up from the ground (½-10 m); it is often placed in a thorny shrub that has rank grass growing through it, or in leafy foliage in a tree, a bush or creeper, supported by multiple stems rather than a single-forked branch; it measures 450 mm high and 260-400 mm wide. Nest material continues to be added during the incubation.
Laying months: mainly Nov-Feb (Oct-Mar). **Clutch size:** 3-4 (2-5); laid at 1-2 day intervals. **Eggs:** 28.1-32.0-38.0 × 23.8-25.1-26.7 mm; mass 67.5-75.1-78.0 g. **Incubation period:** 17-19 days; by both sexes; starts with first-laid egg. **Nestling/fledging period:** 18-20 days; fed by both sexes.

Burchell's Coucal *Centropus burchellii* Gewone Vleiloerie   page 378

Breeds in the s mesic savanna, extending to s Cape along coastal bush; favours wooded thickets mixed with areas of rank, tangled grass or reeds, often along rivers or vleis; also in well-wooded suburban gardens. Its range is essentially a s extension of that of the closely allied White-browed Coucal. Pairs nest solitarily and are widely spaced (400 m apart). **Nest:** a bulky, oval-shaped ball, well hidden despite its size, placed either in leafy foliage of a tree, bush or creeper, or in dense grass/reed growth; typically 1-3 m up from the ground (0,1-5), occasionally at ground level (if on an embankment). It measures 300-380 mm high and 200-300 mm wide, with a circular entrance-hole (100 mm wide) near the top of one side; occasional nests lack a roof. It is built by both sexes with long, coarse strands (up to 1 m length) of dry grass that are roughly woven or curled around to form the ball, with finer grass and leaves lining the cup; further lining is added during the incubation.
Laying months: mainly Oct-Dec (Sep-Jan, occasionally other months). **Clutch size:** 4 (2-5); laid at 1-3 day intervals. **Eggs:** 30.3-34.3-37.6 × 24.5-26.5-28.4 mm. **Incubation period:** 15-16 days; by both sexes; starts with first-laid egg. **Nestling/fledging period:** young leave nest at 14-21 days, before they can fly; young are fed by both sexes.

White-browed Coucal *Centropus superciliosus* Gestreepte Vleiloerie   page 378

Breeds in n mesic savanna. Its nesting habits and nest as described for Burchell's Coucal of which it is often treated as a subspecies.
Laying months: mainly Nov-Dec (Sep-Mar). **Clutch size:** 4 (3-5). **Eggs:** 30.8-34.5-39.0 × 25.5-26.1-28.0 mm; 10.2 g. **Incubation period:** 14-16 days; by both sexes; starts before clutch complete. **Nestling/fledging period:** young leave nest temporarily at 14 days if disturbed, permanently at 18-20 days, before they can fly; young are fed by both sexes.

Coppery-tailed Coucal *Centropus cupreicaudus* Grootvleiloerie   page 378

Breeds on floodplains and rivers in n Botswana, Caprivi and ne Zimbabwe, especially in *Phragmites* reedbeds intergrown with rank grass, forbs or creepers. Pairs nest solitarily and are territorial year-round. **Nest:** a thick-walled, oval- or conical-shaped ball, made with dry grass, with a side entrance hole, well hidden in reeds or thick undergrowth ½-1 m up; usually over water; it measures 350 mm (height) × 250 mm (width and breadth), with an internal chamber, 250 mm wide at the entrance and 200 mm at the cup. The entrance hole, which in some nests has a runway leading from it into the vegetation, measures about 110 × 125 mm across.
Laying months: Jan-Mar. **Clutch size:** 2-4. **Eggs:** 35.7-36.5-37.8 × 27.7-28.3-28.6 mm. **Incubation period:** not recorded. **Nestling/fledging period:** young leave nest at 17 days, before they can fly.

Black Coucal *Centropus grillii* Swartvleiloerie   page 378

A breeding visitor arriving Nov-Dec, to dambos and seasonally wet, rank grassland in n mesic savanna; favours areas of old grass (not burnt the previous summer), 1-2 m tall. Pairs and polyandrous trios nest in territories of 5-10 ha; in polyandrous trios, adjacent nests may be <25 m apart. **Nest:** a well-hidden oval-shaped ball of coarse dry grass-blades with live grass incorporated into the walls, especially the roof, placed 100-450 mm up in rank grass, either over moist ground or on a grassed-over termite island in water; the cup is lined with green leaves which continue to be added during the incubation. It measures 225-300 mm high and 175-225 mm wide, with an 80 mm-wide side entrance hole. ♂s incubate and care for the young without ♀ assistance.
Laying months: mainly Jan-Feb (Dec-Mar). **Clutch size:** 4 (2-6); laid at 1-day intervals. ♀ may lay 6 clutches/season. **Eggs:** 25.9-29.5-31.8 × 20.0-23.6-25.7 mm; mass 7.2-7.6-8.1 g. **Incubation period:** 14 days; by ♂ only; begins with first-laid egg. **Nestling/fledging period:** young leave nest if disturbed at 11 days old, permanently at 18-20 days; fly at 28 days; brooded and fed by ♂.

Green Malkoha *Ceuthmochares aereus* Groenvleiloerie   page 378

Breeds in lowland, coastal and riparian forest. Nesting habits are poorly known. Pairs nest solitarily and are widely spaced. **Nest:** a small (150 mm in diameter), flimsy saucer, made of pieces of twigs with foliage attached, tendrils, grass and other plant material, the cup lined with green leaves. It is well hidden in densely foliaged creepers or where stems of different trees intertwine, 2-15 m up, and is easily overlooked as being an accumulation of caught-up plant debris.
Laying months: Oct-Dec. **Clutch size:** 2-4. **Eggs:** 27.8-30.3-31.9 × 21.0-23.0-25.9 mm. **Incubation period:** not recorded. **Nestling/fledging period:** not recorded; young are fed by both sexes.

Senegal Coucal

White-browed Coucal

Burchell's Coucal

Burchell's Coucal

Coppery-tailed Coucal

Black Coucal

Green Malkoha

Cuckoos

CUCKOOS, COUCALS, MALKOHAS Family Cuculidae Worldwide 147 species; 24 breed in Afrotropics (11 more in Madagascar), 17 in southern Africa; 11 are southern African members of the so-called 'Old World' cuckoos that parasitise the nests of other birds; coucals, malkohas and 'New World' cuckoos don't, instead building their own nests and rearing their young themselves.

The 11 cuckoos here, as well as being parasitic, vary in their mating systems, in the hosts they select and in the strategies they use to get their eggs into hosts' nests. Some species are monogamous, others promiscuous; some are host-specific, others parasitise a range of hosts; some lay eggs that closely match those of their hosts; others lay eggs that are conspicuously different; some lay a single egg per host-nest, others lay several; some remove host-eggs when they lay, others don't; in some, the cuckoo nestling evicts its host's eggs, in others it doesn't. These cuckoos do, however, share the trait of having shorter incubation periods than their hosts, and of laying their eggs in host nests while the hosts are laying their own clutch. The cuckoo eggs thus hatch ahead of their hosts' and this advantage usually results in the demise of the host's brood.

Black Cuckoo *Cuculus clamosus* Swartkoekoek   page 379

A breeding visitor arriving in late Sep in the savanna belt, from the semi-arid west to the mesic east; also in montane forest, extending via this habitat into s Cape. ♂s are probably promiscuous. Its hosts in southern Africa are the 4 *Laniarius* shrikes (Crimson-breasted Shrike and Southern, Tropical and Swamp boubous); in the case of the Crimson-breasted Shrike, an estimated 14-36% of all nests are parasitised seasonally. The ♀ cuckoo lays one egg per host-nest (rarely two) and she removes a host egg from the nest while doing so. The cuckoo egg closely matches the eggs of this group of shrikes (being similar in coloration and markings) but is sometimes distinguishable by being marginally longer, more blunt on the obtuse end, and having finer speckling. ♀s lay 'clutches' of 4-5 eggs on successive or alternate days, estimated to total up to 22 eggs/season. Because of its shorter incubation period, the cuckoo egg usually hatches before those of its host and the young cuckoo evicts the host eggs from the nest.
Laying months: Oct-Apr, peaking in Feb-Mar (Namibia) and Nov-Dec elsewhere. **Eggs:** 23.5-24.9-27.3 × 17.0-18.0-19.1 mm; mass 5.0 g; egg ground colour either white or washed with blue or green, variably speckled with shades of red-brown and underlying grey, mainly at the blunt end and sometimes forming a ring of markings. **Incubation period:** 14 days. **Nestling/fledging period:** 20-21 days; fledged chick remains with foster parents for a further 19-43 days.

Red-chested Cuckoo *Cuculus solitarius* Piet-my-vrou   page 378

A breeding visitor arriving in Sep in mesic savanna and montane forest, extending in grassland and karoo edge where alien or other woodland provides habitat; a familiar bird in the wooded suburbs of many cities. ♂s are probably promiscuous. The primary hosts of this cuckoo in southern Africa are robin-chats, thrushes, chats and wagtails. Numerous other species (e.g. see photograph page 349) are occasionally parasitised; these and others like them are probably parasitised as a result of egg-dumping rather than specific host selection. The Cape Robin-Chat is the most widely recorded host, with 14.5-22% of its nests parasitised seasonally. Cape Wagtail is the second-most frequently recorded host, followed by 8 robins, robin-chats and scrub-robins (White-starred and Swynnerton's Robins; Bearded and White-browed Scrub Robins; Heuglin's, Chorister, Red-capped and White-throated robin-chats) and 6 thrush/chat species (Kurrichane, Olive, Karoo Thrushes, Cape Rock Thrush, Boulder Chat, African Stonechat). Other regular hosts are Mountain Wagtail and African Dusky Flycatcher. The cuckoo lays one egg per host-nest (rarely two) and it removes a host egg from the nest. Its egg frequently does not closely match the eggs of the species it parasitises (see photographs opposite), yet there is, apparently, no rejection of the foreign egg by these hosts. One ♀ is estimated to lay about 20 eggs/season. Because of its shorter incubation period, the cuckoo egg usually hatches before those of the host and the young cuckoo evicts the host's eggs from the nest.
Laying months: mainly Nov-Dec (Oct-Jan). **Eggs:** 22.8-24.6-25.9 × 17.2-18.3-19.6 mm; two types occur; one is unmarked, glossy and chocolate- or olive-brown; the other is a speckled egg, in which the ground colour ranges between olive-green, pale blue and buff, and the speckling is various shades of brown. **Incubation period:** 12-14 days. **Nestling/fledging period:** 17-21 days; fledged chick remains with foster parents for a further 20-25 days.

African Cuckoo *Cuculus gularis* Afrikaanse Koekoek   page 378

A breeding visitor arriving in late Sep in the savanna belt, its range extending from the semi-arid west to the mesic east. ♂s are probably promiscuous. This cuckoo has a single host in southern Africa, the Fork-tailed Drongo. It lays one egg per host-nest and removes one or more host-eggs. Fork-tailed Drongos lay a range of egg colour-types and the cuckoo egg closely matches the most common of these egg-types (one having a ground-colour of pinkish-white, speckled or blotched with red-brown). Cuckoo eggs laid in nests with this egg-type are accepted, but in non-matching clutches the cuckoo egg is evicted by the host. Because of its shorter incubation period, the cuckoo egg usually hatches before those of the host and the young cuckoo evicts the host's eggs from the nest.
Laying months: mainly Oct-Nov (Sep-Dec). **Eggs:** 23.1-24.2-25.0 × 16.8-17.8-18.2 mm. **Incubation period:** not known accurately; between 11-17 days. **Nestling/fledging period:** 23 days.

Barred Long-tailed Cuckoo *Cercococcyx montanus* Langstertkoekoek

A scarce, localised summer visitor to lowland and riparian forests. No hosts have yet been proven in the region: East Coast Akalat, African Broadbill and Chestnut-fronted Helmetshrike have been named as potential hosts but none have been confirmed to date. A captive bird in Tanzania laid a white egg measuring 23 × 17 mm that was finely speckled with red in a zone around the broad end.

full-grown nestling in Crimson-breasted Shrike nest	**Black Cuckoo**	egg in Crimson-breasted Shrike nest
egg in Boulder Chat nest	**Red-chested Cuckoo**	egg in Kurrichane Thrush nest
fledged chick being fed by Cape Wagtail	**Red-chested Cuckoo**	fledged chick being fed by Karoo Thrush
egg in nest of Fork-tailed Drongo	**African Cuckoo**	full-grown nestling in Fork-tailed Drongo nest

Great Spotted Cuckoo *Clamator glandarius* Gevlekte Koekoe page 379

A breeding visitor arriving in mid-Oct in the savanna, from the semi-arid west to mesic east. Occurs in pairs and probably territorial and monogamous. Its primary hosts in southern Africa are starlings and crows, with at least eight starling species (Common Myna, Pied, Burchell's, Meves', Cape Glossy, Greater Blue-eared, Red-winged and Pale-winged Starlings) and two crow species (Pied and Cape Crows) as confirmed hosts. Estimates of the percentage of host-nests parasitised by this cuckoo range between 13% (in Pied Crows), 10% (in Cape Crows) and 5% in Pied Starlings. ♀s usually lay more than one egg/host-nest, mostly 2-3 (1-13 recorded) and no host-eggs are removed in the process, though they might be inadvertently damaged. The cuckoo pair work together to parasitise a nest, the ♂ luring the hosts away, while the ♀ slips in to lay, taking about 10 sec for this. When laid in a crow nest, the cuckoo egg is easily distinguished by its smaller size from the crow eggs; in the case of Cape Crow it is also differently coloured. But in nests of larger starlings the cuckoo's egg may closely match those of the host in size, colour and markings. With the possible exception of Cape Crow, none of the host species reject the eggs of this cuckoo. The cuckoo nestlings, which normally hatch out before those of the host, do not evict host-eggs, and mixed broods (of host and cuckoo chicks) are occasionally reared in the same nest. More usually, however, the first-hatched young (the cuckoo/s) have a size advantage which results in the last-hatched young (of the host) being trampled or starved, and only cuckoo chicks are raised.

Laying months: mainly Oct-Jan (Aug-Mar); peaks Feb-Mar in Namibia. **Eggs:** 29.0-33.4-37.0 x 21.0-24.5-27.0 mm; mass 9.3 g; greenish-blue variably speckled, spotted or blotched with shades of red-brown and underlying shades of grey; eggs a close colour-match for Pied Crow, less so for starling eggs. **Incubation period:** 14-15 days. **Nestling/fledging period:** 22-26 days; fledged chick remains with foster parents for up to 33 days.

Levaillant's Cuckoo *Clamator levaillantii* Gestreepte Nuwejaarsvoël page 378

A breeding visitor arriving in late Oct in the savanna belt, from the semi-arid west to the mesic east. Occurs in pairs and is probably monogamous. Its sole hosts in southern Africa are babblers and 4/5 of the region's babblers are known to be parasitised (Arrow-marked, Bare-cheeked, Hartlaub's, Southern Pied). It lays one (rarely two) eggs per host-nest and removes one or more of the host-eggs from the clutch. The cuckoo egg closely matches the unmarked blue babbler egg in size and colour. An estimated 7½% of Arrow-marked Babbler nests/season are parasitised, and some babbler groups are parasitised more than once in a season; Arrow-marked Babblers do, on occasion, abandon a parasitised nest. Because of their shorter incubation period, the cuckoo nestlings usually hatch first, but they do not evict host-eggs and mixed broods of cuckoo and host young are frequently raised.

Laying months: Oct-May. **Eggs:** 24.2-26.6-28.6 x 19.0-20.6-22.3 mm; unmarked turquoise-blue, matches host eggs in size and colour, recognisable by different texture, finely pitted and slightly glossy. **Incubation period:** 11-12 days. **Nestling/fledging period:** 13-16 days; fledged chick remains with foster parents a further 3-5 weeks.

Jacobin Cuckoo *Clamator jacobinus* Bontnuwejaarsvoël page 378

A breeding visitor arriving in early Oct in the savanna belt, from the semi-arid west to the mesic east, extending into grassland where alien woodland provides habitat. ♂s are probably polygamous or promiscuous. This cuckoo has five main hosts in southern Africa: the Common Fiscal and 4 bulbuls (Dark-capped, Red-eyed, Cape Bulbuls, Sombre Greenbul). Because it lays a plain white, easily recognised egg, it has also been recorded parasitising many other unrelated species, some probably victims of egg-dumping rather than selection. Among these are Fork-tailed Drongo, Terrestrial Brownbul, Chestnut-vented Titbabbler, Cape Grassbird, Fiscal Flycatcher, Southern Boubou, Bokmakierie, Black-backed Puffback, Southern Tchagra, Brown-crowned Tchagra (illustrated in photos opposite), Golden-breasted Bunting, Speckled Mousebird, African Paradise Flycatcher, Fiscal Flycatcher, Cape White-eye, Cape Wagtail; also, apparently Southern Pied Babbler)). In one study area, 16% of Cape Bulbul nests were parasitised, 13% of Sombre Greenbul nests and 12% of Dark-capped Bulbul nests. Usually one egg per host-nest is laid (less often 2-3, rarely up to 7) no host-eggs are removed from the clutch. Although its egg is conspicuously different, none of its regular hosts reject these eggs from their nests. The cuckoo eggs usually hatch ahead of the eggs of the host, but the young cuckoos do not evict the host's eggs. Mixed broods (of cuckoo and host together) rarely survive, however, as the first-hatched young (the cuckoos) have a size advantage which results in the last-hatched (host young) being trampled or starved, and only cuckoo chicks are usually raised. ♀s lay 'clutches' of about 4 eggs, each egg at 2-day intervals, with an estimated 25 eggs laid in a 10-week breeding season.

Laying months: mainly Nov-Dec (Oct-Apr). **Eggs:** 23.0-26.0-28.5 x 19.0-21.6-24.0 mm; mass 5.35-7.95 g. **Incubation period:** 11 days (11-12). **Nestling/fledging period:** 17 days.

Thick-billed Cuckoo *Pachycoccyx audeberti* Dikbekkoekoek page 378

Apparently resident, breeding in mesic savanna and lowland and riparian forest. ♂s are probably promiscuous or polyandrous. Has a single host in southern Africa, Retz's Helmetshrike. The ♀ cuckoo lays one egg (rarely two) per host-nest and removes one or more host-eggs when laying; adult cuckoos have also been recorded removing host-chicks from nests later in the breeding cycle. Parasitism of the host's nest is achieved by the ♀ cuckoo forcibly knocking the host off its nest and returning to lay before the helmetshrike returns. In one 5-year study, 50% of the host-nests were parasitised. The cuckoo's egg closely matches the helmetshrike's egg in size, colour and markings and is essentially indistinguishable from those of the host. Because of its shorter incubation period, the cuckoo egg normally hatches first and the young cuckoo evicts the host-eggs from the nest. Cuckoo nestlings void a foul-smelling fluid if they are handled, and when they fledge they are twice the size of their foster parents (see right-hand photograph).

Laying months: mainly Oct-Nov (Sep-Apr). **Eggs:** 22.5-23.7-25.4 x 17.2-17.6-18.0 mm; ground colour variable, from pale cream to pale blue-green, marked with large spots and blotches of shades of pale brown, grey and lilac, mainly in a zone near the blunt end of the egg; a close colour match, but egg more rounded than egg of host. **Incubation period:** 13 days. **Nestling/fledging period:** 28-30 days; fledged chick remains with foster parents for up to 50 days.

fledged chick being fed by Red-winged Starling | Great Spotted Cuckoo | chick in nest of Red-winged Starling

Levaillant's Cuckoo — egg in nest of Arrow-marked Babbler | Jacobin Cuckoo — egg in nest of Dark-capped Bulbul

small chick in nest of Brown-crowned Tchagra | Jacobin Cuckoo | large chick in nest of Brown-crowned Tchagra

egg/s in nest of Retz's Helmetshrike | Thick-billed Cuckoo | full-grown nestling in Retz's Helmetshrike nest

Cuckoos

Diederik Cuckoo (Diderick Cuckoo) *Chrysococcyx caprius* Diederikkie — page 379

A common breeding visitor arriving in late Sep; widespread and absent only from arid areas. ♂s are probably promiscuous. This cuckoo has more recorded host species (>24) than any other southern African cuckoo. Weavers, sparrows and Southern Red Bishops constitute the main hosts, but host preference varies regionally and a commonly used host in one area may not be parasitised in another (e.g. Southern Red Bishop is a common host in the grassland region, but is not parasitised in sw Cape). The 6 most frequently recorded hosts are: Southern Masked, Cape and Village Weavers, Cape Sparrow, Southern Red Bishop and Cape Wagtail. At least five other weavers are commonly parasitised, two other sparrows, one or more widowbird species and a variety of warblers, robin-chats, chats, flycatchers and others. Except in possible instances of egg-dumping, this cuckoo and Klaas's Cuckoos do not overlap in their choice of hosts in the region. Parasitism levels vary seasonally, regionally and between hosts, ranging between 1-66% of host-nests in an area being parasitised. The ♀ cuckoo lays one egg per host-nest and removes a host-egg from the clutch while doing so. There are several 'tribes' or gentes of ♀s, each laying her own specific egg-type and a ♀ lays a similarly coloured and marked egg through her lifetime. One ♀ Diederik Cuckoo gentes lays weaver-type eggs (white, pink or blue with speckles and blotches), another lays sparrow-type eggs (cream, mottled with diffuse brown and grey markings); a third lays Red Bishop-type eggs (plain blue) and a fourth lays plain white eggs. A ♀ recognises which host/s lay an egg-type matching hers (perhaps through being originally raised by those hosts), and she selects her nests to be parasitised accordingly. Cuckoo and host-eggs can be so closely matched to be undetectable to the human eye. Because of its shorter incubation period the cuckoo egg usually hatches ahead of the host's eggs and the just-hatched cuckoo nestling invariably evicts other eggs or nestlings in the nest, using its back to push these out of the nest (as shown in the right-hand photograph opposite). ♀s are estimated to lay 20-24 eggs/season.

Laying months: mainly Nov-Jan (Oct-Mar); peaking earliest in winter-rainfall region and latest in Namibia. **Eggs:** 18.9-22.0-24.9 × 9.8-14.8-16.0 mm; mass 1.5-2.5-3.5 g. very variable, including both unmarked eggs (white or blue) and marked eggs that have variable ground colours (ranging from white, cream, blue, green) and variable markings (speckling, spotting, blotching, streaking in shades of brown and grey, and evenly spread or concentrated on the blunt end). **Incubation period:** 11-12 days. **Nestling/fledging period:** 20-22 days.

Klaas's Cuckoo *Chrysococcyx klaas* Meitjie — page 379

A breeding visitor arriving in late Sep in the savanna belt, from the semi-arid west to the mesic east. ♂s are probably promiscuous. This cuckoo is known to parasitise at least 18 species in southern Africa, but three groups – sunbirds (11 species), batises (3 species) and warblers (4 species) – constitute its main hosts, and in different regions the host-pool usually comprises a sunbird, a batis and a warbler, e.g. in s Cape it is Greater Double-collared Sunbird/Cape Batis/Bar-throated Apalis; in Namibia, Dusky Sunbird/Pririt Batis/Yellow-bellied Eremomela. Measured levels of parasitism of host species range between 1-8%. This cuckoo lays one egg per host-nest and removes a host-egg from the clutch. Its eggs vary considerably in colour and markings, although individually a ♀ lays a consistent egg type through her lifetime; it is thought that individual ♀s specialise in parasitising particular host species where their eggs match best. Egg-matching varies: in some cases the match is so close as to make the cuckoo egg undetectable to the human eye; more usually, the colour and markings match, but the size does not (the cuckoo egg being larger), and occasionally, neither size nor colour/markings match. Given its shorter Incubation period, the cuckoo egg usually hatches before the eggs of the host; the just-hatched cuckoo nestling invariably evicts other eggs or nestlings from the nest. ♀ lays 'clutches' of 3-4 eggs, one on every alternate day, an estimated 24 eggs/season. Eggs of Klaas's and Diederik cuckoos are often similar in colour and markings, and they overlap marginally in size (but Diederik eggs are mostly larger). Because there is no overlap in their preferred hosts, a cuckoo egg in a nest can be identified as belonging to Diederik or Klaas's on the basis of the host's identity; nestlings of the two can be distinguished by the difference in their bill colour (red-orange in Diederik, horn-coloured in Klaas's).

Laying months: Feb-Apr in Namibia, mainly Oct-Jan elsewhere (Sep-Jun). **Eggs:** 18.0-18.7-20.2 × 12.2-13.1-13.8 mm; variable, both in ground colour (from white to greenish-white, pale pink or pale blue) and markings (speckled and spotted with shades of brown, either concentrating on the blunt end or in a ring near the blunt end). **Incubation period:** 11-12 days. **Nestling/fledging period:** 19-21 days; fledged chick remains with foster parents for up to 25 days.

African Emerald Cuckoo *Chrysococcyx cupreus* Mooimeisie — page 379

A breeding visitor arriving in Sep in coastal, lowland, riparian and montane forests. ♂s are probably promiscuous. Breeding habits are not well known and only two hosts have been proven in southern Africa: Green-backed Camaroptera and Barratt's Warbler. White-starred Robin and Yellow-throated Woodland Warbler have been found with cuckoo eggs in their nests thought to belong to this species, but neither have been confirmed by hatching. In parasitised camaroptera nests, mostly a single egg is laid per nest and a single host-egg is removed. The cuckoo's egg (unmarked white) matches the Camaroptera's egg in colour but is substantially larger (see photograph opposite). ♀s lay 'clutches' of 3-4 eggs on successive or alternate days, laying an estimated total of about 20 eggs/season. Many reported host records (of fledged young attended by foster parents) are questionable given the similarity between the juveniles of this and Klaas's Cuckoo. Young Emerald Cuckoos can be distinguished from young Klaas's by lacking a buff-coloured flare behind the eye (which is present in Klaas's) and by having bolder and generally greenish barred underparts; in Klaas's the underparts are finely barred and bronzy, The young Diederik Cuckoo has an orange-red bill, whereas young Emerald Cuckoos have horn-coloured bills.

Laying months: Oct-Jan. **Eggs:** 19.3-20.7-21.8 × 13.9-14.5-15.0 mm. Either unmarked white to very pale blue, or white, freckled and blotched with brown in a ring of markings concentrated near the blunt end. **Incubation period:** 16 days. **Nestling/fledging period:** >22 days.

le cuckoo trapped in tunnel of Lesser Masked Weaver nest   Diederik Cuckoo   cuckoo nestling (left) evicting weaver nestling (right)

egg in nest of Cape Batis   Klaas's Cuckoo   chick in nest of Cape Batis    chick in nest of Olive Sunbird

egg in nest of Green-backed Camaroptera   African Emerald Cuckoo   full-grown nestling in nest of Green-backed Camaroptera

Owls

OWLS Families **Tytonidae** (worldwide 18 species) and **Strigidae** (worldwide 202 species); 31 of these breed in the Afrotropics, 12 in southern Africa. Monogamous; pairs nest solitarily; the two grass-nesting owls make rudimentary nests on the ground, the other species don't construct nests, but lay in tree- and rock-cavities, in old nests of other birds, or on the ground; eggs unmarked white, elliptical or near-spherical, 2-18/clutch; ♀ incubates, both sexes rear young; incubation periods are unusually long (>28 days); young are semi-altricial and nidicolous.

Western Barn Owl *Tyto alba* Nonnetjie-uil   page 380

Breeds widely throughout southern Africa. Pairs nest solitarily, usually spaced >1 km apart, but during rodent irruptions adjacent nests can be within 50 m of each other. **Nest:** eggs are laid in a cavity (usually one >300 mm wide) or dark place of some sort – very commonly uses man-made structures: in lofts and chimneys in old buildings and farm outbuildings; in mine shafts, watertowers, grain silos, haystacks and in nest boxes; natural sites include Hamerkop nests (which are commonly used where available), cavities in trees (especially large baobabs), and holes and crevices in rock faces and earth banks. The nest becomes a thick bed of pellets that accumulate from long useage; sites are usually occupied year-round as daytime roosts when not breeding and are reused for nesting in successive years, often for decades. Breeding output variable, dependent on rodent abundance, large clutches (up to 19) are laid in high rodent years, whereas in low rodent years either no breeding is attempted or smaller clutches (5-6) are laid.
Laying months: a mainly winter breeder, peaks in Mar-May (in summer-rainfall areas), Aug-Sep (in winter-rainfall areas); but may lay in any month; double-brooded when prey is abundant. **Clutch size:** 5-6 (2-19; very variable according to prey availability); laid at 1-3 day intervals. **Eggs:** 36.0-39.1-43.1 × 28.9-31.3-34.5 mm; 17.3-20.3-23.9 g. **Incubation period:** 31 days (29-34); by ♀ only, fed on nest by ♂; begins when first egg is laid. **Nestling/fledging period:** 50 days (45-55); young brooded and fed by ♀, later fed by both sexes.

African Grass Owl *Tyto capensis* Grasuil   page 380

Breeds sparsely in grasslands and moist savannas, restricted to areas of tall, thick grass, usually along drainage lines and in unburnt and ungrazed areas. Pairs nest solitarily and are widely spaced, seldom within 150 m of each other; sites chosen may be damp or dry underfoot, but not wet; the pair roost in separate sites during the day and one of their roost sites is usually used for breeding. **Nest:** eggs are laid on the ground on a thin pad of grass-stems (thicker if on damp ground), typically at the end of one or more roofed passageways, 1-2 m in length, that lead through the grass; these passages distinguish its nest from that of the Marsh Owl, which often nests alongside it in suitable habitat. Sites are sometimes reused in successive years. The ♀, which incubates without ♂ assistance, sits tight when incubating, only flying off at the last moment when approached.
Laying months: mainly Feb-May (Nov-Aug). **Clutch size:** 4 (2-6); laid at 2-day intervals. **Eggs:** 37.4-41.1-45.0 × 30.0-32.7-36.0 mm. **Incubation period:** 32 days; by ♀ only; probably begins before clutch is completed. **Nestling/fledging period:** young leave nest at 28-35 days; fly at 49-52 days; young brooded by ♀, fed by both sexes.

Marsh Owl *Asio capensis* Vlei-uil   page 380

Breeds widely in rank grassland and vleis in mesic and semi-arid savannas, often alongside African Grass Owl but more tolerant of aridity and heavier grazing on its habitat, so more widely distributed. It nests and roosts (during the day) on the ground, sometimes in communal roosts of 10-75 birds. Pairs nest solitarily, though, usually >200 m apart (adjacent nests rarely within 30 m of each other). **Nest:** a saucer-shaped pad of green and dry grass-stems, about 300 mm in diameter and 25-50 mm thick which is added to through the incubation. It is placed in thick grass on the ground (or it can be over shallow water), concealed from above by a canopy of plant-stems pulled over to form a camopy; it does not have an extensive network of tunnels leading to it (as does the African Grass Owl nest). There is no reuse of nest sites. The ♀, which does the incubation without ♂ assistance, often calls from the nest at dusk (uttering a short rasping croak). If approached while incubating or brooding young, the ♀ flies up and circles around, sometimes calling, and occasionally engaging in an injury-feigning display on the ground.
Laying months: mainly Mar-May (Feb-Oct, rarely in other months); sometimes relays after an earlier failure. **Clutch size:** 3-4 (2-6); laid at 2-3 day intervals. **Eggs:** 37.9-40.0-43.0 × 32.4-34.1-36.0 mm. **Incubation period:** 27-28 days; mainly or entirely by ♀; begins before clutch is completed. **Nestling/fledging period:** young leave nest at about 14-18 days; fly at about 35-40 days; young brooded and fed by ♀, later fed by both sexes.

African Wood Owl *Strix woodfordii* Bosuil   page 380

Breeds in coastal, lowland, riparian and montane forest and in densely wooded mesic savanna. Pairs are territorial and nest solitarily; along ribbons of riparian forest they are spaced about ½-1 km apart. **Nest:** lays in a tree cavity, usually a rot-hole about 200-250 mm wide that has formed where a branch has broken off a main trunk; depth variable, typically about 250 mm deep (60-510 mm); height above ground is also very variable, between 0.6-3.0 m. Preferred cavities are usually in living trees; sites are often reused in successive years, some in known use for decades; it also nests in artificial boxes erected for the owls and, occasionally, on old eagle or hawk platform nests. Although highly vocal before nesting, these owls become secretive once incubation commences, and may go undetected even when nesting in a garden where there is frequent activity around the nest tree.
Laying months: mainly Aug-Oct (Jul-Nov, rarely in other months); may relay after an early failure. **Clutch size:** 2 (1-3); laid at a 1-4 day interval. **Eggs:** 40.0-43.4-46.0 × 35.5-37.6-40.5 mm. **Incubation period:** 31 days; probably by ♀ only; begins when first egg is laid. **Nestling/fledging period:** young start 'branching' from 21 days, fly from 30-37 days; young brooded and fed by ♀; later fed by both sexes.

nesting in Hamerkop nest   Western Barn Owl   nesting in owl box (left) chimney (right)

African Grass Owl

Marsh Owl

African Wood Owl

Spotted Eagle-Owl *Bubo africanus* Gevlekte Ooruil
page 380

Breeds widely throughout southern Africa, from the arid west to the mesic east. Pairs nest solitarily and, in suitable habitat, are spaced about ½-2½ km apart. **Nest:** eggs are laid on bare ground, but the sites they choose are very diverse; they often nest on hillsides or ridges among rocks or in flat open country in the arid west they frequently lay under a shrub; hollows in the walls of deep dongas (as in left-hand photograph) are commonly used, as are tree cavities, or a bowl formed in a crotch of a tree where branches diverge, or where leaves have caught up on a branch to form a bed; man-made sites (on ledges in quarry walls and buildings, in haystacks, flood debris, window boxes) are also widely used; also the top of Hamerkop and Sociable Weaver nests and, very occasionally, old birds of prey nests. Selected nest sites are invariably open above and are not in an enclosed hole as a Barn Owl would choose. Sites are commonly reused in successive years. Where habituated to people, these owls often become bold when nesting and may attack humans if their nests or young are approached.
Laying months: mainly Aug-Oct (Jul-Nov, rarely in other months); may relay after early failure; rarely double-brooded. **Clutch size:** 2-3 (1-6, occasional large clutches when rodents abundant); laid 1-4 day intervals. **Eggs:** 47.1-49.0-54.2 x 39.1-41.0-44.4 mm. **Incubation period:** 32 days (29-33); by ♀ only, fed by ♂; begins when first egg is laid. **Nestling/fledging period:** young wander from nest at about 3 weeks; fly at about 40 days; young brooded and fed by ♀; later fed by both sexes.

Cape Eagle-Owl *Bubo capensis* Kaapse Ooruil
page 380

Breeds in open, rocky, usually treeless landscapes (karoo, Namib, grassland, fynbos), where cliffs provide suitable nesting and roosting sites. **Nest:** eggs are laid in a scrape on bare ground on a shelf on a rock face or on a steep rocky scree under an overhanging boulder; favoured sites are on a shelf, some way up a vertical cliff with an overhanging roof, screened in front by low vegetation; sheltered rocky ravines are preferred to exposed escarpment faces. Pairs nest solitarily, usually >2 km apart. Sites are often reused annually, some known to have been occupied for decades; at such sites the shelf becomes carpeted with the fine bones and hair of prey (this is often referred to as an 'ossuary'); nest scrapes, 280-380 mm wide and 25 mm deep, are often placed in this debris (as shown in the nest opposite). Breeding sites are often given away by the distinctive whitewashing left by these owls (their faeces are especially viscous) on the surrounding rocks and, when they have nestlings, by the downy feathers that get caught up in the vicinity of the nest. Pairs do not breed every year.
Laying months: mainly May-Jun (Apr-Sep); peaks later in w and e Cape. **Clutch size:** 2 (1-3); laid at least a 2-day interval. **Eggs:** 50.6-53.0-54.8 x 42.0-44.0-46.8 mm (South Africa, race *capensis*); 55.0-57.5-60.0 x 44.0-46.5-49.1 mm (Zimbabwe, race *mackinderi*). **Incubation period:** 34-38 days; mainly by ♀, ♂ sitting briefly when she leaves to feed; begins when first egg is laid. **Nestling/fledging period:** young leave nest (on foot) at about 4-6 weeks; fly at about 10-11 weeks; young brooded and fed by ♀; later fed by both sexes.

Verreaux's Eagle-Owl *Bubo lacteus* Reuse-ooruil
page 380

Breeds widely in both semi-arid and mesic savannas, with isolated pairs in the s Cape; favours areas with tall, scattered trees including aliens such as eucalypts. Pairs nest solitarily and are widely spaced, rarely <4 km apart, and typically 10-20 km apart. **Nest:** sites used vary, but the most frequently used are old birds of prey nests, crow nests, and the tops of the nests of Hamerkop, Sociable Weaver and Red-billed Buffalo Weaver; more than 15 species of raptor nests have been recorded used, those of Wahlberg's Eagle being the most frequent; active nests of these eagles are sometimes usurped by the owls. Nest height is variable, from 3-5 m up for those on top of Hamerkop or Sociable Weaver nests, to >15 m up when a tree-top eagle or vulture nest is used; large hollows or crotches in tree trunks are also sometimes used (see right-hand photograph), and one was recorded on top of a tree orchid. Sites may be reused in successive years. Examination of a nest with young sometimes elicits a noisy distraction display from the parent bird which dances about on a nearby branch, waving its wings and making grunting squawks. Nestlings may feign death when examined.
Laying months: mainly Jun-Aug (Mar-Sep); pairs do not breed every year. **Clutch size:** 2 (1-2); laid at a 2-3 day interval. **Eggs:** 58.0-62.8-67.3 x 48.0-51.2-54.0 mm; mass 93-102 g. **Incubation period:** 38-39 days; mainly or entirely by ♀, fed by ♂; begins when first egg is laid. **Nestling/fledging period:** 62-63 days; young brooded and fed by ♀; later fed by both sexes; second-hatched chick usually dies of starvation.

Pel's Fishing Owl *Scotopelia peli* Visuil
page 380

Breeds along low-lying tropical rivers and floodplains where there is a tall, dense forest fringe; largest population (about 100 pairs) is in the Okavango. Pairs breed solitarily and, in optimum habitat, are spaced at intervals of 2-5 km. **Nest:** eggs are laid in a large rot-hole cavity or in a spacious crotch where multiple branches diverge in a large tree, usually one standing <25 m from a river and always within 200 m of it; favoured nest trees are *Ficus sycomorus* and *Diospyros mespiliformis*; twice reported breeding on top of old Hamerkop nests. The nest site is typically 4-5 m up from the ground (3-12) in a cavity about 300-400 mm in diameter and those in rot-holes may be ½-1 m down from the entrance. No material is added and the eggs are laid on fallen leaves, fish-scales, bones and other accumulated debris. Sites are commonly reused in successive breeding attempts; pairs usually do not attempt to breed in the year after rearing a chick. Parent may perform a striking distraction display, wailing loudly and flopping from branch to branch if nest is approached.
Laying months: mainly Feb-Apr (Jan-Jun). **Clutch size:** 2 (1-2); laid at up to a 5-day interval. **Eggs:** 58.6-61.3-65.1 x 49.2-51.3-53.5 mm; mass 85 g. **Incubation period:** about 33-38 days; by ♀ only, fed by ♂; starts with first-laid egg. **Nestling/fledging period:** 68-70 days; young brooded by ♀; second-hatched chick usually dies of starvation, only one nestling normally raised per attempt.

nesting in a donga   Spotted Eagle-Owl   nesting in a hollow tree (centre), on a rocky hillside (right)

Cape Eagle-Owl

using old Tawny Eagle nest   Verreaux's Eagle-Owl   nesting in the bowl of a large tree

Pel's Fishing Owl

Pearl-spotted Owlet *Glaucidium perlatum* Witkoluil
page 380

Breeds widely in well-wooded savanna from the semi-arid west to the mesic east. Pairs nest solitarily and, in continuous habitat, are spaced at intervals of about ½-1 km. **Nest:** uses a hole in a tree, often the old hole of a Bearded, Bennett's or Golden-tailed Woodpecker; natural cavities (e.g. rot-holes where branches have broken off) are also used, as well as artificial nest-boxes, and, rarely, a hollow metal pipe. Nest hole is typically one in the main trunk of a largish tree, 1-6 m up from the ground, with an entrance hole about 50 mm in diameter and a chamber 230-350 mm deep. Such holes are often reused by the owls in successive years and, in between, by other hole-nesting species. The eggs are laid on a bed of wood chips; if grass or leaves are found in the nest they were brought there by previous occupants. The pair duet frequently in the vicinity of the nest hole in the two months preceding laying, and in the 2-3 weeks before laying (during which time the ♂ feeds the ♀), she perches for long periods near the hole, uttering, from time to time, a quiet 'piep' soliciting note. Once incubation commences, the pair seldom call and they are easily overlooked. The ♀ incubates without ♂ assistance; if the nest is inspected with a light, she is easily overlooked as her speckled back can be mistaken for the floor of an empty hole. She emerges briefly at dusk, usually when the ♂ arrives with prey.

Laying months: mainly Oct (Aug-Nov); single-brooded and does not usually relay if earlier clutch fails. **Clutch size:** 3 (2-4); laid at 2-day intervals. **Eggs:** 28.0-30.8-33.8 x 23.8-25.6-27.2 mm. **Incubation period:** 28-29 days by ♀ only, fed by ♂; begins when clutch is completed. **Nestling/fledging period:** 28-30 days; young brooded and fed by ♀; later fed by both sexes.

African Scops Owl *Otus senegalensis* Skopsuil
page 380

Breeds widely in tall, open woodland in both semi-arid and mesic areas; requires standing dead trees such as mopane and leadwood to provide its favoured nest sites. Pairs nest solitarily and are widely spaced. **Nest:** uses a hole in a tree, typically a natural cavity 200-500 mm deep that has a vertical entrance, either one open at the top from a break in the stem (two photographs on the right), or in a cavity accessed where two branches split (top right photograph); the nest cavity is usually 3-5 m above the ground (1-9 m) and sites in dead trees or dead branches in trees are commonly used. Nests boxes (with side entrances) are used by the birds in parts of their range; there is also a record of it nesting on the ground among rocks at the base of a koppie (Namibia). Nest holes are frequently reused in successive years. Before laying, the ♂ can be heard calling at times during the day close to the nest hole. The ♀ covers the eggs continuously during the day, her head facing downwards (see photograph opposite) so that she is easily overlooked.

Laying months: mainly Oct (Jun-Nov). **Clutch size:** 2-3 (2-4); laid at 2-day intervals. **Eggs:** 28.0-29.6-32.2 x 23.7-25.5-27.0 mm. **Incubation period:** 20-24 days; by ♀ only, fed by ♂; begins before clutch is completed. **Nestling/fledging period:** 25-28 days; young brooded and fed by ♀; later fed by both sexes.

African Barred Owlet *Glaucidium capense* Gebande Uil
page 380

The two widely separated races of this species (*ngamiense* and *capense*) occur in different habitats: *ngamiense* favours tall, dense mesic woodland in northern savannas, especially riparian woodland and tall mopane; *capense* lives in densely wooded, euphorbia-dominated thickets on steep hillslopes in the e Cape. The nesting habits of *ngamiense* are well known, but a nest of *capense* has not yet been described. In *ngamiense*, pairs nest solitarily and they are widely spaced. **Nest:** eggs are laid in a cavity in a tree, usually in a rot-hole in the main trunk where a branch has broken off, about 4-6 m up; cavity depth varies between 150-300 mm in depth with at entrance hole at least 70 mm wide; woodpecker holes do not appear to be used, probably because their entrances (<55 mm wide in all woodpeckers in the region) are too narrow.

Laying months: mainly Sep-Oct (Jul-Dec). **Clutch size:** 3, less often 2. **Eggs:** 30.0-32.9-34.0 x 26.0-27.6-28.0 mm. **Incubation period:** 28-34 days; by ♀ only; begins before clutch is completed. **Nestling/fledging period:** 32-33 days; young brooded and fed by ♀; later fed by both sexes.

Southern White-faced Owl *Ptilopsis granti* Witwanguil
page 380

Breeds widely across the savanna belt, from the semi-arid west to the mesic east; thornveld is its preferred habitat. Pairs nest solitarily and are spaced at intervals of 1-5 km, their spacing probably at least partly affected by nest site availability. **Nest:** disused stick nests in trees of small birds of prey (especially Gabar Goshawk, Shikra, Black-shouldered Kite), crows (Pied or Cape) or Grey Louries are most frequently used; also recorded being used are flattened old nests of sparrows, Scaly-feathered Finches, Wattled Starlings, Magpie Shrikes and Lesser Galagos. They may also nest in hollows in tree stumps and trunks, and in a crotch in a tree between two or more diverging branches where a flat base >200 mm wide is available which will support the eggs. Sites range in height between 2-13 m up. If they remain intact long enough, nest sites may be reused in successive years (though most stick-nests fall apart before this). In the weeks before laying, ♂s call frequently in the general nesting area but once incubation commences they become silent and there is then little evidence of their presence. The ♀ incubates without ♂ assistance during the day and she sits tight, crouched low and with eyes closed, if approached.

Laying months: mainly Aug-Oct (Jun-Nov, rarely in other months). **Clutch size:** 2-3, rarely 4; laid at about 1-3 day intervals. **Eggs:** 37.0-38.8-41.4 x 30.4-32.3-33.3 mm. **Incubation period:** 30 days; mainly by ♀ (♂ takes short turns when she leaves to feed); begins when first egg is laid. **Nestling/fledging period:** young become 'branchers' at 23-25 days, fly at 30-33 days; brooded and fed by ♀; later fed by both sexes.

Pearl-spotted Owlet nest interior African Scops Owl

Pearl-spotted Owlet African Scops Owl

African Barred Owlet

using old nest of Grey Lourie Southern White-faced Owl

Nightjars

NIGHTJARS Family Caprimulgidae Worldwide 92 species; 22 breed in Afrotropics, 6 in southern Africa; 5 are monogamous (and in these both sexes incubate and brood the young); 1 (Pennant-winged Nightjar) is polygynous and, in its case, all parental care is by the ♀. Nightjars make no nest and lay their eggs on the ground; some species lay on particular substrates e.g. Freckled Nightjar lays on rock surfaces, Fiery-necked Nightjar on leaf litter, Swamp Nightjar in thick grass. They rely on their cryptic plumage to conceal themselves during the day; sitting tight when approached and they are not easily flushed, especially so when they are incubating eggs or brooding chicks; their eggs are distinctively elliptical in shape and are shades of buff, pink or salmon in colour, marbled with darker markings of the same colour; when not covered by the parent they are surprisingly conspicuous; where known, the ♂ incubates during the night and the ♀ during the day; chicks are semi-altricial and nidicolous, and move away from the nest site within 1-2 weeks of hatching, well before they can fly. The 6 species are early summer nesters, and egg-laying is mainly timed to coincide with the week after full-moon. Nightjar nests are usually only chanced upon, and identifying which species is involved is seldom easy; there are, however, consistent differences between the size and coloration of the eggs of the different species by which the identity can be ascertained.

Fiery-necked Nightjar *Caprimulgus pectoralis* Afrikaanse Naguil   page 381

Breeds in woodland under the canopy of trees or tall shrubs; most plentiful in miombo woodland (1 pair/3 ha), less so in other broad-leafed woodlands, in coastal bush, fynbos and in plantations of eucalypts and wattles. **Nest:** none made, eggs are laid on the ground where there is a bed of leaf litter. It does not nest in open, treeless country and, given its preference for nesting on leaf litter, is generally found on unburnt ground; spring fires are a particular threat to its eggs and young. Clutches laid in successive years are often found in the vicinity of a previous year's site. Before laying, ♂s call frequently at night from a few favoured call sites in the vicinity of the nest, but they become virtually silent once incubation commences. During the day, when the ♀ incubates or broods the young, the ♂ usually sits within 5-10 m of her. The incubating bird reacts to intruders by flattening its body and narrowing its eye-lids to slits, flushing when intruder <3 m away; it may perform an injury-feigning display when flushed off nestlings. Rarely, eggs are moved from where they were originally laid to a new position.
Laying months: mainly Sep-Nov (Aug-Dec); laying occurs during full moon; usually lays replacement clutch after early failure; sometimes double-brooded. **Clutch size:** 2 (rarely 1); laid at a 1-day interval. **Eggs:** 23.5-27.3-30.0 × 18.0-20.0-21.4 mm; mass 4.9-5.9-6.8 g; paler than eggs of other local species; ivory to pink ground-colour (rarely plain white); either unmarked, or lightly marked with freckling/marbling of darker pink or shades of light brown. **Incubation period:** 16-18 days; by both sexes, ♂ at night, ♀ in the day; begins when first egg is laid. **Nestling/fledging period:** young move (walk) away from nest site at 5 days; fly weakly at 16 days, strongly at 18 days; young brooded and fed by both sexes.

Rufous-cheeked Nightjar *Caprimulgus rufigena* Rooiwangnaguil   page 381

A breeding summer visitor; this is the region's most widespread nightjar, breeding in both open treeless country, especially the semi-arid areas (karoo, Kalahari, arid grassland), and in mesic woodlands, including miombo; also in eucalypt plantations. **Nest:** none made, eggs are laid on the ground, either on stony ground, among short, scattered forbs in treeless country or, in wooded habitat, favouring areas where a fire has swept through, leaving short, blackened grass tufts and fire-burnt debris in which the incubating bird blends closely; upland sites rather than along vlei edges and valley bottoms are preferred. May nest in leaf litter, but not as dependent on this as the Fiery-necked Nightjar. Pairs breed solitarily and clutches laid in successive years are often found in the vicinity of a previous year's site. Before laying, ♂s call frequently at night in the vicinity of the nest site, but they become virtually silent once incubation commences. Incubating bird reacts to intruders by flattening body and narrowing eye-lids to slits, flushing when intruder <3 m away; may perform an injury-feigning display when flushed off nestlings.
Laying months: mainly Sep-Nov (Aug-Jan). **Clutch size:** 2 (rarely 1); laid at a 2-day interval. **Eggs:** 23.9-27.2-30.0 × 18.4-20.0-21.6 mm; mass 4.1-5.7-7.2 g; pinkish-cream ground-colour (rarely plain white); mottled with pale brick and underlying lilac, sometimes salmon, spread evenly over whole egg (the mottled markings are the distinctive feature of this species' eggs). **Incubation period:** 15-17 days; by both sexes, ♀ during the day; begins when first egg is laid. **Nestling/fledging period:** 18-20 days; young brooded and fed by both sexes.

Swamp Nightjar *Caprimulgus natalensis* Natalse Naguil   page 381

Breeds in open grassland usually adjoining wet ground of some sort – a floodplain, lagoon, river or other wetland; preferred nesting areas are treeless and densely covered with grass (such as *Ichmaeum* or *Echinochloa*); they rarely lay on burnt ground, and if a fire sweeps the area before they breed, they select an unburnt remnant in which to nest. They are assumed to be monogamous (as most nightjars) but there is one recorded instance of 2 simultaneously active nests 10 m apart; this suggests that a polygynous trio was involved in case. **Nest:** none made, eggs are laid on bare ground between or under grass-tufts. The incubating bird is easily overlooked; it sits tight if approached, only flushing when almost trodden on; the eggs are conspicuous when they are not covered by the bird. Once the eggs have hatched, the parent bird may leave the chicks unattended and instead sit a few metres from them. At the onset of breeding, ♂s call frequently at night in the general nesting area. Birds flushed from eggs or small nestlings may perform an injury-feigning display as they leave.
Laying months: mainly Sep-Oct (Aug-Dec). **Clutch size:** 2. **Eggs:** 28.0-30.0-31.9 × 20.8-21.5-22.5 mm; mass 8.1-8.2 g; large size and flesh-pink ground-colour (either unmarked or faintly marked with grey and brown) distinguishes these eggs from those of other nightjars. **Incubation period:** <20 days; by both sexes, apparently ♀ during the day, ♂ at night. **Nestling/fledging period:** 21-22 days; young brooded and fed by both sexes.

Fiery-necked Nightjar

Rufous-cheeked Nightjar (FOUR ABOVE)

Swamp Nightjar

Freckled Nightjar *Caprimulgus tristigma* Donkernaguil   page 381

Breeds in rocky, hilly country, its range extending right across the region from the arid and semi-arid west through to the mesic east; favours extensive exposures of rock outcrop on granites, sandstones, quartzites, schists and other rock-types, in both open country and in woodland; often around the bases of hills where large, isolated boulders provide favoured nesting sites. Pairs nest solitarily; in ideal habitat they occur at a density of about 1 pair/5½ ha. **Nest:** none made, eggs are laid in a hollow on a rock surface, sometimes where pebbles or wind-blown debris has accumulated, otherwise on the bare rock; a lichen-covered surface is usually selected, and it is often on a boulder that stands apart from other rock outcrops. Sites can be completely exposed to the sun or be shaded by trees; eggs may be moved if the hollow used temporarily fills with rainwater. Pairs commonly lay in successive years in the same spot. The incubating bird blends well with its surroundings and, if approached, flattens itself and closes its eyelids down to slits, flushing only when almost touched; it often performs an injury-feigning display if flushed off chicks.

Laying months: mainly Sep-Nov (Aug-Dec); eggs laid between full moon and last quarter; usually lays a replacement clutch after an early failure; sometimes double-brooded. **Clutch size:** 2 (rarely 1); laid at a 1-day interval. **Eggs:** 27.5-29.4-31.1 x 20.0-21.2-22.6 mm; mass 5.8-6.1 g; the eggs of this nightjar differ from those of other nightjars in the region by lacking any pink or rufous colouration: they are ashy-white in ground-colour with streaking and blotching of darker shades of grey. **Incubation period:** 18½-20 days; by both sexes, ♀ during the day, ♂ at night; begins when first egg is laid. **Nestling/fledging period:** 19-20 days; young brooded and fed by both sexes.

Square-tailed Nightjar *Caprimulgus fossii* Laeveldnaguil   page 381

A breeding resident in some parts of its range and migratory or nomadic in others. Pairs nest solitarily, doing so both in woodland and in more open country such as along vlei edges, in clearings in acacia bush, areas recently swept by fire, old agricultural lands and even in ploughed fields. **Nest:** none made, eggs are laid on bare, open ground which can be both on pale-coloured sandy soils and on dark clay substrates; may nest in successive years close to a previously used site. Incubating bird reacts to intruders by flattening body and narrowing eye-lids to slits, only flushing when almost trodden on.

Laying months: mainly Sep-Nov (Aug-Dec); eggs laid between full moon and last quarter; usually relays after an early failure. **Clutch size:** 2 (rarely 1). **Eggs:** 24.5-27.0-31.1 x 18.5-20.0-21.5 mm; mass 4.5-5.7-7.0 g; eggs darker than those of other nightjars in the region as a result of being well marked (blotched or smeared) with shades of brown. **Incubation period:** about 14-17 days; by both sexes, but mainly by the ♀. **Nestling/fledging period:** young brooded and fed by both sexes; mobile within 24 hrs of hatching; fly weakly at 17-19 days.

Pennant-winged Nightjar *Macrodipteryx vexillarius* Wimpelvlerknaguil   page 381

A breeding visitor to northern savanna areas, arriving in Sept, ♂s displaying from then through to late Nov-early Dec, whereafter they shed their pennants and depart in Feb-Mar. Nests in and along the verges of broad-leafed woodland, especially miombo, in both hilly and flat country. ♂s call each evening from display arenas, these being clearings in the woodland, and they use somewhat elevated positions – mounds or stones – from which to call. **Nest:** none made, eggs are laid on the ground, either among leaf litter, or in burnt plant debris (twigs, leaves, etc) in areas that have been recently swept by fire. ♂s play no role in incubation and parental care, and are almost certainly polygynous, displaying and calling, and then mating with ♀s that are attracted. Semi-colonial nesting has been recorded (in Zambia, not yet in southern Africa) in which 4 ♀s had simultaneous nests 6-20 m apart. ♂s may lie up, during the day, in the vicinity of a nesting ♀. As with other nightjars, nests are not easily located as the incubating bird blends well with its surroundings and sits tight on the eggs if approached, only flushing when almost trodden on.

Laying months: mainly Oct-Nov (Sep-Dec); eggs usually laid at full moon. **Clutch size:** 2 (rarely 1); laid at a 1-day (rarely 2-day) interval. **Eggs:** 26.4-30.8-34.4 x 20.4-22.0-23.6 mm; 6.0-7.8-9.2 g; larger than the eggs of other nightjars in the region except Freckled, and differing from the eggs of that species by being pinky-salmon in colour, and not grey. **Incubation period:** 15-18 days; by ♀ only; begins when first egg is laid. **Nestling/fledging period:** not recorded.

Freckled Nightjar (FOUR ABOVE)

Square-tailed Nightjar (THREE ABOVE)

Pennant-winged Nightjar

SWIFTS, SPINETAILS Family Apodidae Worldwide 102 species; 20 breed in Afrotropics, 11 in southern Africa; nesting habits of these species mostly poorly known; nest and eggs of 1 (Scarce Swift) undescribed; breeds colonially or solitarily; nest a shallow open saucer (enclosed in some species) built of feathers and other wind-borne material glued together and to the nest site, with saliva; nests reused in successive years; occurrence much dependent on nest sites which vary between species; an exposed drop for the bird to become airborne is required; monogamous; sexes share nest-building, incubation and care of young; incubation and nestling periods are unusually long; eggs elliptical, white, unmarked, 2/clutch; nestlings are altricial and nidicolous.

Mottled Spinetail *Telacanthura ussheri* Gevlekte Stekelstert   page 381

Breeds solitarily or in small colonies (2-5 pairs) in low-lying hot areas where large baobabs, in which it nests, are well represented. **Nest:** a half-cup, made from short twigs, leaf petioles, pieces of bark, fragments of rotting wood, bits of feather quill, and often grains of sand, firmly cemented together and attached with saliva, >5 m up, on an inside vertical wall of a hollow chamber in the main trunk of a large old baobab; access may be from an entrance at ground level or much higher up the trunk; elsewhere in Africa it is known to nest in buildings and in chimneys. The nest is more substantial than that of Böhm's Spinetail, measuring 104 mm across the back wall (where attached to the tree), 45-82 mm wide (from back wall to outer rim) and 25-40 mm thick at its thickest point (against the tree); cup depth 32 mm. Nest sites and nests are reused in successive years.
Laying months: Nov-Apr. **Clutch size:** 1-2. **Eggs:** 20.6-21.1-21.4 x 13.8-13.9-14.3 mm. **Incubation period:** not recorded. **Nestling/fledging period:** not recorded.

Böhm's Spinetail *Neafrapus boehmi* Witpensstekelstert

Breeds solitarily in low-lying hot areas where large baobabs, in which it typically nests, are well represented; elsewhere in Africa known to also nest in disused mine shafts, wells, deep pits. **Nest:** attached to a vertical wall inside a hollow chamber in a baobab, a very flimsy-looking, but rigid half-cup, made with short, dry twigs and/or decayed wood chips that are firmly cemented together, and to the wall of the tree, with saliva; it measures 60-80 mm across the back wall (where attached to the site), 55-70 mm wide (from back wall to outer rim), 30 mm thick and cup depth 25 mm; structurally similar to, but much smaller than the nest of a Mottled Spinetail. Nests are reused in successive years, or a new nest may be built on top of an older nest.
Laying months: mainly Oct-Mar (Aug-May). **Clutch size:** 3, less often 2. **Eggs:** 18.0-19.1-19.8 x 11.9-12.5-13.0 mm; white, unmarked (egg not illustrated). **Incubation period:** 17-20 days. **Nestling/fledging period:** 38-42 days, but nestling may leave nest at 4 weeks and cling to wall away from nest.

Mottled Swift *Tachymarptis aequatorialis* Bontwindswael   page 381

Breeds colonially (<25 pairs/colony), less often solitarily, in hilly, granite country in c and e Zimbabwe, typically in walls and roofs of overhangs on granite dwalas, especially in crevices resulting from peeling-off slabs of rock. **Nest:** a saucer-shaped half-cup made of feathers, leaves, grass fragments and other wind-borne debris, cemented together, and to the rock, with saliva; placed at the back of a narrow, usually vertical crevice about 200 mm wide, 6-30 m up from the cliff base; it measures 80-100 mm across the back wall (where attached), 60-87 mm wide (from back wall to outer rim), 22-48 mm thick (thinnest at the outer rim), with a shallow (20 mm) depression in which the eggs are laid. Nests are reused in successive years; within-colony laying is not synchronised.
Laying months: mainly Sep (Jun-Jan). **Clutch size:** 1-2, rarely 3. **Eggs:** 28.5-29.5-31.1 x 18.7-19.1-19.5 mm. **Incubation period:** not recorded; by both sexes. **Nestling/fledging period:** young fully feathered but not flying at 28 days.

African Black Swift *Apus barbatus* Swartwindswael   no nest photo   page 381

Breeds solitarily or colonially on cliffs or in deep gorges in mountainous areas, sometimes alongside Alpine Swifts; only one report of nesting on a man-made structure. Nesting habits are poorly known. **Nest:** a half-cup made of grass stubble, fragments of plants, thistle down, feathers, etc., cemented together and to the rock face, with saliva; it is placed deep inside a vertical or horizontal fracture in a vertical rock face, often beneath an overhang; the nest measures 120-135 mm across the back wall (where attached to the rock), 60 mm wide (from back wall to outer rim) and 95 mm thick (at it thickest point), eggs are laid in an unlined 20 mm depression; sites are reused annually. Tall *Washingtonia* palms may also provide nest sites, but confirmation of this is required.
Laying months: mainly Sep-Oct (Sep-Feb). **Clutch size:** 2, rarely 1. **Eggs:** 25.1-25.7-26.1 x 18.0-18.1-18.2 mm. **Incubation period:** not recorded. **Nestling/fledging period:** not recorded.

Bradfield's Swift *Apus bradfieldi* Muiskleurwindswael

Breeds in the semi-arid to arid west. Nesting habits poorly known. Pairs nest solitarily or in small colonies, attaching the nest to the walls or back of a narrow vertical or horizontal crevice in a rock face; apparently also nests in old opencast mine workings (e.g. Kimberley 'big hole') and in the crowns of tall *Washingtonia* palms. **Nest:** a half-cup made with grass fragments, twigs, small feathers and other wind-borne material, cemented together and to the nest site, with saliva; it measures 100-120 mm outside diameter, 87 mm cup diameter, and the nest is 35-70 mm thick from front to back; the eggs are laid in an unlined depression 24 mm deep.
Laying months: Aug-May (Namibia). **Clutch size:** 2. **Eggs:** 26.5-27.4 x 16.8-17.0 mm; white, unmarked (egg not illustrated). **Incubation period:** not recorded. **Nestling/fledging period:** not recorded.

Scarce Swift *Schoutedenapus myoptilus* Skaarswindswael   no nest or egg photo

A summer visitor (Aug-Mar) to the e highlands of Zimbabwe; suspected to nest in crevices on cliffs; nest and eggs undescribed.
Laying months: Dec-Jan suspected.

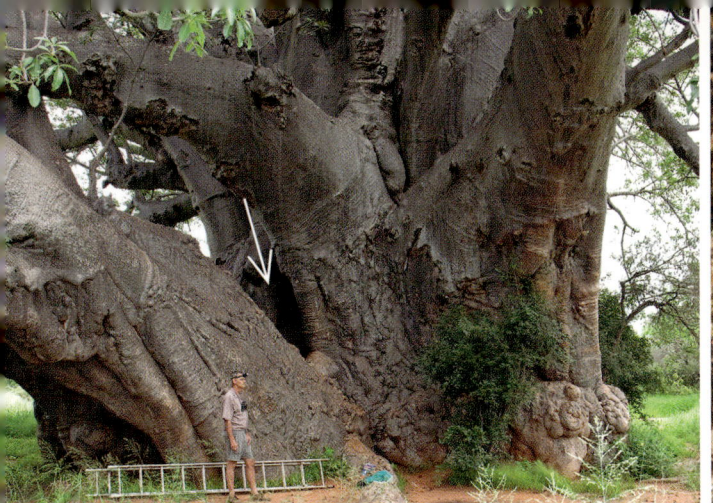

breeding site in large old baobab   **Mottled Spinetail**   nestling clinging to wall of baobab alongside nest

Mottled Swift   nests in rock crevice (TWO ABOVE)    **Böhm's Spinetail**

nesting at the base of palm fronds   **Bradfield's Swift**   nesting in rock crevice

African Palm Swift *Cypsiurus parvus* Palmwindswael   page 381

Breeds solitarily or colonially (max 100 nests/colony), mostly in the leaves of tall fan-leafed palms, especially *Hyphaene*, *Washingtonia*, *Borassus*; not in pinnate-leafed palms (*Phoenix*, *Raphia*); now (since the 1940s) also nests regularly on man-made structures (on metal girders of bridges, under open-thatched roofs). **Nest:** a small pad of feathers attached to the underside of a down-hanging palm leaf, usually one of a cluster forming a fringing skirt around the trunk; 2-15 m up from the ground; usually well hidden, accessed by the birds from directly below. It is made of soft, short feathers (10-30 mm) and some plant down, glued together, and to the leaf, with saliva. Nests measure 45-120 mm in vertical length and 45-55 mm in maximum width; the eggs rest on a protruding lip of feathers at the base of the structure and are attached to the nest with saliva as they are laid. Both sexes build, taking 10 days or less, collecting wind-borne material; further material is added during incubation. The incubating bird clings vertically to the nest, holding its brood patch against the eggs; at night its mate clings alongside it. Colonies are occupied year-round in warmer areas.
Laying months: all months, peaking in Oct-Jan; multiple-brooded. **Clutch size:** 2, rarely 1; laid at a 2-day interval. **Eggs:** 18.2-19.3-21.0 x 9.9-12.3-13.8 mm. **Incubation period:** 20 days (18-22); by both sexes, in shifts of 10-20 min (occasionally >3 hrs); begins when clutch is complete. **Nestling/fledging period:** 31 days (29-33); young brooded and fed by both sexes, 16-27 visits/day.

Little Swift *Apus affinis* Kleinwindswael   page 381

Breeds colonially (usually <30 pairs, occasionally 100s) wherever suitable nest sites are available. **Nest:** an enclosed bowl with a narrow entrance hole near the top of one side, measuring 150-180 mm horizontally and 80-100 mm vertically; made with feathers, some grass and other debris and cemented together with saliva to form a rigid wall 5-15 mm thick which encloses a spacious internal chamber. External appearance shaggy and colour (black, white or shades of grey) depends on feathers used; interior smoothly finished. Nests usually built in clusters touching each other; most are on man-made structures – under high bridges and on the walls of tall buildings (watertowers, grain silos, multi-storey factories, office, residential buildings). Both sexes build, collecting wind-swept material on the wing. Colonies are occupied year-round, used as night-time roosts when not breeding. Once recorded nesting with African Palm Swifts in leaves of a fan-palm (*Washingtonia*) and occasionally uses the nest of a tunnel-building swallow.
Laying months: mainly Sep-Dec (Aug-May); double-brooded. **Clutch size:** 2 (1-3); laid at a 1-3 day interval. **Eggs:** 21.0-23.0-25.4 x 14.2-14.7-15.3 mm. **Incubation period:** 21-23 days (20-26); begins before clutch is completed; shared equally by both sexes, in shifts of ½-2 hrs. **Nestling/fledging period:** 38-39 days (36-40); young brooded and fed by both sexes.

Horus Swift *Apus horus* Horuswindswael   page 381

A breeding resident in parts of its range, a summer visitor in others; usually breeds colonially (2-10 pairs), often within colonies of other tunnel-nesting colonial birds. **Nest:** a saucer-shaped pad of feathers, fragments of grass, plant down and other wind-borne debris, held together by saliva and placed at the end of a tunnel in an earth bank, often one excavated by a bee-eater, Pied Starling, Brown-throated Martin. Nest sites mostly in vertical sandbanks along rivers, in donga walls, mine-tailings, sand quarries and road cuttings. Dimensions of tunnel used very variable; ½-2 m in length, 35-100 mm in diameter; those suspected to have been excavated by the swifts themselves are <2 m long with wide, flat, slit-like entrance holes; the nest saucer measures 100-140 mm in diameter. Sites are commonly reused in successive years and are occupied as night-time roosts when not nesting.
Laying months: all months recorded, but mostly in the second half of summer. **Clutch size:** 2-3, rarely 4. **Eggs:** 21.1-22.8-24.3 x 13.8-15.1-16.3 mm. **Incubation period:** 28 days. **Nestling/fledging period:** about 6 weeks; young fed by both sexes.

White-rumped Swift *Apus caffer* Witkruiswindswael   page 381

A breeding summer visitor, present Aug-Apr, its occurrence much dependent on nest site availability; most pairs nest solitarily, less often in small colonies (2-20 pairs); some may be assisted by helpers. **Nest:** mainly uses enclosed swallow nests (striped and Red-breasted), also Little Swift and South African Cliff Swallow, typically usurping occupants of newly built nests and adding a characteristic lining of feathers to the entrance tunnel; nests are reused for successive broods and in successive years; occasionally, open (half-cup) swallow nests (e.g. of Wire-tailed Swallow) are used. Also nests, occasionally, in a horizontal crack in a rock face, or in the eaves of a building, making a shallow saucer-shaped nest of feathers, fragments of grass, plant down and other material held together with saliva. Most breeding sites are on man-made structures, especially under house eaves and bridges.
Laying months: mainly Sep-Jan (Aug-Apr); double or triple-brooded. **Clutch size:** 2 (1-3, rarely 4 or 5; >2 probably laid by 2 ♀s); laid at a 1½-3 day interval. **Eggs:** 21.6-23.1-26.1 x 13.4-14.9-16.2 mm. **Incubation period:** 22½ days (21-25); begins when second egg is laid; shared equally by both sexes. **Nestling/fledging period:** 42-46 days (35-53); young brooded and fed by both sexes.

Alpine Swift *Apus melba* Witpenswindswael   no nest photo   page 381

Breeds on tall cliffs in gorges and on mountains, often in colonies, frequently alongside African Black Swifts; a few instances known of their nesting on buildings (in vertical ducts 20 stories up and in a concrete silo). **Nest:** a compact half-cup of feathers, grass, plant down and aerial debris cemented together, and to the rock, with saliva; usually placed at the back of a vertical crack in the rock face; extensive cracks may contain several nests; size variable according to width of crack; typically 110-120 mm across the back wall (where attached to the rock), 70-100 mm wide (from back wall to outer rim) and 70-90 mm high with a shallow (20 mm) unlined cup. Extensive cracks may support several nests. Sites and nests are reused in successive years. Both sexes build the nest, gathering the material used in flight (Europe). Colonies are occupied year-round, used as night-time roosts when not breeding.
Laying months: Sep-Jan. **Clutch size:** 1-2. **Eggs:** 28.0-30.7-32.3 x 17.3-19.4-20.3 mm. **Incubation period:** 20 days (17-23); begins when clutch is completed. by both sexes. **Nestling/fledging period:** 45-55 days; young brooded and fed by both sexes (all this data from Europe).

African Palm Swift

Little Swift

African Palm Swift

nest tunnels in old mine tailings

Horus Swift

nest at end of tunnel

tunnel of striped swallow nest lined with feathers by swifts

White-rumped Swift

MOUSEBIRDS Family Coliidae Worldwide 6 species; all endemic to Afrotropics, 3 breed in southern Africa; gregarious but disperse into pairs (or pairs with helpers) to breed; monogamous, both sexes building (some assisted by helpers), incubating and rearing the young; nest an open cup; eggs oval-shaped, unmarked white or white with scrolled markings; 2-3/clutch; nestlings are altricial and nidicolous; if threatened, the young temporarily flee into the branches well before they can fly; they are continuously brooded by a parent even when close to fledging; their faeces are eaten by the parents.

White-backed Mousebird *Colius colius* Witkruismuisvoël   page 381

Breeds in semi-arid and arid areas, nesting in thornveld and along tree-lined watercourses, around farmsteads, in orchards and gardens. Pairs nest solitarily, some with helpers, sometimes in close proximity (e.g. 17 nesting along 1 km of watercourse). **Nest:** a cup-shaped bowl of twigs and plant-stems (often using green twigs of *Asparagus* sp.), with a roughly finished exterior, bulkier than those of the other two mousebirds; cup warmly lined using plant down, soft seedheads, cobweb, wool; placed in a shrubby, usually thorny, tree or bush and concealed in thick foliage, in mistletoe or in a mass of dead branches; sometimes on top of an old nest (Cape Sparrow, Bokmakierie); typically 1½-3 m (½-7) up from the ground; outside diameter 120-150 mm; cup diameter 60-85 mm, depth 25-45 mm. Nest built by both sexes, helpers may assist. Incubating bird sits tight, reluctant to leave if approached.

Laying months: all months but mainly Sep-Jan; earlier in winter-rainfall region (Sep-Oct). **Clutch size:** 3 (2-4, rarely 7-8, laid by >1 ♀); laid at 1-2 day intervals. **Eggs:** 19.0-21.2-23.3 × 15.0-16.3-17.6 mm; mass 3.2 g. **Incubation period:** 11-13 days; by both sexes; begins when first egg is laid. **Nestling/fledging period:** 15 days (11-20), but young temporarily leave nest from 9-10 days if disturbed; young brooded and fed by both sexes; sometimes helpers assist.

Speckled Mousebird *Colius striatus* Gevlekte Muisvoël   page 381

Breeds in wooded thickets, forest verges, parks, gardens, often in alien vegetation, mainly in the more mesic east. Pairs and polygynous trios, some with helpers, nest solitarily, or, sometimes, within 10 m of each other. **Nest:** an open cup built with stems of forbs and shrubs (often using green *Asparagus* fronds or *Helichrysum* sp.) which are curled around into a roughly finished bowl with a warm inner lining of plant down, *Usnea*, grass ends or wool; pieces of green leaf often form part of the lining; the nest is placed in a shrubby tree or bush, often a thorny species and usually concealed in thick foliage, in mistletoe (*Loranthus*, *Viscum*) or among multiple converging branches; it is typically 1-4 m (½-7) up from the ground, occasionally built on top of an old nest, or the nest of another bird. The nest measures: outside diameter 120-135-150 mm; inside diameter 60-74-85 mm; nest height 45-85-120 mm; cup depth 25-42-50 mm. Both sexes build and continue adding nest-lining during the incubation; nests are occasionally reused for two successive clutches. Incubating bird sits tight, reluctant to leave if approached.

Laying months: mainly Sep-Jan (Jul-Apr, rarely other months); peaks earlier in winter-rainfall areas (Aug-Nov). **Clutch size:** 3 (2-7, larger clutches probably laid by >1 ♀); laid at 1-2 day intervals. **Eggs:** 19.5-20.8-24.2 × 14.6-16.6-18.4 mm; mass 2.7 g. **Incubation period:** 13 days (12-15); by both sexes, sometimes by helpers, in shifts of ½-2 hrs; begins when first egg is laid. **Nestling/fledging period:** 17 days (15-20); young temporarily flee nest from 10-11 days if disturbed; brooded and fed by both sexes.

Red-faced Mousebird *Urocolius indicus* Rooiwangmuisvoël   page 381

Breeds widely across the region in any wooded country, including gardens and in introduced vegetation in formerly treeless areas. Pairs, sometimes assisted by a helper, nest solitarily; occasionally as close as 10-30 m apart. **Nest:** an open cup, smaller and flimsier that those of the other mousebirds, the base built with dry twigs, so resembling a dove nest from below; the cup is warmly lined with plant down, cobweb, *Usnea*, wool or moss; it is placed in a tree or shrub, usually well inside a smallish, isolated, thorny or thickly foliaged tree; typically 2-3½ m off the ground (1-8). This species does not add green leaves to the nest lining nor does it build the nest exterior with rough forb stems as the other two mousebirds do. The nest measures: outside diameter 100-120-150 mm; inside diameter 45-67-90 mm; nest height 60-70-90 mm; cup depth 20-35-55 mm. Both sexes build, assisted by a helper if present, and further nest-lining is added during the incubation. The incubating bird sits tight, reluctant to leave if the nest is approached.

Laying months: mainly Sep-Jan (Aug-Apr, rarely in other months). **Clutch size:** 2-3 (2-7, larger clutches probably laid by >1 ♀); laid at 1-2 day intervals. **Eggs:** 18.7-21.3-24.0 × 14.4-15.8-17.0 mm; 2.9 g. **Incubation period:** 13 days (10½-15); by both sexes; sometimes assisted by helper; begins when first egg is laid. **Nestling/fledging period:** 14-20 days; young temporarily leave nest from 10 days if disturbed; brooded and fed by both sexes.

TROGONS Family Trogonidae Worldwide 42 species, 3 breed in Afrotropics, 1 in southern Africa. Monogamous; incubation and nestling care is shared by the sexes; nests in a tree cavity; eggs short oval in shape; white, unmarked; 3/clutch; young are altricial and nidicolous.

Narina Trogon *Apaloderma narina* Bosloerie   page 381

Breeds in coastal, lowland, riparian and montane evergreen forests. Pairs nest solitarily, usually >150 m apart. **Nest:** a natural tree cavity is used, usually a rot-hole where a branch has broken off the main stem of a living tree; it typically has an upward-slanting entrance (75-104-120 mm in diameter) and is usually 3-5 m above the ground (1½-16). The cavity is unlined, 250-600 mm deep; holes are often reused in successive years (>13 years once recorded). While breeding, the birds are secretive and silent in the vicinity of the nest and the parent attending the nest is not easily flushed, making a threatening, hissing display if the hole is inspected. **Laying months:** mainly Nov-Dec (Oct-Feb). **Clutch size:** 3 (2-4). **Eggs:** 25.9-28.3-31.0 × 21.2-23.0-23.8 mm. **Incubation period:** 16-17 days; by both sexes; by ♂ 10h00-17h00, by ♀ the rest; starts with first-laid egg. **Nestling/fledging period:** 26½ days (25-28, Kenya); young brooded and fed by both sexes.

Speckled Mousebird

White-backed Mousebird

Red-faced Mousebird

Narina Trogon (FOUR ABOVE)   female brooding inside nest chamber

Rollers

ROLLERS Family Coraciidae Worldwide 12 species; 7 breed in Afrotropics, 4 in southern Africa. Monogamous, the sexes sharing incubation and parental care (where known); they nest in an unlined cavity in a tree, occasionally in a rock face, termite mound or metal pipe; eggs broad-oval to spherical in shape, glossy white, unmarked; 2-4/clutch; nestlings are altricial and nidicolous.

Purple Roller *Coracias naevius* Groottroupant   page 381

Breeds widely across the savanna region, from the semi-arid west (where most common) to the mesic east, in open woodland in flat or hilly country. Nesting habits are poorly known. Pairs nest solitarily and are widely spaced (usually >1 km apart). **Nest:** typically uses a natural hole in a large tree, 2-12 m up from the ground; often in baobabs, where they occur together; the nest tree may be alive or dead, and the cavity may be so shallow that the incubating bird's head is visible; some nests have vertical entrances, others enter the cavity from the side; no lining is added, the eggs being laid on the bare substrate; also breeds (in the west) in cavities in rock faces and these may be used alternately with Monteiro's Hornbills; occasional nests have been recorded in a hole in the wall of an abandoned farm building, or in a pipe; woodpecker holes are apparently too small for this species to enter. Sites are regularly reused in successive years.
Laying months: mainly Sep-Oct (Aug-Jun); in Namibia probably lays opportunistically in any month in response to rain. **Clutch size:** 3 (2-4). **Eggs:** 31.0-34.5-36.7 x 25.8-28.5-29.3 mm. **Incubation period:** not recorded. **Nestling/fledging period:** not recorded; young fed by both sexes.

Racket-tailed Roller *Coracias spatulatus* Knopsterttroupant   page 381

Breeds in tall woodland, typically in miombo, mopane, *Baikiaea* or in tall riparian acacia. Nesting habits are poorly known. Pairs nest solitarily, sometimes, apparently, assisted by a helper, and they are widely spaced. **Nest:** uses a hole in a tree, either a natural cavity or one excavated by a large woodpecker, usually 6-7 m up from the ground. The birds are unobtrusive while nesting and are easily overlooked.
Laying months: mainly Oct (Sep-Dec). **Clutch size:** 2-3. **Eggs:** 29.6-31.8-34.7 x 23.7-25.7-26.6 mm. **Incubation period:** not recorded. **Nestling/fledging period:** not recorded.

Lilac-breasted Roller *Coracias caudatus* Gewone Troupant   page 381

Breeds widely across the savanna region, from the semi-arid west to the mesic east, favouring open woodland with scattered tall trees. Pairs nest solitarily and are widely spaced. **Nest:** a cavity in a tree is used; where holes excavated by Bearded and Bennett's Woodpeckers are available, they are the most frequently used sites, these having an entrance about 50-55 mm in diameter and a cavity 200-300-450 mm deep (right-hand photograph illustrates such a nest). Natural cavities are also used and these sometimes have vertical, rather than side entrances. Holes selected can be in living or dead trees, in vertical stems or in the underside of a sloping branch, and at variable heights above the ground, though usually between 2-4 m (1½-14 m). The eggs are laid on whatever debris has accumulated in the floor of the nest; where grass or leaves are present, this has usually been put there by a previous occupant, not by the rollers. Occasionally, a hollow metal pole (e.g. a crossbar on a transmission-line tower) is used, a nest box or a cavity in a large termite mound. Holes are often reused in successive years (>16 years in one case). The pair takes occupation of its intended nest-hole a few weeks before laying, and during this period they are especially vocal and demonstrative, often chasing off other hole-nesting birds and displaying aerially. Once incubation begins, they become relatively quiet and unobtrusive near the nest.
Laying months: mainly Oct (Aug-Feb); single-brooded. **Clutch size:** 3 (2-4). **Eggs:** 28.4-31.4-34.0 x 21.5-25.4-28.5 mm. **Incubation period:** 22 days (17-25); by both sexes, mostly ♀, sometimes fed by ♂ while incubating. **Nestling/fledging period:** 26 days (22-35); young fed by both sexes.

Broad-billed Roller *Eurystomus glaucurus* Geelbektroupant   page 381

A breeding visitor (Sep-Apr) to mesic savannas in the n and e, and riparian forest fringes. Nesting habits are poorly known. Pairs nest solitarily, defending a territory of about 15-30 ha around the nest site. **Nest:** a natural cavity in a tree is used, typically a rot-hole in the main trunk of a large baobab, fig, acacia or *Newtonia* which stands clear of other trees. It is usually situated well above the ground (5-15 m up), with an entrance hole (75-130 mm in diameter) that leads into the nest cavity either from the side or from directly above; the cavity is typically 300-380 mm deep; no nest lining is added, the eggs being laid on the bare substrate; one recorded nest was in a cavity in the wall of a farm building (Zimbabwe). Holes are frequently reused in successive years, and many are used alternately with other hole-nesting birds. Pairs are noisy and conspicuous in their nesting areas.
Laying months: mainly Oct-Nov (Sep-Dec). **Clutch size:** 2-3 (2-4). **Eggs:** 30.2-32.5-33.7 x 24.3-26.0-26.6 mm. **Incubation period:** not recorded. **Nestling/fledging period:** not recorded; young fed by both sexes.

Purple Roller

Racket-tailed Roller

Lilac-breasted Roller

Broad-billed Roller

Kingfishers

KINGFISHERS Family Alcedinidae Worldwide 95 species; 17 breed in Afrotropics, 10 in southern Africa; are monogamous, solitary breeders, one species occasionally nesting semi-colonially. Seven species excavate nest tunnels in earth banks, 3 use holes in trees; nest excavation, incubation and nestling care shared by the sexes; 2 species are occasional cooperative breeders; eggs broad-oval to spherical in shape; white, unmarked; 3-4/clutch; nestlings altricial and nidicolous; faeces are not removed, resulting in nests becoming fouled and strong-smelling.

Grey-headed Kingfisher *Halcyon leucocephala* Gryskopvisvanger   page 382

A breeding summer migrant to northern savanna areas. Pairs nest solitarily, but may be <100 m apart (Kenya). **Nest:** a tunnel is excavated by both sexes into a low (<1 m usually) earth bank, either along a stream or gulley, in the wall of a pit, a sand quarry, an irrigation channel or other man-made excavation; in some areas the roofs of aardvark holes are the most frequently used sites. The tunnel is usually shallower than that of a Brown-hooded Kingfisher, about 600 mm long (0,31-1,24 m); its entrance 50-60-76 mm in diameter, widening into a chamber 150 mm wide. Eggs are laid on the bare floor of this, or on a bed of chitinous insect-remains. The pair call and display around the nest site prior to laying but become silent and secretive once incubating.
Laying months: mainly Oct-Nov (Sep-Dec). **Clutch size:** 4 (2-5); parasitised by Greater Honeyguide. **Eggs:** 22.7-24.6-28.2 x 19.1-21.6-24.1 mm. **Incubation period:** 20 days. **Nestling/fledging period:** not recorded; young fed by both sexes.

Brown-hooded Kingfisher *Halcyon albiventris* Bruinkopvisvanger   page 382

Breeds widely in mesic parts of e southern Africa, its occurrence much dependent on nest site availability. Pairs nest solitarily, and remain year-round in the same area, using the nest tunnel as a night-time roost. **Nest:** a tunnel excavated by both sexes into a 1-4 m high earth bank, either a bank along a river or donga, in a pit, a road cutting, or in some other man-made excavation; rarely uses the roof of an aardvark hole; the nest-hole is usually placed close to the top of the bank; it is often used for successive years, or a new one is excavated close by. The tunnel extends horizontally into the bank for about 1 m (0,6-1,2), widening at the end into a circular chamber 225-240-300 mm across and 150 mm high; at the entrance it measures about 70 mm wide and 50 mm high. The chamber is unlined but chitinous remains of insects accumulate once the eggs hatch; large nestlings are vociferous when being fed and their churring calls can be heard from 30 m away.
Laying months: mainly Oct (Sep-Dec); lays a replacement clutch after an early failure. **Clutch size:** 4 (2-6). **Eggs:** 24.2-27.7-30.1 x 22.6-24.5-26.6 mm. **Incubation period:** 14 days; by ♀ only; sometimes fed by ♂. **Nestling/fledging period:** not recorded; young fed by both sexes.

Striped Kingfisher *Halcyon chelicuti* Gestreepte Visvanger   pages 179, 382

Breeds throughout the savanna. Pairs nest solitarily and are widely spaced. **Nest:** a hole in a tree, usually one excavated by a barbet (especially Black-collared and Crested Barbet) or woodpecker; natural tree cavities are also used, as are artificial nest-logs attached to tree trunks; occasionally uses a hole under the eaves of a building or a striped swallow nest. Tree holes are typically about 5 m up (1½-10) and the cavity about 140-250 mm deep with an entrance hole 45-70 mm in diameter. No lining is added, the eggs being laid on whatever debris has accumulated on the nest floor. Holes may be reused for second or replacement clutches, and for nesting in successive seasons; they are also used year-round for night-time roosts.
Laying months: mainly Sep-Nov (Sep-Feb); peaks earlier in the north; relays after early failure; sometimes double-brooded. **Clutch size:** 3-4 (2-6); laid at 1-day intervals; parasitised by Lesser Honeyguide (Kenya). **Eggs:** 22.8-24.5-27.0 x 19.5-21.1-23.1 mm. **Incubation period:** not recorded; by both sexes, ♀ at night. **Nestling/fledging period:** not recorded; young fed by both sexes.

Woodland Kingfisher *Halcyon senegalensis* Bosveldvisvanger   page 382

A breeding visitor to mesic savannas, arriving in November. Pairs nest solitarily and are widely spaced, adjacent nests once within 40 m of each other. **Nest:** occupies holes in trees, either those excavated by larger woodpeckers (especially Bearded); less often in a natural cavity formed in a rot-hole in a tree trunk. Nest-holes are usually in a main trunk or a large branch, usually 3½-5 m up from the ground (1,2-9). An entrance hole >44 mm in diameter is needed for access (45-60 mm is typical); depth of the cavity 150-400 mm. The eggs are laid on whatever debris has accumulated in the floor of the nest; in some there is a thick layer of chitinous remains of insects, accumulated during a previous occupation. Nest-holes are often reused in successive years. In West Africa (nowhere yet in southern Africa), this species has been recorded nesting in tree termitaria and in a Little Swift nest. Very vocal on arrival in their nesting areas, calling frequently near the intended nest, but becoming quiet once incubation begins; nest change-overs, or feeding visits to the nest, are done silently and unobtrusively. Large nestlings, however, often call noisily from the nest when hungry.
Laying months: mainly Dec-Jan (Oct-Mar); lays replacement clutch after early failure. **Clutch size:** 3 (2-4), laid at 1-day intervals. **Eggs:** 25.0-27.8-30.5 x 22.1-24.1-25.6 mm. **Incubation period:** 17 days; by both sexes, with frequent (about 40 mins) change-overs; ♀ at night. **Nestling/fledging period:** at least 22 days; young brooded and fed by both sexes.

Mangrove Kingfisher *Halcyon senegaloides* Manglietvisvanger

Breeds along wooded fringes of estuaries in e Cape, and in lowland woodland/forest in c Mozambique. Nesting habits are poorly known. **Nest:** in Mozambique tree termitaria, 3-10 m up from the ground, are used for nest sites (see photographs opposite), whereas in e Cape 3 reported nests were in woodpecker or barbet holes in trunks of forest trees, 4-5 m up from the ground.
Laying months: Oct-Jan. **Clutch size:** 3 (East Africa). **Eggs:** not illustrated; about 25 x 24 mm, white, unmarked (East Africa). **Incubation period:** not recorded. **Nestling/fledging period:** not recorded, young fed by both sexes.

Grey-headed Kingfisher | nest tunnel dug in roof of aardvark hole

Brown-hooded Kingfisher | Striped Kingfisher

Woodland Kingfisher | Mangrove Kingfisher | in nest of tree ants

Kingfishers

African Pygmy Kingfisher *Ispidina picta* **Dwergvisvanger**   page 382

A breeding visitor to mesic woodlands in e southern Africa, arriving in early/mid-Oct and laying about 20 days later. Pairs nest solitarily, sometimes within 200 m of each other. **Nest:** a tunnel excavated into a low earth bank; it can be in a road cutting, in a shallow pit or in a stream bank; away from banks it is commonly excavated into the roof of an aardvark hole. The tunnel is 300-450-600 mm long, with an entrance 35 mm wide x 35-60 mm high. The tunnel inclines upwards before enlarging into an unlined nest chamber, 100-130 mm wide; both sexes excavate the nest tunnel.

Laying months: mainly Oct-Dec (Sep-Mar). **Clutch size:** 4 (3-6). **Eggs:** 16.0-18.0-19.3 x 14.3-15.7-16.5 mm. **Incubation period:** 18 days (in captivity); by both sexes, alternating in 2-hr shifts. **Nestling/fledging period:** 18 days (in captivity); young brooded and fed by both sexes.

Malachite Kingfisher *Alcedo cristata* **Kuifkopvisvanger**   page 382

Breeds widely across southern Africa wherever there are streams, rivers, dams, pans, estuaries, lagoons, floodplains or irrigation channels with suitable nesting sites nearby. Pairs nest solitarily. **Nest:** a tunnel in an earth bank, excavated by both sexes, usually overhanging water and rarely >200 m from it. A low (<1 m) bank along a river or stream is most frequently used, but it can be in the wall of a dry donga, in a road cutting or run-off drain, in a pit, in the roof of an aardvark burrow or in soil compacted onto the roots of a fallen tree. The tunnel is about ½ m in length (0.25-1.2 m), has an entrance diameter of about 40 mm and it inclines gently upwards before broadening into a chamber about 90 mm wide; eggs are laid on the bare floor of the nest chamber, but fish scales and bones accumulate here after the chicks hatch; the chamber and tunnel become increasingly soiled from nestlings' faeces which eventually ooze from the entrance hole as a foul-smelling fluid (as illustrated in the photograph opposite). Nest holes are sometimes reused for successive broods and in successive years.

Laying months: mainly Aug-Nov (Aug-Mar), except on Botswana floodplains (mainly May-Oct) where dictated by flood regime; sometimes double/multiple-brooded. **Clutch size:** 4 (3-6), laid at 1-day intervals. **Eggs:** 17.0-18.8-20.5 x 15.0-15.6-16.7 mm. **Incubation period:** 14-16 days; by both sexes; begins when clutch is complete. **Nestling/fledging period:** 22-25 days; young brooded and fed by both sexes.

Giant Kingfisher *Megaceryle maxima* **Reusevisvanger**   page 382

Breeds on larger rivers, estuaries, lagoons, lakes and dams where nest sites are available. Pairs nest solitarily and are widely dispersed in one instance adjacent nests were 4,3 km apart. **Nest:** a tunnel, excavated by both sexes, into the side of a high (1-6 m) earth bank, usually overhanging water, but occasionally in a bank, sand quarry, road cutting or other site up to 1.6 km from water. The tunnel is usually >2 m up from the foot, and in the upper third of the bank. Its entrance measures 90-130 mm in diameter and it is 0.9-1.8-2.5 m long; it is horizontal or slopes gently upward, ending at an enlarged chamber 200-380-600 mm wide, 450 mm long and 230-270-300 mm high. The eggs are laid here on bare soil, but fish bones and scales accumulate once there are nestlings. One nest tunnel was completed in 7 days. Sites can be reused in successive years, or a new tunnel may be dug close to a previous nest.

Laying months: mainly Aug-Oct (Jul-Nov, rarely in other months). **Clutch size:** 3-4, rarely 5; laid at about 2-day intervals. **Eggs** 40.7-45.0-51.0 x 33.2-35.1-36.7 mm; mass 31.8 g. **Incubation period:** at least 25-27 days; by both sexes, with 3-4 change-overs day. **Nestling/fledging period:** 37 days; young brooded and fed by both sexes.

Half-collared Kingfisher *Alcedo semitorquata* **Blouvisvanger**   page 382

Breeds along perennial, wooded, clear-water streams and rivers. Pairs nest solitarily, at densities of about a pair/km of river. **Nest:** a tunnel, excavated by both sexes, into a low alluvial bank at the water's edge; a bank 1-1½ m high (0.3-4.5) is preferred, facing onto the river and screened or concealed to some extent by overhanging vegetation or tree roots. The tunnel is 0.4-1.1 m in length either horizontal or gently inclined upward, widening into a nest chamber. Its entrance is about 50 mm wide and 70 mm high. Eggs are laid on a bare soil floor, or on a bed of fish bones and scales accumulated during a previous occupation. Nest-holes may be used for successive broods and in successive years. Tunnels become fouled and smelly from the faeces of the nestlings, and parents splash-bath to clean themselves after nest visits.

Laying months: mainly Sep-Oct (Aug-Nov, rarely in other months); double-brooded. **Clutch size:** 3-4 (2-6). **Eggs:** 21.0-24.1-25.5 x 18.0-20.6-22.3 mm. **Incubation period:** at least 16 days; shared equally by both sexes, in alternating shifts of 1-2 hrs. **Nestling fledging period:** 27 days; young brooded and fed by both sexes.

Pied Kingfisher *Ceryle rudis* **Bontvisvanger**   page 382

Breeds on most freshwater and coastal wetlands (estuaries, lagoons, rivers, lakes and dams). Pairs, some with helpers, nest solitarily or, in a few places, semi-colonially (up to 10 pairs nesting within 25 m of each other). **Nest:** a tunnel excavated by both sexes into a vertical earth bank, usually a river bank, less often in a gravel pit, or cutting; occasionally up to 1 km from the nearest water; rarely in a low rise in otherwise flat terrain. The tunnel takes 3-4 weeks to dig (11-77 days) and it is excavated by both sexes. Tunnels measure about 60 mm in diameter and are 0.8-1.2-2.4 m long, sloping gently upward before reaching an unlined, widened chamber about 300 mm long, 200 mm wide and 130 mm high. Tunnels are usually positioned in the least accessible positions available: over water wherever possible, in a high bank, and near the top of the bank. Holes are regularly reused for successive clutches.

Laying months: all months, but mainly Aug-Nov (Jul-Feb) except on Botswana floodplains (May-Jun peak) where dictated by flood regime; relays after early failure. **Clutch size:** 4 (1-7); laid at 1-day intervals. **Eggs:** 24.7-29.0-32.8 x 21.0-23.1-24.4 mm. **Incubation period:** 18 days; by both sexes, mostly ♀; begins when first egg is laid. **Nestling/fledging period:** 24-29 days; young brooded and fed by both sexes, sometimes helpers assist.

African Pygmy Kingfisher

Malachite Kingfisher

Giant Kingfisher

Half-collared Kingfisher

Malachite Kingfisher

Pied Kingfisher

BEE-EATERS Family Meropidae Worldwide 26 species; 17 breed in Afrotropics, 6 (perhaps 7 with Bohm's) in southern Africa; 2 species nest colonially, 1 of these in very large colonies; 2 species can nest colonially or solitarily, and 2 are solitary nesters. All species nest in tunnels excavated into the ground, mostly into vertical banks; all are monogamous (where known) and the sexes share nest excavation, incubation and nestling care; eggs are broad oval to spherical in shape, white, unmarked, 4-5/clutch; several species are parasitised by Greater Honeyguide; nestlings are altricial and nidicolous. Nestling faeces are not removed by the parents but are voided against the walls of the nest chamber; pellets containing chitinous insect-remains are regurgitated onto the floor.

Swallow-tailed Bee-eater *Merops hirundineus* Swaelstertbyvreter   page 382

Breeds widely across the savanna belt, extending marginally into the n karoo; the western race *M. h. hirundineus* nests widely and commonly in semi-arid savanna, especially Kalahari thornveld, whereas the eastern race *M. h. furcatus* nests sparsely in mesic woodlands, especially miombo. The nesting habits of both are poorly known. Pairs nest solitarily, occasionally assisted by a helper. **Nest:** a tunnel, dug by both sexes, into the side of a low sandbank, typically a vertical bank that is <1 m high (0.15-1.5); nests may also be dug into the sloping sides of low sandy mounds and, occasionally, into flat ground; aardvark holes, trenches, pits and road embankments, where present, are commonly used. The nest tunnel is 80-100 cm in length and is straight, widening at the end into a nest chamber; those on flat ground slant downwards at a shallow angle.
Laying months: mainly Oct (Aug-Feb), peaking later in Namibia. **Clutch size:** 3-4; laid at 1-day intervals; sometimes parasitised by Greater Honeyguide. **Eggs:** 19.7-20.8-21.9 x 17.0-18.1-19.1 mm. **Incubation period:** not recorded. **Nestling/fledging period:** not recorded; young fed by both sexes, sometimes assisted by a helper.

White-fronted Bee-eater *Merops bullockoides* Rooikeelbyvreter   page 382

Breeds in savanna, especially in areas dissected by streams and rivers that provide nesting banks. A colonial nester and a cooperative breeder, colonies comprising about 10-20 (rarely >100) nesting pairs. The birds often remain year-round in the general area of the colony, roosting in the nests at night when not breeding. Colonies are mostly located in high (2-12 m), vertical banks in alluvial soil, either along rivers, in erosion gulleys, in sand quarries, road cuttings or in some other man-made embankment. Many sites are reused year after year and where they occur in the same breeding range as Southern Carmine Bee-eaters, colonies of the two are often found alongside one another. **Nest:** is a tunnel that extends for about 1 m (0,3-1,2) into the bank, widening at the end into a nest chamber about 200-230 mm across; tunnels do not usually bend to the left or right, but they may incline gently upwards before dipping down into the nest chamber, or they are horizontal from the entrance to the chamber. Tunnels of adjacent pairs are typically close together (150-300 mm apart). The members of a colony have a complex social structure; most pairs (58% in Kenya) have one or more helpers and there is a high incidence (16% in Kenya) of members of the colony parasitising one another's nests; perhaps for this reason, birds that are incubating are reluctant to leave their nests if a colony is disturbed.
Laying months: early summer, mainly Aug-Oct (Aug-Dec, occasionally other months). **Clutch size:** 3-4 (2-6); laid at daily intervals; sometimes parasitised by Greater Honeyguide. **Eggs:** 19.1-22.1-25.0 x 17.0-18.6-21.5 mm. **Incubation period:** 22 days (20-26); by both sexes, assisted by helpers; starts with 2nd- or 3rd-laid egg; incubation shifts last about 25 min (3-180 min). **Nestling/fledging period:** 26 days (20-28, occasionally up to 42 days); young fed by both sexes, assisted by helpers.

Little Bee-eater *Merops pusillus* Kleinbyvreter   page 179, 382

Breeds in mesic and semi-arid savannas. Pairs nest solitarily, although a pair may, occasionally, nest in a bank alongside other bee-eater species at a colony. **Nest:** a tunnel dug into an earth bank, often in the roof of an aardvark hole or in the wall of a pit, a trench, a road cutting or some other shallow embankment. Man-made pits in sandy soils in woodland are often occupied by these bee-eaters within days of their being dug. Rarely, the tunnel may be located in gently sloping or even in flat ground. It is 0.5-0.7-1.3 m long with an entrance hole about 40-50 mm in diameter, and is usually straight and horizontal, widening terminally to about 100 mm at the nest chamber; eggs are laid on a bare soil floor. Both sexes dig the tunnel, and newly excavated holes are recognisable by the fresh mound of soil that accumulates directly below them. Holes may be reused for replacement clutches after an early failure, but they are not reused in successive years.
Laying months: mainly Sep-Nov (Aug-Feb); peaks later (Nov) in the south of its range than the north (Oct); single-brooded, but may relay after an early failure. **Clutch size:** 4 (2-6); frequently parasitised by Greater Honeyguide. **Eggs:** 17.0-18.7-20.7 x 14.4-15.7-17.0 mm. **Incubation period:** 18-20 days (Nigeria); by both sexes; begins when first egg is laid. **Nestling/fledging period:** 23 days (22-24, Nigeria); young fed by both sexes.

Böhm's Bee-eater *Merops boehmi* Roeskopbyvreter

Breeds in tropical savannas, its range narrowly entering southern Africa in the lower Zambezi River valley, east of Tete in Mozambique; there are few records of it from this area and, to date, none of it breeding within southern African limits. North of the Zambezi it breeds on flat ground in open woodland. Its nesting habits are poorly known.

Swallow-tailed Bee-eater

White-fronted Bee-eater

Swallow-tailed Bee-eater

Little Bee-eater

adult at nest entrance

Böhm's Bee-eater

Bee-eaters

Southern Carmine Bee-eater *Merops nubicoides* Rooiborsbyvreter   page 382
A breeding visitor to northern savanna areas (Caprivi, n Botswana, n Zimbabwe, n Mozambique), arriving at traditionally used nesting sites in Aug-Sep and dispersing from these in Dec. Colonial, nesting in large, densely packed colonies of 100s to 1000s of pairs. Most of the larger colonies are located in high, extensive, sandy banks along the edges of large flowing rivers (Kavango, Chobe, Zambezi and others); 30 such colonies are known along the 230 km length of the Zambezi river downstream of Kariba Lake in Zimbabwe; some colonies are in banks well away from water and several are on flat ground in alluvial soils on river terraces. Most sites are reused in successive years, or positions change marginally as older banks erode and collapse and new ones are cut. At long-used colonies the banks become honeycombed with tunnels, with as many as 60 tunnels/m^2 entering the bank. **Nest:** a tunnel that extends into the bank for about 1½ m (1.1-3.7), widening at the end into a nest chamber; some tunnels remain straight and horizontal from the entrance to the chamber, others curve upward or left or right in an irregular fashion; at its entrance, the tunnel has a diameter of about 60 mm. In colonies situated on flat ground, nest tunnels are dug downward into the soil at a shallow angle. Both sexes excavate. Breeding sites are very conspicuous and quite spectacular during the months (Aug-Nov) that they are active.
Laying months: mainly Sep-Oct (Aug-Dec). **Clutch size:** 3 (2-5); laid at 1-2 day intervals; begins with first-laid egg (in captivity). **Eggs:** 23.9-26.4-28.4 × 20.8-22.1-23.4 mm. **Incubation period:** 20-21 days, by both sexes, with frequent change-overs (in captivity). **Nestling/fledging period:** not recorded; young fed by both sexes.

Olive Bee-eater *Merops superciliosus* Olyfbyvreter   page 382
Breeds in the northern savanna where resident in part of its range (coastal Mozambique), but apparently less consistently present in other areas (Namibia, Zimbabwe). Nesting habits are poorly known. Colonial, nesting in groups of 10-60 pairs, rarely 100s; occasionally nests alongside Southern Carmine and White-fronted bee-eaters. Breeds in vertical sand banks, either along large rivers, in coastal dunes (Mozambique), in road cuttings and sand quarries; sometimes in flat ground in alluvial soils on river terraces. **Nest:** a tunnel, 0.9-1.6 m long with an entrance diameter of 80 mm, extending horizontally into vertical banks, inclined on flat ground, and widening to a chamber where the eggs are laid on bare soil. Both sexes excavate the tunnel.
Laying months: Sep-Dec. **Clutch size:** usually 4 (2-4). **Eggs:** 23.3-25.3-27.5 × 20.5-22.2-23.0 mm. **Incubation period:** not recorded. **Nestling/fledging period:** not recorded.

European Bee-eater *Merops apiaster* Europese Byvreter   page 382
A summer visitor to southern Africa, comprising a large non-breeding population that moves into the region (mainly into the mesic east) from the Palearctic, and a much smaller population that over-winters in the tropics and moves south, mainly into the semi-arid west (w, e and n Cape) to breed, arriving here in Sep where it reoccupies regularly used breeding sites. Some pairs nest solitarily, but they are more usually found in colonies of 10-30 pairs (rarely as many as 100). Most nesting sites are in vertical banks, either along (usually dry) watercourses or, more frequently, they are man-made (trenches, road cuttings, sand quarries, pits, etc); some are in the sides of sloping ridges rather than on a vertical bank and, occasionally, they are in flat ground; nest banks are sometimes shared with Pied Starling, Banded and Brown-throated martins, and other tunnel-nesters. **Nest:** a tunnel, excavated by both sexes, about 1½ m long (0,7-2) and, in banks, it is either horizontal or gently inclined upwards, leading into a widened nest chamber at the end. The tunnel is about 65-70 mm in diameter (and may be wider than this at the entrance) and the chamber is about 130-200 mm across; eggs are laid on bare soil or on the chitinous remains of insects that accumulate in tunnels that have been used previously.
Laying months: mainly Nov (Sep-Jan, rarely other months); single-brooded; may relay after an early failure. **Clutch size:** 4-6 (2-7) (South Africa); laid at 1-2 day intervals (Europe). **Eggs:** 23.7-25.8-28.0 × 20.0-21.8-23.0 mm; mass 6 g. **Incubation period:** 20 days (13-28) (Europe); begins before clutch is completed; by both sexes. **Nestling/fledging period:** 30-31 days (Europe); young brooded and fed by both sexes, sometimes helpers assist (Europe).

Southern Carmine Bee-eater a breeding colony in a river bank (above) and on flat ground (below)

Olive Bee-eater

European Bee-eater

European Bee-eater

Hoopoe, Woodhoopoes, Scimitarbill

HOOPOES & WOODHOOPOES Families Upupidae & Phoeniculidae Two related families that worldwide comprise 12 species; 10 breed in Afrotropics, 4 in southern Africa. Monogamous; 2 (woodhoopoes) live year-round in family groups of 3-12 birds and are cooperative breeders; 2 (hoopoe, scimitarbill) do not usually have nest helpers; all are hole-nesters; eggs oval to elliptical in shape, unmarked turquoise-blue to olive, finely pored, 3-6/clutch; nestlings are altricial and nidicolous.

African Hoopoe *Upupa africana* Hoephoep   page 382

Breeds widely in woodland, savanna, grassland, shrubland and in many suburban environments; absent only from evergreen forest and the most arid regions. Pairs nest solitarily, occasionally assisted by a helper. **Nest:** a hole of some sort is used; ideal sites are those that have a narrow entrance (<50 mm wide) which leads into a wider, enclosed chamber (>150 mm across); natural cavities in trees are most frequently used, especially those in the gnarled old trunks of trees such as willows. Holes in the ground are also often used, especially subterranean chambers of disused termitaria; other sites include inside a heap of brick or stone rubble, in the eaves or a wall cavity of a building; or in a nest box; holes of barbets and woodpeckers are seldom used. Tree holes range in height from ground level to about 8 m up. The eggs are laid on the floor of the cavity, and accumulated debris in the hole is cleaned out by the pair before laying. Sites are regularly reused in successive years. Except for short daily breaks, the ♀ remains in the nest hole continuously through the incubation and she is fed regularly by her mate; after the young hatch, she leaves the hole to assist in feeding them. If a nest is closely examined, the ♀ (and later the young) utter loud snake-like hissing sounds: coming from the dark interior of the hole it is often an effective deterrent to getting too close! The ♀ and young discharge a foul-smelling gland secretion if handled. Nest cavities become increasingly odorous as the nestlings grow and defecate in the nest.
Laying months: mainly Sep-Nov (Aug-Dec, occasionally other months); sometimes multiple-brooded. **Clutch size:** 4-6 (2-7); laid at 1-2 day intervals; commonly parasitised by Greater Honeyguide. **Eggs:** 22.2-25.3-27.6 x 15.8-17.2-18.5 mm. **Incubation period:** 15-16 days; by ♀ only, fed by ♂ 5-8x/hr; begins when first egg is laid. **Nestling/fledging period:** 29 days (26-32); young brooded by ♀, fed by both sexes.

Green Woodhoopoe *Phoeniculus purpureus* Rooibekkakelaar   page 382

Breeds widely in any tall woodland (except evergreen forest). Lives year-round in family groups (comprising a pair assisted by 1-10 helpers); group density in suitable habitat 15-50 ha/group. **Nest:** a hole in a tree is used, either a natural cavity or a hole made by a woodpecker or barbet; it is typically 4-5 m up from the ground (½-9); frequently in a dead tree; cavity depth variable, usually 400-600 mm deep with an entrance >40 mm in diameter; in natural holes the entrance may be an elongated slit rather than the usual round, woodpecker-type hole; some holes are accessed from a vertical entrance; occasionally nests in a pipe or a wall cavity in a building; eggs are laid on the bare substrate without addition of a lining. Holes are regularly reused in successive years and are used as night-time roosts. Once incubation begins, the ♀ remains in the nest most of the day, fed at regular intervals by her mate and helpers; she leaves the nest and assists in feeding the young once they hatch. If handled, the young are liable to discharge a foul-smelling gland secretion; their nests also become increasingly foul-smelling as their faeces are not removed by the parents, but instead discharged onto the inside walls of the nest; when nearly fledged, the chicks squirt their faeces out through the entrance.
Laying months: mainly Sep-Nov with second peak in Mar-May from second broods; all months recorded. **Clutch size:** 3-4 (2-5, rarely 6); laid at 1-day intervals; occasional host to Greater and Lesser honeyguides. **Eggs:** 22.2-24.9-29.2 x 16.0-17.3-18.9 mm; mass 2.6-3.6 g. **Incubation period:** 17-18 days; by ♀ only, fed by ♂, assisted by helpers; begins before clutch is completed. **Nestling/fledging period:** 28-30 days; young brooded by ♀, fed by both sexes, assisted by helpers.

Violet Woodhoopoe *Phoeniculus damarensis* Perskakelaar

Breeds in arid woodlands in n Namibia. Closely related to the Green Woodhoopoe and nesting habits closely similar; it also lives year-round in family groups (a pair plus 1-9 helpers) which defend permanent territories. **Nest:** uses a natural cavity or old woodpecker hole in a tree. Once incubation begins, the ♀ remains in the nest most of the day, being fed at regular intervals by her mate and by helpers; she leaves the nest and assists in feeding the young once they hatch.
Laying months: Dec-Apr. **Clutch size:** 4. **Eggs:** about 26 x 18 mm; similar to eggs of Green Woodhoopoe (not illustrated). **Incubation period:** not recorded; by ♀ only, fed by ♂ and helpers. **Nestling/fledging period:** not recorded; young fed by family group.

Common Scimitarbill *Rhinopomastus cyanomelas* Swartbekkakelaar   page 382

Breeds in woodland and savanna; most common in semi-arid areas. Pairs nest solitarily and are widely dispersed. **Nest:** a hole in a tree is used, usually a natural cavity in the main trunk <2 m up from the ground (½-5); nest cavity 250-450 mm in depth, with a narrow entrance (about 38 mm), just sufficient to admit the bird; old woodpecker or barbet holes are occasionally used, also holes in walls of buildings; eggs are laid on the unlined floor of the cavity. Holes are sometimes reused in successive years, or for second clutches. Once incubation begins, the ♀ remains in the nest most of the day, being fed at regular intervals by her mate; a solitary ♂ seen carrying food is probably en route to a nest to feed his partner. The ♀ leaves the hole about a week after the young have hatched and thereafter she assists in feeding the brood. If handled, the young are liable to discharge a foul-smelling gland secretion; they also perform a threatening display that simulates the striking action of a snake.
Laying months: most months recorded, but mainly Sep-Nov (Aug-Feb); peaking earlier in Zimbabwe (Sep) and later in Namibia; sometimes double-brooded. **Clutch size:** 3 (2-4); laid at 1-day intervals; infrequent host of Greater Honeyguide. **Eggs:** 20.0-21.5-23.5 x 14.5-15.7-16.7 mm. **Incubation period:** 13-14 days; by ♀ only, fed by ♂; ♀ leaves nest to feed herself <30 mins/day; begins before clutch is completed. **Nestling/fledging period:** 23 days (21-24); young brooded by ♀, fed by both sexes.

nesting in a tree cavity — African Hoopoe — nesting in a hole in the ground

Green Woodhoopoe

Violet Woodhoopoe

Common Scimitarbill

Hornbills

HORNBILLS & GROUND HORNBILLS Families **Bucerotidae** and **Bucorvidae** Worldwide 61 species; 29 breed in Afrotropics, 10 in southern Africa. Monogamous, nesting in solitary pairs or (Ground Hornbills) in cooperative family groups. All are hole-nesters, mostly using tree cavities, a few also nesting in cavities in rock faces and in earth banks. Hornbills have the near-unique feature, while breeding, of the ♀ confining herself to the nest for the incubation and part of the nestling period and becoming entirely dependent on her mate for food during this time. In most instances she seals herself into the nest-hole, using her faeces mixed with nest debris to plaster up the nest entrance, leaving just a narrow slit through which the ♂ is able to pass her food. While thus confined she undergoes a complete moult of her wing and tail feathers, becoming temporarily flightless. In most species the nest hole has a hollow 'chimney', extending up the trunk beyond the entrance, which is used by the ♀ and nestlings as a retreat if the nest is threatened from the outside. When the nestlings begin feathering (at about 3 weeks of age) she breaks out of the nest to assist the ♂ with feeding the brood and the young reseal themselves in. Southern Ground Hornbill is an exception as the ♀ does not seal herself in, nor does she moult while on the nest; she does, however, remain confined to the nest-hole and is fed by her group. Eggs are elliptical in shape; dull white, unmarked, pitted with fine pores; 2-5/clutch; they are laid at irregular intervals (1-5 days between eggs); nestlings hatch asynchronously and are altricial and nidicolous.

Crowned Hornbill *Tockus alboterminatus* Gekroonde Neushoringvoël   page 383

Breeds in coastal, lowland and riparian forest and woodland/forest mosaics. Pairs nest solitarily; one nesting density of 28 pairs in 440 ha of e Cape valley bushveld reported. **Nest:** a hole in the trunk of a large tree, typically a natural cavity formed at a rot-hole where a branch has broken off; height above the ground variable, between 1½-12 m. A nest cavity with an internal width >180 mm is needed by the ♀; it is usually <100 mm deep with an entrance hole 48-90 mm wide and 65-400 mm high which the ♀ seals to a narrow (12 mm wide) vertical slit, using her faeces and food remains; some holes have hollow 'chimneys' above the entrance into which the ♀ moves if threatened. While confined for 10 weeks in the cavity, the ♀ is fed by the ♂; she sheds her wing and tail feathers then, defecates out through the nest-slit and pushes out her moulted feathers; their accumulation on the ground below is a tell-tale sign of an occupied nest. The ♂ also brings bark fragments to the nest throughout the nesting cycle. The ♀ emerges when oldest chick is 25-30 days old; the chicks then reseal the entrance, breaking out a few weeks later when they fledge. Nest sites are regularly reused in successive seasons.

Laying months: mainly Oct-Nov (Sep-Jan). **Clutch size:** 3-4 (2-5); the first laid 7-14 days after confinement, the others at 2-4 day intervals. **Eggs:** 36.5-39.3-41.5 x 25.5-27.8-30.4 mm. **Incubation period:** 26 days (25-27); by ♀ only; fed by ♂; begins when first egg is laid. **Nestling/fledging period:** 50 days (46-55); young brooded by ♀; fed by both sexes.

Bradfield's Hornbill *Tockus bradfieldi* Bradfieldse Neushoringvoël   page 383

Breeds in tall woodland in semi-arid northern savannas. Pairs nest solitarily and are widely spaced. Nesting habits are poorly known. **Nest:** a natural cavity in a tree is used, typically 3-7 m up from the ground and in the main trunk of a large (400-500 mm diameter) tree; inside cavity width about 220 mm, entrance hole >50 mm wide, depth 190-270 mm down from the entrance. In arid areas holes in rock faces are probably used more frequently than the single record of this suggests. The ♀ seals herself into the hole for the duration of the incubation and part of the nestling period and is fed by the ♂ then. Nest holes are reused in successive seasons.

Laying months: mainly Nov (Sep-Apr). **Clutch size:** 3. **Eggs:** 39.1-40.9-43.0 x 26.5-26.8-27.0 mm. **Incubation period:** at least 28 days, by ♀, fed by ♂. **Nestling/fledging period:** at least 47 days; ♀ emerges when chicks are about 32 days old and assists ♂ feeding the brood; young reseal the nest, breaking out a few weeks later when they fledge.

Monteiro's Hornbill *Tockus monteiri* Monteirose Neushoringvoël   page 383

Breeds in arid, rugged, hilly country along the Namibian escarpment. Pairs nest solitarily, a pair/15 ha at one site, a pair/11-14 ha in another area with supplementary nest boxes. **Nest:** selected by the ♀, typically in a hole in a rock face, less often in a tree; nest boxes, where they have been erected, are commonly used. Rock holes used are usually in low (3-50 m) cliffs where box-shaped cavities have formed in bedded sedimentary rocks; the hole selected is usually 2-4 m up from the base of the cliff. Rock cavities are very variable in their dimensions, between 170-600 mm in depth, 70-380 mm in height and 60-320 mm in width (at the entrance). Holes used in trees are also usually close to the ground (0.2-2 m up), in the main trunk or in a stump, often using an *Acacia* or *Boscia* sp.; their entrance- and cavity-dimensions are equally variable. Holes are regularly reused in successive years and those in rocks retain their partially plastered walls for use in the next breeding season. Given the nature of rock cavities, few of these sites have 'chimneys'. The ♀ seals herself into the hole 4-11 days before laying the first egg, plastering up the entrance with her faeces mixed with debris found in the nest, leaving a single narrow slit through which the ♂ feeds her. During the time that she is enclosed, the ♂ brings her food at intervals during the day, including snail shells, as well as a variety of items that are probably used for nest lining (bark, leaves, grass, seed pods, snail shells). She breaks out from the nest when the oldest chick is about 22 days old; the young then reseal the entrance, breaking out a few weeks later when they fledge.

Laying months: mainly Jan-Mar (Oct-Mar); relays after an early failure; single-brooded. **Clutch size:** 4-5 (2-8); first egg laid 1-4-15 days after confinement, others laid at 2-9 day intervals. **Eggs:** 34.1-40.3-45.8 x 21.6-27.4-31.9 mm; mass 12.7-16.8-21.9 g. **Incubation period:** 24-27 days; by ♀ only; fed by ♂; begins when first egg is laid. **Nestling/fledging period:** 44-46 days; young brooded by ♀; fed by both sexes.

Crowned Hornbill

Crowned Hornbill

Bradfield's Hornbill (TWO ABOVE)

Monterio's Hornbill

Hornbills

Southern Yellow-billed Hornbill *Tockus leucomelas* Geelbekneushoringvoël   page 383

Breeds widely in savanna areas. Pairs nest solitarily, rarely within 100 m of each other. **Nest:** uses a hole in a tree, either a natural cavity, or one excavated by a woodpecker; holes can be in living or dead trees, in trunks or side branches, and in vertical stems or in the underside of a sloping branch; they are typically 2-5 m up from the ground (0,75-12), the entrance hole 40-60 mm in diameter, leading into a cavity 200-300 mm wide and 100-300 mm deep; most holes have a hollow 'chimney' above the entrance into which the ♀ retreats if threatened; nest-boxes are also used where available. The ♀ seals herself into the hole 4-5 days before laying the first egg, plasters up the entrance with her faeces, leaving a single narrow vertical slit (5-15 mm wide) through which the ♂ passes her food. She lays eggs at irregular (1-4 day) intervals, shedding her wing and tail feathers in this period. Holes are regularly reused in successive years (at least 16 years recorded in one case). The ♀ is fed by the ♂ for 7 weeks while she is immobile; he also brings her dry plant material – leaves, twigs, bark – presumably used for nest lining. She defecates through the slit and pushes her moulted feathers out here, leaving characteristic tell-tale signs of occupation on the ground below the nest-hole. In areas where this species occurs alongside Southern Red-billed and African Grey hornbills, active nests of the three are usually indistinguishable unless the ♀ can be seen in the nest, or the ♂ is seen attending the nest.

Laying months: mainly Oct-Dec (Sep-Mar), but later (Jan-Feb) in Namibia; sometimes double-brooded. **Clutch size:** 3-4 (2-6); laid at 1-4 day intervals. **Eggs:** 31.5-36.9-41.0 x 21.3-26.0-28.5 mm. **Incubation period:** 24 days; by ♀ only; begins when first egg is laid. **Nestling/fledging period:** 45 days (42-47); young brooded by ♀; fed by both sexes.

African Grey Hornbill *Tockus nasutus* Grysneushoringvoël   page 383

Breeds widely in deciduous woodland. Pairs nest solitarily, adjacent nests seldom closer than 250 m apart; typical densities are a pair/22-63 ha. **Nest:** a hole in a tree is used, usually in the main stem, either in a natural cavity or in an old woodpecker hole; typically 2-4 m up from the ground (0,7-9). In the arid west occasional nests are in cavities in rock faces. Tree cavities measure 150-230-320 mm in diameter, 0-80-200 deep, and have an entrance hole 50-85-200 mm high and 25-40-80 mm wide; most holes have a hollow 'chimney' above the entrance into which the ♀ retreats if threatened; nest-boxes may be used. The ♀ enters the hole 7-11 days before laying the first egg and seals herself in, plastering up the entrance with her faeces, but leaving a narrow (10-15 mm) vertical slit through which the ♂ passes her food and dry plant material (especially pieces of bark) which are used for nest lining. She lays her clutch of eggs at irregular intervals and sheds her wing and tail feathers. He feeds her for 6-8 weeks until she re-emerges. While confined, she defecates through the slit and pushes her moulted feathers out here, leaving characteristic tell-tale signs of occupation on the ground below the nest-hole. Holes are commonly reused in successive years and are often used alternately with other hole-nesting birds.

Laying months: mainly Oct-Nov (Sep-Dec); peaks later (Dec-Mar) in arid west. **Clutch size:** 3-4 (3-5); laid at 1-7 day intervals. **Eggs:** 34.2-37.3-40.0 x 25.0-26.2-28.3 mm. **Incubation period:** 25 days (24-26); by ♀ only; begins when first egg is laid. **Nestling/fledging period:** 45½ days (43-49); young brooded by ♀; fed by both sexes.

Damara Hornbill *Tockus damarensis* Damara Rooibekneushoringvoël

Breeds in arid savanna. Pairs nest solitarily. **Nest:** a hole in a tree is used, similar in all respects to nest-hole used by Southern Red-billed Hornbill. The ♀ seals herself in, plastering up the entrance with her faeces, leaving a single narrow vertical slit through which the ♂ feeds her. She lays her first egg 0-4-11 days after confinement and leaves the nest after 43-46 days when the oldest chick is about 18 days old.

Laying months: Feb-Mar. **Clutch size:** 4 (3-8); laid at 1-3-11 day intervals. **Eggs:** 32.0-35.6-38.4 x 23.6-25.0-27.5 mm; mass 10.2-12.7-18.8 g; unmarked white (not illustrated). **Incubation period:** 24-27 days; by ♀ only; begins when first egg is laid. **Nestling/fledging period:** 18-45 days; young brooded by ♀; fed by both sexes.

Southern Red-billed Hornbill *Tockus erythrorhynchus* Rooibekneushoringvoël   page 383

Breeds in savanna, favouring areas with a sparse ground cover. Pairs nest solitarily at a density of about a pair/10 ha in good habitat. **Nest:** a hole in a tree is used, either a natural cavity or an old woodpecker hole; it is typically 2-4 m up from the ground (0,3-9), with a cavity 200-250 mm deep and an entrance hole 30-50 mm wide; most holes are hollow above the entrance (having a 'chimney') into which the ♀ retreats if threatened; nest-boxes are also used. The ♀ enters the nest-hole a week (rarely up to 24 days) before laying the first egg and seals herself in, plastering up the entrance with her faeces, but leaving a single narrow (10-15 mm wide) slit through which the ♂ feeds her. Other exterior holes or cracks in the stem containing the nest chamber are also plastered up, usually just before she goes in. She lays her clutch of eggs at irregular intervals and sheds her wing and tail feathers in this period. The ♂ feeds her during the day for the 6-9 weeks that she is sealed in; he also passes green leaves and other plant material to her, this being used for nest lining. She defecates through the slit and pushes her moulted feathers out here, leaving characteristic tell-tale signs of occupation on the ground below the nest-hole. Holes are commonly reused in successive years and are often used alternately with other hole-nesting birds.

Laying months: mainly Oct-Dec (Sep-May); sometimes double-brooded. **Clutch size:** 3-5 (2-7); laid at 2-4 day intervals. **Eggs:** 31.8-37.1-40.9 x 23.0-26.2-29.0 mm. **Incubation period:** 24 days (23-25); by ♀ only; begins when first egg is laid. **Nestling/fledging period:** 45 days (39-50); young brooded by ♀; fed by both sexes.

Southern Yellow-billed Hornbill

African Grey Hornbill (THREE ABOVE)

Damara Hornbill

Southern Red-billed Hornbill

Silvery-cheeked Hornbill *Bycanistes brevis* Kuifkopboskraai page 383

Breeds in tall lowland and riparian forest in Mozambique and e Zimbabwe. Few nests have been recorded in the region and little is known here of its nesting habits; most of the information given here is from Tanzania. Pairs nest solitarily. **Nest:** a large natural hole high up (15-25 m) in the main trunk of a tall forest tree (e.g. *Craibia brevicaudata*, *Khaya nyassica*) is used; the entrance hole measures 320-375 x 200-250 mm and this, when plastered up, is sealed to a vertical slit 125-250 x 20-50 mm. Plastering is done by both sexes using mud pellets collected and brought to the site by the ♂. The ♀ remains in the nest for the duration of the incubation and nestling periods and she and the young are fed by the ♂, mainly on regurgitated fruit; at intervals he also brings bark and small sticks to the nest. Nest holes are regularly reused in successive years.

Laying months: Sep, Oct, Apr (e Zimbabwe). **Clutch size:** 1-2, perhaps also 3 rarely. **Eggs:** 51.9-53.1-53.6 x 36.4-37.1-38.2 mm. **Incubation period:** 40 days (Tanzania); by ♀ only, fed by ♂. **Nestling/fledging period:** 77-80 days (Tanzania); ♀ remains sealed in the nest until the young fledge; fed by the ♂ making 12-18 feeding visits/day (Tanzania).

Trumpeter Hornbill *Bycanistes bucinator* Gewone Boskraai page 383

Breeds in or close to lowland, coastal or riparian forest. Pairs nest solitarily, occasionally assisted by a helper; a reported nesting density of 4 prs in a 240 ha e Cape coastal forest. **Nest:** a hole is used, usually one in a tree, occasionally in a rock face; tree holes are usually in the main stem of a large tree (such as a baobab, fig, *Khaya nyassica* or *Acacia xanthofloea*), where a cavity has formed at a rot-hole; height above the ground variable, from 2-15 m up (once 40 m); the cavity is typically 300-450 mm wide inside, 120-200 mm deep, with an entrance at least 60 mm wide (usually 100-150 mm wide, 100-300 mm high); tree holes commonly have an inside 'chimney' that extends up the trunk from the entrance. Rock cavities used have a max entrance size 300 x 200 mm, probably because of constraint of plastering closed a larger hole. ♀ seals herself in using her faeces, plastering the entrance closed, leaving a narrow vertical slit 150-240 mm high and 20 mm wide. Holes are commonly reused in successive years, some in known use for decades; holes are, on occasion, used alternately with Crowned Hornbill. The ♀ remains in the nest for the duration of the incubation and nestling periods (for a 94-day period by one in captivity), fed at infrequent intervals by the ♂, some pairs assisted by a helper. The ♂ is secretive while breeding and is very cautious when approaching the nest; he may range 3-8 km from the nest in search of food to bring the ♀.

Laying months: mainly Oct-Nov (Sep-Jan); single-brooded. **Clutch size:** 2-3 (rarely 4); first egg laid 10-15 days after confinement, others laid at 2-3 day intervals. **Eggs:** 45.0-48.4-51.8 x 34.0-35,0-36.8 mm. **Incubation period:** 24 days; by ♀ only, fed by ♂; starts with first-laid egg. **Nestling/fledging period:** >50 days; ♀ and young fed by ♂; ♀ emerges when young leave.

Southern Ground Hornbill *Bucorvus leadbeateri* Bromvoël page 383

Breeds in savanna and in forest-grassland mosaics. Monogamous, but nests in family groups (a pair with 1-3, rarely up to 9 helpers). Groups are territorial year-round; group density about 1/100 km² in South Africa, 1/20 km² in n Zimbabwe. **Nest:** a large hole or bole in a tree is the most frequently used site, but cavities in rock faces or in the walls of embankments or dongas are also used. Tree holes used vary between 2-9 m up from the ground, usually in the main stem of a large tree (e.g. *Combretum imberbe*, *Diospyros mespiliformis*, *Lannea discolor*, *Schotia* sp., marula, fig, baobab, mopane) which may stand alone, or be among other trees in riparian woodland or evergreen forest; dead trees are often used. A large cavity is required, it measures 260-370-700 mm internal width, 450-600 mm deep (from entrance lip to bowl) and the entrance is about 500 x 300 mm in diameter. Holes used in rock faces and donga walls are usually larger, the nest chamber here about 900 mm wide. Sites are commonly reused in successive years, some in known use for decades. Before laying, the cavity is thickly lined with leaves, dry grass and other plant material and this continues to be added during the nesting cycle. The dominant ♀ in the group lays in the nest and she remains there throughout the incubation, being fed at intervals during the day by her group. She does not seal herself in and does not undergo the extensive moult that ♀s of other hornbills do when confined to the nest. Family groups do not breed every year and overall annual recruitment is very low (average of 1 young/group/9 years).

Laying months: mainly Oct-Nov (Aug-Jan); pairs do not breed every year. **Clutch size:** 2 (1-2, rarely 3); laid 3-14 days apart; only one chick is reared per breeding attempt, the second-hatched invariably succumbing to starvation. **Eggs:** 67.3-73.9-79.0 x 46.9-51.3-55.7 mm; second-laid egg is invariably smaller than the first. **Incubation period:** 37-43 days; by ♀ only; begins when first egg is laid; she leaves nest briefly 3-4x/day to feed and is fed by mate and helpers 4-9x/day. **Nestling/fledging period:** 86 days; young brooded by ♀; fed by both sexes, assisted by helpers.

Silvery-cheeked Hornbill

Southern Ground Hornbill   nesting in hole in bank

Trumpeter Hornbill

nesting in hole in baobab   Southern Ground Hornbill

Barbets

BARBETS Family Lybiidae Worldwide 42 species; all endemic to Afrotropics, 8 breed in southern Africa. Tinkerbirds are diminutive barbets that do not differ in their nesting habits. Monogamous, several are cooperative breeders; both sexes incubate and brood and feed the nestlings. Nest is a hole, excavated into a dead tree-stem; often reused, and as night-time roost; eggs broad-oval to elliptical in shape, white, unmarked; 3-5/clutch; nestlings are altricial and nidicolous; the larger species are frequently parasitised by honeyguides which lay matching white eggs only distinguishable by being smoother-shelled and more glossy than barbet eggs and, in some cases, differ in size. Nest holes of the larger barbets are used by a wide range of other hole-nesting birds. One species, the Green Tinkerbird *Pogonolius simplex*, has been excluded from this account – it has only once been recorded in the region (specimen collected at Inhambane, s Mozambique, Jan 1958) and its nest and eggs are unknown.

White-eared Barbet *Stactolaema leucotis* Witoorhoutkapper — page 382

Breeds in coastal, lowland and riparian forests and in moist woodlands up the eastern side of the region. Pairs and family groups (pair plus 1-6 helpers) nest solitarily, sometimes within 50 m of each other, even in the same tree on occasion. **Nest:** a hole is excavated in the dead stem of a soft-wood tree, often a dead branch in a living tree, height above ground very variable (1-20 m); nest cavity is 85-140 mm wide inside, 300-460 mm deep (once 710 mm); entrance hole usually oval-shaped (55-60 mm wide and 38-40 mm high), leading into the stem at right angles for some distance before descending into the nest chamber; eggs are laid on a floor of wood chips. Nest-holes may be reused, and they are used as night-time roosts. Holes excavated by Black-collared Barbets may be taken over. Both sexes, and helpers when present, excavate the nest-hole; one took 8 weeks to complete.
Laying months: mainly Oct-Dec (Aug-Mar). **Clutch size:** 4-5 (3-6). **Eggs:** 22.1-23.4-25.1 x 17.0-17.8-18.4 m; occasionally parasitised by Lesser Honeyguide, suspected by Scaly-throated Honeyguide. **Incubation period:** 14-18 days; by both sexes, assisted by helpers. **Nestling/fledging period:** 39 days; young brooded and fed by both sexes, assisted by helpers.

Black-collared Barbet *Lybius torquatus* Rooikophoutkapper — pages 179, 382

Breeds widely in mesic savanna, its range now extending widely into former grassland areas as a result of urbanisation and alien tree introduction. Pairs nest solitarily, some assisted by helpers; adjacent nests can be <100 m apart in suburban gardens. **Nest:** a hole, excavated by both sexes, helpers sometimes assisting; placed in a dead branch or trunk of a tree (100-250 mm diameter), especially one where decay is advanced; uses both vertical stems and the underside of sloping branches; usually 1-4 m up from the ground (½-6); entrance hole measures 35-40 mm across, entering branch at right-angles for 30-90 mm before descending into chamber, 140-300-480 mm deep; eggs are laid here on a bed of wood chips. Nest logs attached to trees in gardens are commonly used; holes are often reused for second broods and, if they survive that long, in successive years; reused nests are usually deepened by the birds; they are also used as night-time roosts when the birds are not nesting.
Laying months: mainly Oct-Nov (Sep-Feb, rarely in other months); often double-brooded. **Clutch size:** 3-4 (2-5, rarely 7-8 probably laid by two ♀s). **Eggs:** 21.2-24.4-27.1 x 16.1-17.6-18.5 mm; frequently parasitised by Lesser Honeyguide, occasionally by Greater Honeyguide. **Incubation period:** 18½ days; by both sexes, sometimes assisted by helpers; begins when first egg is laid. **Nestling/fledging period:** 34 days (33-36); young brooded and fed by both sexes, some assisted by helpers.

Acacia Pied Barbet *Tricholaema leucomelas* Bonthoutkapper — page 382

Breeds widely across southern Africa, from arid west to mesic east, in the savanna, fynbos, karoo and grassland regions where introduced trees have provided nesting sites and extended its range. Pairs nest solitarily and are usually widely spaced. **Nest:** a hole excavated by both sexes, in the stem of a decayed soft-wood tree, typically in a stump or in the underside of a sloping or horizontal branch, usually close to the ground, about 1-3 m up (½-7 m); the selected branch is often just thick enough to contain the nest cavity (90-120 mm inside); entrance hole is typically oval-shaped (33-38 mm wide and 30-32 mm high), sometimes uniformly circular, about 32 mm in diameter; it leads into the stem at right angles for about 50 mm before descending into the nest chamber, which is 100-200-320 mm deep; eggs are laid here on a bed of wood chips. Nest-holes are often reused for second broods and, if they survive that long, in successive years; reused nests are usually deepened by the birds. Occasionally breeds in old nests of a striped swallow.
Laying months: mainly Sep-Dec (Jul-May); peaking earlier (Sep-Oct) in sw Cape, and later (Feb-Mar) in arid west; sometimes double-brooded. **Clutch size:** 3 (2-4; records of 5 possibly included honeyguide eggs); frequently parasitised by Lesser Honeyguide, rarely by Greater Honeyguide. **Eggs:** 20.0-22.0-24.0 x 14.5-16.0-17.7 mm; in parasitised nests Lesser Honeyguide eggs are not distinguishable from those of the barbet by size, but they are by their smoother and glossier shell. **Incubation period:** 14-15 days; by both sexes. **Nestling/fledging period:** about 35 days; young brooded and fed by both sexes.

Whyte's Barbet *Stactolaema whytii* Geelbleshoutkapper — page 382

Breeds in primary miombo woodland in e Zimbabwe and w Mozambique; favours areas with granite koppies and associated fig trees. Nests in family groups (a pair plus 1-6 helpers), with adjacent nests frequently <100 m apart. **Nest:** a hole is excavated in a dead trunk or branch of a soft-wood tree; it may be a dead limb in a living tree, or in a wholly dead stump, and either a vertical stem is used, or the underside of a sloping branch; holes are 1-10 m up from the ground and several holes from previous years may be in the same branch; branches used are typically 150-300 mm in diameter, the nest chamber is about 350 mm deep; the eggs are laid on a bed of wood chips. Nest-holes are used as night-time roosts year-round, with 9 birds recorded sleeping in a nest with eggs in one instance; holes originally excavated by Black-collared Barbets are occasionally taken over.
Laying months: mainly Sep-Oct (Sep-Jan). **Clutch size:** 4-5 (3-6). **Eggs:** 22.9-24.3-25.0 x 17.5-18.6-19.4 mm. **Incubation period:** not recorded. **Nestling/fledging period:** 49 days; young fed by pair and helpers.

White-eared Barbet

Black-collared Barbet

Acacia Pied Barbet

Whyte's Barbet

Yellow-fronted Tinkerbird *Pogonolius chrysoconus* Geelblestinker   page 382

Breeds in mesic savanna, favouring broad-leafed woodlands. Pairs nest solitarily. **Nest:** a hole is excavated by both sexes in a thin (100 mm diameter) dead branch in a soft-wood tree, usually in a dead stub in a living tree; typically 3-4 m (1½-6) up from the ground, either in a vertical stem, or in the underside of a sloping branch. The entrance hole is tiny (22 mm in diameter) and leads in at right-angles before descending into a chamber, about 75-100 mm deep; eggs are laid here on a bed of wood chips. Nest-holes are occasionally reused for second clutches but they usually do not survive beyond the season; holes in successive seasons are sometimes excavated close to previous nests; they are used as night-time roosts when the birds are not breeding. The position of nests containing well-grown young is often given away by the persistent food-begging call of the chicks from the hole.
Laying months: mainly Sep-Dec (Aug-Feb, rarely other months); sometimes double-brooded. **Clutch size:** 3 (2-4). **Eggs:** 16.0-17.7-19.8 x 13.0-14.1-16.1 mm. **Incubation period:** not recorded; by both sexes. **Nestling/fledging period:** not recorded (at least 21 days); young brooded and fed by both sexes.

Red-fronted Tinkerbird *Pogonolius pusillus* Rooiblestinker   page 382

Breeds in a narrow range along the e coast from e Cape to s Mozambique in coastal and lowland forest and other wooded habitats. Pairs nest solitarily. **Nest:** a hole, excavated by both sexes, in a thin (80-100 mm diameter) dead branch, usually 1-3 m up from the ground (1-6 m); easily overlooked, being either in the underside of a sloping branch, or facing directly onto one or more nearby branches; several holes may be started in a stem before one is completed. The entrance is 21-25 mm in diameter and it leads in at right-angles for about 37 mm before descending into a chamber about 50-55 mm wide and 100-130 mm deep; eggs are laid here on a bed of wood chips. Nest holes are probably never reused, given the decayed state of branches used for nest sites.
Laying months: mainly Oct-Nov (Aug-Dec). **Clutch size:** 3 (2-4). **Eggs:** 18.5-19.0-19.7 x 13.7-14.0-14.4 mm. **Incubation period:** not recorded. **Nestling/fledging period:** not recorded; young fed by both sexes.

Green Barbet *Stactolaema olivacea* Groenhoutkapper

Restricted, in southern Africa, to a single forest in n KwaZulu-Natal (Ongoye), where an estimated 200-300 pairs breed within an area of 2600 ha. Pairs nest solitarily in the forest interior. **Nest:** a hole, excavated by both sexes, usually in the main trunk of a dead tree in an advanced stage of decay; typically 4-5 m up (one at 18 m), usually situated where the trunk emerges above the foliage of under-canopy saplings; favours trunks that stand close to large-leafed, sub-canopy trees (e.g. *Tabernaemontana ventricosa*) in which the nesting birds perch, well concealed, on their approach to and departure from the nest; preferred nest trees usually have a large girth (>300 mm diameter), are smooth-surfaced and barkless; nest-holes have a 50 mm-wide entrance, leading into a cavity about 150 mm wide and 250-280 mm deep; the eggs are laid here on a bed of wood chips. During the nestling period the chicks utter a continual whurring sound that is audible from up to 40 m away. Holes are probably seldom reused, given the decayed state of the stumps selected for nests.
Laying months: Nov-Jan (Ongoye). **Clutch size:** 5 (Ongoye). **Eggs:** 23.5-24.4-24.8 x 17.2-17.4-17.9 mm (Malawi); white, unmarked (not illustrated). **Incubation period:** 18 days (Ongoye); by both sexes. **Nestling/fledging period:** 39 days (Ongoye); young brooded and fed by both sexes.

Yellow-rumped Tinkerbird *Pogonolius bilineatus* Swartblestinker   page 382

Breeds in and adjacent to coastal, lowland and riparian forest. Pairs nest solitarily. **Nest:** excavated by both sexes; a hole in a dead branch, usually in the underside of a sloping, thin (85-105 mm diameter) branch some distance up from the ground (1½-10 m); seldom as close to the ground as a Red-fronted Tinkerbird's nest. The entrance hole is tiny (22-25 mm in diameter) and it leads in at right-angles for about 25 mm before descending into a chamber, about 45-50 mm in diameter and 37-250-1000 mm deep; eggs are laid here on a bed of wood chips. Nest-holes seldom survive for reuse but the next season's hole is sometimes excavated in the same branch. Holes may be used as night-time roosts when the birds are not breeding. Well-grown nestlings often give away their presence by their persistent calling from the nest-hole.
Laying months: mainly Nov-Jan (Sep-Mar); sometimes double-brooded. **Clutch size:** 3-4 (2-5). **Eggs:** 17.8-19.2-19.8 x 13.7-14.1-14.7 mm; in Kenya recorded hosting Scaly-throated Honeyguide (which had to widen nest entrance to gain entry). **Incubation period:** about 12 days (Kenya); by both sexes. **Nestling/fledging period:** 25 days; young brooded and fed by both sexes.

Crested Barbet *Trachyphonus vaillantii* Kuifkophoutkapper   page 382

Breeds in well-wooded mesic savanna, its range much extended into the grassland region as a result of urbanisation and the widespread introduction of alien trees. Pairs nest solitarily and are widely spaced; it is not a cooperative breeder. **Nest:** a hole in a tree, excavated by both sexes; it is invariably in dead wood, either in a main trunk or side branch, often a dead branch within a living tree, and is as likely in a vertical stem as in the underside of a sloping branch; typically 1½-4½ m up (rarely >7 m). Some nests have vertical- rather than side-entrance holes; the latter measures 45-50 mm wide and it enters the stem at right-angles before it descends to the chamber 60-80 mm wide and about 300-400 mm deep; eggs are laid here on a bed of wood chips. Nest logs attached to trees in gardens are commonly used; holes are often reused for successive broods and, if they survive, in successive years; reused nests are usually deepened by the birds; holes are also used as night-time roosts when the birds are not nesting.
Laying months: mainly Sep-Dec (Aug-Mar, rarely in other months); regularly double- or multiple-brooded. **Clutch size:** 3-4 (2-5), laid at 1-day intervals. **Eggs:** 22.4-26.4-29.1 x 17.1-19.4-21.7 mm; occasionally parasitised by Greater and Lesser honeyguides. **Incubation period:** 15 days (14-16); by both sexes; begins before clutch is completed. **Nestling/fledging period:** 29 days (27-31); young brooded and fed by both sexes.

Yellow-fronted Tinkerbird

Red-fronted Tinkerbird

Green Barbet

Yellow-rumped Tinkerbird

Crested Barbet

Honeyguides

HONEYGUIDES Family Indicatoridae Worldwide 17 species; 15 breed in Afrotropics, 6 in southern Africa. Breeding habits of many are poorly known; all are polygynous, ♂s calling in summer from call-sites to attract ♀s. All are parasitic, some parasitising just a single species, others having multiple hosts. ♀s lay 1egg/host nest (rarely two) and they may or may not damage or remove host eggs when doing so; eggs are oval, white, unmarked (also pale blue in one); most match the host egg and are distinguishable either by size difference or by shell texture (honeyguide egg glossier, with denser pore structure). Honeyguide chick is born with sharp hooks at the tip of its upper and lower mandibles and it bites nest siblings to death; hooks disappear after 1-2 weeks.

Greater Honeyguide *Indicator indicator* Grootheuningwyser

Breeds widely across the mesic savanna, extending into the grasslands, karoo and fynbos where riparian woodland or alien vegetation especially eucalypts, and availability of hosts, permit. During summer (Sep-Mar) ♂ Greater Honeyguides maintain call-sites to which ♀s are attracted to mate; sites are reoccupied annually, some in known use for decades (one since 1930). At least 29 host species have been recorded, the most frequent being species that nest in tunnels in earth banks (Pied Starling, Ant-eating Chat, White-fronted, Little and other bee-eaters, martins, kingfishers). Second-most frequent are tree hole-nesters (barbets, woodpeckers, African Hoopoe, Green Woodhoopoe, tits, starlings) and the third are swallows that build tunnel nests. There is overlap in hosts used by this and Lesser and Scaly-throated honeyguides and a suspected honeyguide egg in a host-nest can only be identified once it has hatched and the nestling is well grown. ♀s lay 1 egg/host clutch (rarely 2); host eggs not removed but may be damaged during laying. A ♀ lays an estimated 21 eggs/season. Very occasionally, two honeyguide nestlings are reared in one nest.
Laying months: mainly Oct-Nov (Sep-Jan). Eggs: 21.0-24.3-26.0 × 17.1-18.8-20.0 mm; mass 5.2 g. **Incubation period:** not recorded. **Nestling/fledging period:** about 38 days.

Scaly-throated Honeyguide *Indicator variegatus* Gevlekte Heuningwyser

Breeds in coastal, lowland, riparian and montane forest. Breeding habits are poorly known in the region. ♂s call through the breeding season from traditionally used call-sites (some of these in known use for decades) to which ♀s are attracted. Recorded hosts in southern Africa are 4 woodpecker species (Cardinal, Olive, Golden-tailed, Knysna) and Black-collared Barbet. ♀s lay 1egg/host-nest.
Laying months: Sep-Jan. Eggs: 20.0-21.3-22.8 × 16.5-16.9-18.0 mm; mass 4.2-4.8 g. **Incubation period:** est. 18 days (Malawi). **Nestling/fledging period:** 27-35 days (Malawi).

Lesser Honeyguide *Indicator minor* Kleinheuningwyser

Breeds widely, but largely absent from the arid west. ♂s maintain a call-site during summer to which ♀s are attracted to mate. Primary hosts in southern Africa are barbets (especially Black-collared and Acacia Pied barbets) but numerous other hole-nesters have also been recorded, including White-eared and Crested barbets, Red-throated Wryneck, Golden-tailed and Olive woodpeckers, Green Woodhoopoe, Striped Kingfisher, Little Bee-eater, Common, Cape Glossy, Pied and Violet-backed starlings, Yellow-throated Petronia; also White-throated Swallow and Cape Rock Thrush – some of these, perhaps, were cases of misidentification with Greater Honeyguide. The ♀ lays 1 egg/host nest (rarely more) and it may remove or damage a host egg in the process. A ♀ is estimated to lay 18-20 eggs/season at an average interval of 5 days between eggs.
Laying months: mainly Oct-Dec (Sep-Feb). Eggs: 20.0-21.5-24.0 × 16.1-17.0-19.6 mm; mass 2.9 g. **Incubation period:** 12 days. **Nestling/fledging period:** 37-38 days.

Pallid Honeyguide *Indicator meliphilus* Oostelike Heuningwyser

A scarce resident in n lowland forests in Mozambique and e Zimbabwe. Breeding habits are essentially unknown. Possible hosts include Golden-rumped Tinkerbird (East Africa) and White-eared Barbet (e Zimbabwe). Circumstantial evidence of White-eared Barbets being a host in the region include a report of the honeyguide worrying a nesting pair of these barbets in Nov, and a clutch of barbet eggs, collected in Jan, which included a smaller egg (21 × 17 mm) that may or may not have been laid by this honeyguide.

Brown-backed Honeybird *Prodotiscus regulus* Skerpbekheuningvoël

Breeds in wooded habitats in mesic savanna and grassland. Breeding habits are poorly known; the eggs have not yet been described and virtually all breeding records refer to recently fledged young being attended by foster-parents. In all recorded cases, small warblers and cisticolas that make enclosed nests have been the hosts involved; Neddicky is the most frequently recorded one; also Tinkling Levaillant's, Lazy, Wailing, Rattling cisticolas; Tawny-flanked, Black-chested and Karoo prinias, and Grey-backed Camaroptera. Other named hosts lack unequivocal evidence. Three honeybird nestlings were reported in one parasitised nest.
Laying months: Nov (Nov-Feb). Eggs: no data. **Incubation period:** not recorded. **Nestling/fledging period:** estimated 17-21 days.

Green-backed Honeybird *Prodotiscus zambesiae* Dunbekheuningvoël

Breeds in n savanna in miombo woodland. It parasitises a single host, the Yellow White-eye, in a short (2 month) breeding season when the ♂ maintains a display territory from which he calls and performs aerial flights to attract ♀s. She lays 1 egg/host nest (occasionally 2) and removes one or more host eggs. Individual ♀s either lay a blue or a white egg as do ♀ Yellow White-eyes and in most cases, the honeybird ♀ seeks out a host-nest with an egg matching its own. Two honeybirds are occasionally raised in the same nest. The incidence of parasitism of white-eye nests varies between 3-27%.
Laying months: Sep-Oct (Zimbabwe). Eggs: 14.3-14.9-15.2 × 11.5-11.9-12.1 mm; white or blue, unmarked; indistinguishable from eggs of host (Yellow White-eye) unless texture is closely examined: the white-eye egg is smooth-shelled with scattered pores, the honeyguide egg has a rougher texture (resembling an orange skin) with closely packed pores. **Incubation period:** <13 days. **Nestling/fledging period:** 20-22 days.

Greater Honeyguide (left egg)
parasitising
Violet-backed Starling (two right eggs)

Greater Honeyguide (left egg)
parasitising
Little Bee-eater (two right eggs)

Greater Honeyguide (left egg)
parasitising
Cape Glossy Starling (two right eggs)

Scaly-throated Honeyguide (left egg)
parasitising
Golden-tailed Woodpecker (two right eggs)

Lesser Honeyguide (left egg)
parasitising
Black-collared Barbet (two right eggs)

Lesser Honeyguide (left egg)
parasitising
Striped Kingfisher (two right eggs)

Green-backed Honeybird (left egg)
parasitising
African Yellow White-eye (two right eggs)

Woodpeckers

WOODPECKERS, WRYNECKS Family Picidae Worldwide 225 species; 29 breed in Afrotropics, 10 in southern Africa. They are monogamous; nest solitarily; both sexes incubate and share parental care; are renowned for excavating their nest-holes in the trunks of trees; unlike barbets, several species excavate their holes in hard wood and these endure for years, even decades, and provide secondary nest sites to many other hole-nesting birds; one species (Ground Woodpecker) instead makes a tunnel in an earth bank, and one (Red-throated Wryneck) doesn't excavate a nest-hole for itself, but uses an existing hole; eggs are oval-shaped, glossy white, unmarked, 2-3/clutch; nestlings are altricial and nidicolous. Most species are parasitised by one or more species of honeyguide.

Olive Woodpecker *Mesopicos griseocephalus* Gryskopspeg   page 383

Breeds, in South Africa (race *M. g. griseocephalus*, extending from w Cape to the Soutpansberg), in montane forest, extending marginally into adjacent non-forested wooded habitats that include gardens, tall fynbos and alien plantations. A second population that occurs widely across tropical Africa (race *M. g. ruwenzori*) reaches its s limit in e Caprivi and nw Zimbabwe and here is restricted to riparian forest. Pairs nest solitarily and, in montane forest, nest at densities of a pair/40-60 ha. **Nest:** a hole is excavated into a dead tree stem, usually a large, decayed, barkless vertical trunk of a soft-wood tree (e.g. *Xymalos monospora*) standing slightly apart from others in the forest. Nest height very variable, usually 4-10 m up from the ground (1½-18 m); several holes, reflecting previous years' nestings, may be found in the same trunk or branch. The nest-hole's entrance is oval-shaped, vertical axis longer than horizontal axis, about 47 x 43-44 mm, which leads into a cavity where the eggs are laid on a bed of wood chips. A new nest-hole is usually excavated each breeding season. Both sexes, but mainly the ♂, excavate the nest and the sound of their tapping at this time of the year often pinpoints the nest site.
Laying months: mainly Sep-Oct (Aug-Nov, rarely in other months). **Clutch size:** 2-3. **Eggs:** 23.3-24.2-26.2 x 17.6-18.2-18.8 mm; mass 4.3 g. Occasionally parasitised by Scaly-throated Honeyguide. **Incubation period:** 15-16 days (Malawi); by both sexes. **Nestling/fledging period:** 24-26 days (Malawi); young brooded and fed by both sexes.

Green-backed Woodpecker *Campethera cailliautii* Gevlekte Speg   page 383

Breeds in lowland forest, riparian forest and in associated lowland woodlands (including miombo); a tropical species that narrowly extends into southern Africa in c Mozambique and e Zimbabwe. Nesting habits are poorly known. Pairs nest solitarily. **Nest:** a typical woodpecker-type hole is excavated in a dead trunk or in a main branch of a forest tree, usually high up (7-15 m above the ground); both sexes excavate; holes are not normally reused in successive years.
Laying months: Sep-Feb. **Clutch size:** 2-3. **Eggs:** 22.6-23.9-24.7 x 18.0-18.2-18.4 mm. **Incubation period:** not recorded; by both sexes. **Nestling/fledging period:** not recorded; young brooded and fed by both sexes; food is carried in the crop and regurgitated to the nestlings.

Bearded Woodpecker *Thripias namaquus* Baardspeg   page 383

Breeds widely across the savanna belt from the semi-arid west to the mesic east and extending narrowly into e Cape; favours tall open woodland. Pairs nest solitarily and are widely spaced (>100 ha/pair). **Nest:** a hole is excavated into a substantial branch or trunk of a large tree, typically a stem 150-300 mm in diameter and at a height of 3-5 m (1,6-8 m) above the ground; partly or wholly dead trees are favoured nesting sites, especially old, dead, barkless, hard-wood trunks; the hole can be excavated into a vertical stem or in the underside of a sloping branch and no particular orientation is selected; the entrance hole is larger than those of other woodpeckers in the region, characteristically oval-shaped, vertical axis longer than horizontal, about 77 x 55 mm across. The nest chamber is 300-380-500 mm deep and the eggs are laid in it on a bed of wood chips. Nest-holes are often reused in successive years, usually deepened each time used, and any lining material brought in by other occupants (starlings, etc) is removed. If a new hole is excavated, it is frequently in the same branch, or near to a previously used hole; branches occasionally have several (3-10) such holes in them. Both sexes excavate, taking 30-40 days to complete a nest. Nest-holes excavated into hard wood may last for years, even decades.
Laying months: mainly May-Aug (Apr-Dec); single-brooded. **Clutch size:** 2 (1-3, rarely 4); laid at a 1-day interval. **Eggs:** 24.1-25.5-28.0 x 17.5-19.1-20.3 mm; mass 4.8 g. **Incubation period:** 13 days; by both sexes, in shifts of 18-70 min. **Nestling/fledging period:** 27 days; young brooded and fed by both sexes.

Cardinal Woodpecker *Dendropicos fuscescens* Kardinaalspeg   page 383

The region's most common woodpecker, breeding widely across the savanna belt and extending into grassland, karoo and fynbos wherever riparian vegetation or introduced trees provide habitat. Pairs nest solitarily and are widely spaced. **Nest:** a hole is excavated into a thinnish (120-230 mm diameter), usually dead, stub or stem of a tree, often on the underside of a sloping branch and typically about 2 m up from the ground (0,9-4 m); the nest entrance is oval-shaped, vertical axis longer than horizontal, about 44 x 37 mm, leading into a chamber 100-190-250 mm deep, where the eggs are laid on a bed of dry wood chips. A new nest-hole is excavated each year, seldom in the vicinity of a previous year's nest. Both sexes excavate, completing a nest in 13-21 days; nesting birds often call in the vicinity of the nest while excavating but become quiet and unobtrusive once incubation commences.
Laying months: mainly Aug-Oct (Jul-Dec, occasionally other months); single-brooded. **Clutch size:** 2 (1-3); laid at a 1-day interval; occasionally parasitised by honeyguides, including Lesser and Scaly-throated. **Eggs:** 18.2-21.0-23.0 x 15.0-16.1-17.2 mm. **Incubation period:** 12½ days; by both sexes; begins when clutch is completed. **Nestling/fledging period:** 27 days; young are brooded and fed by both sexes.

Olive Woodpecker

Green-backed Woodpecker

Bearded Woodpecker

Cardinal Woodpecker

Woodpeckers

Ground Woodpecker *Geocolaptes olivaceus* **Grondspeg** page 383

Breeds in rock- and boulder-strewn hills and mountains, usually in treeless country in the grassland, karoo and fynbos regions where a suitable nest site (an earth bank) is available. Pairs nest solitarily and (in family groups after breeding) are territorial year-round, at densities of a pair/21-70 ha. **Nest:** a tunnel is excavated into a vertical earth bank, typically 1-2 m in height (2-6 m recorded), either along a river, in the wall of a donga, in a road cutting or in the wall of a gravel pit; rarely in a termite mound, in the crumbling earth wall of an abandoned farmhouse, or in a deep crevice between rocks. The hole is usually excavated into the upper part of the bank, and in road cuttings or gravel pits it is often in the thin soil layer just below the top of the bank. It is ½-1 m in length, about 70-80 mm in diameter, and it widens at the end to a chamber about 150 mm across; nest tunnels usually slope gently upwards and, in hard substrates, often have an uneven, irregular passage, swinging left or right (to avoid rocks) before widening into the chamber. Tunnels are not routinely reused in successive years; more usually, the pair excavate a new tunnel each season, often in the same bank; both sexes exacavate, doing this at any time of the year; tunnels are also used as night-time roosts. Sometimes nests in banks alongside Pied Starlings (and other bank hole-nesters), and here a tunnel originally excavated by the starlings may also be used.
Laying months: mainly Aug-Sep (Jul-Dec); single-brooded. **Clutch size:** 3 (2-4). **Eggs:** 24.4-27.9-30.2 x 20.2-21.8-22.9 mm; 1 record of parasitism by Great Spotted Cuckoo. **Incubation period:** not recorded; by both sexes, alternating in ½-2½ hr shifts. **Nestling/fledging period:** not recorded; young brooded and fed by both sexes.

Golden-tailed Woodpecker *Campethera abingoni* **Goudstertspeg** pages 179, 383

Breeds widely across the savanna belt, from the semi-arid west to the mesic east, extending into coastal and lowland forest in the east and into the grassland and karoo where riparian growth along rivers provides habitat. Pairs nest solitarily and are widely spaced. **Nest:** a hole is excavated in a dead tree, typically in the main stem of a tree about 150-300 mm in diameter, often close to the ground (<2 m up, range ½-5 m), and commonly excavated into the underside of a sloping trunk, rather than in a vertical stem; the entrance hole is circular, 50-53 mm in diameter and it leads into the nest cavity, 200-380 mm deep; the eggs are laid here on a bed of wood chips. A new nest-hole is usually made each season; less often an existing hole is reused; new holes are sometimes excavated into the same branch used previously. Both sexes excavate, completing a hole in 2-3 weeks. Nestlings often give the position of a nest away by their continuous, low churring food-begging call, audible from 30 m away.
Laying months: mainly Sep-Nov (Aug-Dec); single-brooded. **Clutch size:** 2-3, rarely 4; occasionally parasitised by Greater, Lesser and Scaly-throated honeyguides. **Eggs:** 22.5-24.6-26.5 x 17.3-18.4-19.5 mm. **Incubation period:** 13 days; shared equally during the day by both sexes, by ♂ at night. **Nestling/fledging period:** 22-25 days; young brooded and fed by both sexes.

Knysna Woodpecker *Campethera notata* **Knysnaspeg** page 383

Breeds in a narrow range across s and e Cape in riparian and coastal forest, euphorbia thickets and valley bushveld. Pairs nest solitarily and are widely spaced. **Nest:** a hole is excavated in a dead branch, stub or trunk of a tree, often in a *Mimusops*, *Erythrina*, *Schotia* or *Euphorbia*; a stem about 150-300 mm in diameter is favoured; sisal stems attached to a branches are also used; the nest varies in height between 1.2-6 m up from the ground; the nest entrance is circular, about 45 mm in diameter, and it leads into a chamber 150-300 mm deep where the eggs are laid on a bed of wood chips; existing holes are regularly reused in successive years; if not, a new hole is sometimes excavated in the same branch. Nestlings frequently make a continuous, low churring sound which often gives away the presence of the nest.
Laying months: mainly Oct (Aug-Nov); single-brooded. **Clutch size:** 2-4; parasitised by Greater and Scaly-throated honeyguides. **Eggs:** 22.7-23.5-24.5 x 17.5-18.1-18.7 mm; mass 3.9 g. **Incubation period:** not recorded. **Nestling/fledging period:** not recorded; young fed by both sexes; food carried to nest in crop and regurgitated to nestlings.

Bennett's Woodpecker *Campethera bennettii* **Bennettse Speg** page 383

Breeds widely across the savanna belt from the semi-arid west to the mesic east, favouring open woodland with tall, scattered trees. Pairs nest solitarily and are widely spaced. **Nest:** pairs may excavate their own nest-hole, but as often they occupy an existing hole originally made by some other woodpecker. When excavating their own hole (both sexes doing this), it is typically 2-4 m up from the ground (2-8) in a vertical or sloping, live or dead tree trunk, with a circular entrance hole 45-47 mm in diameter which leads into a chamber 230-330-460 mm deep; the eggs are laid on a bed of wood chips or on whatever nest material was brought in by previous occupants. The same hole may be reused for successive broods, and in successive years, and, as shown opposite, holes used by this species frequently have a dilapidated appearance.
Laying months: mainly Oct-Dec (Aug-Feb); usually relays after an early failure; rarely double-brooded. **Clutch size:** 3 (2-6); laid at 1-day intervals; reported clutches >4 probably include undetected honeyguide eggs. **Eggs:** 21.4-23.7-28.1 x 16.6-18.3-20.2 mm; mass 4.7 g. **Incubation period:** 15-18 days; by both sexes, shared equally. **Nestling/fledging period:** 26-27 days; young brooded and fed by both sexes; food is carried in the crop and regurgitated to nestlings.

Speckle-throated Woodpecker *Campethera scripticoricauda* **Tanzaniese Speg** page 383

Closely related to Bennett's Woodpecker and perhaps conspecific, this species narrowly enters southern Africa in e Mozambique where it occurs in lowland forest and tall miombo woodland; breeding has not yet been recorded here. Its nesting habits are poorly known but probably do not differ from those of Bennett's Woodpecker. **Nest:** a hole excavated in a dead tree branch or palm trunk.
Laying months: Oct-Nov (Malawi). **Clutch size:** 3. **Eggs:** 26.5-27.1-27.4 x 19.7-20.2-20.5 mm. **Incubation period:** not recorded. **Nestling/fledging period:** not recorded.

Ground Woodpecker

Ground Woodpecker

Golden-tailed Woodpecker

Knysna Woodpecker

Bennett's Woodpecker

Red-throated Wryneck *Jynx ruficollis* **Draaihals** page 383

Breeds in South African grasslands where scattered trees (acacias, *Protea caffra*, eucalypts, willows and other introduced aliens) provide nesting and roosting sites. Pairs nest solitarily and are territorial year-round at densities of a pair/8-35 ha; adjacent nests usually >300 m apart. **Nest**: a hole in a tree is used, either a natural cavity or, more often, an old woodpecker or barbet (Black-collared or Crested barbet) hole; it also uses nest boxes and hollow, vertical, metal fence posts, and once reported using the closed chamber of a Greater Striped Swallow nest. Nest holes are typically 3-4 m (½-9) up from the ground, and the cavity is 200-300-800 mm deep. While they do not excavate holes for themselves, they probably peck out the interior walls of the cavity to provide wood chips that form the base of the nest on which the eggs are laid. Holes are commonly reused for successive broods, they are less often used in successive seasons and are sometimes used as night-time roosts outside the breeding season. The birds are most vocal in the 1-2 months before laying, but once incubation commences they become relatively quiet.
Laying months: mainly Oct (Aug-Feb); sometimes double- or multiple-brooded. **Clutch size**: 3-4 (2-6); reported clutches >4 probably include undetected honeyguide eggs; laid at 1-day intervals. **Eggs**: 19.8-21.5-23.5 × 15.1-16.6-17.5 mm; mass 3.5 g; occasionally parasitised by Lesser Honeyguide. **Incubation period**: 13 days (12-14); by both sexes; begins before clutch is completed. **Nestling/fledging period**: 25 days (25-26); young brooded and fed by both sexes.

PITTAS Family Pittidae Worldwide 32 species; 2 breed in Afrotropics, 1 in southern Africa. Monogamous; pairs nest solitarily; both sexes build a domed nest of twigs in a tree or creeper; both sexes share the incubation and parental care; eggs broad-oval in shape; cream with dark spots, 3/clutch; nestlings are altricial and nidicolous.

African Pitta *Pitta angolensis* **Angolapitta** page 383

A summer-breeding visitor to lowland and riparian forest and dense deciduous thickets in e Zimbabwe and c Mozambique, arriving in Nov-Dec. The birds display and call conspicuously in the first few weeks of its arrival which coincides with the first summer rains, then become largely silent once breeding is underway. Pairs nest solitarily in the dense, dark thickets they inhabit and adjacent pairs may breed within 150 m of each other. **Nest**: a large enclosed ball of twigs placed 2-8 m up from the ground, built in the fork of a sapling or in the thorny foliaged branches of *Acacia ataxacantha*, *Ziziphus*, *Ximenia*, *Dicrostachys cinerea* or some other thorny tree. The nest is widest at its base (250 × 350 mm) and has a broad shelf below the entrance hole that serves as a landing platform. Overall, the nest is 180-200 mm high, and it encloses an interior nest chamber that is about 100 mm in diameter and 80 mm in height. The nest entrance is 70-80 mm wide and 60 mm high and the nest contents are easily visible from outside. Dry twigs up to 300 mm long and 5 mm thick, tendrils and long petioles are used to construct the nest, coarse material being used in the base, and finer material, including dry leaves, used in the roof; the nest-cup is lined with pieces of leaf and leaf-stalk. It is a bulky, untidy, dark-coloured nest that is usually easily visible. Nests often survive long after breeding is completed and the old nests can be easily located in winter when the nest tree has shed its foliage. Nests are built by both sexes and they are frequently placed near a previous year's nest.
Laying months: mainly Nov-Dec (Nov-Jan). **Clutch size**: 3 (2-4). **Eggs**: 24.8-27.6-29.1 × 21.9-23.3-25.0 mm; mass 7.2-7.7-8.2 g. **Incubation period**: not recorded; by both sexes, with brief change-overs 2x/day, in early morning and late afternoon. **Nestling/fledging period**: not recorded.

BROADBILLS Family Eurylaimidae Worldwide 20 species; 4 breed in Afrotropics, 1 in southern Africa. Monogamous; pairs nest solitarily; nest an enclosed pouch, suspended from a twig; both sexes build the nest, ♀ incubates, both sexes feed young; eggs oval-shaped, white, unmarked, slightly glossy, 2-3/clutch; nestlings are altricial and nidicolous.

African Broadbill *Smithornis capensis* **Breëbek** page 383

Breeds in coastal-, dune- and riparian forests at low altitudes, also deciduous thickets, favouring dark sites under a close canopy. Pairs nest solitarily, in optimum habitat, 100-150 m apart. **Nest**: distinctive and unlike the nest of any other southern African bird, an oval-shaped ball with a trailing tail below that gives it the appearance of some debris that has caught onto a branch; it is built within a metre or two of the ground (1.2-2.8 m), attached to a horizontal twig that extends out from the main stem of a sapling, usually hanging clear of foliage and frequently suspended over a small stream or gully. The nest is firmly attached to the twig along its entire roof length. and it measures about 110 mm high, 80-90 mm wide and 85-120 mm from front-to-back; it has a large, roughly triangular-shaped entrance hole that faces out from the nest tree, this measuring 45-60 mm high and 35-45 mm wide; the nest-cup inside is about 60 mm down from the lower lip of the entrance. The tail that trails below the nest is variable in length, between 140-660 mm. Nest materials used also vary between nests and areas and their choice results in nests being variably coloured; some are made entirely with *Usnea* lichen and these are pale green (see centre photograph); others are made from flakes of bark, dry leaves, grass, tendrils, twigs, rootlets and are brownish nests (left photograph), or they are made from fibres of *Marasmius* fungus and these are black; cobweb is used sparsely to bind the nest together; the nest-cup is sometimes lined with finer material. Nests are frequently built in the vicinity of a past nest and sometimes rebuilt on the same twig. Both sexes build, and material from old nest may be recycled for use in the the new nest.
Laying months: mainly Nov (Sep-Feb). **Clutch size**: 2-3, occasionally 1. **Eggs**: 19.0-21.7-23.6 × 14.5-15.4-16.1 mm; mass 2.6-2.8 g. **Incubation period**: 16-17 days; by ♀ only, leaves nest every ½-2 hrs to feed. **Nestling/fledging period**: not recorded; young fed by both sexes.

Red-throated Wryneck

Red-throated Wryneck

African Pitta

African Broadbill

BATISES, WATTLE-EYES & ALLIES Family Platysteiridae Worldwide 32 species; all endemic to Afrotropics, 8 breed in southern Africa. Batises and their allies (*Platysteira*, *Bias*, *Lanioturdus*) were previously grouped with the flycatcher family Muscicapidae, but DNA evidence shows they comprise a family of their own with the closest affinity to helmetshrikes and bushshrikes. Monogamous; the ♀ in most species plays the greater role in the nesting cycle (building, incubating, brooding young); ♂ provisions her and the nestlings; nest is a small well-camouflaged cup on a branch; eggs oval-shaped, white, buff, pale green-blue, speckled or blotched with red-brown; 2/clutch; nestlings are altricial and nidicolous; batises are regular hosts to Klaas's Cuckoo.

Cape Batis *Batis capensis* Kaapse Bosbontrokkie   page 384

Breeds in montane and lowland forest, including small, isolated patches of relict forest and scrub-forest. Pairs nest solitarily, are territorial year-round and nest at a density of about a pair/0.3-1.0 ha. **Nest:** a small, neat, thick-walled cup, somewhat globular in shape (i.e. the sides bulge out at the middle), placed in a tree or sapling from close to the ground to the mid-canopy of a large tree (0.8-9½ m); favoured nest sites are lichen-covered branches about 30-50 mm thick; the nest is made with shreds of bark and other fibrous plant material, bound into a firm-walled structure with cobweb; the outer walls are covered with pieces of grey lichen and these effectively camouflage the nest when built on a lichen-covered branch; the cup is neatly lined with fine grass ends. Nests show little variation in size. It measures: outside diameter 60-80 mm; cup diameter 50 mm; cup depth 30 mm; nest height 50 mm. The nest is frequently built on or close to the site of a previous year's nest; it is built mainly or entirely by the ♀, and can remain empty for 15 days before the first egg is laid; the ♀ is fed frequently by the ♂ during this time and she solicits food from him by uttering a characteristic food-begging call.
Laying months: mainly Oct-Dec (Aug-Jan); peaks a month earlier in sw Cape than elsewhere; may relay after an earlier nest loss. **Clutch size:** 2 (1-3); laid at 1-2 day interval. **Eggs:** 16.3-18.0-21.0 × 12.6-13.9-15.2 mm; parasitised by Klaas's Cuckoo which closely matches the host egg in size and colour. **Incubation period:** 18 days (17-21); begins when clutch is completed; by ♀ only; she leaves nest briefly (2-7-12 min) at about 2-hr intervals to feed. **Nestling/fledging period:** 16 days; young brooded by ♀ only; fed by both sexes.

Pririt Batis *Batis pririt* Priritbosbontrokkie   page 384

Breeds widely across the arid savanna and across the karoo into desert where acacia thornveld along watercourses provides habitat. Pairs nest solitarily and are widely spaced. **Nest:** a small, neat, cup-shaped structure, typical of a batis, but distinctive in having higher nest walls clad on the outside with small, rough shards of tree bark (rarely with lichen, unlike other batises); it is placed on a branch, often a dead one, at no great height, typically 1½-3 m (0.7-8 m) up from the ground. It is made of fibrous, dry shreds of plant material curled around to form the bowl and firmly bound together with cobweb. It measures: outside diameter 60 mm; cup diameter 40 mm; nest height 30 mm. It is built by both sexes, but mainly by the ♀, accompanied by the ♂; while nest-building and through the incubation she makes a characteristic food-begging call and she is fed by the ♂; she lays up to 5 days after nest completion.
Laying months: lays opportunistically in response to rainfall in extreme arid areas; otherwise mainly Oct-Mar, peaking earlier in the south than the north. **Clutch size:** 2 (rarely 1, 3 or 4; larger clutches reported possibly from undetected eggs of Klaas's Cuckoo); laid at 1-day interval. **Eggs:** 15.7-16.5-18.1 × 12.0-12.7-13.3 mm; infrequently parasitised by Klaas's Cuckoo which matches the host egg in size but is larger. **Incubation period:** 17 days; by ♀ only, fed by ♂; starts with 2nd-laid egg. **Nestling/fledging period:** 16 days (15-18); young brooded by ♀ only, fed by both sexes.

Chinspot Batis *Batis molitor* Witliesbosbontrokkie   page 384

Breeds in the mesic east of the savanna belt, extending into e Cape; occurs commonly in both acacia thornveld and broad-leafed woodland. Pairs nest solitarily, are territorial year-round, and occur at densities of about a pair/5-15 ha. **Nest:** a small neat cup, made with shreds of weed bark and other fibrous plant material, firmly bound together with cobweb; the outer walls are invariably clad with pieces of grey lichen and, rarely, also with flakes of bark; it is built on the branch of a tree or sapling, mostly 3-5 m up from the ground (1-10 m), typically on a horizontal, dead, lichen-covered branch where the nest's lichen cladding matches the substrate. The nest measures: outside diameter 55 mm; cup diameter 40-42 mm; cup depth 22-26 mm; nest height 30-40 mm. It is built by both sexes in 3-4 days but it may remain empty for a further 10-14 days before laying. Some are built close to the site of a previous year's nest. The ♀ utters a characteristic food-begging call and is fed by the ♂ during nest-building and through the incubation.
Laying months: mainly Sep-Dec (Aug-Feb, once May); peaks earlier in Zimbabwe (Sep-Oct) than further south (Oct-Nov); usually relays after an early loss; occasionally double-brooded. **Clutch size:** 2, rarely 3 or 4 (perhaps undetected eggs of Klaas's Cuckoo?) laid at a 1-day interval. **Eggs:** 15.4-17.3-19.0 × 11.9-13.0-14.2 mm; occasionally parasitised by Klaas's Cuckoo. **Incubation period:** 17 days (16-18); begins when clutch is completed; by ♀ only; she leaves nest briefly (6-16 min) at about ½-hr intervals to feed. **Nestling/fledging period:** 17 days (16-18); young brooded by ♀ only; fed by both sexes.

Pale Batis *Batis soror* Mosambiekbosbontrokkie   no nest photo   page 384

Breeds in lowland woodlands and riparian forest in Mozambique and e Zimbabwe. Pairs nest solitarily, living in territories <3 ha in size. **Nest:** a small, deep cup, resembling that of a Chinspot Batis, placed in a forked branch (30-40 mm in diameter) of a tree typically 4-6 m up in woodland (4-10 m); higher in riparian forest (14-37 m); horizontal and dead branches are favoured; it is built with thin shreds of tree bark, bound with cobweb, the outer walls thickly decorated with lichen; the cup is finely lined with plant fibres. The nest measures: outside diameter 64 mm; cup diameter 39 mm; cup depth 20 mm; it is built by the ♀, escorted by the ♂.
Laying months: mainly Sep (Aug-Nov). **Clutch size:** 2. **Eggs:** 15.2-16.3-17.2 × 12.1-12.5-13.6 mm. **Incubation period:** not recorded; by ♀ only, fed by ♂. **Nestling/fledging period:** not recorded; young fed by both sexes, but mainly by the ♀.

Cape Batis

Pririt Batis

Chinspot Batis (THREE ABOVE)

Wattle-eye, Batis, Shrike, Flycatcher

Black-throated Wattle-eye *Platysteira peltata* Beloogbosbontrokkie   page 384

Breeds in coastal mangroves and lowland, coastal and riparian forest, extending up larger rivers into drier habitats. Pairs nest solitarily and are widely spaced. **Nest:** a small, rather shallow cup, built of thin, pliable strips of inner bark and fibrous plant material, with a small amount of cobweb used to strengthen the nest walls and bind the nest to the branch; it is placed in a slender fork of a tree or sapling; in places (e.g. mangrove swamp) it nests close to the ground, <2 m up, usually in a spindly, sub-canopy sapling, whereas in riparian forest it may be as high as 12 m up in the mid-stratum of a large tree, often among thick foliage and trailing creepers. Little or no lichen is used to decorate the nest walls and the nest is not usually built on a lichen-covered branch; it relies on its smallness and position among foliage, rather than being camouflaged, for concealment. It measures: outside diameter 50 mm; nest thickness 25 mm; an old African Paradise Flycatcher nest has also been recorded being used. The nest is built by both sexes, but mainly by the ♀, fed by the ♂ then and while incubating; during this period she often utters a characteristic food-begging call. Nests in successive years are frequently built close to a previous year's nest.
Laying months: mainly Oct-Dec (Aug-Feb); usually relays after an early loss. **Clutch size:** 2; rarely 1 or 3. **Eggs:** 16.5-17.9-18.5 x 13.0-13.3-14.3 mm. **Incubation period:** 18 days (16-18); by ♀ only; fed by ♂ on nest. **Nestling/fledging period:** 16 days (14-16); young brooded and fed by both sexes.

Woodward's Batis *Batis fratrum* Woodwardse Bosbontrokkie   page 384

Breeds in lowland, riparian and coastal forests from n Zululand through Mozambique. Pairs nest solitarily and are widely spaced. Nesting habits are poorly known. **Nest:** a small, shallow cup placed in a creeper or on a thin, forked branch at no great height (about 0,8-2,8 m up from the ground), well below the forest canopy; it is made of shredded dry plant material, fine, dark rootlets, tendrils, lichens, pieces of dead leaf, loosely bound together and to the nest branch, with cobweb; its outside walls are sparingly decorated with fragments of bark and leaf. One nest measured: cup diameter 45 mm; cup depth 13 mm.
Laying months: Oct-Nov. **Clutch size:** 2, less often 3. **Eggs:** 16.3-18.1-19.3 x 12.4-13.1-14.1 mm; mass 1.8 g; one record of parasitism by Red-chested Cuckoo, probably a case of egg-dumping. **Incubation period:** not recorded; by ♀ only. **Nestling/fledging period:** not recorded; young brooded by ♀, fed by both sexes.

White-tailed Shrike *Lanioturdus torquatus* Kortstertlaksman   page 384

Breeds along the Namibian escarpment and adjacent areas in mopane and combretum woodlands; favours the bases and slopes of hills and drainage lines in the more arid areas. Pairs nest solitarily, occasionally with 1 helper (1/40 pairs); territorial year-round; nests of adjacent pairs typically ½ km apart (100 m - 1.3 km). **Nest:** a deep, thick-walled, compact open cup, typically 1-2 m up from the ground (0.4-8 m), usually in a dead or dying branch of a living tree; placed either in a fork or on a lateral branch about the same thickness as the nest; *Combretum apiculatum* is a favoured nest tree, with *Acacia* sp. and *Commiphora* sp. also being used. The nest is made with fibrous shreds of tree bark interwoven with cobweb; the exterior has a smooth finish and this and its pale colour blend with the (dead) branch on which it is usually placed. The nest-cup is neatly lined with fine, darker-coloured strands of dry grass. The nest measures: outside diameter 70-85 mm; cup diameter 50-60 mm; cup depth 30-40 mm; nest height 50-80 mm. It is built mostly by the ♀ and is completed in about 6 days; nests in successive years are only rarely placed near a previous year's nest.
Laying months: mainly Feb-Mar (Sep-Apr); double-brooded; relays after early nest loss. **Clutch size:** 2-3; laid at 1-day intervals. **Eggs:** 20.2-20.4-20.9 x 15.4-15.8-16.8 mm. **Incubation period:** 15 days; mainly by ♀, fed by ♂; starts with second-laid egg. **Nestling/fledging period:** 20 days; young brooded by ♀; fed by both sexes.

Vanga Flycatcher (Black-and-white Shrike-Flycatcher) *Bias musicus* Witpensvlieëvanger   page 384

Breeds in tall lowland and riparian forest in c Mozambique and e Zimbabwe. Pairs nest solitarily and are widely spaced. Few nests have been recorded in southern Africa and its nesting habits here are poorly known. **Nest:** a small, shallow cup, placed in a fork in the upper branches of a tall forest tree (e.g. *Newtonia buchananii*, *Khaya anthotheca*), 19-38 m above the ground (whereas in w Africa it may nest as low as 1,2 m up). It is made with pliable shreds of inner bark, curled around to form the nest bowl, with the outside walls thickly and smoothly plastered and bound to the branch with cobweb; in this respect it much resembles the nest of a helmetshrike but it is smaller and shallower. It measures: outside diameter 76 x 83 mm; cup diameter 53 mm; cup depth 18 mm; nest height 28 mm (w African nests are reportedly larger and deeper than this). The nest is built by the ♀ over a period of about a week, when she is accompanied on nest-building trips by the ♂ which frequently calls and displays at this time.
Laying months: Sep-Dec; occasionally double-brooded; may relay after clutch loss (w Africa). **Clutch size:** 2; laid at 1-day intervals (w Africa). **Eggs:** 19.0-19.1-19.2 x 15.2-15.2-15.3 mm. **Incubation period:** 18-19 days (w Africa); shared equally by both sexes during day, in 10-29-71 min shifts; ♀ at night (w Africa). **Nestling/fledging period:** 18-23 days (w Africa); young brooded and fed by both sexes.

Black-throated Wattle-eye

Woodward's Batis

White-tailed Shrike

Vanga Flycatcher

Helmetshrikes

HELMETSHRIKES Family Prionopidae Worldwide 8 species; all endemic to Afrotropics, 3 breed in southern Africa. Previously included in the diverse shrike family, DNA evidence shows the helmetshrikes to comprise a family of their own, more closely related to batises and bushshrikes than true shrikes. The helmetshrikes are best known for being obligate cooperative breeders, living year-round in family groups that comprise a pair plus 1-10 helpers; monogamous, but both sexes and the helpers share in incubation and nestling care; the helpers are not necessarily offspring of the dominant pair. The nest is an open cup, its exterior thickly plastered with cobweb so that it resembles the branch supporting it. Eggs are oval-shaped, white to pale turquoise with spots and blotches of red, brown and grey; 3-4/clutch; the nestlings are altricial and nidicolous. One species is commonly parasitised by the Thick-billed Cuckoo.

White Helmetshrike (White-crested Helmetshrike) *Prionops plumatus* Withelmlaksman   page 384

Breeds mainly in mesic broad-leafed woodlands, especially in miombo. Invariably a cooperative breeder, the pair assisted by about 4-5 (1-8) helpers. Territorial while breeding, at a density about a group/20 ha in miombo; the group has a single active nest at a time. **Nest:** a neat, deep, open cup, placed on a stout (about 80 mm diameter), horizontal or sloping branch, usually at a fork in the mid-stratum of a tree; it is usually about 5 m up from the ground (2-10 m) and blends well with the supporting branch as the outside walls are thickly plastered to a smooth finish with cobweb so that they resemble a swelling on the branch. The nest is made largely or entirely with pliable strips and shreds of inner-bark, coarser pieces being used at the base and finer pieces for the walls and cup lining; the cobweb applied to the outside walls also binds the nest to the branch. The nest measures: outside diameter 81-84-90 mm; cup diameter 63-68-71 mm; cup depth 24-26-28 mm; nest height 35-50-65 mm. Both sexes build the nest with some (<25%) assistance from helpers; it can be completed in 4 days but may remain unused for 1-11-21 days before the first egg is laid. The same nest tree and even nest position may be reused in a subsequent seasons. During the incubation and nestling periods the group visit the nest at intervals (for nest change-overs or to feed nestlings) and they draw attention to themselves and to the nest by calling frequently during these trips.
Laying months: mainly Sep-Nov (Aug-Apr); peaks earlier (Sep-Oct) in Zimbabwe than South Africa (Oct-Nov); relays after an early nest failure. **Clutch size:** 4 (2-5, rarely 7-9, probably laid by 2 ♀s); laid at 1-day intervals. **Eggs:** 18.5-20.6-23.5 x 14.5-16.0-18.0 mm. **Incubation period:** 17 days (16-21); by both sexes, assisted by helpers. **Nestling/fledging period:** 20 days (17-22); young brooded and fed by both sexes, assisted by helpers.

Retz's Helmetshrike *Prionops retzii* Swarthelmlaksman   pages 378, 384

Breeds in tall, broad-leafed woodlands in mesic savanna. Almost invariably a cooperative breeder (35/36 observations), the pair assisted by 3-5 (1-8, rarely more) helpers. Territorial while breeding, at a density about a group/20 ha; the group has a single active nest at a time. **Nest:** a broad open cup built in the upper branches of a tree on a stout (about 50 mm diameter), 2- or 3-pronged fork. It is usually placed higher up than the nest of a White Helmetshrike, typically about 7 m (3-17) from the ground and its nest also differs from that species by being less smoothly finished and having a shallower, broader cup. It is made with pliable shreds of inner-bark, leaf petioles and shreds of grass that are curled around to form the bowl and roughly plastered on the outside and bound to the branch with cobweb. The nest measures: outside diameter 100-110 mm; cup diameter 70-77 mm; cup depth 15-30 mm; nest thickness 35-50 mm. It is built by all members of the group and can be completed in 6-8 days. While building, and during the incubation and nestling periods, the group visit the nest at intervals and they draw attention to themselves, and the nest site, by their frequent calling during these trips.
Laying months: mainly Sep-Nov (Aug-Mar); relays after early nest failure; occasionally double-brooded. **Clutch size:** 3-4 (2-5). **Eggs:** 22.1-23.7-25.8 x 15.6-17.1-18.1 mm; ; commonly parasitised by Thick-billed Cuckoo (55% of 29 nests in Zimbabwe) which lays an egg that is a close match to the host's but it is usually more rounded (23.7 x 17.6 mm), more chalky in texture, and less well marked. **Incubation period:** 17-20 days; by both sexes, assisted by helpers; begins when clutch is complete. **Nestling/fledging period:** 20 days; young brooded and fed by both sexes, assisted by helpers.

Chestnut-fronted Helmetshrike *Prionops scopifrons* Stekelkophelmlaksman

Breeds in lowland and low-altitude riparian forest. Invariably a cooperative breeder, the pair assisted by about 5 (2-10) helpers. Nesting habits are poorly known. Family groups nest solitarily and are widely spaced. **Nest:** an open cup, broadly similar to the nests of other helmetshrikes, placed on a thickish (35-75 mm diameter) horizontal or sloping branch, usually at a fork, in the mid- to upper- canopy of a tree, 4½-12-21 m above the ground. It is made of pliable shreds of inner-bark and other fine plant material and the outer walls are thickly plastered to a smooth finish with cobweb which also binds the nest to the branch; this continues being added to nest during incubation. The nest measures: cup diameter 62 x 65 mm; cup depth 25 mm (Kenya); it is built by the pair assisted by helpers. While building and during the incubation and nestling periods the nest is frequently visited by the group and they draw attention to themselves and to the nest by their frequent calling.
Laying months: Oct-Dec. **Clutch size:** 3. **Eggs:** 19.0-19.5-20.0 x 15.2-15.3-15.3 mm; (not illustrated); very pale greyish-turquoise liberally spotted and flecked with lavender, brick and grey, concentrated in a zone near the blunt end (Kenya). **Incubation period:** not recorded; by both sexes and helpers, in shifts of 18-72-167 min. **Nestling/fledging period:** not recorded; young fed by both sexes and helpers.

White Helmetshrike

Retz's Helmetshrike nest contains a Thick-billed Cuckoo chick

White Helmetshrike (TWO ABOVE)

Retz's Helmetshrike

Chestnut-fronted Helmetshrike

Bushshrikes

BUSHSHRIKES Family Malaconotinae Worldwide 50 species; all endemic to Afrotropics, 17 breed in southern Africa. A diverse family that includes boubous, tchagras, puffbacks and brubrus; all are monogamous; nest-building, incubation and nestling care is shared by the sexes in all but a few (in Black-backed Puffback and Grey-headed Bushshrike incubation is by the ♀ only); the nest is an open cup, placed in a tree or bush, its architecture and finish varying from species to species; eggs short-oval to sub-elliptical; white, pale blue or pale green, variably speckled, scrolled, streaked or blotched in shades of red, brown and grey; 2-4/clutch; nestlings are altricial and nidicolous; boubous are regular hosts to Black Cuckoo and several other species are incidentally parasitised by Jacobin Cuckoo.

Grey-headed Bushshrike *Malaconotus blanchoti* Spookvoël page 384

Breeds mainly in mesic savannas, especially in tall woodland. Pairs nest solitarily and are widely spaced. **Nest:** a broad, shallow, open bowl, placed in the mid- or upper-branches of a leafy tree, typically 4-5 m (1,2-12) up from the ground; it is usually hidden in a cluster of thick foliage and twigs, often in a clump of mistletoe (*Viscum* or *Loranthus* sp.) or, occasionally, on an old nest (e.g. that of a dove, Grey Lourie or small accipiter). The base of the nest is made with pencil-thick, branched twigs, often lichen-covered, and these extend untidily from the base and sides, giving the nest some resemblance, when seen from below, to the nest of a small bird of prey. The cup is a shallow bowl, neatly lined with brown-coloured rootlets, fine creeper-stems or leaf petioles. The nest measures outside diameter 150-160-200 mm; cup diameter 70-88-100 mm; cup depth 45-50 mm; nest height 90 mm. Both sexes build taking 10 days to complete a nest. The ♂ calls frequently in the general nesting area at the start of breeding but becomes silent once incubation commences.
Laying months: mainly Sep-Nov (Sep-Feb, rarely in other months); relays in new nest after early clutch loss. **Clutch size:** 3 (2-4). **Eggs:** 26.5-29.4-32.1 x 19.3-20.6-21.8 mm. **Incubation period:** 18 days (15-21); by ♀ only, fed by ♂ on the nest. **Nestling/fledging period:** 22 days (20-24); young brooded and fed by ♀, provisioned by ♂.

Olive Bushshrike *Telophorus olivaceus* Olyfboslaksman page 384

Breeds in montane and coastal forest, in forest verges and in forest/woodland mosaics, nesting well below the forest canopy. Pairs nest solitarily and are widely spaced. **Nest:** a shallow cup, placed in a fork on thin, horizontal branches in a dense thorny bush or creeper (e.g. *Heterophylla* or *Scutia*), usually about 3 m (½-6) up from the ground and well concealed in foliage. It is made mainly with long, thin pieces of creeper tendril, also rootlets, *Usnea* or stems of fine grass that are curled around to form a shallow bowl with no particular nest lining added; the eggs can usually be seen from below through the floor of the nest. It measures: outside diameter 120-140 mm; cup diameter 65-95 mm; cup depth 20-25 mm; nest height 32-40 mm, and is built by both sexes. Both sexes incubate and nest change-overs are often initiated by the ♂ calling from the nest.
Laying months: mainly Nov (Sep-Feb). **Clutch size:** 2, rarely 1. **Eggs:** 19.4-21.6-23.0 x 14.3-15.9-17.0 mm. **Incubation period:** 18 days; by both sexes. **Nestling/fledging period:** 16-17 days; young brooded and fed by both sexes.

Orange-breasted Bushshrike *Telophorus sulfureopectus* Oranjeborsboslaksman page 384

Breeds in mesic savannas, favouring acacia-dominated woodlands, often along drainage lines. Pairs nest solitarily and are widely spaced. **Nest:** a flimsy, dove-nest like structure; a thin saucer of dry, branched twigs and curly tendrils that protrude in all directions giving the nest an untidy appearance, usually placed in the mid-canopy of a thorny tree (*Acacia tortilis* is much favoured), and within a tangle of thin, horizontal branches, either on a fork or where two or more stems cross; it is typically 3-6 m (1,8-10) up from the ground; the cup is sparsely lined with finer tendrils and the eggs are often visible through the nest from below. Although not hidden in thick foliage, the nest is easily overlooked because of its small size and its position inside the tree. It measures: outside diameter 100 mm; cup diameter 65 mm; cup depth 12 mm; nest height 38 mm, and is built by both sexes, sometimes close to the position of the previous season's nest. The pair are largely silent while nesting but nest change-overs are often initiated by the ♂ calling from the nest.
Laying months: mainly Oct-Dec (Sep-Mar, rarely in other months); sometimes double-brooded. **Clutch size:** 2, rarely 3. **Eggs:** 19.5-22.0-24.0 x 14.0-16.1-18.0 mm. **Incubation period:** reported as 13-14 days but probably longer than this; by both sexes shared equally in alternating shifts of about 1-1½ hrs. **Nestling/fledging period:** reported as 12-14 days but probably longer than this; young brooded and fed by both sexes.

Black-fronted Bushshrike *Telophorus nigrifrons* Swartoogboslaksman no nest photo page 384

Breeds in the canopy of tall montane and riparian forest. Pairs nest solitarily, are territorial year-round, and nest at a density of a pair/6-9 ha of forest (Malawi). Nesting habits are poorly known and few nests have been found anywhere in its range. **Nest:** a small flimsy, saucer-shaped platform, made of thin, dark-coloured, branched twigs and tendrils, placed high up (12-20 m), inside tangled mats of vine and creeper in the canopy of the forest; the shallow nest-cup is sparsely lined with finer tendrils, rootlets or some wisps of *Usnea*. The nest is not easily seen from the ground. It measures: outside diameter 80-180 mm; cup diameter 45 mm; cup depth 9-15 mm; nest height 40-57 mm. It is built by one or both sexes.
Laying months: mainly Oct-Nov (Oct-Feb). **Clutch size:** 2. **Eggs:** 23.1-23.3-23.5 x 17.1-17.3-17.3 mm. **Incubation period:** not recorded; by both sexes. **Nestling/fledging period:** not recorded; young fed by both sexes.

Grey-headed Bushshrike

Olive Bushshrike

Orange-breasted Bushshrike

Tchagras

Marsh Tchagra *Bocagia minuta* Vleitjagra — page 385

Restricted, in southern Africa, to a small area in c Mozambique and e Zimbabwe; breeds here in valley bottoms where tangles of rank grass, reeds, tall weedy growth, scattered bushes and creepers grow in damp conditions. Pairs nest solitarily and are widely spaced. **Nest:** a neat, deep cup placed in a tree sapling or leafy forb, usually <1 m up from the ground; typically in a 2- or 3-pronged vertical fork in the main stem, and concealed by the dense, tangled undergrowth that surrounds it. The nest is much like that built by other tchagras, being loosely constructed, made mainly from dry, brown-coloured, fine plant fibres (rootlets, leaf petioles, fern shredding), bound together sparingly with cobweb, and lined with rootlets. It differs from the nests of other tchagras by frequently being decorated with one or two pieces of discarded snake skin, or a few snake-skin scales, which are attached to the outside walls. The nest measures: outside diameter 70-90-96 mm; cup diameter 64-70-75 mm; cup depth 38-45-52 mm; nest height 61-80-110 mm. It is built by both sexes.

Laying months: Nov-Mar. **Clutch size:** 2, less often 3. **Eggs:** 19.5-22.5-26.5 x 15.5-17.0-19.0 mm. **Incubation period:** not recorded; by both sexes, but mostly the ♀. **Nestling/fledging period:** not recorded; young fed by both sexes.

Brown-crowned Tchagra *Tchagra australis* Rooivlerktjagra — page 385

Breeds widely across the savanna belt, from the semi-arid west to the mesic east; often found alongside the larger Black-crowned Tchagra, but is more frequently found in xeric vegetation (such as thornveld) than that species. Pairs nest solitarily, spaced at a density of about a pair/4-20 ha. **Nest:** a small, neatly-finished, thin-walled cup, typically placed about 1 m (0,2-3,6) up from the ground, usually in a forked main stem of a sapling tree, or against its trunk where several twigs branch off. Some nests are in dead or leafless trees and they are often poorly concealed; made largely (or entirely) with dry leaf petioles and bound together, and to the supporting twigs, with a small amount of cobweb; grass is not used in the nest. The nest-cup is finely lined with rootlets. The nest measures outside diameter 80-90-1000 mm; cup diameter 55-63-68 mm; cup depth 20-30-45 mm; nest height 40-50-70 mm. Both sexes build the nest, completing it in 6-7 days. During this period the ♂ frequently performs his singing aerial display in the vicinity of the nest and he continues with such displays into the incubation. Incubating birds often sit tight on the nest if approached.

Laying months: mainly Oct-Dec (Sep-Apr) in the east of its range but Dec-Mar in the west. **Clutch size:** 2-3, rarely 4; laid at 1-day intervals. **Eggs:** 19.19.4-21.7-25.3 x 14.9-16.3-18.3 mm; occasionally parasitised by Jacobin Cuckoo. **Incubation period:** 15 days (14-17); starts with first-laid egg; by both sexes, but mainly ♀, fed on nest by ♂. **Nestling/fledging period:** 14 days (13-16); young brooded and fed by both sexes.

Black-crowned Tchagra *Tchagra senegalus* Swartkroontjagra — page 385

Breeds mainly in the mesic savannas where commonly found alongside the Brown-crowned Tchagra. Pairs nest solitarily, spaced at a density of about a pair/20-25 ha. **Nest:** a shallow, thin-walled cup, placed in a forked main stem of a young sapling, or against its trunk where several twigs branch off; in second-growth habitats it commonly nests on top of a cut-off stump from which new twigs are regenerating; most are close to the ground, usually 1-1½ m (0,6-5,4) up; it is usually concealed by foliage but some are quite exposed. The base of the nest is made with dry, brown-coloured leaf petioles and the upper part, including the lining, is made with fine rootlets, creeper tendrils or other fine plant-stems. The nest is characteristically brown-coloured from the material used, and its exterior is lightly bound together, and to the supporting branch, with cobweb. It is very like the Brown-crowned Tchagra's nest but is larger. It measures: outside diameter 95-100-125 mm; cup diameter 70-75-85 mm; cup depth 30-37-40 mm; nest height 65-70-75 mm. Both sexes build the nest, completing it in about 7 days.

Laying months: mainly Oct-Dec (Aug-Apr). **Clutch size:** 2-3, rarely 4. **Eggs:** 21.9-24.6-27.5 x 17.0-18.0-19.4 mm; eggs are distinguishable from those of Three-streaked Tchagra by their larger size and twirled ('chinese character') markings. **Incubation period:** 15 days (12-17); by both sexes, but mainly ♀. **Nestling/fledging period:** 14 days (13-16); young brooded and fed by both sexes.

Southern Tchagra *Tchagra tchagra* Grysborstjagra — page 385

Breeds in a narrow range, mainly coastal, from the w Cape to Mpumalanga, frequenting tangled thickets associated with scrub forest, forest edge and fynbos, extending into grassland and semi-arid karoo along densely bushed river courses. Pairs nest solitarily and are widely spaced. **Nest:** a broad, shallow cup, placed low down, usually <1 m (0.3-3) up from the ground; it is well hidden in a matted tangle of thin branches, among creeper stems, or placed in a cactus, in the crown of a euphorbia tree, in mistletoe, or on the leaf of an *Aloe ferox*; a bush standing somewhat apart from the main thicket is often selected. The nest is flimsily made with fine plant-stems (grass runners, forbs, thin twigs) and lined with rootlets. In contrast to nests of other tchagras, cobweb is not used in the nest. The nest measures: outside diameter 110-130 mm; cup diameter 70-100 mm; cup depth 25-50 mm. It is sometimes built on the site of a previous year's nest. When incubating, the bird on the nest often sits tight if approached.

Laying months: mainly Oct-Nov (Aug-Jan); earlier in sw Cape than elsewhere. **Clutch size:** 2, rarely 1 or 3. **Eggs:** 22.9-24.3-26.7 x 17.0-18.4-19.7 mm; occasionally parasitised by Jacobin Cuckoo. **Incubation period:** 16 days; role of sexes not recorded. **Nestling/fledging period:** 14½ days (13-16); young fed by both sexes.

Marsh Tchagra

Brown-crowned Tchagra

Black-crowned Tchagra

Southern Tchagra

Bushshrikes

Black-backed Puffback *Dryoscopus cubla* Sneeubal page 384

Breeds in mesic savanna and evergreen forest. Pairs nest solitarily and are widely spaced. **Nest:** a small, compact, open cup built in the upper leafy canopy of a tree, usually in a central position, and mostly in a smooth-barked, two- or three-pronged upright fork. In deciduous woodland nests are typically 5-6 m (3-8) up, whereas in evergreen forest, they can be 15 m from the ground. The nest is built with pliable strips of inner-bark that are curled around to form the nest bowl and these are also used to line the cup, sometimes together with leaf petioles. Cobweb is used copiously to bind the nest to the branch and the outer walls are smoothed off with cobweb, blending its surface with the supporting branch. The nest measures: outside diameter 75-85 mm; cup diameter 55-60 mm; cup depth 32-35 mm; nest depth 50-55 mm. It is built by the ♀, accompanied by the ♂ while building; nest building takes place mainly in the early morning and a nest takes about 11 days to complete.

Laying months: mainly Sep-Dec (Aug-Apr, rarely in other months), peaking in Oct in Zimbabwe and in Nov elsewhere; relays after early failure. **Clutch size:** 2-3; laid at 1-day intervals. **Eggs:** 19.2-22.2-24.4 x 14.9-15.9-17.7 mm; rarely parasitised by Jacobin Cuckoo. **Incubation period:** 14 days (13-14½); by ♀ only; begins when clutch is complete; ♀ is fed on nest by ♂. **Nestling/fledging period:** 17-18 days; young brooded by ♀; fed by both sexes.

Brubru *Nilaus afer* Bontroklaksman page 384

Breeds in both mesic and semi-arid savannas, favouring any tall woodland (broad-leafed, mopane or acacia). Pairs nest solitarily and are spaced at a density of about a pair/30 ha in broad-leafed woodland. **Nest:** little more than a shallow rim, just sufficient to contain the eggs, built on a gently up-sloping branch at a fork; it is usually placed in the upper branches of a tree, typically 5-7 m (2½-13) from the ground. Trees used are often leafless when the birds start nest-building. The walls and thin base of the nest are built mainly from dry leaf petioles which are bound together and to the supporting branch with cobweb, and the outside is plastered with lichen which enhances its camouflage. The nest measures: outside diameter 65-75-89 mm; cup diameter 38-43-45 mm; cup depth 19-20 mm; nest height 25-50 mm. Both sexes share equally in building, and the nest can be completed in 2-5 days. A pair frequently builds several nests early in the breeding season before one is used. The pair is especially vocal during this nest-building period and often duet in the nest tree; the incubation is shared, and duetting often occurs at change-overs.

Laying months: mainly Sep-Nov (Aug-Feb); peaks earlier in Zimbabwe than elsewhere; single-brooded; relays after early failure. **Clutch size:** 2, rarely 1 or 3; laid at 1-day interval. **Eggs:** 18.6-20.2-22.3 x 14.3-15.4-16.8 mm. **Incubation period:** 19 days; by both sexes, shared equally in shifts of about 40 min; begins when first egg is laid. **Nestling/fledging period:** 21-22 days; young brooded and fed by both sexes.

Bokmakierie *Telophorus zeylonus* Bokmakierie page 384

Breeds in the fynbos, karoo and grassland regions, favouring open country with scattered shrubs. **Nest:** a bulky open cup placed in the centre of a densely foliaged shrub or a bushy tree usually < ½ m up (0-6 m); katbos (*Asparagus* sp.) is much favoured in the karoo while in suburban environments hedges, cyprus trees or discarded piles of cut branches are often used. The shell is built with coarse stems of forbs (especially *Helichrysum* sp.), rough grass blades, shreds of bark, fine twigs, rootlets, etc.; the cup is lined with finer material, often rootlets. The nest measures: outside diameter 127-180 mm; cup diameter 80-90 mm; cup depth 38-58 mm; nest height 75-100 mm. Pairs frequently nest in successive years in the vicinity of a previously used nest (even building on top of the old nest) and, occasionally, a second clutch is laid in the same nest in one season. The nest is built by both sexes and can be completed within 2-3 days. The pair duet frequently in the vicinity of the nest during this period but become relatively silent once incubation starts.

Laying months: mainly early summer, peaking in Jul-Sep in the winter-rainfall region and Aug-Nov elsewhere; occasionally in other months; double-brooded; relays after early failures. **Clutch size:** 3 (2-5, once 6); laid at 1-day intervals. **Eggs:** 22.6-25.6-29.3 x 16.5-19.3-20.8 mm; occasionally parasitised by Jacobin Cuckoo. **Incubation period:** 16 days (14-19); shared evenly by both sexes; begins when clutch is completed. **Nestling/fledging period:** 18 days (15-21); young brooded and fed by both sexes.

Gorgeous Bushshrike *Telophorus quadricolor* Konkoit page 384

Breeds in and on the fringes of coastal, lowland and riparian forests, frequenting dense, tangled thickets and undergrowth which can be virtually impenetrable to humans. Pairs nest solitarily and are widely spaced. **Nest:** a loosely built, shallow cup, placed low down, typically 1-1½ m (0,6-1,6) up, well hidden in the outer, matted branches of a thorny bush, among a tangle of vines or in thick bracken. The base is loosely made with long (120 mm) dead twigs about as thick as a match, and with long curly tendrils, while the nest-cup is lined with fine tendrils. There is no binding used to consolidate the nest and it is liable to disintegrate if lifted from its supporting twigs. The nest measures: outside diameter 100-150 mm; cup diameter 65-100 mm; cup depth 15-20 mm; nest height 40-50 mm. Nest may be built within 3 m of a previous year's nest; is usually located close to where the ♂ is most frequently heard calling. The birds utter a distinctive low growling alarm call when they have nestlings.

Laying months: mainly Oct-Dec (Oct-Feb). **Clutch size:** 2. **Eggs:** 22.4-23.3-24.6 x 15.9-16.9-18.3 mm. **Incubation period:** not recorded; by both sexes. **Nestling/fledging period:** not recorded; young fed by both sexes.

Black-backed Puffback

Brubru

Bokmakierie

Gorgeous Bushshrike

Boubous

Tropical Boubou *Laniarius major* Tropiese Waterfiskaal page 385

Breeds in the northern savannas, frequenting tangled thickets and bush clumps along drainage lines, along the bases of hills and on forest edges; also in wooded gardens. Pairs nest solitarily and are widely spaced; its nesting habits are similar to those of its sibling species, the Southern Boubou. **Nest:** a shallow cup, placed in the lower branches of a thicket, usually among thin multi-twigged stems or where branches criss-cross, typically about 3 m up (½-15). It is built with pieces of dry twig, bark or coarse grass which form the base, and tendrils and rootlets are used to line the cup. It is bound together, and to the supporting twigs, with a small amount of cobweb. Both sexes build, the ♀ taking the greater share. Both sexes incubate and at nest change-overs the pair duet briefly, initiated by the incubating bird.
Laying months: mainly Sep-Nov, but most months recorded. **Clutch size:** 2, rarely 3; laid at a 1-day interval. **Eggs:** 22.3-24.7-26.8 x 16.7-18.2-19.1 mm; parasitised by the Black Cuckoo which lays an egg that is a close match in size and colour to its host's. **Incubation period:** 15 days (14-16); by both sexes. **Nestling/fledging period:** 15 days (14-16); young brooded and fed by both sexes.

Southern Boubou *Laniarius ferrugineus* Suidelike Waterfiskaal pages 379, 385

Breeds widely in a variety of wooded habitats along the e side of South Africa and s Mozambique, frequenting scrub-forest, forest edge, tangled thicket and bush clumps; often in well-wooded gardens. Pairs nest solitarily, are territorial year-round, nesting at densities of a pair/4-10 ha. **Nest:** a shallow open cup, placed in the lower branches of a thicket, usually supported by 2 or more sloping branches crossing each other, or crossing a main trunk, typically about 2 m (½-8) up from the ground; the base of the nest is made from strands and stems of rough, pliable material (strips of dry bark and thin twigs), curled around to form the nest bowl and bound to the supporting twigs with a few wisps of cobweb; the rim of the nest and the cup lining uses finer material, usually long, fine rootlets. The nest measures: outside diameter 115-130 mm; cup diameter 66-78 mm; cup depth 35-40 mm; nest height 55-70 mm. It is built by the ♀ only or by both sexes, in about 6 days. The pair become quiet while nesting but usually duet briefly at nest change-overs.
Laying months: mainly Oct-Nov (Aug-Feb, once May); peaks a month earlier (Sep) in the winter-rainfall region than elsewhere; sometimes double-brooded; usually relays after an early failure. **Clutch size:** 2-3; laid at 1-day intervals. **Eggs:** 22.0-24.6-27.4 x 16.0-18.1-19.2 mm; frequently parasitised by Black Cuckoo, rarely by Jacobin Cuckoo; egg of Black Cuckoo (but not Jacobin Cuckoo) closely matches that of its host. **Incubation period:** 16-17 days; by both sexes. **Nestling/fledging period:** 16-17 days; young brooded and fed by both sexes.

Swamp Boubou *Laniarius bicolor* Moeraswaterfiskaal page 385

Breeding range in southern Africa restricted to the floodplains of n Botswana, the Caprivi and nw Zimbabwe where it frequents dense tangles of riparian vegetation. Nesting habits are poorly known. Pairs nest solitarily and are widely spaced. **Nest:** a loosely constructed open cup, placed in dense vegetation among the criss-crossing, thin, sloping branches near the edges of the thicket, 1-4 m up from the ground; in gardens, bouganvillea is a favoured site. It is made of long, thin, pliable twigs that are curled around to form a bowl with rootlets and tendrils used to line the cup; little or no cobweb is used. The nest measures: outside diameter 110-130 mm; cup diameter 70-75 mm; cup depth 45 mm; nest height 60 mm. Pair duet briefly at nest change-overs.
Laying months: mainly Sep-Nov (Aug-Mar, once in Jun) (Botswana). **Clutch size:** 2. **Eggs:** 23.0-23.7 x 19.8-19.9 mm; one record of parasitism by Black Cuckoo. **Incubation period:** not recorded; by both sexes. **Nestling/fledging period:** not recorded; young fed by both sexes.

Crimson-breasted Shrike *Laniarius atrococcineus* Rooiborslaksman pages 379, 385

Breeds widely across the semi-arid savanna, where largely confined to acacia thornveld. Pairs nest solitarily, are territorial year-round and nest at densities of a pair/2½-12 ha. **Nest:** an open cup, distinctive for being built largely or entirely with pliable shreds of inner-bark; it is almost always built in a thorny tree (*Dicrostachys cinerea*, *Acacia tortilis*, *A. nilotica*, *A. karoo* are favoured), and is usually placed in a lower forked branch of a smallish, isolated tree about 2-3 m up (1-8 m), either in a fork in the main stem, or on a side branch up against the main stem; less often, it is placed away from the centre of the tree. The nest is built with 212-477 pieces of material that are curled around to form a bowl; most nests are built with strands of inner-bark only, but some have a few rootlets added in the lining; a small amount of cobweb is used to hold the outside walls together and to bind the nest to the supporting branch. The nest measures: outside diameter 100-130 mm; cup diameter 60 mm; cup depth 40 mm; nest height 50 mm. Both sexes build, working mostly in the early morning and the nest is completed in 4-6 days, but it may only be laid in 3-14 days later; in some cases several nests are built before a clutch is laid, and material from one nest is recycled to the next. Failed nests are often pulled apart by the birds, possibly for recycling. During the incubation and early nestling periods the pair is relatively silent and unobtrusive; they do sometimes duet briefly when making nest change-overs
Laying months: mainly Oct-Nov (Aug-Mar) in east of range; Jan-Mar in the west; sometimes double-brooded; usually relays after earlier failures. **Clutch size:** 2-3; laid at 1-day intervals. **Eggs:** 22.0-23.7-25.5 x 16.3-17.5-19.7 mm; frequently parasitised by Black Cuckoo which lays an egg that closely matches those of its host. **Incubation period:** 16½ days (16-17); usually begins when clutch is completed; by both sexes, in ½-1 hr shifts. **Nestling/fledging period:** 19 days (18-20); young brooded and fed by both sexes.

Tropical Boubou

Southern Boubou

Swamp Boubou

Crimson-breasted Shrike

Shrikes

SHRIKES Family Laniidae Worldwide 33 species; 14 breed in Afrotropics, 4 southern Africa. Monogamous; 2 are cooperative breeders; nest is an open cup placed in a tree or bush; nest site and architecture varies between species; both sexes build the nest and feed the nestlings, but (where known) only the ♀ incubates and broods the young; eggs are oval-shaped; well-marked, white buff or pale green in ground-colour with speckles and blotches; 3-4/clutch; nestlings are altricial and nidicolous. One (Common Fiscal) is parasitised by the Jacobin Cuckoo.

Common Fiscal *Lanius collaris* Fiskaallaksman   pages 378, 385

Breeds widely and commonly in open or lightly wooded country, mostly in the grassland, karoo and fynbos regions; it occurs locally in savanna, mainly in agricultural areas. Pairs nest solitarily, spaced at a density of a pair/½-10 ha. **Nest:** a bulky, open cup, placed in a forked branch of a tree or shrub, often in a lone-standing tree and usually a thorny one if available (e.g. *Acacia*, *Ziziphus*, *Pyracantha* are much-used); it is typically 2-3 m up from the ground (0.6-6 m, one at 15 m). The base of the nest is made with coarse stems or plant material (often *Helichrysum* or *Stoebe*) that give the nest a rough exterior, while around human habitation rags, string, wool and such debris is often used; the cup is neatly lined with rootlets or fine shreds of grass. The nest is sometimes well hidden, but as often is not. It measures: outside diameter 100-130-180 mm; cup diameter 65-75-90 mm; cup depth 35-50-75 mm; nest height 65-95-120 mm. It is built by both sexes and may be completed within 3 days, but completed nests often remain empty for several weeks before the first egg is laid. The pair sometimes builds a succession of nests before laying in one, and nest material is recycled from one to the next. Nests are occasionally reused for successive broods, and the same site (or nest tree) is sometimes used annually (once recorded for 14 successive years). The ♂ feeds his mate during the incubation and early part of the nestling periods and during this time the ♀ begs noisily from the nest.

Laying months: mainly Sep-Oct (Aug-Dec, rarely in other months); peaks earlier in the winter-rainfall region (Aug-Oct); often double-brooded. **Clutch size:** 4 (2-5, rarely 6 or 8, probably laid by >1 ♀); laid at 1-day intervals; occasionally parasitised by Jacobin Cuckoo (2% of nests). **Eggs:** 19.6-23.5-28.5 x 15.6-17.7-19.9 mm. **Incubation period:** 14-15 days (12-16½); by ♀ only; begins when clutch is completed. **Nestling/fledging period:** 18-19 days (14-21); young brooded by ♀ only; fed by both sexes.

Magpie Shrike *Urolestes melanoleucus* Langstertlaksman   page 385

Breeds in acacia savanna, favouring open areas with a short ground cover and scattered, well-spaced trees. Pairs or family groups (pair plus 1-10 helpers) nest solitarily, spaced at a density of about a group/70 ha. **Nest:** a roughly constructed bulky cup, usually built in a thorn tree, typically 3-5 m (2½-10) up, and either inside the thick foliage of a shrubby acacia or in the upper, outer branches of a tall spreading tree (such as *Acacia tortilis*). It is typically built with fine, brown-coloured plant stems, often using the fine, thorny stems of an *Asparagus* sp. for this; in their absence, blades and stems of dry grass are used; the cup is neatly lined with pale brown rootlets that match the colour of the eggs. From below, the nest looks much like an old sparrow or finch nest. It measures: outside diameter 165-180 mm; cup diameter 95-100 mm; cup depth 50-60 mm; nest height 110-160 mm. Both sexes build, completing a nest in 5 days. Most nesting pairs have one or more helpers, and these assist the ♂ in feeding the ♀ during the incubation; she solicits from them by calling from the nest from time to time, sounding much like a nestling in this respect.

Laying months: mainly Oct-Dec (Aug-Mar); sometimes double-brooded. **Clutch size:** 3-4, rarely 2, 5 or 6 (perhaps laid by 2 ♀s) laid at 1-day intervals. **Eggs:** 23.1-26.8-29.9 x 18.3-19.7-20.7 mm. **Incubation period:** 16 days; by ♀ only; begins when clutch is completed. **Nestling/fledging period:** 15-19 days; young brooded by ♀ only; fed by both sexes, assisted by helpers.

Southern White-crowned Shrike *Eurocephalus anguitimens* Kremetartlaksman   page 385

Breeds across the savanna belt, from the semi-arid west to the mesic east, favouring open woodland where there are scattered tall trees. Pairs or family groups (3-6 birds/group) nest solitarily and are widely spaced. **Nest:** a smoothly finished broad cup, usually built in a large tree that stands out above others in the vicinity, characteristically placed near the outer extremity of one of the lower branches where there is a clear drop to the ground; about 5 m up (2-18). The nest is made mainly with stems of fine, shredded grass; its outside walls and rim thickly and smoothly plastered with cobweb, which also binds it to the branch – the nest has the appearance of being made with *papier-mâché*. It measures: outside diameter 115-120 mm; cup diameter 85-95 mm; cup depth 40-47 mm; nest height 80-90 mm. Both sexes build the nest, assisted, when present, by helpers.

Laying months: mainly Oct-Dec (Sep-Apr), later in Namibia (mainly Jan-May). **Clutch size:** 3-4 (2-5, rarely 7-10 eggs, probably laid by more than 1 ♀). **Eggs:** 23.0-27.2-30.0 x 17.0-21.3-22.8 mm. **Incubation period:** 20 days reported, but seems too long; mainly by ♀, assisted by helpers. **Nestling/fledging period:** 19-20 days; young fed by both sexes, assisted by helpers.

Souza's Shrike *Lanius souzae* Souzase Laksman   page 385

A species of broad-leafed woodlands of tropical Africa, its range extending narrowly into the Caprivi where it breeds locally and in small numbers. Pairs nest solitarily and are widely spaced. **Nest:** a small, neat cup placed in a forked branch in the main stem, or on a side limb, or where two branches cross close to the main trunk, in a smallish, well-foliaged tree (including *Strychnos spinosa* and *Pterocarpus angolensis*), about 5 m (2½-6½) up. The base of the nest is made with leaf petioles, pieces of shredded bark and plant fragments, bound with cobweb that strengthens the walls and secures the nest to the branch, and the cup is neatly lined with fine tendrils, rootlets and/or fine shreds of grass. The nest is usually well camouflaged and easily overlooked. It measures: outside diameter 80-90 mm; cup diameter 55-60 mm; cup depth 35 mm; nest height 55 mm. Both sexes build the nest.

Laying months: Aug-Dec, but mainly Oct (Zambia); Nov (Caprivi). **Clutch size:** 2-3, rarely 4. **Eggs:** 19.0-20.8-21.9 x 15.9-16.3-17.0 mm. **Incubation period:** at least 11 days; by ♀ only, fed by ♂; commences before completion of the clutch (Caprivi). **Nestling/fledging period:** 20 days (Caprivi).

Common Fiscal

Magpie Shrike

Southern White-crowned Shrike

Souza's Shrike

Cuckooshrikes

CUCKOOSHRIKES Family Campephagidae Worldwide 92 species; 10 breed in Afrotropics, 3 in southern Africa. Monogamous; pairs nest solitarily; nest-building and incubation by the ♀ in Black Cuckooshrike but shared in the other 2 species. Nest a small, inconspicuous cup placed in the upper branches of a tree; eggs oval-shaped, bluish-green with dark speckles; 2/clutch; nestlings are altricial and nidicolous.

Black Cuckooshrike *Campephaga flava* Swartkatakoeroe   page 385

A breeding summer visitor to the mesic savanna, especially broad-leafed woodland, arriving in late Sep; its range extends into s Cape in valley bushveld and forest verges. Pairs nest solitarily, at a density of about a pair/30 ha in broad-leafed woodland. **Nest:** a small, inconspicuous, shallow-rimmed saucer placed in a multiple fork or saddle in the upper branches of a well-foliaged tree, usually 5-7 m (3½-9 m) up from the ground; a branch at least 60 mm in diameter is selected and usually one that has grey lichen growing on it. The nest is made with leaf petioles, lichen, *Usnea* and cobweb and its outer walls are smoothed with cobweb and covered with lichen, resulting in the nest blending well with the branch; from below it appears to be a swelling on the branch. It measures: outside diameter 90-100; cup diameter 40-60 mm; cup depth 13-25 mm. The ♀ builds the nest and is accompanied by the ♂ on material-collecting trips; he sings and often perches prominently near the nest during this period. Nests started early in the season are often abandoned before being used.
Laying months: mainly Nov-Dec (Oct-Jan, rarely in Sep and Feb). **Clutch size:** 2, rarely 1 or 3; laid at a 1-day interval. **Eggs:** 21.5-23.8-25.9 x 16.2-17.3-18.4 mm. **Incubation period:** 20 days; by ♀ only; she is fed on nest by the ♂ and she also leaves for short periods to feed. **Nestling/fledging period:** 22 days (20-23); brooded by ♀; fed by both sexes.

White-breasted Cuckooshrike *Coracina pectoralis* Witborskatakoeroe   page 385

Breeds in tall broad-leafed woodland, especially miombo and mopane. Pairs nest solitarily, spaced at a density of about a pair/ 20 ha (in miombo, Zimbabwe). **Nest:** a slight, shallow-rimmed cup, built in a sloping widely-forked branch, usually one festooned with lichen in the upper branches of a large tree (especially a *Brachystegia* sp. where these occur) about 6-15 m off the ground. It is easily overlooked. The base of the nest is built with leaf petioles and leaf-ribbing, with grey lichen providing most of the wall material and it is held together and loosely attached to the branch with a little cobweb. A layer of *Usnea* is used to line the nest-cup and this extends beyond the cup, spilling loosely over the rim and enhancing the camouflaged effect of the nest. The nest measures: outside diameter 100-114 mm; cup diameter 83 mm; cup depth 38 mm. One nest was reportedly built by the ♂ only and it took 6 days to complete; confirmation of the roles of the sexes in this would be nice.
Laying months: mainly Sep-Nov (Aug-Dec); single-brooded. **Clutch size:** 2, rarely 1; laid at a 1-day interval. **Eggs:** 26.1-27.3-30.0 x 18.9-19.5-20.1 mm. **Incubation period:** 23 days; by both sexes. **Nestling/fledging period:** 24 days; brooded and fed by both sexes.

Grey Cuckooshrike *Coracina caesia* Bloukatakoeroe   page 385

Breeds in Afromontane forest. Pairs nest solitarily and are widely spaced. Nesting habits are poorly known. **Nest:** a small, shallow-rimmed cup nest of lichen bound together with cobweb, and placed on a lichen-covered, forked branch high up (15-20 m) in the leafy canopy of a forest tree (*Eugenia capensis*, *Milletia sutherlandii*). Both sexes build the nest. They call at the nest while doing so (a wispy 'swee' note) and the incubating bird, if disturbed off the nest, may utter this call as it leaves.
Laying months: Nov-Dec, Sep in s Cape. **Clutch size:** 2, less often 1. **Eggs:** 26.2-27.5-29.9 x 19.2-19.3-19.5 mm. **Incubation period:** not recorded; by both sexes. **Nestling/fledging period:** not recorded; young fed by both sexes.

Black Cuckooshrike (THREE ABOVE)

White-breasted Cuckooshrike

Grey Cuckooshrike

Orioles, Drongos

ORIOLES Family Oriolidae Worldwide 32 species; 8 breed in Afrotropics, 3 in southern Africa. Monogamous; where known sexes share incubation and nestling care; nest a woven, deep, open cup suspended, hammock-style, between two or more horizontal twigs; eggs oval; white or pink with dark red spots; 2-3/clutch; nestlings are altricial and nidicolous.

Black-headed Oriole *Oriolus larvatus* Swartkopwielewaal   page 386

Breeds in woodland in mesic savanna, in evergreen forest and, where it has spread into grassland and karoo, in eucalypts, poplar and other aliens. Pairs nest solitarily and are widely spaced. **Nest:** a deep, open-cup slung between twigs in an outer branch of a tree, well concealed in foliage; the nest is suspended, hammock-style, from the twigs, its rim flush with them; nest height variable, mostly 6-9 m up from the ground (2,8-20 m), with those built in eucalypts being particularly high. The nest is loosely knitted together using dry, pliable pieces of grass and/or shreds of pliable inner bark; coloured baling string is sometimes used around farmsteads, and *Usnea* moss where available; some cobweb is used in attaching it to the branch. The nest measures: outside diameter 80-93-100 mm; cup diameter 65-68-70 mm; nest height 60-70-80 mm; cup depth 55 mm; the cup is usually round, but some are strongly oval-shaped. One bird (probably the ♀) does most or all the building, completing a nest in 9 days; it may nest in successive years close to a previous nest site.
Laying months: mainly Oct-Nov (Sep-Feb), peaking earlier in the north (Oct) than the south (Nov). **Clutch size:** 3, less often 2; laid at 1-day intervals. **Eggs:** 26.1-28.9-32.7 × 16.7-20.2-22.3 mm. **Incubation period:** 14-16 days; by both sexes. **Nestling/fledging period:** 15-18 days (14-20); young brooded mainly by ♀, fed by both sexes.

African Golden Oriole *Oriolus auratus* Afrikaanse Wielewaal   page 386

A breeding summer visitor to northern mesic woodlands, arriving is Sep. Pairs nest solitarily and are widely spaced. **Nest:** a deep, open-cupped nest placed in the canopy of a well-foliaged tree, 7-9 m (5-13) up from the ground; it is slung between the twigs of a thin, horizontal forked branch, the rim level with these twigs and the nest bowl suspended, hammock-style, beneath the fork; it is built with dry grass and strands of pliable inner bark, a small amount of cobweb binding it to the branch; *Usnea* is seldom used; it measures: cup diameter 80-90 mm; nest height 75 mm; cup depth 50-55 mm; cup usually round, but some strongly oval-shaped.
Laying months: mainly Oct (Sep-Dec, rarely Jan-Mar). **Clutch size:** 2-3, rarely 4. **Eggs:** 26.0-28.5-32.9 × 19.2-20.5-21.8 mm; the eggs of this species and the Black-headed Oriole are distinguished by their having different ground-colours: pinkish-buff in the former and white in the latter. **Incubation period:** 16-17 days; role of sexes unrecorded. **Nestling/fledging period:** 15 days; young brooded mainly or entirely by ♀, fed by both sexes.

Green-headed Oriole *Oriolus chlorocephalus* Groenkopwielewaal   page 386

Restricted in southern Africa to montane forest on Mt Gorongosa, c Mozambique. Nesting habits are poorly known. **Nest:** a suspended deep open cup built with *Usnea*; one being built on Gorongosa in Dec was about 20 m up in the canopy of a forest tree.
Laying months: Dec. **Clutch size:** 2. **Eggs:** not recorded. **Incubation period:** not recorded. **Nestling/fledging period:** not recorded.

DRONGOS Family Dicruridae Worldwide 25 species; 4 breed in Afrotropics, 2 in southern Africa. Monogamous; both sexes build the nest, incubate and share nestling care; nest is a shallow open cup suspended between twigs in a tree; eggs oval, very variably coloured and marked; 3/clutch; nestlings are altricial and nidicolous.

Fork-tailed Drongo *Dicrurus adsimilis* Mikstertbyvanger   pages 378, 386

Breeds widely across the savanna, from the semi-arid west to the mesic east, extending into the grassland, karoo and fynbos regions where alien trees (especially eucalypts) have been introduced. Pairs nest solitarily, at densities of a pair/11-30 ha. **Nest:** a shallow open cup suspended between two twigs, characteristically near the extremity of an upper, horizontal forked branch of a tree, 4-6 m (2.2-17) up from the ground (highest in eucalypts); often selects an outer dead branch of a fire-blackened tree; occasionally nests on a radio mast or television antenna. It is built from petioles, rootlets and thin pliable plant stems, coarser material in the base and walls, finer pieces lining the cup; it is firmly attached to the branch and bound together with cobweb. In some nests the floor is so thinly made that the eggs or nestlings can be seen through it from below. The nest measures: outside diameter 100-103-110 mm; cup diameter 70-75-80 mm; nest height 44-50-68 mm; cup depth 32-35-40 mm. Both sexes build, completing a nest in about 4 days.
Laying months: mainly Sep-Nov (Aug-Jan); peaks earlier in Zimbabwe (Sep-Oct) than elsewhere (Oct-Nov); single-brooded, but relays after early failure. **Clutch size:** 3 (2-4); laid at 1-day intervals. **Eggs:** 21.2-24.3-28.3 × 16.7-18.2-20.1 mm; colour very variable; commonly parasitised by African Cuckoo which lays an eggs that closely matches the drongo's white, speckled egg type, but is smaller (21 × 17 mm). **Incubation period:** 16 days (15-18); by both sexes; begins when clutch is completed. **Nestling/fledging period:** 17-18 days (16-22); young brooded and fed by both sexes.

Square-tailed Drongo *Dicrurus ludwigii* Kleinbyvanger   page 386

Breeds in lowland, coastal, riparian and montane forest. Pairs nest solitarily and are widely spaced. **Nest:** a shallow, open, cup suspended between two thin twigs of a horizontal forked branch, often in a subcanopy broad-leafed sapling standing in a glade overhanging a stream or a road; height above ground variable, often <5 m, but some much higher (2½-25 m). It is made from dry, curled leaf petioles and pieces of lichen held together and to the supporting twigs with cobweb. It measures: outside diameter 64-77-85 mm; cup diameter 51-56-60 mm; nest height 33-38-45 mm; cup depth 20-24-28 mm. Both sexes build, and material may be recycled from an earlier nest to its replacement.
Laying months: mainly Oct-Nov (Sep-Jan, once in Apr); may relay after earlier failure. **Clutch size:** 3, less often 2. **Eggs:** 20.1-21.1-22.8 × 15.0-15.7-16.5 mm; mass 2.3-2.4 g. **Incubation period:** not recorded. **Nestling/fledging period:** 14 and 22 days recorded.

Black-headed Oriole

African Golden Oriole

Green-headed Oriole

Fork-tailed Drongo

Square-tailed Drongo

'Flycatchers'

'FLYCATCHERS' DNA evidence has shown that none of the 4 species below are flycatchers (Muscicapidae) in the traditional sense; 2 (Blue-mantled, African Paradise flycatchers) are 'monarchs' (Monarchidae), 2 (White-tailed and Fairy flycatchers) are 'fairy flycatchers' (Stenostiridae). Their grouping here more or less reflects their currently perceived place in the systematic order.

Blue-mantled (Crested) Flycatcher *Trochocercus cyanomelas* Bloukuifvlieëvanger — page 386

Breeds in montane, coastal and lowland forests. Pairs nest solitarily, spaced at a density of about a pair/1 ha (Malawi). **Nest:** cup-shaped, much like that of African Paradise Flycatcher, placed in a fork in a small, thin-stemmed sapling (diameter about 10 mm), 1-2 m up from the ground (rarely to 8 m), usually where some foliage disrupts the outline of the nest. It is made of shreds of dry, fibrous plant material (bark, weed-stems), neatly smoothed with cobweb around the rim but left shaggy around the lower walls; the cup is neatly lined with fine leaf petioles or grass strands. Unlike the nest of the African Paradise Flycatcher its outer walls are not adorned with lichen. It measures: outside diameter 57-65 mm; cup diameter 45 mm; cup depth 25-28 mm; nest height 50-90 mm. The incubating bird often sits tight, allowing a close approach.
Laying months: mainly Oct-Dec (Sep-Jan). **Clutch size:** 2; rarely 3. **Eggs:** 15.8-16.8-17.9 × 12.2-12.7-13.0 mm. **Incubation period:** not recorded; by both sexes in shifts of about 45 min. **Nestling/fledging period:** not recorded; young fed by both sexes.

African Paradise Flycatcher *Terpsiphone viridis* Paradysvlieëvanger — page 386

Breeds widely in southern Africa, especially in mesic savanna and evergreen forest; found especially along rivers, streams and gullies and in copses of tall, dense trees; a common and well-known breeding bird in wooded gardens. Pairs nest solitarily, adjacent nests usually spaced 50-100 m apart, but sometimes within 10 m of each other. **Nest:** a delicate little cup, attractively decorated with pieces of lichen and usually attached to an up- or down-sloping twig in the lower canopy of a shady tree. Away from gardens the birds commonly nest along streams, their nest overhanging the watercourse, and away from water the nest is typically in a shaded glade. It is not hidden in foliage and relies on its disruptive pattern for concealment. It is typically 2-4 m (1½-10) up from the ground and is made of thin, dry, pliable strips of whatever fibrous plant material, usually inner bark, is available, bound together and to the branch with cobweb; the outer walls are characteristically decorated with pieces of grey lichen. It measures: outside diameter 65-70 mm; cup diameter 45-50 mm; cup depth 30-40 mm; nest height 50-90 mm. Both sexes build the nest, completing it in 2-9 days. It is often built close to the site of a previous year's nest and occasionally at the same spot. During nest-building there is much vocal activity in the vicinity of the nest but the pair become relatively silent once incubation begins, when they call briefly only during nest change-overs.
Laying months: mainly Oct-Dec (Sep-Mar); peaks earlier (Oct-Nov) in the winter-rainfall region than elsewhere (Nov-Dec); rarely double-brooded; relays 1-5x after earlier clutch losses. **Clutch size:** 3 (1-3, rarely 4; small clutches are usually replacements); laid at 1-day intervals. **Eggs:** 17.3-18.8-21.5 × 13.0-14.1-15.1 mm; occasionally parasitised by Diederik, Jacobin and Red-chested Cuckoo. **Incubation period:** 15 days (11-19); begins when first egg is laid; shared equally by both sexes, in alternating day shifts of about 30-45 min. **Nestling/fledging period:** 14 days (10-16); young brooded and fed by both sexes.

Fairy Flycatcher *Stenostira scita* Feevlieëvanger — page 386

Breeds in arid shrublands in karoo and fynbos, and especially favours the wooded watercourses in such areas. Pairs nest solitarily, adjacent nests about 200 m apart along drainage lines. **Nest:** a small, thick-walled open cup placed in a tree or bush usually < 1 m (0,2-2,3) up from the ground; it is usually buried deep within a thick tangle of dead, thorny branches or in the heart of a multi-stemmed, densely foliaged shrub, often visible from only one angle, and usually difficult to spot. It is warmly insulated, made from finely shredded grass, weed-stems or bark, bound together with cobweb and lined with wool, animal hair, plant down and, sometimes with feathers. Some nests lack outside decoration while others have the outer walls adorned with shards of bark or a few pieces of lichen. It measures: outside diameter 64-70 mm; cup diameter 32-38 mm; cup depth 25-38 mm; nest height 50-55 mm. The nest is built by the ♀ in about 4 days. She is fed frequently by the ♂ during the nest building and incubation periods, and she utters a characteristic food-begging call (a buzzing sound) when approached by the ♂.
Laying months: Jul-Dec; peaking earlier in winter-rainfall areas (Aug-Sep) than in summer-rainfall areas (Oct-Nov). **Clutch size:** 2-3. **Eggs:** 14.5-15.2-16.9 × 10.8-11.5-12.7 mm. **Incubation period:** 17-18 days; probably by ♀ only; fed by ♂ on nest. **Nestling/fledging period:** not recorded.

White-tailed (Crested) Flycatcher *Elminia albonotatus* Witstertvlieëvanger — page 386

Breeds in montane forests in e Zimbabwe and c Mozambique. Pairs nest solitarily, spaced at a density of a pair/1-2 (Malawi). **Nest:** small, deep, open cup, placed below the forest canopy, typically 1-2 m (½-6½) up from the ground in a fork in the thin vertical stem of a forest sapling (especially *Peddia* or *Xymalos*), usually positioned where it is surrounded by some foliage. The nest is distinctive in its shape and its colouration – shaped like a cone or goblet and it encases the twigs that support it, some of the nest material also extending down the stem below the nest. It is made mainly, sometimes entirely, with green moss which is closely woven to give the nest exterior a soft, felted texture and the appearance of being a wad of green moss caught up in a fork. In a few nests there may be some pieces of lichen added to the outside walls, but this is unusual. The nest-cup is lined with fine hair-like fibres. It measures: outside diameter 70 mm; cup diameter 40 mm; cup depth 30 mm; nest height 70-95 mm and is built by the ♀ over a period of about 11 days. The pair call frequently at the nest during nest-building but become relatively silent once incubation commences, calling only if the nest is threatened or when the ♂ arrives to feed the ♀.
Laying months: mainly Nov-Dec (Oct-Jan). **Clutch size:** 2, rarely 3. **Eggs:** 14.2-15.5-16.3 × 11.7-12.4-13.1 mm. **Incubation period:** 17 days; by ♀ only, fed on nest by ♂. **Nestling/fledging period:** 12 days; young brooded by ♀, fed by both sexes.

Blue-mantled Flycatcher

African Paradise Flycatcher (LEFT & TWO ABOVE)

Fairy Flycatcher (TWO ABOVE)

White-tailed Flycatcher

CROWS Family Corvidae Worldwide 127 species; 9 breed in Afrotropics, 4 in southern Africa; 1 a recent colonist from Asia (House Crow, since 1972). Monogamous, sexes share nest-building, incubation and nestling care to varying degrees according to species; nest a large, bowl-shaped platform of twigs; built in a tree, on a utility pole or on a cliff face; eggs oval, pale blue or pink with dark speckling, 4-5/clutch; nestlings are altricial and nidicolous; 2 species are parasitised by Great Spotted Cuckoo.

Cape Crow *Corvus capensis* Swartkraai   page 386

Breeds widely in the region, most common in mesic grasslands, the Kalahari and Namib, but absent from much of the karoo and savanna regions. Pairs nest solitarily, adjacent nests usually spaced >2 km apart. **Nest:** a broad, open bowl made of dry twigs, built in the upper fork of a tree or in the top cross-bars of an electricity transmission tower or telephone pole; in some areas potholes in cliff faces may also be used. Tree nests vary in height above the ground between 1,3-30 m, those in eucalypts and pines (which are commonly used) are higher (10-20 m up) than those placed in indigenous acacias or other trees (3-6 m up). The nest is built with both thorny and non-thorny twigs that are firmly interlocked to make a rigid structure; occasional nests are built partly or wholly from pieces of wire. Set in the top of the bowl of sticks is a deep cup, thickly and smoothly lined with a dense, felted mat of material which may comprise wool, plant down, finely shredded grass, animal hair, dried animal dung, string or another similar material. The nest measures: outside diameter 280-380 mm; cup diameter 200 mm; nest height 200 mm; cup depth 100 mm. Although nests often remain intact for several years, they are not reused by the crows which instead build a new nest each year, often placing it close to a previous one, and sometimes on top of it. It is built mainly by ♀ with material brought by ♂. Old nests are commonly taken over by kestrels.

Laying months: mainly Sep-Nov (Jul-Jan); peaks earlier in s and e Cape (Aug-Sep) than further north (Oct); relays after early failure; single-brooded. **Clutch size:** 4 (2-6); laid at 1-2 day intervals. **Eggs:** 40.0-45.4-53.5 x 27.6-31.1-34.3 mm; mass 17-18.6-20 g; frequently (10%) parasitised by Great Spotted Cuckoo which lays a smaller (33.4 x 24.5 mm), non-matching egg. **Incubation period** 18-19 days; by both sexes; begins before clutch complete. **Nestling/fledging period:** 36-39 days; young brooded, fed by both sexes.

Pied Crow *Corvus albus* Witborskraai   pages 379, 386

Breeds widely in the region but absent from much of the Kalahari and the Namibian interior. Pairs nest solitarily, are widely spaced and adjacent nests are mostly >200 m apart. **Nest:** a broad, open bowl made of twigs, indistinguishable from nest of Cape Crow: usually built in a tree, but electricity-transmission towers, top crossbars of telephone poles, windmills, etc. are commonly used; ledges and potholes in cliff faces also provide occasional nest sites; in trees the nest is placed in a high forked branch, often just below the top of the tree; height above the ground varies according to the tree used (3-30 m), those in eucalypts and pines (which are commonly used nest trees) being higher (10-20 m) than those in other trees. It is made of dry twigs and sticks, tightly knitted together; occasional nests are built partly or wholly from pieces of wire. Set in the top of this coarsely made shell is a deep cup, thickly and smoothly lined with a dense, felted mat of material which may comprise wool, plant down, finely shredded grass, animal hair, dried animal dung, string or another similar material. The nest measures: outside diameter 400-620 mm; cup diameter 210-250 mm; nest height 200-290 mm; cup depth 100 mm. Nests are occasionally reused in successive years but more usually a new nest, in the vicinity of a previous one, is built, by both the sexes, in 11-12 days. Old nests are frequently used by kestrels and other birds of prey.

Laying months: mainly Sep-Oct (Jul-Dec, once Apr); relays after early failure; single-brooded. **Clutch size:** 4 (1-7); laid at 1-day intervals. **Eggs:** 39.0-44.7-50.1 x 26.2-30.5-33.0 mm; mass 20-23-24 g; frequently (13%) parasitised by Great Spotted Cuckoo which lays a colour-matching, but much smaller egg (33.4 x 24.5 mm). **Incubation period:** 18-19 days; by both sexes, but mostly ♀; begins before clutch is completed. **Nestling/fledging period:** 38 days (35-43); young brooded and fed by both sexes.

House Crow *Corvus splendens* Huiskraai   page 386

First recorded in Durban in 1972 and Cape Town in 1977, their arrival in the region probably the result of ship-assisted passage from Asia or East Africa; breeding populations are well established in both areas. In Durban, pairs nest solitarily or semi-colonially and these are virtually all associated with human settlements; adjacent nests can be within 30 m of each other, but not more than 1 nest/tree. **Nest:** a broad, open bowl of dry twigs, with a deep cup, thickly lined with dry grass and plant-stems, placed in the upper branches of eucalypts, casaurinas, araucarias, mangos and suburban trees, 5-13-26 m up from the ground. The nest measures: outside diameter 200-350-470 mm; cup diameter 130-160-200 mm; cup depth 70-90-150 mm. In India, both sexes collect nest material and the ♀ builds the nest.

Laying months: mainly Oct-Nov (Oct-Jan); may relay after early failure. **Clutch size:** 4 (3-5). **Eggs:** 33.4-37.0-41.6 x 24.1-26.9-29.7 mm; mass 9.5-13.1-17.5 g. **Incubation period:** 16-17 days (India); by both sexes, but mostly ♀; begins before clutch is completed. **Nestling/fledging period:** 27-31-38 days; young fed by both sexes.

White-necked Raven *Corvus albicollis* Withalskraai   page 386

Breeds in hilly and mountainous country in South Africa and Zimbabwe it is restricted, while breeding, to the vicinity of cliffs which provide nest sites. Pairs nest solitarily and are widely spaced. **Nest:** a broad, open bowl of sticks placed on a cliff face or an abandoned quarry face, 2½-90 m up from the base; usually inaccessibly placed in a pothole or in a sheltered recess rather than on an exposed ledge. It is built with dry twigs and sticks, tightly knitted together; the cup, set in the top of the stick mass, is thickly lined with dry grass, animal hair, wool and other fluffy material. Nests are often reused in successive years and these become increasingly large, sometimes filling the pothole in which they are built. One nest measured: outside diameter 680 mm; cup diameter 210 mm; nest height 300 mm; cup depth 50 mm. Both sexes build or refurbish the nest.

Laying months: mainly Sep-Oct (Jul-Nov, rarely in other months); single-brooded. **Clutch size:** 4 (2-5). **Eggs:** 45.0-51.0-56.9 x 31.6-33.3-35.0 mm. **Incubation period:** 21 and 26 days recorded. **Nestling/fledging period:** 38 days; young fed by ♀.

Cape Crow

Pied Crow

House Crow

White-necked Raven

TITS

TITS Family Paridae Worldwide 59 species; 15 breed in Afrotropics, 7 in southern Africa. Monogamous, some are cooperative breeders, others not; where known, ♀ builds nest, incubates and broods young, fed by ♂ and helpers (if present); builds a warmly lined cup in a tree cavity, or cavity in walls, rocks, etc; also uses nest boxes; eggs oval; white or pink with red-brown speckles 3-5/clutch; nestlings are altricial and nidicolous; nestlings and incubating ♀ make a snake-like hissing and lunge when nest hole is examined; 2 species are occasionally parasitised by Greater Honeyguide.

Southern Black Tit *Parus niger* Gewone Swartmees page 380

Breeds in deciduous woodland in the mesic savannas also, locally, in evergreen forest. Pairs or family groups (pair plus 1-4 helpers) are territorial year-round, nest solitarily, a pair or group/28-45 ha. **Nest:** uses a natural cavity in a tree, less often a woodpecker or barbet hole, a hollow metal pole (e.g. a fence post), or a nesting box. The most usual site is a natural cavity in a tree trunk where narrow (35-50 mm wide) entrance hole (a knot or crack) gives access into a hollow core; nest-holes are typically about 2 m up from the ground (0.9-5), and the nest 150-270-610 mm down from the entrance; hollows deeper than this are usually partly filled with leaves, bark, etc. The nest is a compact, cup-shaped pad (6-9 cm thick) typically made with shredded plant fibre, plant down and animal hair. Nest holes are only infrequently reused in successive seasons. Only the ♀ builds the nest and she is accompanied while doing this by her mate; it takes about 15 days to complete. While incubating she is fed at the nest by her mate but she also leaves the nest unattended for short periods to feed. She sits tight while incubating and, if the nest is inspected, she performs a hissing display that simulates a snake striking. The birds are secretive and unobtrusive in the vicinity of the nest.
Laying months: mainly Oct-Nov (Aug-Jan), starting earlier in the north (Sep in Zimbabwe) than in south (Oct in e Cape); single brooded; may relay after an early failure. **Clutch size:** 4 (3-6). **Eggs:** 16.6-18.0-20.7 x 13.0-13.9-14.6 mm; occasionally parasitised by Greater Honeyguide. **Incubation period:** 15 days; by ♀ only, in shifts of 34-47-63 min, fed by ♂, sometimes assisted by helpers. **Nestling/fledging period:** 23 days (22-24); brooded by ♀, fed by both sexes, assisted by helpers when present.

Carp's Tit *Parus carpi* Ovamboswartmees page 380

Breeds in semi-arid and arid woodlands in central and northern Namibia, especially in mopane and acacia savanna; often in rugged hilly country and, in arid regions, restricted to wooded watercourses. Pairs nest solitarily and are widely spaced. **Nest:** a shallow cup of soft, felted plant material and animal hair placed in a tree cavity a few metres up from the ground; mostly uses natural cavities, less often a woodpecker or barbet hole, hollow metal pipe (e.g. road sign pole, fence post) or nest box; the nest can be as deep as 400 mm down in a tree cavity, as much as to 2 m down in a metal pipe.
Laying months: mainly Feb-Apr (Jan-Jul). **Clutch size:** 4 (2-5). **Eggs:** 16.0-17.5-18.0 x 13.0-13.7-14.0 mm. **Incubation period:** 13-15 days; by ♀ only, leaving at intervals to feed; fed by ♂ at nest. **Nestling/fledging period:** 18 days; young brooded by ♀, fed by both sexes.

Grey Tit *Parus afer* Piet-tjou-tjou-grysmees no nest photo page 380

Breeds in open, scrub in the karoo and fynbos, also in agricultural landscapes and in the Lesotho highlands. Pairs or family groups nest solitarily and are widely dispersed. **Nest:** a shallow-cupped pad of fine grass, animal hair, wool, feathers and other soft material placed in a cavity; sites chosen range from clefts or hollows in the walls of dongas, embankments, rock faces and tree stumps, to man-made sites that include narrow drain pipes, crevices in bridges and old buildings, and hollow fence posts (up to 2 m deep in these); also recorded using the closed nest of a Greater Striped Swallow. The nest is built by both sexes in 14 days.
Laying months: mainly Aug-Sep (Jul-Oct) in s Cape and karoo; Nov-Jan in Lesotho highlands. **Clutch size:** 3-4 (2-5). **Eggs:** 18.9-19.2-19.5 x 14.5-14.6-14.6 mm. **Incubation period:** 14 days; by ♀, fed by ♂. **Nestling/fledging period:** 20 days; young fed by both sexes, assisted by helpers if present.

Miombo Tit *Parus griseiventris* Miombogrysmees page 380

Breeds in miombo and teak woodlands in Zimbabwe. Nesting habits are poorly known. Pairs nest solitarily and are widely dispersed. **Nest:** uses a natural cavity in a tree 0.4-5 m up from the ground; holes of woodpeckers or barbets, or hollow metal fence posts, are infrequently used. Preferred nest cavities have a narrow entrance hole (25-35 mm), either a thin crack or a circular hole, which leads into a hollow core in which the nest is built, usually about 300 mm down. The nest is a compact, cup-shaped pad of finely felted plant material, animal hair and/or other fine debris. The birds are secretive and unobtrusive when nesting.
Laying months: mainly Sep (Aug-Dec). **Clutch size:** 3-4, rarely 5. **Eggs:** 16.8-18.2-18.5 x 13.2-13.5-14.9 mm. **Incubation period:** not recorded. **Nestling/fledging period:** not recorded; young fed by both sexes.

Ashy Tit *Parus cinerascens* Akasiagrysmees page 380

Breeds in arid and semi-arid savanna, especially in thornveld. Pairs nest solitarily and are widely dispersed. **Nest:** a shallow-cupped pad of soft plant material is built at the bottom of a cavity in a tree, usually a natural hole 1-3 m up from the ground, in a dead trunk or stem; entrance usually narrow, leading in to a hollow core from the side or top; old woodpecker and barbet holes are also regularly used, also hollow metal fence posts and metal rafter pipes. Deep holes may be partly filled with dry flakes of animal dung and the nest pad built on top of this; nests are mostly built with shredded grass, animal hair, plant down, feathers and other soft material.
Laying months: Sep-Feb; mainly Sep-Oct in Zimbabwe; Oct-Nov in S Africa and Nov-Feb in Namibia; probably opportunistic in arid regions. **Clutch size:** 4-5 (3-6). **Eggs:** 17.0-18.6-19.7 x 12.0-13.8-14.2 mm; mass 2.02-2.10-2.23 g; occasionally parasitised by Greater Honeyguide. **Incubation period:** 14-15 days; by ♀ only; starts with third-laid egg; ♀ leaves to feed at 45-min intervals; also fed by ♂ at nest. **Nestling/fledging period:** 20-22 days; young brooded by ♀, fed by both sexes.

Southern Black Tit

Southern Black Tit

Carp's Tit

Miombo Tit

Ashy Tit (LEFT & TWO ABOVE)

Tits, Penduline Tits

Rufous-bellied Tit *Parus rufiventris* Rooipensmees
This and the next species are treated as races by some authorities and as separate species by others. Rufous-bellied Tits breed in mopane, teak and other broad-leafed woodlands in ne Namibia. Nesting habits are poorly known but they are unlikely to differ from those of Cinnamon-breasted Tit.

Cinnamon-breasted Tit *Parus palludiventris* Vaalpensmees   page 386
This and the previous species are treated as races by some authorities and as separate species by others. Cinnamon-breasted Tits breed in miombo woodland in ne Zimbabwe and w Mozambique. Pairs nest solitarily and are widely spaced. Nesting habits are poorly known. **Nest:** built in a hole in a tree, usually in the main trunk in a natural cavity with a small entrance hole (30-40 m across) through a knot or crack, either entering from the side or the top; one cavity used was about 350 mm deep and 50-60 mm wide inside. Nests are usually within 2 m of the ground but occasionally up to 7 m. The nest, a warmly lined cup, is built on the floor of the cavity, made from finely shredded pieces of grass, bark other plant material and animal hair. Nest material continues to be added during the incubation.
Laying months: Sep-Dec (Zimbabwe), Nov (Namibia). **Clutch size:** 3-4. **Eggs:** 15.8-17.6-19.5 × 12.8-14.3-14.6 mm. **Incubation period:** not recorded; incubating ♀ is fed on the nest by the ♂. **Nestling/fledging period:** not recorded; young fed by both sexes.

PENDULINE TITS Family Remizidae Worldwide 12 species; 6 breed in Afrotropics, 2 in southern Africa. Monogamous; sexes share nest-building, incubation and nestling care; infrequent cooperative breeders; nest is one of the more remarkable structures built by a bird; it is a finely-knitted, durable woolly pouch suspended in a tree or bush, used as a night-time roost outside the breeding season; eggs oval; tiny; white, unmarked; 4-5/clutch; nestlings are altricial and nidicolous.

Cape Penduline Tit *Anthoscopus minutus* Kaapse Kapokvoël   page 386
Breeds throughout the semi-arid and arid areas in karoo, savanna and fynbos. Pairs or, infrequently (20%), family groups (pair plus 1-2 helpers) nest solitarily, spaced at about a pair/10 ha, adjacent nests usually >700 m apart. **Nest:** a small, enclosed bag, built in a shrub or tree, occasionally on a fence wire; 1-3 m up from the ground in the karoo (where nests are mostly in low bushes), higher (up to 7 m) in thornveld, where it is usually placed in tree-tops. It is oval-shaped, long axis vertical, attached to a twig from its roof; its entrance (through a short spout) leads into the nest from near the top of one side, and beneath this is a lip on which the bird perches on its arrival at the nest; above the lip is an indentation into the nest wall that is commonly referred to as a 'false-entrance'; the nest spout closes automatically when the bird leaves the nest. The nest is densely woven from plant down (e.g. *Tarchonanthus camphoratus Eriocephalus* sp. and others) and/or animal down (sheep's wool where available), and cobweb, making it durable and weather-proof. The finely felted texture of the nest is achieved by the birds repeatedly pulling at the material, teasing it and jabbing it back into the nest wall. Nests vary in size and finish and, although cobweb is invariably an important component, other materials used differ between nests and areas. The exterior of the nest measures about 130-150 mm in height and 60-80 mm in width and the internal cavity is about 90-110 × 50-60 mm. The entrance spout, which is inclined downwards, is thin-walled and 20-25-60 mm long and 20-30 mm in diameter. Both sexes build, taking 20-26-35 days to complete the nest, though replacement nests are finished more rapidly (13-20 days); material continues to be added during the incubation. Nests are often reused for successive broods and as night-time roosts by family groups outside of the breeding season. They are often easily visible from a distance, being light-coloured (but black when built with wool from karakul sheep!), and they lack any form of camouflage, often in the upper branches of a leafless tree.
Laying months: mainly Jul-Oct in winter-rainfall region and Oct-Jan elsewhere (Jul-Apr); often double-brooded. **Clutch size:** 4-5 (3-7; occasionally 10-12, probably laid by more than one ♀); laid at 1-day intervals. **Eggs:** 13.2-14.1-14.9 × 9.3-9.8-10.9 mm. **Incubation period:** 14½ days (13½-15); shared equally by both sexes. **Nestling/fledging period:** 19 days (16-22); brooded and fed by both sexes; second broods are often assisted by young from the first brood.

Grey Penduline Tit *Anthoscopus caroli* Gryskapokvoël   page 386
Breeds widely in mesic savannas, in a range that is largely non-overlapping with that of the Cape Penduline Tit; favours broad-leafed (including miombo) and mixed woodlands. Pairs, with occasional instances of 1 helper, nest solitarily and are widely spaced. **Nest** much resembles that of the Cape Penduline Tit, a small weather-proof bag, attached by its roof to the uppermost twigs of a tree. It is also made of cobweb, plant down and other woolly material which is knitted into a blanket-like fabric; the nest is oval-shaped (long axis vertical) with a spout entrance pointing downwards out from near the top of one side of the nest with a ridge below this on the outer wall which serves as a perch to the incoming bird; above this is an indentation into the nest wall that is commonly referred to as a 'false-entrance'. The nest differs from that of the Cape Penduline Tit in generally being smaller and having a less shaggy finish especially to the underside of the nest. The nest measures: height 120-130 mm; width 65-75 mm; entrance spout 30-40 mm long and 25 mm in diameter; the spout is thin-walled and closes automatically. A further difference from Cape Penduline Tit is that the nest is usually placed at a greater height, typically 5-10 m up from the ground, usually well-hidden in foliage in the topmost twigs of a leafy tree. Both sexes build the nest and they continue to work on it throughout the nesting cycle. The same tree is sometimes used for a nest site in successive years.
Laying months: mainly Sep-Nov (Aug-Jan, rarely in other months). **Clutch size:** 4-5 (2-8). **Eggs:** 12.6-14.2-16.6 × 8.5-9.5-10.0 mm. **Incubation period:** not recorded. **Nestling/fledging period:** 22-26 days; fed by both sexes.

Rufous-bellied Tit

Cinnamon-breasted Tit

Cape Penduline Tit

Grey Penduline Tit

LARKS Family Alaudidae Worldwide 98 species; 67 breed in Afrotropics, 31 in southern Africa. These small, ground-living birds, nearly a third of the world's species represented in the region, are among southern Africa's most interesting bird families; many are desert-living and show interesting adaptations for surviving and breeding in sometimes extreme arid environments; some are sedentary, others highly mobile, moving into and out of areas in response to rainfall; in many, the ♂s perform distinctive aerial displays at the start of breeding and, of course, they exhibit great variety and ingenuity in their nests. Where known (and many are poorly known), they are monogamous, but at least one is an occasional cooperative breeder (Spike-heeled Lark); parental roles vary between species – shared in some, mainly by the ♀ in others; eggs are oval-shaped, whitish with a dense speckling of brown and grey; 1-3/clutch; nestlings are altricial and nidicolous, but they leave the nest well before they can fly.

Monotonous Lark *Mirafra passerina* Bosveldlewerik page 387

Breeds widely but erratically in the semi-arid savannas; it is highly nomadic, seldom nesting in the same area in successive years but instead moving into, and breeding, where good rains have fallen. Favours open mopane, acacia or combretum savanna or scrub where scattered tufts of annual grasses have emerged following the rains, on otherwise bare or stony ground. Breeding is initiated by ♂s arriving at the site and singing incessantly, even through the night; in optimum conditions 5-10 ♂s may be heard singing simultaneously; ♀s follow, and commence breeding within 10 days of their arrival. Nesting density is about a pair/½-2 ha. **Nest:** a deep cup set into the ground with a domed roof and a side entrance, placed between or against grass tufts. It is built by the ♀ and is made of dry grass blades, culms and roots, with live grass stems from the tuft incorporated into the walls and roof of the nest. She lays her clutch before the nest is complete (2 days after starting the nest) and continues adding nest lining during the incubation. ♂s are initially promiscuous, becoming monogamous as the cycle progresses.
Laying months: mainly Jan (Oct-Mar). **Clutch size:** 2-4, laid at 1-day intervals. **Eggs:** 18.5-20.6-24.4 x 13.5-14.5-15.8 mm. **Incubation period:** 12-13 days; by ♀ only; begins before clutch is complete. **Nestling/fledging period:** young fed by both sexes; nestlings leave the nest when 8-9 days old, before they can fly.

Melodious Lark *Mirafra cheniana* Spotlewerik page 387

Breeds in open semi-arid grasslands in a fragmented range centering on the transition zone between the grassland and karoo; it nests on mid- or upper-slopes (away from bottomlands) where the grass cover (usually *Themeda*) has not been heavily grazed or trampled; in ideal conditions a density of several pairs per hectare may be found. **Nest:** built between grass tufts and set well into the ground (in a depression about 25-35 mm deep); it is cup-shaped with a partly or wholly domed roof and a side entrance; the dome is more peaked than those built by other dome-nesting larks. It is made of dry blades and stems of grass, with coarser material being used outside and finer material for the interior and cup lining. The nest measures: outside diameter 75-80 mm; cup diameter 50-80 mm; cup depth 25-35 mm; nest height (ground to peak) 100-125 mm. The entrance is about 50 mm in width and height and has a lower protruding lip or 'doormat' of grass stems. It is built by the ♀, and during this period the ♂ sings and displays aerially for lengthy periods in the day. A bird flushed off the nest usually returns quickly, flying back, accompanied by its mate, hovering in the vicinity then settling on the ground close to the nest.
Laying months: mainly Nov-Jan (Sep-Mar). **Clutch size:** 3 (2-4). **Eggs:** 17.8-19.5-21.6 x 13.8-14.4-15.4 mm. **Incubation period:** not recorded; by ♀ only. **Nestling/fledging period:** not recorded; nestlings fed by both sexes.

Rufous-naped Lark *Mirafra africana* Rooineklewerik page 387

Breeds widely in the savanna and grassland regions, favouring open or lightly wooded country with a rather sparse grass cover. Pairs are sedentary, nest solitarily and are widely dispersed. **Nest:** cup-shaped, with a partly or wholly domed roof and a side entrance, built between grass tufts and set well into the ground in a scrape about 25 mm deep; it is usually well concealed. It is made of dry blades, shreds and stems of grass, in which coarse, old, weathered material is used for the exterior, and finer material is used to line the nest-cup; some nests are substantial, thick-walled structures, while others are relatively flimsy. The nest measures: outside diameter 100-130 mm; cup diameter 60-70 mm; cup depth about 25 mm; nest height (ground to peak) 80-90 mm. The entrance to the nest is about 60 mm wide and high. ♂s sing frequently in the nesting area before egg-laying, but become relatively quiet once incubation commences.
Laying months: mainly Oct-Jan (Sep-Mar, rarely in other months). **Clutch size:** 2-3, rarely 4. **Eggs:** 20.2-22.2-24.7 x 14.9-15.8-18.2 mm. **Incubation period:** 14-15 days. **Nestling/fledging period:** young leave the nest at 10-11 days, before they can fly; brooded by ♀ only, fed by both sexes.

Flappet Lark *Mirafra rufocinnamomea* Laeveldklappertjie page 387

Breeds in mesic savanna, favouring grassy areas between scattered trees. Pairs nest solitarily and are widely dispersed. **Nest:** cup-shaped, set in a shallow scrape between grass or forb tufts, with a three-quarter domed roof and a side entrance; it is made of dry blades and stems of grass, and has living grass stems pulled over and incorporated into the roof with finer grass stems and rootlets used to line the nest-cup. The nest measures: outside diameter about 110 mm; cup diameter 60 mm; nest height (ground to peak) about 110 mm. The nest's entrance, which has a lower protruding lip or 'doormat', is about 60 mm wide and 70 mm high.
Laying months: mainly Nov-Feb (Oct-Apr). **Clutch size:** 2-3. **Eggs:** 18.5-20.8-22.4 x 13.7-14.8-16.1 mm. **Incubation period:** not recorded. **Nestling/fledging period:** young leave nest at 11 days, before they can fly.

Monotonous Lark

Melodious Lark

Rufous-naped Lark

Flappet Lark

Cape Clapper Lark *Mirafra apiata* Kaapse Klappertjie

Breeds in fynbos and karoo where dwarf shrubs dominate the vegetation. Nesting habits are poorly known. It is a sedentary species and pairs nest solitarily. **Nest:** a shallow cup with a partly domed roof accessed by a side entrance. The cup is set in the ground between, or at the base of grass or forb tufts, well concealed from above. It is made from dry grass, lined with rootlets. ♂s sing and perform aerial displays, usually in early morning and evening, throughout the breeding cycle.
Laying months: mainly Sep-Oct (Aug-Nov). **Clutch size:** 2-3. **Eggs:** 21.1-21.5-22.0 x 15.2-15.4-15.6 mm. **Incubation period:** not recorded. **Nestling/fledging period:** not recorded.

Eastern Clapper Lark *Mirafra fasciolata* Hoëveldklappertjie   page 387

Breeds in open, mainly semi-arid grasslands, favouring sandy or stony areas where the grass cover is fairly sparse. Pairs are sedentary and nest solitarily, although numerous ♂s may be found displaying within an area of a few hectares. **Nest:** cup-shaped with a partly or wholly domed roof and a side entrance, placed on the ground among scattered grass tufts, built between two or more tufts or between stones. It is made of dry blades and stems of grass, in which coarser, old weathered material is used for the exterior, and finer grass stems are used to line the nest-cup; some nests are substantial, thick-walled structures, while others have thin transparent walls and wide entrances. The nest measures: outside diameter about 90-100 mm; cup diameter 60 mm; cup depth about 20 mm; nest height (ground to peak) 80-90 mm. The entrance to the nest is about 60 mm wide and high. ♂s sing and perform aerial displays in the nesting area throughout the breeding cycle.
Laying months: Sep-Mar, peaking in Oct-Dec in S Africa and Dec-Mar in Namibia and Botswana. **Clutch size:** 2-3. **Eggs:** 20.0-22.3-24.5 x 14.9-15.4-16.2 mm. **Incubation period:** not recorded. **Nestling/fledging period:** young leave nest at 11 days, before they can fly.

Sabota Lark *Calendulauda sabota* Sabotalewerik   page 387

Breeds widely across the savanna belt, from the semi-arid west to the mesic east and extending southwards into the karoo along drainage lines with trees and grass; favours open, grassy woodland, especially thornveld. Pairs nest solitarily and are widely spaced. **Nest:** a cup, usually but not invariably, with a domed roof set into a scrape in the ground against, or between, grass tufts or stones; it is made of dry blades and stems of grass, using coarser material for the walls and roof, and finer material to line the cup. Some nests are substantial, thick-walled and thick-roofed structures with a small, concealed entrance, whereas others are relatively flimsily made and have a wide entrance. The nest measures: cup diameter 65-75 mm; cup depth 30-40 mm. The incubating bird usually sits tight, only flushing off the nest when closely approached; on flying off it may feign injury in flight, settle on a tree and call agitatedly, using a range of mimicked notes of other birds' alarm calls.
Laying months: mainly Oct-Dec in S Africa and Zimbabwe, Feb-Mar in Namibia. **Clutch size:** 2-3, rarely 4. **Eggs:** 18.6-20.6-23.0 x 13.9-14.8-15.5 mm. **Incubation period:** not recorded. **Nestling/fledging period:** not recorded; young fed by both sexes.

Rudd's Lark *Mirafra ruddi* Drakensberglewerik   page 387

Breeds in a narrow range along the eastern, high-lying watershed of South Africa's grassland region; favours flat to undulating ground on mid- to upper-slopes where the grass cover is dense, but short. Pairs nest solitarily and are widely spaced (mostly >100 m between adjacent nests). **Nest:** well-hidden, a deep cup with a domed roof and tunnelled side entrance, placed in a scrape in the ground and set between short, thick grass tufts: it is made of dry blades and shreds of grass, using coarser, old material for the walls and roof, and finer material to line the cup; it is a substantially built nest, being thick-walled and thick-roofed. It measures: nest length (including tunnel entrance) 80-90-120 mm; nest width 70-75-100 mm; nest height (ground to top of dome) 40-55-80 mm; cup diameter 65-75-85 mm; cup depth 20-30-35 mm; nest entrance 45-50-55 mm wide and 30-45-60 mm high. The nest is built by the ♀ and it takes 2-4 days to complete; nest material is collected from within 10 m of the nest; eggs are laid 1-9 days after completion. After nest failure a replacement nest is started within 2-3 days, <50 m from failed nest. ♂s perform aerial song displays mainly before egg-laying; once incubation commences they are less demonstrative.
Laying months: mainly Jan-Feb (Oct-Mar); relays up to 4 x after earlier failures; single-brooded. **Clutch size:** 3 (2-4), laid at 1-day intervals. **Eggs:** 19.9-21.5-23.1 x 14.3-15.4-16.1 mm; mass 2.4 g. **Incubation period:** 14 days (13-15), by ♀, in shifts of 1-16-59 min; the nest is attended by the female for 56% of day. **Nestling/fledging period:** nestlings leave the nest at 11-13-15 days, before they can fly; they are brooded by the ♀, fed by both sexes.

Fawn-coloured Lark *Calendulauda africanoides* Vaalbruinlewerik   page 387

Breeds on sandy soils in savanna, primarily in semi-arid savanna or scrub; this is the ubiquitous lark of the Kalahari sandveld. Pairs nest solitarily and are widely spaced; in ideal conditions at a density of several pairs per hectare. **Nest:** cup-shaped, with a domed roof and a side entrance (occasionally, nests lack the domed roof); it placed on the ground and set against, or between, grass tufts or small forbs; faces s or e in most Kalahari nests. The nest is made of dry blades and stems of grass, using coarser, usually old (grey-coloured) weathered grass for the walls and roof, and finer material, including rootlets, to line the cup. The nest measures: outside diameter 90 mm; cup diameter 65-70 mm; cup depth 20-40 mm; entrance 55 mm wide and 55 mm high, with a variable amount of nest material laid in front of the entrance in the form of a 'doormat'. When building the nest, the scrape is made first, followed by the roof and side-walls, and it is completed by adding lining material to the scrape.
Laying months: mainly Oct-Mar (Aug-Apr); opportunistic in the more arid areas in response to rainfall. **Clutch size:** 2-3, rarely 4. **Eggs:** 17.2-20.7-23.4 x 11.9-14.6-15.6 mm. **Incubation period:** 12 days, incubation starts with last-laid egg. **Nestling/fledging period:** 12-14 days; fed by both sexes.

Cape Clapper Lark

Eastern Clapper Lark

Sabota Lark

Rudd's Lark

Fawn-coloured Lark

Red Lark *Calendulauda burra* **Rooilewerik** page 387

Breeds in a narrow range in Bushmanland (N Cape), red-backed forms (*M. b. burra*) occurring mainly on red sand dunes and sandy plains, and brown-backed forms (*M. b. harei*) on shale soils; both frequent areas that have a sparse covering of bushman grass (*Stipagrostis* sp.) and scattered shrubs such as *Rhygozum*. Pairs nest solitarily and are widely dispersed. Its nesting habits are poorly known and few nests have been recorded. **Nest:** cup-shaped, with a domed roof that extends as a hood over a side entrance; placed against the base of a grass tuft or between two tufts; well concealed. It is made with dry blades and stems of grass (mainly *Stipagrostis* sp.) with coarser, weathered material being used in the roof and walls and finer grass ends used to line the cup (in one case with some pieces of reptile skin added). The nest measures: nest length (entrance to back wall) about 180 mm; nest width 75-90 mm; cup diameter 75 x 85 mm (width x length); cup depth 25 mm; height of entrance 60 mm. When breeding the birds are wary, and they walk, rather than fly, to and from their nests. ♂s frequently sing and display aerially in the general nesting area.
Laying months: mainly Oct (Aug-May). **Clutch size:** 2-3. **Eggs:** 22.7-23.0-23.3 x 16.5-16.6-16.8 mm. **Incubation period:** not recorded. **Nestling/fledging period:** not recorded; young fed by both sexes.

Karoo Lark *Calendulauda albescens* **Karoolewerik** page 387

Breeds in flat, open, dwarf shrubland in the karoo and fynbos (including renosterveld and strandveld) where there is a sparse, low cover of shrubs, forbs and grass. Pairs nest solitarily and are widely spaced. **Nest:** a lined scrape in the ground, set between, or against, one or more low shrubs or grass tufts; it is cup-shaped with a partially or completely domed roof and a side entrance. The walls and roof are made of dry stems and blades of grass and/or fine-stemmed forbs, with softer material, including rootlets, *Stipagrostis* grass-awns and woolly seeds of *Eriocephalus*, used to line the cup. The nest-cup has a diameter of about 100 mm and a depth of about 30 mm. It is built by the ♀, accompanied by the ♂.
Laying months: mainly Aug-Nov (Jul-May), but probably nests opportunistically in any month in response to rains. **Clutch size:** 2-3, rarely 4. **Eggs:** 21.5-22.4-24.0 x 14.6-15.9-17.0 mm. **Incubation period:** not recorded. **Nestling/fledging period:** not recorded; young leave nest before they can fly; fed by both sexes.

Dune Lark *Calendulauda erythrochlamys* **Duinlewerik** page 387

Breeds in the sand desert of the Namib where it is the only permanently resident passerine. Pairs nest solitarily and are dispersed in territories of 2-4 ha on the sparsely vegetated sandy hummocks formed along the lower slopes of dune ridges. **Nest:** is cup-shaped with a domed roof, having a side entrance that usually faces out towards the e or s; it is built against the base of a grass tuft and is well concealed. It is made of dry blades and stems of grass, principally *Stipagrostis sabulicola*, with coarser material being used outside and finer material inside; some cobweb is used to bind the nest walls. The cup is lined with fine, plant fragments plus variable amounts of mammal hair, reptile skin or feathers. The nest measures: outside diameter 110-121-145 mm; nest height 115-129-160 mm; cup diameter 55-69-100 mm. The entrance hole is very variable in size (60-100 mm in width and 55-100 mm in height), some having a low, overhanging dome, others being virtually open-cupped. The nest is built by the ♀ over a period of 7-9 days and material from one nest may be recycled for another. During nest building, ♂s frequently sing and display aerially, but they become silent once the incubation commences. The ♀ sits tight while incubating and is not easily flushed; when she is forced off the nest she is undemonstrative. Once the chicks have hatched, however, both parents hover and call anxiously above any intruder that approaches the nest.
Laying months: mainly Jan-Feb (Aug-Apr); usually relays after an early nest failure; sometimes double-brooded. **Clutch size:** 2 (rarely 1); laid at a 1-day interval. **Eggs:** 20.1-22.0-23.7 x 14.3-15.9-17.5 mm. **Incubation period:** 13-14 days; by ♀ only; nest is left unattended when she feeds. **Nestling/fledging period:** 12-14 days; brooded by ♀ only, fed by both sexes.

Barlow's Lark *Calendulauda barlowi* **Barlowse Lewerik** page 387

This recently recognised species (described in 1998) has a narrow range extending from Port Nolloth to Luderitz and the same distance inland. It occurs here in arid scrubland on both sandy and stony substrates. Its nesting habits are poorly known. **Nest:** two nests are described as being 'domed structures on the sand with the domes woven into the bushes under which they were placed'; a third nest with young in coastal dunes (this one illustrated in the photographs opposite) was a cup 72 x 80 mm wide and 44 mm deep, not domed, placed under a 40 cm shrub, its base built with small twigs.
Laying months: Aug-Oct. **Clutch size:** 2. **Eggs:** 23 x 17 mm. **Incubation period:** not recorded. **Nestling/fledging period:** 13 days; young fed by both sexes.

Red Lark

Karoo Lark

Dune Lark

Barlow's Lark

Benguela Long-billed Lark *Certhilauda benguelensis* **Kaokolangbeklewerik**   no nest or egg photo

Breeds in nw Namibia in semi-arid and arid dwarf shrublands. Its nesting habits are poorly known. ♂'s sing and perform aerial displays in the nesting area during the nesting period. **Nest:** a shallow cup of dry grass and forb leaves set into the ground at the base of a plant.
Laying months: Apr-May. **Clutch size:** 2-3. **Eggs:** sizes not recorded. **Incubation period:** not recorded. **Nestling/fledging period:** not recorded.

Karoo Long-billed Lark *Certhilauda subcoronata* **Karoolangbeklewerik**

Breeds across the central karoo into central Namibia frequenting stony and rocky areas in dwarf shrubland. Nesting habits are poorly known. ♂'s sing and perform aerial displays in the nesting area during the nesting period. **Nest:** a neat cup of twigs, lined with fluffy *Eriocephalus* seeds, set into the ground at the base of a plant or stone, usually facing s or e. Adults bringing food to nestlings land >5 m from the nest and approach from there on foot; they leave the same way.
Laying months: Aug-Apr; main laying period varies regionally from Aug-Oct (sw Cape), to Oct-Dec (karoo), to Jan-Apr (Namibia). **Clutch size:** 2-3. **Eggs:** 23 x 16 mm. **Incubation period:** not recorded. **Nestling/fledging period:** not recorded; young fed by both sexes.

Cape Long-billed Lark *Certhilauda curvirostris* **Weskuslangbeklewerik**   no nest photo   page 387

Breeding range restricted to the w coastal plain of w Cape where it frequents coastal scrub, strandveld, renosterveld and other dwarf shrubland, also fallow croplands. Pairs nest solitarily at densities of about a pair/10 ha. Nesting habits are poorly known. ♂'s perform aerial displays over nesting area during the breeding season. **Nest:** a cup set in the ground between grass tufts, dwarf shrubs or stones, made with dry grass and lined with finer material.
Laying months: Aug-Oct. **Clutch size:** 3. **Eggs:** 23.2-24.0-24.9 x 16.6-17.1-17.5 mm. **Incubation period:** not recorded. **Nestling/fledging period:** not recorded.

Agulhas Long-billed Lark *Certhilauda brevirostris* **Overberglangbeklewerik**   no nest or egg photo

Breeding range restricted to the s Cape between the Agulhas plain and Worcester where it frequents areas of low scrub and fallow croplands. Nesting habits are poorly known. ♂'s perform aerial displays over nesting area during the breeding season. **Nest:** a cup set in the ground, hidden between dwarf shrubs and made with dry grass, lined with rootlets and finer grass leaves.
Laying months: Sep-Oct. **Clutch size:** 2-3. **Eggs:** 22.3-23.5-24.6 x 16.0-17.0-18.3 mm. **Incubation period:** not recorded. **Nestling/fledging period:** not recorded.

Eastern Long-billed Lark *Certhilauda semitorquata* **Grasveldlangbeklewerik**   page 387

Breeds in open highveld grasslands where there are areas of rocky outcrop. Pairs nest solitarily and are widely spaced. **Nest:** a broad shallow, open cup placed against a rock, under a partly projecting stone, or against a low shrub or grass tuft; the open side of the nest is fringed by a broad apron of pebbles laid around one side. The cup is made with shreds of dry grass and lined with finer grass stems and rootlets; it measures about 70 mm across and is 40 mm deep. The pebble apron that encircles the exposed side of the nest is built of 15-30 mm diameter stones; in some nests they form a close-packed rim extending from the edge of the nest for 70-80 mm, while in others they may be scattered loosely next to the nest. The nest is built by the ♀, accompanied by the ♂. ♂'s perform aerial song displays mainly before egg-laying; once incubation commences they are less demonstrative.
Laying months: mainly Oct-Nov (Sep-Jan). **Clutch size:** 2-3. **Eggs:** 21.6-22.1-22.9 x 15.8-16.4-17.0 mm. **Incubation period:** not recorded. **Nestling/fledging period:** not recorded; young fed by both sexes.

Short-clawed Lark *Certhilauda chuana* **Kortkloulewerik**   page 387

Breeds in flat, open, semi-arid savanna, especially scrub thornveld where the grass cover is sparse and has been subject to heavy grazing. Pairs are sedentary, and they nest solitarily at densities of a pair/ ¾-10 ha; in one instance, two adjacent nests were 33 m apart. **Nest:** a shallow open cup set into the ground against a low shrub, forb, grass tuft or thorn tree sapling; in se Botswana most nests were situated on the n side of the plant and they were poorly shaded; it is loosely made, using mainly blades and shreds of dry grass, with finer material, including rootlets, used for the lining. The nest measures: outside diameter 83-107-140 mm; cup diameter 65-71-80 mm; cup depth 20-35-42 mm. The nest is built by the ♀ in 5-14 days; she is accompanied by the ♂ then and she continues to add material through the incubation. ♂'s sing and perform aerial displays in the nesting area throughout the nesting period; while she is incubating he perches on a tree near the nest and warns the ♀ when there is a threat to the nest.
Laying months: Sep-Mar; mainly Dec-Feb in Limpopo, Oct-Nov in se Botswana; relays after early failures (up to 5x/season); multi-brooded. **Clutch size:** 2 (1-3), laid at a 1-day interval. **Eggs:** 18.7-21.4-23.8 x 14.5-15.7-16.8 mm; mass 2.1-2.7-3.2 g. **Incubation period:** 16 days (14-16); by ♀ only. **Nestling/fledging period:** young leave nest at 11-12 days before they can fly; brooded and shaded by ♀; fed by both sexes; fledged young fed by parents for up to 4 weeks.

Karoo Long-billed Lark

Eastern Long-billed Lark

Eastern Long-billed Lark

Short-clawed Lark (LEFT & TWO ABOVE)

Dusky Lark *Pinarocorus nigricans* Donkerlewerik

A non-breeding visitor to southern Africa, present between Nov-Apr; however, in Apr 2010 a pair were recorded building a nest (see photograph opposite) in mixed savanna in se Botswana, suggesting that further attention to this bird's status in the region is needed. Little is known of its nesting habits in its known breeding range in Angola and Zambia; it lays there in Aug-Oct; the nest is an open cup placed on the ground under a clod or plant tuft, about 100 mm in diameter and 60 mm deep. It lays 2 eggs.

Gray's Lark *Ammomanopsis grayi* Namiblewerik page 387

Restricted to the gravel plains of the Namib Desert, this species breeds in flat, open areas that are covered with light-coloured gravel pebbles and stones and, after rains, with scattered tufts of *Stipagrostis* grass. It is gregarious and nomadic. Pairs and occasional trios nest solitarily, but nests may be loosely aggregated. **Nest:** a deep, open cup, placed in a scrape in the ground, usually situated against the shaded side of a stone or grass tuft, but sometimes completely exposed. The rim of the nest lies level with (or slightly above) the ground surface and the cup is surrounded by an flat apron of small pebbles (5-10 mm diameter) which extend beneath the nest as a loose foundation across the bottom of the nest scrape. The nest lining lies above this; it is a thick-walled, well-insulated pad of light-coloured, finely-shredded pieces of grass and soft grass (*Stipagrostis*) inflorescences; in one nest described no material was added to a bare scrape in the ground. The width of the nest (including the pebble apron) is 60-100-150 mm across; the cup diameter is about 60 mm in diameter, and the cup depth about 35-50 mm. The incubating bird sits low in the nest, its back level with the ground and its pale colouring blending well with the surroundings. During the breeding period ♂s perform aerial song displays in the nesting area before sunrise and after sunset.

Laying months: mainly Mar-Jul, but probably breeds opportunistically in any month in response to rain. **Clutch size:** 2-3. **Eggs:** 19.8-21.2-22.4 x 14.6-15.3-16.0 mm. **Incubation period:** 12-13 days. **Nestling/fledging period:** young leave nest at about 10 days before they can fly; fed by both sexes.

Large-billed Lark *Galerida magnirostris* Dikbeklewerik page 387

Breeds widely in the karoo, in semi-arid grasslands and in low fynbos; also in fallow or harvested lands; it favours areas with low shrubby vegetation or low grass cover and may nest on both flat ground and on relatively steep slopes. Pairs nest solitarily and are widely spaced. **Nest:** an open cup, placed on the ground and inside thick grass or other low vegetation, or against the side of a small shrub (mostly on its shaded side in the karoo); nests are usually well concealed by surrounding foliage. It is made with dry stems of forbs and other plants, shreds of dry grass and rootlets, the cup lined with finer stems and rootlets and, in some cases, with plant down (*Eriocephalus*), wool or a few feathers; some nests are substantial while others are little more than a lining added to the floor of a scrape. The cup is 60-70 mm wide and 30-38 mm deep. Birds flushed off nests sometimes perform an injury-feigning display as they fly from the nest. ♂s sing frequently from the nesting area in the earlier stages of the breeding period.

Laying months: mainly Aug-Oct (Jul-Dec, rarely to Apr). **Clutch size:** 2-3 (1-4). **Eggs:** 20.9-23.2-25.7 x 15.4-16.6-17.4 mm. **Incubation period:** 16 days. **Nestling/fledging period:** not recorded; fed by both sexes.

Spike-heeled Lark *Chersomanes albofasciata* Vlaktelewerik page 387

Breeds widely across the grasslands and karoo of southern Africa, everywhere in open, treeless landscapes. Pairs, and occasionally family groups (pair plus 1 helper), nest solitarily and they are widely spaced. **Nest:** an open cup set into a scrape in the ground and made from fine blades and shreds of dry grass or, in arid areas, from thin stems of forbs. Rootlets may or may not be used in the cup lining. Nests in arid areas differ from those in mesic habitats by having an extended apron of nest material (that may include twigs, pebbles, clods of earth, etc.) added to the open side of the nest; in mesic grasslands the nest is usually encircled by short, densely spaced grass tufts and this apron is absent. Nests in arid areas are mostly located on the s and e sides of tussocks or small shrubs where they are most shaded from the sun. The nest-cup measures about 65 mm in diameter and 25-30 mm in depth. It is built by both sexes and takes about 5 days to complete, eggs being laid 3-4 days after this.

Laying months: mainly Aug-Nov, but all months recorded, especially in arid areas where breeding occurs in response to rainfall. **Clutch size:** 2-3, rarely 4 or 5; laid at 1-day intervals. **Eggs:** 19.2-20.9-22.5 x 13.7-14.8-16.3 mm; mass 2-2.1 g. **Incubation period:** 12-13 days; by ♀ only, fed at the nest by the ♂; may start before clutch is complete. **Nestling/fledging period:** young leave the nest at about 8-12 days before they can fly; they are fed by both sexes, occasionally assisted by helpers.

Red-capped Lark *Calandrella cinerea* Rooikoplewerik page 387

Breeds widely in short, open grassland, especially where burnt, heavily grazed or mowed, and commonly found on edges of pans, airfields, road verges and other short-grass habitats. Pairs nest solitarily; in ideal conditions, 2-4 pairs/ha, and adjacent nests may be within 25-30 m of each other. **Nest:** a deep, open cup, set into the ground, usually against a grass tuft or between tussocks, in some cases against a mound of dry cow-dung or a stone; other nests are not close to any such protective feature (as shown in photograph opposite). The base of the nest is made of coarse shreds and blades of dry grass, and the cup is lined with finer pieces of grass and rootlets. Nests commonly have a built-up rim or ramp on their open side which consists of shreds of cow-dung, clods of earth, grass stubble or pebbles. The nest measures: outside diameter 70-80 mm; cup diameter 50-60 mm; cup depth 25-35 mm cup depth. ♂ perform aerial song displays over the nesting area, mainly before egg-laying. The nest is built mainly by the ♀ in 4-5 days.

Laying months: all months recorded, but mainly Sep-Nov in the south of its range and Jul-Sep in the north (Zimbabwe); regularly double-brooded. **Clutch size:** 2 (2-4); laid at a 1-day interval. **Eggs:** 17.0-21.2-23.3 x 13.2-15.1-16.8 mm. **Incubation period:** 14 days (12-15); by ♀ only, fed by ♂; starts when clutch completed. **Nestling/fledging period:** 12 days (9-18); young fed by both sexes.

Dusky Lark

Gray's Lark

Large-billed Lark

Spike-heeled Lark

Red-capped Lark

Pink-billed Lark *Spizocorys conirostris* **Pienkbeklewerik** page 387

Breeds widely in open, short, semi-arid to mesic grasslands, on grass-covered dunes, and in old lands. Nomadic over much of its range and it can be found nesting prolifically in an area one year but not the next. Pairs nest solitarily but adjacent pairs may nest <50 m apart. **Nest:** an open cup placed in a scrape in the ground, usually against the s or e side of a grass tuft to maximise shading, or between tussocks; rarely away from any plant cover; it is made of blades and shreds of dry grass, with coarser material forming the base and finer material, including rootlets and pieces of mammal hair, lining the cup: 700-800 pieces of material have been counted in a nest. The rim of the nest is somewhat raised above the level of the ground and, especially in nests in arid areas, there is an apron of material extending beyond the rim of the nest on its open side. The nest is usually poorly concealed. Its dimensions are: outside diameter 65-74-90 mm; cup diameter 50-53 -55 mm; cup depth 30-35-40 mm.
Laying months: all months, breeding opportunistically in response to rains, with a slight Apr-Jul peak. **Clutch size:** 2 (1-3). **Eggs:** 16.1-18.2-20.6 x 12.7-13.6-14.4 mm. **Incubation period:** 12 days (11-13); begins with first-laid egg. **Nestling/fledging period:** young leave nest before they can fly at about 10 days; fed by both sexes.

Botha's Lark *Spizocorys fringillaris* **Vaalrivierlewerik** page 387

Breeds in a restricted range in the eastern highveld in open, short, mesic grassland, favouring heavily grazed, upland situations typically on clay soils where grass cover is dense and shortly cropped; often in the vicinity of areas where stock is concentrated; breeding density up to 6 pairs/ha and adjacent nests may be <20 m apart (and once 3 m apart). **Nest:** an open cup placed in a scrape in the ground and surrounded and concealed by short, closely spaced grass tufts. It is made of shreds of dry grass with a fine grass or mammal-hair lining; it lacks the extended nest rim (or 'ramp') found in other *Spizocorys* lark nests. Some nests are wholly exposed above while others are well concealed by the surrounding grass. It measures: outside diameter 78-86-100 mm; cup diameter 51- 58-63 mm; cup depth 31-34-45 mm. It is built in 3 days. The incubating bird usually sits tight if approached; when flushed it flies up and circles, calling in flight. The birds are confiding and quickly return to their nests.
Laying months: Oct-Jan; apparently single-brooded but will relay 5 days after clutch loss. **Clutch size:** 2 (2-3), laid at a 1-day interval. **Eggs:** 17.2-18.7-19.7 x 12.6-13.8-14.5 mm; mass 1.9 g. **Incubation period:** 13 days; by both sexes, in shifts of <1 hour. **Nestling/ fledging period:** 13 days (11-15); young brooded and fed by both sexes.

Sclater's Lark *Spizocorys sclateri* **Namakwalewerik** page 387

Breeds in the arid karoo; highly nomadic, moving between sites in response to rainfall. It nests in exposed positions on flat, open gravel- and pebble-covered terraces; pairs nest solitarily and are usually widely spaced (but adjacent nests once reported to be 7 m apart). **Nest:** an open cup set into the soil in a scrape about 45-50 mm deep; its rim lies flush with the ground surface and the cup is thickly lined with finely shredded pieces of dry grass and grass inflorescences. The nest-cup is characteristically encircled by an apron of flat pebbles up to 80 mm wide (as shown in the right hand photograph opposite) and a large number (59-160-253) of pebbles are collected and brought to the site by the birds for this purpose; their function is uncertain. In addition, one or more pebbles are frequently placed in the nest-cup alongside the single egg or chick. The cup has a diameter of 47-52-59 mm and a depth of 21-28-35 mm. The incubation, and care of the nestling, is shared equally by the sexes and they change-over frequently during the day, probably in response to high ambient temperatures; if approached, the incubating or brooding bird may sit tight, even allowing itself to be touched. When flushed, it quickly returns to the nest.
Laying months: mainly Aug-Nov (Apr-Nov), often breeding at the driest time of the year, even during droughts. **Clutch size:** 1. **Eggs:** 19.9-21.2-23.4 x 14.2-14.8-15.5 mm; mass 3.1 g. **Incubation period:** 13 days (11-13); by both sexes, with frequent (11-26-65 min) change-overs. **Nestling/fledging period:** young leaves nest at 11 days (10-14) before it can fly; brooded and fed by both sexes.

Stark's Lark *Spizocorys starki* **Woestynlewerik** page 387

Breeds on arid or semi-arid open plains in the karoo and fringes of the Namib Desert. It is a gregarious, nomadic species which moves about and nests in response to rainfall. Pairs nest solitarily but, when conditions are optimum, occur at high densities (2-6 pairs/ha) when dozens of ♂s can be simultaneously seen or heard from one point displaying in the air. **Nest:** an open cup set into a scrape in the ground, usually against a low tuft of *Stipagrostis* or other grass, or against a stone; it is placed on the most shaded (s or e) side. The nest-cup is lined with fine stems of grass (including their soft inflorescences) and it is encircled on its open side with an apron of pebbles, small clods of soil and, in some cases some pieces of sand-encrusted spider-web. The nest-cup has a diameter of 45-56- 64 mm and a depth of 25-35-38 mm. Nests containing nestlings blend particularly well with their backgrounds as the young have a dappled plumage and wisps of down which match the grass inflorescences used in the nest lining. Incubating birds may perform an injury-feigning display when flushed from the nest. Stark's Larks commonly nest in association with the two nomadic sparrow-larks and the Lark-like Bunting.
Laying months: mainly Mar-May (Mar-Aug, sometimes in other months in response to rainfall). **Clutch size:** 2-3, rarely 4. **Eggs:** 17.2-19.0-20.7 x 12.0-14.2-14.9 mm. **Incubation period:** 12 days (11-13); by both sexes. **Nestling/fledging period:** young leaves nest at 10 days before they can fly; brooded and fed by both sexes.

Pink-billed Lark

Botha's Lark

Sclater's Lark

Stark's Lark

Black-eared Sparrow-Lark *Eremopterix australis* Swartoorlewerik
page 387

Breeds in arid and semi-arid karoo, sporadically moving into adjacent areas; favours flat, open landscapes, especially on sandy soil that have a short, sparse grass cover (after rains) and scattered, low shrubs. It is a gregarious, nomadic species which moves about and nests in response to rainfall. Pairs nest solitarily or in loose aggregations in which adjacent nests are spaced 20-50 m apart. **Nest**: an open cup placed in a scrape in the ground, its rim usually level, or only slightly raised above the ground surface. It is usually placed against a low shrub (e.g. *Rhigozum*), always on its most shaded side; in winter, though, nests are occasionally exposed and away from such protection. The nest-cup is thickly lined with fine stems of grass (and especially with their soft inflorescences), and with plant petioles; it measures about 52 mm in diameter and 33 mm in depth. The nest-cup is encircled on its open side by a rim (that can extend 50 mm beyond the edge of the cup) of short, dry twigs overlain by soil-encrusted webs of the buckspoor spider (*Seothyra* sp.); the use of this unusual item is a consistent feature in this lark's nest. The nest is built by the ♀ in 4-5 days; ♂s assist in collecting the web used for the rim. Where their ranges overlap, this species commonly nests alongside Stark's Lark, Grey-backed Sparrow-Lark and/or Lark-like Bunting.

Laying months: all months: breeds opportunistically at any time in response to rainfall, and a rainfall event of 40-50 mm triggers breeding. **Clutch size:** 2-3 (1-3, rarely 4); laid at 1-day intervals. **Eggs:** 16.7-18.4-20.6 x 12.3-13.4-14.9 mm. **Incubation period:** 10½ days (8-11½); shared equally by both sexes, starts when clutch completed. **Nestling/fledging period:** young leave nest at 8-10 days (7-12) before they can fly; they fly at 15-20 days; brooded and fed by both sexes.

Chestnut-backed Sparrow-Lark *Eremopterix leucotis* Rooiruglewerik
page 387

Breeds in the semi-arid savannas, and in the western (more arid) half of the grassland region where it favours flat, open or sparsely wooded ground underlain by heavy soils (clayey or loamy) where the ground cover is shortly grazed, burnt or cleared; the birds are especially attracted to recently harvested agricultural lands. It is nomadic in some areas, resident in others, and is usually gregarious when nesting. Pairs nest solitarily but adjacent nests may be as close as 3 m apart. **Nest:** an open cup placed in a scrape in the ground, typically against a clod of earth, a stone, grass tuft or weed stem and it is usually situated on the most shaded (s or e) side. The cup is lined with shreds of dry grass, some with rootlets as well, and coarser stems of grass may extend in an apron beyond the rim of the nest. It measures about 50 mm in diameter and 30 mm in depth. Both sexes build the nest and continue to add material to it during the incubation period.

Laying months: mainly Mar-Aug, but all months recorded; sometimes double-brooded. **Clutch size:** 2 (1-3); laid at a 1-day interval. **Eggs:** 16.9-19.1-21.1 x 12.3-13.7-15.0 mm. **Incubation period:** 11 days; by both sexes, in shifts of ½-3 hrs, usually 1 hr. **Nestling/fledging period:** young leaves nest at 10-12 days before they can fly; brooded and fed by both sexes.

Grey-backed Sparrow-Lark *Eremopterix verticalis* Grysruglewerik
page 387

Breeds in a variety of open, arid or semi-arid habitats in the karoo, Kalahari and Namib; favours flat, open landscapes (plains, pans etc.) with a short grass cover and scattered shrubs. It is a highly gregarious, nomadic species which moves about and nests in response to rainfall. Pairs nest solitarily but in prime conditions can occur at high densities (12 pairs/ha) and adjacent nests may be within a few metres of one another. **Nest:** an open cup, placed either in a scrape in the ground or raised above ground level (when possibly too hard to excavate) by having a ramp of pebbles, small soil clods or short twigs built up around the cup. It is usually placed against a grass tuft, a low shrub, a stone or clod of earth, always on the most shaded (s to e) side; in winter, more nests tend to be placed in exposed positions away from such shelter. The nest-cup is lined with fine stems of grass (and especially with their soft inflorescences) and sometimes plant down (e.g. seeds of *Eriocephalus* sp.) or wool; it measures about 54 mm in diameter and 30 mm in depth. The pebble/clod/twig apron encircling the open side of the nest can extend at least 100 mm beyond the nest rim and pieces up to 20 mm in size may be used; as many as 235 such items were used in one case. The nest is built by the ♀, sometimes accompanied by the ♂, over a period of 4-5 days. Parent may feign injury when disturbed at nest. Where their ranges overlap, this species commonly nests in close proximity to Stark's Lark, Black-eared Sparrow-Lark and/or Lark-like Bunting.

Laying months: all months recorded, breeding opportunistically in response to rainfall. **Clutch size:** 3 (1-5); Clutch size correlates with rainfall; laid at 1-day intervals. **Eggs:** 16.9-19.3-21.4 x 12.3-13.9-16.4 mm. **Incubation period:** 10 days (9-11); by both sexes, starts before clutch completed. **Nestling/fledging period:** young leave nest (on foot) at 8-10 days (7-12½), before they can fly; brooded and fed by both sexes, the ♀'s share 2-3x that of ♂; first fly at 15-20 days.

Black-eared Sparrow-Lark

Chestnut-backed Sparrow-Lark

Grey-backed Sparrow-Lark

Wagtails

WAGTAILS, PIPITS, LONGCLAWS Family Motacillidae Worldwide 68 species; 30 breed in Afrotropics, 17 in southern Africa. These species are monogamous; none are cooperative breeders; all build open-cupped nests; eggs are oval-shaped, white or light buff variably speckled and blotched, 2-4/clutch; nestlings are altricial and nidiculous. Wagtails, longclaws and pipits differ in aspects of the nesting behaviour.

Wagtails (3 species) mostly nest near water, usually above ground-level, both sexes share nest-building, incubation and parental care and they are commonly parasitised by Red-chested Cuckoo and sometimes by Diederik Cuckoo.

Longclaws (3 species) and pipits (11 species) all nest at ground-level like larks, and conceal their nests in grass; none are parasitised by cuckoos and, where known, ♀s build the nest and incubate, with both sexes sharing feeding of nestlings. Pipits are a notoriously difficult group of birds to identify, and the nests of most of the local species are, in the absence of the parent birds, essentially indistinguishable. In most pipit species the ♂s sing and/or perform aerial display flights over the nesting area early in the breeding cycle.

Cape Wagtail *Motacilla capensis* Gewone Kwikkie   page 388

Breeds widely across the region, always close to water (estuaries, streams, pans, dams, river edges) bordered by open ground, from the coast to high-altitude mountain streams; also commonly nests in urban and suburban environments. Pairs nest solitarily, spaced at about a pair/13-40 ha in natural habitats. **Nest:** an open-cupped bowl, very variably placed from ground-level to about 7 m up; in man-made environments it nests on ledges and cavities in buildings, bridges, hedges, shrubs, creepers, pot-plants, etc; in natural conditions the nest is typically built along a stream bank, in a donga wall or on vegetated dune, where it is well hidden in an overhanging grass tuft. The nest is a substantial bowl, untidily built with rough pieces of dry grass and forbs, with a deep central cup, finely lined with rootlets and finely shredded grass, hair and/or feathers. The nest measures: outside diameter 200 mm; cup diameter 55-65 mm; cup depth 45-50 mm. Nests and nest sites may be reused for successive clutches and in successive years, but it is more usual for a new nest to be built for each nesting attempt. Both sexes build the nest in 2-10-28 days.

Laying months: all months, but peak varies regionally; mainly in Jul-Oct in winter-rainfall region and Aug-Dec elsewhere; relays after earlier failures; multi-brooded (in one case 8 clutches laid in 12 months). **Clutch size:** 3 (1-4, rarely 5-8, these probably laid by >1 ♀); laid at 1-day intervals, in early morning. **Eggs:** 18.6-21.0-25.5 x 14.0-15.4-16.8 mm; mass 2.3-2.5-2.7 g; parasitised by Red-chested and Diederik cuckoos. **Incubation period:** 14 days (13½-15½); by both sexes. in 7-45 min shifts, those of ♀ longer. **Nestling/fledging period:** 15½ days (14-21); young brooded and fed by both sexes.

African Pied Wagtail *Motacilla aguimp* Bontkwikkie   page 388

Breeds along, or close to, larger rivers, estuaries, large dams. Pairs nest solitarily and are widely spaced. **Nest:** a bulky, open-cupped bowl built in a variety of sites, usually over water or surrounded by water; it is often placed in caught-up driftwood or flood debris, in trees, bushes, reed-clumps standing in rivers and dams, in crevices or sheltered ledges on rocks, earth banks, tree stumps. Man-made sites close to water also often used, e.g. moored boats, cavities in walls, niches and ledges in buildings, roofs and bridges. The base is roughly made from stems of dry grass or weeds, flood debris, roots, string, rags or other coarse material; the deep open cup is neatly finished with a lining of fine grass, roots, hair or feathers. The nest measures: outside diameter 170 mm, cup diameter 55-60 mm, cup depth 40 mm. Nests or nest sites are frequently reused in successive broods and seasons. Both sexes build or refurbish the nest.

Laying months: mainly Sep-Oct (Aug-Apr), peaks a month earlier in the n than the s; multi-brooded. **Clutch size:** 3 (2-4, rarely 5), laid at 1-day intervals. **Eggs:** 19.4-21.8-24.9 x 14.6-15.9-16.6 mm; frequently parasitised by Red-chested Cuckoo, occasionally by Diederik cuckoo. **Incubation period:** 13 days (13-14); by both sexes, but mostly by ♀. **Nestling/fledging period:** 15-18 days; young fed by both sexes.

Mountain Wagtail *Motacilla clara* Bergkwikkie   page 388

Breeds along flowing rivers and streams, especially in hills and mountains, usually where forested. Pairs nest solitarily, are territorial year-round, and are spaced along rivers and streams at intervals of a pair/ 0.4-1.2 km. **Nest:** an open-cupped bowl, usually placed over water, often over a pool or close to a waterfall, 1-5 m up from the water on a rock-face ledge, in a crevice, at the base of a plant stem or behind a grass tuft; less often used are cavities in overhanging tree trunks, caught-up flood debris; ledges and cavities on man-made structures (bridge, pump house, beneath house roof, etc.) are occasionally used. The nest looks like a wad of caught-up flood debris, often with material trailing below it; it is built of dead leaves, twigs, roots, grass stems and other rough material and is secured to the site by being built with wet material. In the top of this bowl is a neatly finished, open cup, lined with rootlets and thin grass stems. It measures: outside diameter 120-240 mm; nest thickness 70-150 mm; cup diameter 55-60 mm; cup depth 60 mm. Pairs have 4-5 sites that are repeatedly used over the years; old nests are refurbished, or new ones built from scratch by both sexes in 4-8 days, (refurbishing an old nest taking 2-4 days); the nest may stand empty for 1-5-10 days before the first egg is laid. The birds are secretive while nesting, leaving the nest silently if disturbed, and calling minimally during nest change-overs.

Laying months: mainly Sep-Dec (Aug-May); lays 1-4 clutches per season; multi-brooded. **Clutch size:** 2-3 (rarely 1 or 4); laid at 1-day intervals. **Eggs:** 17.4-20.2-21.9 x 14.2-15.1-16.0 mm; 2.1-2.4-2.8 g; occasionally parasitised by Red-chested Cuckoo. **Incubation period:** 13-14 days; by both sexes, ♀ at night; daytime shifts 3-60 mins; eggs seldom left unattended. **Nestling/fledging period:** 14-18 days; young fed by both sexes.

Cape Wagtail

African Pied Wagtail

Cape Wagtail

Mountain Wagtail (LEFT & TWO ABOVE)

Longclaws

Yellow-throated Longclaw *Macronyx croceus* Geelkeelkalkoentjie page 388

Breeds in mesic savanna, mostly at lower altitudes (<900 m above sea-level) in shortish, dense grass among low, scattered trees. Pairs nest solitarily and are widely spaced. **Nest:** a shallow open cup, placed on the ground or a few cm above it in short, usually densely matted grass; it is set into a hollow in the ground or in a grass tuft, some nests quite exposed from above, others entirely covered by overhanging grass, these having a short passageway by which the bird reaches the nest. The base of the nest is built with dry stems and blades of grass while the cup is neatly lined with fine rootlets. The nest measures: outside diameter 100-120-145 mm; cup diameter 75-85-100 mm; cup depth 35-55-60 mm. It is built by the ♀, accompanied by ♂ while collecting material. The incubating bird usually leaves the nest at a distance when approached, flying off silently; with recently hatched chicks it may sit tight, leaving at the last moment and performing an injury-feigning display as it flies off.
Laying months: mainly Nov-Jan (Sep-Mar). **Clutch size:** 3 (2-4). **Eggs:** 22.4-24.1-26.3 × 17.1-18.2-19.3 mm; the light ground-colour and fine markings distinguish the eggs of this species from those of other longclaws in the region. **Incubation period:** 13-14 days; mainly or entirely by ♀. **Nestling/fledging period:** 16-17 days; young fed by both sexes.

Cape Longclaw *Macronyx capensis* Oranjekeelkalkoentjie page 388

Breeds in open grassland and short fynbos from sea-level to 2400 m; also breeds locally in mesic savanna where restricted to grassy fringes of wetlands, old lands and other treeless habitats. **Nest:** a shallow open cup, placed on or within a few cm of the ground in short (<400 mm) dense grass; often in damp situations; in shortly grazed areas, the nest will usually be placed in the longest grass available. Pairs nest solitarily and are widely spaced. The nest is usually well hidden between two or more grass tufts, often completely encircled by grass which folds over the top of the nest, screening it from view. It is a deep, neatly lined, open cup, often asymmetrically shaped; its base is built from coarse, rough, dry grass stems and the cup is lined with rootlets. It measures: outside diameter 150 mm; cup diameter 80-85-90 mm; cup depth 40-55-65 mm. It is built by the ♀, accompanied by ♂ during nest-building trips. The incubating bird often sits tight when the nest is approached, flying off silently at the last moment.
Laying months: all months recorded, but mainly Aug-Oct (Jul-Jan) in winter-rainfall region; Oct-Jan (Aug-Apr) in summer-rainfall areas; relays after early clutch failure. **Clutch size:** 3-4 (2-4); laid at 1-day intervals. **Eggs:** 22.4-24.4-26.7 × 16.5-17.8-18.9 mm. **Incubation period:** 13-14 days; probably by ♀ only. **Nestling/fledging period:** 14 days (9-14); young fed by both sexes.

Rosy-throated Longclaw *Macronyx ameliae* Rooskeelkalkoentjie page 388

Breeds in mesic grasslands on the coastal plain from n KwaZulu-Natal northwards, and in n mesic savannas in seasonally wet dambos and floodplains; everywhere restricted to damp ground on fringes of wetlands. Pairs nest solitarily and are widely spaced. **Nest:** a shallow open cup, placed in short (<300 mm), usually dense, grass growing in a slightly raised, dry position close to marshy ground. It is set into a hollow in the grass, either at ground level, or a little above it, usually well concealed by overhanging grass. The base of the nest is made with dry stems of grass while the cup is neatly lined with fine rootlets. It measures: outside diameter 100 mm; cup diameter 75-80 mm; cup depth 35-55 mm. It is built by the ♀ and she is accompanied by ♂ while collecting material.
Laying months: mainly Nov-Feb (Sep-Mar). **Clutch size:** 3 (2-4). **Eggs:** 21.1-22.4-23.8 × 15.5-16.3-17.3 mm. **Incubation period:** 13-14 days; by ♀ only. **Nestling/fledging period:** 16 days; young fed by both sexes.

Yellow-throated Longclaw (LEFT & TWO ABOVE)

Cape Longclaw

Rosy-throated Longclaw

Pipits

African Pipit *Anthus cinnamomeus* Gewone Koester page 388

Breeds widely in the region in most open, treeless, short-grass habitats, from sea-level to an altitude of about 2200 m, in both flat and hilly (but not mountainous) country and in natural grasslands as well as those created or maintained by agricultural activity. Pairs nest solitarily and, in ideal habitat, adjacent nests are within 50-100 m of each other. **Nest:** an open cup, placed on the ground, usually set into a shallow scrape or hollow against a tuft of grass or a low plant (but seldom against rocks or earth clods); usually well hidden, even when the grass cover is very short, as there is invariably a fringe of overhanging grass that screens the nest from view. Its base is made from shredded pieces of dry grass and root stubble and its cup lined with finer stems of grass and rootlets. The open side of the nest (opposite the supporting grass tuft) typically has an extended rim. The nest measures: outside diameter 100-130 mm; cup diameter 60-70 mm; cup depth 30-45 mm. There is no reuse of nests. The nest is built mainly or entirely by the ♀, accompanied by ♂, and it takes 3-4 days to complete. The incubating bird often sits tight when the nest is approached, flying off silently at the last moment; it may perform an injury-feigning display, especially when there are eggs close to hatching or when small nestlings present.
Laying months: mainly Sep-Nov (Aug-Jan) in winter-rainfall region, but Oct-Dec (Aug-Feb, rarely in other months) elsewhere; relays after earlier failures. **Clutch size:** 3 (2-4, rarely 5); laid at 1-day intervals. **Eggs:** 18.8-20.7-23.4 x 13.9-15.3-16.9 mm. **Incubation period:** 13-14 days (12-15); mainly or entirely by ♀. **Nestling/fledging period:** 12 days (11-17); young brooded by ♀, fed by both sexes.

Long-billed Pipit *Anthus similis* Nicholsonse Koester page 388

Breeds on rocky hillsides that have a cover of short grass; found both in open grasslands and in lightly wooded or bushed country; occurs from sea-level up to altitudes of about 2400 m, and found in both semi-arid and mesic regions. Pairs nest solitarily and are widely spaced. **Nest:** an open cup, placed on the ground, usually on a slope and situated against the underside of a sloping rock, or wedged between a rock and a thick grass tuft; some nests are quite exposed and easily visible, while others are well concealed by a fringe of overhanging grass. Its base is made from shredded pieces of dry grass and dry fibre from the stems of *Xerophyta* or other plants; the cup is neatly lined with fine grass stems and rootlets. It measures: outside diameter 130 mm; cup diameter 70 mm; cup depth 40 mm. The nest is built mainly or entirely by one bird (possibly the ♀) which is accompanied by its mate while building.
Laying months: mainly Oct-Dec (Aug-Dec, rarely in other months). **Clutch size:** 3 (2-4). **Eggs:** 20.1-21.1-22.5 x 14.8-15.9-16.6 mm. **Incubation period:** not recorded. **Nestling/fledging period:** 13-14 days; young fed by both sexes.

Kimberley Pipit *Anthus pseudosimilis* Kimberleykoester

Breeds in flat and hilly country in open, treeless, grassy karoo. Nesting habits are poorly known. Pairs nest solitarily and are widely spaced. **Nest:** an open cup, placed on the ground, set into a shallow scrape or hollow against or between tufts of grass, or against a clod of earth, usually well hidden by a fringe of overhanging grass. Its base is compactly made with shredded pieces of dry grass and it has an extended rim on the approach-side to the nest; the cup is lined with fine strands of grass and rootlets. It measures: outside diameter 150 mm; cup diameter 50-75 mm; cup depth 45-55 mm.
Laying months: Oct-Dec. **Clutch size:** 3 (2-4). **Eggs:** 22 x 16 mm; not illustrated. **Incubation period:** not recorded. **Nestling/fledging period:** 16 days; young fed by both sexes.

Mountain Pipit *Anthus hoeschi* Bergkoester page 388

Breeds in highlands of Lesotho and ne Cape, mainly above 2300 m altitude, nesting on flat, undulating or even steep-sloping (30-40°) ground that has a short grass/shrub cover; southern slopes and recently burnt or shortly grazed areas are favoured. Nesting habits are poorly known. Pairs nest solitarily and are widely spaced. **Nest:** an open cup, placed on the ground, set into a shallow scrape or hollow on the down-slope side of a tuft of grass and concealed to a greater or lesser extent by overhanging grass stems. The base is made with coarse dry stems and pieces of grass, the cup lined with finer grass strands and rootlets; the open side of the nest has a wide, extended rim. The nest measures: outside diameter 110-120 mm; cup diameter 55-60 mm; cup depth 50-55 mm. The nest is built by one bird (possibly the ♀) which is accompanied by its mate while building. The incubating bird may sit tight when the nest is approached, flying off (silently) at the last moment.
Laying months: Nov-Jan. **Clutch size:** 2-3. **Eggs:** 21.4-22.5-23.5 x 15.4-15.8-16.2 mm. **Incubation period:** not recorded **Nestling/fledging period:** not recorded.

Wood Pipit *Anthus nyassae* Boskoester page 388

Breeds in n mesic savanna in broad-leafed woodlands, especially miombo; unlike the closely related Long-billed Pipit, it is not confined to rocky hillsides for breeding habitat. Nesting habits are poorly known. Pairs nest solitarily and are widely spaced. **Nest:** an open cup, placed on the ground and set into a shallow scrape or hollow against the side of a grass tuft, usually well hidden by overhanging grass and with an extended rim. Its base is made from pieces of dry grass and plant stems; the cup is lined with finer stems of grass and rootlets. It measures: cup diameter 60-65 mm; cup depth 45 mm. Adult may perform broken-wing distraction display when flushed from a nest with young.
Laying months: mainly Sep-Nov (Jul-Feb). **Clutch size:** 2-3; laid at 1-day intervals. **Eggs:** 19.0-21.7-24.0 x 14.5-15.6-17.5 mm. **Incubation period:** not recorded. **Nestling/fledging period:** not recorded.

African Pipit

Long-billed Pipit

Kimberley Pipit

Mountain Pipit

Wood Pipit

Pipits

Plain-backed Pipit *Anthus leucophrys* Donkerkoester   page 388

Breeds in grassland, grassy karoo and semi-arid savanna in open, mainly treeless country with a short grass cover and stretches of bare ground; frequents both hilly and flat landscapes; often on recently burnt grassland, on exposed margins of floodplains and estuaries, and on cultivated lands; absent from arid areas and mesic savanna. Pairs nest solitarily and are widely spaced. **Nest:** an open cup, placed on the ground and set into a shallow scrape or hollow against or between tufts of grass, or against a clod of earth. It is usually well hidden by a fringe of overhanging grass. Its base is compactly made with shredded pieces of dry grass and the cup is lined with fine strands of grass and rootlets. The nest measures: outside diameter 120-130 mm; cup diameter 50-95 mm; cup depth 45- 57 mm.
Laying months: mainly Oct-Nov (Aug-Jan). **Clutch size:** 3 (2-4). **Eggs:** 19.3-21.5-24.8 × 14.3-15.6-16.6 mm. **Incubation period** <14 days; starts with first-laid egg. **Nestling/fledging period:** 16 days; young fed by both sexes.

Buffy Pipit *Anthus vaalensis* Vaalkoester   page 388

Breeds widely in semi-arid and mesic savanna, in grassland and grassy karoo; favours open, treeless areas where there is a cover of short grass, areas of bare ground, and scattered rocks or termitaria to provide perches; found in both hilly and flat country. Pairs nest solitarily and are widely spaced. **Nest:** a bulky, roughly finished open cup, placed on the ground, set into a shallow scrape or hollow against a tuft of grass, or on the underside of a sloping rock, usually well concealed. Its base is made from shredded pieces of dry grass and other plant stems, the cup is lined with finer stems of grass and rootlets. It measures: cup diameter 60-70 mm; cup depth 38-44 mm.
Laying months: mainly Sep-Nov (Jul-Feb). **Clutch size:** 2-3. **Eggs:** 20.4-22.0-24.4 × 14.9-15.3-17.2 mm. **Incubation period:** 14 days. **Nestling/fledging period:** not recorded; young fed by both sexes.

African Rock Pipit *Anthus crenatus* Klipkoester   page 388

Breeds on open, grassy, rock-strewn hillsides in hilly and mountainous areas in the karoo and grassland regions, at altitudes up to 2800 m. Pairs nest solitarily and are spaced, in ideal habitat, at a density of a pair/15 ha (Lesotho). **Nest:** a shallow, untidily finished open cup, usually situated well up from the base of the hill-slope and placed against or inside a thick grass tuft growing among rocks; it is usually well hidden. Its base is made with pieces of dry grass, twigs and roots, and the nest-cup is lined with fine shredded dry grass. The nest measures: outside diameter 110-140 mm; cup diameter 70-80 mm; cup depth 15-30 mm. It is built by one of the pair (possibly the ♀), accompanied on nest-building trips by its mate.
Laying months: mainly Nov (Oct-Jan) in summer-rainfall area; Aug in winter-rainfall region. **Clutch size:** 3 (2-3). **Eggs:** 20.7-21.5-22.2 × 14.9-15.3-15.9 mm. **Incubation period:** >12 days. **Nestling/fledging period:** 12-13 days; young fed by both sexes.

Long-tailed Pipit *Anthus longicaudatus* Langstertkoester   no nest or egg photo

Nest and nesting habits have not yet been described; it is currently considered to be a non-breeding visitor to the region.

Plain-backed Pipit

Plain-backed Pipit

Buffy Pipit

Buffy Pipit

African Rock Pipit

Pipits

Bushveld Pipit *Anthus caffer* Bosveldkoester
page 388

Breeds in mesic savanna in hilly, well-wooded country, especially in open glades where there is a ground cover of short grass and areas of bare ground. Pairs nest solitarily and, in ideal habitat, adjacent nests may be <100 m apart. **Nest:** a small, thick-walled cup placed on, or close to the ground, set into a shallow scrape or hollow against or inside a short, thick tuft of grass, often one that is partly moribund, its colour matching that of the nest; most nests are entirely concealed from view from above by overhanging plant material. The base of the nest is made from dry, shredded pieces of grass and its cup is lined with finer stems of grass and rootlets. It measures: outside diameter 80 mm; cup diameter 50-60 mm; cup depth 30-45 mm. The nest is built mainly or entirely by 1 bird (possibly the ♀) which is accompanied by its mate while building. The incubating bird often sits tight when the nest is approached, flying off silently at the last moment and usually settling in a tree.
Laying months: mainly Nov-Feb (Oct-Mar). **Clutch size:** 3 (2-3). **Eggs:** 16.5-18.5-21.4 x 13.1-14.0-14.5 mm. **Incubation period** >14 days. **Nestling/fledging period:** not recorded; young fed by both sexes.

Striped Pipit *Anthus lineiventris* Gestreepte Koester
page 388

Breeds in mesic savanna on the slopes of well-wooded, grassy, rock- and boulder-strewn hillsides. Pairs nest solitarily and are widely spaced. **Nest:** a large, open cup, placed on the ground, well hidden beneath or within a dense tuft of grass, often a partly moribund tuft which overhangs the nest and conceals it from view. The nest site is usually on a level terrace, often at the base of a boulder; it is larger than the nests of other pipits in the region, built with dry grass and forb stems, root stubble, twigs and fragments of dead leaf and moss or lichen where available; the cup is lined with fine grass stems and rootlets. The open side of the nest may have an extended rim. The nest measures: outside diameter 120-140 mm; cup diameter 90-95 mm; cup depth 50 mm. The incubating bird sits tight when the nest is approached, flying off silently at the last moment; it may perform an injury-feigning display when leaving.
Laying months: mainly Oct-Dec (Sep-Jan). **Clutch size:** 3 (2-3). **Eggs:** 22.6-23.9-24.9 x 16.5-17.1-17.5 mm. **Incubation period:** not recorded. **Nestling/fledging period:** not recorded; young fed by both sexes.

Short-tailed Pipit *Anthus brachyurus* Kortstertkoester
page 388

Breeds in mesic grasslands from the coastal plain (from KwaZulu-Natal northwards) to uplands in the interior; sparse and localised mainly on grassy hillsides. Nesting habits are poorly known. Pairs nest solitarily and are widely spaced; 4-5 nesting pairs recorded in 30-40 ha at one site. **Nest:** a small, deep, open cup, placed on the ground in short (about 230 mm), dense grass, against or between grass tufts and usually screened from view by an overhanging fringe of grass stems that conceal the nest-cup. Its base is made from dry pieces of grass and its cup is finely lined with shredded dry grass stems and rootlets. It measures: outside diameter 80-110 mm; cup diameter 50-65-90 mm; cup depth 40-50 mm.
Laying months: mainly Nov (Oct-Feb). **Clutch size:** 2-3. **Eggs:** 16.1-17.3-18.4 x 13.2-13.3-14.3 mm. **Incubation period:** not recorded. **Nestling/fledging period:** 13 days; young fed by both sexes.

Yellow-breasted Pipit *Hemimacronyx chloris* Geelborskoester
page 388

Breeds in upland grasslands 1900-2400 m above sea-level, favouring undulating or rolling, submontane country with a short (150-300 mm), dense, grass cover. Monogamous, with occasional instances of polygyny recorded. Pairs nest solitarily, adjacent nests usually >100 m apart (rarely within 20 m of each other). **Nest:** a deep, neatly lined, open cup placed on the ground, usually set into a shallow scrape or hollow between two or more short grass tufts that entirely encircle the nest; it lacks an open side that is typical of the nest of many other pipit species. It is well hidden, even in short grass, as it is screened above by an overhanging fringe of grass. A minimal foundation to the nest is made from rough, dry stems of grass, and the cup is lined with fine grass strands and rootlets. The nest measures: cup diameter of 55-65 mm; cup depth 40-55 mm. It is built by the ♀, accompanied by ♂ during nest-building trips. The incubating bird often sits tight when the nest is approached, flying off silently at the last moment; it may perform an injury-feigning display when it leaves.
Laying months: Nov-Feb. **Clutch size:** 3 (2-4). **Eggs:** 19.2-20.7-22.4 x 15.2-15.8-16.6 mm. **Incubation period:** 14 days; by both sexes in shifts of 30-35 min. **Nestling/fledging period:** 14 days; young brooded and fed by both sexes.

Bushveld Pipit

Striped Pipit

Short-tailed Pipit

Yellow-breasted Pipit

BULBULS, GREENBULS, BROWNBULS Family Pycnonotidae Worldwide 145 species; 66 breed in Afrotropics, 9 in southern Africa. Monogamous; ♀ builds nest, incubates, broods nestlings; both sexes feed young; nest an open cup in a tree or shrub; eggs oval, white, buff or pink, speckled or blotched, some beautifully so; 2-3/clutch; nestlings are altricial and nidicolous.

African Red-eyed Bulbul *Pycnonotus nigricans* Rooioogtiptol   page 388

Breeds widely in semi-arid and arid savanna, in the karoo, and in wooded areas in semi-arid grasslands; nests in thornveld, riverine bush, scrub thickets; often in gardens. Pairs nest solitarily, adjacent pairs usually >50-100 m apart. **Nest:** similar to that of Dark-capped Bulbul; cup-shaped; placed in the fork of a smallish tree or shrub, usually 2-3 m up (1-4 m); it is usually in an outer branch well concealed in leafy foliage. It is made from pliable stems of dry weed, grass, rootlets or other fibrous material that are curled round to form the nest-bowl, in some cases using cobweb to hold the nest together. The cup is lined with fine rootlets, with the occasional addition of such exotic materials as shreds of tissue paper. Nests measure: outside diameter 90-119-120 mm; nest height 69 mm; cup diameter 60-65 mm; cup depth 50 mm. The ♀ builds nest, while ♂ sings from nearby perch.
Laying months: Sep-Mar, peaking in Oct-Dec in the east; Dec-Feb in the west; sometimes double-brooded. **Clutch size:** 3 (2-3); laid at 1-day intervals. **Eggs:** 20.5-22.0-25.0 x 15.5-16.3-17.3 mm; regularly parasitised by Jacobin Cuckoo. **Incubation period:** 12 days (11½-13); by ♀ only. **Nestling/fledging period:** 12 days; young fed by both sexes.

Dark-capped Bulbul *Pycnonotus tricolor* Swartoogtiptol   pages 378, 388

Breeds mainly in mesic savanna and in grassland regions wherever there is wooded habitat; abundant in man-transformed habitats throughout its range. Pairs nest solitarily. **Nest:** an open cup placed in leafy foliage in a tree or shrub, usually 2-4 m up (2-12) and usually well concealed among leaves. It is a fairly rigid and thick-walled nest built with different materials in different areas, mostly using long fine stems and inflorescences of dry grass with coarser material curled round to form the outer bowl and finer grass ends used in the lining; in some, shreds of bark, leaf petioles, tendrils or rootlets are used. A small amount of cobweb binds the nest to its supporting twigs. Nests measure: outside diameter 110-120 mm; cup diameter 60-75 mm; nest height 44-58 mm; cup depth 37-40 mm. It is built by the ♀ in 8-10 days. Despite being a common bird, its nest is not easily found, even in much-frequented gardens, and it is often only at the end of summer when trees lose their foliage that their old nests are revealed.
Laying months: mainly Sep-Dec (Aug-Apr). **Clutch size:** 3 (2-3, once 6 probably laid by 2 ♀s); laid at 1-day intervals. **Eggs:** 19.8-22.9-26.9 x 14.0-16.7-19.5 mm; mass 2.85-2.95-3.16 g; commonly parasitised by Jacobin Cuckoo. **Incubation period:** 13 days (12-15); begins when clutch is completed; by ♀ only, fed on nest by ♂. **Nestling/fledging period:** 13 days (11-16); young fed by both sexes.

Cape Bulbul *Pycnonotus capensis* Kaapse Tiptol   page 388

Restricted to the w and e Cape where it breeds in fynbos, heath, riverine bush, scrub, and in gardens. Pairs nest solitarily, spaced about a pair/1-2 ha. **Nest:** similar to that of Dark-capped Bulbul; an open cup placed in the leafy foliage of a small tree or shrub (rooikrans commonly used where it occurs), either in a thin-twigged fork or at the outer end of a horizontal branch, usually <1½ m up (0,3-4). It is made with twigs, rootlets and grass stems, with coarser material used at the base and finer material inside; some nests have woolly or downy material or some other decoration added to the lining. Nests measure: outside diameter 110 mm; cup diameter 65 mm; nest height 65 mm; cup depth 45 mm. The ♀ builds the nest, completing it in 4½ days (2-10); she builds mostly in the morning, and the ♂ sings nearby while she builds; egg-laying begins 1-4 days after nest completion.
Laying months: mainly Sep-Nov (Aug-Mar); relays up to 8x/season after early failures; sometimes double-brooded. **Clutch size:** 3 (2-5); laid at 1-day intervals. **Eggs:** 20.6-23.6-28.7 x 15.8-17.1-19.0 mm; commonly (up to 35% in e Cape) parasitised by Jacobin Cuckoo. **Incubation period:** 12 days (11-13½); by ♀ only, leaving eggs briefly unattended 20-40x/day to feed. **Nestling/fledging period:** 13 days (11-15); young brooded by ♀ only; fed by both sexes.

Stripe-cheeked Greenbul *Arizelocichla milanjensis* Streepwangwillie   page 389

Breeds in forest in highlands of e Zimbabwe and w Mozambique. **Nest:** an open cup, typically placed in a well-foliaged, subcanopy tree sapling, often one entwined with creeper, about 3-5 m (2-7 m) up from the ground, usually well hidden. It is more substantial than those of other bulbuls, made mainly from dry grass stems, with tendrils, petioles, small twigs, shredded bark, pieces of dead or skeletonised leaf, moss and/or *Usnea* incorporated to varying degrees; the cup is lined with fine grass ends. Nests measure: outside diameter 120-130 mm; cup diameter 65 mm; nest height 65-80 mm; cup depth 30 mm. ♀ sits tight while incubating.
Laying months: mainly Nov-Dec (Oct-Mar). **Clutch size:** 2, rarely 1. **Eggs:** 24.3-25.1-26.0 x 17.5-17.8-18.1 mm. **Incubation period:** not recorded; by ♀ only. **Nestling/fledging period:** not recorded.

Sombre Greenbul *Andropadus importunus* Gewone Willie   page 389

Breeds in coastal scrub, riparian thickets and evergreen forest. Pairs nest solitarily. **Nest:** a shallow, open cup placed in a thickly foliaged tree or shrub, often one standing isolated, 1½-2½ m up from the ground (1-4 m), typically in a leafy outer branch or main fork of a sapling. Nest material varies from place to place: fine stems of dry grass most commonly used, but some nests made from *Usnea*, others from petioles, rootlets and/or shreds of bark; it is attached to the branch with some cobweb. It measures: outside diameter 113 mm; cup diameter 63 mm; nest height 81 mm; cup depth 37 mm. It is built by the ♀, while the ♂ sings nearby. Despite being locally abundant birds, they are secretive while nesting and their nests are easily overlooked; birds flushed off nests may feign injury.
Laying months: mainly Oct-Dec (Sep-Apr). **Clutch size:** 2, rarely 3; laid at a 1-day interval. **Eggs:** 20.7-24.0-27.0 x 14.5-16.8-19.3 mm; mass 3.4-3.8 g; frequently parasitised by Jacobin Cuckoo. **Incubation period:** 13 days (12-13½); by ♀ only, fed on the nest by ♂. **Nestling/fledging period:** 13 days (10½-14); young brooded and fed by both sexes.

African Red-eyed Bulbul

Dark-capped Bulbul

Cape Bulbul

Stripe-cheeked Greenbul

Sombre Greenbul

Yellow-bellied Greenbul *Chlorocichla flaviventris* Geelborswillie page 389

Breeds in lowland, coastal, riparian and sand-forest, and in riparian thickets that extend into drier areas along drainage lines. Pairs nest solitarily. **Nest:** an open cup, placed in the fork of a leafy tree or shrub, usually 2-3 m (1-4) off the ground, and either in the canopy of a sapling, or along an outer, horizontal branch, or among creepers; most are well concealed in foliage. It is rather flimsily made, some being so transparent that the eggs can be seen from below through the nest floor. It is built from pliable stems of weedy plants and grasses, incorporating petioles, tendrils, small twigs and rootlets. The cup is lined with finer pieces of the same material and some cobweb is used to attach it to the supporting branches. The nest measures: outside diameter 85-100 mm; cup diameter 55-75 mm; nest height 45-50 mm; cup depth 25-35 mm. The nest is reportedly built by both sexes, in about 7 days.
Laying months: mainly Oct-Dec (Sep-Mar). **Clutch size:** 2 (1-3). **Eggs:** 21.6-24.8-27.1 × 15.9-17.1-18.0 mm. **Incubation period:** 14 days; starts with first-laid egg; by ♀ only; she is fed on the nest by the ♂ and she also leaves nest unattended for short periods to feed. **Nestling/fledging period:** 16-18 days; young brooded and fed by both sexes.

Terrestrial Brownbul *Phyllastrephus terrestris* Boskrapper page 389

Breeds in montane, coastal, lowland and riparian forests, extending into savanna areas along riparian thickets. Pairs nest solitarily. **Nest:** a shallow, flimsy cup, placed in dark, thick tangles, usually ½-2 m up, where criss-crossing branches and stems provide nest sites. It is made with dark-coloured material, usually dark brown petioles, skeletonised leaves or dark, stringy tendrils, and although not usually hidden in foliage, it is inconspicuous given its dark colour and the dark background. It measures: outside diameter 85-90 mm; cup diameter 50-65 mm; nest height 35-60 mm; cup depth 22-30 mm. It is frequently placed close to (<2 m) the site of a previous year's nest. Unlike other bulbuls, both sexes are reported to build the nest and to share the incubation. The incubating bird sits tight and is not easily flushed from the nest; once off the nest, however, it scolds loudly and draws attention to itself.
Laying months: mainly Oct-Dec (Sep-Apr). **Clutch size:** 2, less often 3; laid at a 1-day interval. **Eggs:** 19.2-22.8-27.4 × 14.0-16.1-19.0 mm. **Incubation period:** 13 days; by both sexes. **Nestling/fledging period:** not recorded; young fed by both sexes.

Tiny Greenbul *Phyllastrephus debilis* Kleinboskruiper page 388

Breeds in lowland forest in c Mozambique and adjacent e Zimbabwe. Nesting habits are poorly known. Pairs nest solitarily. **Nest:** a small, open cup (the size of a white-eye nest), placed about 1 m up (0.4-3) from the ground in dense shrubbery in the forest under-storey. It is typically slung between the twigs of a horizontal fork or where two or more horizontal twigs cross each other; often alongside a few large, dead leaves caught-up in the adjacent branches which draw attention away from the nest. It is built with fine, dark-coloured fibrous plant strands (such as roots of *Marasmius* forest fern) and tendrils; the cup is lined with fine plant stems; fragments of dead leaf may be incorporated into the nest walls. Nests are often asymmetrically shaped (their long axis parallel to the supporting twigs): outside diameter 62-70 mm; cup diameter 37-50 mm; nest height 40-60 mm; cup depth 22 mm.
Laying months: Oct-Jan. **Clutch size:** 2. **Eggs:** 17.5-18.3-18.9 × 13.0-13.3-13.7 mm. **Incubation period:** not recorded. **Nestling/fledging period:** not recorded.

Yellow-streaked Greenbul *Phyllastrephus flavostriatus* Geelstreepboskruiper page 389

Breeds in montane and lowland forest. Pairs nest solitarily, at densities of about a pair/2-3 ha (Malawi). **Nest:** an open cup, placed low down, usually only about 1-2 m up from the ground, in shrubby undergrowth close to the forest floor. It is slung between horizontal twigs of a forest sapling, the upper rim of the nest level with the stems that support it; a couple (2-3) of large dead leaves are often built into the nest wall, loosely encasing it (shown in photograph opposite). The nest is built with dark-coloured rootlets, petioles and black, fibrous strands of forest fern (*Marasmius androsaceus*); cobweb is used to attach the nest to its supporting twigs and to the encasing leaves; the cup is neatly lined with fine forest grass inflorescences or rootlets. Nests are often noticeably asymmetrical in shape, being longest in the direction parallel to the supporting twigs and this is reflected in the nest dimensions: outside diameter 60-110 mm; cup diameter 45-63 mm; nest height 63-80 mm; cup depth 25-45 mm. The incubating bird sits tightly on the nest approached and is not readily flushed.
Laying months: mainly Nov-Dec (Oct-Mar). **Clutch size:** 2, rarely 3. **Eggs:** 21.0-22.7-23.9 × 15.4-16.5-17.0 mm; mass 3.3-3.4 g. **Incubation period:** not recorded; by ♀ only. **Nestling/fledging period:** not recorded.

NICATORS Family Nicatoridae Worldwide 2 species; both endemic to Afrotropics, 1 in southern Africa. Uncertain whether monogamous or polygynous; song behaviour of ♂ and size dimorphism between sexes (♂ larger) suggest latter; nest a small saucer in a sapling; eggs oval, greyish, heavily speckled, 2/clutch; nestlings altricial and nidicolous.

Eastern Nicator *Nicator gularis* Geelvleknikator page 389

Breeds widely in coastal, lowland, riparian and sand-forest. Nesting birds are widely spaced. Despite it being common in parts of its range, its nesting habits are poorly known and relatively few nests have been recorded in the region. **Nest:** a small, flimsy, dove-like nest, a saucer-shaped platform of dry twigs placed about 1 m up from the ground in a forked branch of a sapling, in a tangle of dead branches, or among the stems of a mat of creepers. It is made of thin, dry twigs with a few curly dry tendrils forming the cup lining; it does not resemble the nest of any bulbul species, and is closest in appearance to nest of an Orange-breasted Bushshrike. It has an outside diameter of about 100-150 mm, cup diameter 75 mm.
Laying months: Nov-Jan. **Clutch size:** 2, rarely 1 or 3. **Eggs:** 24.7-25.6-27.0 × 16.6-17.3-19.5 mm. **Incubation period:** not recorded; by ♀ only. **Nestling/fledging period:** not recorded.

Yellow-bellied Greenbul

Terrestrial Brownbul

Tiny Greenbul

Yellow-streaked Greenbul

Eastern Nicator

Saw-wings, Swallow, Martins

SWALLOWS, MARTINS Family Hirundinidae Worldwide 88 species; 34 breed in Afrotropics, 16 in southern Africa. Monogamous; nest-building, incubation and nestling-care shared by sexes to varying degrees; 10 species build mud nests (build a half-cup, 2 a closed bowl with a spout entrance, 5 a closed bowl with a long tunnel entrance), 6 nest in tunnels in banks o in flat ground; eggs oval; unmarked, white in tunnel-nesters and closed-nest species, speckled in 4/5 open-cup nesting species 3-4/clutch; nestlings are altricial and nidicolous.

Black Saw-wing *Psalidoprocne holomelas* Swartsaagvlerkswael — page 38

Breeds in coastal, lowland, riparian and montane forest/grassland mosaics, also in clearings in timber plantations. Pairs nest solitaril occasionally 2-3 pairs loosely colonial. **Nest:** a tunnel is excavated into an earth bank, usually a bank < 1 m high; erosion gulleys, roo of aardvark burrows and banks along the verges of streams, road cuttings, embankments, drainage ditches and pits provide usual nes sites; occasionally uses a drainage hole in a concrete bridge-support; once reported using the disused nest tunnel of a Giant Kingfishe Tunnels are usually close to the top of the bank, the entrance sometimes concealed by overhanging vegetation. They are typicall 0.3-0.6 m in length, 25-35 mm in diameter, widening into a chamber at the end, about 100 mm across, where a saucer-shaped nes pad of dry grass, rootlets, *Usnea* or moss is built. Both sexes excavate, both collect nesting material, and both build.
Laying months: mainly Oct-Dec (Sep-Mar). **Clutch size:** 2 (1-3). **Eggs:** 17.9-19.1-20.7 x 11.9-13.0-14.3 mm. **Incubation perioc** 14-15 days. **Nestling/fledging period:** 25-27 days; young fed by both sexes.

Eastern Saw-wing *Psalidoprocne orientalis* Tropiese Saagvlerkswael — page 38

Breeds in mosaics of grassland and montane or lowland forest or mesic woodland. Pairs nest solitarily, but adjacent nests can be a close as 10-20 m apart. **Nest:** a tunnel is excavated into a ½-5 m high earth bank; either vertical or inclined banks are used; nests ar often in road cuttings, but any excavation or stream bank may provide the nest site. Nesting banks are commonly reused in successiv years. The tunnel is about 0,4-0,8 m long and it slopes gently upward before widening into a chamber at the end, about 75 mm wid and 70 mm high where a saucer-shaped nest, made of shreds of dry grass, lined with *Usnea*, is built.
Laying months: mainly Oct-Dec (Jul-Apr). **Clutch size:** 2. **Eggs:** 18.3-18.4 x 12.0-12.2 mm. **Incubation period:** 19 days (Tanzania) **Nestling/fledging period:** 24-27 days (Tanzania); young fed by both sexes.

Grey-rumped Swallow *Pseudohirundo griseopyga* Gryskruisswael — page 38

Breeds in mesic savanna in winter. Pairs nest solitarily, sometimes within 50-100 m of each other. They nest in bare, open, flat groun with a short grass cover (from being grazed or burnt), often on seasonal vleis or floodplains that have dried up, fallow lands, recentl harvested fields, airfields or sports grounds. **Nest:** is placed at the bottom of a gerbil or other rodent tunnel, often just wide enoug (33-38 mm across) to admit the bird and 0.6-1.2 m in length; it may slant gently downwards or enter the ground steeply, and twis and turn before reaching a widened chamber at the end where a nest pad of dry grass is built, about 115 mm across and 50 mr thick; disused passages in subterranean termite nests or other exiting cavities in the ground may also be used, and occasionally ol bee-eater and kingfisher tunnels. Only one of the pair (possibly ♀) builds; while breeding, both sexes sleep in the nest-hole at nigh
Laying months: mainly Jul-Aug (Jul-Nov). **Clutch size:** 3-4 (1-5). **Eggs:** 14.3-16.0-17.6 x 11.0-11.9-12.9 mm; mass 1.4 g. **Incubatio period:** not recorded. **Nestling/fledging period:** not recorded.

Brown-throated Martin *Riparia paludicola* Afrikaanse Oewerswael — page 38

Breeds in open country, mostly close to water (rivers, dams, estuaries, pans, floodplains) where it nests in sandbanks, usually alon rivers or fringing open water, also in sand excavations, mine workings, road cuttings, extensive donga walls, etc. Pairs nest solitaril on occasion, but more usually do so in colonies, typically 6-12 pairs/colony, occasionally 100s where space permits. **Nest:** a tunne about 35-38 mm in diameter, excavated into the wall of a vertical bank of alluvial soil; it is about ½ m (300-800 mm) long and straigh inclining gently upwards, and widening at the end to a chamber about 75-87 mm wide and 75 mm high; a shallow cup-nest of dr grass and feathers is built in the chamber. Both sexes excavate the nest-tunnel over a period of 2-3 weeks; some nesting banks ar shared with bee-eaters, Pied Starlings and other hole-nesters, and in these the martins may occupy burrows originally dug by thes species. Holes may be reused in successive years and they are used as night-time roosts by the pair when not breeding.
Laying months: mainly Jun-Sep, but all months recorded. **Clutch size:** 3 (2-4). **Eggs:** 15.3-16.9-18.7 x 10.5-12.2-13.8 mm; mas 1.22-1.36-1.56 g. **Incubation period:** 12 days; mainly by ♀, joined by ♂ in burrow at night. **Nestling/fledging period:** 20-25 days young fed by both sexes.

Banded Martin *Riparia cincta* Gebande Oewerswael — page 38

Breeds in an extensive, but fragmented range across s Africa in open grasslands or where bush has been cleared for cultivation. Pair nest solitarily and are widely dispersed. **Nest:** a tunnel is excavated into a vertical sandbank; favoured sites are sandbanks about 1-3 n high in dry dongas, along river- or stream-edges, in pits, cuttings, road embankments and, where they occur, in the roofs of aardvar holes; once recorded nesting in a plastic drain pipe and in an indentation in the wall of a very hard bank. The tunnel is about 450-90 mm long and 50 mm wide at the entrance; it is straight, inclining gently upwards and widening at the end into a nest chamber abou 150 mm in diameter. Here, a saucer-shaped nest of dry fragments and shreds of grass, using coarser material at the base and fine grass for the lining, is built. Tunnel nests originally excavated by Pied Starlings or some other hole-nester are also frequently used, an vigorous competition with Ant-eating Chat for nest sites in aardvark holes commonly occurs.
Laying months: Aug-Mar, but mainly Sep-Oct (s Cape) and Nov-Feb (elsewhere). **Clutch size:** 3 (2-4). **Eggs:** 19.4-21.3-24.3 14.5-15.0-16.0 mm; occasionally parasitised by Greater Honeyguide. **Incubation period:** not recorded. **Nestling/fledging period** 21-24 days; young fed by both sexes.

Black Saw-wing

Eastern Saw-wing (TWO ABOVE)

Grey-rumped Swallow

Brown-throated Martin

Banded Martin

Wire-tailed Swallow *Hirundo smithii* Draadstertswael page 389

Breeds widely in mesic savanna, but mainly confined to the vicinity of permanent water. Pairs nest solitarily and are widely dispersed. **Nest**: a half-cup of mud pellets built against a vertical wall, close to a roof when available; usually placed over water, and mostly on a man-made structure; road bridges crossing streams and rivers are commonly used, also dam walls, water towers, boat-houses, rocks over water, or trunks of partly submerged trees. The nest is flatter than those of other cup-nesting swallows (twice as wide as high); the cup is lined with grass, rootlets and a few feathers. The nest measures: 100-120-150 mm across the top and is 40-60-100 mm high. Nests are reused for successive clutches and in successive years. Both sexes build, completing a nest in 7 days.
Laying months: year-round, peaking in Aug-Oct and Feb-Apr; often double- or multiple-brooded. **Clutch size**: 3 (1-3, rarely 4) laid at 1-day intervals. **Eggs**: 17.0-18.4-19.5 × 12.5-12.9-14.2 mm. **Incubation period**: 17 days (14-19); by ♀ only; she frequently leaves eggs left unattended to feed (>40% of the day); begins when clutch is completed. **Nestling/fledging period**: 19 days (15-24); young brooded by ♀, fed by both sexes; young continue using nest as roost after fledging.

Blue Swallow *Hirundo atrocaerulea* Blouswael page 389

A breeding visitor, arriving in Sep-Oct; breeding range is fragmented; restricted to mountainous mistbelt grasslands from s KwaZulu-Natal to e Zimbabwe. Pairs nest solitarily, most >150 m apart. **Nest**: a half-cup, made of a mud/grass mix, attached to a vertical or sloping wall. Most are in dark subterranean holes in the ground, 1-8 m below ground-level; either naturally formed (sink holes along subterranean drainage lines), holes dug by aardvarks, or old prospecting pits and mine workings; in Zimbabwe occasionally nests in farm outbuildings. Nests are typically attached to the underside of a sloping earth wall, often one that is damp and clad with moss. The grass and mud-mix used gives the nest an untidy, straggly exterior; the cup is lined with fine grass and rootlets, and several conspicuous white feathers are added before laying. The nest measures: 115-120-150 mm across (at the top) and 60-80-140 mm high; the cup is 60-80-90 mm wide and 30-40-50 mm deep. Nests are commonly reused for successive broods and in successive years, or a new nest is built close by; occasional nests are built on top of old ones. Both sexes build or refurbish the nest.
Laying months: mainly Nov-Jan (Sep-Mar); relays after early failure; multiple-brooded. **Clutch size**: 3 (1-4) laid at 1-day intervals. **Eggs**: 17.3-18.5-19.6 × 12.5-13.1-13.8 mm. **Incubation period**: 15 days (14-17); by ♀; she leaves nest unattended up to 4x/hr to feed; begins when clutch is completed. **Nestling/fledging period**: 22 days (20-26); young brooded by ♀, fed by both sexes.

White-throated Swallow *Hirundo albigularis* Witkeelswael page 389

A breeding summer visitor, arriving in Aug; nests widely and commonly in grassland, karoo and fynbos, much scarcer further north; mostly nests close to permanent water. Pairs nest solitarily, seldom <50-100 m apart. **Nest**: a thick-walled half-cup made of mud pellets, attached to a vertical wall, especially man-made brick and concrete structures and those overhanging water – bridges, pump-houses, boat-sheds, dam walls; also on rock faces overhanging streams and rivers. Less often nests some way from water in farm buildings, wells, silos, discarded tanks, etc. Little or no grass is included in the mud-mix used; the cup is thickly lined with fine grass overlaid with feathers. The nest measures: 100-120 mm across the top and 90-120 mm high; occasional nests are placed on flat shelves under bridges. Nests are commonly reused in successive years, or a new nest is built close to a previous one.
Laying months: mainly Sep-Dec (Aug-Mar); often double- or multiple-brooded. **Clutch size**: 3 (1-4, rarely 5); laid at 1-day intervals. **Eggs**: 18.1-20.0-23.0 × 12.9-14.2-15.8 mm. **Incubation period**: 16 days (15-18). **Nestling/fledging period**: 22 days (18-25); young fed by both sexes; young sleep in nest for about 12 days after fledging.

Pearl-breasted Swallow *Hirundo dimidiata* Pêrelborsswael page 389

A summer visitor in s and e Cape, where it breeds mainly in open, agricultural landscapes; resident in mesic savannas, nesting here in woodland, often far from water. Pairs nest solitarily and are widely dispersed. **Nest**: a half-cup of mud, lined with fine grass and rootlets (not feathers), attached to a sloping or vertical wall just beneath an overhang or ceiling; seldom nests on buildings in the north, instead using a sidewall inside a porcupine, aardvark or some other hole in the ground, 2-5 m below the surface; by contrast, in s Cape it commonly nests on the walls of buildings. The nest measures: outside diameter 110-135 mm (across the top) and 45-75 mm high; cup diameter 95 mm; cup depth 30 mm. Both sexes build, taking 3-4 weeks to complete a nest. Nests are commonly reused.
Laying months: mainly Sep-Dec (Aug-Apr); double- or multiple-brooded. **Clutch size**: 3 (2-3, rarely 4, once 6 perhaps laid by 2 ♀s) laid at 1-day intervals. **Eggs**: 14.8-17.3-19.5 × 11.3-12.6-14.0 mm. **Incubation period**: 17 days (16-18); by ♀ only; begins when clutch is completed. **Nestling/fledging period**: 20 days (18-23); young brooded by ♀, fed by both sexes; young continue using nest as roost up to 2 weeks after fledging.

Rock Martin *Ptyonoprogne fuligula* Kransswael page 389

Breeds widely from the arid west to the mesic east, mostly associated with cliff-faces in mountainous terrain, but increasingly nesting in towns and villages, especially in arid areas, using buildings, bridges and other man-made structures for this purpose. Pairs nest solitarily and are widely dispersed. **Nest**: a half-cup, made of mud pellets attached to a vertical surface, usually just beneath an overhang or ceiling. It is a flattish nest compared with those of most other cup-nesting swallows, its width being 2-3x its height; the nest-cup is lined with fine pieces of grass above which is laid a lining of feathers. It measures 50 mm across the top and 50-70 mm in height; the cup is 75 mm across and 25 mm deep. It is built by both sexes, completed in about 20 days, and a single nest is normally reused for successive clutches in the same season and commonly refurbished for use in successive years.
Laying months: Aug-Mar, occasionally in other months; double- or multiple-brooded. **Clutch size**: 2-3 (rarely 5 or 6, probably laid by more than one ♀); laid at 1-day intervals. **Eggs**: 17.1-21.0-23.5 × 12.0-14.2-15.3 mm; mass 1.65 g. **Incubation period**: 20 days (17-29); shared equally by both sexes with frequent change-overs. **Nestling/fledging period**: 26 days (22-29); young brooded and fed equally by both sexes; young continue using nest as roost up to 3 weeks after fledging.

Wire-tailed Swallow

Blue Swallow

White-throated Swallow

Pearl-breasted Swallow

Rock Martin

Greater Striped Swallow *Cecropis cucullata* Grootstreepswael page 389
A breeding visitor, arriving in Aug; nests widely in grassland, karoo and fynbos; sparsely in savanna. Pairs nest solitarily. Nests are mostly on man-made brick and concrete structures (under bridges, in road culverts, house eaves, in derelict machinery, old mine workings); natural sites mostly on undersides of sloping rocks. **Nest:** built with mud pellets, an closed bowl with a long horizontal entrance tunnel; bowl thickly lined with dry grass and feathers. It measures 200 x 200 mm (exterior width x height), tunnel 70-230 mm long, 35-50 mm wide. Nests are reused for successive clutches and in successive years; many are taken over by other species, especially White-rumped Swift, forcing the swallows to build another nest. Both sexes build the nest in 14-19 days.
Laying months: mainly Oct-Feb (Aug-Apr) in most of its range but Sep-Nov in sw Cape; multiple-brooded. **Clutch size:** 3 (2-4, rarely 5); laid at 1-day intervals. **Eggs:** 19.1-21.7-24.5 x 13.6-15.1-16.5 mm. **Incubation period:** 17-18 days (16-20); by ♀ only; at night ♂ sleeps in nest with her. **Nestling/fledging period:** about 26 days (23-30); young brooded by ♀, fed by both sexes.

Lesser Striped Swallow *Cecropis abyssinica* Kleinstreepswael page 389
A breeding visitor to mesic savannas, arriving in Aug. Pairs nest solitarily, but occasionally 2-10 pairs under a single bridge. Most nests on man-made structures (under bridges, in road culverts, house eaves); also beneath rock overhangs; in n savanna frequently uses underside of sloping tree trunks. **Nest:** built with mud pellets, an enclosed bowl with a horizontal entrance tunnel; bowl lined with dry grass and feathers. Bowl measures 130-150 mm wide, 120-150 mm high; tunnel 70-120 mm (60-250) long and 30-40 mm wide and high. Nests are reused for successive clutches and, if they survive, in successive years; many are taken over by White-rumped Swift and others. Both sexes build, taking 13-23 days to complete the nest; lining is added throughout the incubation.
Laying months: mainly in Oct-Jan (Sep-Mar) in south/central savanna; Apr-Aug in northern savanna; double- or triple-brooded. **Clutch size:** 3 (2-4). **Eggs:** 17.3-19.7-21.8 x 12.5-13.9-15.4 mm. **Incubation period:** 14-21 days; by ♀ only. **Nestling/fledging period:** 19 days (17-20); young fed by both sexes; young continue using nest as roost for up to 3-4 weeks after fledging.

Red-breasted Swallow *Cecropis semirufa* Rooiborsswael page 389
A breeding summer visitor to savanna and semi-arid grasslands. Pairs nest solitarily, adjacent nests >150 m apart. Most recorded nests are in road culverts, 450-750 mm in diameter, less often in low (<1 m) square bridges; it rarely nests on buildings; natural sites are in cavities in the ground, including wash-away holes, holes dug by mammals, and the interior of broken termitaria. **Nest:** a gourd-shaped, thick-walled, closed bowl of mud pellets with a long entrance tunnel; bowl is lined with feathers, hair, grass, sometimes sheep's wool. The nest measures: 145-200-270 mm wide; 63-105-145 mm high; walls 5-18-20 mm thick; tunnel length 140-220 mm (90-370), 35-40-47 mm wide. Nests are reused for successive broods and in successive seasons; those in culverts are susceptible to flooding. Both sexes build, taking 13-21-35 days; both add lining through the incubation.
Laying months: Aug-Apr, mainly Nov-Dec (S Africa), Nov-Feb further north; double-brooded; relays after failure. **Clutch size:** 3-4 (1-8, >4 laid by 2 ♀s); laid at 1-day intervals. **Eggs:** 19.6-22.2-25.2 x 14.0-15.5-16.6 mm; mass 2.4-2.8-3.4 g. **Incubation period:** 20 days (18-23); by ♀ only; eggs unattended for >80% of the day; begins with last-laid egg. **Nestling/fledging period:** 24 days (23-25); young fed by both sexes.

Mosque Swallow *Cecropis senegalensis* Moskeeswael page 389
Breeds in n savannas, especially where large boababs or leadwoods provide nesting sites. Pairs nest solitarily. Nesting habits are poorly known. **Nest:** built with mud pellets, it is a thick-walled closed bowl with an entrance tunnel; typically placed inside a tree cavity, 6-8 m up, rarely in pipes, house eaves or rafters. One nest in a baobab cavity measured 150 x 230 mm (nest-chamber width) with a 75 mm long entrance tunnel, entering the chamber from above. The nest is lined with grass and feathers; both sexes build.
Laying months: Aug-Apr; sometimes double-brooded. **Clutch size:** 2-4. **Eggs:** 21.0-21.7-22.1 x 14.0-14.7-15.0 mm. **Incubation period:** not recorded. **Nestling/fledging period:** not recorded.

South African Cliff Swallow *Petrochelidon spilodera* Familieswael page 389
Breeds widely in South African grassland and grassy karoo. Colonial, 10-900 pairs/colony. Most colonies are on man-made brick and concrete structures, especially road bridges with vertical walls and a horizontal ceiling, 2-3 m above water. Ancestrally, breeding was probably restricted to rock overhangs and deeply eroded dongas. **Nest:** a gourd-shaped shell of mud pellets, with a short entrance spout; adjacent nests usually touching, their entrance holes 20-50-100 mm apart. Nest size very variable: exterior measures 140-184-210 mm in total length, 77-90-126 mm high; interior chamber 130 mm across, 80 mm deep; entrance spout 35 mm long 25-30-37 mm wide and 34-43-57 mm high. Nests are reused for successive clutches and in successive years, and are roosted in at night. Older nests often become heavily infested with parasites, causing a new nest to be built. Both sexes build, completing the mud shell in 5-7 days. Lining (plant down, wool and feathers, but not grass) is added during egg-laying and start of incubation.
Laying months: mainly Nov-Dec (Aug-Feb); multiple-brooded. **Clutch size:** 2-3 (1-4), second clutches smaller than first clutches laid at 1-day intervals. **Eggs:** 18.5-20.8-24.7 x 12.9-14.1-15.0 mm; mass 1.5-2.2-2.6 g. **Incubation period:** 14 days (14-16); shared equally by both sexes with frequent change-overs (at 9-min intervals on average); begins when first egg is laid. **Nestling/fledging period:** 24½ days (23-26); young brooded and fed by both sexes; young continue using nest as roost after fledging.

Common House Martin *Delichon urbica* Huisswael page 389
A summer visitor, arriving in Sep; mainly non-breeding, with <10 reports of breeding at widely scattered localities between 1892-1985, none sustained; nesting habits in the region virtually unknown. In Europe mostly colonial, 2-5 pairs/colony, rarely 100s. **Nest:** a gourd-shaped shell of mud, lined with grass and feathers, placed against a wall below an overhang. It measures: 143 mm deep, 178 mm wide, 106 mm from back-wall to entrance; no tunnel is added, access through the space 66 mm wide, 24 mm high, between ceiling and nest-bowl. Both sexes build, completing shell in 8-10-18 days; lining added during egg-laying and early incubation (Europe).
Laying months: Sep-Jan (southern Africa). **Clutch size:** 3-5 (Europe); laid at 1-day intervals. **Eggs:** 19 x 13 mm (South Africa). **Incubation period:** 14-16 days (Europe); by both sexes; begins when clutch is completed (Europe). **Nestling/fledging period:** 22-32 days (Europe); young brooded and fed by both sexes (Europe).

Greater Striped Swallow

Red-breasted Swallow

Lesser Striped Swallow

Mosque Swallow

South African Cliff Swallow

Common House Martin

Reed Warblers

WARBLERS Recent DNA evidence has transformed the warbler landscape from the once-familiar catch-all family that embraced a wide spectrum of small insectivorous birds to the current arrangement in which 7 local families are now recognised in its place. These are the Acrocephalidae, Cettiidae, Cisticolidae, Locustellidae, Macrosphenidae, Phylloscopidae and Sylviidae; combined they comprise 473 species worldwide, of which 183 breed in the Afrotropics, 60 in southern Africa.

REED WARBLERS Family Acrocephalidae (below) are the first of these. Worldwide 55 species; 6 breed in Afrotropics, 4 in southern Africa. Monogamous; parental care is shared by sexes; the nest is an open cup supported by reed- or weed-stems, mostly over water; eggs oval; white or pink, finely speckled, 2-3/clutch; nestlings are altricial and nidicolous.

Lesser Swamp Warbler *Acrocephalus gracilirostris* Kaapse Rietsanger   page 390

Breeds widely on wetlands (estuaries, lakes, dams, rivers, floodplains) where there is emergent vegetation (especially *Phragmites* reedbeds) growing in water. Pairs nest solitarily, but are often clustered in restricted habitat; adjacent nests here may be 5-10 m apart. **Nest:** a deep, firm-walled, cylindrical open cup, invariably placed above water and attached to 2-3 vertical stems about 1 m up (½-2). The supporting stems are typically reeds or bulrushes, but other aquatic plant stems may be used, including sedges, sapling trees and arum lilies. The nest is built with strips and shredded pieces of dry grass, sedge or reed blade; these are wrapped around the supporting stems to form 'handles' and are loosely woven to form the nest walls; the cup is lined with finer shreds of the same material, and some nests are lined with feathers, even dragonfly wings. The nest is placed well below the canopy of the supporting plants and, when in reeds, nests are usually to be found where the reed growth is most dense. The nest measures: outside diameter (including nest 'handles') 100-110 mm; (excluding handles 85 mm); cup diameter 50-55 mm; cup depth 40-50 mm; nest thickness 70-90 mm. The nest is built by ♀ only, while the ♂ sings nearby.
Laying months: Jul- May; mainly Aug-Dec in winter-rainfall region, Oct-Mar elsewhere. **Clutch size:** 2-3 (1-4); laid at 1-day intervals. **Eggs:** 18.1-19.4-22.1 x 13.0-14.2-15.3 mm. **Incubation period:** 14 days (13-14); by both sexes. **Nestling/fledging period:** 12 days (10-14); young fed by both sexes.

Greater Swamp Warbler *Acrocephalus rufescens* Rooibruinrietsanger   page 390

Restricted to n savanna in areas of papyrus in floodplains associated with the Kavango, Kwando, Linyanti, Chobe and upper Zambezi rivers. Pairs nest solitarily, spaced at a density of about a pair/0,06 ha (Zambezi River). **Nest:** a deep, open cup, invariably placed over water and usually built into the leafy crown of a papyrus plant; also in stems inside 'gomoti' fig thickets standing in water (Okavango). The nest is 1-2½ m above the water, placed beneath the papyrus canopy; it is built with long, thin shreds of papyrus and other leaves loosely and coarsely woven to form the nest walls, with a finely finished interior, the cup lining being fine shreds of the same material. The nest measures: outside diameter 83-92 mm; cup diameter 49-61 mm; cup depth 45-48 mm; nest thickness 45-61 mm; in some cases the nest-cup is asymmetrical (oblong rather than circular in cross-section).
Laying months: mainly Nov-Dec (Aug-Apr). **Clutch size:** 2-3; laid at 1-day intervals. **Eggs:** 20-21 x 15-16 mm. **Incubation period** >14 days; by both sexes. **Nestling/fledging period:** 14 days; young fed by both sexes.

African Reed Warbler *Acrocephalus baeticatus* Kleinrietsanger   page 390

Breeds widely in s Africa and likely to be present wherever there is suitable habitat; it favours marshy areas, especially tall sedges (*Cyperus, Carex*), reedbeds (*Typha, Phragmites*) or tall, thick herbaceous growth close to water. Pairs and occasional trios (pair plus 1 helper in 12% of cases) nest solitarily but may be <50 m apart in optimum habitat. Nests may be over water (e.g. in *Phragmites* reeds), over marshy ground, or over dry ground; occasionally, nests in fields of maize away from water or in the down-hanging branches of willows; the hairy willow-weed (*Epilobium hirsutum*) provides favoured nest sites. **Nest:** a small version of the Lesser Swamp Warbler nest; a firm-walled, cylindrical cup attached to two or more vertical stems (typically about 5 mm thick) of emergent vegetation (reed, sedge, etc), ½-1½ m up (0.3-3) from the ground or water. It is built of strips and shredded pieces of dry grass, sedge or reed blade which are wrapped around the supporting stems to form 'handles'. The cup is lined with finer shreds of the same material. The nest is always hidden from view below the canopy of the plant growth. It measures: outside diameter 70 mm; cup diameter 50 mm; cup depth 40 mm; nest thickness 70 mm.
Laying months: Aug-Apr, peaking earlier in winter-rainfall region (Oct-Nov) than elsewhere (Nov-Jan); sometimes double-brooded. **Clutch size:** 2-3; laid at 1-day intervals. **Eggs:** 16.0-17.6-18.7 x 12.4-13.2-14.5 mm. **Incubation period:** 12½-14 days; shared equally by both sexes. **Nestling/fledging period:** 12-13 days; young brooded and fed by both sexes, some assisted by a helper.

Dark-capped Yellow Warbler *Iduna natalensis* Geelsanger   page 390

Breeds in rank vegetation and bracken in damp areas, usually along streams; commonly in forest/grassland mosaics. Pairs nest solitarily and are widely spaced. **Nest:** a deep open cup, much like the nest of Lesser Swamp and African Reed warblers but not usually placed over water: it is most usually attached to two or more thin vertical stems of bracken, reed or some herbaceous plant, or it is built into a low fork in a shrubby tree (such as *Leucosidea sericea*); usually <1 m (0.3-1.3 m) above the ground; it is thick-walled, built entirely from long strips and shreds of dry grass which are curled around and woven to form the nest; coarser material, especially strips of leaf blade, is used in the base and walls, and finer material, including grass inflorescences, in the rim and cup lining. It is usually well concealed by surrounding rank growth. Nest measures: outside diameter 65-90 mm; cup diameter 42-45 mm; cup depth 38-40 mm; nest thickness 65-90 mm; in some cases the nest-cup is asymmetrical (oblong rather than circular in cross-section). One nest took 10 days to build.
Laying months: mainly Nov-Dec (Sep-Feb). **Clutch size:** 2 (2-3). **Eggs:** 16.6-18.0-19.0 x 11.8-13.4-14.2 mm. **Incubation period:** 12 days; by both sexes, but mostly by ♀. **Nestling/fledging period:** 14-16 days; young fed by both sexes.

Lesser Swamp Warbler

Greater Swamp Warbler

African Reed Warbler

Dark-capped Yellow Warbler

Warblers

'LEAF' WARBLERS Family Phylloscopidae Worldwide 77 species; 7 breed in Afrotropics, 1 in southern Africa. Mainly represented in Palearctic and Asia with a single species in the region. Monogamous; nestlings are altricial and nidicolous.

Yellow-throated Woodland Warbler *Phylloscopus ruficapillus* Geelkeelsanger   page 390

Breeds in montane forest, nesting on or close to the ground. Nesting habits are poorly known. Pairs nest solitarily and are widely spaced. **Nest:** a small domed structure with a side entrance, typically placed on a moss-covered, sloping bank, often close to a stream and among ferns, *Crocosmia*, or *Oplismenus* grass; it is built mainly or entirely with green moss so that it blends closely with its surroundings; cup is lined with fine strands of dry grass and a few feathers. It measures 80-100 mm across, the side entrance 35 mm wide. Some nests are placed in low growth off the ground (<15 cm) and one was recorded using in a weaver nest.
Laying months: mainly Oct-Nov (Oct-Dec). **Clutch size:** 3 (2-3). **Eggs:** 15.1-16.1-16.3 × 11.0-12.1-12.8 mm. Parasitism by African Emerald Cuckoo reported once. **Incubation period:** 17 days. **Nestling/fledging period:** 16 days; young fed by both sexes.

'BUSH' WARBLERS Family Cettiidae Worldwide 39 species; 7 breed in Afrotropics, 1 in southern Africa. Most species found in Asia, 1 in the region. Nest a ball, encased in leaves, placed in a tree; nesting habits poorly known; nestlings altricial and nidicolous.

Livingstone's Flycatcher *Erythrocercus livingstonei* Rooistertvlieëvanger   page 390

Breeds in lowland and riparian forest in n Zimbabwe and adjacent Mozambique. Nesting habits are poorly known. Pairs nest solitarily adjacent nests spaced 75-150 m apart. **Nest:** an oval-shaped shell of dry leaves that encases a deep, neatly lined cup-nest; placed in leafy foliage in the mid- to upper-canopy of a tall deciduous tree (e.g. *Combretum hereroense*, *Pterocarpus brenanii*), about 8 m (5-11) up from the ground. It is built into a cluster of leaves or seeds near the end of a lateral branch and is well concealed; the leaf shell is made up of numerous, overlapping, old, dry leaves (one built with 160 leaves of *Grewia flavescens*) firmly attached to each other with small gum-spots of cobweb; the leaves are not stitched or rivetted together as in camaropteras. The entrance is near the top of one side, and the nest-cup fills the base of the nest; it is made with finely shredded pieces of inner bark that extend up the sidewalls as far as the entrance hole; no plant down is used and cobweb use is minimal. One nest measured 110 mm (overall height), 50 mm (external width), entrance 30 × 40 mm in diameter.
Laying months: Jan-Feb (Zimbabwe). **Clutch size:** 2-3. **Eggs:** 13.6-14.0-14.3 × 10.3-10.6-10.9 mm. **Incubation period:** not recorded. **Nestling/fledging period:** not recorded.

'AFRICAN' WARBLERS Family Macrosphenidae Worldwide 18 species; 18 breed in Afrotropics, 6 in southern Africa. This newly named family includes crombecs (below), Rockrunner, Cape Grassbird, Moustached Warbler (all page 272) and Victorin's Warbler (page 252). Crombecs are monogamous; the sexes share parental duties; the nest an open pouch suspended from a twig; eggs long ovals, white with speckles, 2/clutch; nestlings are altricial and nidicolous.

Red-faced Crombec *Sylvietta whytii* Rooiwangstompstert   page 390

Breeds in n mesic savanna, mainly in miombo and *Baikiaea* woodland; also in lowland forest. Pairs nest solitarily and are widely spaced. **Nest:** a small, deep-cupped bag, open above, built in a tree (e.g. *Combretum molle*, *Brachystegia boehmii*), usually one that is leafless or covered with seedpods, characteristically placed on the tree's outer edge near the end of a down-hanging branch; it is slung between the twigs of a forked stem 2-4 m (1½-5½) above the ground. The nest wall is made from shreds of inner-bark and leaf petioles, held together with cobweb, its exterior extensively decorated with wood-flakes, caterpillar faeces and other debris that hangs loosely, attached with cobweb; the cup is lined with fine shreds of bark. The nest measures: 93 mm in height; 37 mm inside width of entrance; 42 mm cup depth (from lip of entrance to base of nest). It differs from the Long-billed Crombec nest by having a shorter back-wall, is usually higher up, and is placed at the edge of a tree. Some nest sites are reused in successive years.
Laying months: mainly Sep-Nov (Aug-Dec). **Clutch size:** 2 (1-3). **Eggs:** 16.6-17.8-19.6 × 11.1-12.2-13.0 mm. **Incubation period:** 13-14 days; by both sexes but mainly by ♀. **Nestling/fledging period:** 14-17 days; young fed by both sexes.

Long-billed Crombec *Sylvietta rufescens* Bosveldstompstert   pages 379, 390

Breeds widely across s Africa from arid west to mesic east, in savanna, karoo and fynbos; most common in wooded habitats dominated by acacias. Pairs nest solitarily, spaced at densities of a pair/3-20 ha. **Nest:** a small, deep-cupped bag built inside a tree or bush-clump, mostly <1 m up from the ground (½-4½), placed close to the trunk in an open space and suspended from near the end of a trailing twig. It is open above with a distinctly raised lip around the lower rim of the nest opening; the nest wall is made from shreds of inner-bark, leaf petioles, plant down and fine fibrous grass ends, held together and to the supporting twigs with cobweb. The nest's exterior is decorated with loosely hanging flakes of wood, fragments of bark, caterpillar faeces, cobweb litter; near human habitation such items as cigarette stubs made be incorporated, and here the nest is sometimes placed in a sheltered position against a wall; the cup is lined with fine dry grass ends or plant down. It differs from the Red-faced Crombec nest by having a longer back wall and by its location inside a tree rather than at its edge. The nest measures: 110-120-170 mm in height; 50-60 mm external width; 30-36 mm entrance width (internal); 40-45 mm cup depth (internal). Some nest sites are reused in successive years; it is built in 7-10 days but laying may only occur as late as 18 days after completion.
Laying months: mainly Oct-Dec (Aug-Mar, occasionally in other months) in summer-rainfall areas, Aug-Oct in s Cape; usually relays after an earlier failure. **Clutch size:** 2 (rarely 1 or 3); laid at a 1-day interval. **Eggs:** 17.1-18.6-20.9 × 11.0-12.4-13.7 mm; occasionally parasitised by Klaas's Cuckoo. **Incubation period:** 14 days; begins when clutch is completed; by both sexes. **Nestling/fledging period:** 14 days; young fed by both sexes.

Yellow-throated Warbler

Red-faced Crombec

Livingstone's Flycatcher (TWO ABOVE)

Long-billed Crombec

Warblers

'GRASSBIRDS' Family Locustellidae Worldwide 55 species; 11 breed in Afrotropics, 4 in southern Africa. Monogamous; nesting habits are poorly known; in 1, the ♀ builds and incubates, both sexes feed the young; nest an open cup on, or close to the ground, well hidden in vegetation; eggs oval; white with speckles, 2-3/clutch; nestlings are altricial and nidicolous.

Broad-tailed Warbler (Fan-tailed Grassbird) *Schoenicola brevirostris* Breëstertsanger — page 390

Breeds along e escarpment grasslands and in n mesic savanna in areas of thick, rank grass, often along edges of vleis, in seepages and in grassy levees bordering streams and rivers. Pairs nest solitarily at densities of about a pair/ 1½ ha (Tzaneen). **Nest:** an open cup, well hidden in dense grass (*Imperata*, *Hyparrhenia* spp. favoured), either placed in the heart of a tuft or between densely packed stems 150-200 mm up from the ground; it is not visible from above unless the grass is parted right above the nest; sometimes over dry ground but more often in a damp place, or above shallow water. The nest-cup is lined with fine shreds of grass and it is supported by a broad, loosely built bowl of uncompacted coarse blades and stems of dry grass. The nest measures: outside diameter 75-90 mm; cup diameter 45-60 mm; cup depth 25-50 mm; nest height 65-120 mm. It is built mainly or entirely by ♀ in 4 days. **Laying months:** mainly Dec-Feb (Nov-Mar). **Clutch size:** 2-3; laid at 1-day intervals. **Eggs:** 17.9-18.4-19.0 x 13.4-13.8-15.0 mm. **Incubation period:** not recorded. **Nestling/fledging period:** not recorded; young fed by both sexes.

Little Rush Warbler *Bradypterus baboecala* Kaapse Vleisanger — page 390

Breeds widely in wetlands in dense beds of sedge or bulrush (*Carex*, *Cyperus*, *Typha*). Pairs nest solitarily; in ideal habitat, can occur at a density of 10 pairs/ha. **Nest:** well concealed in rank vegetation, always over water or boggy ground, and usually <1 m up (0,2-1,2). It is an open cup, placed in the heart of a sedge or reed tuft, or in a deep recess between sheaves of fallen *Typha* stems, the nest often in the shape of a deep 'V'. Its base consists of coarse, dry pieces of sedge, grass or reed leaves, held together by the supporting stems and in this is set the deep nest-cup which is neatly lined with fine strands of dry plant material. It measures about: outside diameter 75 mm; cup diameter 45-50 mm; cup depth 38-50 mm; nest thickness 75-90 mm. **Laying months:** mainly Oct-Jan (Jul-Mar) in summer-rainfall region, Aug-Sep in winter-rainfall area. **Clutch size:** 2 (2-3). **Eggs:** 17.6-19.0-20.6 x 12.9-13.8-14.6 mm. **Incubation period:** 12-14 days. **Nestling/fledging period:** 12-13 days; young fed by both sexes.

Barratt's Warbler *Bradypterus barratti* Ruigtesanger — page 390

Breeds in and on the verges of montane forest and scrub forest, often along drainage lines where they nest on the forest floor. Nesting habits are poorly known. Pairs nest solitarily and are widely spaced. **Nest:** an open cup, placed on or close to the ground (<0.3 m up), well hidden within the tangle of dead branches, creepers, nettles, *Begonia*, grass and other ground-layer growth on the forest floor. The nest is a substantial bowl, 120 mm wide, of coarse dry plant stems, dry grass blades and leaves set into the ground or supporting substrate; the cup, 52 mm wide, 55 mm deep, is finely lined with hair-thin shreds of plant material. **Laying months:** mainly Nov (Oct-Dec). **Clutch size:** 2. **Eggs:** 19.6-20.5-21.4 x 14.5-15.5-16.5 mm; two records of parasitism by African Emerald Cuckoo. **Incubation period:** not recorded. **Nestling/fledging period:** not recorded; young fed by both sexes.

Knysna Warbler *Bradypterus sylvaticus* Knysnaruigtesanger — page 390

Breeds in forest in s Cape, in dense thickets, often along drainage lines. Pairs nest solitarily, about a pair/½ ha, adjacent nests 50-60 m apart. **Nest:** a well-concealed, deep cup either on the ground or close to it in thick, tangled vegetation (in bramble thickets or below branches or foliage of a fallen tree). The base is a bulky, uncompacted and loosely constructed bowl made from large and small dry leaves and stems of dry grass; the cup is set in this and it is neatly lined with fine, fibrous plant material. The nest measures: outside diameter 120-135-150 mm; cup diameter 55-58-65 mm; cup depth 30-55-70 mm; nest thickness 90-120-150 mm. It is built by the ♀ in 8 days, material collected <5 m from the nest. While she builds, the ♂ sings from a perch 3-5 m away. Both sexes utter a low purring alarm note if disturbed close to the nest. **Laying months:** Sep-Nov; single-brooded, but lays 1-2 replacements for failed clutches. **Clutch size:** 2-3. **Eggs:** 19.6-20.7-21.5 x 13.7-14.4-14.9 mm. **Incubation period:** 16 days (16-19); by ♀ only, starts with last-laid egg; leaves nest at 30-40 min intervals to feed. **Nestling/fledging period:** 13 days (12-14); young fed by both sexes.

'AFRICAN' WARBLERS Family Macrosphenidae Worldwide 18 species; 18 breed in Afrotropics, 6 in southern Africa (see others on pages 250, 272). Monogamous; ♀ builds and incubates, young fed by both sexes; nest an open cup on the ground well hidden in vegetation; eggs oval; white, finely speckled, 2/clutch; nestlings are altricial and nidicolous.

Victorin's Warbler *Cryptillas victorini* Rooiborsruigtesanger — page 390

Breeds in mountain fynbos, especially on s-facing slopes; mainly along streams and in seepages in dense vegetation (in restios, ericas, grass, etc). Pairs nest solitarily at a density of about 1 pair/6 ha. **Nest:** an open cup placed on or close to the ground (<0.3 m up) well hidden in dense undergrowth. It consists of a broad, loosely constructed base of dry grass, dead leaves, *Protea* bark and other plant material, curled around to form a bowl in which the deep nest-cup is set; this is neatly lined with fine, dry plant stems. The nest measures: outside diameter 100-120 mm; cup diameter 45-50 mm; cup depth 38-40 mm. Nest-building is done mainly but not entirely by the ♀, mostly between 07h00-11h00, and the nest takes 16 days to complete; most material is collected <5 m from the nest. The ♂ sings during nest-building; she remains silent, but both may call briefly close to the nest immediately after feeding nestlings; both sexes utter a low, purring alarm note if disturbed near the nest. **Laying months:** mainly Sep-Oct (Aug-Nov). **Clutch size:** 2. **Eggs:** 19.9-20.8-21.9 x 15.0-15.4-15.9 mm. **Incubation period:** 21 days; by ♀ only; starts when clutch completed. **Nestling/fledging period:** 18-19 days; young fed by both sexes.

Broad-tailed Warbler

Little Rush Warbler

Barratt's Warbler

Knysna Warbler

Victorin's Warbler

Cisticolas

CISTICOLAS Family Cisticolidae Worldwide 160 species; 124 breed in Afrotropics, 41 in southern Africa. DNA evidence has extended the limits of the family from cisticolas and prinias to also include apalises, camaropteras, eremomelas, wren-warblers and others; in terms of nesting habits, they are a diverse group; most are monogamous, but at least one is polygynous; nature of parental care varies between species; nests are ball-shaped or open-cupped, placed on the ground in some, up to treetop height in others; eggs oval-shaped; very variably coloured and marked, polychromatic in many species; 2-5/clutch; many are parasitised by Cuckoo-Finch and/or Brown-backed Honeybird, several by cuckoos as well; nestlings are altricial and nidicolous.

Red-faced Cisticola *Cisticola erythrops* Rooiwangtinktinkie   page 39

Breeds in mesic savannas in areas of tall grass, scattered bush and rank growth, usually on the margins of rivers, streams, lakes and reedbeds. Pairs nest solitarily and are widely spaced. **Nest:** similar to the nests built by Singing Cisticola and camaropteras, i.e. an oval ball encased in several large leaves that are drawn together to form a shell; ½-1½ m up from the ground in a broad-leafed sapling or herb (e.g. *Combretum apiculatum*, *Pseudarthria*, *Solanum* sp.). It is usually encased by 3-8 large leaves, one of which forms the roof of the nest and partly conceals the entrance. The nest inside is loosely woven using coarse, dry grass blades and a sparse lining of plant down is added to the nest-cup. It is roughly finished and the leaf cladding may only partially cover the enclosed nest made of dry grass; occasionally, nests lack a roof altogether. The ♀ continues to add plant down to the nest during the incubation.
Laying months: mainly Dec-Feb (Oct-Apr). **Clutch size:** 3 (2-4). **Eggs:** 16.0-17.7-18.8 x 11.6-12.8-13.5 mm; eggs lack variability of other cisticolas, being glossy-blue marked with shades of red-brown. **Incubation period:** 12-16 days; by ♀ only. **Nestling/fledging period:** 14 days; young fed by both sexes.

Singing Cisticola *Cisticola cantans* Singende Tinktinkie   page 39

Breeds in bracken, briar and forest-edge scrub in e highlands of Zimbabwe and adjacent Mozambique. Pairs nest solitarily and are widely spaced. **Nest:** unlike those of most cisticolas, it is an oval-shaped ball encased by broad green leaves of a growing plant that are stitched into the walls of the nest, resembling the nest built by a camaroptera but larger and less finely finished; it is placed ½-1 m up from the ground in a broad-leafed sapling or herb. The leaves are stitched in place with cobweb which is pushed through pinprick-sized holes made in the leaf and 'rivetted' (by tying a knot) on the outside; it may be encased by a single large leaf folded into a cone or, more usually, 2-4 leaves are used. The encased nest is made with coarse, dry blades of grass, shreds of bark and/or other dry plant material and thickly lined inside with light-coloured plant down. It measures: outside height 140 mm; outside width 75 mm; cup depth (from lower rim of entrance) 50 mm. The ♀ continues to add plant down to the nest during the incubation.
Laying months: mainly Dec-Jan (Nov-Apr). **Clutch size:** 3 (2-4). **Eggs:** 15.9-17.0-19.5 x 11.9-12.3-13.1 mm; eggs are variably coloured and marked but less so than those of most other cisticolas; they are always spotted and never unmarked nor finely speckled. **Incubation period:** 12-14 days; by ♀ only; begins before clutch is completed. **Nestling/fledging period:** 16 days; young fed by both sexes.

Lazy Cisticola *Cisticola aberrans* Luitinktinkie   page 39

Breeds in mesic savanna on rocky, wooded, grass-covered hillsides or along streams. Pairs nest solitarily and are widely spaced. **Nest:** an oval-shaped ball, longest on its vertical axis, placed low down (100-150 mm up from the ground), usually built into a thick old grass tuft among rocks, under a fallen branch or grown into a low shrub; usually well concealed. It is made with broad and fine strips of dry old grass and other plant material, loosely bound together and to the grass tuft with cobweb. The entrance hole faces out sideways from near the top of one side; inside, the nest is well lined with white plant down. It measures: 115 mm high; 65-70 mm wide. The nest of this species is much like those of other cisticolas that build oval-shaped ball nests and, where several of these species overlap in range, it is differences in their preferred breeding habitats that serve to distinguish them rather than the nests they make. The nest is built by the ♀; one took 19 days from start to the laying of the first egg.
Laying months: mainly Oct-Jan (Sep-Mar). **Clutch size:** 3-4 (2-4); laid at 1-day intervals. **Eggs:** 15.2-17.0-17.9 x 11.1-12.3-12.5 mm; very variable in colour and markings; parasitised by Brown-backed Honeybird. **Incubation period:** 13 days; by ♀ only. **Nestling/fledging period:** 13 days; young fed by both sexes, but mostly by the ♀.

Rattling Cisticola *Cisticola chiniana* Bosveldtinktinkie   page 39

Breeds widely in savanna areas, favouring acacia-dominated habitats with a good ground-cover of grass. Pairs nest solitarily and are spaced at densities of about a pair/4 ha. **Nest:** an oval-shaped ball, longest on the vertical axis, placed 150-300 mm (50-500) up from the ground, built into a dense, low shrub (e.g. *Helichrysum* sp.), into a thick grass tuft or in thick grass growing through a sapling or fallen branches; it is usually well concealed. It is made with blades and shreds of dry old grass, loosely bound together and to the supporting plant stems with a small amount of cobweb; nests in grass tufts sometimes have live stems pulled over and around them but these are not incorporated into the roof as they are in the nests of some cisticolas. The interior is lined with fine grass stems and the lower walls and floor are thickly lined with plant down. The entrance hole faces out sideways from near the top of one side; it is unconcealed and is usually the only part of the nest visible outside the tuft. It measures: 95-110 mm high; 60-75 mm wide; entrance 23-45 mm wide. The nest of this species is much like those of the Neddicky and Tinkling Cisticola, and where they occur together the identity of the nest owners needs to be established to identify it. The ♀ continues to add plant down to the nest during the incubation.
Laying months: mainly Nov-Jan (Oct-Apr). **Clutch size:** 3-4 (2-5); laid at 1-day intervals. **Eggs:** 14.7-16.9-18.8 x 10.9-12.4-13. mm; very variable in colour and markings; parasitised by Cuckoo-Finch and Brown-backed Honeybird. **Incubation period:** 13-14 days; by ♀ only. **Nestling/fledging period:** 14 days; young fed by both sexes.

Red-faced Cisticola

Singing Cisticola

Lazy Cisticola

Rattling Cisticola

Tinkling Cisticola *Cisticola rufilata* Rooitinktinkie page 391

Breeds in semi-arid savanna; favours areas with short, scattered trees and large, scattered grass tufts; often in regenerating woodland. Pairs nest solitarily and are widely spaced. **Nest:** an oval-shaped ball, longest on the vertical axis, placed low down (100-300 mm up from the ground), in a tuft of coarse grass (e.g. *Eragrostis pallens*, *Hyperthelia dissoluta*), sometimes growing beneath a sapling, or built in a sapling ingrown with rank grass; not usually well concealed. It is made with coarse and fine blades and stems of dry old grass loosely bound together and to the supporting plant stems with cobweb; there is minimal incorporation of the live stems in the walls and roof. The nest interior is well lined with white plant down. The nest measures: 90-130 mm high; 75 mm wide; entrance 25-38 mm wide. It is not readily distinguishable from the nest of a Rattling Cisticola alongside which it occurs in parts of its range. The ♀ continues to add plant down to the nest during the incubation.
Laying months: mainly Dec-Jan (Sep-Mar). **Clutch size:** 3-4 (2-5). Eggs: 16.0-17.0-18.8 × 11.4-12.6-12.9 mm; variable in colour and markings, but less so than other cisticolas; parasitised by Brown-backed Honeybird. **Incubation period:** not recorded; by ♀ only. **Nestling/fledging period:** not recorded; fed by both sexes.

Grey-backed Cisticola *Cisticola subruficapilla* Grysrugtinktinkie page 391

Breeds widely in the karoo and fynbos in low shrubland. Pairs nest solitarily and are widely spaced. **Nest:** an oval-shaped ball, longest on the vertical axis, placed low down (50-170 mm up from the ground, max 0.8 m) in a short, densely foliaged shrub (e.g. *Helichrysum* sp.), a grass tuft or low-growing forb where it is usually well hidden. It is made with thin (1 mm) strands and shreds of dry old grass, dry tendrils of *Clematis* and other plants, loosely bound together and to the supporting plant stems with cobweb. The lower walls and floor inside this shell are thickly lined (5-10 mm) with white plant down. The entrance hole faces out sideways from the top of one side and has a distinct lower lip. The nest measures: 105-120-140 mm in height; outside diameter 75-85 mm; inside diameter 65 mm; entrance 30-40 mm wide. It is similar to the nest of Neddicky but differs by usually being larger, and having an outer shell made with finer blades of nest material; where it meets Wailing Cisticola, the nests of the two species are indistinguishable. It is built in 6 days and plant down continues to be added to the nest lining during the incubation.
Laying months: mainly Aug-Sep (Jul-Dec) in winter-rainfall parts of range; Aug-Feb, peaking Oct-Nov in summer-rainfall areas. **Clutch size:** 3-4 (2-5); laid at 1-day intervals. Eggs: 14.2-15.9-17.1 × 10.6-11.9-13.0 mm; very variable in colour and markings. **Incubation period:** 13 days (12½-14). **Nestling/fledging period:** 14 days (11½-16).

Wailing Cisticola *Cisticola lais* Huiltinktinkie page 391

Breeds in hilly and mountainous country in open, treeless, rocky grassland. Pairs nest solitarily; adjacent nests may be <50 m apart. **Nest:** an oval-shaped ball, longest on the vertical axis, placed low down (70-150 mm up from the ground), usually in a short, dense grass tuft, less often in a densely foliaged forb or shrub; it is usually well concealed. It is made with strands and shreds of dry old grass and other plant material, loosely bound together and to the supporting plant stems with cobweb; nests in grass tufts incorporate live stems in their walls and these are drawn over to form the roof. The lower walls and floor inside the dry-grass shell are well lined with white plant down. It measures: 110 mm high; entrance 40-48 mm wide. The nest of this species is much like those of other cisticolas that build oval-shaped ball nests and, where several of these species overlap in range, it is differences in their preferred breeding habitats that serve to distinguish them rather than the nests they make. The ♀ continues to add plant down to the nest during the incubation.
Laying months: mainly Nov-Jan (Sep-Mar). **Clutch size:** 3 (2-5). Eggs: 15.3-17.2-19.2 × 11.5-12.9-14.0 mm; very variable in colour and markings. **Incubation period:** not recorded. **Nestling/fledging period:** not recorded.

Short-winged Cisticola *Cisticola brachyptera* Kortvlerktinktinkie page 391

Breeds in lowland broad-leafed woodland, palm savanna, forest edge and second growth where such habitats have been cleared for agriculture. Pairs nest solitarily and are widely spaced. **Nest:** a neat, compact, oval-shaped ball, longest on its vertical axis, placed 75-300 mm up from the ground, well concealed in a thick, green (recent growth) grass tuft or where grass is intergrown with weedy vegetation. It is made with broad strips of coarse grass, bound together and to the grass tuft with a small amount of cobweb. The entrance hole faces out sideways from near the top of one side; inside, the nest is well lined with light-coloured plant down. It measures: 90-100 mm in height; 65 mm wide (external); entrance 25 mm across.
Laying months: Nov-Mar (Zimbabwe). **Clutch size:** 2-4. Eggs: 15.2-16.0-17.0 × 10.0-11.8-12.2 mm; variable in colour and markings. **Incubation period:** 14 days; by ♀ only (E Africa). **Nestling/fledging period:** 17 days; young fed by both sexes (E Africa).

Croaking Cisticola *Cisticola natalensis* Groottinktinkie page 391

Breeds in mesic grassland and open savanna in areas of dense grass; can be dry or damp underfoot. Pairs nest solitarily at densities of about a pair/1 ha. **Nest:** a spherical ball, usually <100 mm (50-300) up from the ground, built into a green (growing) grass tuft. It is made of both live grass blades, drawn over to form the domed roof, and strips of dry grass curled round and bound together, and to the live stems, with cobweb. The nest interior is lined with finer grass ends, the cup with white plant down, which continues to be added during the incubation. The entrance hole is located midway up one side of the nest. The nest resembles those of Ayres' and Cloud cisticolas but is much larger; also similar to those of some widows, being distinguished from these by the use of plant down in the nest lining. It measures: 100-130 mm outside diameter; entrance 25-40 mm wide. Nests are well concealed, but given away by the domed roof formed by bent-over grass stems. Several nests may be built before one is selected for use.
Laying months: mainly Dec-Feb (Oct-Apr). **Clutch size:** 3-4 (2-5). Eggs: 16.0-18.7-20.6 × 12.4-13.7-14.7 mm; variable in colour and markings; parasitised by Cuckoo-Finch. **Incubation period:** 18 days; by ♀ only. **Nestling/fledging period:** 13-16 days.

Tinkling Cisticola

Grey-backed Cisticola   Wailing Cisticola   Short-winged Cisticola

Croaking Cisticola

Cisticolas

Levaillant's Cisticola *Cisticola tinniens* Vleitinktinkie page 39

Breeds widely in open, treeless habitats where there is tall grass and weedy growth, especially along streams and vlei margins; usually but not invariably associated with water. Pairs nest solitarily and are widely spaced. **Nest:** an oval-shaped ball, longest on its vertical axis, placed low down, usually 200-300 mm (70-900) up from the ground; it is typically in a thick, leafy grass-tuft or near the base of a broad-leafed plant, well hidden in foliage. It is made with blades and shreds of dry grass and weed stems, rootlets and other plant material, loosely bound together and to the supporting vegetation with a small amount of cobweb; the living foliage is loosely incorporated into the walls of the nest. The interior is lined with fine grass stems, and the lower walls and floor becoming increasingly thickly lined (by the ♀) with plant down as the incubation progresses. The entrance hole faces out sideways from near the top of one side; it is unconcealed and is usually the only part of the nest visible. Occasional nests lack a roof, remaining as deep, open cups. The nest measures: 120-130 mm height; 70-76 mm external width; entrance 20-40 mm wide.
Laying months: mainly Aug-Nov (Jun-Apr) in winter-rainfall region; Nov-Feb (Aug-May) elsewhere. **Clutch size:** 4 (2-5); laid at 1-day intervals. **Eggs:** 13.8-16.0-17.6 x 10.9-12.0-13.3 mm; very variable in colour and markings; parasitised by Cuckoo-Finch. **Incubation period:** 13-14 days; begins when clutch is completed. **Nestling/fledging period:** 14-15 days; young fed by both sexes.

Rufous-winged Cisticola *Cisticola galactotes* Swartrugtinktinkie page 39

Breeds along e margin of s Africa in marshy rank grass, sedges and reeds bordering on open water. Pairs nest solitarily and are widely spaced. **Nest:** an oval-shaped ball, longest on its vertical axis, built in rank vegetation, usually in a thick grass or a sedge tuft, 0.25-1.2 m up, usually over water or wet ground; it is built with shreds of grass and other dry plant material, lightly bound together and to the supporting plant stems with cobweb, and incorporating live stems into the nest walls. The entrance hole faces out sideways from near the top of one side. The nest is most solidly built in its lower half and, rarely, the upper section may be missing, resulting in an open cupped nest. Plant down is mostly, but not invariably, used to line the nest. It measures: 100 mm high; 70-90 mm wide; entrance 30 mm wide. The nest is built mainly by the ♀ and she continues to line it during the incubation.
Laying months: mainly Nov-Jan (Oct-May). **Clutch size:** 3 (2-4). **Eggs:** 15.9-17.2-18.3 x 11.5-12.7-13.3 mm; the terra-cotta colour of the egg is unique among the region's cisticolas; it also lays a pink, densely speckled egg which is rare here, but common in East Africa. **Incubation period:** not recorded. **Nestling/fledging period:** 14-17 days (Kenya); young fed by both sexes.

Luapula Cisticola *Cisticola luapula* Luapulatinktinkie no nest or egg photo

Breeds in flooded grass in the floodplain systems in the Caprivi and Okavango. Nesting habits are poorly known. Pairs nest solitarily, about a pair/2 ha. **Nest:** a well-hidden oval ball, longest on its vertical axis, placed over water, 0.35-0.38 m above water, usually half way up a dense, coarse-stemmed, standing grass-tuft. It is built with dry grass blades and incorporates living leaves of grass stems into the nest shell. It measures: 88-124 mm high; 65-84 mm wide; 61-84 mm front-to-back; entrance oval 35 x 75 mm wide. It is built by the ♀ in about 5 days and she continues adding plant-down to the nest during the incubation.
Laying months: Nov-Apr. **Clutch size:** 2-3. **Eggs:** 16.1-16.4-17.4 x 11.8-12.3-12.7 mm; egg (not illustrated) is pale salmon-pink heavily speckled or stippled uniformly with grey and dark red-brown. **Incubation period:** not recorded. **Nestling/fledging period:** not recorded.

Chirping Cisticola *Cisticola pipiens* Piepende Tinktinkie page 39

Breeds in the floodplain systems of Caprivi and Okavango in stands of dense, tall grass, reeds and papyrus growing in water. Pairs nest solitarily and are widely spaced. **Nest:** an oval- to pear-shaped ball, longest on its vertical axis, placed over water, 0.45-0.90 m above water or marshy ground, well hidden in dense, coarse-stemmed, standing grass. It is loosely built with broad shreds of dry grass and/or reed leaf, incorporating living leaves of grass stems that support it into the nest walls; a small amount of cobweb may be used to bind the nest together and to these stems. It measures: 110-140 mm high; 60-65 mm wide; 50-75 mm front-to-back; 35-45 mm entrance width. The nest is lined with plant down which is added throughout the incubation. Both sexes build the nest.
Laying months: mainly Jan-Mar (Oct-Apr). **Clutch size:** 3-4. **Eggs:** 14.8-17.6-19.1 x 12.0-12.7-13.0 mm. **Incubation period:** 14 days; by both sexes in 15-min shifts. **Nestling/fledging period:** 16 days; young fed by both sexes.

Neddicky *Cisticola fulvicapilla* Neddikkie page 39

Breeds widely in the savanna, grassland and fynbos regions, mainly in mesic areas and where there is grass and tree cover; it has extended its range in the grasslands as a result of the introduction of alien woody vegetation here. Pairs nest solitarily and are spaced at a density of about a pair/5-10 ha. **Nest:** a smallish, oval-shaped ball, longest on its vertical axis, placed close to the ground (about 150 mm up, rarely >300 mm) in a thick grass tuft or, less usually, into a low shrubby bush (*Asparagus*, *Helichrysum* sp.); it is built with shreds of dry grass, bound together and to the grass tuft with a small amount of cobweb; inside, the nest is well lined with white plant down. The entrance hole faces out sideways from near the top of one side; it is unconcealed and is usually the only part of the nest visible outside the tuft. Occasionally, nests are found that lack a roof. The nest measures: 90-100 mm high; 65-75 mm wide (external); entrance 30-40 mm across. The Neddicky builds a smaller nest than other cisticolas that overlap in range (Grey-backed, Wailing, Rattling, Lazy, Tinkling) but this is not sufficient to identify a nest without identifying its owners. The nest is built by the ♀ and nest-lining material continues to be added during the incubation.
Laying months: Sep-Mar (rarely in other months); peaks in Sep (sw Cape); Oct-Nov (e Cape, KwaZulu-Natal); Nov-Jan (n South Africa, Zimbabwe, Botswana). **Clutch size:** 3 (2-5; rarely 7, probably laid by more than one ♀); laid at 1-day intervals. **Eggs:** 13.8-15.2-16.9 x 10.5-11.5-12.6 mm; very variable in colour and markings; parasitised by Brown-backed Honeybird, Cuckoo-Finch and Klaas's Cuckoo. **Incubation period:** 12-15 days. **Nestling/fledging period:** 12-15 days.

Levaillant's Cisticola

Rufous-winged Cisticola

Chirping Cisticola   Neddicky

Cisticolas

Zitting Cisticola *Cisticola juncidis* Landeryklopkloppie   page 391
Breeds widely in open grassy areas, especially in mesic grasslands in knee-height grass; often but not invariably on damp ground. Adjacent nests may be <50 m apart. **Nest:** the nest differs from those of other cisticolas by being a pear-shaped 'soda-bottle' with a vertical entrance, its outer walls incorporating the leaves of the grass tuft in which it is built; it is placed 100-250 mm up from the ground in a living, broad-leafed grass tuft; a shell of 13-34 grass blades is bound together with cobweb, encasing a warmly lined interior. The nest measures: 130-180 mm in height (external); outside width (at the base) 60-65-70 mm; inside width 50 mm; distance from nest floor to entrance 100-130 mm; entrance 25-35 mm across. The ♀ continues adding plant down through the incubation. In Europe ♂s are polygynous, building up to 18 nest shells/season; ♀s select and line one and undertake all subsequent parental care.
Laying months: mainly Oct-Dec (Aug-Feb) in winter-rainfall region, Nov-Feb (Oct-Mar) elsewhere; sometimes double-brooded. **Clutch size:** 4 (2-5, rarely 6); laid at 1-day intervals. **Eggs:** 13.3-15.1-16.5 x 10.4-11.4-12.4 mm; mass 1.1 g; very variable colour and markings; parasitised by Cuckoo-Finch. **Incubation period:** 13 days (12-15); by ♀ only; begins when clutch is completed. **Nestling/fledging period:** 13-14 days (11-15); fed mainly by ♀, sometimes by ♂.

Desert Cisticola *Cisticola aridula* Woestynklopkloppie   page 391
Breeds in open, semi-arid grasslands with a poor basal cover, often in old croplands. Adjacent nests sometimes <20 m apart. **Nest:** a pear-shaped oval with a tapering roof and an upward-angled entrance; placed close to the ground (its base 100-150 mm up) in a grass tuft from which a few stems are drawn together and incorporated into the nest wall; lacks the elongated entrance neck of Zitting Cisticola's nest and by being built mainly with dry plant material rather than with living stems. The nest walls are flimsy and transparent, bound together and to the grass tuft with sparse cobweb; the cup is more substantial, being thickly lined with white plant down. Nests vary in their degree of concealment, some easily visible, others very well concealed. It measures: 110-115 mm in height (external); outside width (at the base) 60-65 mm; inside depth (nest floor to entrance) 60 mm; entrance 30 mm wide. One nest took 4 days to build (from start to laying of first egg). The ♀ continues lining the nest during the incubation.
Laying months: mainly Nov-Feb (Oct-Apr); relays after earlier failure. **Clutch size:** 3-4 (2-5); laid at 1-day intervals. **Eggs:** 13.9-15.0-15.9 x 10.8-11.3-12.0 mm; very variable in colour and markings; parasitised by Cuckoo-Finch. **Incubation period:** 14 days. **Nestling/fledging period:** 13 days.

Cloud Cisticola *Cisticola textrix* Gevlekte Klopkloppie   page 391
Breeds in open highveld grassland, in the grassy karoo and in restio-dominated fynbos, often nesting in places where the grass is so short (from burning or grazing) that it appears incapable of hiding a nest. Pairs nest solitarily and are widely spaced. **Nest:** a small spherical ball with a circular side entrance, placed almost at ground level in or between tufts, 20-30 mm up from the ground (0-50 mm); the shell is made of blades of dry grass loosely bound together with cobweb, live stems bent over and woven into the roof; the interior is lined with white plant down which continues being added through the incubation. The nest is usually well concealed and measures: 70-75 mm outside diameter; 110-130 mm high; internal diameter 55 mm; entrance 25-30 mm wide. Ayres' Cisticola's nest is similar and, where the two species occur side-by-side, their nests can only be distinguished by identifying the owners.
Laying months: mainly Sep-Oct (Aug-Nov) winter-rainfall region, Nov-Jan (Oct-Mar) elsewhere. **Clutch size:** 3-4 (2-5); laid at 1-day intervals. **Eggs:** 14.0-15.7-17.8 x 10.8-11.6-12.5 mm; very variable in colour and markings; parasitised by Cuckoo-Finch. **Incubation period:** 14 days. **Nestling/fledging period:** 15 days.

Pale-crowned Cisticola *Cisticola cinnamomeus* Bleekkopklopkloppie   page 391
Breeds in mesic grassland and in dambos in mesic n savanna; favours short (300-400 mm), open grass, often, but not invariably over damp ground in depressions or bordering vleis. Pairs nest solitarily, are widely spaced. **Nest:** an oval-shaped (longest on vertical axis) ball, built close to the ground (50-150 mm up) in a grass or sedge tuft, its walls and roof incorporating live stems of the supporting plant in the nest shell, these stems giving the roof a peaked look and concealing the entrance. The shell is made of strips and shreds of dry grass that are bound together and to the live stems with cobweb, while the interior of the nest is sparsely lined with white plant down. It measures: 150-160 mm in height; outside diameter 60-70 mm; entrance, which faces out sideways from near the top of one side, 25-40 mm wide. The ♀ continues adding plant down to the nest during the incubation.
Laying months: mainly Dec-Jan (Nov-May). **Clutch size:** 3-4 (2-6); laid at 1-day intervals. **Eggs:** 14.3-15.3-17.6 x 10.0-11.3-12.0 mm; variable colour and markings; parasitised by Cuckoo-Finch. **Incubation period:** >12 days. **Nestling/fledging period:** 12-14 days; young fed by both sexes.

Ayres' Cisticola (Wing-snapping Cisticola) *Cisticola ayresii* Kleinste Klopkloppie   page 391
Breeds in mesic grasslands, mainly in upland areas and usually the most common nesting grassland bird where it is found; also occurs locally in dambos and other isolated grasslands in the n mesic savanna. Adjacent nests may be <10 m apart. **Nest:** a small spherical ball, placed in short, thick, often wiry grass, which may or may not have been burnt the previous winter. It is set inside or between green grass tufts, 0-50 mm up from the ground; the shell is made of blades of dry grass curled around to form a ball, loosely bound together with sparse cobweb with live grass blades bent over and woven into the roof; usually very well concealed, with the roof structure and small side entrance hole all that's visible of the nest. The interior of the nest is lined with white plant down. It measures: outside diameter 70-75 mm; inside diameter 40-45 mm; entrance 20-35 mm wide. Where it occurs alongside Cloud Cisticola, the nests of the two can't be distinguished without identifying the owners. Completed nests may remain unused for up to 2 weeks before eggs are laid. The ♀ continues adding plant down to the nest during the incubation.
Laying months: mainly Nov-Jan (Oct-Mar). **Clutch size:** 4 (2-5). **Eggs:** 13.2-15.1-16.5 x 10.5-11.5-12.0 mm; very variable colour and markings; parasitised by Cuckoo-Finch. **Incubation period:** 11-14 days; by ♀ only. **Nestling/fledging period:** 14-15 days.

Zitting Cisticola

Desert Cisticola

Cloud Cisticola

Pale-crowned Cisticola

Ayres' Cisticola

Warblers, Prinias

Rufous-eared Warbler *Malcorus pectoralis* Rooioorlangstertjie   page 390
Breeds in semi-arid and arid karoo and arid savanna. Pairs nest solitarily and are widely spaced. **Nest:** a small, oval-shaped ball placed about ½ m (0.2-1.2) up from the ground in the centre of a low, thorny shrub (e.g. *Rhigozum, Pteronia, Osteospermum, Galenia, Rosinia*). It is typically well concealed and is thick-walled but loosely built from long strands and shreds of dry plant material (stems and lengths of bark stripped from milkweed and other forbs) that are curled around to form the walls and secure the nest to its supporting twigs. The entrance, about 34 mm in diameter, is near the top of one side. The nest is not 'knitted' in the way that prinia nests are. Inside, it is warmly lined with plant down, and this continues to be added during the incubation. If disturbed at the nest, the bird may flee by running from the nest on the ground, rather than flying off.
Laying months: lays opportunistically in response to rainfall, but mainly Oct-Mar (rarely in other months) in summer-rainfall areas, Aug-Sep in winter-rainfall region. **Clutch size:** 3-4 (7 recorded were probably laid by >1 ♀). **Eggs:** 14.2-15.5-17.1 x 10.5-11.4-12.3 mm. **Incubation period:** 12-13 days. **Nestling/fledging period:** 11-13 days; young fed by both sexes.

Namaqua Warbler *Phragmacia substriata* Namakwalangstertjie   page 390
Breeds in the arid karoo along the margins of dry watercourses, usually within 10 m of a drainage line (rarely >50 m), in thickets of *Acacia* or *Rhus* trees mixed with clumps of reed or bullrush. Pairs nest solitarily, about 100 m apart. **Nest:** a deep, open-cupped nest, similar to that of a *Bradypterus* warbler, usually <1 m (0.3-1.5) up from the ground and well hidden in the heart of a reed or bullrush clump, in caught-up drift debris, or in the midst of a thorny-leafed shrub (e.g. *Galenia* sp.) or thistle (e.g. *Berkeya* sp.); it is entirely different to the oval-shaped, closed nest woven by prinias, loosely and untidily made with pieces of dry plant material (leaves, grass, shreds of bullrush, weed-stems, rootlets, etc.). The deep cup is warmly lined with fluffy seed-heads, feathers and rootlets. The nest measures: outside diameter 60-100 mm; cup diameter 40 mm; cup depth 40 mm; nest height 70-90 mm.
Laying months: mainly Sep-Oct (Aug-Apr). **Clutch size:** 3 (2-4). **Eggs:** 14.2-16.5-17.1 x 10.5-11.5-12.7 mm. **Incubation period:** 16 days. **Nestling/fledging period:** 15 days.

Tawny-flanked Prinia *Prinia subflava* Bruinsylangstertjie   page 390
Breeds widely in mesic savanna, nesting in areas of rank grass and weeds, especially second-growth in regenerating woodland, along streams and rivers, and on the margins of damp ground. **Nest:** a typical prinia-type oval- to pear-shaped ball (its vertical axis longest) with an entrance near the top of one side; it is usually <1 m up from the ground (½-2½) and is built in a leafy shrub, sapling or tall tuft of grass or sedge, often over shallow water or damp ground; in contrast to the Black-chested Prinia, it shows no preference for nesting in thorny bushes. Occasionally, the disused nest of a Southern Red Bishop (shown in photograph opposite) or widowbird may be used. The nest is finely 'knitted' from thin lengths of green blades of grass; newly built nests are green, but they soon fade to a dry-grass colour. The nest is either unlined, or it is sparsely lined with grass ends, but not with plant down. It measures: 95-110 mm in height; 55-65 mm in width (external); entrance is 25-35 mm wide. Structurally, the nest is probably indistinguishable from that of the next species. It is built by both sexes.
Laying months: mainly Nov-Feb (Aug-Apr, occasionally other months); relaying up to three replacement clutches after earlier failures. **Clutch size:** 3 (2-5); laid at 1-day intervals. **Eggs:** 14.1-16.0-17.9 x 10.5-11.4-12.8 mm; very variable in colour and markings; occasionally parasitised by Cuckoo-Finch and Brown-backed Honeybird. **Incubation period:** 14 days (13-17); by both sexes, but mainly the ♀. **Nestling/fledging period:** 14-15 days (13-18); young fed by both sexes.

Black-chested Prinia *Prinia flavicans* Swartbandlangstertjie   page 390
Breeds in semi-arid and arid savannas, in northern parts of the karoo and in western parts of the grassland region; favours acacia-dominated woodland and scrub, and is common in second growth, road verges and gardens. Pairs nest solitarily and are spaced at densities of a pair/2-8 ha. **Nest:** a typical prinia-type oval- to pear-shaped ball with an entrance near the top of one side, typically about 1 m off the ground (0.2-2.2), built into the twigs or stems of a small tree or shrub, usually one that stands alone; small acacias and thorny *Asparagus* sp. bushes are much favoured. The nest is finely 'knitted' from thin lengths of green blades of grass; newly built nests are green, but they soon fade to a dry-grass colour. The nest is not usually lined. It measures: 95-115 mm in height; 60-65 mm in width (external); entrance hole is 30 mm wide. Structurally, the nest is probably indistinguishable from that of the previous species. It is built by both sexes, starting at the floor and working upwards (as shown in the photograph opposite), taking 11-12 days to complete.
Laying months: Aug-May (occasionally in other months); peaks in Nov-Jan in the east of its range, but Dec-Mar in the west; usually relays after an earlier failure; sometimes double-brooded. **Clutch size:** 3-4 (2-6). **Eggs:** 13.7-16.0-17.8 x 10.5-11.6-12.4 mm; very variable in colour and markings; occasionally parasitised by Cuckoo-Finch. **Incubation period:** 14-15 days (12-16). **Nestling/fledging period:** 14 days (11-14); young fed by both sexes.

Rufous-eared Warbler | Namaqua Warbler

Tawny-flanked Prinia | using old nest of Southern Red Bishop

Black-chested Prinia | a nest being 'knitted'

Karoo Prinia *Prinia maculosa* **Karoolangstertjie**   page 390

Breeds in fynbos, karoo and coastal bush in low shrubland. Pairs nest solitarily and are spaced at densities of about a pair/2 ha. **Nest:** a typical prinia-type nest, oval- to pear-shaped (vertical axis longest) with an entrance near the top of one side, built in a low, well-foliaged shrub (such as *Erica, Senecio, Helichrysum*), attached to 3-4 thin inside twigs, usually about ½ m up from the ground (0.2-1.2); seldom builds the nest in a protea or in a dead plant. It is finely 'knitted' with thin lengths of green blades of grass; newly built nests are green but they soon fade to a dry-grass colour. The cup is thickly lined with plant down (usually *Eriocephalus* sp.) which continues to be added during the incubation. The nest measures: 90-110-130 mm in height; 40-70-90 mm in width; entrance is 30-40 mm in diameter. It is built by both sexes in 4-14 days, and laying commences 2-6 days after its completion. Rarely, the old nest of a widowbird may be used, or a previously used nest is reused for a second clutch.
Laying months: mainly Oct-Nov (Aug-Dec, rarely in other months) in summer-rainfall areas, Aug-Sep in winter-rainfall region; relays after earlier failure, rarely double-brooded. **Clutch size:** 4 (2-5); laid at 1-day intervals (rarely 2). **Eggs:** 15.2-16.4-17.6 × 10.8-11.7-12.5 mm; very variable in colour and markings; occasionally parasitised by Diederik and Klaas's cuckoo and Brown-backed Honeybird. **Incubation period:** 13½ days (12-17); begins when clutch is completed; by ♀ only; she leaves nest 2-3x/hr to feed. **Nestling/fledging period:** 12½ days (10-14); young fed by both sexes.

Drakensberg Prinia *Prinia hypoxantha* **Drakensberglangstertjie**   page 390

Breeds in mesic grasslands, often on the verges of montane forest, in areas of bracken, forest scrub and other rank growth, especially along drainage lines. Pairs nest solitarily and are widely spaced. **Nest:** a typical prinia-type knitted oval- to pear-shaped ball with a side-top entrance, placed in bracken or a leafy sapling, bush or weed, typically about 1 m (0.3-1.2) up from the ground; usually well concealed. It is 'knitted' with thin lengths of green blades of grass which rapidly fade to a dry-grass colour. Nests may or may not be lined with plant down. The nest measures: about 120 mm in height; 70 mm in width; entrance is 25-30 mm in diameter. As happens with many nests of other prinias, the growth of the plant supporting the nest often distorts the nest's original shape before the nest cycle is completed.
Laying months: mainly Nov-Jan (Oct-Feb). **Clutch size:** 3 (2-4). **Eggs:** 15.0-16.4-17.5 × 11.0-11.9-12.0 mm; eggs are very variable in colour and markings; occasionally parasitised by Brown-backed Honeybird. **Incubation period:** 14 days. **Nestling/fledging period:** 15 days; young fed by both sexes.

Roberts' Warbler (Roberts's Warbler) *Oreophilias robertsi* **Woudlangstertjie**   page 390

Breeds in bracken-briar thickets along the margins of montane forest in the highlands of e Zimbabwe and adjacent Mozambique. Nesting habits are poorly known. **Nest:** a thin-walled, oval-shaped ball with a side-top entrance, placed in a shrub, low dense thicket or leafy weed, typically about 1 m up from the ground. It is a loosely built, thin-walled structure, made with dry grass ends that are bound together, and to the supporting twigs, with cobweb. Green moss is incorporated into the outer walls of some nests; the interior is lined with fine, hair-like strands of grass, curled around to form the cup. It lacks the characteristic knitted wall structure of a prinia nest. It measures: about 150-160 mm in height; 70-75 mm in width; entrance is 45 mm wide and 60-80 mm high. (In the upper centre photograph opposite the nest-entrance has been temporarily widened to show the eggs).
Laying months: mainly Oct-Dec (Sep-Feb). **Clutch size:** 2, less often 3. **Eggs:** 16.3-17.4-18.0 × 12.2-12.7-13.1 mm. **Incubation period:** not recorded. **Nestling/fledging period:** not recorded; both sexes feed the young.

Red-winged Warbler *Heliolais erythroptera* **Rooivlerksanger**   page 390

Breeds in the grassy understorey of lowland deciduous woodland, especially miombo, and in second growth where such habitat has been cleared for agriculture. Nesting habits are poorly known. Pairs nest solitarily and are widely spaced. **Nest:** a thin-walled, oval-shaped ball, with a side-top entrance, placed about ½ m up from the ground, in the stems of a leafy shrub, well concealed in rank undergrowth; it is loosely constructed with fine strands of dry, old grass, held together with a little cobweb and the cup is lined with soft grass inflorescences. It lacks the finely knitted structure of a prinia nest.
Laying months: Oct-Jan. **Clutch size:** 2-3. **Eggs:** 16.5-17.5-19.0 × 12.0-12.4-13.0 mm. **Incubation period:** not recorded. **Nestling/fledging period:** not recorded.

Karoo Prinia

Drakensberg Prinia

Roberts' Warbler (LEFT & TWO ABOVE)   Red-winged Warbler

Apalises

Bar-throated Apalis *Apalis thoracica* Bandkeelkleinjantjie   pages 379, 390

Breeds in montane forest and forest scrub (from sea-level in s Cape to highland forests in the interior), in thickets and riparian galleries in mesic savanna, extending into the grassland and karoo where introduced or riparian trees provide habitat; it is a regular garden bird in wooded suburban habitats. Pairs nest solitarily and are widely spaced. **Nest:** a small, oval-shaped ball placed in thick foliage about 1-2 m (0.1-3) up from the ground; it is often in a leafy shrub or sapling (e.g. azalea, bouganvillea, *Diospyros whyteana*, *Scutia myrtina*) growing beneath a canopy of taller trees, some are built in trailing creepers, suspended from a branch end, or in a grass tuft or root mat beneath an overhanging bank. The nest is loosely made, built typically with pieces of green moss, fine plant fibres (often *Asparagus sp.*), strands of *Usnea*, grey lichen and/or fine grass stems. The interior is usually well lined with plant down, but in some this is lacking; some nests are decorated outside with a few pieces of such unusual items as spider egg-capsule. The nest measures 95-110-130 mm high; 60-70-75 mm wide; entrance near the top of one side, 30-40 mm in diameter. It is built by one bird (possibly the ♀), accompanied by its mate. The same sites are sometimes reused in successive seasons.
Laying months: mainly Sep-Dec (Aug-Mar) in summer-rainfall areas, Aug-Oct (Jul-Jan) in winter-rainfall region; often double-brooded. **Clutch size:** 3 (2-4); laid at 1-day intervals. **Eggs:** 15.5-17.2-19.1 x 11.2-12.2-13.5 mm; frequently parasitised by Klaas's Cuckoo. **Incubation period:** 15 days (14-17); by both sexes. **Nestling/fledging period:** 16 days (13-18); young fed by both sexes.

Rudd's Apalis *Apalis ruddi* Ruddse Kleinjantjie   page 390

Breeds from n KwaZulu-Natal to c Mozambique in deciduous woodland, coastal, sand and riparian forest; most common in dense acacia thickets. Pairs nest solitarily, adjacent nests spaced about 80 m apart. **Nest:** a small, oval-shaped ball with an entrance hole near the top of one side, placed about 1 m up (0.2-3) from the ground, in a densely twigged, leafy bush (e.g. *Maytenus, Gymnosporia*) that stands a little apart from others. Some nests are built largely or entirely with *Usnea*, and placed within *Usnea*-draped branches, while others are made of finely shredded brown-coloured bark, pieces of green moss, grey lichen, fine grass stems and other plant fibres. It is held together and to the supporting twigs with cobweb; the nest-cup inside is lined with plant down. Nests vary in their degree of concealment, some being very difficult to see while in others the nest material does not blend with its surroundings and the nest is conspicuous. It measures: about 95-100 mm high; 65-70 mm wide; entrance is about 25-32 mm in diameter. Built (reportedly, but seems unlikely) by the ♂ alone in 8-12 days; it may stand empty for 16 days before laying.
Laying months: mainly Oct-Nov (Sep-Jan). **Clutch size:** 2 (1-3). **Eggs:** 16.0-16.9-17.8 x 11.6-12.2-12.8 mm. **Incubation period** not recorded. **Nestling/fledging period:** not recorded; young fed by both sexes.

Yellow-breasted Apalis *Apalis flavida* Geelborskleinjantjie   page 390

Breeds in riparian woodland in mesic savanna and in lowland, coastal and riparian forest. Pairs nest solitarily and are widely spaced. **Nest:** a small, oval-shaped ball with an entrance hole near the top of one side, placed 1-3 m (rarely to 5 m) up, usually well hidden in a densely foliaged shrubby tree. Nest sites are more variable than those of other apalises: a lichen-festooned tree is a favoured site (as shown in the photograph opposite) and the nest may be built largely or entirely with this material; others are built in the top of a weed, or suspended from a trailing, leafy branch, and old nests of weavers, waxbills and Collared Sunbird are sometimes used. Nests are bound together and to the supporting twigs with cobweb and their interior is warmly lined with plant down. The nest measures: 85-100 mm in height; 55 mm in width; entrance hole is 35-40 mm across. The incubating bird usually sits tight if the nest is approached, only flying off at the last moment.
Laying months: mainly Oct-Dec (Sep-Feb, occasionally in other months). **Clutch size:** 3 (2-3); laid at 1-day intervals. **Eggs:** 14.2-15.8-17.7 x 10.0-11.3-12.0 mm; very variable in colour and markings; parasitised by Klaas's Cuckoo (in Kenya). **Incubation period** 13 days (12-14); by both sexes (Kenya). **Nestling/fledging period:** 15-17 days (Kenya); young fed by both sexes.

Chirinda Apalis *Apalis chirindensis* Gryskleinjantjie

Restricted to montane forest in e highlands of Zimbabwe and adjacent Mozambique. Nesting habits are poorly known: 3 nests have been described from Vumba (e Zimbabwe) but eggs, clutch size, young, parental roles in the breeding cycle, and more, awaits description. **Nest:** three nests at Vumba were all located inside forest, one suspended from the underside of a lichen- and *Usnea*-clad twig; they were 4, 10 and 20 m up from the ground; oval-shaped with an entrance at the top of one side, built with *Usnea*, lichen, epiphytic liverwort, fine grass stems, skeletonised leaves and seed heads and bound together with cobweb. In one report both sexes brought and added down-lining to the nest.
Laying months: not recorded; nest-building in Nov-Dec (Vumba). **Clutch size:** not recorded. **Eggs:** not recorded. (not illustrated) **Incubation period:** not recorded. **Nestling/fledging period:** not recorded; young fed by both sexes.

Black-headed Apalis *Apalis melanocephala* Swartkopkleinjantjie   no nest or egg photo

Range extends narrowly into c Mozambique and e edge of Zimbabwe from tropical Africa; not yet recorded breeding in the region; frequents lowland and riparian forest. **Nest:** an oval-shaped ball with a side entrance, placed 5-7 m up from the ground, well hidden in the outer foliage of a tree (Malawi). It is built with fine grey lichen and a small amount of *Usnea*, forming walls about 13 mm thick, loosely bound and attached to the supporting twigs with a little cobweb. The nest-cup is thickly lined with white-coloured plant down.
Laying months: Oct-Nov (Malawi). **Clutch size:** 2-3 (Malawi). **Eggs:** 15.3-15.4-15.7 x 11.4-11.8-12.0 mm; (not illustrated) pale greenish, boldly marked all over with spots and a few speckles of dull to bright chestnut, with underlying spots, blotches and speckles of faint purplish slate, in some cases so faint as to be almost imperceptible (Malawi). **Incubation period:** not recorded. **Nestling/fledging period:** not recorded.

Bar-throated Apalis

Rudd's Apalis

Yellow-breasted Apalis

Chirinda Apalis

Warblers

Green-backed Camaroptera *Camaroptera brachyura* Groenrugkwêkwêvoël   pages 379, 392

Breeds commonly in coastal, lowland, riparian and montane forest. Pairs nest solitarily, adjacent nests spaced 50-100 m apart. **Nest**: a small, ball-shaped structure placed close to the ground, usually <1 m up (0.1-1.5, rarely 6 m), well hidden in the foliage of a low, broad-leafed shrub (often *Isoglossa woodii*, *Monoanthotaxus* or a *Microsporium* fern frond); sometimes in a broad-bladed grass. Living leaves (5-6) encase the nest, held together with spiderweb by 'rivetting' thread through pinprick-sized holes made in the leaf. The interior is thickly lined with fine, dry, pliable plant stems, soft, downy plant seeds and cobweb; little of the nest shows through the leaf casing except where the entrance hole is at the top of one side. The nest measures: outside height 100-115 mm; outside width 69-76 mm; entrance diameter 25-40 mm. The nest is built mainly by one of the pair (possibly ♀), taking 9-17 days to complete. When alarmed at the nest, the pair make their characteristic 'bleating' call.
Laying months: mainly Oct-Dec (Sep-Feb, rarely in other months). **Clutch size:** usually 3 (2-4); laid at 1-day intervals. **Eggs:** 14.0-17.0-18.6 × 10.8-12.3-13.5 mm; unlike those of next species its eggs are unmarked white; it is parasitised by the Emerald Cuckoo which lays a matching but larger white egg. **Incubation period:** 14-15 days; begins before clutch is completed; mostly or entirely by one parent, probably the ♀. **Nestling/fledging period:** 14-15 days; young fed by both sexes.

Grey-backed Camaroptera *Camaroptera brevicaudata* Grysrugkwêkwêvoël   page 392

Breeds in semi-arid and mesic savannas, favouring thickets, often along drainage lines, at the base of hills or on termitaria. Pairs nest solitarily and are widely spaced. **Nest:** similar to that of the previous species; usually <0.3 m up from the ground (seldom >1 m up), well hidden in foliage of a broad-leafed shrub, a sapling/coppicing tree, occasionally in a broad-bladed grass; 5-6 living leaves enclose the small, ball-shaped nest, drawn together and rivetted in place with cobweb; the interior is lined with fine, dry, grass ends or hair-like plant fibres, sometimes a little plant down; entrance is at the top of one side; it is more transparent and lacks the thicker down padding usually found in Green-backed Camaroptera nests; some nests are poorly enclosed by leaves so most of the lining is visible. The nest measures: outside height 75-90 mm; outside width 55-65 mm; cup depth (measured from lower rim of entrance) 40 mm; entrance diameter 35-40 mm. Birds give away their nesting area by alarming with a characteristic 'bleating' call.
Laying months: mainly Nov-Dec (Sep-Apr). **Clutch size:** 2-3 (2-4). **Eggs:** 15.5-16.9-18.0 × 11.5-12.2-12.5 mm; parasitised by Brown-backed Honeybird; unlike those of Green-backed Camaroptera, eggs are variable in coloration and markings. **Incubation period:** 13 days. **Nestling/fledging period:** 14-15 days.

Barred Wren-Warbler *Calamonastes fasciolatus* Gebande Sanger   page 392

Breeds in semi-arid savanna, especially acacia thornveld. Pairs nest solitarily and are widely spaced. **Nest:** an oval-shaped ball, usually <½ m up from the ground (0.15-2½), placed in a low, broad-leafed shrub, sapling or coppiced leaf growth (e.g. *Rhus pyroides*, *Ziziphus mucronata*, *Fadogia* sp.); a compact nest, entrance at the top of one side, with 10-15 living leaves firmly rivetted together to form the outer shell which virtually encases the nest, leaving just the entrance-hole clear. The interior is thickly lined with light coloured plant down, cobweb and a small amount of fine grass, knitted to a blanket-like consistency. The entrance-hole has a firm lower rim and is usually partly covered above by a leaf that projects over the entrance. It is very like the nest of the next species, mainly differing by being closer to the ground. Wren-warbler nests differ from those of camapteras by their thicker-walled interior which have a felted, blanket-like texture. The nest measures: outside height 90-95-100 mm; outside width 60-65-70 mm; cup depth (measured from lower rim of entrance) 50 mm; entrance diameter 35-45 mm.
Laying months: mainly Nov-Jan (Nov-Mar); relays after earlier failure. **Clutch size:** 3 (2-4); laid at 1-day intervals. **Eggs:** 15.2-17.1-19.4 × 11.0-12.3-13.5 mm. **Incubation period:** not recorded. **Nestling/fledging period:** not recorded.

Stierling's Wren-Warbler *Calamonastes stierlingi* Stierlingse Sanger   page 392

Breeds in mesic savanna in broad-leafed woodlands. Pairs nest solitarily at densities of about a pair/3-6 ha. **Nest:** similar to that of previous species but usually placed higher, typically about 3 m up from the ground (0.5-6.2), and in the foliage of a broad-leafed tree rather than a low shrub. It is a compact, oval-shaped ball with an entrance-hole at the top of one side; living leaves virtually encase the nest, leaving just the entrance-hole clear, attached using strands of cobweb pushed through pinprick-sized holes in the leaf, 'rivetted' in place on the inside and outside with a small knot of thread. The interior is thickly lined with plant down, cobweb and a small amount of fine grass, knitted to give a blanket-like consistency. The nest measures: outside height 100 mm; outside width 65-90 mm (wider from front-to-back that left-to-right); entrance diameter 25-30 mm; wall thickness 16-19 mm.
Laying months: mainly Oct-Dec (Sep-Mar); relays after earlier failure. **Clutch size:** 2-3, rarely 4. **Eggs:** 15.5-17.8-19.0 × 11.5-12.5-13.1 mm. **Incubation period:** not recorded. **Nestling/fledging period:** not recorded.

Cinnamon-breasted Warbler *Euryptila subcinnamomea* Kaneelborssanger   page 392

Breeds in arid karoo on boulder-strewn hillsides, especially where dissected by ravines. Pairs nest solitarily, at densities of about a pair/1-2 ha. **Nest:** a substantial, oval-shaped ball placed inside the foliage of a densely branched, hillside shrub (*Restio*, *Serruria*, Asteraceae), in a dry old grass tuft; once in aloe and crassula; 0.2-1 m above the ground. It is thick-walled, the exterior built with dry plant material, especially old grass, built into a hollow in the supporting plant rather than being woven into the twigs. The interior of the nest is thickly lined with white plant down (especially *Eriocephalus* sp.) and cobweb. The nest entrance is near the top of the most exposed side of the nest. The nest measures: outside height 115-130-190 mm; outside width 90-100-140 mm; entrance diameter 30-45 mm; wall thickness 20 mm; nest depth (from lower rim of entrance to cup) 50 mm.
Laying months: mainly Jul-Aug (Jul-Mar); breeds opportunistically in response to rainfall. **Clutch size:** 3 (2-4). **Eggs:** 18.2-18.3-18.4 × 13.1-13.2-13.3 mm. **Incubation period:** not recorded. **Nestling/fledging period:** not recorded.

Green-backed Camaroptera

Grey-backed Camaroptera

Barred Wren-Warbler

Stierling's Wren-Warbler

Cinnamon-breasted Warbler

Burnt-necked Eremomela *Eremomela usticollis* **Bruinkeelbossanger**   page 390

Breeds widely across the savanna belt from the semi-arid west to the mesic east; largely restricted to areas of thornveld, especially *Acacia tortilis* savanna. Pairs (some perhaps with occasional helpers) nest solitarily, spaced at a density of about a pair/17 ha. **Nest:** small, thin-walled cup, placed about 5 m (3-6) up from the ground in the uppermost canopy branches of an acacia (e.g. *A. erioloba, A. tortilis, A. karoo*), where it is supported by two or more thin, upright twigs. It is attached to these with fine, light-coloured web and is well hidden in the foliage; given its small size and colour, it is easily overlooked. The nest is made of fine silky plant material and its outside walls are adorned with small, broken-up pieces of praying mantis egg capsule, tiny pieces of caterpillar faeces and other debris, giving the nest exterior a rough texture and a mottled pale green colour. It is bound together with cobweb. The nest measures: outside diameter 52 mm; cup diameter 36 mm; cup depth 35 mm; nest height 41 mm. One nest was built by one bird accompanied by its mate, in 8 days. The pair sings frequently in the nest tree (and from the nest), both during nest-building and at change-overs during incubation and while brooding young. Pairs build a new nest for successive broods, and this is often placed close to a previously used nest.

Laying months: mainly Nov (Sep-Apr); relays after earlier failures; sometimes double or triple-brooded. **Clutch size:** 2 (2-3, rarely 4). **Eggs:** 14.0-15.9-17.3 x 10.5-11.7-12.6 mm. **Incubation period:** not recorded; by both sexes. **Nestling/fledging period:** not recorded; young brooded and fed by both sexes.

Karoo Eremomela *Eremomela gregalis* **Groenbossanger**   page 390

Breeds in the semi-arid and arid karoo on low shrub-covered plains and hillsides. Pairs or family groups (pair plus 1-4 helpers) nest solitarily, spaced at a density of about a pair or group/5 ha. **Nest:** an open cup, placed 0.3-0.5 m up from the ground, built inside a low shrubby plant (e.g. *Pteronia, Galena, Euphorbia*), where it is secured in a fork formed by branches coming off the main stem. It is thick-walled (20-40 mm thick) and has a roughly built exterior, made with thin, dry stems of grass, pliable twigs and/or shredded pieces of forb stems; by contrast, the nest-cup is smoothly lined with a thick layer of light-coloured plant down (e.g. *Eriocephalus, Chrysocoma*). No cobweb is used in the nest's construction. The nest measures: outside diameter 78-120 mm; cup diameter 40 mm; cup depth 52 mm; nest height 71 mm. The nest is built by all group members and may be used as a night-time roost by the group when not breeding.

Laying months: mainly Aug-Oct but most months recorded, and it probably lays opportunistically in response to rainfall. **Clutch size:** 3 (2-4). **Eggs:** 14.4-15.3-16.3 x 10.9-11.2-11.5 mm. **Incubation period:** not recorded. **Nestling/fledging period:** not recorded; young fed by pair plus helpers.

Yellow-bellied Eremomela *Eremomela icteropygialis* **Geelpensbossanger**   page 390

Breeds widely in savanna and karoo, favouring semi-arid, open woodland or shrubland. Pairs nest solitarily and are widely spaced. **Nest:** a small, deep, thin-walled, open cup, much like the nest of a white-eye; it is placed in a lone-standing sapling or bush, typically about 1-1½ m (0.6-2.7) up from the ground and characteristically slung between the twigs of a horizontal, forked branch, its rim level with the twigs that support it; usually away from the centre of the tree. It is built with fine strands of dry grass, shreds of bark, plant down and/or other plant fibre, held together with spider web. The cup is lined with fine grass-ends. In some nests the exterior is decorated with a few small leaves, spider cocoons or other objects. The nest measures: outside diameter 50-55-60 mm; cup diameter 36-38-40 mm; cup depth 25-39-52 mm; nest height 50-55-60 mm. The incubating bird often sits tight on the nest approached, only flying off at the last moment.

Laying months: mainly Sep-Nov (Aug-Apr). **Clutch size:** 2, less often 3; laid at a 1-day interval. **Eggs:** 14.3-15.8-18.0 x 10.4-11.4-12.2 mm; parasitised by Klaas's Cuckoo (3 of 12 nests in Namibia). **Incubation period:** 14 days (13-15); begins when first egg is laid. **Nestling/fledging period:** 15-16 days; young fed by both sexes.

Green-capped Eremomela *Eremomela scotops* **Donkerwangbossanger**   page 390

Breeds in mesic savanna, especially in miombo and other broad-leafed woodlands. Pairs or family groups (pair plus 2-5 helpers) nest solitarily spaced, in miombo, at a density of about a pair or group/20 ha. **Nest:** a small, thin-walled open cup, placed in the leafy upper/outer branches of a tall tree (*Brachystegia spiciformis* is commonly used), 6-8 m up from the ground. It is suspended between two or more thin, forked twigs and is well hidden in foliage. It is built with fine, fibrous plant material and down, bound together and attached to the twigs with cobweb, the outside walls commonly festooned with dried flowerbuds or sepals. The nest measures: outside diameter 50 mm; cup diameter 38 mm; cup depth 35 mm; nest height 55 mm. The nest is built by both sexes, assisted by helpers, and the members of the group share the incubation and brooding and feeding the nestlings.

Laying months: mainly Sep-Nov (Aug-Feb). **Clutch size:** 3 (2-5). **Eggs:** 14.3-16.0-17.0 x 10.0-11.7-12.5 mm. **Incubation period:** not recorded; by both sexes, assisted by helpers. **Nestling/fledging period:** not recorded; young brooded and fed by both sexes, assisted by helpers.

Burnt-necked Eremomela

Karoo Eremomela

Yellow-bellied Eremomela

Green-capped Eremomela

ROCKJUMPERS Family Chaetopidae Worldwide 2 species; both endemic to southern Africa; closely related (were previously treated as subspecies); have allopatric ranges; nesting habits similar; both monogamous; cooperative breeders (pair plus 0-2 helpers); build an open nest on the ground; eggs oval, white, unmarked, 2-3/clutch; nestlings are altricial and nidicolous.

Drakensberg Rockjumper *Chaetops aurantius* Oranjeborsberglyster   page 392
Breeds on the grass- and shrub-covered slopes and crests of rock- and boulder-strewn hills and mountains. Pairs or family groups (pair plus 1-2 helpers) nest solitarily at a density of about a pair or group/30 ha (Lesotho). **Nest:** an open cup, placed on or close to the ground, typically inside a dense grass tuft (especially *Merxmuellera* in c Lesotho), less often under it, or under a shrub (e.g. *Chrysocoma*) or under a small, projecting rock. It is a bulky nest, usually well hidden, made mainly or entirely with grass, using coarse material for the base and finer material inside; most nests are warmly lined with *Otomys*-, sheep- or goat-hair. The nest measures outside diameter 140-150-180 mm; cup diameter 85 mm; cup depth 40-50-60 mm. Both sexes build the nest.
Laying months: mainly Oct-Nov (Aug-Feb, once May). **Clutch size:** 3, rarely 2. **Eggs:** 24.2-26.5-27.9 x 18.6-19.7-20.7 mm. **Incubation period:** not recorded; by both sexes. **Nestling/fledging period:** not recorded; young fed by both sexes.

Cape Rockjumper *Chaetops frenatus* Kaapse Berglyster   page 392
Breeds in s Cape mountains on slopes and crests of rocky hills covered with sparse, low-growing fynbos. Pairs or family groups (pair plus 1-2 helpers) are territorial year-round, spaced at a density of a pair or group/4-11 ha. **Nest:** a bulky open cup, placed on the ground, mostly under a rock slab (62%) or next to a rock (15%), otherwise under a tuft of grass or some other low vegetation; most face nnw to e, away from the prevailing se winds. The nest is roughly built with stems of dry grass and forbs, coarser material used at the base and finer material to line the cup. The nest measures: outside diameter 93-153-220 mm, nest height 24-53-95 mm, cup diameter 50-65-126 mm, cup depth 23-34-50 mm. It is built by both sexes in 3-7 days, further lining added over next 5-10 days before egg-laying. The birds regularly breed in the same areas in successive years and sometimes reuse the same nest site.
Laying months: mainly Sep-Oct (Jul-Jan); single-brooded, but relays after early nest failure. **Clutch size:** 2; laid on successive days. **Eggs:** 25.4-26.3-26.8 x 19.6-19.8-20.2 mm. **Incubation period:** 20 days (19-21); by both sexes, ♂ in shifts of 28-65-125 mins, ♀ shifts 33-44-59 mins. **Nestling/fledging period:** 19½ days (18-21); young fed by both sexes.

'AFRICAN' WARBLERS Family Macrosphenidae Worldwide 18 species; all restricted to Afrotropics, 6 in southern Africa. This newly named family includes the three species below plus crombecs (page 250) and Victorin's Warbler (page 252). Monogamous; in one of the 3 species below the ♀ builds and incubates, both sexes feed young (not known in other two); nest an open cup on the ground well hidden in vegetation; eggs oval, white with speckles, 2-3/clutch; nestlings are altricial and nidicolous.

Moustached (Grass) Warbler *Melocichla mentalis* Breëstertgrasvoël   no nest photo   page 392
Restricted to lowland forest/grassland mosaics in e Zimbabwe and adjacent Mozambique where it frequents densely tangled bracken, grass/scrub, mostly on the edges of marshes and streams. Nesting habits are little known. **Nest:** an open cup, built with long, coarse strands of dry grass that are curled around to form the bowl in which the cup, lined with finer grass stems and rootlets, is set. The nest is placed close to the ground (150-300 mm up), well hidden in a tuft of tall, densely matted grass. It measures: outside diameter 90-100 mm; cup diameter 65-80 mm; cup depth 50 mm; nest thickness 65 mm.
Laying months: Jan (Zimbabwe). **Clutch size:** 2-3. **Eggs:** 21.5-22.3-23.5 x 15.3-16.0-16.5 mm. **Incubation period:** not recorded, mainly by ♀. **Nestling/fledging period:** not recorded.

Cape Grassbird *Sphenoeacus afer* Grasvoël   page 392
Breeds in grassland and fynbos, favouring sloping ground close to streams and seepages where there is a dense cover of tall, rank grass or *Restio*. Pairs nest solitarily and are widely spaced. **Nest:** a deep, open cup, well hidden in a grass tuft, in a tangle of *Restio* or some other dense cover; placed 100-400 mm up from the ground. It is built with long stems and blades of grass that are curled around to form the nest-bowl, while the cup is well lined with finer stems of grass and other plant material. The nest measures outside diameter 80-110 mm; cup diameter 50-60 mm; cup depth 40-50 mm; nest thickness 75 mm. It is built by the ♀; she is secretive while incubating and often slips unseen off the nest when approached.
Laying months: mainly Oct-Dec (Jul-Dec) in summer-rainfall areas, earlier (Jul-Oct) in s Cape; sometimes double-brooded. **Clutch size:** 2-3; laid at 1-day intervals. **Eggs:** 20.0-22.0-24.0 x 14.8-15.8-17.0 mm. **Incubation period:** 16 days (14-18); by ♀ only. **Nestling/fledging period:** 14 days (14-16); young fed by both sexes.

Rockrunner *Achaetops pycnopygius* Rotsvoël   page 392
Breeds in semi-arid and arid, hilly country along the Namibian escarpment; favours sparsely wooded, rocky slopes that have grass cover. Nesting habits are poorly known. Pairs nest solitarily and are widely spaced. **Nest:** an open cup placed in or beneath a dense grass tuft on a hillslope; well hidden. The base of the nest is made with coarse stems of dry grass, the cup lined with finer pieces of soft dry grass and, in some cases, with rootlets; the rim of the nest may extend outwards on its approach side for about 50 mm. One nest measured: outside diameter 89 x 140 mm (the long axis includes the 'ramp'); cup diameter 63 x 76 mm; cup depth 57 mm; nest thickness 89 mm. The nest is well hidden and is not easily found, given the bird's secretiveness while breeding.
Laying months: mainly Jan-Mar (Nov-Apr). **Clutch size:** 2-3. **Eggs:** 20.9-21.4-22.7 x 15.0-15.4-16.5 mm. **Incubation period:** 15 days. **Nestling/fledging period:** not recorded; young fed by both sexes; they leave the nest before they can fly.

Drakensberg Rockjumper

Drakensberg Rockjumper

Cape Rockjumper

Cape Grassbird

Rockrunner

Babblers, Bush Blackcap

BABBLERS Family Timaliidae Worldwide 326 species (most in Asia); 34 breed in Afrotropics, 6 in southern Africa. Monogamous, group-living birds comprising a pair with 1-12 helpers; all participate in nest-building, incubation and nestling care; nest an open cup; eggs oval; unmarked, blue; 2-3/clutch; nestlings are altricial and nidicolous. Parasitised by Levaillant's Cuckoo.

Hartlaub's Babbler *Turdoides hartlaubii* Witkruiskatlagter
page 392

Breeds in n Namibia and ne Botswana in riparian thickets and reedbeds, typically associated with floodplains. Family groups (pair plus 1-6-13 helpers) are territorial year-round and widely spaced. **Nest:** a bulky open cup, well hidden in foliage or among dense twigs in a tangled thicket, in a bank of caught-up driftwood or in a reed-clump, 1-4 m up from the ground. The bowl is made from coarse dry grass stems and thin pliable twigs, with the inner cup lined with finer material. The nest measures: outside diameter 120-150-200 mm; cup diameter 70-90 mm; cup depth 40-70 mm; nest height 90-120 mm. It is built by the pair, assisted by the helpers.
Laying months: mainly Aug-Feb (Jul-Apr); probably double-brooded. **Clutch size:** 3 (2-4). **Eggs:** 25.0-26.0-27.3 × 18.2-18.7-19.5 mm; parasitised by Levaillant's Cuckoo. **Incubation period:** not recorded. **Nestling/fledging period:** 18 days; young brooded and fed by both sexes and helpers.

Arrow-marked Babbler *Turdoides jardineii* Pylvlekkatlagter
pages 378, 392

Breeds in mesic savanna, favouring a patchy habitat with thickets. Family groups (pair plus 1-6-12 helpers) are territorial year-round, a group/10-64 ha. **Nest:** a bulky, open cup, mostly 2-4 m up from the ground (0.15-7) and well hidden in a densely foliaged tree or shrub, often against the trunk, or placed where a branch has coppiced, in mistletoe, tucked between several closely spaced stems, sometimes in rank grass or *Asparagus* which has invaded the branches of a sapling, in reeds, in driftwood, or behind bark peeling from an old trunk; occasionally in old nests of other birds. The base is made with stems and blades of dry grass and forbs curled around to form a bowl; the cup is lined with finer plant material, mostly rootlets or fine grass stems. The nest measures: outside diameter 165-205 mm; cup diameter 75 mm; cup depth 50 mm; nest height 95-115 mm. It is built by all members of the group.
Laying months: mainly Oct-Nov (Sep-Apr, but all months recorded in Zimbabwe); relays after early failure; usually double-brooded. **Clutch size:** 3 (2-5). **Eggs:** 22.0-25.3-28.4 × 17.4-18.8-20.3 mm; infrequently (7-8% of nests) parasitised by Levaillant's Cuckoo. **Incubation period:** 16 days (14-17); by both sexes and helpers. **Nestling/fledging period:** 19 days (18-21); brooded and fed by both sexes and helpers.

Southern Pied Babbler *Turdoides bicolor* Witkatlagter
page 392

Breeds in semi-arid savanna, especially in acacia thornveld. Family groups (pair plus 1-6-12 helpers) are territorial year-round, at densities of a group/35-50 ha. **Nest:** a bulky, open cup built in a dense acacia or other thorn tree, typically well hidden in a multiple fork 3-4 m (2-6) up from the ground. It is built with coarse dry stems and blades of grass and pliable forb stems, curled around to form a bowl; the cup is lined with finer plant material, mostly rootlets or fine grass. The nest measures: outside diameter 170-250 mm; cup diameter 70-100 mm; cup depth 60 mm. It is built by the pair and helpers, and takes up to 26 days to complete.
Laying months: mainly Nov-Jan (Aug-Apr); relays after early failure; double-brooded. **Clutch size:** 3 (2-5). **Eggs:** 23.5-26.0-27.5 × 18.0-19.0-20.1 mm; infrequently parasitised by Levaillant's Cuckoo, occasionally by Jacobin Cuckoo. **Incubation period:** 16 days. **Nestling/fledging period:** 16 days; young fed by both sexes and helpers.

Bare-cheeked Babbler *Turdoides gymnogenys* Kaalwangkatlagter
no nest or egg photo

Breeds in semi-arid savanna in nw Namibia, frequenting wooded hills and dry watercourses. Family groups (pair plus 1-4-9 helpers) nest solitarily, about 1.7 km between groups. **Nest:** a bulky, open cup like those of other babblers, the bowl being made of coarse dry grass and other plant stems and the cup lined with finer material. It is placed in multiple fork of a shrubby tree, 2-3 m up from the ground. One nest measured: outside diameter 125 mm; cup diameter 80 mm; cup depth 50 mm.
Laying months: mainly Sep-Jan (also May, Jul). **Clutch size:** 2-3. **Eggs:** 25.2-26.6 × 18.2-20.2 mm; (not illustrated) unmarked blue; parasitised by Levaillant's Cuckoo. **Incubation period:** not recorded. **Nestling/fledging period:** >16 days; young fed by both sexes and helpers.

Black-faced Babbler *Turdoides melanops* Swartwangkatlagter
no nest photo   page 392

Breeds in n Namibia and nw Botswana in semi-arid woodland and savanna dominated by *Baikiaea*, *Commiphora*, *Acacia* or *Terminalia prunioides*. Nesting habits are poorly known. Family groups (pair plus 1-5 helpers) nest solitarily and are widely spaced. **Nest:** a bulky open cup resembling those of other babblers; it is built with coarse dry grass and other plant stems, the cup lined with finer material. Two nests were in *Commiphora* trees, 1½ and 5 m up from the ground.
Laying months: Oct-Dec, Mar (n Namibia). **Clutch size:** 2-3. **Eggs:** 25.0-26.8-29.2 × 18.3-19.0-20.0 mm. **Incubation period:** not recorded. **Nestling/fledging period:** not recorded.

Bush Blackcap *Lioptilus nigricapillus* Rooibektiptol
page 392

Breeds in, and on the verges of montane forest. Nesting habits are poorly known. Pairs nest solitarily at densities of about a pair/10 ha. **Nest:** an open cup similar to that built by a bulbul, 2-5 m off the ground, in the upper, leafy branches of a sub-canopy tree (e.g. *Rhamnus*, *Halleria*, *Buddleja*), often on the forest fringe. It is built with fine, pliable stems of dry plant material – forbs, grass, leaf petioles, tendrils; the cup is lined with finer pieces of the same; moss or lichen is not used. It measures: outside diameter 105-110 mm; cup diameter 60 mm; nest height 55 mm, cup depth 40 mm. Both sexes build the nest.
Laying months: mainly Nov (Oct-Jan). **Clutch size:** 2. **Eggs:** 22.1-23.0-24.3 × 15.8-16.4-17.0 mm. **Incubation period:** not recorded. **Nestling/fledging period:** not recorded; young brooded and fed by both sexes.

Hartlaub's Babbler

Arrow-marked Babbler (LEFT & TWO ABOVE)

Bush Blackcap

Southern Pied Babbler

Titbabblers, Hyliota, Creeper

'SYLVIID BABBLERS' Family Sylviidae Worldwide 28 species; 6 breed in Afrotropics, 3 in southern Africa – the titbabblers and Bush Blackcap. Monogamous; nest a small cup; eggs oval, white, finely speckled; 2-3/clutch; nestlings altricial and nidicolous.

Chestnut-vented Titbabbler (Chestnut-vented Warbler) *Parisoma subcaeruleum* Bosveldtjeriktik — page 392

Breeds widely in semi-arid and arid savanna and, in the karoo, in thornveld along drainage lines. Pairs nest solitarily, usually >50 m apart. **Nest:** a small, thin-walled cup supported by two or more thin twigs, typically well hidden in a thorny, well-foliaged bush (e.g. *Maytenus*, *Karissa*) or in a lone-standing sapling, 1-2 m above the ground (up to 5½ m). The nest is loosely made with dry leaf petioles and fine twigs, loosely held together and to the supporting twigs with cobweb; smaller and thinner-walled than the nest of Layard's Titbabbler; the cup is lined with hair-thin dry grass stems, rootlets and/or creeper tendrils. The nest measures: outside diameter 70-80 mm; cup diameter 45-50 mm; cup depth 25-35 mm; nest height 45-50 mm.

Laying months: mainly Sep-Nov (Aug-Apr) in summer-rainfall areas; later in the arid west in response to rains (Feb-Apr); earlier in sw Cape (Sep); relays after early failure; sometimes double-brooded. **Clutch size:** 2-3 (2-4); laid at 1-day intervals. **Eggs:** 16.3-18.2-20.3 x 12.6-13.8-14.8 mm; mass 1.57-1.66-1.78 g; occasionally parasitised by Diederik and Jacobin Cuckoos. **Incubation period** 14 days (13-16); by both sexes. **Nestling/fledging period:** 14-15 days; young brooded and fed by both sexes.

Layard's Titbabbler (Layard's Warbler) *Parisoma layardi* Grysjeriktik — page 392

Breeds in semi-arid and arid shrubland in the karoo and arid fynbos, mainly on hillslopes; also in alpine scrub in Lesotho. Pairs nest solitarily and are widely spaced. **Nest:** a small, deep-cupped nest supported in a forked branch among foliage, ½-2 m up from the ground in a shrubby bush, often *Rhigozum obovatum*; superficially like the nest of Chestnut-vented Titbabbler, but thicker-walled (20-25 mm versus 10 mm), deeper-cupped and well-insulated. Its shell is made with thin, pliable, plant fibres (*Helichrysum*, *Asclepias* other plants) and rootlets, bound together and to the supporting twigs with a small amount of cobweb. The cup is thickly lined with plant down and it has a warm, woolly appearance. One nest measured: outside diameter 90 x 85 mm; cup diameter 45 mm; cup depth 40 mm. During the early stages of the nesting cycle the ♂ sings frequently in the vicinity of the nest.

Laying months: mainly Aug-Nov (Jun-Dec, occasionally in other months). **Clutch size:** 2 (2-3). **Eggs:** 17.2-18.3-19.2 x 12.7-13.7-14.7 mm. **Incubation period:** not recorded. **Nestling/fledging period:** <15 days; young fed by both sexes.

HYLIOTAS Family Hyliotidae Worldwide 4 species; all endemic to Afrotropics, 2 breed in southern Africa. A small family variously included in flycatchers and warblers in past classifications, now accorded family status on current DNA evidence. Nesting habits not well known. Monogamous; eggs oval, white, finely speckled; 2-3/clutch; nestlings are altricial and nidicolous.

Yellow-bellied Hyliota *Hyliota flavigaster* Geelborshyliota — no nest or egg photo

Range narrowly extends from tropical Africa into c Mozambique; breeding not yet recorded within the region. Nesting habits are poorly known. **Nest:** two in Malawi were small open cups, structurally similar to nest of Southern Hyliota, about 4 m up from the ground in miombo woodland in the fork of a tree; built with thin, hairy flower-stalks, flower-heads and grey and green-coloured foliaceous lichen. One measured: outside diameter 65 mm; cup diameter 40 mm; nest height 50 mm; cup depth 20 mm.

Laying months: Oct-Nov (Zambia, Malawi). **Clutch size:** 2. **Eggs:** 17 x 14 mm; (not illustrated) similar to eggs of Southern Hyliota, differ by having a more pronounced zone of markings which form a ring close to the blunt end and by these markings (speckles and spots) being larger. **Incubation period:** not recorded. **Nestling/fledging period:** not recorded.

Southern Hyliota *Hyliota australis* Mashonahyliota — page 392

Breeds in broad-leafed woodlands, especially miombo. Pairs nest solitarily and are widely spaced. **Nest:** a small, deep, thick-walled cup placed at a fork on a thickish (50 mm diameter) branch, typically one covered with lichen, 7-8 m (4-12½) up from the ground in the upper branches of a mature tree; somewhat globular in shape (inside diameter at the rim less than middle of nest), built with grey lichen and *Usnea*, shreds of bark, short pieces of fine grass, fine seedheads, moth egg-cases, bound together and to supporting branch with cobweb; exterior closely matches the supporting branch; cup lined with fine bark shreds and grass fibres and sometimes a few small feathers or green leaves. The nest measures: outside diameter 57 mm; cup diameter 30 mm; cup depth 35 mm.

Laying months: mainly Sep-Nov (Aug-Mar). **Clutch size:** 3 (2-4). **Eggs:** 15.0-17.5-20.0 x 11.5-13.1-14.6 mm. **Incubation period:** not recorded. **Nestling/fledging period:** not recorded.

CREEPERS Family Certhiidae Worldwide 10 species; 1 breeds in Afrotropics, 1 in southern Africa. Monogamous; nest a well-concealed shallow cup on a branch; eggs oval, 3/clutch; nestlings are altricial and nidicolous.

Spotted Creeper *Salpornis spilonotus* Boomkruiper — page 392

Breeds in tall miombo woodland. Pairs nest solitarily and are widely spaced. **Nest:** a small, well disguised, lichen-covered cup, placed in an acute-angled, two-pronged, vertical fork of an upright, lichen-covered tree stem; less often on a sloping or horizontal branch; nest built in mid- to upper-canopy, 5-7 m (4-15) up from the ground; at the time the nest is built the tree used is usually devoid of foliage; msasa trees (*Brachystegia spiciformis*) are commonly selected. The nest is made of numerous small pieces of plant material – bits of petiole, bark and dry leaf, dry flower-buds – and both its exterior and interior surfaces are then covered with pieces of grey lichen; these and the nest are bound with cobweb. The nest measures: outside diameter 70-85 mm; cup diameter 40-50 mm; cup depth 17-25 mm; nest height 45-55 mm. The incubating bird sits tight on the nest if approached, its long beak pointing upwards. If flushed, it may give an injury-feigning display. At times it may call from the nest while incubating.

Laying months: mainly Sep (Aug-Nov). **Clutch size:** 3 (2-3). **Eggs:** 17.2-18.3-20.3 x 12.0-13.3-14.4 mm. **Incubation period:** not recorded; by ♀, fed on nest by ♂. **Nestling/fledging period:** not recorded; brooded and fed by both sexes.

Chestnut-vented Titbabbler

Layard's Titbabbler

Southern Hyliota

Spotted Creeper

WHITE-EYES Family Zosteropidae Worldwide 104 species; 12 breed in Afrotropics, 3 in southern Africa. Monogamous; nest a small cup, well hidden in foliage; sexes share nest-building, incubation, nestling care; eggs oval; unmarked, pale blue or white 2-3/clutch; one species is a common host to Green-backed Honeybird; nestlings are altricial and nidicolous.

Cape White-eye *Zosterops virens* Kaapse Glasogie   page 392

Largely confined to South Africa, breeding in fynbos, savanna, forest; also in grassland and karoo where riparian bush and introduced trees provide habitat. Pairs nest solitarily and are widely spaced. **Nest:** a small deep cup, placed in leafy foliage in a tree or bush, 1-3 m (0.25-10) up from the ground; sites vary, from garden shrubs to forest canopy. Nest well-concealed among leaves, typically slung, hammock-style, between two or more horizontal twigs. Also, rarely, builds inside an old weaver nest. Nest material varies, forest nests often built with *Usnea*, whereas in drier habitats grass, bark shreds stripped from forbs, tendrils, rootlets and other pliable, dry material is used; near human habitation cotton, wool, string, etc. often incorporated; fine grass ends, hair, plant down used to line the cup. Cobweb binds the nest together and to supporting twigs. The nest measures: outside diameter 65-70-75 mm; cup diameter 37-45-50 mm; cup depth 35-40-45 mm; nest height 50-52-60 mm. Both sexes build, completing the nest in 5-10 days.
Laying months: mainly Oct-Dec (Aug-Feb, occasionally in other months); relays following an earlier failure. **Clutch size:** 2-3 (1-4) laid at 1-day intervals. **Eggs:** 14.6-16.8-19.1 x 10.9-12.3-13.6 mm; eggs unmarked pale blue or white; blue colour-type more common than white. **Incubation period:** 10-12 days; by both sexes with frequent change-overs; begins when clutch is completed. **Nestling/fledging period:** 12-13 days; young brooded and fed by both sexes.

Orange River White-eye *Zosterops pallidus* Gariepglasogie   no nest or egg photo

Breeds across the karoo, commonly along tree-lined watercourses or in copses of indigenous or exotic trees. Nests and nesting habits are poorly known but probably closely match those of sibling Cape White-eye.
Laying months: Oct-Mar. **Clutch size:** 3. **Eggs:** 16.9-17.2 x 12.5 mm; unmarked blue. **Incubation period:** not recorded. **Nestling/fledging period:** not recorded.

African Yellow White-eye *Zosterops senegalensis* Geelglasogie   pages 179, 392

Breeds widely in n mesic savanna in any wooded habitat, including gardens. Pairs nest solitarily and are widely spaced. **Nest:** an open cup, placed in leafy foliage in a tree or sapling (commonly in *Brachystegia spiciformis*), typically 3-5 m (1-8) up from the ground, highest in forests. Like the Cape White-eye's nest, it is usually slung, hammock-style between two or more horizontal twigs. Materials used vary, some built with *Usnea*, others with shredded pieces of pliable bark, fine dry grass shreds, fine petioles and moss; the cup is lined with fine grass fibres, shreds of bark, sometimes plant down. Cobweb binds the nest together and to supporting twigs; it measures outside diameter 52-55 mm; cup diameter 40-43 mm; cup depth 24-27 mm; nest height 28-36 mm. Both sexes build, completing it in a week. Commonly nests alongside White Helmetshrikes (either in the same tree or in an adjacent tree).
Laying months: mainly Sep-Oct (Aug-Feb). **Clutch size:** 3 (2-4). **Eggs:** 13.2-15.3-16.9 x 11.3-11.7-12.0 mm; unmarked blue or white (ratio 1:1 Zimbabwe); commonly parasitised by Green-backed Honeybird. **Incubation period:** 11-12 days; by both sexes. **Nestling/fledging period:** 13-14 days; young brooded and fed by both sexes.

SUGARBIRDS Family Promeropidae Worldwide 5 species; all endemic to Afrotropics; 2 endemic to southern Africa. Recent DNA evidence has extended the sugarbird family to include 3 tropical African species. Monogamous; ♀ builds nest and incubates both sexes feed young; nest an open cup; eggs oval; cream with dark markings; 2/clutch; nestlings altricial and nidicolous.

Cape Sugarbird *Promerops cafer* Kaapse Suikervoël   page 392

Breeds in s Cape fynbos, especially on mountain slopes and where taller proteas dominate (*P. repens, P. lepidocarpodendron, P. coronata, P. neriifolia, P. longifolia* and others). Pairs nest solitarily at densities of a pair/1-2 ha. **Nest:** an open cup, usually built in a protea tree, occasionally in a *Leucadendron, Erica, Rhus* or some other woody plant, usually in a forked branch 1-1½ m (½- 4) up from the ground, and hidden to a greater or lesser extent by foliage. The base is made from dry stems of heather, grass, bracken or something similar, curled around to form a bowl with a roughly finished exterior; the cup is neatly lined, using silky, brown-coloured plant down collected from dead protea flowerheads. The nest measures: outside diameter 100-135-180 mm; cup diameter 55-70-80 mm; cup depth 40-60-70 mm; nest thickness 60-110-190 mm. It is built by the ♀ in 3-10 days.
Laying months: mainly Apr-May (Mar-Aug, occasionally other months); peaks later (May) on Cape Peninsula than elsewhere sometimes double-brooded. **Clutch size:** 2, rarely 1; laid at a 1-2 day interval. **Eggs:** 21.4-23.4-25.0 x 16.5-17.5-18.7 mm. **Incubation period:** 17 days; by ♀ only; begins when clutch is completed; ♀ leaves nest about 3x/hr to feed, off 30% of day. **Nestling/fledging period:** 18 days (17-21); young brooded by ♀, fed by both sexes.

Gurney's Sugarbird *Promerops gurneyi* Rooiborssuikervoël   page 392

Breeds in stands of tall protea (especially *P. gaguedi, P. roupelliae, P. subvestita*) in mountainous escarpment areas. Pairs nest solitarily, a pair/2 ha, adjacent nests 100-200 m apart. **Nest:** an open cup, usually in a protea tree, well concealed by foliage, often in an isolated, thickish sapling and placed in old flower bract or in a multiple fork, on the w or sw side of the tree, typically 2-3 m (1-8) up from the ground. Nest base is built with a rough-stemmed forb (*Erica, Helichrysum, Stoebe*); the neatly lined nest cup is characteristically lined with fluffy, brown-coloured protea seeds (these identify this species' nest, even when breeding is long finished). The nest measures: outside diameter 100-125 mm; cup diameter 50-58 mm; cup depth 40-44 mm; nest thickness 100 mm. It is built by the ♀ in 5-10 days.
Laying months: Sep-Jul, varying regionally according to peak flowering times of proteas. **Clutch size:** 2, rarely 1. **Eggs:** 20.9-22.3-23.4 x 16.0-16.7-17.5 mm; mass 2.35 g. **Incubation period:** 16-17 days; by ♀ only; begins when clutch is completed. **Nestling/fledging period:** 21-23 days; young brooded by ♀, fed by both sexes.

Cape White-eye

African Yellow White-eye

Cape Sugarbird

Gurney's Sugarbird

Starlings

STARLINGS Family Sturnidae Worldwide 118 species; 47 breed in Afrotropics, 16 in southern Africa; 2 of these (Common Myna, Common Starling) are introductions from Asia and Europe. Two are colonial breeders (Wattled, Pied starlings), the others nest solitarily; monogamous; in 3 species occasional cooperative breeding occurs; sex roles in nesting cycle varies; in most, sexes share nest-building and feeding young; incubation by ♀ in most species, shared in some; nest a cup, placed in a tree cavity in most species, a few using rock cavities instead; eggs oval, either unmarked or faintly speckled white (Wattled Starling) or pale blue, unmarked, or speckled with red; 2-4/clutch; 5 species are parasitised by Great Spotted Cuckoo, 4 by Greater and/or Lesser honeyguide; nestlings are altricial and nidicolous.

Common Starling *Sturnus vulgaris* Europese Spreeu   page 393

Breeds widely in southern South Africa in cities, towns, villages, farmsteads and on offshore islands. Pairs nest solitarily or semi-colonially. **Nest:** placed in a cavity, often in the roof of a building with access via a hole; also in pipes, holes in walls, trees, banks (including Pied Starling burrows), rock faces and on offshore islands in thick bushy trees. Woodpecker and barbet nest-holes are occasionally usurped; also, once, the nest of a Little Swift. Nest is a large, untidy structure, the base built with stems of dry grass, weeds, twigs and debris such as paper, rags, string; set in this is the nest-cup which is lined with feathers, wool, hair and other soft material. It measures: about 100 mm in diameter and 95 mm deep; where not restrained by space, nests may become very large (e.g. 500-600 mm wide, 250 mm high). It is built mainly or entirely by the ♀ (Europe). Nest sites are regularly reused in successive seasons.
Laying months: mainly Sep-Nov (Jul-Dec, rarely in other months). **Clutch size:** 4-5 (3-7); laid at 1-day intervals. **Eggs:** 27.5-29.6-32.9 x 19.7-21.3-22.4 mm; mass 7.0 g. **Incubation period:** 15 days; by ♀ only; begins before clutch is completed. **Nestling/fledging period:** 21-22 days; young brooded by ♀, fed by both sexes.

Common Myna *Acridotheres tristis* Indiese Spreeu   page 393

Breeds abundantly in many towns and cities across e side of South Africa, extending narrowly into s Zimbabwe and e Botswana. Pairs nest solitarily. **Nest:** built in a hole, mostly under the eaves or roof of a building or in a pipe, broken street light, nest box, electrical installation; a hole in a tree is only occasionally used. It is a bulky mass of twigs, leaves, grass, roots and all kinds of human-derived debris (rags, string, plastic, paper, wool, etc) and, where not confined by space, a large volume of nest material accumulates (in one case sufficient to fill a wheelbarrow!). Set in this untidy base is a deep, open cup which is lined with finer material. It is built by both sexes. Nest sites are regularly reused in successive seasons.
Laying months: mainly Oct-Dec (Sep-Feb). **Clutch size:** 4 (2-5, rarely 6); laid at 1-day intervals. **Eggs:** 26.3-29.2-32.9 x 20.2-21.5-22.5 mm; occasionally parasitised by Great Spotted Cuckoo. **Incubation period:** 17-18 days (Asia); by both sexes. **Nestling/fledging period:** 22-24 days (Asia); young fed by both sexes.

Wattled Starling *Creatophora cinerea* Lelspreeu   page 393

Breeds widely but erratically in semi-arid savanna and karoo; colonial, seldom nesting twice in the same place; breeding is triggered by a surge in insect availability, especially by mass hatchings of brown locust; when this happens, nesting gets underway rapidly and is well synchronised; if the food supply fails, entire colonies may be abruptly abandoned. Colonies comprise 10s to 1000s of nests, and in the largest colonies these can be spread across several km. **Nest:** a ball or oval about ½ m in diameter, built of dry, thorny twigs; each contains 1-3 (and occasionally up to 8) individual nest chambers, each one accommodating a single nesting pair; there can be 1-12 such nests/tree. Nests are usually built in thorny trees and are placed 2-8 m up from the ground; occasionally, nests may be built in eucalypts or on telephone pole cross-bars. The nest chamber has a side funnel entrance leading to a cavity 100-150 mm in diameter, lined with dry grass, leaves and some feathers. Both sexes build and continue adding material during the incubation. Old nests can remain intact for years before disintegrating.
Laying months: opportunistic in response to rain but mainly Sep-Nov in winter-rainfall region, Dec-Mar elsewhere. **Clutch size:** 3-4 (2-5, rarely 8, probably laid by >1 ♀). **Eggs:** 24.9-28.3-32.1 x 18.3-20.5-22.0 mm. **Incubation period:** 11 days; by both sexes. **Nestling/fledging period:** 13-16 days; young fed by both sexes.

Pied Starling *Lamprotornis bicolor* Witgatspreeu   page 393

Nests widely in the karoo, grassland and fynbos where earth-banks provide nest sites. Pairs, some assisted by 1-5 helpers, nest in colonies (3-20 pairs/colony; occasionally solitary or in larger colonies); many sites are reused annually, some in known use for decades. **Nest:** a tunnel is excavated into the vertical wall of an earth bank at the end of which is built an untidy bowl; sites are typically along rivers, in dongas, in road- or rail-cuttings, or in the sides of gravel pits or ditches; some banks are shared with bee-eaters, sandmartins or Ground Woodpecker. Favours banks >3 m high; in some extensive banks there can be >100 nest holes, of which only a small proportion are likely to be simultaneously active. The tunnel is about 1 m (0,3-1½) long, shorter in ferricrete or rocky substrates; 80-100 mm in diameter at its entrance, usually inclined gently upwards, and widening at the end into a chamber 150-200 mm across. The nest bowl is made of coarse grass, feathers, roots and often human-derived debris (string, cotton, plastic, paper, etc), occasionally sloughed snake-skin. Both sexes excavate the tunnel and build the nest. Tunnels are commonly reused for successive broods and in successive seasons. It occasionally also nests in hay bales, under roof eaves and in tree cavities.
Laying months: mainly Sep-Nov (Aug-Feb, rarely other months); usually double-brooded. **Clutch size:** 4 (2-6, rarely 7-11, probably laid by >1 ♀). **Eggs:** 26.9-30.3-35.3 x 19.6-21.3-22.5 mm; mass 7.2 g; occasionally parasitised by Great Spotted Cuckoo and Greater Honeyguide. **Incubation period:** 14 days; by ♀ only; begins before clutch is completed. **Nestling/fledging period:** 25 days (21-27); young fed by both sexes, assisted by helpers.

Common Starling

Common Myna

Wattled Starling

Wattled Starling

Pied Starling

Starlings

Greater Blue-eared Starling *Lamprotornis chalybaeus* Groot-blouoorglansspreeu   page 393
Breeds widely in mesic savannas. Pairs nest solitarily and are widely spaced. **Nest:** a hole in a tree is used, either a natural cavity or an old barbet/woodpecker hole; the cavity is typically 300-400 mm deep with an entrance leading in from the side or top; its height above ground ranges between 1-6 m (rarely up to 13 m); hollow metal fence posts and nest boxes are also used. The nest is a shallow-cupped pad of dry grass and/or feathers and, occasionally, pieces of sloughed snake skin are added to the lining. Both sexes build; holes are sometimes reused in successive years.
Laying months: mainly Sep-Nov (Aug-Jan). **Clutch size:** 3-4 (2-5). **Eggs:** 26.4-27.9-30.6 x 18.3-19.6-20.7 mm; occasionally parasitised by Great Spotted Cuckoo and Greater Honeyguide. **Incubation period:** 14 days (13-17); by ♀ only. **Nestling/fledging period:** 23 days; young fed by both sexes.

Cape Glossy Starling (Cape Starling) *Lamprotornis nitens* Kleinglansspreeu   pages 179, 393
Breeds widely in mesic and semi-arid savannas, extending into the grassland and karoo where trees are present. Pairs or occasional trios (pair plus 1 helper) nest solitarily and they are widely spaced. **Nest:** a hole in a tree is used, either a natural cavity or an old barbet/woodpecker hole; it is typically 2-3 m (1-7) up from the ground in a main stem, the cavity 250-300-550 mm deep, with an entrance at least 42 mm wide; hollow metal fence posts and nest boxes also provide frequent nest sites and, in fence posts, the nest may be >1 m down from the entrance of the pipe. Deep holes like this are sometimes partially filled with coarse, dry material (twigs, dung, etc). The nest is a shallow-cupped pad of dry grass and/or feathers; some include mammal hair in the lining and, occasionally, pieces of sloughed snake skin. Holes may be reused in successive years (one reported to be in use for >20 years).
Laying months: mainly Oct-Nov (Sep-Mar, rarely in other months). **Clutch size:** 3 (2-4, rarely 5-6, perhaps laid by >1 ♀); laid at 1-day intervals. **Eggs:** 25.4-28.1-32.5 x 19.0-20.0-22.5 mm; eggs are blue, 90% of clutches are speckled with red-brown, and 10% are unmarked; parasitised by Great Spotted Cuckoo and Greater Honeyguide. **Incubation period:** 15-17 days; by ♀ only. **Nestling/fledging period:** 20 days (19-23); young fed by both sexes, sometimes assisted by helpers.

Burchell's Starling *Lamprotornis australis* Grootglansspreeu   page 393
Breeds in open, tall-tree, semi-arid savanna. Pairs nest solitarily and are widely spaced. **Nest:** a hole in a tree is used, either a natural cavity or a large woodpecker hole; it is usually in the main stem of a mature tree which can be living or dead and is typically 4-5 m (1,2-5,7) up from the ground; nest cavities are about 450 mm deep and 80-100 mm across inside, with an entrance hole >50 mm wide. Occasional nests are in hollow metal fence posts, cavities in the walls of buildings, or in holes in rock faces. The nest is a saucer, 30-50 mm thick, made of dry and/or green grass; deep holes may be partly filled with coarse dry debris (twigs, dung, etc). Material in the nest from a previous occupancy is usually cleaned out before the new nest is made. Both sexes build and holes are commonly reused in successive years.
Laying months: mainly Oct-Nov (Sep-Apr) in east of range, Jan-Mar in the west; sometimes double-brooded. **Clutch size:** 3 (2-4). **Eggs:** 27.5-29.4-32.7 x 19.8-20.7-22.5 mm; occasionally parasitised by Great Spotted Cuckoo and Greater Honeyguide. **Incubation period:** 14 days; by ♀ only. **Nestling/fledging period:** 20-24 days; young fed by both sexes.

Meves' Starling (Meves's Starling) *Lamprotornis mevesii* Langstertglansspreeu   page 393
Breeds in hot, low-lying, tall-tree savannas. Pairs nest solitarily, but occasionally 2-3 pairs may nest simultaneously in the same tree; it infrequently nests cooperatively (pair plus 1-2 helpers). **Nest:** a natural cavity in the main trunk of a tree is used; hollow metal fence posts or ventilation pipes are occasionally used; it is typically 4-5 m (1-10) up from the ground, often in a knot-hole where a branch has broken off; an entrance >50 mm wide leading into a cavity 300-400 mm deep is favoured; old woodpecker holes or nest boxes are sometimes used. The nest is a shallow cup of dry grass, rootlets, baobab fibre or other plant material and debris accumulated in the hole from previous use is cleaned out before the new nest is made. Holes are commonly reused in successive years.
Laying months: Nov-Apr; sometimes double-brooded. **Clutch size:** 3-4 (2-5). **Eggs:** 24.0-26.7-30.0 x 18.2-19.9-20.7 mm; occasionally parasitised by Great Spotted Cuckoo and Greater Honeyguide (see photograph opposite). **Incubation period:** 18 days; by ♀ only. **Nestling/fledging period:** 23 days; young fed by both sexes, sometimes assisted by helpers.

Black-bellied Starling *Notopholia corruscus* Swartpensglansspreeu   page 393
Breeds in forests and woodland along the eastern coastal plain. Pairs nest solitarily and are widely spaced. **Nest:** a hole in a tree is used, either a natural cavity or an old barbet/woodpecker hole, at a height between 2½-6 m up from the ground; holes in buildings are also used occasionally. A shallow-cupped pad of dry grass, leaves, feathers and hair is built in the base of the cavity.
Laying months: Oct-Jan. **Clutch size:** 3 (2-4). **Eggs:** 24.2-25.7-27.2 x 17.9-19.0-19.8 mm; eggs are usually unmarked, but some clutches are faintly speckled. **Incubation period:** not recorded; by ♀ only. **Nestling/fledging period:** not recorded; young fed by both sexes.

Miombo Blue-eared Starling *Lamprotornis elisabeth* Klein-blouoorglansspreeu   page 393
Breeds in miombo woodland, sometimes nesting alongside the closely similar Greater Blue-eared Starling. Pairs nest solitarily and are widely spaced. **Nest:** a hole in a tree is used, either a natural cavity or old barbet/woodpecker hole; it is typically 1½-5 m up from the ground in a cavity 200-380 mm deep with 40 mm wide entrance hole. Deep holes may be partially filled with coarse, dry material (twigs, dung, etc). The nest is a shallow-cupped pad of dead leaves, dry grass and a few feathers.
Laying months: mainly Sep-Oct (Sep-Nov). **Clutch size:** 4 (2-5). **Eggs:** 25.9-26.8-27.4 x 18.6-19.0-19.3 mm; eggs are invariably unmarked. **Incubation period:** not recorded. **Nestling/fledging period:** not recorded; young fed by both sexes.

Greater Blue-eared Starling

Cape Glossy Starling

Burchell's Starling

Meves' Starling feeding nestling Greater Honeyguide

Black-bellied Starling

Miombo Blue-eared Starling

Starlings, Oxpeckers

Violet-backed Starling *Cinnyricinclus leucogaster* Witborsspreeu   pages 179, 393
Breeds in savanna, especially in broad-leafed woodlands. Pairs, or occasional trios (pair plus 1♂ helper), nest solitarily and are widely spaced. **Nest:** mostly uses a natural cavity in the main trunk of a living tree, typically 1-3 m (1-10) up from the ground, 230-450 mm deep and 70-100 mm wide; barbet and woodpecker holes are also also used, and hollow metal fence posts occasionally. Deep holes often partly filled with dry dung and other material to reduce depth. The nest is a shallow cup built of grass and twigs by both sexes, and it is characteristically lined with green leaves (see right-hand photograph); these are added throughout the incubation.
Laying months: mainly Oct-Dec (Oct-Feb); peaks later (Feb) in arid west. **Clutch size:** 3 (2-4). **Eggs:** 22.9-24.5-26.7 x 15.5-17.4-19.2 mm; mass 3.5-3.6 g; occasionally parasitised by Greater and Lesser honeyguides. **Incubation period:** 13-14 days; by ♀ only, she leaves the nest unattended at intervals to feed. **Nestling/fledging period:** 20-22 days; young brooded by ♀, fed by both sexes, occasionally assisted by a helper.

Red-winged Starling *Onychognathus morio* Rooivlerkspreeu   pages 379, 393
Breeds widely where cliffs are present, or in towns, villages and farms where man-made structures provide nest sites. Pairs nest solitarily, usually widely spaced, but occasionally semi-colonial. **Nest:** a bulky, cup-shaped bowl placed in a sheltered site (e.g. pothole) on a cliff; in urban areas and on farms it uses roof eaves, creeper-covered walls, open-roof cross-beams, pigeon lofts, tank-stands, here, often aggressive towards humans. The nest is made with grass, twigs, roots, leaves, rags; wet mud mixed with plant material often used in the base to secure nest to the site; the cup is lined with fine grass or animal hair. It measures: outside diameter 200-240 mm; cup diameter 90 mm; cup depth 70 mm; thickness 70-100 mm. Both sexes build or refurbish the nest; it is often reused.
Laying months: mainly Oct-Dec (Sep-Mar, rarely other months); 1-4 broods/season. **Clutch size:** 3 (2-4, rarely 5); laid at 1-day intervals. **Eggs:** 21.8-33.8-38.6 x 20.3-23.2-28.5 mm; occasionally parasitised by Great Spotted Cuckoo. **Incubation period:** 14 days; mainly or entirely by ♀. **Nestling/fledging period:** 22-25 days (19-28); young fed by both sexes.

Pale-winged Starling *Onychognathus nabouroup* Bleekvlerkspreeu   no nest photo   page 393
Breeds in semi-arid and arid shrubland and savanna where rock-faces (>3 m high) are available for nest sites; also in cities, towns and villages. Pairs nest solitarily or semi-colonially (e.g. 9 pairs nesting along 150 m length of cliff). **Nest:** typically at the back of a deep, narrow crevice (>1 m deep) in a vertical rock face; occasionally on man-made structures (much less so than Red-winged Starling); nest a bulky, open-cupped bowl, made with stems of dry grass and forbs, lined with finer plant stems. Unlike Red-winged Starling, no mud is used. Both sexes build or refurbish the nest; nests are often reused for successive clutches and in successive years.
Laying months: mainly Oct-Dec in the south, Feb-Apr in the north (Namibia); sometimes double-brooded. **Clutch size:** 3 (2-5). **Eggs:** 29.2-31.4-35.2 x 20.7-21.7-23.0 mm; occasionally parasitised by Great Spotted Cuckoo. **Incubation period:** not recorded; by ♀ only. **Nestling/fledging period:** not recorded; young fed by both sexes.

Sharp-tailed Starling *Lamprotornis acuticaudus* Spitsstertglansspreeu   no nest or egg photo
Breeds in broad-leafed woodland in ne Namibia. Nesting habits virtually unknown. **Nest:** active nests have been found in Caprivi in holes in the main trunks of large *Burkea africana* and *Baikiaea plurijuga* trees, 6-8 m up from the ground.
Laying months: Nov-Mar (Caprivi). **Clutch size:** not recorded. **Eggs:** not recorded. **Incubation period:** not recorded. **Nestling/fledging period:** not recorded; young fed by both sexes.

OXPECKERS Family Buphagidae
Worldwide 2 species; both endemic to Afrotropics, both breed in southern Africa; monogamous; breeds cooperatively (pair plus 1-5 helpers); sexes share incubation, nest-building; feeding nestlings shared by group; eggs oval, pink with speckles, 2-3/clutch; nestlings are altricial and nidicolous.

Yellow-billed Oxpecker *Buphagus africanus* Geelbekrenostervoël   page 393
Breeds in savanna; largely confined to large wildlife conservation areas or rural areas with no stock-dipping. Pairs, some assisted by 1-2 helpers, nest solitarily and are widely spaced. **Nest:** typically in a natural cavity in a tree, 3-6 m up from the ground; cavity size variable, 380-500 mm deep, 90-100 mm wide inside; rarely in a hollow metal post or wall cavity. Nest a shallow cup about 50 mm thick, base made with coarse dry grass, cup thickly lined with mammal hair; built by both sexes assisted, if present, by helpers.
Laying months: mainly Oct (Sep-Mar). **Clutch size:** 2-3; laid at 1-day intervals. **Eggs:** 23.4-24.6-26.6 x 16.6-17.1-18.0 mm. **Incubation period:** >13 days; begins with first-laid egg. **Nestling/fledging period:** 25-32 days; young fed by both sexes assisted by helpers.

Red-billed Oxpecker *Buphagus erythrorhynchus* Rooibekrenostervoël   page 393
Breeds widely in savanna; original range much fragmented as a result of tick-control poisons used on stock. Nests cooperatively (pair plus 1-5 helpers), groups are widely spaced. **Nest:** a tree cavity is mostly used, typically about 8 m (1.2-15) up from the ground in a tree, with a top- rather than side-entrance; cavities measure: 170-350-800 mm (once 1.8 m!) deep, 90-140-170 mm wide, entrance 70-90 mm wide. Deep cavities often partially filled with twigs, dung, grass; occasionally in metal pipes, stone walls, holes in rocks. The nest is a pad (60-80-100 mm across, 25-30-45 mm deep) of grass, rootlets and mammal hair collected directly off animals they're feeding on; completed by the group in about 6 days, further lining added during incubation. Sites are regularly reused.
Laying months: mainly Nov-Dec (Oct-Mar); sometimes 2 or 3 broods/season. **Clutch size:** 3 (2-4, rarely 5); laid at 1-day intervals. **Eggs:** 22.5-24.0-26.5 x 15.8-17.2-18.6 mm. **Incubation period:** 12-13 days; by both sexes (not assisted by helpers); begins with first-laid egg. **Nestling/fledging period:** 30 days (26-32); young brooded by both sexes; fed by both sexes assisted by helpers.

Violet-backed Starling

Red-winged Starling

Yellow-billed Oxpecker

Red-winged Starling

Red-billed Oxpecker

THRUSHES Family Turdidae Worldwide 184 species; 31 breed in Afrotropics, 7 in southern Africa. Monogamous; pairs nest solitarily; nest-building, incubation shared by sexes in some species, by ♀ in others; nest an open cup placed in a tree; eggs oval-shaped, blue in most species with speckles and blotches, 2-3/clutch; nestlings are altricial and nidicolous; 3 species are occasionally parasitised by Red-chested Cuckoo.

Spotted Ground Thrush *Zoothera guttata* Natallyster — page 393

Breeds in coastal and low-altitude forest from e Cape to Zululand, favouring forest with an open understorey and scattered saplings. Pairs nest solitarily, 1 pair/5-10 ha. **Nest:** a bulky, bowl-shaped cup, typically placed in a forked branch of a free-standing sapling 1½-3 m up from the ground; occasional nests placed in crowns of *Dracaena* (as in right-hand photograph opposite). The nest is often conspicuous, resembling a wad of debris caught on a branch, and it is roughly made from damp material including leaves, twigs, tendrils and other forest-floor debris, its moisture securing it firmly; the cup is lined with skeletonised leaves and rootlets. The nest measures: outside diameter 130-140-180 mm; cup diameter 75-80-88 mm; thickness 75-80 mm; cup depth 38-44-59 mm.
Laying months: mainly Oct-Dec (Sep-Mar); relays up to 5x after earlier failures. **Clutch size:** 2 (1-3); laid at a 1-day interval. **Eggs:** 23.3-26.8-28.7 × 17.6-19.7-20.8 mm. **Incubation period:** 13½-14 days; by ♀ only; it starts the night before the last egg is laid. **Nestling/fledging period:** 13-14 days; young fed by both sexes.

Orange Ground Thrush *Zoothera gurneyi* Oranjelyster — page 393

Breeds in montane forest from e Cape to e Zimbabwe. Pairs nest solitarily, 1 pair/ha; adjacent nests may be <75 m apart. **Nest:** a bulky, bowl-shaped cup, 1-2 m up from the ground (0.3-3.7), built in a sapling, often on a drainage line; also nests in crowns of tree-ferns, in vine-entwined tree trunks, or in folds in their trunks, or on moss-covered earth banks; it is built mainly or entirely with green moss, with dead or skeletonised leaves often used in the base; the cup is lined with fine, dark-coloured fibrous fern rootlets. No mud is used. Nests are often conspicuous, but easily overlooked as being a cluster of growing moss. It measures: outside diameter 140-200 mm; cup diameter 75-90 mm; nest height 100-110 mm; cup depth 45-60 mm. It is built by the ♀.
Laying months: mainly Nov-Dec (Oct-Jan); relays 1-3x after earlier failures. **Clutch size:** 2 (1-3); laid at a 1-day interval. **Eggs:** 24.0-28.0-31.2 × 19.2-20.3-21.8 mm. **Incubation period:** 15 days; by ♀ only; begins when clutch is complete. **Nestling/fledging period:** 17 days (15-19); young brooded by ♀; fed by both sexes.

Kurrichane Thrush *Turdus libonyana* Rooibeklyster — page 393

Breeds widely in mesic savanna, extending into grassland where alien tree introductions provide habitat. Pairs nest solitarily, a pair/1-2 ha in miombo and mature broad-leafed woodland, adjacent nests sometimes <25 m apart. **Nest:** a bulky, deep-cupped bowl, 3-5 m up from the ground (1½-17), in a main fork in a tree. Some nests are conspicuous, others are hidden in mistletoe or tree orchids; occasionally nests on an old dove or other birds' nests, in roof gutters, pot plants, even in a rain gauge. The base is made from coarse plant material (dry grass, *Helichrysum* stems) giving the exterior a rough appearance, and strands of nest material often trail below the nest; wet leaves, moss, sometimes mud, is used to consolidate the nest. The cup is neatly lined with fine rootlets. The nest measures: outside diameter 140-145-150 mm; cup diameter 65-75-80 mm; thickness 70-75-80 mm; cup depth 35-45-50 mm; it is occasionally reused for successive clutches. It is built by the ♀, and can be completed in <2 days.
Laying months: mainly Sep-Dec (Aug-Mar, occasionally other months); double-brooded; may relay up to 7x after earlier failures. **Clutch size:** 3 (2-4); laid at 1-2 day intervals. **Eggs:** 22.3-26.5-30.0 × 17.0-19.3-21.3 mm; mass 4.8-5.2-5.6 g; occasionally parasitised by Red-chested Cuckoo (which lays a non-matching egg that is not evicted). **Incubation period:** 13 days (12-15); by ♀ only; begins the evening before the clutch is completed. **Nestling/fledging period:** 13-15 days (12-16); young brooded mostly or entirely by ♀; fed by both sexes.

White-chested Alethe *Pseudalethe fuelleborni* Witborswoudlyster — page 394

Breeds in lowland forest in c Mozambique. Pairs nest solitarily, about 1 pair/1.6 ha. **Nest:** a flimsy cup, placed 1½-6 m up from the ground in a deep recess in the trunk of a forest tree, some in the base of ferns growing on trunks, among entwining lianas, or on the top of a stump. It is built with moss and lined with dark-coloured rootlets; the cup measures 70 mm across, 40 mm deep.
Laying months: Oct-Nov (Mozambique). **Clutch size:** 2-3. **Eggs:** 25.5-26.2-26.9 × 17.7-18.0-18.2 mm. **Incubation period:** not recorded; by ♀ only. **Nestling/fledging period:** not recorded; young fed by both sexes.

Groundscraper Thrush *Turdus litsitsirupa* Gevlekte Lyster — page 393

Breeds across the savanna belt from arid west to mesic east and extends into grassland where alien tree introductions provide habitat. Pairs nest solitarily, about 1 pair/15 ha. **Nest:** a bowl-shaped cup, 3-5 m up from the ground (2-9, rarely up to 16), in 3- or 4-pronged fork of a tree. The nest base is characteristically built with long, pliable stems of rough plant material (especially *Helichrysum* spp.), curled around to form the bowl, some nests made entirely with one plant type, others using coarse grass, weeds, twigs, string and other material; the cup is usually lined with rootlets, but some lack this. The nest measures: outside diameter 150 mm; cup diameter 70-90 mm; thickness 90 mm; cup depth 55 mm. Both sexes build; completed nests may remain unused for 2-weeks before laying. Pairs frequently build their nest in the same tree being used by Fork-tailed Drongos, and nests of the two may be <4 m apart.
Laying months: mainly Sep-Nov (Aug-Mar), peaks earlier in Zimbabwe; relays 1-2x after early failures. **Clutch size:** 3 (2-4); laid at 1-day intervals. **Eggs:** 24.7-27.5-31.9 × 18.0-20.3-22.4 mm. **Incubation period:** 14-15 days; by both sexes. **Nestling/fledging period:** 16 days; young brooded and fed by both sexes.

Spotted Ground Thrush

Orange Ground Thrush

Kurrichane Thrush

White-chested Alethe (TWO ABOVE)

Groundscraper Thrush

Olive Thrush *Turdus olivaceus* **Olyflyster**   page 394

Breeds in montane forest and in s Cape, in copses, orchards, plantations of alien vegetation, and suburban gardens. Pairs nest solitarily, 1 pair/6 ha in forest, but at much higher density in suburban Cape Town (12-17 pairs/ha). **Nest:** a large, deep bowl, typically placed in a multi-pronged fork of a large tree, 5-6 m up (1½-22 m). It is built with a variety of material, including string, rag, coarse grass, weed stems, strips of bark, leaves, twigs; mud is often, but not invariably, incorporated; when used it forms a hard rim to the nest; the cup is lined with rootlets or other fine material. Forest nests are usually built with moss, are closer to the ground (2-4 m up) and are usually placed in an upper fork of a sapling. It measures: outside diameter 140-150 mm; cup diameter 80-90 mm; thickness 70-80 mm; cup depth 40-50 mm. It is built by the ♀; old nests are occasionally reused.

Laying months: all months, but mainly Sep-Dec, peaking earlier (Sep-Oct) in s Cape than elsewhere (Oct-Dec); sometimes double-brooded. **Clutch size:** 2-3, rarely 4; laid at 1-day intervals; occasionally parasitised by Red-chested Cuckoo (which lays a non-matching egg that is not evicted). **Eggs:** 28.0-29.9-31.5 x 20.6-21.6-23.6 mm. **Incubation period:** 14 days; by ♀ only; she leaves nest unattended for periods of ½-49 min to feed. **Nestling/fledging period:** 16 days; young brooded by ♀, fed by both sexes.

Karoo Thrush *Turdus smithi* **Geelbeklyster**   page 394

Breeds across the karoo, e highveld and s savanna; alien vegetation has extended its habitat widely into treeless areas; it is common in most towns and gardens in its range. Pairs nest solitarily, 2 pairs/ha in a suburban environment. **Nest:** a large, deep bowl placed in the fork of a tree or shrub, usually well concealed by the foliage, 4-5 m up (1½-8 m); some garden nests are built in creepers or under house eaves. The nest is made of coarse dry grass, weed stems, strips of bark, leaves and twigs; mud is often, but not invariably, incorporated, forming a hard rim to the nest; the cup is lined with finer material, usually rootlets. The nest measures: outside diameter 150 mm; cup diameter 80 mm; thickness 80 mm; cup depth 45 mm. It is built by the ♀.

Laying months: mainly Sep-Nov (Aug-Feb); double-brooded; relays after earlier nest failures. **Clutch size:** 2 (1-4); laid at a 1-day interval. **Eggs:** 29.6 x 21.9 mm; occasionally parasitised by Red-chested Cuckoo (which lays a non-matching egg that is not evicted). **Incubation period:** 14 days; by ♀ only. **Nestling/fledging period:** 16 days; young brooded by ♀, fed by both sexes.

FLYCATCHERS, PALM THRUSHES, CHATS, ROBIN-CHATS, SCRUB ROBINS, ROCK THRUSHES, AKALATS
Family Muscicapidae Worldwide 297 species; 107 breed in Afrotropics, 42 in southern Africa. The Old World Flycatcher family Muscicapidae has been extended as a result of DNA evidence to include the above-named groups that were formerly assigned to thrushes. Where known, they are monogamous, territorial, non-cooperative breeders; they build cup-shaped nests on or close to the ground; the ♀ builds the nest and incubates, sexes share feeding of young; eggs oval-shaped, very variably coloured and marked; 2-4/clutch; nestlings are altricial and nidicolous; several, especially robin-chats are frequently parasitised by cuckoos.

White-starred Robin *Pogonocichla stellata* **Witkoljanfrederik**   page 394

Breeds in montane forest. Pairs nest solitarily at densities of a pair/½-3 ha. **Nest:** ball-shaped, consisting of a deep cup covered by a domed roof with a small side-entrance; most nests (75%) placed on the ground, usually on a slope, among ferns or lianas, or against the side of a moss-covered rock or fallen tree trunk. It is built with dead leaves, moss, tendrils and similar debris found on the forest floor; cup lined with soft skeletonised leaves, fine plant inflorescences and/or animal hair. It measures 110-155-230 mm wide, 75 mm high, with a cup diameter 50-65-85 mm and cup depth 25-40-50 mm; entrance round or elliptical (about 50 mm across), in some cases concealed by an overhanging extension of the roof; built by the ♀ in 7 days or less; lays 2-8 days after completion.

Laying months: mainly Nov (Oct-Jan); single-brooded; relays after early failure. **Clutch size:** 3 (2-3); laid at 1-day intervals; an occasional host (<10%) of Red-chested Cuckoo (lays a non-matching egg which is not evicted); one record of parasitism by African Emerald Cuckoo. **Eggs:** 19.6-22.0-24.0 x 14.8-16.0-17.2 mm; mass 2.7-3.0-3.2 g. **Incubation period:** 17 days (16-18); by ♀ only; begins when clutch complete. **Nestling/fledging period:** 14 days (13½-15½); young brooded by ♀, fed by both sexes.

Swynnerton's Robin *Swynnertonia swynnertoni* **Bandkeeljanfrederik**   page 394

Breeds in montane forest in e Zimbabwe and on Mt Gorongosa. Pairs nest solitarily; adjacent nests may be <75 m apart. **Nest:** rather bulky, thrush-like bowl with a wide flat rim, typically placed about 1 m (0.3-2) off the ground in a sapling, where one or more side branches diverge from the main trunk; also nests in crowns of *Dracaena*, in trailing creepers, in hollows on broken-off stumps or rot-holes in tree trunks; some are conspicuous, others well concealed. It is built with skeletonised leaves, moss, rootlets, fine plant stems and other material, the cup is neatly lined with fine, dark-coloured plant stems and fibres. The nest measures: outside diameter 80-100-140 mm, cup diameter 50-54-60 mm; cup depth 25-32-40 mm. It is built by the ♀ in 7-10 days.

Laying months: mainly Nov-Dec (Oct-Jan); probably double-brooded. **Clutch size:** 2, rarely 3; laid at a 1-day interval. **Eggs:** 19.4-20.6-22.5 x 14.2-14.9-16.5 mm. **Incubation period:** 15-16 days; by ♀ only; she leaves the nest at frequent (15 min) intervals for short periods (10 min) to feed. **Nestling/fledging period:** 14 days; young brooded by ♀ only; fed by both sexes.

East Coast Akalat *Sheppardia gunningi* **Gunningse Janfrederik**   page 394

Breeds in lowland forest where there is thick leaf litter. Pairs nest solitarily, at a density of about 1 pair/0.6 ha. Nesting habits little known. **Nest:** a small cup, placed on the ground at the base of a sapling, set into the leaf litter, its rim level with the litter surface; thin-walled half-dome closes the back of the nest; built with green moss, skeletonised leaves, cup lined with black rootlets.

Laying months: Oct (Mozambique). **Clutch size:** 2-3. **Eggs:** 18.7-19.5-20.4 x 15.2-15.3-15.4 mm (Kenya); eggs are white, spotted and blotched with russet-brown, concentrating on the blunt end of the egg (not illustrated). **Incubation period:** not recorded. **Nestling/fledging period:** not recorded; young fed by both sexes.

Olive Thrush

Karoo Thrush   note the mud used in the rim of the right nest, none used in the left nest

White-starred Robin

Swynnerton's Robin

East Coast Akalat

Robin-Chats

Cape Robin-Chat *Cossypha caffra* Gewone Janfrederik page 394

Breeds in montane forest, forest margins, scrub-forest, fynbos and, in semi-arid areas, in thickets along watercourses; also occurs widely where alien vegetation provides habitat in grasslands; a familiar garden bird across its range. Pairs are territorial year-round; in suburban sw Cape 1-15 pairs/ha. **Nest:** a bulky open cup placed in a variety of sites; often in a recess in an earth bank, in a hollow stump, in a niche in a tree trunk, in flood debris, or in a densely foliaged shrub; creeper-covered walls or hanging fern baskets are often used in gardens; height above ground 0-1.1-3.7 m. Nest base is built with twigs, pieces of bark, moss, grass, leaves, etc. into which a deep cup is set, finely lined with animal hair, rootlets, shreds of grass or bark. The nest measures: outside diameter 75-150-250 mm; cup diameter 55-65-75 mm; cup depth 40-50-70 mm. It is built by the ♀ in 4-14 days from material gathered within 25 m of the nest. Previously used nests are sometimes refurbished for second clutches, and sites are often reused in successive years. **Laying months:** mainly Oct-Nov, except in winter-rainfall region where it peaks in Aug-Oct; most months recorded; sometimes double-brooded; relays 1-4x after early failures. **Clutch size:** 2-3; laid at 1-day intervals; commonly parasitised by Red-chested Cuckoo (which lays a non-matching egg that is not evicted). **Eggs:** 18.8-23.0-26.1 x 13.5-16.5-18.3 mm; mass 3.6 g. **Incubation period:** 16 days (14-19); by ♀ only; begins when clutch is completed. **Nestling/fledging period:** 16 days (14-18); young brooded by ♀, fed by both sexes, ♀ doing the larger share.

White-throated Robin-Chat *Cossypha humeralis* Witkeeljanfrederik pages 378, 394

Breeds in mesic savanna in copses of thicket, commonly on termitaria. Pairs nest solitarily and are widely spaced. **Nest:** an open cup placed on the ground under a tree- or bush-canopy where there is a thick accumulation of dead leaf-, twig- and bark-litter. It is set in the litter, its rim level with the litter surface, usually against a tree stem, aloe, stone or some object that screens it from view in that direction; sometimes built inside rusted pots and tins; the open side of the nest has an apron of coarse, dry twigs arranged like a necklace around the cup which is sparingly lined with petioles, shreds of bark or fine twigs; the nest blends well into its surroundings especially with nestlings. It measures: outside diameter 90-150-230 mm; cup diameter 50-65-75 mm; cup depth 20-40-50 mm. Sites are occasionally reused in successive years. Nesting birds utter a characteristic alarm call (a squeaky 'si-tuu' note). **Laying months:** mainly Oct-Nov (Sep-Jan); relays after early nest failure. **Clutch size:** 3 (2-4); laid at 1-day intervals; frequently parasitised by Red-chested Cuckoo. **Eggs:** 18.0-20.9-23.3 x 13.0-15.1-16.0 mm. **Incubation period:** 14-15 days; by ♀ only; begins when clutch is completed. **Nestling/fledging period:** 13-14 days; young brooded by ♀, fed by both sexes.

Heuglin's Robin-Chat (White-browed Robin-Chat) *Cossypha heuglini* Heuglinse Janfrederik page 394

Breeds in mesic savanna in evergreen thickets, especially along watercourses; a familiar garden bird. Pairs nest solitarily, about 1 pair/ ha. **Nest:** a deep, open, neatly lined cup; typically placed in a rot-hole or cleft in the trunk of a large tree; also in hollow tops of stumps in creepers and vines, root mats on banks and, occasionally, on the ground; usually 1-2 m up (rarely up to 8 m up). The nest base is roughly made of twigs, leaves, moss, grass and other bulky material, the cup finely lined with rootlets, leaf midribs and fine plant fibres. Nest size variable according to site, some merely a lined cup. It measures: outside diameter 75-150-230 mm; cup diameter 55-65-75 mm; cup depth 25-40-50 mm. Nest built by ♀ in <1 week; sites are often reused in successive years. **Laying months:** mainly Oct-Nov (Sep-Jan, rarely in other months); relays after early nest failures. **Clutch size:** 2, rarely 3; laid at a 1-day interval. **Eggs:** 20.8-23.0-26.0 x 15.1-16.6-18.2 mm; occasionally parasitised by Red-chested Cuckoo. **Incubation period:** 14-15 days; by ♀ only; begins when clutch is completed. **Nestling/fledging period:** 15 days (13-17); young brooded by ♀; fed by both sexes.

Chorister Robin-Chat *Cossypha dichroa* Lawaaimakerjanfrederik page 394

Restricted to s and e South Africa where it breeds in montane and mid-altitude forest. Pairs are territorial year-round, spaced at densities of about 1 pair/ha. **Nest:** an open cup, typically placed higher above the ground than those of other robin-chats, often >5 m up (1½-12½); most are in rot-holes or crevices in tree trunks, less often in a hollow on the top of a stump or behind loose bark. The nest is built with dark-coloured plant material, especially rootlets, skeletonised leaves, moss, leaf midribs or petioles and this often matches the chocolate-coloured eggs. The nest measures: outside diameter 75-100-140 mm; cup diameter 65-75-100 mm; cup depth 25-40-50 mm. It is built by the ♀; sites are frequently reused in successive years. **Laying months:** mainly Nov (Oct-Dec). **Clutch size:** 3 (2-3). **Eggs:** 23.0-24.5-28.8 x 18.1-18.8-19.9 mm; mass 4.6 g; egg colour variable – most (40%) are chocolate-brown, 30% are olive-green and 10% intermediate; it is infrequently parasitised by Red-chested Cuckoo. **Incubation period:** >15 days. **Nestling/fledging period:** 14 days; young brooded by ♀; fed by both sexes.

Red-capped Robin-Chat *Cossypha natalensis* Nataljanfrederik page 394

Breeds in lowland, coastal and riparian forest, favouring dense, shrubby undergrowth where lianas occur abundantly. Pairs are territorial, at densities of a pair/0.2-0.8 ha. **Nest:** a cup, usually placed on a broken-off stump or in a rot-hole/crevice in a tree trunk typically 1½ m up (rarely >4 m); also nests in creepers, dense thickets and in recesses in banks. Nest size variable according to site, those in hollow stump-tops little more that a cup lining, whereas nests in exposed sites (on ledges, etc.) are more substantial. The nest base is built with dead leaves, twigs, bark fragments, roots; cup neatly lined with fine leaf midribs, rootlets and/or tendrils. The nest measures: outside diameter 70-140-255 mm; cup diameter 55-65-80 mm; cup depth 25-45-55 mm; built by ♀ in <5 days. **Laying months:** mainly Oct-Nov (Sep-Jan); single-brooded; relays after an early failure. **Clutch size:** 3 (2-4); occasionally (2%) parasitised by Red-chested Cuckoo. **Eggs:** 20.0-22.4-24.9 x 15.0-16.5-18.0 mm; egg-colour variable – mostly (48%) olive, overlaid with brown, 25% unmarked olive-green, 21% chocolate-brown, 6% turquoise-blue. **Incubation period:** 14½ days (14-15); by ♀ only; starts when clutch is completed. **Nestling/fledging period:** 11-12 days; brooded by ♀; young fed by both sexes.

Cape Robin-Chat

a Red-chested Cuckoo nestling in the nest   White-throated Robin-Chat

Heuglin's Robin-Chat

Chorister Robin-Chat   Red-capped Robin-Chat

Scrub Robins

Bearded Scrub Robin   *Erythropygia quadrivirgata*   Baardwipstert   page 394
Breeds in riparian and sand forests and in forested thickets in mesic savanna. Pairs nest solitarily and are widely spaced. **Nest:** an open cup placed about 1½ m (1-3) up from the ground, typically built in the hollow top of a broken-off, decaying stem; otherwise in a tree rot-hole or in the fold of a gnarled tree trunk (*Gardenia volkensii* is often used); the nest-cup is usually sufficiently close to the lip of the cavity for the incubating bird to see out. Nest sites often face onto a clearing or path. Nest size is variable according to site, those in narrow cavities being little more than a lined cup, whereas more spacious sites support a substantial nest, built from rootlets, dead leaves, shreds of bark, *Usnea* or green moss; the cup is lined with rootlets, tendrils, animal hair or petioles. The nest measures: outside diameter 65-90-100 mm; cup diameter 45-55-70 mm; cup depth 30-45-65 mm.
Laying months: mainly Oct-Nov (Sep-Dec). **Clutch size:** 3 (2-3); laid at 1-day intervals; frequently (25% of nests) parasitised by Red-chested Cuckoo which lays a matching egg. **Eggs:** 18.2-20.3-21.9 × 13.8-14.8-15.9 mm. **Incubation period:** 11-14 days; by ♀ only; begins when clutch is completed. **Nestling/fledging period:** 15-17 days; young brooded by ♀ only, fed by both sexes.

Brown Scrub Robin   *Erythropygia signata*   Bruinwipstert   page 394
Breeds mainly in coastal forest, locally in montane forest, especially along drainage lines. Pairs nest solitarily and are widely spaced. **Nest:** an open cup, usually about 1 m up from the ground (0.8-2½), placed in a natural cavity in a tree trunk or in a hollow in the top of a rotting stem; occasionally in a hollow metal pole; some nests are situated in near-darkness, deep (300-400 mm down) inside tree cavities (as in opposite photograph). The nest is made of moss, strands of dark 'forest fibre', dead leaves, fine twigs, rootlets and animal hair; some comprise little more than a thin nest-lining laid on the cavity floor. The nest measures: outside diameter 70 mm; cup diameter 65 mm; cup depth 60 mm.
Laying months: mainly Nov (Oct-Jan). **Clutch size:** 3, rarely 2. **Eggs:** 21.6-22.6-24.0 × 16.1-16.5-17.0 mm. **Incubation period:** 14-15 days, by ♀ only. **Nestling/fledging period:** 14-16 days; young fed by both sexes.

White-browed Scrub Robin   *Erythropygia leucophrys*   Gestreepte Wipstert   page 394
Breeds widely across the savanna belt from the semi-arid west to the mesic east. Pairs nest solitarily at densities of a pair/0.7-5 ha. **Nest:** a deep open cup, placed close to, but not on the ground, typically 100-200 mm up, in a tuft of rank grass, open above; tufts are usually chosen growing at the base of saplings or stumps, between fallen branches or against an aloe, and in a shaded position. The base of the nest is made from stems and blades of coarse grass; the cup is lined with fine rootlets. The nest measures: outside diameter 80-110-200 mm; cup diameter 50-55-60 mm; cup depth 35-45-50 mm. It is built by the ♀ in 4-5 days. She is unobtrusive while incubating, but both parents become vocal and alarm noisily once the eggs have hatched.
Laying months: mainly Sep-Nov (Sep-Jan); relays after early nest failure. **Clutch size:** 3 (2-4); laid at 1-day intervals; occasionally parasitised by Red-chested and Diederik cuckoo (both lay non-matching eggs which are not evicted). **Eggs:** 17.1-20.0-21.8 × 13.2-14.2-15.5 mm; mass 1.9-2.1-2.0 g. **Incubation period:** 12 days (Kenya); by ♀ only; begins when clutch is completed. **Nestling/fledging period:** 11-12 days; young brooded by ♀ only, fed by both sexes.

Kalahari Scrub Robin   *Erythropygia paena*   Kalahariwipstert   page 394
Breeds in semi-arid savanna, especially in thornveld. Pairs are territorial, at densities of a pair/0.7-1.3-4.3 ha. **Nest:** a deep, open cup, similar to that of White-browed Scrub Robin but the site chosen is quite different: this species does not use a grass tuft, but places its nest inside a low, thorny bush (those often used are *Acacia, Gymnosporia, Lycium* spp.), about 350 mm up (0.15-1.5 m). It is well hidden, built with blades and stems of old dry grass, using coarser material for the base and finer material inside; the cup is lined with fine grass stems, sometimes animal hair. The nest measures: outside diameter 80-103-125 mm; cup diameter 44-55-65 mm; cup depth 33-48-59 mm, height 57-69-76 mm. It is built by the ♀, accompanied by the ♂, in 5-7 days.
Laying months: mainly Oct-Nov (Jul-Mar, occasionally other months). **Clutch size:** 2 (1-4); laid at a 1-day interval; occasionally parasitised by Diederik Cuckoo. **Eggs:** 18.3-20.2-23.4 × 13.8-14.6-15.6 mm; mass 2.1-2.3-2.5 g. **Incubation period:** 12½ days (12-13), by ♀ only; in shifts of 2-240 mins; starts when the clutch is completed. **Nestling/fledging period:** 12 days (11-13); young brooded by ♀, fed by both sexes.

Karoo Scrub Robin   *Erythropygia coryphaeus*   Slangverklikker   page 394
Breeds in the karoo and fynbos in open, often treeless shrubland. Pairs, some with one or more helpers, nest solitarily and are widely spaced. **Nest:** a deep, open cup typically (>90%) placed on the ground, well concealed under a small shrub or fallen branch, in a heap of flood debris, a recess in a gully bank; occasional nests are built in a dense shrub, up to 1 m above the ground. The nest consists of a roughly built base made of pieces of twig, dry plant stems, old leaves, bark fragments, grass and root stubble, with a ramp extending from approach side of the nest which can be up to 220 mm wide. The cup is thickly lined with fine plant stems, rootlets and/or animal hair, including sheep's wool. The nest measures: outside diameter 100-114-125 mm; cup diameter 50-60-75 mm; cup depth 40-48-55 mm; thickness 70 mm. It is built by the ♀ in 5-6 days, sometimes assisted in nest material gathering, by helpers.
Laying months: Jul-Jan, peaking in Aug in winter-rainfall region, in Oct-Nov elsewhere; relays up to 4× after early failures; sometimes double-brooded. **Clutch size:** 3 (2-4); laid at 1-day intervals; occasionally parasitised by Diederik Cuckoo. **Eggs:** 16.6-19.7-22.0 × 13.5-14.6-16.0 mm; mass 2.1-2.3-2.6 g. **Incubation period:** 13-15 days; by ♀ only, frequently fed by ♂; begins when the clutch is completed. **Nestling/fledging period:** 14 days (13-17); young fed by both sexes and helpers, when present.

Bearded Scrub Robin   Brown Scrub Robin

White-browed Scrub Robin

Kalahari Scrub Robin

nest built in a roll of discarded fencing wire   Karoo Scrub Robin

Palm Thrushes, Stonechats, Wheatears

PALM THRUSHES, STONECHATS, WHEATEARS Family Muscicipadae The 5 species here are monogamous and territorial, one is an occasional cooperative breeder; all build open cup-shaped nests; where known, the ♀ builds the nest and incubates, sexes share feeding of young; eggs oval-shaped, variably coloured, 2-3/clutch; nestlings are altricial and nidicolous.

Rufous-tailed Palm Thrush *Cichladusa ruficauda* Rooistertmôrelyster   page 394

Breeds in *Hyphaene* palm savanna along the Kunene River in n Namibia. Nesting habits are poorly known. Pairs nest solitarily and are widely spaced. **Nest:** a half-cup, attached to a vertical-hanging palm frond, to the base of a palm frond, to a rock face, crevice in a baobab trunk, or against the wall or under the eaves of a building or bridge. It is a bulky, thick-walled mud nest incorporating grass and other plant material with a deep open cup on top about 100 mm in diameter and 50 mm deep. Both sexes build the nest.
Laying months: Aug-May. **Clutch size:** 3 (2-4). **Eggs:** 23.7-23.9-24.1 × 16.2-16.3-16.5 mm. **Incubation period:** not recorded. **Nestling/fledging period:** not recorded; young fed by both sexes.

Collared Palm Thrush *Cichladusa arquata* Palmmôrelyster   page 394

Breeds in lowland woodlands where tall palms (*Hyphaene, Borassus, Phoenix*) occur widely; often along larger rivers. Pairs nest solitarily and are widely spaced. **Nest:** a bulky cup, typically built in the leafy crown of a palm tree, 15-20 m up from the ground, usually in a concave fold of a leaf-frond, either where this grows out from under another frond, or where two fronds overlap; it is well hidden. Such nests are broader at the base than the cup (150 mm where attached to the leaf and 85-105 mm at the cup), 50-80 mm thick with a cup diameter of 60-70 mm and cup depth of 25 mm. Buildings are occasionally used, where the nest is an open half-cup built with mud and shredded palm fibre, attached like a swallow nest to a wall (as in the photograph opposite), to the underside of a thatched roof or placed on a cross-beam or pillar. The cup is finely lined with shredded grass, petioles and tendrils. It is built mainly by the ♀ with some ♂ assistance; nests are often reused in successive years.
Laying months: mainly Oct-Nov (Sep-Mar); relays after earlier failures; sometimes double-brooded. **Clutch size:** 2-3. **Eggs:** 22.0-25.4-27.0 × 15.0-16.4-17.6 mm. **Incubation period:** 13 days; by both sexes. **Nestling/fledging period:** 20 days; young brooded and fed by both sexes.

African Stonechat *Saxicola torquatus* Gewone Bontrokkie   page 394

Breeds in mesic savanna, grassland and fynbos in areas of rank grass, often close to water. Pairs, occasionally with a ♂ helper, nest solitarily and are widely spaced. **Nest:** a deep, open cup placed on or close to the ground (<0.4 m up); typically well hidden with vegetation concealing it from above; it is usually inside or at the base of a dense grass tuft, less often under a clod of earth, or at the base of a leafy forb. It is made of dry grass and weed stems, with coarse material forming the base; the cup is lined with fine grass rootlets and, occasionally, with wool or feathers. The nest measures: outside diameter 100 mm; cup diameter 50-60 mm; cup depth 35-50 mm. It is built by the ♀ without ♂ assistance.
Laying months: mainly Aug-Oct (Jul-Jan); peaking earliest (Aug) in the winter-rainfall region; sometimes double-brooded. **Clutch size:** 3-4 (2-5); laid at 1-day intervals. **Eggs:** 17.4-18.9-20.4 × 13.2-14.2-15.6 mm. **Incubation period:** 14-15 days; by ♀ only; begins when clutch is completed; she leaves eggs unattended for short (20-min) periods to feed. **Nestling/fledging period:** 13-16 days; young brooded by ♀; fed by both sexes.

Mountain Wheatear *Oenanthe monticola* Bergwagter   page 394

Breeds in open, hilly, rocky country in grassland, karoo and along the Namibian escarpment; often nests in dongas and derelict buildings. Pairs nest solitarily and are widely spaced. **Nest:** a flattish heap of coarse material into which is set a deep cup; usually hidden under a rock on a hill-slope or in a deep recess between rocks; also uses crevices in donga walls and road- and river-embankments especially where screened by overhanging grass. Man-made sites are also commonly used – ledges under roof overhangs, drainwater pipes, window-sills and wall cavities in derelict buildings. The base of the nest is made from twigs, pieces of bark, small clods of earth, pebbles, grass stubble, moss and/or rootlets; the cup is thickly and warmly lined with sheep wool or felted plant down. The nest measures: outside diameter 100-200 mm; cup diameter 50-80 mm; nest thickness 40-70 mm; cup depth 20-35 mm. Nests are usually reused for successive clutches and sites are often reused in successive years. The nest is built by the ♀ in 4-14 days.
Laying months: mainly Sep-Nov (Jun-Mar) in much of its range; in arid areas nests opportunistically in response to rain; relays up to 4x after earlier failures; multi-brooded. **Clutch size:** 3 (2-4); laid at 1-day intervals; occasionally parasitised by Diederik Cuckoo. **Eggs:** 20.9-23.5-26.4 × 15.8-16.8-19.0 mm. **Incubation period:** 13 days; by ♀ only; she leaves the nest about 6x/day to feed. **Nestling/fledging period:** 14-16 days; young brooded mostly by ♀; fed by both sexes.

Capped Wheatear *Oenanthe pileata* Hoëveldskaapwagter   page 394

Breeds widely in open, treeless, usually flat country; often in grasslands that have been recently burnt; resident in some areas, seasonal or erratically present in others. Pairs nest solitarily and are widely spaced. **Nest:** a substantial cup placed below the ground mostly at the end of a rodent burrow where it widens into a chamber; the entrance is via a small hole (50-100 mm wide) on the surface that leads along a tunnel ½-1 m in length to the chamber; occasionally, nests are placed under discarded railway sleepers or in the eaves of a building. The nest is built from shredded stems of dry grass, leaves, rootlets, animal hair; the cup is warmly lined. The nest measures: outside diameter 110-120 mm; cup diameter 60-65 mm; depth 55 mm; cup depth 35 mm.
Laying months: mainly Aug-Sep (Jul-Jan); earlier (Sep-Jan) in winter-rainfall region, later (Sep-Nov) in Botswana; sometimes double-brooded. **Clutch size:** 3 (2-5). **Eggs:** 20.9-23.4-27.0 × 15.5-17.4-20.4 mm. **Incubation period:** not recorded. **Nestling/fledging period:** not recorded; young fed by both sexes.

Rufous-tailed Palm Thrush

Collared Palm Thrush

African Stonechat

Mountain Wheatear

Capped Wheatear

Mountain Wheatear

Buff-streaked Chat *Campicoloides bifasciata* **Bergklipwagter**   page 395

Breeds in hilly, open, mesic grassland, mainly on rock- and boulder-strewn slopes. Pairs and occasionally trios (pair plus 1 ♂ helper) nest solitarily and are widely spaced. **Nest:** an open cup, placed on the ground against the down-slope side of a large (usually ½-1 m diameter) rock or boulder; some nests are well concealed, tucked deep under a lip of rock or screened from view by grass tufts, whereas others are easily visible from above. The base of the nest is made with coarse plant material, mainly dry grass- and root-stubble; the cup is finely lined with rootlets and/or animal hair. The nest measures: cup diameter 75 mm; cup depth 45 mm. The nest is built mainly or entirely by the ♀. Nest sites are sometimes reused in successive years; replacement or second-brood nests are usually <50 m from a previously used nest.
Laying months: mainly Oct-Nov (Sep-Feb); often double-brooded. **Clutch size:** 3 (2-4). **Eggs:** 21.0-22.7-25.3 × 15.3-16.7-17.3 mm; mass 4 g. **Incubation period:** not recorded; by ♀ only; she leaves the nest at regular intervals to feed, with average shifts of 36 mins on the nest and 14 mins off the nest; **Nestling/fledging period:** 16 days; young are fed by both sexes, but mostly by the ♀.

Sickle-winged Chat *Cercomela sinuata* **Vlaktespekvreter**   page 395

Breeds in karoo shrubland and arid grassland, mostly on open, treeless plains; also in the treeless highlands of Lesotho. Pairs nest solitarily, spaced at a density of about a pair/10 ha (Lesotho). **Nest:** an open cup placed on the ground under a thick grass tussock or low shrub; less often under a rock or a clod of earth, occasionally in a hole in a stone wall. The nest is usually not visible from above except via the narrow opening used by the bird to gain access. It is a substantial bowl, made mainly or entirely of soft, shredded grass, into which is set a neatly lined cup, with animal hair or wool used for this. The nest measures: outside diameter 100-125 mm; cup diameter 50-65 mm; nest thickness 50 mm; cup depth 30-35 mm.
Laying months: mainly Oct-Jan (Aug-Mar) and Aug-Nov in winter-rainfall region. **Clutch size:** 2-3, rarely 4. **Eggs:** 18.5-20.1-22.5 × 13.6-14.7-15.6 mm. **Incubation period:** not recorded; by ♀ only. **Nestling/fledging period:** not recorded; young fed by both sexes.

Karoo Chat *Cercomela schlegelii* **Karoospekvreter**   page 395

Breeds in the semi-arid and arid karoo and along the fringes of the Namib desert, in open, treeless plains where the ground is sparsely covered with low shrubs or succulents. Pairs nest solitarily and are widely spaced, adjacent nests usually >250 m apart. **Nest:** an open cup placed on the ground at the base of a low shrub (e.g. *Pteronia pallens, Galenia fruticosa*), a grass tuft or rock; a s or se aspect is favoured. It is a bulky nest, not usually well hidden, the base built with dry twigs and dry plant stems into which is set a wide, shallow cup, thickly lined with shredded grass, the fluffy seeds of *Eriocephalus* sp. and/or animal hair; sheep wool, even if available, is not usually used. The nest measures: outside diameter 200-250 mm, cup diameter 60-70 mm, cup depth 40 mm. It is apparently built by ♀ only, in about 8 days. Sites are sometimes reused in successive years.
Laying months: mainly Aug-Mar, but may nest opportunistically in any month in response to rainfall; relays after an early nest-failure. **Clutch size:** 2-3, rarely 4. **Eggs:** 19.1-20.7-24.0 × 14.3-15.4-16.5 mm. **Incubation period:** not recorded. **Nestling/fledging period:** not recorded; young fed by both sexes.

Tractrac Chat *Cercomela tractrac* **Woestynspekvreter**   page 395

Breeds in karoo and in the Namib desert in arid, open, treeless plains with extensive bare ground or gravel and a sparse cover of low shrubs. **Nest:** an open cup placed at ground level under a low bush or rock; a se or e aspect is favoured. It is a bulky nest, usually easily visible; its broad base is built with twigs and dry plant stems into which is set a shallow, warmly lined cup, made mainly of shredded grass, plant down (*Eriocephalus*), animal hair or wool. It measures: outside diameter 130-180 mm; cup diameter 55-65 mm, cup depth 40 mm.
Laying months: mainly Sep-Oct (Aug-Apr); most breeding occurs opportunistically in response to rainfall. **Clutch size:** 2-3. **Eggs:** 19.5-21.8-22.6 × 15.0-16.1-16.9 mm. **Incubation period:** 14 days; reportedly by both sexes. **Nestling/fledging period:** 18 days.

Familiar Chat *Cercomela familiaris* **Gewone Spekvreter**   page 395

Breeds widely where there is broken ground – along rocky outcrops, hills, scarps, in erosion dongas; also around old mine workings, abandoned buildings and farmsteads; most common in semi-arid areas. **Nest:** cup-shaped, placed in a cavity or recess of some kind – in a rock-face or earth wall, in a disused starling or bee-eater burrow in a bank, in a cleft in a Sociable Weaver nest mass, in a partly broken swallow or martin nest; many nests use man-made sites: holes in walls, under the eaves of roofs, in disused machinery, in pipes and even inside buildings on ledges or among equipment. The nest has a substantial foundation of clods of soil, pebbles, pieces of bark, coarse twigs or other bulky material on which is built a base of finely shredded grass, hair, wool, string, shreds of cloth, carpet sweepings, rootlets, etc.; the pebbles or clods of soil are a characteristic feature and up to 361 have been counted in a single nest; the nest-cup is deep and warmly lined, typically using animal hair. Nests are very variable in size according to site but the nest cup measures 65 mm in diameter and is about 32 mm deep. Both sexes build, completing a nest in 2-13 days. Nests are sometimes reused for successive broods and nest sites are commonly reused in successive years.
Laying months: mainly Aug-Dec (Jun-Apr); in arid areas nesting occurs opportunistically in response to rainfall; sometimes double-brooded. **Clutch size:** 3 (2-4); laid at 1-day intervals. **Eggs:** 18.0-20.4-23.6 × 14.1-15.1-16.6 mm. **Incubation period:** 14 days (13-15), starts with second-laid egg. **Nestling/fledging period:** 13½-15 days; young fed by both sexes.

Buff-streaked Chat

Sickle-winged Chat

Karoo Chat

Tractrac Chat

Familiar Chat — nest built in a cupboard; note the collection of pebbles

Ant-eating Chat *Myrmecocichla formicivora* **Swartpiek**   page 394

Breeds widely in karoo, grassland and open, semi-arid savanna; also in fallow lands. Pairs and family groups (pair plus 1-2 helpers) nest solitarily and are widely spaced. **Nest:** a tunnel is excavated in an earth bank, characteristically located in the roof of an aardvark hole; may also be in the wall of a donga, sandpit or road cutting; once recorded using an old Greater Striped Swallow nest with a broken-off tunnel. The tunnel is 0.3-0.9-1.5 m long and 55-79-120 mm in diameter at the entrance; it widens at the end into a chamber where a bowl-shaped nest of dry grass and rootlets is built. Both sexes excavate, completing a tunnel in 8-10 days, and both sexes build the nest. Nest-holes are not usually used for successive broods in the same season, but they may be reoccupied in successive seasons. **Laying months:** mainly Oct-Nov (Aug-Apr); relays after early nest-failure; double-brooded. **Clutch size:** 3-4 (2-7); occasionally parasitised by Greater Honeyguide. **Eggs:** 21.7-23.9-28.5 × 16.5-17.9-19.4 mm; mass 3.8-4.1-4.2 g. **Incubation period:** 14½ days (14-15); by ♀ only; begins with 2nd last or last-laid egg; she leaves the eggs unattended at intervals during the day to feed. **Nestling/fledging period:** 16½ days (15-18); young brooded by ♀; fed by both sexes, sometimes assisted by helpers.

Herero Chat *Namibornis herero* **Hererospekvreter**   page 395

Restricted to the arid Namibian escarpment, breeding on and at the base of wooded rocky slopes of hills and inselbergs; highest densities on w and sw facing slopes. Pairs nest solitarily, spaced about ½ km apart (250-800 m). **Nest:** a small, compact cup placed in a twiggy, multiple-stemmed fork in a lower, outer branch of a lone-standing tree, typically 1-2 m above ground (1-4); *Maerua schinzi* is a frequently used nest tree; dead trees are rarely used. The nest is built from dry plant fibres, shredded inner bark and rootlets, some bound with a little cobweb or plant down; it has a roughly finished exterior while the cup is finely and neatly lined with plant down and/or animal hair; the nest has an overall whitish appearance and is poorly concealed. It measures: outside diameter 80-106 mm; cup diameter 50-70 mm; cup depth 30-59 mm; nest thickness 60 mm. It is built by both sexes in 3-4 days and material from an earlier nest may be recycled to the new nest. **Laying months:** Feb-Mar; linked to rainfall, and may not nest in years when rains fail; single-brooded; may relay (within a week) after an early nest failure. **Clutch size:** 2, less often 3; laid at a 1-2 day interval. **Eggs:** 20.1-22.0-23.2 × 15.1-16.1-16.6 mm. **Incubation period:** < 16 days, by both sexes, ♀ taking the greater share. **Nestling/fledging period:** 14 days (12-16); young fed by both sexes.

Arnot's Chat *Thamnolaea arnoti* **Bontpiek**   page 395

Breeds in n savannas in deciduous woodland, especially in miombo and mopane where there is an open understorey. Pairs or family groups (pair plus 1-3 helpers) nest solitarily, are territorial year-round and are spaced at a density of a group/15 ha. **Nest:** a shallow cup, placed in a small cavity in a tree, usually a knot-hole in a main trunk, 1-2 m (1-4) up from the ground; old woodpecker nest-holes are occasionally used. The nest is seldom deep (most < 100 mm down from the entrance) and deeper cavities are often partly filled with dry animal dung, twigs, leaves and other material to bring the base closer to the entrance. The nest is built with dry grass stems, rootlets, leaf petioles, leaves and other dry plant material, with a central cup, neatly lined with finer petioles and strands of grass. It measures: cup diameter 55-80 mm; cup depth 40 mm. Pairs often breed in the same area in successive years, and nest sites are frequently reused. **Laying months:** mainly Oct-Nov (Aug-Dec). **Clutch size:** 3 (2-4); laid at 1-day intervals. **Eggs:** 20.9-22.6-24.0 × 16.0-16.8-17.5 mm. **Incubation period:** 13-14 days; by ♀ only. **Nestling/fledging period:** 21-22 days; young fed by both sexes, sometimes assisted by helpers.

Mocking Cliff Chat *Thamnolaea cinnamomeiventris* **Dassievoël**   page 395

Breeds in mesic savanna and grassland on rocky wooded hillsides with cliffs, or in deep ravines. Pairs nest solitarily and are widely spaced. **Nest:** an open cup-shaped pad, characteristically built in the nest chamber of a tunnel-nesting swallow (Greater and Lesser Striped swallows' nests are mostly used); the cliff chats both usurp active swallow nests and use their dilapidated old nests; usually the nest's entrance tunnel is broken to gain access; less often, an open-cupped Rock Martin nest may be taken over, or the nest is placed on a protected ledge or cavity in a rock-face, or on a building or bridge. The loosely built base of the nest is made with dry grass blades and stubble, twigs, rootlets, and the cup is warmly lined with fibrous plant material and animal hair. The nest measures: outside diameter 120 mm; cup diameter 75-85 mm; cup depth 30 mm. Both sexes build the nest, taking about 7 days to complete it. **Laying months:** mainly Sep-Nov (Aug-Dec); rears up to three broods/season. **Clutch size:** usually 3 (2-4); laid at 1-day intervals. **Eggs:** 23.3-25.8-29.9 × 17.0-18.1-19.1 mm. **Incubation period:** 14 days; by ♀ only; she leaves nest at frequent intervals to feed; or warm day eggs covered only 20% of time. **Nestling/fledging period:** 17-21 days; young fed by both sexes.

Boulder Chat *Pinarornis plumosus* **Swartberglyster**   pages 378, 395

Breeds on, and at the base of, boulder-strewn hillsides in n savanna woodlands. Pairs nest solitarily, spaced at a density of about a pair/80 ha. **Nest:** a shallow, open cup placed on the ground at the base of a boulder, in some cases well hidden in a crevice between adjacent rocks; in others quite exposed and easily visible. It is set in the leaf litter and comprises little more than a sparse lining of brown leaf petioles which, combined with the colouring of the eggs or nestlings, blends well with the surroundings. The nest measures: 88-96-110 mm in diameter; 35-46-54 mm in depth. Nesting birds give away their presence by uttering a characteristic squeaky alarm call. **Laying months:** mainly Oct-Nov (Sep-Jan). **Clutch size:** 3 (2-4); laid at 1-day intervals. **Eggs:** 24.8-26.8-32.7 × 17.6-18.9-19.9 mm; mass 4.1-4.8-5.5 g; frequently (20% of nests) parasitised by Red-chested Cuckoo which lays a matching egg. **Incubation period:** 13-14 days. **Nestling/fledging period:** young leave nest at 16-20 days before they can fly; young fed by both sexes.

in roof of aardvark burrow — Ant-eating Chat

Herero Chat

Arnot's Chat

Mocking Cliff Chat — LEFT & RIGHT using striped swallow nests with the tunnel removed

Boulder Chat

Rock Thrushes

Sentinel Rock Thrush *Monticola explorator* Langtoonkliplyster   page 395
Breeds in open, hilly, rocky country in grassland or low mountain fynbos. Pairs nest solitarily and are widely spaced. **Nest:** a broad, shallow bowl with a central cup, placed on the ground, usually well hidden under a boulder or slab of rock or, less often, under a dense tuft of grass. Nests are rarely on flat ground, usually on hillslopes and may be anywhere on the slope (high or low) and facing any direction. The nest is made entirely of blades of dry grass, the cup being lined with shreds of finer grass and rootlets. It measures outside diameter 95-150-200 mm; cup diameter 72-77-88 mm; cup depth 40-70 mm. Sites are frequently reused in successive years. The nest is built by the ♀ without ♂ assistance; he sings frequently in the area while she builds. While incubating, the ♀ may sit tight if the nest is approached, only flying off at the last moment; usually, though, she is warned by ♂ and leaves the nest surreptitiously. **Laying months:** mainly Oct-Nov (Sep-Jan); sometimes double-brooded. **Clutch size:** 3 (2-4). **Eggs:** 24.2-26.5-28.5 x 18.3-19.1-20.4 mm. **Incubation period:** about 14-15 days; by ♀ only. **Nestling/fledging period:** about 16-18 days; young brooded by ♀ only, fed by both sexes.

Cape Rock Thrush *Monticola rupestris* Kaapse Kliplyster   no nest photo   page 395
Breeds in rocky, usually mountainous country, especially in ravines. **Nest:** a substantial, bowl-shaped structure placed in a crevice or sheltered ledge on a cliff, 3-20 m up from the base; recesses in man-made sites are also commonly used; these include sheltered ledges in outbuildings, bridges and electricity substations. The nest is substantially larger than those built by other rock thrushes in the region: its base consists of a mass of dry grass stems, weed stalks, twigs and rootlets and set in this is a broad, deep cup, lined with finer material, including animal hair; cup measures: diameter 100 mm, depth 50 mm. Nest sites are frequently reused in successive years. **Laying months:** mainly Nov-Dec (Sep-Feb) in summer-rainfall areas, Sep-Nov in the winter-rainfall region; sometimes double-brooded. **Clutch size:** 3 (2-4). **Eggs:** 25.5-27.3-29.8 x 19.1-19.8-20.7 mm; occasionally parasitised by Red-chested Cuckoo. **Incubation period:** 14-16 days; by ♀ only. **Nestling/fledging period:** 16-17 days; young fed by both sexes.

Pretoria Rock Thrush *Monticola pretoriae* Pretoriakliplyster
Treated by some authorities as a subspecies of Short-toed Rock Thrush (*Monticola breviceps pretoriae*) and by others as a separate species, this bird breeds at low densities in sparsely wooded, rocky, hilly country. **Nest:** placed on the ground on a s or e facing rocky, grassy slope under a slab of rock, its entrance sometimes screened by overhanging grass. It is a bulky, cup-shaped nest made of stems and blades of dry grass, sheaths of *Xerophyta*, twigs and roots; the cup is lined with shreds of fine dry grass and rootlets. The nest measures: outside diameter 120-139-160 mm; cup diameter 60-73-80 mm; cup depth 40-50-60 mm, height of nest entrance 110-123-130 mm. It is built by the ♀ in about 5 days; she collects the material from within 20 m of the nest while the ♂ sings from a nearby perch. Successive seasons' nests are usually <100 m from sites used by the pair in the previous year. **Laying months:** Oct-Nov; single-brooded but lays a replacement clutch within 18 days of an earlier nest failure. **Clutch size:** 3, laid at 1-day intervals. **Eggs:** 22.6-24.1-25.5 x 18.0-18.8-19.3 mm. **Incubation period:** 14 days; by ♀ only; she covers eggs for about 83% of the day; the ♂ sings sporadically from nearby while she incubates. **Nestling/fledging period:** not recorded; young brooded by ♀, fed by both sexes.

Short-toed Rock Thrush *Monticola brevipes* Korttoonkliplyster   page 395
Breeds in sparsely wooded, mostly semi-arid country, either in hills or on plains, usually where there is broken ground (rocky outcrops, old mine workings, etc). **Nest:** usually placed on the ground, well hidden under a slab of rock or beneath a thick grass tuft; some are built into the stems or roots of a tree (such as a climbing fig), or in a shrub growing out of a rock face. It is a bulky, cup-shaped nest made of stems and blades of grasses and forbs, the cup being lined with shreds of finer grass, hair or rootlets. The nest measures: outside diameter 120 mm; cup diameter 80 mm; cup depth 60 mm. The nest is built by the ♀ over a period of 4-12 days. **Laying months:** Aug-Mar, peaking later in Namibia (Nov-Mar) than elsewhere in its range (Oct-Nov); sometimes double-brooded. **Clutch size:** 3 (1-4). **Eggs:** 21.6-22.7-24.2 x 16.9-17.5-18.5 mm. **Incubation period:** 13-14 days; by ♀ only. **Nestling/fledging period:** 15-17 days; fed by both sexes.

Miombo Rock Thrush *Monticola angolensis* Angolakliplyster   page 395
Breeds in n savanna in miombo or *Baikiaea* woodland; often but not necessarily in woodland where there are large rock outcrops. **Nest:** an open cup, placed in a shallow hole in a tree stem, usually in a smallish tree, either where the trunk has broken off leaving a shallow bowl on the remaining stump, or in a rot-hole that has formed at the base of a branch; the nest is usually only visible from above and it is typically within 2 m of the ground. Nest size varies according to the size of the cavity; in some, it is little more than a lining of petioles and rootlets (resembling the nest of a Southern Black Flycatcher), whereas other nests are substantial pads of dry grass, twigs and rootlets. Nest sites are commonly reused for successive broods and in successive years. The birds are wary and unobtrusive while breeding. **Laying months:** mainly Sep-Oct (Aug-Dec). **Clutch size:** 3, rarely 4. **Eggs:** 20.4-23.3-26.0 x 16.8-17.4-19.0 mm; eggs usually unmarked blue (as illustrated), but some are finely speckled with brown. **Incubation period:** 14 days (13½-15); by both sexes. **Nestling/fledging period:** 18 days (16-20); young brooded by ♀ only, fed by both sexes.

Sentinel Rock Thrush

Pretoria Rock Thrush

Short-toed Rock Thrush

Miombo Rock Thrush

FLYCATCHERS Family Muscicapidae The 8 species on pages 302-304 comprise the traditional Muscicapid flycatchers, a family that has been much expanded as a result of DNA evidence to include palm thrushes, chats, wheatears, stonechats, robin-chats, scrub robins, rock thrushes and akalats (see pages 288-300). They are monogamous, some are (infrequent) cooperative nesters; where known, the ♀ builds the nest and incubates, both sexes share feeding the young; the nest is an open cup, mostly placed in trees; eggs are oval-shaped, variably coloured and marked; 2-4/clutch; nestlings are altricial and nidicolous; several are infrequently parasitised by Red-chested, Diederik and Jacobin cuckoos.

Marico Flycatcher *Bradornis mariquensis* Maricovlieëvanger   page 395

Breeds in semi-arid savanna, especially in acacia thornveld. Pairs and occasional family groups (pair plus 1-2 helpers) nest solitarily spaced at a pair/36 ha. **Nest:** a small, flimsy, open cup, built in an outer branch midway up a smallish tree, usually an *Acacia* or *Dicrostachys cinerea*; typically 2-3 m (1½-5) from the ground, on a thin horizontal branch where two or more twigs branch upwards. It is made of pieces of dry, shredded grass or weed stems that encase the cup which is lined with a few rootlets and a variable number of feathers. Some nests are so transparent that the eggs are visible through its base. The nest relies on being inconspicuous rather than camouflaged to avoid detection, and even when built in a leafless tree (which is commonly the case) it is easily overlooked. The nest measures: outside diameter 70-80 m; cup diameter 45-50 mm; cup depth 20-25 mm; nest height 37-50 mm. It is built by one bird (possibly the ♀), accompanied by its mate during nest building trips. Nest material from an earlier nest is frequently recycled to build a later replacement. A new nest may be completed and egg-laying started within 8 days of the loss of a previous clutch.
Laying months: mainly Sep-Dec (Aug-Feb, occasionally in other months); later in Namibia than elsewhere; relays up to 5x after earlier failures; sometimes double-brooded. **Clutch size:** 3 (2-3, rarely 4); laid at 1-day intervals. **Eggs:** 18.0-20.2-22.0 x 13.2-14.5-15.7 mm; occasionally parasitised by Diederik Cuckoo. **Incubation period:** not recorded; by one bird (possibly ♀) only, fed by mate on the nest. **Nestling/fledging period:** 14 days; young fed by both sexes, sometimes assisted by helpers.

Pale Flycatcher *Bradornis pallidus* Muiskleurvlieëvanger   page 395

Breeds in mesic savannas in broad-leafed woodland. Pairs nest solitarily, spaced at densities of a pair/15-30 ha; adjacent nests spaced about 400 m apart. **Nest:** a small open cup, typically built in a small tree or sapling that stands apart from larger trees in the woodland; it is placed in the upper, outer twigs where it is hidden by foliage, usually 2-3 m (1½-6) up from the ground. The nest is made of long, fine, dark-coloured stems of weedy plants that are curled around to form the bowl, their ends left trailing untidily from the sides. No cobweb is used in the construction and the nest is held in place by the twigs that support it. The cup is lined with fine rootlets. The nest measures: outside diameter 95-100 mm; cup diameter 55-60 mm; cup depth 25-45 mm; nest height 40-70 mm. It is about 30% larger than the nest of the closely similar Marico Flycatcher and it also differs by not having feathers used to line the cup. The nest is built by the ♀ in about 7 days; she is accompanied by her mate during nest building.
Laying months: mainly Oct-Nov (Aug-Feb); sometimes relays after earlier failure. **Clutch size:** 2-3 (2-4); laid at 1-day intervals. **Eggs:** 17.8-19.8-23.4 x 12.9-14.8-16.5 mm; occasionally parasitised by Diederik Cuckoo. **Incubation period:** 14 days; by ♀ only, starting with last-laid egg; she leaves the nest unattended at intervals to feed, average off-shifts 13 mins; average incubating shifts 19 mins. **Nestling/fledging period:** 17 days; young brooded by ♀, fed by both sexes.

Chat Flycatcher *Bradornis infuscatus* Grootvlieëvanger   page 395

Breeds in arid savanna and karoo shrubland where there are scattered trees. Pairs nest solitarily and are widely spaced; there is one record of 2 active nests in same tree, 2 m apart, attended by a single pair of birds. **Nest:** a large, roughly made bowl, placed in a low bush (especially *Rhigozum*, *Boscia*, *Ziziphus* or *Acacia*), about 1 m up (½-4) and hidden to a greater or lesser extent by foliage. It is much like the nest of a Bokmakierie in appearance, built with dry plant stems, coarse grass and twigs. The nest cup is lined with fine material, including rootlets, and many are also thickly lined with plant down. It measures: outside diameter 100 mm; cup diameter 66 mm; cup depth 45 mm; nest height 60 mm. It takes about 8 days to build.
Laying months: mainly Oct-Jan (Aug-Apr; occasionally in other months in response to rainfall). **Clutch size:** 2-3, rarely 4. **Eggs:** 20.0-23.6-25.9 x 16.2-17.2-18.2 mm. **Incubation period:** 14-15 days; by ♀ only, fed on nest by ♂. **Nestling/fledging period:** 11-14 days; young fed by both sexes.

Fiscal Flycatcher *Sigelus silens* Fiskaalvlieëvanger   page 395

Breeds widely, but mainly within South Africa, in areas with trees in karoo, fynbos, semi-arid savanna and grassland; resident in part of its range, a breeding summer visitor in others. Pairs nest solitarily and are widely spaced. **Nest:** an open cup, placed in a stout forked branch or against the main stem of a tree ½-3½ m (1-7) up from the ground. Much like a miniature version of the nest built by Common Fiscal, having a roughly finished exterior which is built from pliable stems of dry grass and other plants (e.g. *Helichrysum Stoebe*) curled around to form the bowl; rags, string and other debris may be incorporated in nests close to human habitation. The cup is neatly lined with a thick layer of soft plant down and/or feathers. It measures: outside diameter 115-130 mm; cup diameter 65 mm; cup depth 37 mm; nest height 65 mm. It is built by the ♀ and can be completed in 13 days.
Laying months: mainly Sep-Dec (Jul-Mar); double-brooded. **Clutch size:** 3 (2-4); laid at 1-day intervals. **Eggs:** 18.5-21.4-24.2 x 14.4-15.9-17.0 mm; occasionally (4½% of nests) parasitised by Jacobin Cuckoos; rarely by Red-chested Cuckoo. **Incubation period:** 14-15 days; by ♀ only, fed by ♂ on nest; also leaves nest unattended to feed. **Nestling/fledging period:** 16-17 days; young fed by both sexes, but mainly the ♀.

Marico Flycatcher

Pale Flycatcher

Chat Flycatcher

Fiscal Flycatcher

Flycatchers

Southern Black Flycatcher *Melaenornis pammelaina* Swartvlieëvanger — page 395
Breeds widely in mesic savanna, favouring open woodland with a short grass substrate. Pairs nest solitarily at a density of about a pair/12-50 ha. **Nest:** a skimpy open cup, placed in a natural hollow in a tree stem, either where a branch or main stem has broken off, leaving a shallow cavity behind, or in a recess behind a piece of loose bark peeling from a branch; blackened fire-damaged trees are commonly selected, perhaps because they provide added concealment for the incubating bird. The nest is typically 2-3 m (½-9) up from the ground. Less often, the nest is built in the old nest of a bulbul, thrush, babbler or weaver, in eaves of a house, in aloe fronds, in mistletoe, in old machinery, a chimney stack, etc. The shallow nest-bowl is built with thin twigs, leaf petioles or short stems of some other dark-coloured plant material, and rootlets are used to line the cup; some nests are more substantial than others. The nest measures: outside diameter 90-95 m; cup diameter 65-70 mm; cup depth 20-35 mm. The nest is built by one bird (assumed to be the ♀), accompanied by its mate during nest building trips; nest sites are sometimes reused for replacement clutches and in successive years.
Laying months: Aug-Feb, peaking earlier (Sep-Oct) in n savanna than s savanna (Oct-Dec); usually relays following earlier failure. **Clutch size:** 3 (2-3, rarely 4 or 5). **Eggs:** 19.5-21.6-24.3 × 14.7-15.9-17.2 mm; occasionally parasitised by Red-chested Cuckoo. **Incubation period:** 13-16 days; by one bird (possibly ♀) only. **Nestling/fledging period:** 15-19 days; young fed by both sexes.

Ashy Flycatcher *Muscicapa caerulescens* Blougrysvlieëvanger — page 395
Breeds in lowland and coastal forests, mesic savanna and along larger rivers where fringed by riparian forest or tall woodland. Pairs nest solitarily and are widely spaced. **Nest:** an open cup, placed in sites similar to those used by African Dusky Flycatcher: typically in a small hole or recess in a tree trunk, less often in a rock face, and sometimes in a deeply forked branch; it also nests on ledges and in holes in the walls of buildings, and occasionally inside a tree-cavity excavated by a woodpecker; it is usually about 5 m up from the ground (2-15). The nest has a roughly finished exterior, built mainly with fine stringy plant material – moss, tendrils, shredded grass and bark, and debris from the webs of spiders and caterpillars; set in this is a cup, neatly lined with *Usnea* or fine, dry plant fibres (feathers are not used, in contrast to the African Dusky Flycatcher). The nest measures: outside diameter 110-180 mm; cup diameter 45-50 mm; cup depth 25-28 mm; nest height 30 mm. It is built by both sexes. Nests may be reused for successive clutches, even after a failure; nest sites are also sometimes reused in successive years, and occasionally a new nest is built on top of the old one.
Laying months: Sep-Jan, peaking earlier (Sep-Nov) in n areas than further south in its range (Oct-Dec); relays after early nest failure. **Clutch size:** 3 (2-4). **Eggs:** 18.0-19.2-21.4 × 12.3-14.2-15.4 mm; occasionally parasitised by Klaas's Cuckoo. **Incubation period:** 14 days. **Nestling/fledging period:** 14 days; young fed by both sexes.

African Dusky Flycatcher *Muscicapa adusta* Donkervlieëvanger — page 395
Breeds in glades in montane and riparian forest, in mesic woodlands, in plantations, gardens and orchards verging on forest. Pairs nest solitarily, spaced in suitable habitat at about a pair/1-2 ha. **Nest:** an open cup, quite bulky for the size of the bird, and placed in a cavity of some sort; it is most often in a crevice or rot-hole in the trunk of a gnarled old tree, or in a fissure running across the face of a moss- or creeper-covered rock or earth bank; less often, it is in the moss-covered branches of a tree, on a ledge, in a hollow in the wall of a building, in a pot plant or veranda basket; rarely, in the old nest of a canary, Red-winged Starling or Cape Weaver. The site selected is typically 3-5 m up from the ground (1-12). The base of the nest is made with old leaves, moss, *Usnea* and/or other lichen, grass, tendrils, old cobweb debris and feathers, and it has an untidy exterior. Set into this is a deep cup usually, but not invariably lined with feathers. The nest measures: outside diameter 89-116 mm; cup diameter 45-55 mm; cup depth 30-40 mm; nest height 64-95 mm. Both sexes build, completing the nest (in one case) in 22 days; nests may only be laid in 15 days after completion; previous nests or nest sites are regularly reused.
Laying months: mainly Oct-Dec (Sep-Jan); often double-brooded. **Clutch size:** 3 (2-3); laid at 1-day intervals. **Eggs:** 16.4-18.2-19.3 × 12.8-13.4-14.6 mm; occasionally parasitised by Red-chested, Jacobin and Klaas's cuckoos. **Incubation period:** 14-15 days; by ♀ only, fed by ♂; she also leaves the nest at about 3-hr intervals for short feeding spells. **Nestling/fledging period:** 17 days (17-22); young brooded by ♀, fed by both sexes.

Grey Tit-Flycatcher *Myioparus plumbeus* Waaierstertvlieëvanger — page 395
Breeds in mesic savanna, riparian woodland and in lowland forest. Nesting habits are poorly known. Pairs nest solitarily and are widely spaced. **Nest:** a hole in a tree is used, either a natural cavity, or an old woodpecker or barbet hole, 3-10 m up from the ground, usually in a rather thin, unstable-looking dead branch. Nest-holes are mostly shallow (<100 mm deep) and the nest, built at the base of the cavity, is a thin pad of finely shredded dry grass or other plant material, with a cup diameter of 60 mm and cup depth of 25 mm. It is built by both sexes.
Laying months: mainly Oct-Dec (Aug-Jan). **Clutch size:** 2-3. **Eggs:** 17.0-17.2-17.5 × 12.5-13.0-13.3 mm. **Incubation period:** not recorded. **Nestling/fledging period:** not recorded; young fed by both sexes.

Southern Black Flycatcher

Ashy Flycatcher

African Dusky Flycatcher

Grey Tit-Flycatcher

Sunbirds

SUNBIRDS Family Nectariniidae Worldwide 136 species; 82 breed in Afrotropics, 20 in southern Africa (21 if Shelley's Sunbird is proved to nest here). Monogamous; none breed cooperatively; nest is thick-walled, pear- or oval-shaped, longest in its vertical axis; has an entrance at the top of one side leading into a warmly lined chamber; built with dry plant material, bound together, and to nest site with cobweb; nests are suspended from a branch in some, built into twigs in others; size, positioning, whether or not entrance has a hood and how outside walls are decorated, varies between species, in many cases diagnostically. ♀ builds the nest and incubates; ♂ assists in feeding nestlings; eggs long ovals; very variably coloured; 2/clutch in most (1/clutch in one species); nestlings are altricial and nidicolous. Klaas's Cuckoo commonly parasitises many (8 or more) sunbird species.

Malachite Sunbird *Nectarinia famosa* Jangroentjie   page 396

Breeds in montane grasslands, fynbos and fringes of karoo. Pairs nest solitarily and are widely spaced. **Nest:** large, untidy, usually placed in a plant (esp. a *Helichrysum*, bramble or fern) overhanging a stream, gulley, donga, ravine, rock face or pit; usually <2 m up from the ground (0.2-12). Less often it nests in a tree, e.g. in a protea growing on a hillside. It is not suspended, but attached firmly to its supporting twigs at its roof and/or back; has a pronounced hood, no exterior ornaments and no tail of material extending below its base. Some nests built with a single material (e.g. old, dry grass), others use a variety (curly, dry pieces of grass and forb, rootlets, pieces of leaf and/or seed-heads); sparsely bound with cobweb. Cup lining of plant down, fine grass ends or feathers. The nest measures: outside height 135-140 mm; outside width 90-95 mm; entrance width 35-50 mm; nest depth (entrance lip to base of cup) 40-50 mm. Nest built by ♀ in <7- 24 days; nests are occasionally reused, often close to a previous year's nest (10 years in one case). **Laying months:** mainly Oct-Jan (Jun-Mar) in summer-rainfall areas, Jul-Oct in winter-rainfall region; sometimes double- or triple-brooded. **Clutch size:** 2 (1-3); laid at a 1-day interval. **Eggs:** 17.9-19.6-22.2 x 12.8-13.6-15.0 mm; commonly parasitised by Klaas' Cuckoo, infrequently by Red-chested and Diederik cuckoo. **Incubation period:** 13-15 days; by ♀ only. **Nestling/fledging period:** 18-19 days (14-21); young brooded by ♀, fed by both sexes.

Orange-breasted Sunbird *Anthrobaphes violacea* Oranjeborssuikerbekkie   page 396

Breeds in heath and protea shrubland in fynbos, mostly in hilly or mountainous country. Pairs nest solitarily, spaced at densities of 5 pairs/ha. **Nest:** nearly spherical in shape, most <1 m up from the ground (0.1-1.2, rarely up to 10 m), built in a low, shrubby woody plant (*Protea, Leucodendron, Helichrysum, Erica*, renosterbos); most nests face e or se away from the direction of the prevailing wind. Nest not suspended, but firmly built into twigs of nest-tree; lacks a hood, lacks adornments on outside walls, has no 'tail' trailing from its base; compactly built with small dry twiglets of heath, rootlets, fluffy plant seeds, grass in some nests; bound together with copious cobweb. Interior thickly lined with plant down (*Eriocephalus* sp.). It measures: outside height 55-110-150 mm; outside width 60-90-160 mm; entrance width 30-35-50 mm. Nests occasionally reused for successive clutches. Built by the ♀ in about 5-18 days; ♂ accompanies the ♀ on nest-building trips and sings frequently near the nest during this period.
Laying months: mainly Jun-Jul (Apr-Sep, occasionally in other months); relays up to 6x/season for earlier failures; sometimes double-brooded. **Clutch size:** 2 (1-2, rarely 3); laid at a 1-day interval; occasionally parasitised by Klaas's Cuckoo. **Eggs:** 15.1-16.5-18.1 x 11.5-12.4-13.5 mm. **Incubation period:** 14½ days (13-16); begins when clutch is complete; by ♀ only; she leaves nest unattended for short periods 2-3x/hr to feed; is off about 35% of day. **Nestling/fledging period:** 17½ days (14-22); young fed by both sexes; fledged young roost in nest for 5-15 more days.

Bronzy Sunbird *Nectarinia kilimensis* Bronssuikerbekkie   page 396

Breeds in highlands of e Zimbabwe and adjacent Mozambique, in bracken-briar scrub bordering forest. Pairs nest solitarily and are widely spaced. **Nest:** a sunbird-type oval placed 1-2 m up from the ground, typically attached to an upright stem of a thin sapling or shrub (e.g. *Hypericum, Leonotis, Buddleja*; once to two reed-stems) in rank, shrubby growth, often over marshy ground or a stream. Nest exterior roughly finished, smaller than that of Malachite Sunbird, attached to the supporting stem at its roof, some with an elongated extension; has a hood over the entrance; lacks adornments on the outer walls; has little or no tail extending below the nest. It is built with pieces of dry grass, fern, bracken and/or shreds of bark; one was made with pine needles; it is loosely bound together with cobweb; interior is lined with fine grass inflorescences or plant down. It measures: outside height 115-120 mm (up to 200 mm including extended roof); outside width 70-90 mm; entrance width 30-40 mm; nest depth (entrance lip to cup) 40 mm. It is built by the ♀, attended by ♂, in 5-14 days. Nests are sometimes reused for successive clutches.
Laying months: mainly Nov-Dec (Sep-May). **Clutch size:** 1, rarely 2. **Eggs:** 18.9-20.2-21.1 x 12.7-13.5-14.3 mm; occasionally parasitised by Klaas's and Diederik cuckoos. **Incubation period:** 14-16 days; by ♀ only; leaves nest 4-5x/day to feed. **Nestling/fledging period:** 21-22 days; young brooded by ♀, fed by both sexes, ♀ 3x more frequently than ♂.

Copper Sunbird *Cinnyris cupreus* Kopersuikerbekkie   page 396

Breeds in n mesic savanna, in woodland bordering riparian forest, drainage lines and edges of vleis. Pairs nest solitarily and are widely spaced. **Nest:** a sunbird-type oval, shaggy-looking nest, placed 1-2 m up from the ground (½-3), typically attached to a drooping leafy twig growing inside a well-foliaged tree or shrub (e.g. *Cassia, Cussonia, Acacia schweinfurthii*); well concealed. Has a pronounced hood of grass inflorescences, a distinctive tail (120-230 mm) trailing below the base of the nest, and some nests have an extended attachment (up to 150 mm long) between the roof and the supporting branch; outside walls are adorned to varying degrees with lichens or cocoons. It is built with pieces and shreds of dry grass and dead leaf fragments, bound together with cobweb and lined inside with finer grass and plant down. It measures: outside height 120-125 mm (up to 400 mm including extended roof and tail); outside width 70-80 mm; entrance width 30-40 mm. It is built by the ♀.
Laying months: Dec-Mar. **Clutch size:** 2 (1-2); laid at a 1-day interval. **Eggs:** 16.1-17.5-19.2 x 11.0-11.9-12.9 mm; occasionally parasitised by Klaas's Cuckoo. **Incubation period:** 14 days; by ♀ only. **Nestling/fledging period:** 15 days; young brooded by ♀; fed by both sexes.

Malachite Sunbird

Malachite Sunbird

Orange-breasted Sunbird

Bronzy Sunbird

Copper Sunbird

Sunbirds

Olive Sunbird *Cyanomitra olivacea* Olyfsuikerbekkie   page 396
Breeds in and on the fringes of coastal and lowland forest, locally in montane forest. Pairs nest solitarily, spaced at densities of about a pair/1-2 ha. **Nest:** a sunbird-type oval, placed ½-4½ m up from the ground, commonly built over a stream, ditch or gulley, or against the wall of an eroded bank; often nests in patios, garages and outbuildings. It is firmly attached at its roof and upper back to a trailing stem of a tree or creeper; it has a hood and a wispy tail of material trailing 130-240 mm below the bottom of the nest. Nests usually have some large dead leaves or broad, dry grass blades wrapped into the walls, overlaid by fine, fibrous strands of creeper or fern tendril, or black, hair-like stems of a fungus (*Marasmius* sp.). Other materials that may be used in the nest are fine dry grass ends (usually forming the hood), moss and lichen. It is loosely bound together with a small amount of cobweb and lined inside with fine strands of dry grass, tendrils or, in a few cases, with plant down. It measures: outside height 140-180 mm (up to 500 mm including extended roof and tail); outside width 70-90 mm; entrance width 25-40 mm; nest depth (lip of entrance to cup) 30 mm. It is built by the ♀. Nests are frequently built at, or close to the site of previous year's nest.
Laying months: mainly Oct-Dec (Aug-Mar); commonly double-brooded. **Clutch size:** 2 (1-3); laid at a 1-day interval. **Eggs:** 17.4-18.5-20.1 x 11.7-12.8-13.6 mm; frequently parasitised by Klaas's Cuckoo. **Incubation period:** 14 days (13-15); by ♀ only. **Nestling/fledging period:** 14 days (13-16); young fed by both sexes, but mostly by ♀.

Grey Sunbird *Cyanomitra veroxii* Gryssuikerbekkie   pages 379, 396
Breeds in lowland, coastal and riparian forest. Pairs nest solitarily, adjacent nests can be spaced <50 m apart. **Nest:** a distinctively structured sunbird-type oval, usually placed <2 m up from the ground (1.2-5), suspended from the end of a creeper or twig; the attachment at the roof is frequently elongated (see photograph opposite) and some have a trailing tail below the nest resulting in a loosely dangling structure ½ m or more in length; it also has a pronounced hood (projecting up to 85 mm) that forms a flap projecting over the entrance. Typically, it hangs over a small clearing, a path or road; some hang from roots in the caved-in walls of dongas or from inside roofs of outbuildings (garages, garden sheds, etc); some are built alongside active wasp nests. It is built from hair-like plant fibres (grasses, tendrils and often the black fibres of the fungus *Marasmius*) and its outside walls are characteristically clad with dead leaves, pieces of skeletonised leaf and some leaf petioles. Cobweb is used to bind the nest together and the interior is lined with fine dry grass fibre. It measures: outside height 120 mm (with the roof attachment and tail extension each adding up to 200-300 mm to the overall length); outside width 75-80 mm; entrance width 30-40 mm. Nests are frequently built at previous year's sites.
Laying months: mainly Oct-Jan (Sep-Mar). **Clutch size:** 2-3 (1-4); laid at 1-day intervals. **Eggs:** 16.5-17.9-19.0 x 12.2-12.5-13.0 mm; occasionally parasitised by Klaas's Cuckoo. **Incubation period:** not recorded. **Nestling/fledging period:** not recorded.

Amethyst Sunbird *Chalcomitra amethystina* Swartsuikerbekkie   page 396
Breeds widely in mesic savanna, extending marginally into grasslands and karoo where alien trees or riparian woodland permits; a common garden bird in places. Pairs nest solitarily and are widely spaced. **Nest:** a sunbird-type oval, typically placed 3-4 m up from the ground, (1.9-6, rarely to 15), usually attached near the end of a drooping branch in foliage, often hidden inside the tree, sometimes hanging conspicuously below the canopy; exotic trees (eucalypts, pines, etc.) are frequently used; often built close to human activity, e.g. alongside a building, even attached to telephone- and washing-lines. It is firmly attached at its roof and upper back to the supporting branch; it has a well-developed hood of dry grass inflorescences that projects over the entrance hole, and a rounded-off underside with no tail of material trailing below. It is built with fine, dry stems of grass and weeds, bound together with cobweb; some nests remain undecorated outside but others are thickly plastered with grey lichen or pieces of leaf, bark, caterpillar faeces or other debris. Inside, the floor and sides are thickly lined with plant down. It measures: outside height 130-150-170 mm; outside width 65-75-90 mm; entrance width 30-40 mm. Nests are frequently reused for successive clutches and are often built close to the site of a previous year's nest. The ♀ builds the nest in 8-36 days.
Laying months: Aug-Mar, mainly Oct-Dec in South Africa and Sep-Oct in Zimbabwe; often double-brooded. **Clutch size:** 2 (1-3); laid at a 1-day interval. **Eggs:** 17.4-19.3-21.0 x 11.6-12.9-14.0 mm; frequently parasitised by Klaas's Cuckoo. **Incubation period:** 15 days (13-18); by ♀ only; starts with first-laid egg. **Nestling/fledging period:** 16 days (14-18); young fed by both sexes.

Scarlet-chested Sunbird *Chalcomitra senegalensis* Rooiborssuikerbekkie   page 396
Breeds in mesic savanna, extending patchily into the semi-arid west in Namibia; a common garden bird in parts of its range. Pairs nest solitarily, spaced at about a pair/1.7 ha. **Nest:** a sunbird-type oval, usually >5 m up from the ground (1½-9), typically attached to the outer branch of a leafy tree; often suspended over a stream or a gully; frequently close to human habitation, e.g. on verandas, pergolas, attached to telegraph wires, light sockets, against walls of buildings; sometimes built next to active wasp nests, occasionally placed within a cobwebbed nest mass of communal spiders (as illustrated opposite). The nest is firmly attached at its roof and upper back to the supporting branch; it has a well-developed hood of dry grass inflorescences; lacks a trailing tail. It is built with dry, shredded grass and weed stems, pieces of dead leaf and/or shredded bark, bound firmly together with copious amounts of cobweb; the outside walls (and especially the base of the nest) are decorated with loose, dry leaves, pieces of lichen, caterpillar faeces; close to human habitation paper, wool, string, etc. are often used. Interior is lined with plant down, hair and/or feathers. It measures: outside height 130 mm; outside width 75-80 mm; entrance width 35 mm. Nests are frequently built at or close to the site of a previous year's nest. The ♀ builds the nest in 3-6 days. Nests are occasionally reused for successive clutches.
Laying months: mainly Sep-Nov (Aug-Jan, rarely in other months) in the east of its range, but Dec-Apr in Namibia; multi-brooded. **Clutch size:** 2, rarely 3. **Eggs:** 17.1-19.2-20.6 x 12.0-13.2-14.1 mm; frequently parasitised by Klaas's Cuckoo. **Incubation period:** 13-15 days; by ♀ only. **Nestling/fledging period:** 17 days (15-19); young fed by both sexes.

Olive Sunbird

Amethyst Sunbird

Grey Sunbird (TWO ABOVE)　　Scarlet-chested Sunbird

Sunbirds

White-bellied Sunbird *Cinnyris talatala* **Witpenssuikerbekkie** page 396

Breeds widely in mesic and semi-arid savanna; a common garden bird in places. Pairs nest solitarily and are widely spaced. **Nest:** a sunbird-type oval, typically about 1 m (0.2-3) up from the ground, built in a leafy shrub or sapling in woodland; often in a thorny plant (e.g. *Carissa*, *Acacia*) and, where present, commonly in a cactus; in gardens may nest on washlines, in flower pots, etc. The nest is attached to a supporting stem at its roof, some having a substantial roof attachment, others very little; the entrance has a small hood; there is little or no tail of material extending below the nest. The nest is built with dry plant material, including fine grass ends, coarser, old, dry pieces of grass, and numerous dry old leaves and pieces of skeletonised leaf; these are loosely bound together with cobweb to give the nest the appearance of a bunch of dry leaves caught in a cobweb; occasional nests are built into nests of communal spiders (see photograph opposite), or alongside active wasp nests. The inside is thickly lined with plant down (not feathers). It measures: outside height 130 mm (up to 180 mm including the extended roof); outside width 60-75 mm; entrance width 25 mm; nest depth (entrance lip to cup) 35 mm. It is built by the ♀ in 5-8 days, sometimes remaining empty for up to 40 days before the first egg is laid; lining may continue to be added during incubation.
Laying months: mainly Sep-Nov (Jul-Mar); relays 5-12 days after earlier failure; sometimes double-brooded. **Clutch size:** 2 (1-3); laid at a 1-day interval. **Eggs:** 14.3-16.1-17.8 x 10.5-11.4-12.9 mm; occasionally parasitised by Klaas's Cuckoo. **Incubation period:** 13-14 days; by ♀ only; begins with first- or second-laid egg. **Nestling/fledging period:** 14-15 days; young fed by both sexes.

Shelley's Sunbird *Cinnyris shelleyi* **Swartpenssuikerbekkie** page 396

Occurs narrowly in the region along the n borders, in mesic savanna; breeding not yet confirmed in southern Africa; in Zambia it breeds in miombo woodland. Nesting habits are poorly known. **Nest:** a sunbird-type oval, built inside a leafy bush about 4 m up from the ground (1½-10). It is attached firmly at its roof to a twig and the nest may have an extended attachment (40 mm long) between the roof and the supporting branch; it lacks a hood; has a short tail of material (40-50 mm long) trailing below the nest. It is distinctive in being built with cotton-like, pale-coloured cobweb that is mixed with petioles and fine dry pieces of grass and leaf to form a firm-walled, compact nest with a silvery-white appearance; living leaves may be incorporated into the wall, and the outside wall is also adorned with a few pieces of bark and dry seed casings; the interior is lined with feathers. The nest measures: outside height 100-118-125 mm (250 with extended roof and tail); outside width 55-60-70 mm; entrance width 25-30 mm; nest depth (entrance lip to cup) 50 mm. Nests can be reused for second clutches.
Laying months: mainly Sept (Aug-Nov, Zambia). **Clutch size:** 2, rarely 1. **Eggs:** 16.2-17.6-18.7 x 11.1-11.7-12.0 mm; mass 1.2-1.3-1.5 g; not illustrated – pale bluish-grey, flecked, smeared and blotched with lilac-grey, either covering the egg evenly, or forming a ring near the blunt end (Zambia). **Incubation period:** not recorded. **Nestling/fledging period:** not recorded.

Marico Sunbird *Cinnyris mariquensis* **Maricosuikerbekkie** page 396

Breeds widely across the semi-arid savanna, mainly in thornveld, extending locally into thornveld in mesic savanna. Pairs nest solitarily and are widely spaced. **Nest:** a distinctive sunbird-type nest, typically built inside a tree and near the top, some placed in the uppermost twigs; height varies according to the tree, but it is usually 3½-6 m up from the ground (1.8-9); thorny trees (*Acacia*, *Ziziphus* spp.) are mostly, but not invariably, used. The nest is pronouncedly pear-shaped, narrow at the entrance and widest at the nest chamber, and is built with whitish-coloured material which often makes it conspicuous. It is not suspended, but attached firmly at its roof and upper back to an upright, rather than a trailing, twig; it has a short hood and it has no tail of material extending below. It is built mainly with silky white strands of plant seed and cobweb, giving it a smooth exterior; some fine grass ends are used, especially to form the hood, and the outside walls are sparsely adorned with a few pieces of contrasting dark material, usually fragments of bark, bits of dry resin or caterpillar faeces. The inside is thickly lined with feathers. It measures: outside height 120-140 mm; outside width (at widest) 60-65 mm; entrance width 30-40 mm; nest depth (entrance lip to cup) 55 mm. The same nest tree is quite frequently used in successive years and occasionally the nest is built on the same twig. It is built by the ♀ in 6-12 days. Material from one failed nest is often recycled for use in its replacement.
Laying months: mainly Sep-Dec (Aug-Feb); may lay one or more replacement clutches after earlier failures; occasionally double-brooded. **Clutch size:** 2, rarely 3; laid at a 1-day interval. **Eggs:** 16.8-18.4-20.0 x 11.0-12.1-13.6 mm; occasionally parasitised by Klaas's Cuckoo. **Incubation period:** 14 days; by ♀ only, starts with 2nd-laid egg. **Nestling/fledging period:** not recorded; young brooded by ♀, fed by both sexes.

Purple-banded Sunbird *Cinnyris bifasciatus* **Purperbandsuikerbekkie** page 396

Breeds in and on the fringes of coastal, lowland, riparian and sand forest. Pairs nest solitarily and are widely spaced. **Nest:** a distinctively shaped and decorated nest, typically placed at, or near the extremity, of a branch of a smallish thorny tree, often one devoid of leaves, about 3½ m (1.2-4.7) up from the ground, often suspended over the side of a road or watercourse. The nest is narrow, elongated, and pronouncedly pear-shaped (narrow at entrance and wide at chamber); it is suspended from its roof and may have an extended attachment (up to 50 mm long) between roof and supporting branch; it usually has a short tail of material (50-100 mm long) trailing below the nest; it lacks an entrance hood. It is built mainly with grey lichen and petioles, with copious amounts of cobweb binding it together. Outside walls are covered with lichen, and a few pieces of bark, dry leaf or caterpillar faeces are loosely attached, especially in the lower part of the nest. The interior has a thick lining of feathers and/or silky plant down. The nest measures: outside height 110-115 mm (up to 250 mm with extended roof and tail); outside width (at widest) 50-55 mm; entrance width 25-30 mm; nest depth (entrance lip to cup) 35 mm. The nest is built by the ♀, sometimes at the site of the previous year's nest.
Laying months: mainly Sep-Nov (Aug-Dec, occasionally in other months). **Clutch size:** 2 (1-3). **Eggs:** 14.0-16.2-18.1 x 10.5-11.1-12.3 mm. **Incubation period:** not recorded; by ♀ only. **Nestling/fledging period:** not recorded; young fed by both sexes.

White-bellied Sunbird

White-bellied Sunbird  Shelley's Sunbird  Marico Sunbird

Purple-banded Sunbird

Neergaard's Sunbird *Cinnyris neergaardi* Bloukruissuikerbekkie   page 396

Breeds in sand forest and lowland woodland. Nesting habits are poorly known. **Nest:** a sunbird-type oval with a projecting hood; it is characteristically placed in a tree festooned with *Usnea* and, since the nest is built with the same material, it blends closely with its background; may also build the nest in the hanging roots of an epiphytic orchid; the nest is typically 4-6 m up from the ground; Apart from *Usnea* used to build the nest, fibrous bark and tendrils may be incorporated, and cobweb is used to bind it together; the inside is lined with white vegetable down. It is built by the ♀, accompanied by the ♂.
Laying months: Oct-Dev (Sep-Jan). **Clutch size:** 2. **Eggs:** no measurements available. **Incubation period:** not recorded. **Nestling/fledging period:** not recorded; young fed by both sexes.

Southern Double-collared Sunbird *Cinnyris chalybeus* Klein-rooibandsuikerbekkie   page 396

Southern populations (mainly nominate race) breed in shrubland habitats in the karoo and fynbos; northern populations (mainly *Cinnyris c. subalaris*) breed in and on the fringes of forest. Pairs nest solitarily and in fynbos at a density of about a pair/2-10 ha, adjacent nests 130 m part. **Nest:** in fynbos and karoo the nest is built in a densely foliaged bush, usually <1 m up from the ground (0.2-2½); by contrast, in interior forests it is usually higher, up to 10 m above the ground. The nest is compact, thick-walled, lacks a projecting hood over the entrance, and may or may not have a 'tail' of material trailing below it; the outer walls are not usually decorated. Nest material used varies according to location; fynbos/karoo nests mostly built with woolly stems of *Galium tomentosum*; forest nests commonly built with *Usnea*; in both, the nest is bound with cobweb and lined with plant down, fine grass, feathers or other soft material. Rarely, an old nest of a Karoo Prinia may be used. The nest measures: outside height 90-110-130 mm; outside width 60-75-90 mm; entrance width 23-25-30 mm. It is built by the ♀ in 25-30 days (first nest) or 7-16 days (later nests); ♂ accompanies her on nest-building trips and sings frequently near the nest during this period. Nests are occasionally reused, and material from a failed nest may be recycled in its replacement.
Laying months: mainly Jul-Sep (Mar-Nov) in winter-rainfall region, Sep-Nov elsewhere; relays up to 4x/season for earlier failures; sometimes double-brooded. **Clutch size:** 2 (1-3, rarely 4); laid at a 1-day interval. **Eggs:** 14.6-16.3-18.3 x 10.7-11.6-12.8 mm; occasionally parasitised by Klaas's Cuckoo. **Incubation period:** 14-15 days (13-17); by ♀ only; begins when first egg is laid. **Nestling/fledging period:** 16½ days (15-19); young brooded by ♀, fed by both sexes.

Greater Double-collared Sunbird *Cinnyris afer* Groot-rooibandsuikerbekkie   page 396

Breeds on forest edges, in *Protea*, bracken shrubland, sometimes in gardens, usually in hilly or mountainous country. Pairs nest solitarily, a pair/1-3 ha in w Cape forests. **Nest:** an untidy sunbird-type nest, usually 2-3 m up from the ground (1½-7), placed near the top of a well-foliaged shrubby tree or bush (e.g. *Podocarpus, Leucosidea*); it is usually securely built into the foliage, rather than suspended from an outer twig; has a well-developed hood of fine grass-ends that project over the entrance; generally roughly finished, with pieces of nest material hanging loosely from it; may or may not have an extended tail of debris trailing below. It is made of dead plant material – pieces of dry grass, dry leaf, bark shreds, twiglets, seed cases, dry berries – all loosely held together with cobweb. Occasional nests are built with string, pieces of plastic or other human debris. Interior usually lined with feathers; one incorporated 539 feathers in the lining and 1210 other pieces of other material in the walls. The nest measures: outside height 135-150 mm; outside width 60-85 mm; entrance width 30-40 mm; the hood projects 35-60 mm beyond the nest. It is built by the ♀ in 10-24 days; ♂ accompanies her on nest-building trips and sings near the nest during building and incubation. Nests are frequently close to a previous year's site.
Laying months: mainly Jul-Nov (May-Nov, occasionally in other months); multi-brooded. **Clutch size:** 2, rarely 1; laid at a 1-day interval. **Eggs:** 17.0-18.6-20.0 x 11.8-12.4-13.1 mm; frequently parasitised by Klaas's Cuckoo. **Incubation period:** 15-16 days; by ♀ only. **Nestling/fledging period:** 15-16 days; young brooded by ♀, fed by both sexes.

Miombo Double-collared Sunbird *Cinnyris manoensis* Miombo-rooibandsuikerbekkie   page 396

Breeds in n mesic savanna, especially in miombo woodland. Pairs nest solitarily and are widely spaced. **Nest:** a sunbird-type oval, usually placed 2-3 m up from the ground (1.2-8), typically inside the mid-canopy of a leafless to well-foliaged tree; also in saplings, euphorbias, proteas, tree-aloes and on electricity- and telephone-wires. The nest is attached at its roof and upper back to the supporting twig or branch; it may or may not have a hood over the entrance; usually has no tail of material trailing below; built with plant fibres, typically dry, shredded, curly pieces of bark stripped from forbs, pieces of dry leaf, *Usnea* and fine dry grass loosely bound together with cobweb; exterior walls are not usually decorated. Interior is lined with plant down or feathers. It measures: outside height 150 mm; outside width (at widest) 80 mm; entrance width 40 mm. It is built by the ♀, accompanied by ♂.
Laying months: mainly Aug-Nov (May-Dec, occasionally other months). **Clutch size:** 2 (1-3). **Eggs:** 14.6-16.2-18.1 x 10.6-11.5-12.5 mm. **Incubation period:** 14 days (14-16); by ♀ only. **Nestling/fledging period:** 13 days (13-15); young fed by both sexes.

Plain-backed Sunbird *Anthreptes reichenowi* Bloukeelsuikerbekkie   no nest photo page 396

Breeds in Mozambique in coastal, lowland and riparian forest. Nesting habits are poorly known. **Nest:** 0.9-4.7 m up from the ground, and is suspended from a thorny or leafy stem of a well-foliaged tree or sapling growing in a forest glade; location, size and shape resembles nest of Collared Sunbird. It is suspended from its roof and has a well-developed hood that projects over the entrance hole; it does not have a tail of material extending from the base of the nest. It is made with shredded dry grass, bark, lichen and/or other plant material, and is bound together with cobweb. Cocoons may be used to decorate the outside walls. The interior is lined with fine grass and plant down. It measures about: outside height 115 mm; outside width 65 mm; entrance width 30 mm.
Laying months: Jun, Oct-Nov. **Clutch size:** 2 (1-3). **Eggs:** 15.0-15.7-16.2 x 10.4-10.9-11.4 mm. **Incubation period:** not recorded. **Nestling/fledging period:** not recorded.

Neergaard's Sunbird

Southern Double-collared Sunbird     Greater Double-collared Sunbird

Miombo Double-collared Sunbird

Sunbirds

Variable Sunbird *Cinnyris venustus* Geelpenssuikerbekkie page 396
Breeds n mesic savanna and Zimbabwe highlands in bracken-briar scrub and rank, weedy second-growth on forest fringes. Pairs nest solitarily and are widely spaced. **Nest:** a sunbird-type oval resembling the nest of White-bellied Sunbird, similar in size, shape and position; typically 1-1.2 m up from the ground (0.4-3.7), built in a leafy shrub or sapling among tall grass, weeds, creepers, epiphytic orchids; sometimes close to buildings, even placed in a pot-plant (see photograph opposite). It is attached to the supporting stem at its roof and top-back, nest material often wrapped some distance up the stem, making this attachment quite extended; it has a weakly developed hood of soft grass-ends that projects over the entrance hole, a roughly finished exterior, and it lacks adornments on the outer walls; it has no tail extending below the nest. It is built with pieces of dry grass and fine grass inflorescences, and with small dead leaves, pieces of leaf and skeletonised leaf and these are loosely bound together with cobweb. The inside is lined with fine grass-ends, plant down and feathers which form a thick (45 mm) floor to the nest. It measures: outside height 115-120 mm (up to 190 mm including the extended roof); outside width 58-70-78 mm; entrance width 25-30-35 mm; nest depth (entrance lip to cup) 25-30 mm. It is built by the ♀, accompanied by the ♂, in 2-3 weeks.
Laying months: mainly Mar-Jun (Feb-Oct, rarely in other months). **Clutch size:** 2 (1-2). **Eggs:** 13.9-15.1-17.3 x 10.4-11.3-12.1 mm; parasitised by Klaas's Cuckoo (Kenya). **Incubation period:** 14 days; by ♀ only. **Nestling/fledging period:** 15 days (12-16); young fed by both sexes.

Dusky Sunbird *Cinnyris fuscus* Namakwasuikerbekkie page 396
Breeds widely across the karoo and Namib desert fringes in semi-arid and arid shrublands; favours rocky, hilly country and dry watercourses. Pairs nest solitarily but adjacent nests may be <100 m apart. **Nest:** a sunbird-type oval, typically <1 m up from the ground (0.1-1.7), built in a leafy shrub or sapling, often one that is thorny (e.g. an *Acacia, Blepharis, Euphorbia*; cactus *Opuntia* sp.). It is attached to the supporting stem at its roof and top-back, the roof being quite extensive, comprising up to a third of the nest; has little or no hood; usually lacks a tail of material trailing below the nest. It is built with pieces of dry grass and old weed-stems, both fine and coarse, bound together with cobweb; inside thickly lined with plant down and/or mammal hair; the exterior is not decorated. It measures: outside height 110-125 mm; outside width 75 mm; entrance width 30 mm; cup diameter (inside) 40-50 mm. It is built by the ♀ in about 6 days, but may only be laid in up to 12 days later; occasionally reuses a nest for a replacement clutch.
Laying months: opportunistic, related to rainfall: mainly Feb-Mar (Sep-Jun) in Namibia, Aug-Nov (Jun-Jan) in n and w Cape; may relay after early failure. **Clutch size:** 2-3. **Eggs:** 14.0-15.4-16.2 x 10.3-10.9-11.8 mm; frequently (8% of nests) parasitised by Klaas's Cuckoo. **Incubation period:** 12-13 days; by ♀ only. **Nestling/fledging period:** 13-15 days; young fed by both sexes.

Collared Sunbird *Hedydipna collaris* Kortbeksuikerbekkie pages 379, 396
Breeds in and on the fringes of coastal, lowland, riparian and montane forests. Pairs nest solitarily; adjacent nests can be within 50 m of each other. **Nest:** smaller than those of other sunbirds in the region, typically 1½-2 m up from the ground (0.9-6.2), usually attached to the outside foliage of a leafy sapling, shrub or forest creeper, often alongside a path, clearing, or close to a building; some are placed alongside active wasp nests. It is seldom hidden in foliage and is attached at its roof to a supporting twig; has a well-developed hood projecting over the entrance; and most have a tail of loosely attached material trailing below the nest. It is made with fine, dry stems of grass and weeds, fine shreds of bark, strands of *Usnea*, tendrils, *Marasmius* fibres and/or other plant material, bound together with cobweb. Exterior either undecorated or, less often, adorned with a few loosely hanging pieces of bark or dead leaf, lichen, caterpillar faeces or other debris. The interior is lined with plant down. It measures: outside height 90-115-165 mm; outside width 55-70-88 mm; entrance width 20-30 mm. The ♀ builds the nest in 2-17 days.
Laying months: mainly Oct-Dec (Sep-Feb, rarely in other months) occasionally double-brooded. **Clutch size:** 2-3, rarely 1 or 4; laid at 1-day intervals. **Eggs:** 14.5-15.9-17.8 x 10.3-11.2-12.0 mm; occasionally parasitised by Klaas's Cuckoo. **Incubation period:** 14 days; by ♀ only. **Nestling/fledging period:** 14 days; young fed by both sexes, but mostly ♀.

Western Violet-backed Sunbird *Anthreptes longuemarei* Blousuikerbekkie page 396
Breeds in n savanna in miombo and *Uapaca* woodlands. Pairs nest solitarily and are widely spaced. **Nest:** very distinctive in placement and decoration, usually about 6 m up from the ground (3-10), built in a cluster of dead seedpods, often in a leafless tree. It is compact and firmly attached at its roof to a stout twig; it does not have a hood projecting over the entrance nor a tail of material hanging from its base, but, unlike the nest of any other sunbird in the region, the nest's exterior is wholly encased with dead leaves which camouflage it very effectively. It is built with fine plant material, but the casing of dry leaves so covers it that it appears to have been made with leaves and little else. Cobwebs bind the nest and added leaves together and the interior is lined with fine grass stems and plant down. Nest entrances usually face into, rather than out of the nest-tree; occasionally, nests are built into sociable spider nests rather than into a seed cluster. It measures: outside height 150 mm; outside width 100 mm; entrance width 40 mm; nest depth (entrance lip to cup) 50 mm. It is built by the ♀; one nest took a month to complete. Nests are frequently built close to the site of a previous year's nest.
Laying months: mainly Aug-Oct (Aug-Dec). **Clutch size:** 2 (1-3). **Eggs:** 17.9-19.2-21.0 x 12.0-12.8-13.5 mm. **Incubation period:** not recorded. **Nestling/fledging period:** not recorded; young fed by both sexes.

Variable Sunbird

Collared Sunbird

Dusky Sunbird (TWO ABOVE)　　Western Violet-backed Sunbird　　female starting a nest

SPARROW-WEAVER, BUFFALO WEAVER, SOCIABLE WEAVER, SPARROWS, PETRONIAS Family Passeridae

Worldwide 48 species; 24 breed in Afrotropics, 10 in southern Africa, 1 introduced (House Sparrow). Most are monogamous, 1 is poygynous; nests solitarily or colonially; parental care shared in some, by ♀ in others; eggs oval, white variably marked; 3-5 clutch; nestlings are altricial and nidicolous. Sparrows sometimes parasitised by Diederik Cuckoo.

White-browed Sparrow-Weaver *Plocepasser mahali* Koringvoël   page 397

Breeds widely in semi-arid savanna. Pairs and family groups (pair plus 1-5 helpers) build and maintain colonies of about 10-12 nests roosting in these year-round and breeding in one. **Nest:** an untidy retort-shaped ball of dry, straw-like grass, placed in the outer branches of trees, especially acacias, with wide-spreading branches; typically 2-6 m up from the ground and mostly clustered on the w, sw or nw side of the tree, opposite the direction of the prevailing wind. Roosting nests are shaped like an inverted 'U' with entrances leading in at either end; the breeding nest, measuring about 250 mm long and 150 mm wide, has an open entrance at one end, the other end closed and containing the nest-cup which is lined with fine grass, feathers and other soft material. All members of the group participate in nest-building, repairing existing nests and removing old nests; this continues year-round, with surges of activity after rains. A nest takes 5-35 days to complete.

Laying months: mainly Sep-Dec, but all months recorded; in arid areas probably lays opportunistically in response to rainfall; up to 4 broods/season. **Clutch size:** 2 (1-3, occasionally 4); laid at a 1-day interval. **Eggs:** 22.6-24.8-27.6 x 14.6-16.3-17.5 mm; mass 2.2-3.0-4.1 g; occasionally parasitised by Diederik Cuckoo. **Incubation period:** 14 days (13-15); by ♀ only. **Nestling/fledging period:** 22 days (21-23); young fed by both sexes, assisted by helpers.

Sociable Weaver *Philetairus socius* Versamelvoël   page 397

Breeds widely in semi-arid and arid regions where nest sites are available: trees are mostly used for this purpose, but in places the cross-bars of telephone poles, windmill stands or, rarely, rock faces may be used. Pairs (occasionally with helpers) nest colonially, up to 500 birds/colony, adjacent nests 200-500 m apart; these nests are a characteristic feature of arid landscapes where the birds occur. **Nest:** a huge structure – the largest built by any bird in the world – weighing up to a ton and measuring as much as 7 m wide and 4 m high. Most are placed 3-6 m (1½-16) above the ground. The nest mass is built entirely with dry grass stems picked up from the ground, each pair building a nest chamber in the superstructure: the chambers, measuring 105-135 mm wide and 75-105 mm high, are in the underside of the communal nest, each reached via its own tunnel (about 60-70 mm wide, 250 mm long) which leads up from below; the tunnel entrance is protected by having its walls lined with inward-pointing spiked grass stems; the nest-cup is lined with fine grass blades and soft grass inflorescences. As a colony expands, new chambers are added to the edges of the superstructure. Nest chambers are used as year-round roosts when not breeding and are often occupied by Pygmy Falcon, Red-headed Finch, Rosy-faced Lovebird and others. Many colonies support resident cobras that prey on nestlings.

Laying months: all months recorded, laying opportunistically in response to rainfall; may not breed in droughts, but multi-brooded in years of higher-than-average rainfall (when up to 9 clutches/year may be laid). **Clutch size:** 3-4 (2-6); laid at 1-day intervals. **Eggs:** 18.2-21.1-24.5 x 14.0-14.8-15.8 mm; mass 1.9-2.4-3.0 g. **Incubation period:** 14 days (13-15); by both sexes; begins before clutch is completed. **Nestling/fledging period:** 21-24 days; young brooded and fed by both sexes, some assisted by helpers.

Red-billed Buffalo Weaver *Bubalornis niger* Buffelwewer   page 397

Breeds in semi-arid savanna where there are large trees and areas of bare ground. ♂s are polygynous and cooperative breeders. Groups of ♂s (1-5) collectively build a multi-chambered nest and as many as 10 ♂ groups may build such nests in a single tree. These nest-masses are a conspicuous feature in the areas where the birds breed. **Nest:** a loosely knitted, wheelbarrow-sized mass of dry thorny twigs that contains 1-6 (rarely up to 13) chambers (the number is dependent on the number of ♂s in the group); each chamber has a short entrance tunnel leading in from the side; the nesting colonies may be in large trees, 2-15 m up from the ground, in electricity transmission towers (e.g. 137 colonies were counted along a single 15 km transmission line in the lowveld), or in windmill stands. ♂s collect twigs from the ground within 1 km of the colony and build a chamber in about a week; the ♀ selects one, lines it with dry grass, leaves and rootlets, and lays a day or two later. Nest-masses often remain intact for years before disintegrating and they are often used as nest platforms by vultures, Verreaux's Eagle-Owl and other birds of prey.

Laying months: mainly Nov-Mar (Sep-Apr, occasionally in other months); sometimes double-brooded. **Clutch size:** 3 (2-4); laid at 1-day intervals. **Eggs:** 25.4-28.1-32.5 x 19.0-19.8-20.9 mm. **Incubation period:** 14 days; by ♀ only; begins when first egg is laid. **Nestling/fledging period:** 20-23 days; young brooded and fed by ♀ only.

Scaly-feathered Finch (Scaly-feathered Weaver) *Sporopipes squamifrons* Baardmannetjie   page 397

Breeds in semi-arid and arid savanna, favouring areas with scattered, stunted thorn trees, especially second-growth and over-grazed bush. Pairs nest solitarily or semi-colonially (but not usually more than one active nest/tree). **Nest:** an untidy ball of dry, yellow grass placed well inside the thin branches of a dense thorny tree or bush; acacias and *Ziziphus mucronata* are commonly used; it is typically 1-2 m (0.9-4) up from the ground, built with dry grass-ends, each 150-250 mm long, that are curled around to form an enclosed ball, with a short, spout-like entrance formed by the soft inflorescences projecting outwards from one side of the nest. The nest interior (its walls and floor) is thickly lined with feathers (and guineafowl feathers are often used here). The nest measures: about 200 mm long (spout to back-wall, of which the spout is about 80 mm long); 110 mm high; 80-100 mm wide. The entrance, obscured by the fine grass-ends, is about 35 mm in diameter. Occasionally, an old weaver nest is used for breeding. Nests may be reused for successive broods, and they are used as night-time roosts when the birds are not breeding. Both sexes build the nest.

Laying months: mainly Jan-Apr, but all months recorded; breeds opportunistically in response to rainfall. **Clutch size:** 4 (2-5); rarely 6-10 when probably laid by >1 ♀). **Eggs:** 13.9-15.7-17.7 x 10.3-11.3-12.7 mm. **Incubation period:** 10-12 days. **Nestling/fledging period:** 16 days (14-18).

White-browed Sparrow-Weaver

Sociable Weaver

Sociable Weaver

Red-billed Buffalo Weaver

Scaly-feathered Finch

Sparrows

Cape Sparrow *Passer melanurus* Gewone Mossie
pages 379, 397

Breeds widely in the karoo, grassland and fynbos regions, marginally in semi-arid savanna; commonly nests in cities, towns, villages and around farmsteads. Pairs nest solitarily. occasionally semi-colonially (e.g. 5-15 nests/tree reported). **Nest:** an untidy ball of material usually placed in a tree or bush 1½-20 m up from the ground; in man-made environments it nests in hedges, in mesh-wire security fences, pergolas, creepers, drain-pipes against walls, telephone pole cross-bars, under the eaves of houses, in nest-boxes holes in walls and earth banks, and in closed swallow and weaver nests. It measures 250-300 mm across, has a side entrance that leads via a short tunnel into a nest bowl; built with long strands of coarse, dry grass, stems of weedy plants and, in man-modified habitats, with string, rags, cotton and other human debris. The cup is thickly lined with feathers, plant down and other soft materials pieces of aromatic plants are added to the nest lining, and it is suggested that this is done to repel parasites. Both sexes build, and nest maintenance continues year-round; the nest is reused for successive broods and as a year-round night-time roost.

Laying months: all months, but mainly Aug-Nov in winter-rainfall region, Sep-Feb in summer-rainfall areas; multi-brooded. **Clutch size:** 3-4 (2-6, rarely more when probably laid by >1 ♀); laid at 1-day intervals. **Eggs:** 16.5-19.7-22.4 × 13.2-14.3-15.8 mm parasitised by Diederik Cuckoo. **Incubation period:** 12-14 days; by both sexes. **Nestling/fledging period:** 17 days; young brooded and fed by both sexes.

House Sparrow *Passer domesticus* Huismossie
page 397

Breeds widely, virtually wherever there are permanent human settlements – in cities, towns, villages, around farmsteads and on offshore islands. Pairs nest solitarily or semi-colonially. **Nest:** placed in a cavity, typically under the eaves of a building, under a bridge, in a pipe, broken neon signboard, street-lamp, traffic lights, machinery; in an abandoned vehicle; in closed nests of swifts and swallows; rarely in a tree or tree cavity. It is an untidy ball of dry grass, weeds, roots and human debris (wool, string, rags, etc), with a side entrance; its size is dependent on space available. The nest-cup is lined with feathers and/or hair. Both sexes build and continue adding material during the incubation. Nests are reused for successive broods and often in successive years.

Laying months: mainly Sep-Nov (Aug-Dec, less often in other months); up to 4 broods/season. **Clutch size:** 4 (1-6); laid at 1-day intervals. **Eggs:** 19.0-21.5-24.0 × 13.6-15.2-19.7 mm. **Incubation period:** 13 days (11-14); by both sexes, but mostly ♀; begins before clutch is completed. **Nestling/fledging period:** 18 days (14-22); young are brooded and fed by both sexes.

Southern Grey-headed Sparrow *Passer diffusus* Gryskopmossie
page 397

Breeds widely, from the semi-arid west to the mesic east. Pairs nest solitarily and are widely spaced. **Nest:** placed in an enclosed hole of some sort, typically in a natural tree cavity or in an old barbet/woodpecker hole, 1-6 m up from the ground. Other frequently used sites include the enclosed nests of striped swallows and Little Swifts, holes under house eaves, hollow metal fence poles, nest boxes and buffalo weaver nests. The cavity is lined with feathers and pieces of dry grass and the nest-cup is often concealed by all the nest material brought to the site. Both sexes build, and sites are commonly reused for successive broods and in successive years (one site in recorded use for >20 years).

Laying months: mainly Nov-Mar (Sep-Jun, occasionally other months); usually double-brooded. **Clutch size:** 3-4 (2-6). **Eggs:** 17.0-19.2-21.3 × 13.1-14.3-15.2 mm; occasionally (2% of nests) parasitised by Diederik Cuckoo and Greater Honeyguide. **Incubation period:** 12½ days (11-14); by both sexes. **Nestling/fledging period:** 17 days (16-19); young brooded and fed by both sexes.

Northern Grey-headed Sparrow *Passer griseus* Witkeelmossie

A tropical species that narrowly enters southern Africa along the Zambezi River; not yet recorded breeding here. Elsewhere in its range it is monogamous, breeds in cavities, natural holes or woodpecker/barbet holes in trees, or in holes in walls, roofs, thatching in hollow metal pipes, or in nests built by swallows, kingfishers, bee-eaters or swifts; nesting data probably similar to previous species.

Yellow-throated Petronia *Gymnoris superciliaris* Geelvlekmossie
page 397

Breeds in mesic savanna. Pairs nest solitarily and are widely spaced. **Nest:** uses a natural cavity or old barbet/woodpecker hole in a tree; typically in a main stem, usually <200 mm deep and 1½-6 m up from the ground. Occasionally in a hollow metal fence-post or behind loose bark; once in an old waxbill sp. nest. Nest is built with grass, *Usnea* and feathers which often conceal the contents of the nest from view. The ♀ does most or all nest-building, accompanied by her mate, and she adds material through the incubation. Holes may be reused for successive broods and in successive years; some are used as night-time roosts when not breeding.

Laying months: mainly Sep-Nov (Aug-Mar); peaks earlier in Zimbabwe (Sep) than South Africa (Oct); sometimes double-brooded. **Clutch size:** 3-4 (2-5). **Eggs:** 16.9-18.7-20.8 × 12.8-14.2-15.9 mm; occasionally parasitised by Greater Honeyguide. **Incubation period:** 11½ days; by ♀ only. **Nestling/fledging period:** 17-19 days; young fed by both sexes.

Great Sparrow *Passer motitensis* Grootmossie
page 397

Breeds in semi-arid savanna. Pairs nest solitarily and are widely spaced. **Nest:** a large, untidy ball of dry grass with a spout-like side entrance, its lower lip extended to serve as a landing stage; placed 1½-7 m up from the ground in uppermost branches of a smallish, usually thorny, tree. It is made mostly with coarse, dry (straw-like) blades and stems of grass and the cup is thickly lined with feathers; green leaves are added before and during the incubation. It measures about 240 mm in height, 370 mm in length and 300 mm in width; the spout-like side entrance is 150-200 mm long and 60 mm in diameter, nests may or may not have a 'cock's nest' (a cup-like depression) between the entrance and the nest-bowl where the eggs are laid. Both sexes build the nest.

Laying months: Aug-Mar; but mainly Sep-Nov in east of range and Jan-Mar in Namibia. **Clutch size:** 4 (2-6). **Eggs:** 18.5-20.5-22.2 × 14.0-15.0-16.1 mm; occasionally parasitised by Diederik Cuckoo. **Incubation period:** 12-14 days; by both sexes. **Nestling/fledging period:** 15-18 days; young fed by both sexes.

Cape Sparrow | House Sparrow  | Northern Grey-headed Sparrow

using a woodpecker hole | Southern Grey-headed Sparrow | using a striped swallow nest

Yellow-throated Petronia | Great Sparrow

WEAVERS, BISHOPS, WIDOWBIRDS Family Ploceidae Worldwide 108 species; 95 breed in Afrotropics, 24 in southern Africa; well known for their striking, sexually dichromatic plumages (which change seasonally in ♂s), their nest-weaving skills and their polygynous mating systems. Within the family are 3 weaver genera (11 *Ploceus*, 1 *Amblyospiza*, 1 *Anaplectes*) that include in their ranks some of the supreme weavers of nests; all construct intricately woven, suspended structures with a downward-facing entrance (side-facing in 1), some with long tunnel extensions to the entrance. ♂s are polygynous in most species (but monogamous in 3) and they weave the nests and display from these to attract a ♀; the ♀ selects a nest, lines it with soft material, lays and incubates with little or no further ♂ involvement. Some species breed in large multi-♂ colonies, others are solitary. Nests of most weaver species are recognisable by their size differences, by their different architectures and by the materials used. Eggs are oval-shaped, white, blue, pink, unmarked in some species, variably speckled and blotched in others; the eggs in many species are exceptionally variably coloured and marked, possibly as a defence against cuckoo parasitism; 2-3/clutch; nestlings are altricial and nidicolous. Many species are commonly parasitised by Diederik Cuckoo.

Southern Masked Weaver *Ploceus velatus* Swartkeelgeelvink   2nd nest photo page 323   pages 379, 397

Breeds widely in fynbos, karoo, grassland and savanna, often close to human habitation. Nests mostly in single-♂ colonies, occasionally 2-9 ♂s/colony. ♂s are polygynous, pairing with 2-5 ♀s/season. **Nest:** weaver-type, mostly built in trees, 2-12 m up from the ground, in open country often favouring a lone-standing tree; less often in reedbeds, on fence or telephone wires; colonies are often over water. The ♂ strips foliage from the branches at the site and builds a succession of nests,10-25-52/season, displaying at these to visiting ♀s. The ♀ selects a nest, lines it, and while doing so the ♂ adds a narrow entrance-tunnel to the nest. Nests that do not get selected by ♀s are demolished by the ♂ and new nests are built in their place; a nest shell can be completed in a day, and the first egg can be laid within 3 days of the nest being built. The nest is woven from strips, 200-300 mm long, of green reed, palm or grass; it has an interior 'ceiling' of small leaves (e.g. leaves of wattle or acacia) and fine grass ends; the ♀ lines the cup with soft grass ends and feathers before laying. The nest measures: front-to-back (tunnel to chamber) 135-150 mm; in height (roof to base of chamber) 110-140 mm; in width 90 mm; the nest tunnel is usually 10-25 mm long and 30-40 mm wide. Nests are not reused but nesting sites are often reoccupied in successive years.
Laying months: mainly Sep-Jan (Jul-Mar) over most of its range, but Aug-Nov in sw Cape; urban birds start laying 1-2 months before rural birds. **Clutch size:** 2-3 (1-4, rarely 5 or 6); laid at 1-day intervals. **Eggs:** 18.4-20.9-24.5 x 13.0-14.5-19.6 mm; mass 2.0-2.6-3.0 g; very variable in ground-colour and markings; frequently (7% of nests) parasitised by Diederik Cuckoo – cuckoo eggs seldom match closely. **Incubation period:** 12-14 days; by ♀ only; leaves nest unattended for 40% of the day (ave. 7 min on, 5 min off). **Nestling/fledging period:** 16-17 days; young brooded by ♀, fed mostly or entirely by ♀.

Lesser Masked Weaver *Ploceus intermedius* Kleingeelvink   2nd nest photo page 323   page 397

Breeds in savanna, typically in hot, low-lying areas. Colonial, nesting in multiple-♂ colonies of 10-200 nests. ♂s are polygynous, a ♂ pairing with 2-3 ♀s. Breeds mostly in the upper branches of large trees, especially inside large, lone-standing acacias, less often in reedbeds or under house eaves; sometimes within larger colonies of Village Weavers. Each ♂ defends a portion of the colony, builds his nests here and displays to ♀s from these. **Nest:** easily distinguished from nests of other weavers by its small size, its well-developed tunnel (up to 120 mm long) and its distinctively spiky exterior, the result of short ends of woven material being left to protrude rather than being tucked in. It measures: 120-140 mm front-to-back (tunnel to chamber); 80-95 mm in height (roof to base of chamber); 70 mm in width. Unused nests are demolished and replaced. The nest-cup is lined by the ♀ with fine grass ends. Nests are not reused but sites are often reoccupied in successive years.
Laying months: mainly Oct-Jan (Aug-Mar). **Clutch size:** 2-3, rarely 4 or 5; laid at 1-day intervals. **Eggs:** 18.5-21.4-23.5 x 13.9-14.7-15.6 mm; egg colour unusual for a weaver – unmarked white; occasionally parasitised by Diederik Cuckoo. **Incubation period:** 13 days; by ♀ only; leaves nest unattended half the day. **Nestling/fledging period:** 15-16 days; young brooded by ♀, fed mostly by ♀.

Village Weaver *Ploceus cucullatus* Bontrugwewer   2nd nest photo page 323   page 397

Breeds in mesic savanna, mostly near water. A colonial breeder in multiple-♂ (10-300) colonies, sometimes alongside other weaver species (Cape, Yellow or Lesser Masked). ♂s are polygynous, pairing with 1-5 ♀s. Individual ♂s each occupy a section of the colony and build a succession of nests here, usually having 3-5 nests simultaneously, of which 1-2 may be occupied by ♀s at any one time. Nests are usually suspended from the highest branches of large trees 3-10 m up from the ground, usually overhanging water, less often in reedbeds over water. **Nest:** a large, roughly woven weaver-type nest, built by the ♂ from strips, 250-300 mm long, of reed, palm or grass leaves; the nest is thick-walled and has an interior 'ceiling' of sprigs of fine tree leaves; the ♂ builds a nest shell in 9-11-15 hr, using, on average, 384 strips of material for the walls and 326 leaves for the ceiling. He attempts to attract ♀s by displaying from these shells and ones that are not chosen are soon demolished and replaced with a new shell; the ♂ also strips the foliage from the branches around his nests. Once a ♀ has selected a nest, she lines the cup with soft grass-ends (and sometimes a few feathers) before laying; during this period the ♂ adds a short, narrow entrance tunnel to the nest. The nest measures: 130-155-175 mm front-to-back (tunnel to chamber); 130 mm in height (roof to base of chamber); 90-100 mm in width; the nest tunnel is usually about 30 mm long and 35-45 mm in diameter. Nests are not reused and many discarded nests accumulate on the ground below the colony as a result of the continuous replacement of unsuccessful nests. Some breeding sites are reused year after year, whereas other sites are used once and not again.
Laying months: mainly Sep-Feb (Aug-Apr). **Clutch size:** 2-3 (2-5); laid at 1-day intervals. **Eggs:** 20.5-23.1-25.1 x 13.4-14.9-16.9 mm; mass 1.5 g; eggs are very variable in both ground-colour and markings; occasionally (3% of nests) parasitised by Diederik Cuckoo. **Incubation period:** 12 days; by ♀ only, frequently leaving nest unattended (ave. 8 mins on, 9 mins off). **Nestling/fledging period:** 17-21 days; young brooded by ♀, fed by both sexes (but mostly ♀).

Dark-backed Weaver

Spectacled Weaver

Village Weaver

Chestnut Weaver

Cape Weaver

Southern Masked Weaver

Lesser Masked Weaver

Yellow Weaver

Southern Brown-throated Weaver

Golden Weaver

Red-headed Weaver

Cape Weaver *Ploceus capensis* Kaapse Wewer nest photo on page 321 page 398

Breeds in fynbos, grassland and fringes of karoo, commonly in farmland. Breeds colonially, 2-20 ♂s/colony, sometimes alongside other weaver species. ♂s are polygynous, a ♂ pairing with 1-7 ♀s. **Nest:** weaver-type, but larger than those of other weavers, densely woven with a neat finish; usually built in tall trees, often eucalypts, or willows overhanging water, less often in reedbeds; occasionally on fence- or telephone-wires crossing streams; 1-10 m up. Each ♂ defends a portion of the colony and builds multiple nests here, displaying to visiting ♀s from these; the nest selected by the ♀ is lined by her while he adds a narrow entrance tunnel. Nests not selected are demolished and replaced; the ♂ also strips the foliage from the branches around his nests. The nest measures: 170 mm front-to-back (tunnel to chamber); 120 mm in height (roof to base of chamber); 110 mm in width; entrance tunnel about 20-30 mm long. Nests are not reused but breeding sites are commonly reoccupied in successive years.
Laying months: mainly Aug-Oct (Jul-Nov) in winter-rainfall region; Oct-Dec (Aug-Jan) elsewhere. **Clutch size:** 2-3 (2-5); laid at 1-day intervals. **Eggs:** 22.5-25.0-26.7 x 15.7-16.6-17.1 mm; mass 3.6 g; unmarked turquoise blue, some having zones of deeper colouring; commonly parasitised by Diederik Cuckoo. **Incubation period:** 13-14 days; by ♀ only; she frequently leaves the nest unattended (ave. 11 min on, 6 min off). **Nestling/fledging period:** 17 days; young brooded by ♀, fed by both sexes, mostly ♀.

Yellow Weaver (Eastern Golden Weaver) *Ploceus subaureus* Geelwewer nest photo on page 321 page 398

Breeds along e coastal plain, typically in reedbeds bordering rivers, estuaries, lakes, floodplains. Breeds in multi-♂ colonies, 2-20 ♂s/colony and 10-50 nests/colony; often alongside other nesting weavers. ♂s are polygynous. **Nest:** weaver-type, like nest of Southern Masked Weaver but lacks a tunnel extension; typically attached to a single reed-stem, 1½-2½ m above water, often near the reed's extremity where it leans out over open water. Less often, suspended from a drooping branch of tree or palm up to 12 m from the ground. ♂s build a succession of nests, demolishing and replacing those not used; foliage around the nest (in both reeds and trees) is stripped. The nest measures: front-to-back (tunnel to chamber) 165-170 mm; height (roof to base of chamber) 110-115 mm; entrance is 35 mm wide. Nests are not reused but breeding sites are commonly reoccupied in successive years.
Laying months: mainly Sep-Dec (Sep-Feb). **Clutch size:** 2-3, rarely 4. **Eggs:** 21.0-23.0-26.0 x 14.1-15.1-16.3 mm; variable in ground-colour and markings; occasionally parasitised by Diederik Cuckoo. **Incubation period:** not recorded; by ♀ only. **Nestling/fledging period:** 19-22 days (in captivity).

Golden Weaver (Holub's Golden Weaver) *Ploceus xanthops* Goudwewer nest photo on page 321 page 398

Breeds in mesic savanna, mostly in marshy places and along streams and rivers. ♂s usually nest solitarily, having 1-5 nests simultaneously, of which only one is occupied at a time by a ♀; ♂ can be monogamous or polygynous; occasionally 2-3 ♂s breed together. **Nest:** weaver-type, distinctively coarsely woven and with an unusual entrance that lacks an extended tunnel, but is fringed by flowery grass heads that project untidily around the entrance. It is usually suspended from a twig over water, 1-3 m (0.6-6) up; sometimes built on a reed-stem. The ♀ lines the cup with the same soft grasses that project from the entrance. The nest measures: front-to-back (tunnel to chamber) 170-200 mm; in height (roof to base of chamber) 110-150 mm; the entrance hole is about 45 mm in width.
Laying months: mainly Oct-Feb (Sep-Mar, occasionally in other months); breeding season is more extended in Zimbabwe than South Africa; probably double-brooded. **Clutch size:** 2 (1-3). **Eggs:** 22.2-24.1-25.5 x 15.3-16.2-17.3 mm; occasionally parasitised by Diederik Cuckoo; eggs are variable in both ground-colour and markings. **Incubation period:** 14-15 days; by ♀ only. **Nestling/fledging period:** 19-21 days; young fed by both sexes but mostly by ♀.

Southern Brown-throated Weaver *Ploceus xanthopterus* Bruinkeelwewer nest photo on page 321 page 398

Breeds in tropical and subtropical wetlands, typically in reedbeds or papyrus over water, rarely in trees overhanging water. ♂s are polygynous, pairing with 2-3 ♀s; mostly in single-♂ colonies, ♂ building up to 12 nests/season; occasionally in multi-♂ colonies, up to 300 nests/colony. **Nest:** weaver-type, smallish and tightly woven from coarse (2-8 mm wide), green strips of reed with a rough finish; entrance is distinctive – it has no entrance tunnel, instead is cut back so that its rim is level with the lip of the nest-cup, above the level of the base of the nest-bowl. The cup is lined with soft grass ends. The nest measures: front-to-back (tunnel to chamber) 150 mm; height (roof to base of chamber) 130 mm; the entrance has a width of about 25 x 35 mm.
Laying months: Oct-Feb. **Clutch size:** 2-3. **Eggs:** 19.1-21.0-23.0 x 13.9-14.5-15.0 mm; very variable in ground-colour and markings; the common egg types (dark brown and olive-green) are unlike those of any other weaver in the region. **Incubation period:** 14-16 days; by ♀ only. **Nestling/fledging period:** 14-17 days; young brooded and fed by ♀ only.

Chestnut Weaver *Ploceus rubiginosus* Bruinwewer nest photo on page 321 page 398

Breeds in arid savanna in n Namibia. Colonial, nesting in multi-♂ colonies of 10-200 nests. Breeds sporadically in response to rainfall, nesting widely and abundantly in wet summers, but largely absent in dry summers. **Nest:** weaver-type, very distinctive, roughly woven from straw-like lengths of grass, the ends of which protrude to give the nest a shaggy appearance; it is thick-walled and strongly built, usually 2-8 m up from the ground. Colonies are placed in the outside branches of trees, usually acacias, away from water; colonies are conspicuous, especially once the nests have faded from their fresh green colour to a straw-yellow. The nest measures: 150-160-210 mm front-to-back (tunnel to chamber); 120-150-180 mm in height (roof to base of chamber); tunnel entrance (faces vertically downwards) is 30-60-100 mm long. ♂s build the nests and display at these to attract ♀s. The ♀ lines the selected nest, lays, incubates and rears chicks without further ♂ involvement; ♂s abandon the colony before the breeding cycle is completed.
Laying months: mainly Jan-Mar (Dec-May); erratic and opportunistic in response to rainfall. **Clutch size:** 3 (1-6). **Eggs:** 21.5-22.8-24.5 x 14.5-15.7-16.8 mm; mass 2.0-2.6-3.1 g; eggs unmarked, either plain white or turquoise to greenish-blue. **Incubation period:** 11-14 days; by ♀ only. **Nestling/fledging period:** 13-16 days; young brooded and fed by ♀.

Lesser Masked Weaver

Village Weaver

Chestnut Weaver

Yellow Weaver

Southern Masked Weaver

Thick-billed Weaver *Amblyospiza albifrons* Dikbekwewer   page 398

Breeds in reeds, bulrushes or papyrus over water. Polygynous, nesting in colonies, from a single ♂ with one active nest to multi-♂ colonies with >50 nests. **Nest:** distinctive in shape and finish; it is oval-shaped, built between two vertical stems, an entrance on the side; it is densely woven with fine strands of shredded (usually) *Typha* leaf, giving the walls a smooth texture, placed 1-2 m up from the water. New nests are green but soon fade to brown. They measure 165-200 mm high, 100-130 mm wide; nests initially have a wide entrance, 60 x 80 mm across, but this is narrowed by the ♂ to 25-32 mm when a ♀ takes occupation. ♂s break off the stems of reeds growing close to the nests; a succession of nests are built, each taking 2-12 days to complete; many are never used. Sites are commonly reoccupied in successive years, some in known use for decades.
Laying months: Oct-Mar; but mainly Nov-Jan in e, Jan-Mar in w (n Namibia and n Botswana). **Clutch size:** 3 (2-4); laid at 1-day intervals. **Eggs:** 21.1-23.6-26.4 x 15.1-16.2-17.4 mm; mass 2.3-2.7-3.1 g; white or pink, variably marked. **Incubation period:** 15 days (14-16); by ♀ only; begins when clutch complete. **Nestling/fledging period:** 20 days (19-22); brooded and fed by ♀.

Spectacled Weaver *Ploceus ocularis* Brilwewer   nest photo on page 321   pages 379, 398

Breeds in mesic savanna and riparian, coastal and lowland forest. Monogamous, pairs nesting solitarily and widely spaced. **Nest:** weaver-type, but easily recognised by its long tunnel-entrance and very fine weave; it is thin-walled, often transparent, woven from thin lengths of fine grass, leaves of palm or other pliable plant material; occasional nests recorded built of fishing line and horse hair. It is suspended from a twig or creeper, 3-6 m (1½-9) up from the ground, often overhanging a pond, stream or dry gully; the cup is lined with fine plant material which continues to be added during the incubation. It measures: 120 mm front-to-back (tunnel to chamber); 150 mm high (roof to base of chamber); 80 mm wide; tunnel 150-200 mm long (rarely ½-1 m), 45 mm in diameter. It is built mainly or entirely by ♂ in 2-3 weeks; the tunnel may be extended during the incubation. A new nest is built each season, usually close to previous year's nest, even attached to the same twig. Foliage is stripped from the branches surrounding the nest.
Laying months: mainly Oct-Dec (Sep-Mar), peaking earlier in s (Nov) than n (Dec). **Clutch size:** 3 (2-4); laid at 1-day intervals. **Eggs:** 19.0-21.9-23.6 x 13.5-14.8-16.5 mm; mass 1.4-1.7 g; eggs variable in colour and markings; parasitised by Diederik Cuckoo. **Incubation period:** 13-14 days; by both sexes, in ½ hr shifts. **Nestling/fledging period:** 15-19 days; young fed by both sexes.

Dark-backed Weaver *Ploceus bicolor* Bosmusikant   2nd nest photo on page 321   page 398

Breeds in coastal, lowland and riparian forest. Monogamous, pairs nesting solitarily and widely spaced. **Nest:** weaver-type, but easily recognisable by the material used (pliable roots of epiphytes, tendrils from *Asparagus* sp., or fine stems of vines and creepers) and angled entrance-tunnel (about 25° off vertical); nests are green-coloured when new, fading to dark brown. A single nest is built, suspended from a trailing branch or creeper above a clearing, often over a road, path or streambed, 4-6 m (2-15) up from the ground. The exterior is roughly finished with loose ends and loops of material protruding in all directions, the cup is commonly lined with *Usnea*. Both sexes build the nest, completing it in 7-9 days. The nest measures: 165 mm front-to-back (tunnel to chamber); 125 mm in height (roof to base of chamber); 100-110 mm in width; the nest tunnel is usually about 80-100 mm long (up to 330 recorded). A new nest is built each season, usually close to a previous year's nest. Nests are not reused, nor are they pulled down.
Laying months: mainly Nov-Dec (Sep-Feb). **Clutch size:** 3 (2-4). **Eggs:** 20.9-22.7-25.4 x 14.0-15.4-16.6 mm; eggs variably coloured and marked. **Incubation period:** 15-17 days (in captivity). **Nestling/fledging period:** 22 days (in captivity); fed by both sexes.

Red-headed Weaver *Anaplectes melanotis* Rooikopwewer   2nd nest photo on page 321   page 398

Breeds in mesic savanna. Monogamous or polygynous. Pairs or trios usually nest solitarily, building 2-3 nests/season; occasionally in multi-♂ colonies of up to 40 nests. **Nest:** weaver-type, easily distinguished by the material used, the way it is woven, and its long entrance tunnel. It is made from long, pliable pieces of thin, green twig (e.g. *Grewia* sp.) or leaf petioles which are attached at one end, the other left hanging free, giving the nest a dishevelled look, its exterior made up of long, loosely hanging twigs. Twig-ends are attached by stripping loose a section of bark on the twig and using this to tie the twig to other twigs. Nests are built in trees 2-10 m up from the ground; often in large baobabs, commonly alongside Red-billed Buffalo Weaver nests, and sometimes alongside an active eagle nest; also nests on telephone- and electricity-lines, on windmill towers and under house eaves; often close to human habitation. The nest measures: front-to-back (tunnel to chamber) 160-180 mm; height (roof to base of chamber) 140-180 mm; entrance tunnel 150-200 mm long, with inside diameter 60-70 mm. It is built by the ♂, taking 2-3 weeks to complete. Sites are frequently reused in successive years, the new nest often alongside nests built in previous years.
Laying months: Aug-Jan, peaking earlier in n (Sep-Nov) than elsewhere (Oct-Jan). **Clutch size:** 2-3 (1-4); laid at 2-day intervals. **Eggs:** 18.7-20.4-21.9 x 12.9-14.0-14.9 mm; blue, unmarked; occasionally parasitised by Diederik Cuckoo. **Incubation period:** 12-13 days; by both sexes, mostly ♀; nest unattended 40% of day. **Nestling/fledging period:** 17 days (in captivity); young fed by both sexes but mostly by ♀.

Olive-headed Weaver *Ploceus olivaceiceps* Olyfkopwewer

Breeds in *Usnea*-draped, tall miombo woodland in c Mozambique. Nesting habits are poorly known. Monogamous, pairs nesting solitarily and widely spaced. **Nest:** weaver-type, thick-walled and unique in the region for being built entirely with *Usnea*; it is placed 8-18 m up from the ground in the canopy of a *Brachystegia* sp., suspended from an *Usnea*-festooned branch where it blends into its background. The pair builds a single nest/season. The nest measures: 175 mm front-to-back (tunnel to chamber); 125 mm in height (roof to base of chamber); the down-pointing entrance tunnel may be short or up to 140 mm in length.
Laying months: Aug-Oct (Mozambique). **Clutch size:** 2-3 (Malawi). **Eggs:** 20 x 15 mm; (not illustrated) eggs are unmarked and bright turquoise, slightly glossy (Malawi). **Incubation period:** not recorded; by both sexes, mostly ♀; in 30-50 min shifts. **Nestling/fledging period:** not recorded; young fed by both sexes.

Thick-billed Weaver typical breeding site in *Typha* bulrushes; male building (below left), completed nest (below centre)

Thick-billed Weaver

Dark-backed Weaver

Red-headed Weaver

Olive-headed Weaver

Queleas, Bishops

WEAVERS, BISHOPS, WIDOWBIRDS Family Ploceidae The 5 queleas and bishops below form a distinct group of this diverse family; all but the first one are polygynous; some breed in large, multi-♂ colonies, others in single-♂ polygynous groups; all make a roughly woven oval nest of grass with a side entrance and projecting hood (a 'bishop-type nest'); ♂ builds nest, ♀ lines it and undertakes most/all parental care without ♂ assistance; eggs oval, unmarked blue in some, white or blue with speckles in others, 2-4/clutch; nestlings are altricial and nidicolous; one is commonly parasitised by Diederik Cuckoo, others occasionally.

Red-billed Quelea   *Quelea quelea*   Rooibekkwelea   page 398

Breeds mainly in semi-arid savanna, but breeding range has expanded widely since 1960s into small-grain farming areas in grassland and karoo. Has a remarkable breeding cycle, nesting erratically in vast colonies from 10s of 1000s to millions of birds (average is about 300000 nests/colony); breeding is highly synchronised and rapidly completed. Monogamous, sexes share parental roles. Breeds mostly in trees, especially in thorny acacias; such colonies extend over 1-13-80 ha, each tree supporting 50-3000 nests. **Nest:** bishop-type, woven from 600-700 grass strips; has a 'knobbly' texture from numerous fine loops and grass ends left protruding from the walls; placed inside trees, not at edges, 1½-6 m up from the ground; occasionally nests in reedbeds, eucalypts, poplars, even in growing maize. The nest measures: height 90-122-130 mm; width 80-95-100 mm; entrance diameter 40-60 mm. Colonies are rapidly established, ♂s completing nests in 2-3 days, the first egg is laid as soon as nest can support it; hatching commences 15-17 days after the colony's initiation, and the last nestlings fledge, and the colony is abandoned, 35-41 days after nest-building started.
Laying months: mainly Jan-Mar (Nov-Apr); single-brooded (South Africa); breeds erratically in response to rainfall. **Clutch size:** 3 (1-4, rarely 5); laid at 1-day intervals. **Eggs:** 16.1-18.3-21.0 × 11.3-13.2-14.8 mm; plain blue, rarely finely spotted with light brown. **Incubation period:** 10-12 days; begins before clutch is completed; shared equally by both sexes, with frequent change-overs; eggs covered 50-60% of day. **Nestling/fledging period:** young leave nest at 10-13 days; fly 12-14 days; independent at 20-21 days; brooded and fed by both sexes.

Red-headed Quelea   *Quelea erythrops*   Rooikopkwelea   page 398

Breeds erratically and patchily in the region in *Phragmites* reedbeds over water. Colonial, numbering 10-10000 nests/colony; breeding cycle synchronised and rapidly completed. ♂s are probably polygynous, a ♂ paired with 4-5 ♀s. **Nest:** a small, tightly woven bishop-type nest attached to vertical reed-stems ½-3 m up; has the same 'knobbly' texture as the nest of a Red-billed Quelea, distinguishing it from the smooth-surfaced nest of a Southern Red Bishop; it is smaller and narrower than a Red-billed Quelea nest. It measures: 90-110 mm in height; 78-90 mm wide (front to back); 50-58 mm wide (sideways); the entrance diameter is 20 mm high, 30-45 mm wide. ♂ builds, completing a nest in 3 days; it is not lined. Colonies are seldom in the same place in successive years; colonies may be started and aborted before egg-laying.
Laying months: Nov-Mar. **Clutch size:** 2 (1-3, rarely 4). **Eggs:** 17.7-19.4-21.9 × 12.6-13.5-14.4 mm. **Incubation period:** 13 days; by ♀ only; eggs left unattended for long periods. **Nestling/fledging period:** 12-14 days; young fed by both sexes.

Yellow-crowned Bishop (Golden Bishop)   *Euplectes afer*   Goudgeelvink   page 398

Breeds in grassland and savanna in rank grass or sedges over damp or temporarily flooded ground; polygynous, non-colonial, each ♂ building 2-3 nests, 5-15 m apart to attract mates. **Nest:** bishop-type, thin-walled, often transparent, woven into standing grass or sedge, 0.15-0.40 m (rarely to 0.7 m) up; a high proportion face sw. The nest measures: height 140 mm; width (front-to-back) 75 mm; width (across front) 69 mm; entrance diameter 50 mm. ♀ may participate in weaving and she adds a lining of soft grass inflorescences to the cup, continuing this through the incubation.
Laying months: mainly Jan-Feb (Dec-Mar, rarely Nov, Apr, May); relays after an earlier failure. **Clutch size:** 3 (2-4, rarely 6 or 7 when probably laid by >1 ♀); laid at 1-day intervals. **Eggs:** 16.2-17.9-21.7 × 11.9-12.8-13.6 mm; mass 1.4 g. **Incubation period:** 12-14 days (in captivity); by ♀ only. **Nestling/fledging period:** 11-13 days (in captivity); young fed by ♀ only.

Southern Red Bishop   *Euplectes orix*   Rooivink   pages 379, 398

Breeds widely in fynbos, grassland, savanna and karoo; common in agricultural areas; ♂s are polygynous; some nest solitarily, others in multi-♂ (2-20) colonies, ♂ territories in these can be 8 m². Typically nests in reedbeds over water; occasionally in sapling trees, rank grass, sedges or (rarely) in standing maize. **Nest:** bishop-type, loosely woven with shreds of reed leaf or grass blades, usually semi-transparent; built between upright stems, 1-2½ m up. Nests are not concealed but they are built in the tallest reeds available and are placed as far from the edges as possible. The nest measures: height 108-123-140 mm; width (front-to-back) 60-73-83 mm; width (across front) 60-78-97 mm; entrance width 37-56-65 mm; the entrance hood protrudes 27-39-55 mm. ♂ builds 3-8-13 nests/season, each takes 1-3 days; acquires up to 7 partners/season. Sites are commonly reused in successive years.
Laying months: a summer breeder (Aug-Mar), but season varies regionally: earliest in sw Cape (mainly Aug-Oct), latest in Zimbabwe (mainly Dec-Feb), and mainly Nov-Jan in between. **Clutch size:** 3 (1-5); laid at 1-day intervals. **Eggs:** 14.6-19.2-21.6 × 11.8-14.1-15.7 mm; mass 1.73 g; unmarked blue; commonly parasitised by Diederik Cuckoo which also lays an unmarked blue egg in its nest (its egg is more pointed, less glossy than bishop egg). **Incubation period:** 12-13 days; by ♀ only; eggs unattended for 60% of day. **Nestling/fledging period:** 14 days (11-15); young brooded and fed by ♀ only.

Black-winged Bishop   *Euplectes hordeaceus*   Vuurkopvink   no nest photo   page 398

Breeds in lowlands in c Mozambique and adjacent Zimbabwe in areas of rank grass and weeds along drainage lines and in slash-and-burn agriculture. ♂s polygynous, but do not nest in multi-♂ colonies. **Nest:** bishop-type, like that of Southern Red Bishop, 1½-3 m up in rank grass, weeds, reeds or in standing maize; usually over dry ground. ♂ builds 2-4 scattered nests.
Laying months: mainly Feb-Mar (Dec-Apr). **Clutch size:** 3 (2-4). **Eggs:** 17.4-18.6-19.9 × 12.9-13.9-14.4 mm; unmarked blue, some sparsely speckled with liver-brown; occasionally parasitised by Diederik Cuckoo. **Incubation period:** 12-13 days (in captivity); by ♀ only. **Nestling/fledging period:** 11-13 days; young fed by ♀ only.

Red-billed Quelea

Red-headed Quelea

Golden Bishop

Southern Red Bishop

Yellow-rumped Widowbird

Widowbirds

WEAVERS, BISHOPS, WIDOWBIRDS Family Ploceidae Six widowbirds breed in southern Africa; all are polygynous, non-colonial nesters; males defend territories, build multiple nest shells, breed with 1-5 ♀s; nest oval-shaped with a hooded side-entrance and domed roof (this is the 'widowbird-type' nest), made partly from woven-in supporting grass stems; thicker-walled and more substantial than bishop-type nest, placed low down, well hidden, in grass or low shrub; ♀s line the nest, incubate without male assistance; eggs oval; grey or blue, densely speckled; 3-4/clutch; nestlings are altricial and nidicolous; some occasionally parasitised by Diederik Cuckoo.

Yellow-rumped Widowbird (Yellow Bishop) *Euplectes capensis* Kaapse Flap nest photos on page 327   page 398

Breeds in fynbos, grassland, mesic savanna, in rank grass and weeds, often along streams, seepages, forest edges. Males territorial; he builds 2 or more nests usually >25 m apart; mates with 1-4 ♀s/season. **Nest:** widowbird-type, well-hidden in low shrubby growth, placed about ½ m (0.2-1.7) up, over dry, damp or wet ground. It measures: height 130-180 mm; width 130 mm. Those in the winter-rainfall region (race *E. c. capensis*) are much less substantially built than those further north.
Laying months: Aug-Mar, mainly Aug-Oct in winter-rainfall region, Nov-Mar elsewhere; often double-brooded. **Clutch size:** 3 (2-4); laid at 1-day intervals. **Eggs:** 19.9-21.3-23.4 × 14.0-15.0-16.0 mm in sw Cape; smaller (ave 19.6 × 13.9 mm) elsewhere. **Incubation period:** 13-14 days; by ♀ only. **Nestling/fledging period:** 14-15 days; young fed by both sexes, but mostly by ♀.

Fan-tailed Widowbird *Euplectes axillaris* Kortstertflap   page 398

Breeds in mesic grassland and on fringes of tropical wetlands. Male defends a small (0.6 ha) territory, building 1-8 nests/season, these spaced 4-50 m apart. **Nest:** widowbird-type, well-hidden, 0.1-0.2-0.6 m up in dense, shortish grass, *Carex* sedge, *Polyganum* or low shrubs; It measures: height 139 mm; width (front-to-back) 76 mm; width (across front) 64 mm; entrance diameter 51 mm. Easily mistaken for nest of Long-tailed Widowbird but latter is thicker-walled (12 mm vs. 6 mm) and egg markings differ.
Laying months: mainly Nov-Jan (Sep-Mar). **Clutch size:** 3 (2-4); laid at 1-day intervals. **Eggs:** 17.7-19.7-22.4 × 13.3-14.1-15.0 mm; eggs are easily distinguished from those of Long-tailed Widowbird by colour and markings (see page 398). **Incubation period:** 12-13 days; by ♀ only. **Nestling/fledging period:** 15-16 days; young brooded and fed by ♀ only.

Yellow-mantled Widowbird *Euplectes macrourus* Geelrugflap   page 398

Breeds in n mesic savanna in seasonally wet dambos. Males defend a territory of 0.2-1.0-2.7 ha, build 1-27 nest shells/season. **Nest:** widow-bird-type, but lacks a hood; built in shortish (<1 m tall), dense grass, typically 0.4 m (0.15-0.6) up from the ground, usually over damp ground; not camouflaged, but it is concealed by surrounding grass. It measures: outside diameter 90 mm; height 140 mm; entrance diameter 45 mm.
Laying months: mainly Jan (Dec-Mar). **Clutch size:** 2-3, rarely 1. **Eggs:** 16.6-18.9-21.0 × 13.0-13.8-14.2 mm. **Incubation period:** 12-14 days (in captivity); by ♀ only. **Nestling/fledging period:** 15 days (in captivity); young brooded and fed by ♀ only.

Red-collared Widowbird *Euplectes ardens* Rooikeelflap   page 398

Breeds in mesic grassland and savanna, typically in rank grassy areas in hilly country. Males defend small (0.75 ha) territories and build in them several nest shells, 3-50 m apart; mates with 2-3 ♀s/season. **Nest:** widow-bird-type, with a long (45-90 mm) projecting hood; usually 0.5-0.6 m (0.3-2) up from the ground (i.e. higher than nests of other widowbirds), placed in long, thick grass, sometimes in bracken, a shrub or low bush. The nest measures: height 90-100 mm; width 80 mm; entrance diameter 45 mm.
Laying months: Sep-Apr, peaking in Nov-Jan in South Africa, later (Jan-Feb) in Zimbabwe. **Clutch size:** 3 (2-4, rarely more); laid at 1-day intervals. **Eggs:** 17.1-18.9-21.5 × 12.8-13.6-14.6 mm; occasionally parasitised by Diederik Cuckoo. **Incubation period:** 12-15 days; by ♀ only. **Nestling/fledging period:** 14-17 days; young brooded and fed by ♀ only.

White-winged Widowbird *Euplectes albonotatus* Witvlerkflap   page 398

Breeds in mesic savanna and grassland, in tall grass or rank weed growth; often in second-growth, old lands, marshes, along drainage lines. Male defends a small (0.1-0.2 ha) territory, these spaced 50-100 m apart; builds 2 or more nests, 10-25 m apart, mates with 1-4 ♀s/season. **Nest:** widowbird-type, typically ½-1 m (0.3-1.3) up from dry or damp ground, placed in upright stems of tall, thick grass, not camouflaged, but usually concealed by surrounding grass. Nest measures: height 120-140 mm; width (front-to-back) 85 mm; width (across front) 70-75 mm; entrance diameter 40-45 mm; ♀ continues adding lining through the incubation.
Laying months: Nov-Apr (rarely Oct, May); peaking Dec-Feb in south, Jan-Mar further north. **Clutch size:** 2-3, rarely 4; laid at 1-day intervals. **Eggs:** 15.6-18.5-20.0 × 12.1-13.6-14.2 mm; occasionally parasitised by Diederik Cuckoo. **Incubation period:** 12-13 days; by ♀ only. **Nestling/fledging period:** 12 days (11-14); young brooded and fed by ♀ only.

Long-tailed Widowbird *Euplectes progne* Langstertflap   page 398

Breeds in open grassland. Males defend a territory of ½-3 ha, are spaced 50-150 m apart; they build several rudimentary nests ('bowers'), most >25 m apart, to attract ♀s which complete, and line, the nest; 1-5 ♀s/season. **Nest:** widow-bird-type, but lacks a projecting hood, placed close to the ground (mostly 100-200 mm up) in short (300-500 mm), dense grass; usually well hidden; often, but not invariably over damp or wet ground. Nest is thick-walled (12-15 mm) and this (and egg markings) distinguish it from nest of Fan-tailed Widowbirds where they occur together. ♀ continues lining nest through the incubation.
Laying months: mainly Nov-Feb (Sep-Mar), peaking earlier (Oct-Nov) in e Cape. **Clutch size:** 3 (1-4); laid at 1-day intervals. **Eggs:** 19.0-21.6-23.7 × 14.6-15.7-16.6 mm; occasionally parasitised by Diederik Cuckoo. **Incubation period:** 12-14 days; by ♀ only. **Nestling/fledging period:** 15-17 days; young brooded and fed by ♀ only.

Fan-tailed Widowbird

Yellow-mantled Widowbird

Red-collared Widowbird

White-winged Widowbird

Long-tailed Widowbird

Pytilias, Finches

WAXBILLS AND OTHER SMALL FINCHES Estrildidae Worldwide 140 species; 77 breed in Afrotropics, 27 in southern Africa. A group of small finches that includes waxbills, firefinches, mannikins, twinspots, often collectively known as 'estrildids'. Estrildids are popular aviary birds and their nesting habits are mostly known from aviary studies. All are monogamous, most nest solitarily, some are occasionally semi-colonial; the sexes share nest-building, incubation and nestling care. Nest is a closed ball with a side entrance ('retort-shaped'); its size, shape, placement and materials used varies between species (e.g. savanna species use grass, forest species use *Usnea*); some place their nest alongside an active wasp nest; several (at least 7 species) seldom build their own nest, but instead use old nests of weavers, bishops, widowbirds. Eggs oval, unmarked white, 3-6/clutch; nestlings are altricial and nidicolous; nestling's faeces are not removed so nests soon become fouled. At least half the region's estrildids are parasitised by whydahs and indigobirds.

Orange-winged Pytilia *Pytilia afra* Oranjevlerkmelba   page 399

Breeds in n mesic savanna in broad-leafed woodland, especially in areas of shrubby second-growth interspersed with rank grass. Nesting habits are poorly known. **Nest:** a round ball with a wide side entrance, placed in a shrubby tree or bush 1½-3 m up from the ground; similar to that built by Green-winged Pytilia, made with long stems of grass and weeds loosely curled around into a sphere. The interior is lined with feathers.
Laying months: Feb-Apr (Zimbabwe). **Clutch size:** 4 (2-5). **Eggs:** 15.5-16.3-17.9 x 11.7-12.5-13.4 mm; parasitised by Broad-tailed Paradise Whydah, the whydah's egg distinguishable by its larger size (18.1 x 13.3 mm). **Incubation period:** 12-13 days; by both sexes. **Nestling/fledging period:** 21 days (19-22); young fed by both sexes.

Green-winged Pytilia *Pytilia melba* Gewone Melba   page 399

Breeds in the savanna region, mainly in semi-arid thornveld, favouring areas with dense, low, acacia thickets. Pairs nest solitarily and are widely spaced (but once, adjacent nests were 9 m apart). **Nest:** a round ball of grass with a side entrance placed loosely between numerous supporting twigs in a low shrubby tree or sapling, especially an acacia (*Acacia tortilis* is much favoured) and often one with long grass intergrown through it; typically 1-1½ m (½-3½) up from the ground; often well hidden in foliage, or in a cluster of dead, hanging branches. The nest is not woven into the site or woven together, but is formed by curling long (200-300 mm), green, grass inflorescences into a sphere; stems of *Panicum* and *Tricholaena* are commonly used, their soft ends forming the interior. A characteristic of Green-winged Pytilia nests is their use of a few coarse grass blades to form an outside cladding to the nest. The entrance does not have an extended neck, and it may be obscured by projecting grasses. The interior is lined with feathers. It measures: height 130-140 mm; width (front-to-back) 100-130 mm; width (across front) 100-106 mm; entrance diameter 30-50 mm. Grass and feathers continue to be added during the incubation; the ♂ takes a greater share in building. Nests become fouled with droppings and are not reused.
Laying months: mainly Jan-May, but all months recorded, sometimes laying in response to rainfall, irrespective of season. **Clutch size:** 4-5 (2-6); laid at 1-day intervals. **Eggs:** 15.2-16.3-17.7 x 11.7-12.5-13.4 mm; parasitised by Long-tailed Paradise Whydah, the whydah's egg distinguishable by its larger size (18.8 x 13.8 mm). **Incubation period:** 12½ days (12-14); begins before clutch is completed; by both sexes, alternating in shifts of 1½-2 hrs. **Nestling/fledging period:** 19 days (18-21); young brooded and fed by both sexes.

Cut-throat Finch *Amadina fasciata* Bandkeelvink   page 399

Breeds widely across the savanna belt. A monogamous breeder, pairs nesting solitarily or in small, loosely associated groups; when sharing a weaver colony, adjacent pairs may occupy nests 2-3 m apart. **Nest:** almost invariably uses the nest of another bird, building a cup (about 50 mm wide) of fine grass ends and feathers inside the host nest. Sites used vary greatly, but nests of weavers (especially Southern Masked, Lesser Masked, Red-headed and Red-billed Buffalo Weaver) are particularly favoured, and in colonies of these, several pairs may nest semi-colonially; has also been recorded nesting in holes beneath the eaves of buildings, in a woodpecker hole in a tree, a hollow metal fence post and in a Lesser Striped Swallow nest. Both sexes bring lining material to the nest and they share the incubation and nestling care. They are unobtrusive while nesting and easily overlooked; change-overs are infrequent, and the incubating bird sits tightly and is not easily flushed. The nestlings, however, are vociferous when being fed by their parents and often give themselves away by their noisy begging. Both sexes roost in nest at night during the incubation.
Laying months: mainly Feb-Apr (Dec-Aug, occasionally in other months). **Clutch size:** 4 (2-7; larger clutches probably laid by >1 ♀). **Eggs:** 16.0-17.0-18.0 x 12.3-13.0-14.6 mm. **Incubation period:** 12-13 days; by both sexes. **Nestling/fledging period:** 21-23 days; young brooded and fed by both sexes.

Red-headed Finch *Amadina erythrocephala* Rooikopvink   page 399

Breeds widely in semi-arid savanna and grassland. A monogamous breeder, pairs nesting solitarily or, when occupying the nest of a colonial breeder, several pairs may nest within a few metres of each other. **Nest:** uses old nests of other weavers and sparrows (Cape Sparrow, Southern Masked, Village, Chestnut and Sociable Weaver, Red-billed Buffalo Weaver); also, less frequently, the closed nests of Little Swift and South African Cliff Swallow, or under the eaves of a building; these nests are first lined by the finches with grass and feathers before laying. Occasionally, it may build its own nest, an untidy ball of grass and feathers, placed in the branches of a thorny tree.
Laying months: mainly Feb-May (Jan-Oct, but all months recorded). **Clutch size:** 4 (2-6; rarely up to 11, probably laid by >1 ♀); laid at 1-day intervals. **Eggs:** 16.9-18.3-21.3 x 13.2-14.7-15.6 mm. **Incubation period:** 12-14 days; by both sexes. **Nestling/fledging period:** 15-21 days; young brooded and fed by both sexes.

Orange-winged Pytilia

Green-winged Pytilia

Cut-throat Finch   breeding in old Red-headed Weaver nests

Cut-throat Finch   eggs laid in disused Southern Masked Weaver nest

Red-headed Finch   breeding in old weaver nest

Red-faced Crimsonwing *Cryptospiza reichenovii* Rooiwangwoudsysie   page 399

Breeds in and on the edges of montane forest in highlands of e Zimbabwe and w Mozambique. Pairs nest solitarily and are widely spaced. **Nest:** a substantial oval-shaped ball (long axis horizontal) with an entrance at one end and an enclosed nest chamber at the other, large for the size of the bird, placed in a thorny tree or tangle of thorny creepers (often *Gymnosporia, Erythroxylum*), usually 2-3 m (up to 5½) up from the ground in forest, sometimes bordering a clearing or glade, or over a stream or pool. It is built with dark-coloured material, so that it looks old, and blends into the dark under-canopy of the forest; some are built entirely with moss, others incorporate skeletonised leaves, grass blades, vine tendrils and/or fine *Asparagus* stems; lined with feathers and/or fine grass. It measures: 120-150 mm high; 160-200 mm long; 140 mm wide (across entrance); entrance 30-40 mm in diameter. Nests are sometimes built close to previous a years' nest (and even in the same tree). The birds are furtive while breeding and come and go from the nest with minimal calling.
Laying months: Sep-Mar. **Clutch size:** 3-5. **Eggs:** 17.5-17.7-18.1 × 12.9-13.0-13.1 mm. **Incubation period:** not recorded; by both sexes. **Nestling/fledging period:** 21 days; young brooded and fed by both sexes.

Lesser Seedcracker *Pyrenestes minor* Oostelike Saadbrekertjie

Breeds in c Mozambique and e Zimbabwe on the fringes of lowland and riparian forest. Nesting habits are poorly known in the wild. **Nest:** a bulky, oval-shaped ball (long axis horizontal) with a spout-like entrance at one end and an enclosed nest chamber at the other; it is placed in tree or bush, 1½-3 m (rarely to 16 m) up from the ground; one recorded in a banana tree. Nest distinctive from nests of other estrildids by being made entirely from very broad (15 mm wide) strips of grass, loosely curled around to form the nest which is unlined. It measures 225 mm (front to back) and is 175 mm high. Both sexes collect material and build the nest.
Laying months: Feb-May. **Clutch size:** 3. **Eggs:** 17.0-17.1-17.5 × 11.8-12.7-13.0 mm; egg not illustrated. **Incubation period:** 13-15 days (in captivity); by both sexes. **Nestling/fledging period:** 20-23 days (in captivity).

Green Twinspot *Mandingoa nitidula* Groenkolpensie   page 399

Breeds in, and on the edges of coastal and montane forest. Pairs nest solitarily and are widely spaced. **Nest:** a bulky, oval-shaped nest (long axis horizontal) with a short, spout-like entrance at one end and an enclosed nest chamber at the other; it is built in the canopy of a forest tree, 7-9 m (3-15) up from the ground, usually a tree or sapling that stands apart from others and usually well hidden in creeper or dense foliage. It is roughly built from blades of grass, with pieces of skeletonised leaf, rootlets, twigs, *Usnea* and other forest debris incorporated into the structure, lined with fine grass, feathers and other soft material. It measures: 125 mm high; 150 mm long; entrance 40-70 mm in diameter. It is built by both sexes. Occasionally, an old Dark-backed Weaver nest is used, these being lined by the twinspots with fine grass and feathers. Both sexes roost in nest at night during the incubation. The nestlings are noisy when being fed by their parents and their loud begging calls sometimes give their position away.
Laying months: mainly Dec-Apr, also Aug, Oct. **Clutch size:** 4-6. **Eggs:** 15.2-15.9-16.6 × 11.3-12.0-12.3 mm. **Incubation period:** 12-14 days; by both sexes. **Nestling/fledging period:** 21-23 days (in captivity); young fed by both sexes.

Pink-throated Twinspot *Hypargos margaritatus* Rooskeelkolpensie   no nest photo   page 399

Restricted to sand forest and dense undergrowth in mesic woodlands along coastal plain from Zululand to s Mozambique. Little is known of its nesting habits in the wild and few nests have been recorded. **Nest:** an oval-shaped ball (long axis horizontal) with a short tunnel-entrance (40-60 mm wide), placed on the ground, or close to it (<1 m up), well hidden among litter, old grass and fallen twigs and leaves. It is built with decaying and skeletonised leaves, grass inflorescences and probably other plant material and the nest chamber is lined inside with feathers or fine plant fibre.
Laying months: Jan-Apr. **Clutch size:** 3-4. **Eggs:** 15.0-16.2-16.9 × 12.0-12.1-12.2 mm. **Incubation period:** 12-14 days; by both sexes (in captivity). **Nestling/fledging period:** 20-21 days (in captivity).

Red-throated Twinspot *Hypargos niveoguttatus* Rooikeelkolpensie   no nest photo   page 399

Breeds in second growth and on edges of riparian and lowland forest in c Mozambique and n Zimbabwe. Pairs nest solitarily, at a density of a pair/10 ha (Dichwe forest, Zimbabwe). **Nest:** an oval-shaped ball (long axis horizontal) with a short (80 mm) tunnel side entrance leading into a domed nest chamber; it is placed on, or close to the ground (<1 m up), either on a sloping bank, among tree roots, or on a low stem. It is built from small stalks of maiden-hair fern, fine hair-like rootlets and dry moss; its roof is covered with soft, decomposing leaves which camouflage it very effectively; unlike the nests of many other estrildids, grass is not used. Some nests have a partial 'cock's nest'. One nest measured: 120 mm high; tunnel 40 mm wide; interior chamber 90 mm high, 80 mm wide. The nest is built by both sexes.
Laying months: Jan-Jun. **Clutch size:** 3; laid at 1-day intervals. **Eggs:** 14.9-16.0-17.1 × 12.0-12.4-12.8 mm; it is assumed that it is parasitised by Zambezi Indigobird since the ♂s of this species have been recorded imitating the song of this twinspot. **Incubation period:** 12-13 days; by both sexes. **Nestling/fledging period:** 21 days (18-23, in captivity); young fed by both sexes.

Red-faced Crimsonwing

Lesser Seedcracker

Red-faced Crimsonwing

Green Twinspot

Red-billed Firefinch *Lagonosticta senegala* **Rooibekvuurvinkie**   page 399
Breeds widely in mesic savanna, extending marginally into wooded habitats in karoo and grassland; frequents areas with rank grass and thickets; often nests close to human habitation. Pairs nest solitarily and are widely spaced. **Nest:** site chosen and nest is similar to that of Jameson's Firefinch; it is a small round ball with a side entrance, placed from ground level up to about 2 m, well hidden in a low shrub or thicket, or in leaves, twigs and other plant debris accumulated among tufts of grass; around human habitation may nest in garden plants, flower pots, wall creepers, etc. The nest is made from dry stems of grass and dead leaves curled around into a sphere; it rests unattached on the ground or on the stems that support it. The interior is lined with fine grass ends and feathers. It measures: 100 mm high; 90-100 mm wide; entrance 30-35 mm in diameter. It is built by both sexes and material (feathers especially) continue to be added during incubation.
Laying months: mainly Dec-Apr (Dec-Aug). **Clutch size:** 3-4 (2-6); laid at 1-day intervals. **Eggs:** 12.0-13.3-15.1 x 9.9-10.6-12.0 mm; mass 0.84 g; parasitised by Village Indigobird. **Incubation period:** 11-12 days; by both sexes. **Nestling/fledging period:** 18 days (17-20); young brooded and fed by both sexes.

African Firefinch *Lagonosticta rubricata* **Kaapse Vuurvinkie**   page 399
Breeds in n mesic savanna and on fringes of montane and riparian forest. Pairs nest solitarily and are widely spaced. **Nest:** a small, round ball of dry grass and leaves well hidden in thick undergrowth, often in grass entangled in a fallen branch or stump, in cut brush, or in a bracken-briar thicket, ½-2 m up from the ground. The outside shell is made from long coarse blades of dry grass curled around to form a sphere and these encase a more finely lined nest chamber where fine, soft grass ends are used; some nests are also lined with feathers. It has a side entrance and no spout or tunnel leading into the nest. The nest measures: height and width 100-150 mm (wider from front-to-back than across the front); entrance 50 mm in diameter. Both sexes build and continue adding lining during the incubation.
Laying months: mainly Jan-Apr (Nov-Jun). **Clutch size:** 4 (2-5). **Eggs:** 13.9-15.1-16.0 x 10.2-11.5-12.0 mm; mass 1.16 g; parasitised by Dusky Indigobird. **Incubation period:** 11-12 days; by both sexes. **Nestling/fledging period:** 17 days (14-19); young brooded and fed by both sexes.

Jameson's Firefinch *Lagonosticta rhodopareia* **Jamesonse Vuurvinkie**   page 399
Breeds in mesic savanna. Pairs nest solitarily and are widely spaced. **Nest:** a small, round, loosely made ball, usually <½ m up from the ground (0-1,8 m); it is typically sited beneath the canopy of a tree or bush clump where tree litter (leaves, branches, twigs, etc.) has accumulated among rank grass growth and it is well hidden in or under a grass tuft or among dead branches grown through with grass, or in a low, dense shrub (e.g. *Stoebe*); close to human habitation occasional nests are in flower pots, hanging baskets, etc. Shreds of dry grass and dry leaf are used for the walls and roof, this encases an inside chamber lined with soft grass ends (e.g. *Melinis* sp.) curled around the floor, sides and roof. Feathers line the nest-cup. The entrance faces out of one side. The nest measures: height 100-120 mm; width 90-120 mm; entrance diameter 25-40 mm. Both sexes build, and one nest was completed in 4 days; feathers continue to be added during the incubation.
Laying months: mainly Jan-Apr (Dec-May, occasionally in other months). **Clutch size:** 3-4 (2-7); laid at 1-day intervals. **Eggs:** 12.9-14.6-16.2 x 9.9-11.2-12.4 mm; mass 1.04 g; parasitised by Purple Indigobird. **Incubation period:** 12-15 days; by both sexes. **Nestling/fledging period:** 19 days (16-22); young brooded and fed by both sexes.

Brown Firefinch *Lagonosticta nitidula* **Bruinvuurvinkie**   no nest photo   page 399
Breeds in riparian woodland fringing floodplains on the Okavango and along the Caprivi. Pairs nest solitarily and are widely spaced. **Nest:** in southern Africa all recorded nesting to date has been in disused weaver nests (Spectacled, Brown-throated, Golden), these being lined with feathers or fine grass ends. Elsewhere it also builds a firefinch-type nest, ball-shaped with a side entrance, placed close to the ground. Both sexes line the nest, completing this in 5-7 days.
Laying months: mainly Jan-Apr (Oct-Apr). **Clutch size:** 4 (3-6); laid at 1-day intervals. **Eggs:** 14.8-15.7-16.7 x 11.2-11.4-12.0 mm; frequently parasitised (8% of nests) by Village Indigobird. **Incubation period:** 14-16 days; by both sexes. **Nestling/fledging period:** 15-19 days; young fed by both sexes.

Red-billed Firefinch

African Firefinch

Jameson's Firefinch   side view of a disused nest

Violet-eared Waxbill *Uraeginthus granatinus* Koningblousysie
page 399

Breeds widely across the savanna belt, but most abundant in semi-arid savanna. Pairs nest solitarily, are probably territorial year-round, and are spaced at a pair/13-50 ha depending on habitat. **Nest:** an oval-shaped ball (long axis vertical) with a round entrance on one side, placed in the branches of a shrubby tree or sapling, often an acacia, and sometimes where two trees and entwined; typically 1-2 m (½-3) up from the ground. The nest is usually concealed by foliage and its entrance faces into, rather than out from the bush. It is thick-walled and has an outer shell made from stems of old, dry grass that are curled around to form a sphere, their ends protruding untidily in all directions; the interior is lined with finer grass inflorescences (e.g. *Melinis* sp.). Feathers are used to line the cup. The nest measures: 130-140 mm high; 90 mm wide (front-to-back); 90 mm wide (across the front); entrance 30 mm in diameter. Both sexes build the nest and continue to add feathers to it during the incubation.

Laying months: mainly Dec-Apr (Oct-May, occasionally in other months). **Clutch size:** 4 (2-7). **Eggs:** 14.3-15.6-17.0 x 11.0-11.6-13.0 mm; mass 0.6-1.0 g; frequently (33% of nests) parasitised by Shaft-tailed Whydah which may lay 1-5 eggs/nest. **Incubation period:** 12-13 days; by both sexes, shared equally in alternating shifts of 1½-2 hrs. **Nestling/fledging period:** 16-18 days; young brooded and fed by both sexes.

Blue Waxbill *Uraeginthus angolensis* Gewone Blousysie
page 399

Breeds widely across the savanna belt from semi-arid west to mesic east. Pairs nest solitarily or in loosely associated colonies (e.g. 8 nests, 6-26 m apart). **Nest:** a small, oval-shaped to round ball (long axis horizontal) with an enclosed chamber at one end and a short, spout-like entrance at the other; the nest is placed in the thinner branches of a tree, typically 1½-4 m (½-10) up from the ground; thorny trees and shrubs are preferred (especially *Acacia tortilis*; as are lone-standing trees); nests are often conspicuous. Many are placed close to active wasp nests (see photographs opposite). The nest is built with long, green, fine grass ends that are loosely and untidily curled around into a sphere, one end of the grass stem left to project out around the entrance and shape it into a short spout; nest colour soon fades from green to yellow. The cup is lined with feathers. The nest measures: 90-110 mm high; 95-120 mm wide (front-to-back); 95 mm wide (across front); entrance 30-32 mm in diameter. Laying commences before the nest is complete, and grass and feathers continue to be added during the incubation; the ♀ takes a greater share in building and a nest can be completed (start to first egg) in 7 days. An old weaver or sunbird nest is occasionally used, and when it is, it is lined with fine grass and feathers.

Laying months: mainly Jan-Feb (Dec-May, but all months occasionally recorded); in arid areas probably breeds in response to rainfall. **Clutch size:** 3-4 (2-7); laid at 1-day intervals. **Eggs:** 13.3-14.4-16.4 x 9.8-10.8-11.8 mm; occasionally parasitised by Shaft-tailed Whydah. **Incubation period:** 11-12 days; begins before clutch is completed; by both sexes in shifts of 1½-2 hrs. **Nestling/fledging period:** 17-18 days (16-21); young brooded and fed by both sexes.

Grey Waxbill *Estrilda perreini* Gryssysie
no nest photo page 399

Breeds on fringes of coastal, lowland and riparian forest. Pairs nest solitarily and are widely spaced. **Nest:** commonly uses an old nest of a weaver (Dark-backed, Spectacled, Village), lining it with fine grass ends. Less often, it builds its own nest, typically placed in a lone-standing sapling or shrub growing in a glade or open space; it is about 2½ m (1.6-4.7) up from the ground; some are well hidden in foliage, others obvious; they are occasionally placed alongside an active wasp nest. These nests are oval-shaped (long axis horizontal), with a short, spout-like entrance at one side, leading into the nest chamber at the other. They are built with green and dry stems and inflorescences of grass that are curled around into a sphere, with a projection of stem-ends forming a short (50 mm) entrance spout that faces slightly downwards. The interior is lined with soft grass inflorescences (e.g. *Melinis* sp.); feathers are not used. The nest measures: 150-160 mm long (entrance to back of chamber); 100-125 mm wide and high; entrance 45 mm in diameter. Both sexes build the nest with material collected by the ♀.

Laying months: Oct-Apr. **Clutch size:** 4 (2-5). **Eggs:** 13.7-14.6-15.4 x 10.5-11.4-11.5 mm. **Incubation period:** 12 days (in captivity) by both sexes. **Nestling/fledging period:** 19-21 days (in captivity).

Cinderella Waxbill *Estrilda thomensis* Angolasysie

Range narrowly extends into n Nambia from Angola; it breeds here in mopane and riparian bush and scrub along the Kunene River and its adjoining tributaries. Nesting habits are poorly known. **Nest:** a roughly made ball of dry grass, with a side entrance leading in from a short spout, placed 3-5 m up from the ground in the outer branches of a mopane or other leafy tree.

Laying months: Nov-Apr. **Clutch size:** 3-4 (in captivity). **Eggs:** measurements not recorded; egg not illustrated. **Incubation period:** 12½-14 days (in captivity); by both sexes. **Nestling/fledging period:** 17-21 days (in captivity); young fed by both sexes.

Violet-eared Waxbill | Blue Waxbill

building nest alongside wasp nest | Blue Waxbill | a completed nest alongside wasp nest

Cinderella Waxbill

African Quailfinch *Ortygospiza atricollis* Gewone Kwartelvinkie   page 399

Breeds widely in grassland and savanna. Pairs nest solitarily, rarely in loose associations where adjacent nests can be 12-20 m apart. **Nest:** a small, thick-walled ball with a side entrance, placed on the ground between grass tufts; its entrance faces out onto a small (<½ m wide) bare piece of ground, the nest itself being well hidden under or against tufts of grass. The nest shell is made with blades and stems of old, withered grass and fragments of dead leaf, which merges the nest very effectively into its surroundings; the entrance hole does not extend beyond the nest, and is small and inconspicuous. The inner walls are made with fine dry stems and inflorescences of grass, and the nest-cup is lined with feathers, which continue to be added during the incubation. It measures: 115 mm high; 80 mm wide (front-to-back); 110 mm wide (across front); entrance 55 mm in diameter.
Laying months: mainly Jan-Mar (Nov-May, occasionally in other months). **Clutch size:** 4-5 (3-6); laid at 1-day intervals. **Eggs:** 12.7-14.4-16.5 x 10.4-11.1-12.9 mm; mass 0.7 g. **Incubation period:** 15 days; by both sexes. **Nestling/fledging period:** 18-19 days; young brooded and fed by both sexes.

Locust Finch *Ortygospiza locustella* Rooivlerkkwartelvinkie   page 399

Breeds in n mesic and lowland savanna on margins of seasonal vleis, mostly in above-average rainfall years. Pairs nest solitarily and are widely spaced. Its nesting habits, nest and eggs are broadly similar to those of the African Quailfinch: the two species commonly breed in the same areas, and the birds, and their nests, are frequently mistaken for each other. **Nest:** Locust Finches build a round ball-shaped nest which differs from that of the African Quailfinch by usually (but not invariably) being placed above the ground (0.2-0.3 m up) and set into dense tangled grass, or where grass has bent over from its own weight (African Quailfinches invariably build their nests on the ground). Secondly, in Locust Finch nests the walls and roof are uniformly built (from the outside shell to the interior) with fine pieces of soft grass, and the nest lacks the coarse, old-grass exterior that is characteristic of an African Quailfinch nest. The cup is sparsely lined with feathers. One nest measured about 75 mm in diameter and had an entrance about 25 mm wide.
Laying months: Jan-May. **Clutch size:** 5-6 (4-8); laid at 1-day intervals. **Eggs:** 12.3-13.2-14.3 x 9.1-9.7-10.1 mm. **Incubation period:** not recorded; begins before clutch is completed. **Nestling/fledging period:** not recorded; young fed by both sexes.

Magpie Mannikin *Lonchura fringilloides* Dikbekfret   page 399

Breeds in mesic savanna and on the fringes of coastal, lowland, and riparian forest; very localised in the region. Pairs nest solitarily and are widely spaced. **Nest:** an oval-shaped ball (long axis horizontal) built in the leafy foliage of a tree or shrub near the extremity of a branch, often well hidden; usually 2-3 m (1.2-5) up from the ground; has entrance at one end, leading into an enclosed nest chamber at the other. It is built with long, green grass inflorescences or green stems of *Asparagus* sp. curled around to form an untidy, thick-walled sphere with ends projecting outwards in different directions. The entrance may have a short spout (15-35 mm) formed by grass inflorescences extending from the nest around the entrance. Grass inflorescences or *Asparagus* stems are used to line the cup. The nest measures: 130-175-250 mm long (front-to-back); 100-120-130 mm high; 110-120-130 mm wide (across front); entrance 30-50 mm wide, 21-38 mm high. Both sexes build, the nest taking 7-10 days to complete.
Laying months: Oct-Jun. **Clutch size:** 4-5 (2-10; larger clutches probably laid by >1 ♀). **Eggs:** 14.5-15.9-17.8 x 10.2-11.3-12.3 mm. **Incubation period:** 15 days (14-16) (in captivity). **Nestling/fledging period:** 20 days (19-22) (in captivity).

Bronze Mannikin *Lonchura cucullata* Gewone Fret   page 399

Breeds in mesic savanna and on the fringes of coastal and montane forest; common around settlements, in gardens and in second-growth habitats. Pairs nest solitarily or in loosely associated groups (2-3 nests <25 m apart). **Nest:** a thick-walled, untidy grass pear-shaped ball (long axis horizontal) with a side entrance, built in a tree or shrub about 4-5 m (½-12) up from the ground; it is usually concealed in foliage and sometimes placed alongside an active wasp nest (see photograph opposite). It is built with green grass inflorescences (e.g. *Panicum*, *Digitaria*, *Sporobolus*) that are loosely and untidily curled around into a sphere, with spiky ends left projecting untidily in all directions. In some nests the inflorescences extend beyond the entrance, forming a short spout. Newly built nests are green in colour, but they rapidly fade to yellow. The nest chamber is lined with soft grass ends or feathers. Nests are built with 540-650-800 pieces of material. They measure: 140-160-180 mm high; 130-155-170 mm wide (front-to-back); 110-125-130 mm wide (across the front); entrance 40-42-45 mm in diameter. Occasionally, old weaver nests or nests of other waxbills are used for breeding. Both sexes build, ♂ collecting material and ♀ building, completing a nest in 3-14 days. Nests can be used as night-time roosts by family groups and on occasion a thinner-walled nest is built specifically for use as a night-time roost.
Laying months: mainly Nov-Apr (Aug-May). **Clutch size:** 4-5 (2-8); laid at 1-day intervals. **Eggs:** 12.9-14.4-16.1 x 9.6-10.2-12.2 mm; occasionally parasitised by Pin-tailed Whydah. **Incubation period:** 14 days (12-16); begins when clutch is completed; by both sexes. **Nestling/fledging period:** 17 days (15-21); young brooded and fed by both sexes.

Red-backed Mannikin *Lonchura bicolor* Rooirugfret   no nest photo   page 399

Breeds on the fringes of forest, especially in second-growth, often near human habitation. Pairs nest solitarily and are widely spaced. **Nest:** similar to that of Bronze Mannikin in position, placed on an outer branch (often at the extremity) of a tree, usually concealed in foliage, 1½-8 m up from the ground. Oval-shaped (long axis horizontal) with an entrance on one side leading into an enclosed nest chamber at the other, built with green grass inflorescences and/or green stems of *Asparagus* sp. which are untidily curled around into a sphere; grass ends with seed-heads are arranged to project around the entrance, concealing this to some degree. Freshly built nests are green-coloured, but they rapidly fade to yellow. Soft grass inflorescences are used to line the cup. The nest measures: 120-150 mm long (front-to-back); 110 mm high; 110 mm wide (across front).
Laying months: Oct-May. **Clutch size:** 4-5 (2-7). **Eggs:** 12.1-14.4-16.0 x 9.7-10.3-11.1 mm. **Incubation period:** 12-13 days (in captivity); by both sexes. **Nestling/fledging period:** 19 days (17-21) (in captivity).

African Quailfinch

Locust Finch

Magpie Mannikin   nest interior showing clutch

Bronze Mannikin   built alongside an active wasp nest (arrow)

Waxbills

Common Waxbill *Estrilda astrild* Rooibeksysie page 399
Breeds widely across the region, nesting in areas of rank grass, reeds, bracken-briar, farmlands and overgrown gardens. Pairs nest solitarily, a pair/8-10 ha (w Cape). **Nest:** a thick-walled retort-shaped ball of dry grass, with a nest chamber at one end and an extended, tapering entrance spout at the other; placed close to the ground, usually set into a grass tuft, its entrance facing onto a small clearing; occasional nests are higher (but not >3 m), placed in dense shrubbery. Most nests have a false nest (or 'cock's nest'), an open cup lined with feathers, built on top of the main structure. The nest interior is lined with fine grass and some with a few feathers. The nest measures: length 150-175 mm; entrance spout 70-380 mm; height 90-130 mm; width 90-160 mm; entrance diameter 25 mm; the 'cock's nest' is about 65 mm wide. Both sexes build the nest and continue adding lining during the incubation. **Laying months:** mainly Sep-Oct (Aug-Dec) in winter-rainfall region, Dec-Feb (Nov-Mar) elsewhere. **Clutch size:** 4-6 (3-9; larger clutches laid by >1 ♀); laid at 1-day intervals. **Eggs:** 12.5-13.9-16.1 x 9.9-10.6-11.7 mm; mass 0.87 g; commonly parasitised by Pin-tailed Whydah, the whydah egg distinguishable by its larger size (15.5 x 11.7 mm). **Incubation period:** 11-12 days; by both sexes. **Nestling/fledging period:** 17-21 days; young brooded and fed by both sexes.

Orange-breasted Waxbill *Amandava subflava* Rooiassie page 399
Breeds in grassland and mesic savanna, frequenting areas of rank, open grass, sedges and reedbeds, commonly along margins of wetlands. Pairs nest solitarily or semi-colonially. **Nest:** mostly (80%) uses the old nest of a bishop (especially Southern Red Bishop) or widowbird, less often the nest of a prinia, cisticola or weaver; these nests are thickly lined by the waxbill with fine grass-ends and feathers. Less often (20%) it builds its own nest, a small, flimsy round ball with a hooded side entrance, made of strips of grass and lined with feathers; these are placed in sheaves of thick grass or sedge 0.2-1.4 m up from the ground. Self-built nests measure: 84-103-116 mm high; 84-96-115 mm wide (across front); 104-131-152 mm wide (front-to-back); entrance 27-37-47 mm in diameter. Self-made nests are built by the ♂, lined by the ♀; they can be built over dry ground or over water and may, occasionally, be placed in bushes, rather than in grass, usually one standing in water. **Laying months:** mainly Feb-Apr (Jan-Jun, occasionally in other months). **Clutch size:** 5 (3-6; rarely 7-9, probably laid by >1 ♀); laid at 1-day intervals. **Eggs:** 11.8-13.6-15.3 x 9.3-10.2-11.0 mm; mass 0.60-0.77-0.85 g; occasionally parasitised by Pin-tailed Whydah. **Incubation period:** 13-14 days; begins before clutch is completed; shared equally by both sexes, in alternating shifts lasting 18-52-73 mins. **Nestling/fledging period:** 18 days (16-19); young brooded and fed by both sexes.

Swee Waxbill *Estrilda melanotis* Suidelike Swie page 399
Breeds on fringes of montane and coastal forest and planted timber, often in second-growth vegetation, orchards and gardens. Pairs nest solitarily and are widely spaced. **Nest:** a round- to oval-shaped ball with an entrance at one side; built in a tree or bush 2-9 m up from the ground; usually in a foliaged outer branch, often close to buildings or human activity. The outer shell is built with coarse dry blades of grass that are loosely curled around to form a sphere, with finer, soft grass inflorescences forming the inner walls; in some nests these project out of the entrance forming a short spout or hood above the entrance; more neatly finished than nests of most estrildids. The cup is lined with feathers and/or plant down. The nest measures: 100-150 mm high; 90-100 mm wide. The ♂ takes a greater share than the ♀ in building the nest. Both sexes sleep in the nest at night during incubation. **Laying months:** mainly Dec-Jan (Nov-Apr), earlier (Aug-Oct) in winter-rainfall region. **Clutch size:** 4-5 (2-6; rarely more, when laid by >1 ♀); laid at 1-day intervals. **Eggs:** 12.2-13.7-16.3 x 9.9-10.4-11.0 mm; rarely parasitised by Pin-tailed Whydah. **Incubation period:** 12-13 days (in captivity); by both sexes. **Nestling/fledging period:** 19-22 days (in captivity); young fed by both sexes.

Yellow-bellied Waxbill *Estrilda quartinia* Tropiese Swie no nest photo page 399
Breeds in e Zimbabwe highlands in bracken-briar, second-growth, gardens, forest verges. Pairs nest solitarily and are widely spaced. **Nest:** a round- to oval-shaped ball with an entrance near the top of one side, built in a tree or bush about 2-3 m (1½-5) up from the ground; often in a tree standing apart and in an outer branch, some nests concealed in foliage, others exposed. The outer shell is built with coarse dry blades of grass that are loosely curled around to form a sphere, with finer, soft grass inflorescences (and moss in some nests) forming the inner walls. The cup is lined with silky white plant down (in some a few feathers are added). It does not have a projecting spout entrance and it lacks the spiky, untidy look of the nests of many estrildid species. It measures: 100-110 mm high; 90-100 mm wide; entrance 35-40 mm wide. Both sexes build, completing the nest in 7-10 days. **Laying months:** mainly Dec-Jan (Oct-Apr). **Clutch size:** 4-5; laid at 1-day intervals. **Eggs:** 12.9-13.4-14.2 x 10.2-10.4-10.8 mm. **Incubation period:** 12-14 days; by both sexes. **Nestling/fledging period:** 13-16 days; young fed by both sexes.

Black-faced Waxbill *Estrilda erythronotos* Swartwangsysie page 399
Breeds in semi-arid savanna, especially thornveld. Pairs nest solitarily and are widely spaced. **Nest:** distinctively retort-shaped, the spherical nest chamber having its entrance as an extended (75-125 mm) spout that points downwards like a weaver nest; it is typically placed in the upper, thin branches of a thorny tree, usually 4-5 m (3-9) up from the ground. It is bulky and thick-walled, built from fine green grass-ends (which soon fade to yellow); the entrance to the tunnel is concealed by protruding grass-ends. Some nests (<½) have an open cup (or 'cock's nest') built on top of the main structure; its function, apparently, as a decoy to predators away from the nest's real entrance. The nest-cup is lined with fine grass, some with feathers. The nest measures: 180 mm long (across roof, excluding tunnel entrance); 180 mm high (base of chamber to roof); 100 mm wide; entrance tunnel 25 mm in diameter; the false nest is 100 x 65 mm across. Nests are sometimes built in trees used in a previous year. Both sexes share building the nest and they continue lining it during incubation. **Laying months:** mainly Jan-Mar (Dec-Apr, occasionally in other months). **Clutch size:** 4 (2-6). **Eggs:** 13.9-14.8-15.9 x 10.1-10.9-11.4 mm. **Incubation period:** 12 days (in captivity); by both sexes. **Nestling/fledging period:** 22 days (in captivity).

Common Waxbill — entrance temporarily widened to show eggs

using old nest of Southern Red Bishop — Orange-breasted Waxbill — using a self-built nest, faeces of nestlings accumulated at entrance

Swee Waxbill

Black-faced Waxbill

WHYDAHS, INDIGOBIRDS, CUCKOO FINCH Family Viduidae Worldwide 20 species; all endemic to Afrotropics, 9 breed in southern Africa (the list includes Cuckoo Finch which was previously grouped with weavers, and Twinspot Indigobird, nowhere yet recorded breeding). The Vidua finches are parasitic and they have a complex and extraordinary reproductive system; this, coupled with their sexually dimorphic plumages and the seasonal plumage changes undergone by the males, make them an exceptionally interesting bird family. The ♀s of most of the Vidua finches look virtually alike, being buff-coloured with darker streaking and differing mainly in head striping and in the colour of their beaks and feet; in winter, ♂s resemble them, but they assume a strikingly different breeding plumage in summer: indigobirds become glossy-black and whydahs acquire elongated central tail feathers and contrastingly patterned bodies. The Vidua finches do not build nests nor raise their own young but instead lay their eggs in the nests of estrildid finches, most parasitising firefinches and pytilias. They are also polygynous and promiscuous (♂s mate with multiple ♀s and vice versa) and, with a couple of exceptions, each species targets a specific host species. With the exception of Cuckoo Finch (see its species account for details), ♂s set themselves up in summer at call-sites/display-sites from which they attempt to exclude other ♂s, and attract ♀s by singing or performing aerial display flights, or both. Again, with the exception of the Cuckoo Finch, and also the Pin-tailed Whydah, the songs and call-notes used by the ♂'s at these sites are imitations of the song and calls of the particular species that they parasitise (e.g. Long-tailed Paradise Whydah ♂s mimic the song of their host, the Green-winged Pytilia), and it is suggested that the ♂s probably learn these calls from their foster parents when still juveniles under their care. Such songs attract ♀s to the site to mate, these ♀s responding to songs that they, too, learnt while in foster-care. After mating, ♀s seek out nests of the appropriate foster-parent in which to lay their eggs. ♀s can lay as many as 26 eggs per season, laying them in 'clutches' (in which 2-4 eggs are laid on successive days, usually in different host nests) with intervals between each clutch (information based largely on aviary studies). Different ♀s may lay in the same host nest, resulting in as many as five parasite eggs being laid in a single host nest (but usually only 1-2). All the species lay unmarked white eggs that are similar to those of their hosts, some differing slightly in size, shape or texture. The parasite does not consistently remove or damage the host eggs when laying, and nestlings of both host and parasite may be raised together. The nestlings of the parasite mimic the begging calls and begging behaviour of the host nestlings closely, and they match the host chicks in the colouring and pattern of the spots in their mouths and their gape flanges. Occasionally, a ♀ may lay in a host nest of a 'wrong' species, resulting, if a ♂ nestling survives and is raised, in it learning the 'wrong' host song. Or, rarely, she may select the wrong species of ♂ to mate with, resulting in a hybrid. Hybrid ♂s of Long-tailed Paradise Whydah x Purple Indigobird and Shaft-tailed Whydah x Village Indigobird, are entirely black and have long tails and these have, in the past, been described as separate species. The Pin-tailed Whydah differs somewhat from the others by not using vocal mimicry to attract mates and by parasitising more than one host species. Eggs are oval, unmarked white, in most cases larger than those of their hosts; nestlings are altricial and nidicolous.

Pin-tailed Whydah *Vidua macroura* **Koningrooibekkie** page 399

Breeds widely in grassland, savanna, karoo and fynbos. **Host:** mainly Common Waxbill, but regularly targets Orange-breasted Waxbill, less often Swee Waxbill, Bronze Mannikin, Red-billed Firefinch, and occasionally prinias and cisticolas. In summer, adult ♂s establish widely spaced (200-500-1400 m) display sites to which they attract ♀s for mating. These sites are usually centred on a drinking point or concentration of seed (such as on a feeding tray in a garden); the ♂ occupies the site for 90% of the day and attempts to exclude other species from this site by vigorously pursuing them when they approach, while courting and displaying to any ♀ Pin-tailed Whydah that visits. Such ♀s mate fleetingly with him (copulation lasts 1½-6 secs) and thereafter they range widely to lay their eggs in host nests. A ♀ lays 1 egg/day for 2-4 successive days (a 'clutch'), followed by an interval before laying a second clutch; she lays about 25 eggs/season. Host nests may contain more than one whydah egg (up to 5 recorded) as a result of two or more ♀s laying in the same nest. No host eggs are removed, and the host raises its own and the parasite's nestlings together.
Laying months: Aug-Apr; earlier in winter-rainfall region (peaking Sep-Oct) than elsewhere (peaking Dec-Feb). **Eggs:** 14.4-15.5-16.8 x 11.3-11.7-12.5 mm; mass 1.34 g; its egg is larger and heavier than those of any of its hosts. **Incubation period:** 11 days. **Nestling/fledging period:** 17-21 days.

Shaft-tailed Whydah *Vidua regia* **Pylstertrooibekkie** page 399

Breeds in semi-arid and arid, acacia-dominated savannas. **Host:** primarily Violet-eared Waxbill (about 33% of their nests being parasitised); rarely Blue and Black-faced Waxbills. In summer, each ♂ establishes a call site (these spaced at intervals of 50 m - 1½ km apart) to which he attracts ♀s for mating by singing a mixture of notes that includes imitated song and calls of Violet-eared Waxbill. ♀s visit such call-sites, mate with the ♂ in possession of the site and range widely to lay their eggs in appropriate host nests; a ♀ lays 1 egg/day for 3-4 successive days, with an interval before laying the next clutch. Host nests may contain more than one whydah egg (up to 5 recorded) as a result of two or more ♀s laying in the same nest. A host egg may be removed or eaten, and the host raises its own and the parasite's nestlings together.
Laying months: Dec-May. **Eggs:** 16.5-16.7-16.9 x 13.0-13.2-13.4 mm (oviduct eggs smaller, 14.2-15.0 x 11.4-13.2 mm); recognisable in host nest as its egg is larger and rounder than the egg of its host (Violet-eared Waxbill egg 15.6 x 11.6 mm). **Incubation period:** 12-13 days. **Nestling/fledging period:** 16-20 days.

Long-tailed Paradise Whydah *Vidua paradisaea* **Gewone Paradysvink** page 399

Breeds across the savanna belt, from the semi-arid west to the mesic east; mainly in thornveld. **Host:** primary host is Green-winged Pytilia (about 28% of their nests being parasitised), rarely Violet-eared Waxbill. In summer, ♂s maintain display arenas 0.6-1.4-2.8 km apart and sing from here, mimicking the song of the Green-winged Pytilia (assumed to have been learnt as a juvenile while being reared by that host) and they perform bouncing aerial display flights (about 2x/day, each lasting about 20 min) to attract ♀s. ♀s visit these sites, mate with ♂ in possession of the site, and range widely to lay their eggs in appropriate host nests; a ♀ lays up to 22

eggs per season, laying 1/day for 3-4 successive days (i.e. a clutch), with an interval before laying the next clutch. ♀ seeks host nests without ♂ assistance. Host nests may contain more than one whydah egg (up to 3 recorded) as a result of two or more ♀s laying in the same nest. No host eggs are removed, and the host raises its own and the parasite's nestlings together.
Laying months: same as host, mainly Jan-May. **Eggs:** 18.6-18.8-19.5 x 13.0-13.8-14.0 mm; recognisable in host nest as its egg is larger and more pointed than egg of Green-winged Pytilia (16.7 x 12.5 mm). **Incubation period:** 11 days. **Nestling/fledging period:** 16 days (in captivity).

Broad-tailed Paradise Whydah *Vidua obtusa* Breëstertparadysvink

Breeds in n mesic savanna, mainly in miombo and other broad-leafed woodland. Breeding habits in the wild are poorly known. **Host:** only known host is Orange-winged Pytilia. ♂s maintain a display arena and sing from here, mimicking the song of the Orange-winged Pytilia and performing aerial display flights to attract ♀s. The ♀ lays 'clutches' of 3 eggs, 1 egg/day, in host nests, with intervals between 'clutches'.
Laying months: Feb-Apr. **Eggs:** 17.5-18.1-18.5 x 13.0-13.3-14.0 mm; recognisable in host nest as its egg is larger than egg of Orange-winged Pytilia (16.3 x 12.5 mm). **Incubation period:** 12-13 days. **Nestling/fledging period:** 21 days.

Dusky Indigobird *Vidua funerea* Gewone Blouvinkie   page 399

Breeds in mesic savanna and forest edge in coastal, lowland, riparian and montane areas. **Host:** only recorded host is African Firefinch. ♂s advertise from call-sites, singing a mixture of their own notes and imitated notes of the song/calls of the African Firefinch. ♀s visit these call-sites, mate with ♂ in attendance, and lay their eggs in the appropriate host nest; a ♀ usually lays 1 egg/day and a single egg in each host nest but, because more than one ♀ may lay in the same nest, host nests may contain more than one indigobird egg. No host eggs are removed, and the host raises its own, and the parasite's nestlings together.
Laying months: Jan-Apr. **Eggs:** 15 x 12 mm (oviduct egg); egg matches size of host (African Firefinch, 15.1 x 11.5 mm). **Incubation period:** not recorded. **Nestling/fledging period:** not recorded.

Purple Indigobird *Vidua purpurascens* Witpootblouvinkie   page 399

Breeds in mesic savannas. **Host:** only recorded host is Jameson's Firefinch. ♂s advertise from call-sites, singing a mixture of their own notes and imitated notes of the song/calls of the Jameson's Firefinch. ♀s visit these call-sites, mate with ♂ in attendance, and lay their eggs in the appropriate host nest. No host eggs are removed, and the host raises its own and the parasite's nestlings together.
Laying months: Jan-May. **Eggs:** 13.5-14.7-15.4 x 11.6-12.0-12.2 mm (oviduct eggs); egg matches size of host (Jameson's Firefinch, 14.6 x 11.2 mm), recognised by its different texture (has larger pores). **Incubation period:** not recorded. **Nestling/fledging period:** not recorded.

Village Indigobird *Vidua chalybeata* Staalblouvinkie   page 399

Breeds in mesic and semi-arid savannas. **Host:** primary host is Red-billed Firefinch (with about a third of its nests being parasitised); also recorded parasitising Brown Firefinch. In summer ♂s establish themselves at call-sites (80-150-250 m apart) to which they attract ♀s by singing a mixture of their own notes and imitated song and calls of the Red-billed Firefinch. ♀s visit these call-sites, mate with ♂ in attendance, and lay their eggs in the appropriate host nest; a ♀ lays estimated 22-26 eggs per season, laying 1/day for 3-4 successive days (i.e. a 'clutch'), with an interval before laying the next clutch. Each ♀ lays 1 egg/host nest but, because more than one ♀ may lay in the same nest, host nests may contain more than one indigobird egg. No host eggs are removed, and the host raises its own and the parasite's nestlings together. Occasionally, a ♀ may lay in a host nest of the wrong species, evidenced by cases of ♂s, raised by the 'wrong' hosts, mimicking songs of the wrong host (such as Jameson's Firefinch) at their song-post; ♀s may also, occasionally, select the wrong ♂ (e.g. a Shaft-tailed Whydah ♂) to mate with which, if raised successfully, results in a hybrid. Indigobird nestlings recorded in nests of the Brown Firefinch probably belong to this species.
Laying months: Jan-Jun, rarely in other months. **Eggs:** 13.7-14.9-16.3 x 11.5-11.8-12.1 mm; recognisable in host nest as its egg is larger than the egg of its host (Red-billed Firefinch, 13.3 x 10.6 mm). **Incubation period:** 11-12 days. **Nestling/fledging period:** 17-18 days.

Zambezi Indigobird *Vidua codringtoni* Groenblouvinkie

Restricted to mesic woodland and edges of evergreen forest in n Zimbabwe, this indigobird was recognised as a species in 1992 on the basis of ♂s found occupying call-sites and mimicking the songs of Red-throated Twinspot. A parasitised twinspot nest has not yet been recorded, but the song mimicry used by courting ♂s in this indigobird supports the view that this twinspot is this species' host.

Cuckoo-Finch *Anomalospiza imberbis* Koekoekvink   page 399

Breeds in mesic grasslands and grassy areas in savanna. **Host:** cisticolas and prinias; recorded host species include Red-faced, Singing, Rattling, Rufous-winged, Levaillant's Croaking, Zitting, Desert, Cloud, Pale-crowned, Ayres' cisticolas, Neddicky, and Tawny-flanked and Black-chested prinias). ♂ sings from a perch but do not mimic the songs of its hosts. ♀ lays 1 egg/day, about 30/season; 1-2 eggs are laid per host nest and she removes a host egg when laying. Host chicks are seldom raised alongside the young Cuckoo-Finch chicks, but more than one Cuckoo-Finch may be reared in the same nest.
Laying months: Nov-Apr. **Eggs:** 16.1-17.2-18.3 x 12.2-12.7-13.0 mm; mass 1.6 g; eggs are variably coloured and marked: white, pale blue or greenish-blue, either plain or speckled with red-brown; they match cisticola eggs but not prinia eggs. **Incubation period:** 14 days. **Nestling/fledging period:** 18 days.

Canaries

CANARIES Family Fringillidae Worldwide 207 species; 43 breed in Afrotropics, 15 in southern Africa, one introduced from Europe (Common Chaffinch). Monogamous, none are cooperative breeders and they nest solitarily, some occasionally nesting in small, loose colonies; nest an open cup placed in a tree or shrub; ♀ builds the nest and incubates, both sexes share feeding the nestlings; eggs oval, white or pale blue, either unmarked or sparsely speckled; 3-4/clutch; nestlings are altricial and nidicolous.

Common Chaffinch *Fringilla coelebs* Gryskoppie   no nest or egg photo

Breeds in wooded gardens and parks on the Cape Peninsula where it was introduced in 1897. Nesting habits poorly known in South Africa. Pairs nest solitarily, in England at a density of a pair/2 ha. **Nest:** (in Europe) a deep, open cup made of plant stems, well hidden in foliage, 2-10 m up in a leafy tree. It measures: outside diameter 90 mm; cup diameter 53 mm; nest height 71 mm; cup depth 40 mm; it is built by the ♀ in about 7 days. Breeding information given below is based on European birds.
Laying months: Sep-Nov (Cape Peninsula); double-brooded. **Clutch size:** 4-5; laid at 1-day intervals. **Eggs:** 19.7 x 14.0 mm; mass 2 g. **Incubation period:** 12-13 days; by ♀ only. **Nestling/fledging period:** 12-13 days; young brooded by ♀; fed by both sexes

Cape Canary *Serinus canicollis* Kaapse Kanarie   page 399

Breeds in fynbos and mesic grasslands in open, hilly or mountainous country where patches of shrubs, ouhout or alien vegetation provide nest sites; extends into semi-arid karoo along drainage lines and on farmlands. Pairs nest solitarily or semi-colonially: 2-12 pairs can nest in adjacent trees or bushes, nests <25 m apart. **Nest:** a small, thick-walled cup, typically 2-3 m (0.2-20) up from the ground, placed in a multiple fork in a leafy outer branch of a tree or bush. It is built with long, pliable plant stems (e.g. *Helichrysum* sp.) curled around to form a bowl, loosely bound together and to the branch with cobweb; nests in the vicinity of human habitation often incorporate string, cotton, rags, etc. The cup is lined with warm, soft material, usually plant down or sheep's wool. It measures: outside diameter 65-80-89 mm; inside diameter 46-50-56 mm; nest height 46-50-51 mm mm; cup depth 26-30-35 mm; built by the ♀ in 14-22 days. Nests are occasionally reused for a replacement clutch.
Laying months: mainly Nov-Feb (Sep-Apr, rarely in other months); relays after earlier failure. **Clutch size:** 3 (2-5); laid at 1-day intervals. **Eggs:** 15.8-17.2-18.9 x 11.6-12.8-13.6 mm. **Incubation period:** 12-14 days; by ♀ only, fed on nest by ♂. **Nestling/fledging period:** 17 days (15½-18½); young brooded by ♀; fed by both sexes.

Black-throated Canary *Crithagra atrogularis* Bergkanarie   page 399

Breeds widely across the semi-arid grasslands, karoo and savanna, frequenting open or lightly wooded country, especially thornveld. Pairs nest solitarily and are widely spaced. **Nest:** an open cup, built in a tree or bush; typically 3-4 m (1-15) up from the ground. It is usually in a leafy tree or sapling, well concealed in a cluster of leaves near the end of a branch. It is neatly finished, built with dry leaf petioles and shreds of bark stripped from the stems of forbs, or with tendrils and/or dry grass stems, bound together and to the supporting twigs with cobweb or with fibrous strands of plant down. Nests near human habitation may incorporate string, cotton, etc. The cup is lined with soft plant down or sheep's wool. The nest measures: outside diameter 65 mm; cup diameter 40-46-50 mm; nest height 40-46-50 mm; cup depth 25-30-32 mm. It is built by both sexes in about 6 days.
Laying months: mainly Nov-Feb (Sep-Apr, occasionally in other months); relays after earlier failure. **Clutch size:** 3 (2-4); laid at 1-day intervals. **Eggs:** 15.3-16.4-18.0 x 11.0-12.3-13.2 mm. **Incubation period:** 14 days (12-15); by ♀ only. **Nestling/fledging period:** 16 days (15½-17); young brooded by ♀; fed by both sexes.

Yellow-fronted Canary *Crithagra mozambica* Geeloogkanarie   page 399

Breeds in mesic savanna, extending into grassland and karoo where alien trees provide habitat. Pairs nest solitarily, occasionally semi-colonially (e.g. 3 nests built in adjacent trees). **Nest:** a small, compact, open cup, built in a tree or bush, typically 2-4 m up from the ground (<8 m). It is concealed in foliage on a thin outer branch where three or four side twigs provide support. The nest shell is built with shreds of soft bark from the stems of forbs, petioles, finely shredded grass and other plant fibre, and bound together with cobweb and/or with silky strands of plant seed. Nests near human habitation may incorporate string, cotton, etc. The cup is lined with fine, dry, hair-like plant stems: where it breeds alongside Black-throated Canary the linings distinguish the nests of the two (plant-down is used in Black-throated Canary nests). It measures: outside diameter 65-70-75 mm; cup diameter 36-47-51 mm; nest height 45-50 mm; cup depth 30-33 mm. It is built mainly or entirely by one bird (presumed ♀).
Laying months: mainly Dec-Mar (Nov-Apr) in Zimbabwe but Oct-Jan (Sep-Apr) further south. **Clutch size:** 3-4 (2-5); laid at 1-day intervals. **Eggs:** 14.6-16.3-18.5 x 11.1-12.1-13.8 mm; mass 1.5-1.7-2.0 g. **Incubation period:** 13½ days (13-14½); by ♀ only, fed on the nest by ♂. **Nestling/fledging period:** 19 days (16-24); young brooded by ♀; fed by both sexes.

Lemon-breasted Canary *Crithagra citrinipectus* Geelborskanarie   page 399

Breeds along n coastal plain in *Hyphaene* palm savanna. Pairs nest solitarily and are widely spaced. Nesting habits are poorly known. **Nest:** an open cup that differs in its positioning from all other canaries in the region; it is placed in the leaf of an ilala palm, hidden in the deep V formed at the base of a new leaf and only visible from directly above or through the narrow gap between the leaf blades; 1½-7 m up from the ground. It is an open cup, its base an oblong-shaped wad of matted, brown-coloured plant debris (old flower petals covered in cobweb and collected from old palm infloresences) which fill the deep V in the leaf fold. The cup is set in this and is finely lined with long, hair-like fibres shredded from the leaves of the palm. One nest measured: outside diameter 160 x 65 mm; cup diameter 45 x 55 mm. It is built by both sexes.
Laying months: Dec-Feb. **Clutch size:** 3; laid at 1-day intervals. **Eggs:** 15.0-16.0-17.4 x 11.4-11.9-12.0 mm. **Incubation period:** 12-14 days; by ♀ only (in captivity). **Nestling/fledging period:** 14-16 days (in captivity).

Cape Canary

Black-throated Canary

Yellow-fronted Canary

Lemon-breasted Canary

Canaries

Yellow Canary *Crithagra flaviventris* Geelkanarie   page 399
Breeds widely in semi-arid and arid karoo shrublands and in arid grassland and savanna. Pairs nest solitarily and are widely spaced. **Nest:** an open cup, usually placed low down (½-1 m up from the ground, rarely higher than 3 m up) in a shrubby bush (e.g. *Rhigozum*) or low thorn tree; usually placed in the twigs of a multiple fork, near the top of the bush; sometimes poorly concealed. It is built with thin, dry stems and tendrils of shrubs or grass, or rootlets, curled around to form a nest-bowl that is roughly finished outside, but finely and neatly lined inside. Soft white or yellowish-coloured plant down (e.g. *Eriocephalus* sp.) is used to line the cup. The nest measures: outside diameter 90-100 mm; cup diameter 50 mm; cup depth 38 mm. It is built by the ♀ in 3-4 days.
Laying months: all months recorded, but mainly Aug-Sep in winter-rainfall region, Sep-Mar in summer-rainfall areas. **Clutch size:** 3 (2-5); laid at 1-day intervals. **Eggs:** 16.1-18.0-20.6 x 12.2-13.2-14.6 mm. **Incubation period:** 14½ days (12-16); by ♀ only. **Nestling/fledging period:** 16 days (14-19); young brooded by ♀; fed by both sexes.

Brimstone Canary *Crithagra sulphurata* Dikbekkanarie   page 399
Breeds in bracken and scrub on verges of montane and coastal forest. Pairs nest solitarily or semi-colonially, 2-6 pairs sometimes nesting 5-20 m apart. **Nest:** an open cup, typically 1½-2½ m (1-6) up from the ground, usually built in a multiple fork hidden in foliage in a leafy bush or sapling tree. It is built with pliable, dry stems and tendrils of forbs (especially *Helichrysum* sp.), rootlets and/or grass runners that are curled around to form a rough bowl, some nests skimpy and thin-walled, others quite substantial. Inside this shell finer plant material (shredded grass or hair or a few feathers) is used, and a lining of woolly plant down forms the final lining to the cup. The nest measures: outside diameter 90-90-95 mm; cup diameter 50-53-57 mm; cup depth 28-34-38 mm; nest height 50-60-65 mm. It is built by the ♀, accompanied by her mate during nest-building trips. She sits tight while incubating, but if disturbed off the nest she may perform an injury-feigning distraction flight.
Laying months: mainly Aug-Nov (Jul-Mar, occasionally in other months). **Clutch size:** 3 (2-4); laid at 1-day intervals. **Eggs:** 17.4-19.3-21.5 x 13.1-14.0-15.3 mm. **Incubation period:** 14½ days (12½-17); by ♀ only, fed by ♂ on nest; begins before clutch is completed. **Nestling/fledging period:** 16½ days (14-21); young brooded by ♀; fed by both sexes.

Forest Canary *Crithagra scotops* Gestreepte Kanarie   no nest photo   page 399
Breeds in and on the verges of montane forest. Pairs nest solitarily, but there is one record of two nests, 2 m apart, in a tree. Nesting habits of non-captive birds are poorly known. **Nest:** a bulky open cup, well hidden in the leafy foliage of an outer branch of a tree, sapling or bush; between 1-6 m up from the ground. It is commonly built with *Usnea*, but moss and other plant material may be used and the cup is lined with finer plant stems; it is larger than the nests built by Cape or Yellow-fronted canary, its outside diameter 100 mm across, cup diameter about 57 mm. It is built by the ♀ and takes 2 weeks to complete. ♂s may assist in collecting and carrying nest material.
Laying months: mainly Oct-Jan (Sep-Apr); occasionally double-brooded. **Clutch size:** 3-4 (2-4); laid at 1-day intervals. **Eggs:** 16.9-17.3-18.3 x 12.2-12.6-13.3 mm. **Incubation period:** 14 days; by ♀ only (in captivity). **Nestling/fledging period:** 17½ days (15-19, in captivity); young brooded by ♀; fed by both sexes.

Streaky-headed Seedeater *Crithagra gularis* Streepkopkanarie   page 399
Breeds in mesic savanna, in fynbos and in scrub forest; often in hilly country and frequently associated with stands of *Protea* trees. Pairs nest solitarily and are widely spaced. **Nest:** an open cup, typically built in a forked outer branch of a leafy tree, about 3-5 m up (1½-12) from the ground; usually well concealed in foliage; one recorded in the leaves of an *Aloe ferox*. The nest is compact and neatly finished, its exterior made with leaf petioles, short pieces of twig, fragments of leaf or bark, or other dry plant material, bound together, and to the supporting twigs, with a small amount of cobweb. The inside is lined with finer shreds of the same and soft, felted plant down forms the final cup-lining. The nest measures: outside diameter 65-105 mm; nest height 50 mm; cup diameter 50-70 mm; cup depth 26-39 mm. It is built by one bird, assumed to be the ♀.
Laying months: mainly Oct-Jan (Aug-Mar); earlier in winter-rainfall region (Aug-Oct). **Clutch size:** 2-3, rarely 4; laid at 1-day intervals. **Eggs:** 17.0-18.5-21.2 x 12.6-13.8-15.0 mm. **Incubation period:** 14 days (12-15); by ♀ only, fed by ♂ on the nest. **Nestling/fledging period:** 17 days; young brooded by ♀, fed by both sexes.

White-throated Canary *Crithagra albogularis* Witkeelkanarie   page 399
Breeds in semi-arid and arid shrublands of the karoo and fynbos. Pairs nest solitarily, sometimes in loose aggregations (e.g. 3 nests, 30-40 m apart). **Nest:** an open cup built in a shrubby bush, a *Euphorbia*, or in a low thorn tree; typically about 1 m up from the ground (0.6-3.7), concealed among the twigs or stems of a multiple fork. It is built with thin, dry stems and tendrils of forbs or creepers, and/or with bleached dry grass stems, curled around to form a nest bowl that is roughly finished outside, but neatly lined inside. Soft white or yellowish-coloured plant down (especially *Eriocephalus* sp.), occasionally wool, is used to line the cup. The nest measures: outside diameter 120 mm; cup diameter 65-75 mm; cup depth 40 mm. It is built by one bird, assumed to be the ♀.
Laying months: all months recorded, but mainly Aug-Oct (Jul-Nov) in winter-rainfall region and Aug-Apr in summer-rainfall areas. **Clutch size:** 3 (2-5); laid at 1-day intervals. **Eggs:** 17.2-19.8-22.1 x 12.8-14.3-16.6 mm. **Incubation period:** 16 days (13-18); by ♀ only, fed by ♂ on the nest. **Nestling/fledging period:** 16 days (15-17); young fed by both sexes.

Yellow Canary

Brimstone Canary

Streaky-headed Seedeater

White-throated Canary

Cape Siskin *Crithagra totta* Kaapse Pietjiekanarie   page 399

Breeds in mountains of s and w Cape, mostly in fynbos. Pairs nest solitarily and are widely spaced. **Nest:** a bulky cup, built on a rock face, either in a crevice, on a sheltered ledge, or hidden behind grass or a shrub growing out of the face; occasionally in a tree cavity. The nest may be 1-2 m up from the base of the rock, or in a high, inaccessible hole; it is often close to a waterfall or in a moist position. It is built with pliable stems of weeds and grass, rootlets, fragments of dead leaf and other plant material that is curled around to form a bowl; the cup is lined with fine, hair-like plant fibres. It measures: outside diameter 80-115 mm; cup diameter 40-50 mm; cup depth 20-30 mm; nest height 40 mm. It is built by the ♀, accompanied by ♂. Nests sites are frequently reused in successive years.
Laying months: mainly Aug-Nov (Aug-Dec). **Clutch size:** 3-4, rarely 5; laid at 1-day intervals. **Eggs:** 16.4-18.2-19.6 x 12.2-13.1-14.1 mm; occasionally parasitised by Red-chested Cuckoo (as shown in photograph opposite). **Incubation period:** 16-17 days; by ♀ only; begins when third egg is laid. **Nestling/fledging period:** 20 days (17-18 in captivity); young fed by both sexes.

Drakensberg Siskin *Crithagra symonsi* Bergpietjiekanarie   page 399

Breeds in montane grasslands, 2000-2600 m above sea-level. Pairs nest solitarily and are widely spaced. **Nest:** a substantial cup, built on a rock face, wall of an erosion gulley or road cutting, either inside a grass-tuft growing out of the rock or bank, or in a crevice, in a pothole, or on a sheltered ledge, usually 1-4 m up from the base of a low cliff. It is built from fine dry plant material, mainly dark-coloured rootlets, with coarser material used to form the base of the nest. The cup is lined with fine rootlets and other plant fibres, occasionally, sheep's wool. The nest measures: outside diameter 113-120-140 mm; cup diameter 52-54-55 mm; cup depth 25-35-40 mm; nest height 55 mm. Nest sites are frequently reused in successive years and several older nests may be found in the vicinity of one currently in use.
Laying months: mainly Nov-Dec (Nov-Mar). **Clutch size:** 2-4. **Eggs:** 16.4-18.0-19.0 x 12.8-13.4-13.9 mm. **Incubation period:** 17 days (in captivity). **Nestling/fledging period:** 19 days (in captivity).

Black-headed Canary *Crithagra alario* Swartkopkanarie   page 399

Breeds in the karoo in semi-arid and arid shrublands. Pairs nest solitarily, sometimes in loose aggregations, when adjacent nests can be spaced 10-50 m apart. **Nest:** an open cup concealed in the foliage of a low woody shrub or succulent, usually 0.3-0.5 m up from the ground (rarely > 1 m up). The nest's exterior is made with pieces of dry, old stems of grass or some other plant material; its interior is thickly lined with white or yellowish-coloured (e.g. *Eriocephalus* sp.) plant down, sometimes with mammal hair. It measures: outside diameter 70 mm; cup diameter 43-50 mm; cup depth 25 mm. It is built by the ♀ in 4-6 days and she is accompanied by the ♂ during nest-building trips. If flushed from the nest during incubation, the ♀ may perform an injury-feigning distraction flight.
Laying months: mainly Jul-Nov, but all months recorded; probably opportunistic in arid areas, depending on rainfall. **Clutch size:** 3 (2-5); laid at 1-day intervals. **Eggs:** 15.0-17.0-19.1 x 11.5-12.5-13.9 mm. **Incubation period:** 13-14 days (in captivity); by ♀ only. **Nestling/fledging period:** 19½ days (in captivity); young fed by both sexes.

Protea Canary *Crithagra leucoptera* Witvlerkkanarie   no nest photo   page 399

Breeds in tall fynbos, favouring hillslopes and valleys with tall protea growth. Pairs nest solitarily and are widely spaced. **Nest:** an open cup built inside a leafy *Protea* tree (once in a pine), in a forked branch well below the canopy, about 3 m (1½-4½) up from the ground. It is well concealed in a cluster of leaves at a multiple-twigged fork. The nest is compactly made, the outer bowl made from withered stems of forbs or *Helichrysum* sp. curled around to form an untidy bowl, inside of which is a neatly finished cup; this is lined with either plant down (e.g. brown-coloured seeds of *Protea neriifolia*) or fine stems of wiry grass. The nest measures: outside diameter 80-120 mm; cup diameter 53-58 mm; cup depth 35-47 mm; nest height 70-90 mm.
Laying months: Aug-Oct. **Clutch size:** 2-4. **Eggs:** 19.0-20.6-21.7 x 14.4-14.6-14.9 mm. **Incubation period:** 17 days; probably by ♀ only. **Nestling/fledging period:** 14 days; young fed by both sexes.

Black-eared Canary *Crithagra mennelli* Swartoorkanarie   no nest photo   page 399

Breeds in n savanna in miombo woodland. Pairs nest solitarily at a density of a pair/25 ha. Nesting habits are poorly known. **Nest:** a smallish open cup, well concealed by foliage in thin leafy twigs in the upper canopy of a tree or sapling, typically a *Brachystegia* sp.; about 5-6 m (3-9) up, not easily visible from the ground. It is made mainly or entirely with *Usnea* which is used for the walls and the cup lining; in some, leaf petioles and/or rootlets are also incorporated. The nest measures: outside diameter 70-77-90 mm; cup diameter 45-54-70 mm; cup depth 20-27-30 mm; nest height 35-50-70 mm.
Laying months: Nov-Feb (Sep-Mar). **Clutch size:** 3 (2-3). **Eggs:** 17.2-18.2-19.3 x 13.2-13.8-14.4 mm. **Incubation period:** 13 days (in captivity); by ♀ only, fed on nest by ♂. **Nestling/fledging period:** 18 days (in captivity).

Cape Siskin   non-matching brown egg laid by Red-chested Cuckoo

Drakensberg Siskin

Black-headed Canary

Buntings

BUNTINGS Family Emberizidae Worldwide 163 species; 9 breed in Afrotropics, 5 in southern Africa. The majority of this family occur in n, c and s America where they are known as sparrows, juncos, cardinals, towhees or finches. The African members, all of the genus *Emberiza*, are a close-knit group; they are monogamous; gregarious when not breeding; ♀ builds the nest and (in the cases known) does most or all the incubation; nest an open cup placed on the ground or in a low bush; eggs oval, white, scrolled, speckled or mottled with brown; 2-3/clutch; nestlings are altricial and nidicolous. One is infrequently parasitised by Diederik and Jacobin cuckoos.

Lark-like Bunting *Emberiza impetuani* Vaalstreepkoppie   page 399

Breeds widely in the semi-arid and arid karoo, typically in open, sparsely vegetated stony areas. Pairs nest solitarily, but on occasion adjacent pairs can nest <20 m apart. **Nest:** an open cup placed on the ground, usually at base of a rock, less often under a grass tuft or low shrub; it has a broad base of dry twigs into which is set a neatly lined cup of fine grass stems (usually feathery inflorescences of *Stipagrostis* grass) or rootlets. The twiggy base is usually wider (>100 mm) when placed against a bush than a rock. The nest measures: outside diameter 150 mm; cup diameter 53-58-67 mm; cup depth 24-29-39 mm; nest height 70 mm. It is built by the ♀, accompanied by ♂ during nest-building trips. Active nests frequently have one or more incomplete, abandoned nests in their vicinity. **Laying months:** breeds opportunistically in response to rainfall: all months recorded, but mainly Sep-Nov in winter-rainfall areas and Feb-Apr elsewhere. **Clutch size:** 3 (2-4); laid at 1-day intervals. **Eggs:** 15.5-17.8-19.6 x 12.1-13.2-15.3 mm. **Incubation period:** 11-13 days. **Nestling/fledging period:** 12-13 days.

Cinnamon-breasted Bunting *Emberiza tahapisi* Klipstreepkoppie   page 399

A widespread breeding visitor, arriving in Dec, to stony or rocky areas in savanna, grassland and e karoo, nesting on hillsides and koppies, in gravel pits, around mine workings, etc. Pairs nest solitarily, sometimes semi-colonially (e.g. 20 pairs in 6 ha, adjacent nests 20-30 m apart). **Nest:** an open cup placed in a shallow scrape on the ground, typically against the underside of a rock, a grass tuft, a clod of earth or in a crevice on the sloping wall of a donga or old mine working; usually well concealed. The base is made of coarse, dry grass and weed stems that are loosely curled around to form a bowl, some bits straying untidily beyond the rim of the nest; the cup is finely lined with rootlets and grass stems. It measures: outside diameter 90-121-140 mm; cup diameter 50-59-71 mm; cup depth 19-24-28 mm. It is built by the ♀ in 4-13 days, accompanied by the ♂ while building.
Laying months: mainly Jan-Apr (Nov-Jun). **Clutch size:** 3 (2-4). **Eggs:** 16.0-17.9-19.7 x 12.2-13.3-14.0 mm. **Incubation period:** 12-14 days; by both sexes, but mainly by ♀. **Nestling/fledging period:** 14-16 days; young fed by both sexes.

Cape Bunting *Emberiza capensis* Rooivlerkstreepkoppie   page 399

Breeds in open grassland, karoo and fynbos, especially in rocky, hilly areas. Pairs nest solitarily and are widely spaced. **Nest:** a well-concealed open cup, placed in a low shrub or dense grass tuft, usually <300 mm up, but seldom actually on the ground. The nest shrub is often one growing against a rock, at the base of a low cliff, in a depression, or in some other sheltered spot; occasionally in an outbuilding. The base of the nest is roughly built with old, dry stems and blades of grass and weedy plants, and the cup is set into this, neatly lined with fine, hair-like grass, fine rootlets and/or mammal hair; plant down is not usually used. It measures: outside diameter 95-110 mm; nest height 50-60 mm; cup diameter 60 mm; cup depth 40-50 mm. Built by one bird, presumed ♀, in 7 days.
Laying months: all months recorded, but mainly Nov-Apr in summer-rainfall areas, Sept-Oct in winter-rainfall region. **Clutch size:** 3 (2-5). **Eggs:** 17.9-20.3-23.2 x 13.6-15.0-16.4 mm. **Incubation period:** 14½ days (13-16). **Nestling/fledging period:** 10-12½ days; young fed by both sexes.

Cabanis' Bunting (Cabanis's Bunting) *Emberiza cabanisi* Geelstreepkoppie   page 399

Breeds in n savanna in miombo woodland. Pairs nest solitarily and are widely spaced. **Nest:** an open cup, well hidden in leafy foliage of a smallish tree, typically 2½ m (1-6) up from the ground. Bulkier than the nest of Golden-breasted Bunting, its outer shell is built with coarse, dry grass blades, dry stalks of weedy plants, pieces of skeletonised leaf and other plant material; the nest-cup is neatly lined with strands of fine dry grass ends and a few rootlets. It measures: outside diameter 90-100-110 mm; cup diameter 45-50-55 mm; cup depth 32 mm; nest thickness 60-80 mm. It is built by the ♀.
Laying months: mainly Oct-Nov (Sep-Jan, occasionally in other months). **Clutch size:** 2 (1-3). **Eggs:** 17.9-20.2-23.7 x 13.3-14.6-16.0 mm. **Incubation period:** 12-14 days. **Nestling/fledging period:** 16 days (in captivity).

Golden-breasted Bunting *Emberiza flaviventris* Rooirugstreepkoppie   pages 378, 399

Breeds widely across the savanna belt in open woodland and second-growth, extending into grassland and karoo edge, often here in alien vegetation. Pairs nest solitarily and are widely spaced. **Nest:** a rather flimsy open cup built into the leafy twigs of a small, lone-standing tree or shrub, typically 1-1½ m (½-2½) up from the ground. Its outer shell is characteristically made from lengths of old, grey-coloured grass (or shreds of bark or very fine, branched, dry flower-heads of forbs) that are curled around to form a bowl, with pieces left projecting untidily in all directions; the nest rim at the approach side often extends to form a flat lip. The cup is neatly lined with fine hair-like grass ends or rootlets, sometimes also strands of mammal hair. It measures: outside diameter 80-85-90 mm; cup diameter 50-53-55 mm; cup depth 30-35-40 mm; nest thickness 45-53-60 mm. It is built by the ♀, accompanied by the ♂ on nest-building trips; he sings frequently in the vicinity of the nest during the early stages of the breeding cycle.
Laying months: mainly Oct-Dec (Sep-May). **Clutch size:** 2-3, rarely 4 or 5; laid at 1-day intervals; occasionally parasitised by Diederik and Jacobin cuckoos. **Eggs:** 15.5-20.3-22.5 x 13.1-14.3-15.3 mm. **Incubation period:** 12-13 days; by ♀ only. **Nestling/fledging period:** 12-13 days; young brooded by ♀, fed by both sexes.

Lark-like Bunting

Cinnamon-breasted Bunting

Cape Bunting

Cabanis' Bunting Golden-breasted Bunting

352 Ostrich, Guineafowl, Peafowl, Partridge, Francolins

For text on ostrich, guineafowl, peafowl, partridge & francolins see pages 20-22

Chukar Partridge

Coqui Francolin

Crested Francolin

Common Ostrich

Helmeted Guineafowl

Crested Guineafowl

Indian Peafowl

Francolins, Spurfowl, Quails

353

For text on francolins, spurfowl & quail see pages 22-26

Red-winged Francolin

Grey-winged Francolin

Orange River Francolin

Shelley's Francolin

Red-billed Spurfowl

Natal Spurfowl

Cape Spurfowl

Red-necked Spurfowl

Swainson's Spurfowl (2)

Hartlaub's Spurfowl

Blue Quail (2)

Common Quail (3)

Harlequin Quail (3)

Ducks, Geese

For text on ducks & geese see pages 28-34

White-backed Duck

White-faced Duck

Fulvous Duck

Spur-winged Goose

Egyptian Goose

Knob-billed Duck

African Pygmy Goose

Southern Pochard

South African Shelduck

Ducks, Storm Petrel, Penguin, Gannet

355

For text on these ducks see pages 32-34

Yellow-billed Duck

Red-billed Teal

Cape Teal

Hottentot Teal

Cape Shoveler

African Black Duck

Maccoa Duck

For text on storm petrel, penguin & gannet see page 36

Leach's Storm Petrel

African Penguin

Cape Gannet

356　Grebes, Flamingos, Hamerkop, Storks

For text on grebes see page 38

Great
Crested Grebe (2)

Black-necked
Grebe

Little
Grebe

grebe eggs are white when laid but soon become nest-stained as the examples here show

For text on flamingos, storks see page 40

Lesser
Flamingo

Yellow-billed
Stork

Greater
Flamingo

For text on hamerkop see page 54

freshly laid (left)
nest-stained (right)

Hamerkop
(2)

African
Openbill

# Storks, Ibis, Spoonbill 357

For text on these storks, ibis & spoonbill see pages 42-44

Woolly-necked Stork

White Stork

Black Stork

Saddle-billed Stork

Marabou Stork

African Sacred Ibis (2)

African Spoonbill

Ibises, Herons, Egrets

For text on ibises see page 44

Glossy Ibis

Southern Bald Ibis

Hadeda Ibis

Hadeda eggs are very variably marked; this is a middle-of-the-road example

For text on these herons & egrets see pages 46-48

Goliath Heron

Black-headed Heron

Grey Heron

Western Cattle Egret

Purple Heron

Great Egret

Yellow-billed Egret

Little Egret

Herons, Bitterns, Darter, Pelicans

359

For text on these herons, bitterns, darter & pelicans see pages 50-54

Black Heron

Rufous-bellied Heron

Squacco Heron

Green-backed Heron

Little Bittern

Dwarf Bittern

Black-crowned Night Heron

White-backed Night Heron

Eurasian Bittern

African Darter

Pink-backed Pelican

Great White Pelican

Cormorants, Kites, Hawks

For text on cormorants see page 56

Cape Cormorant

White-breasted Cormorant

Bank Cormorant

Reed Cormorant

Crowned Cormorant

For text on kites & hawks see page 58

Yellow-billed Kite (2)

Black-shouldered Kite (2)

Bat Hawk (2)

freshly laid egg left,
well-incubated egg right

African Cuckoo-Hawk

Secretarybird, Vultures

For text on secretarybird & these vultures see page 60

Secretarybird

Palm-nut Vulture

Egyptian Vulture

an authentic Egyptian Vulture egg from South Africa, collected in Oct 1869 in the Malmesbury district, W Cape

Bearded Vulture (2)

freshly laid egg on the left, well-incubated egg on the right, coloured with pigment from breast feathers of incubating bird

Vultures

For text on these vultures see page 62

Cape Vulture

White-backed Vulture

Lappet-faced Vulture (2)

eggs range from unmarked (left) to heavily smeared with brown (right)

Vultures, Eagles

363

For text on these vultures & eagles
see pages 62, 66, 70

eggs range from unmarked (left) to heavily blotched (right)

Hooded Vulture (2)

White-headed Vulture

Long-crested Eagle

African Fish Eagle

364 • **Snake Eagles, Bateleur, Eagle**

For text on these eagles see pages 64-66

Brown
Snake Eagle

Black-chested
Snake Eagle

Western Banded
Snake Eagle

Bateleur

Tawny
Eagle (2)

The snake eagles and Bateleur lay unmarked white eggs, whereas in many other eagles, including Tawny, Verreaux's and Wahlberg's (opposite), eggs can vary from plain white to heavily blotched, as shown in the examples here

Eagles

365

For text on these eagles see pages 68-70

Verreaux's Eagle (2)

Martial Eagle

Crowned Eagle

Ayres' Eagle

Wahlberg's Eagle (2)

366 **Buzzards, Eagles**

For text on buzzards & these eagles see pages 70, 72, 78

buzzard eggs are quite variably marked as examples below show

Jackal Buzzard (2)

Lizard Buzzard (2)

Augur Buzzard (2)

Booted Eagle

Forest Buzzard (2)

African Hawk-Eagle

Sparrowhawks, Goshawks, Harriers

367

For text on sparrowhawks, goshawks & harriers see pages 72-78

Ovambo Sparrowhawk (3)

African Goshawk

Rufous-breasted Sparrowhawk (2)

Shikra (2)

Black Harrier (2)

Black Sparrowhawk

Little Sparrowhawk

their eggs are sometimes faintly marked like this one

African Marsh Harrier

Pale Chanting Goshawk

Dark Chanting Goshawk

Gabar Goshawk

Kestrels, Falcons, Hobby, Osprey

For text on kestrels, falcons, hobby, osprey see pages 60, 80-84

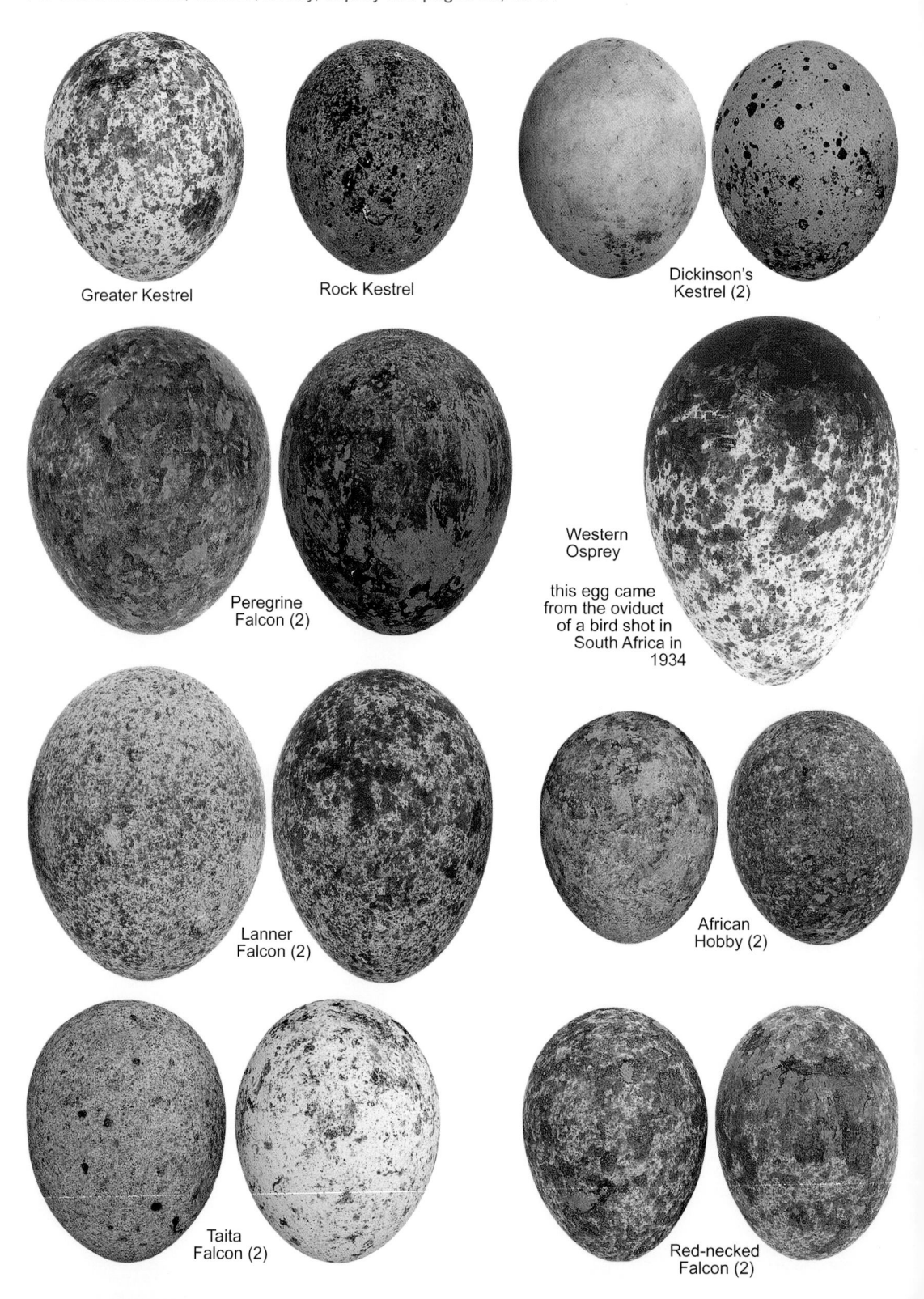

Greater Kestrel

Rock Kestrel

Dickinson's Kestrel (2)

Peregrine Falcon (2)

Western Osprey

this egg came from the oviduct of a bird shot in South Africa in 1934

Lanner Falcon (2)

African Hobby (2)

Taita Falcon (2)

Red-necked Falcon (2)

Harrier-Hawk, Pygmy Falcon, Bustards

For text on harrier-hawk & pygmy falcon see pages 72, 84

African Harrier-Hawk (2)

Pygmy Falcon

For text on these bustards see page 86

Ludwig's Bustard

Kori Bustard

Denham's Bustard (2)

Korhaans, Bustard

For text on korhaans & this bustard see pages 86-90

Karoo Korhaan (2)

Rüppell's Korhaan

the two Karoo Korhaan eggs (above left) are an example of the great variability in shape and colour of korhaan eggs (sometimes even within a clutch)

Blue Korhaan

Red-crested Korhaan

White-bellied Korhaan

Black-bellied Bustard

Southern Black Korhaan

Northern Black Korhaan

Flufftails, Crakes, Rails, Gallinule, Moorhens

For text on flufftails see page 92

Red-chested Flufftail

Buff-spotted Flufftail

Streaky-breasted Flufftail

Striped Flufftail

White-winged Flufftail

For text on crakes, rails, moorhens & gallinule see pages 94-96

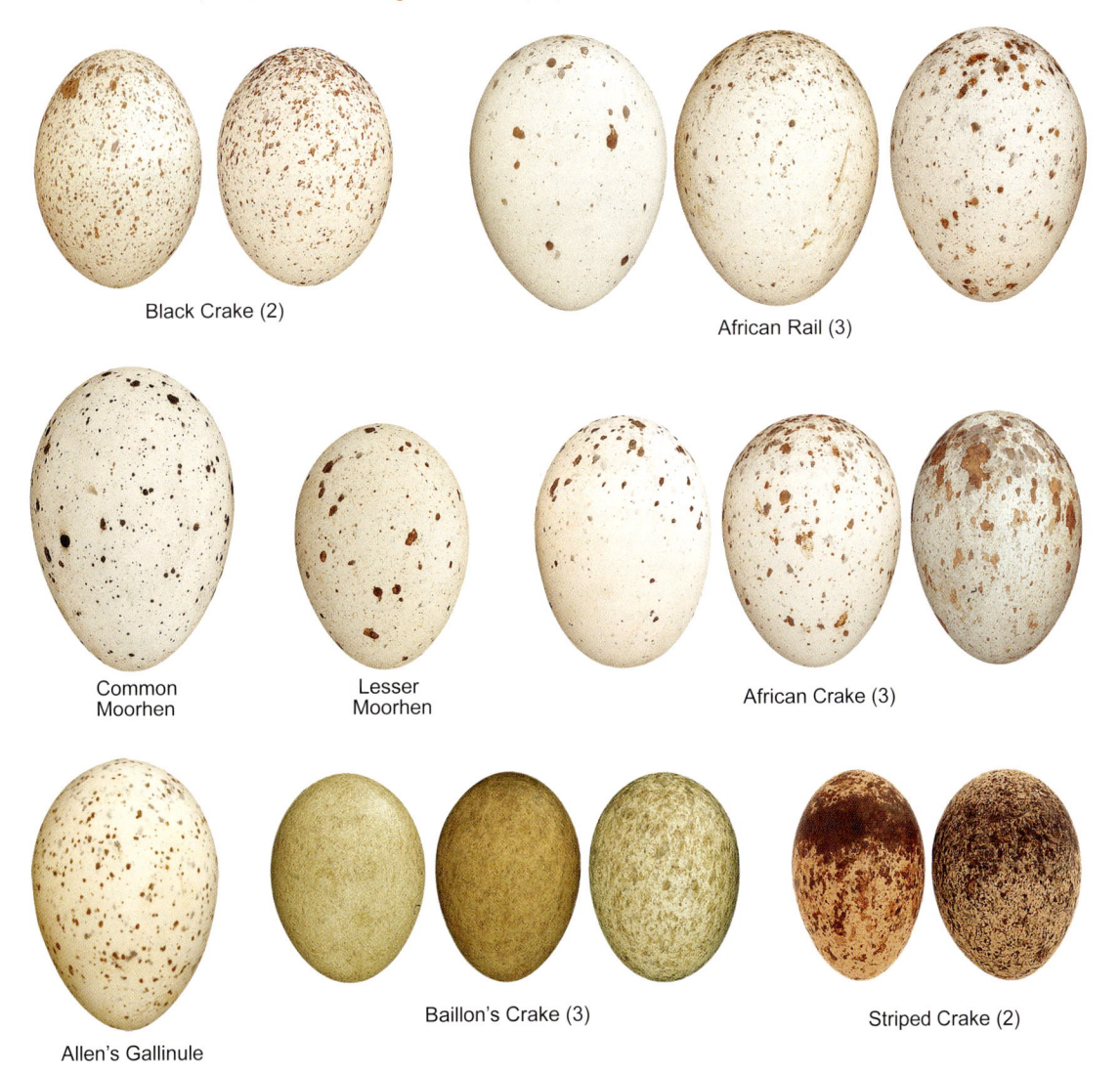

Black Crake (2)

African Rail (3)

Common Moorhen

Lesser Moorhen

African Crake (3)

Allen's Gallinule

Baillon's Crake (3)

Striped Crake (2)

372　　　　　　　　　　Swamphen, Coot, Finfoot, Cranes

For text on swamphen, coot, finfoot & these cranes see pages 96-98, 110

African
Swamphen
(2)

Red-knobbed
Coot (2)

African
Finfoot
(2)

Wattled Crane

Blue Crane

Buttonquails, Dikkops, Stilt, Avocet, Oystercatcher, Crane

For text on buttonquails, dikkops, stilt, oystercatcher & avocet see pages 100-104

Kurrichane Buttonquail (3)

Black-rumped Buttonquail (2)

Spotted Dikkop (2)

Water Dikkop

For text on this crane see page 98

Black-winged Stilt (2)

African Oystercatcher

Pied Avocet (2)

Grey Crowned Crane

Lapwings, Plovers, Jacanas, Painted Snipe, Snipe

For text on lapwings, plovers, jacanas, painted snipe & snipe see pages 104–112

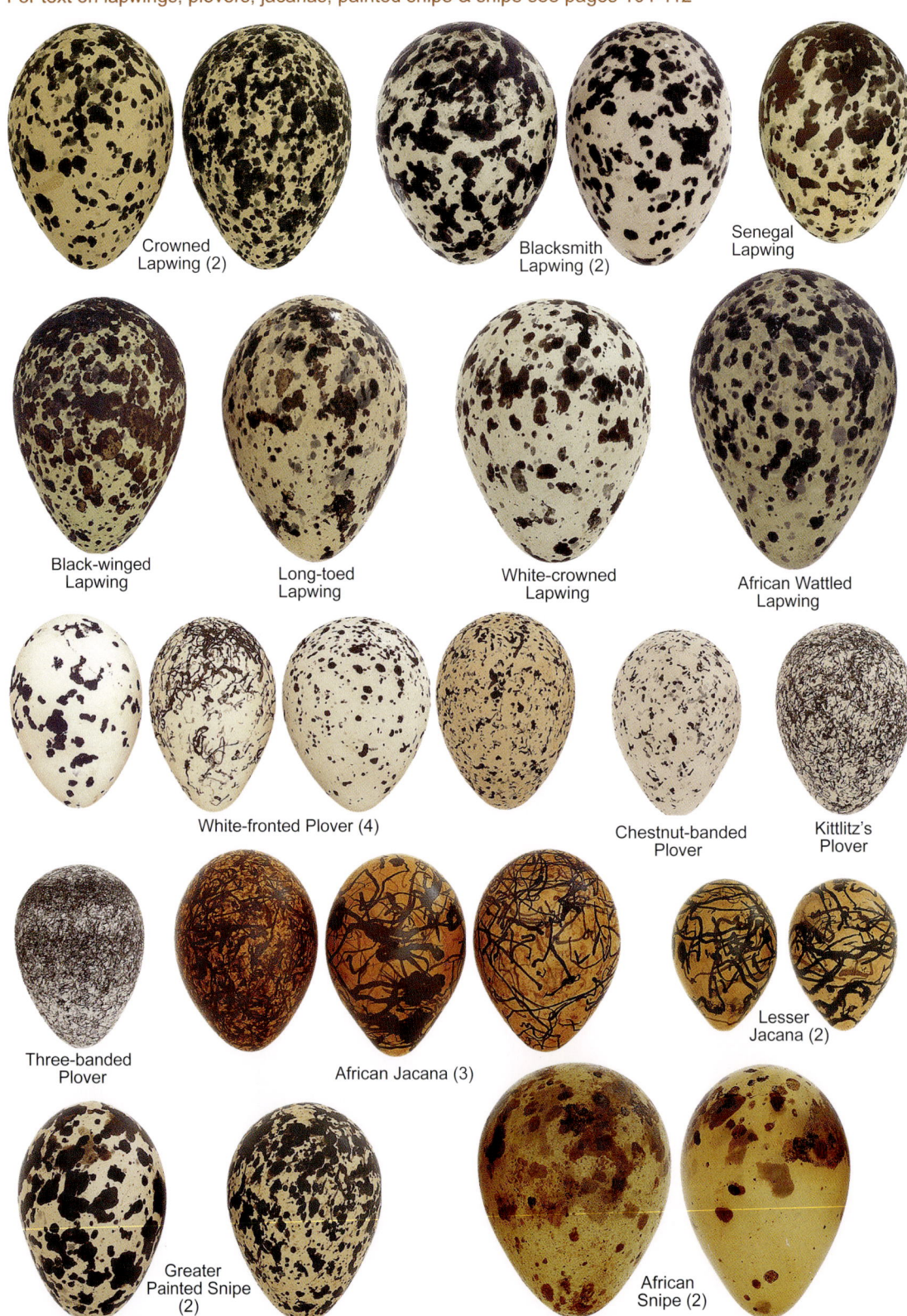

Crowned Lapwing (2)

Blacksmith Lapwing (2)

Senegal Lapwing

Black-winged Lapwing

Long-toed Lapwing

White-crowned Lapwing

African Wattled Lapwing

White-fronted Plover (4)

Chestnut-banded Plover

Kittlitz's Plover

Three-banded Plover

African Jacana (3)

Lesser Jacana (2)

Greater Painted Snipe (2)

African Snipe (2)

Coursers, Pratincoles, Gulls, Tern

For text on coursers & pratincoles see pages 112-114

Burchell's Courser (2)

Temminck's Courser (2)

Double-banded Courser

Three-banded Courser

Bronze-winged Courser (2)

Collared Pratincole

Rock Pratincole (3)

For text on gulls & terns see pages 116-118

Hartlaub's Gull

Grey-headed Gull

Kelp Gull

Caspian Tern (2)

Skimmer, Terns, Sandgrouse

376

For text on terns see page 118

African Skimmer (2)

Whiskered Tern (2)

Damara Tern

Swift Tern (3)

Roseate Tern (2)

Yellow-throated Sandgrouse (2)

For text on sandgrouse see page 120

Double-banded Sandgrouse (2)

Burchell's Sandgrouse (2)

Namaqua Sandgrouse (2)

Pigeons, Doves, Parrots, Lovebirds, Turacos, Lourie

377

For text on pigeons & doves see pages 122-126

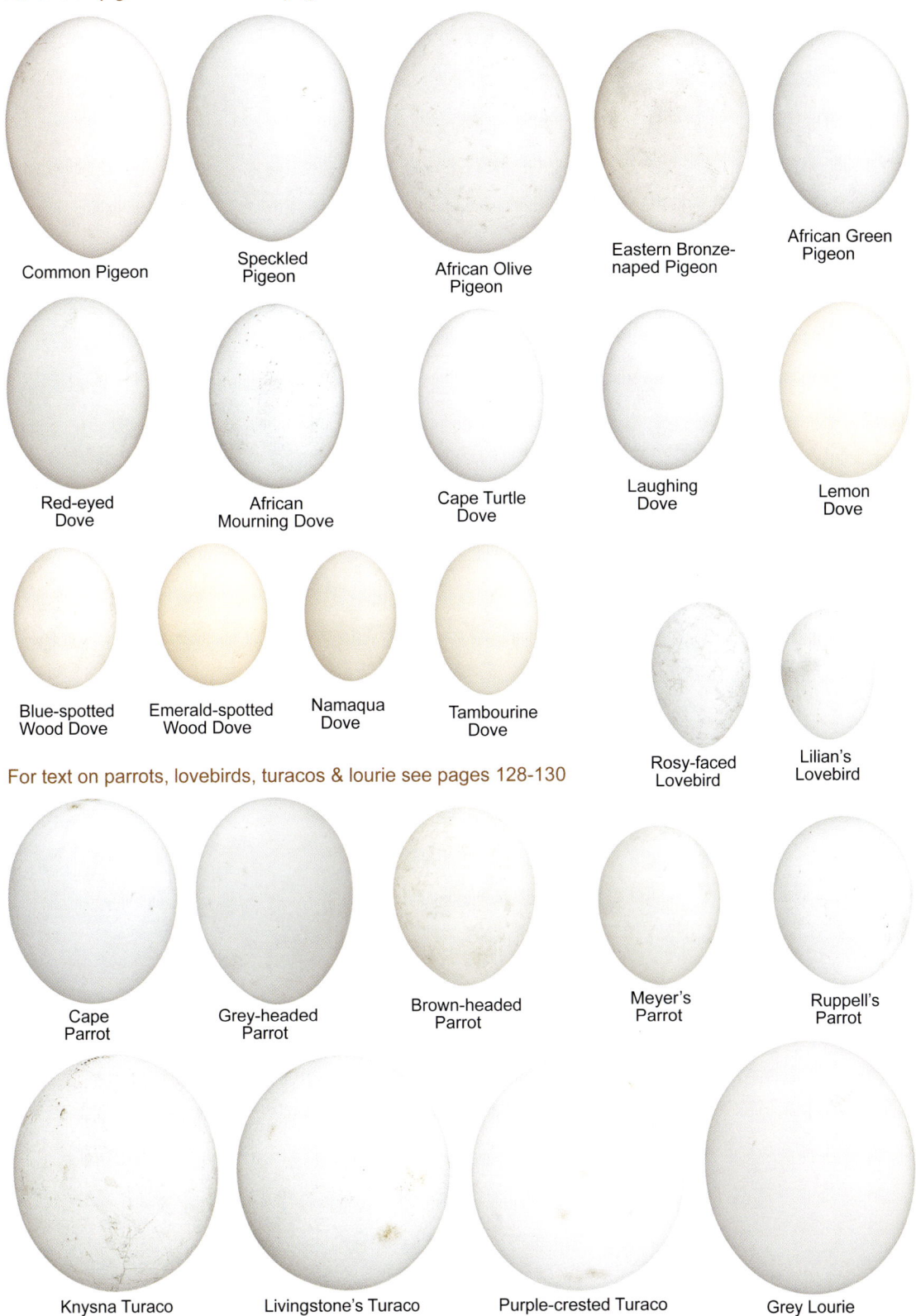

| Common Pigeon | Speckled Pigeon | African Olive Pigeon | Eastern Bronze-naped Pigeon | African Green Pigeon |

| Red-eyed Dove | African Mourning Dove | Cape Turtle Dove | Laughing Dove | Lemon Dove |

| Blue-spotted Wood Dove | Emerald-spotted Wood Dove | Namaqua Dove | Tambourine Dove | Rosy-faced Lovebird | Lilian's Lovebird |

For text on parrots, lovebirds, turacos & lourie see pages 128-130

| Cape Parrot | Grey-headed Parrot | Brown-headed Parrot | Meyer's Parrot | Ruppell's Parrot |

| Knysna Turaco | Livingstone's Turaco | Purple-crested Turaco | Grey Lourie |

Coucals, Malkoha, Cuckoos (& their hosts)

For text on coucals, malkoha & these cuckoos see pages 132-136

Senegal Coucal

Burchell's Coucal

White-browed Coucal

Coppery-tailed Coucal

Black Coucal

Green Malkoha

Red-chested Cuckoo

HOST White-throated Robin-Chat

Red-chested Cuckoo

HOST Boulder Chat

Jacobin Cuckoo

HOST Common Fiscal

African Cuckoo

HOST Fork-tailed Drongo

Jacobin Cuckoo

HOST Golden-breasted Bunting

Thick-billed Cuckoo

HOST Retz's Helmetshrike

Jacobin Cuckoo

HOST Dark-capped Bulbul

Levaillant's Cuckoo

HOST Arrow-marked Babbler

Cuckoos (& their hosts)

For text on these cuckoos see pages 136-138

Great Spotted Cuckoo

HOST Pied Crow

Great Spotted Cuckoo

HOST Red-winged Starling

Black Cuckoo

HOST Crimson-breasted Shrike

Black Cuckoo

HOST Southern Boubou

African Emerald Cuckoo

HOST Green-backed Camaroptera

Klaas's Cuckoo

HOST Long-billed Crombec

Klaas's Cuckoo

HOST Bar-throated Apalis

Klaas's Cuckoo

HOST Grey Sunbird

Klaas's Cuckoo

HOST Collared Sunbird

Diederik Cuckoo

HOST Southern Masked Weaver

Diederik Cuckoo

HOST Southern Red Bishop

Diederik Cuckoo

HOST Cape Sparrow

Diederik Cuckoo

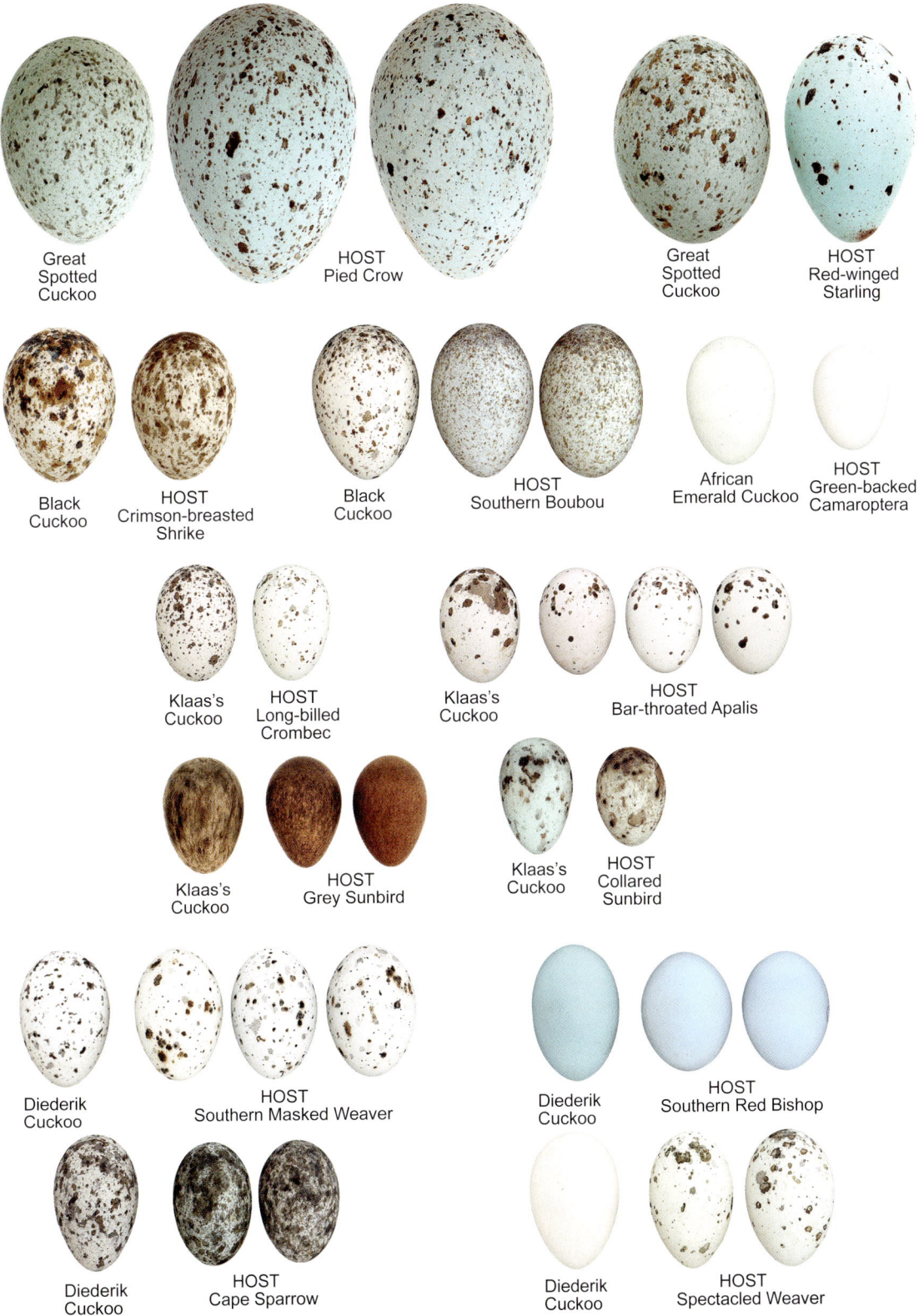

HOST Spectacled Weaver

Owls

For text on owls see pages 140-144

Western Barn Owl

African Grass Owl

Marsh Owl

African Wood Owl

Spotted Eagle-Owl

Cape Eagle-Owl
mackinderi

capensis

Verreaux's Eagle-Owl

Pel's Fishing Owl

Pearl-spotted Owlet

African Scops Owl

African Barred Owlet

Southern White-faced Owl

Nightjars, Swifts, Mousebirds, Trogon, Rollers

For text on nightjars see pages 146-148

Fiery-necked Nightjar (2)

Rufous-cheeked Nightjar (2)

Swamp Nightjar (2)

Freckled Nightjar (2)

Pennant-winged Nightjar (2)

Square-tailed Nightjar (2)

For text on swifts & spinetail see pages 150-152

Alpine Swift

Mottled Swift

African Black Swift

White-rumped Swift

Horus Swift

Little Swift

African Palm Swift

Mottled Spinetail

For text on mousebirds & trogon see page 154

White-backed Mousebird

Speckled Mousebird

Red-faced Mousebird

Narina Trogon (2)

For text on rollers see page 156

Purple Roller

Racket-tailed Roller

Lilac-breasted Roller

Broad-billed Roller

Kingfishers, Bee-eaters, Hoopoe, Woodhoopoe, Scimitarbill, Barbets

For text on kingfishers see pages 158-160

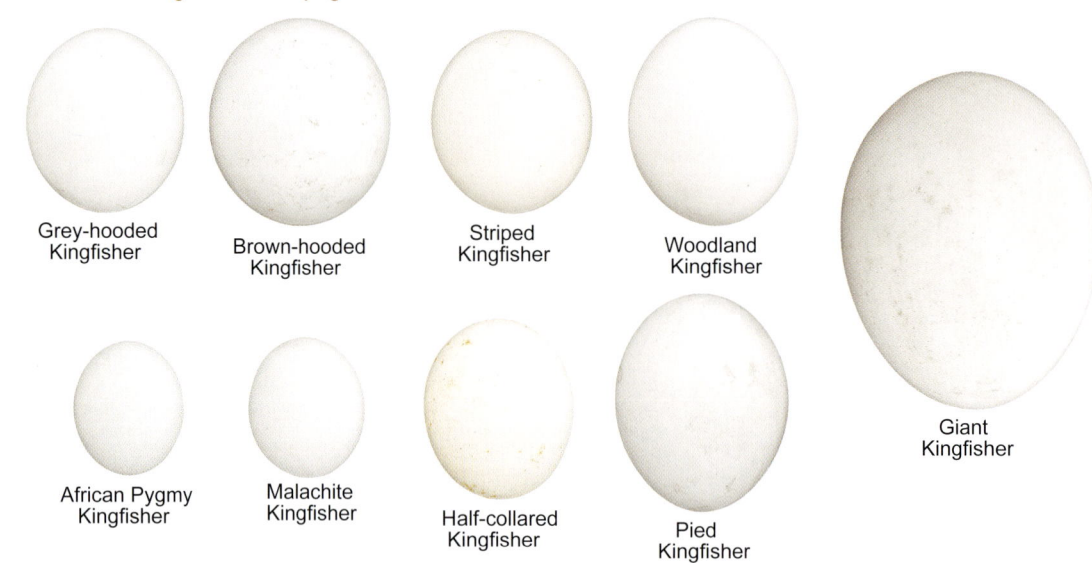

Grey-hooded Kingfisher

Brown-hooded Kingfisher

Striped Kingfisher

Woodland Kingfisher

Giant Kingfisher

African Pygmy Kingfisher

Malachite Kingfisher

Half-collared Kingfisher

Pied Kingfisher

For text on bee-eaters see pages 162-164

Swallow-tailed Bee-eater

White-fronted Bee-eater

Little Bee-eater

Southern Carmine Bee-eater

Olive Bee-eater

European Bee-eater

For text on hoopoe, woodhoopoe & scimitarbill see page 166

African Hoopoe (3)

Green Woodhoopoe (2)

Common Scimitarbill

Crested Barbet

For text on barbets see pages 174-176

White-eared Barbet

Black-collared Barbet

Acacia Pied Barbet

Whyte's Barbet

Red-fronted Tinkerbird

Yellow-fronted Tinkerbird

Yellow-rumped Tinkerbird

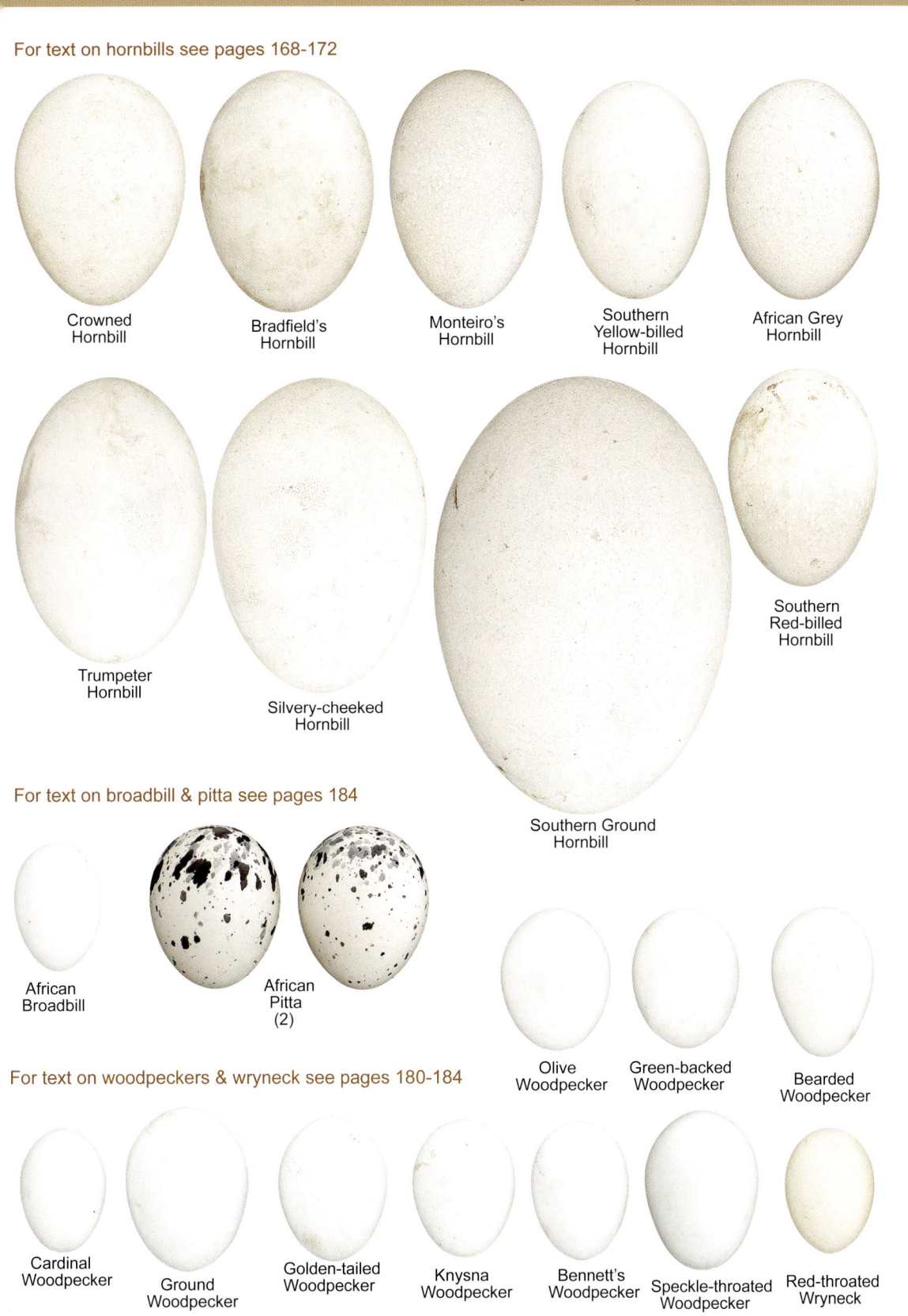

Hornbills, Broadbill, Pitta, Woodpeckers, Wryneck

For text on hornbills see pages 168-172

| Crowned Hornbill | Bradfield's Hornbill | Monteiro's Hornbill | Southern Yellow-billed Hornbill | African Grey Hornbill |

| Trumpeter Hornbill | Silvery-cheeked Hornbill | Southern Ground Hornbill | Southern Red-billed Hornbill |

For text on broadbill & pitta see pages 184

| African Broadbill | African Pitta (2) |

For text on woodpeckers & wryneck see pages 180-184

| Olive Woodpecker | Green-backed Woodpecker | Bearded Woodpecker |

| Cardinal Woodpecker | Ground Woodpecker | Golden-tailed Woodpecker | Knysna Woodpecker | Bennett's Woodpecker | Speckle-throated Woodpecker | Red-throated Wryneck |

Batises, Helmetshrikes, Bushshrikes

For text on batises & allied species see pages 186-188

Cape Batis (3)

Pririt Batis

Chinspot Batis (3)

Pale Batis

Black-throated Wattle-eye

Woodward's Batis (2)

White-tailed Shrike

Vanga Flycatcher

For text on helmetshrikes see page 190

White Helmetshrike (3)

Retz's Helmetshrike (4)

For text on these bushshrikes, bokmakierie, puffback & brubru see pages 192, 196

Grey-headed Bushshrike (4)

Olive Bushshrike (3)

Orange-breasted Bushshrike (2)

Black-fronted Bushshrike

Gorgeous Bushshrike (2)

Bokmakierie (2)

Black-backed Puffback (3)

Brubru (3)

Bushshrikes, Shrikes, Cuckooshrikes

For text on tchagras & boubous see pages 194, 198

Southern Tchagra (2)

Brown-crowned Tchagra (3)

Black-crowned Tchagra (3)

Marsh Tchagra

Crimson-breasted Shrike (4)

Swamp Boubou (2)

Southern Boubou (5)

Tropical Boubou (2)

For text on these shrikes see page 200

Common Fiscal (3)

Souza's Shrike

Magpie Shrike

Southern White-crowned Shrike (2)

For text on cuckooshrikes see page 202

Black Cuckooshrike (2)

White-breasted Cuckooshrike (2)

Grey Cuckooshrike

386   Orioles, Drongos, Flycatchers, Tits, Penduline Tits, Crows, Raven

For text on orioles & drongos see page 204

Black-headed Oriole   African Golden Oriole   Green-headed Oriole   Square-tailed Drongo (3)

Fork-tailed Drongo (7)

For text on monarch flycatchers see page 206

Blue-mantled Flycatcher   African Paradise Flycatcher (2)   Fairy Flycatcher (2)   White-tailed Flycatcher (2)   Cape Penduline Tit   Grey Penduline Tit

For text on tits & penduline tits see pages 210–212

Grey Tit   Ashy Tit   Miombo Tit   Southern Black Tit (3)   Carp's Tit   Cinnamon-breasted Tit

For text on crows & ravens see page 208

Cape Crow   Pied Crow   White-necked Raven   House Crow

Larks

387

For text on larks see page 214-226

Monotonous Lark

Melodious Lark (3)

Rufous-naped Lark (3)

Flappet Lark (2)

Eastern Clapper Lark (2)

Sabota Lark (3)

Gray's Lark

Rudd's Lark (2)

Fawn-coloured Lark (3)

Red-capped Lark (3)

Large-billed Lark (3)

Cape Long-billed Lark

Eastern Long-billed Lark

Short-clawed Lark

Spike-heeled Lark (2)

Red Lark (2)

Karoo Lark (2)

Dune Lark

Barlow's Lark

Pink-billed Lark (2)

Botha's Lark (2)

Sclater's Lark

Stark's Lark

Chestnut-backed Sparrow-Lark (3)

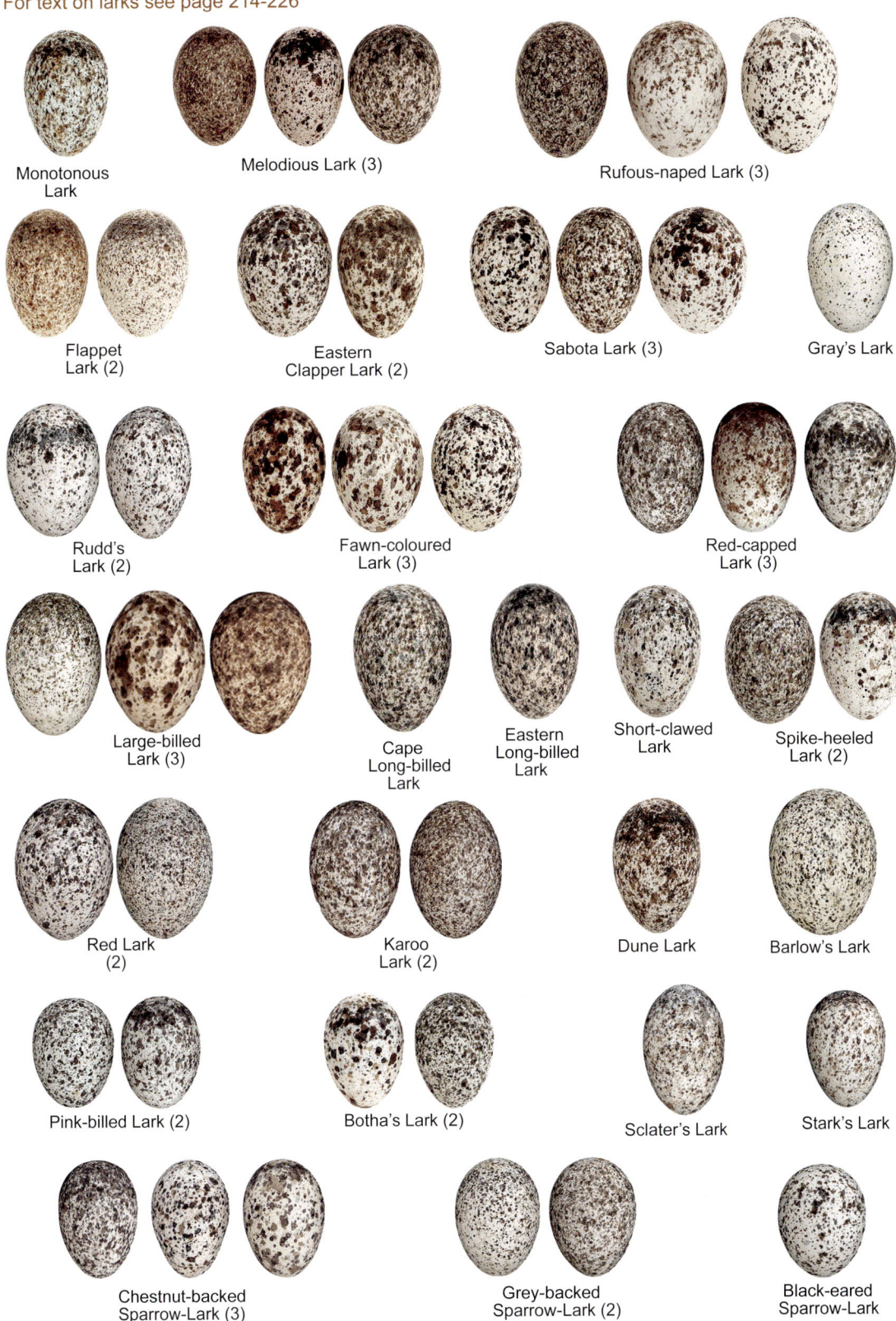

Grey-backed Sparrow-Lark (2)

Black-eared Sparrow-Lark

Wagtails, Longclaws, Pipits, Bulbuls, Greenbul

For text on wagtails, longclaws & pipits see pages 228-236

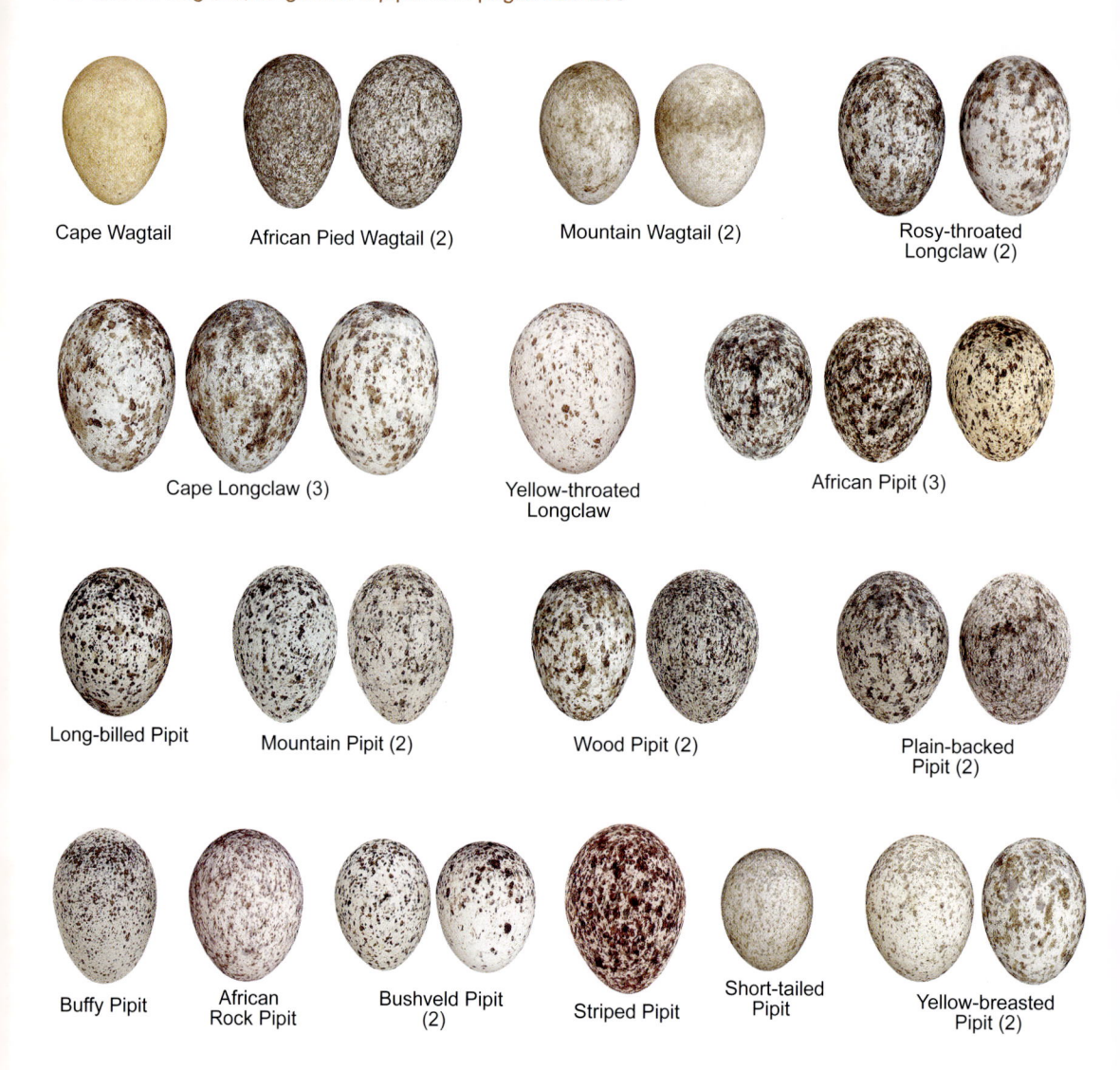

Cape Wagtail

African Pied Wagtail (2)

Mountain Wagtail (2)

Rosy-throated Longclaw (2)

Cape Longclaw (3)

Yellow-throated Longclaw

African Pipit (3)

Long-billed Pipit

Mountain Pipit (2)

Wood Pipit (2)

Plain-backed Pipit (2)

Buffy Pipit

African Rock Pipit

Bushveld Pipit (2)

Striped Pipit

Short-tailed Pipit

Yellow-breasted Pipit (2)

For text on bulbuls & this greenbul see pages 238-240

Cape Bulbul

African Red-eyed Bulbul

Dark-capped Bulbul (3)

Tiny Greenbul (2)

Greenbuls, Brownbul, Nicator, Saw-wings, Swallows, Martins

For text on these greenbuls, brownbuls & nicator see pages 238-240

Stripe-cheeked Greenbul (3)

Sombre Greenbul (3)

Yellow-streaked Greenbul (2)

Terrestrial Brownbul (3)

Yellow-bellied Greenbul (3)

Eastern Nicator (2)

For text on saw-wings, swallows & martins see pages 242-246

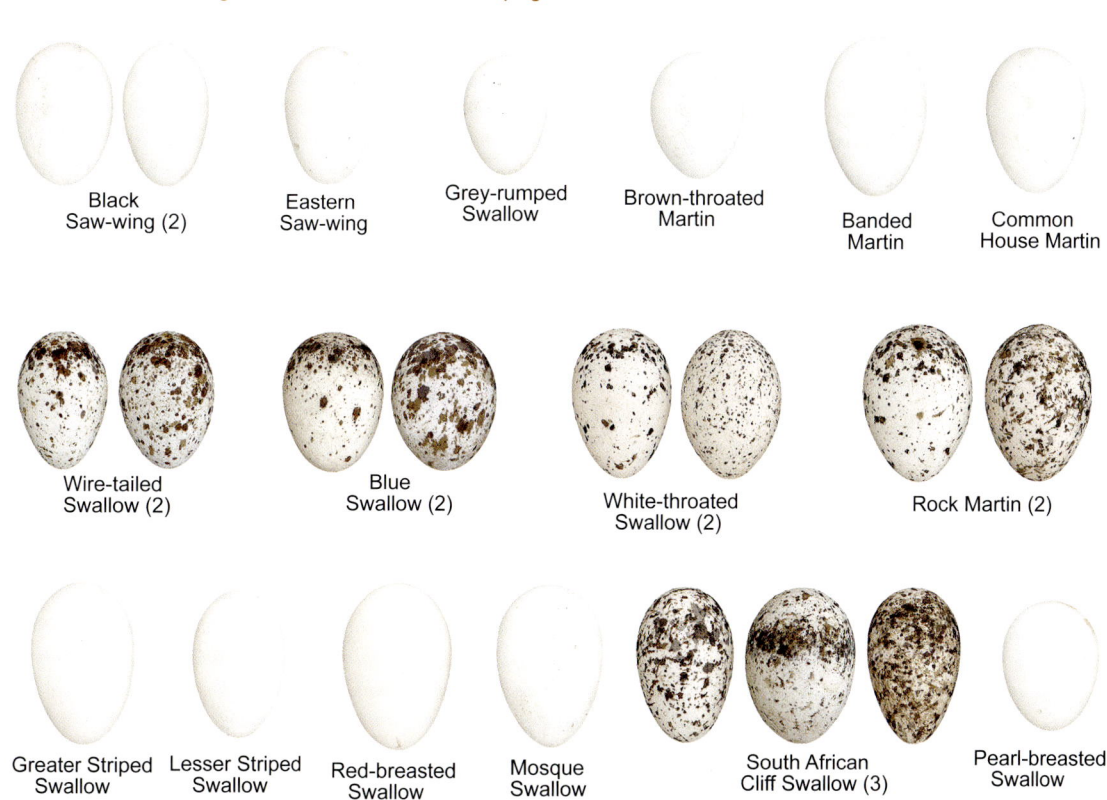

Black Saw-wing (2)

Eastern Saw-wing

Grey-rumped Swallow

Brown-throated Martin

Banded Martin

Common House Martin

Wire-tailed Swallow (2)

Blue Swallow (2)

White-throated Swallow (2)

Rock Martin (2)

Greater Striped Swallow

Lesser Striped Swallow

Red-breasted Swallow

Mosque Swallow

South African Cliff Swallow (3)

Pearl-breasted Swallow

Warblers, Crombecs, Prinias, Eremomelas, Apalises

For text on these warblers, flycatcher & crombecs see pages 248-252

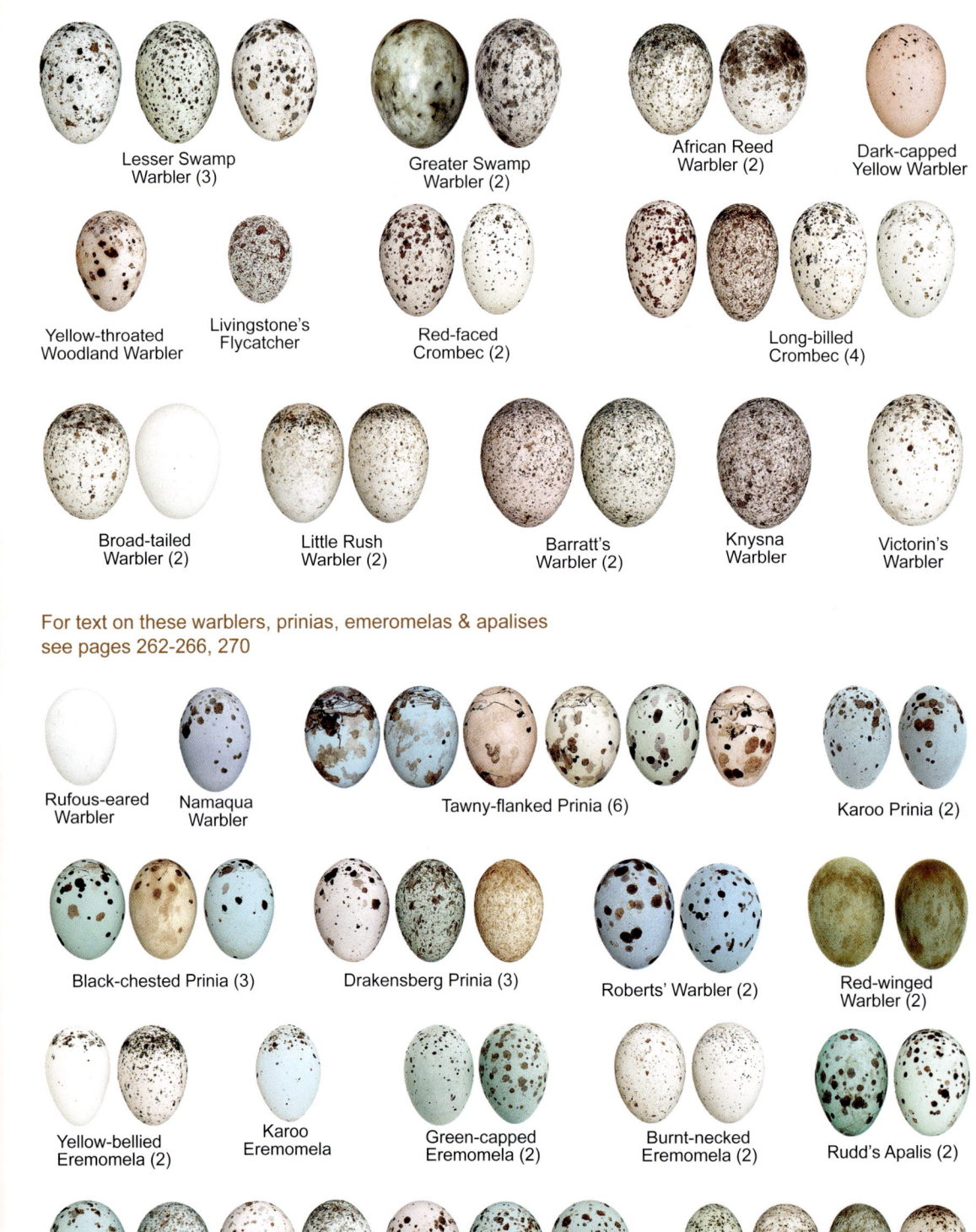

Lesser Swamp Warbler (3)

Greater Swamp Warbler (2)

African Reed Warbler (2)

Dark-capped Yellow Warbler

Yellow-throated Woodland Warbler

Livingstone's Flycatcher

Red-faced Crombec (2)

Long-billed Crombec (4)

Broad-tailed Warbler (2)

Little Rush Warbler (2)

Barratt's Warbler (2)

Knysna Warbler

Victorin's Warbler

For text on these warblers, prinias, emeromelas & apalises see pages 262-266, 270

Rufous-eared Warbler

Namaqua Warbler

Tawny-flanked Prinia (6)

Karoo Prinia (2)

Black-chested Prinia (3)

Drakensberg Prinia (3)

Roberts' Warbler (2)

Red-winged Warbler (2)

Yellow-bellied Eremomela (2)

Karoo Eremomela

Green-capped Eremomela (2)

Burnt-necked Eremomela (2)

Rudd's Apalis (2)

Bar-throated Apalis (7)

Yellow-breasted Apalis (7)

Cisticolas

For text on cisticolas see pages 254-260

Red-faced Cisticola (3)

Singing Cisticola (2)

Lazy Cisticola (2)

Chirping Cisticola (2)

Rattling Cisticola (6)

Tinkling Cisticola (3)

Short-winged Cisticola (2)

Croaking Cisticola (5)

Neddicky (6)

Rufous-winged Cisticola (2)

Levaillant's Cisticola (8)

Grey-backed Cisticola (3)

Wailing Cisticola (6)

Zitting Cisticola (5)

Desert Cisticola (4)

Cloud Cisticola (9)

Ayres' Cisticola (6)

Pale-crowned Cisticola (5)

Warblers, Rockjumpers, Babblers, Creeper, Sugarbirds, White-eyes

For text on camaropteras, wren-warblers, rockjumpers & allied species see pages 268-272

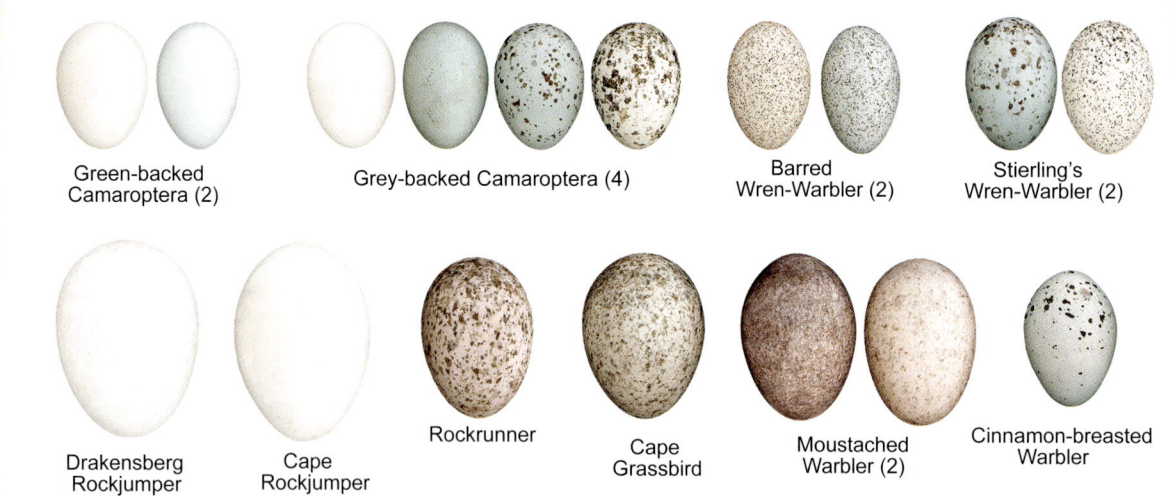

Green-backed Camaroptera (2)

Grey-backed Camaroptera (4)

Barred Wren-Warbler (2)

Stierling's Wren-Warbler (2)

Drakensberg Rockjumper

Cape Rockjumper

Rockrunner

Cape Grassbird

Moustached Warbler (2)

Cinnamon-breasted Warbler

For text on babblers see pages 274

Southern Pied Babbler

Hartlaub's Babbler (2)

Black-faced Babbler (2)

Arrow-marked Babbler (2)

For text on bush blackcap, titbabblers, hyliota & creeper see pages 274-276

Bush Blackcap (2)

Chestnut-vented Titbabbler (2)

Layard's Titbabbler

Southern Hyliota

Spotted Creeper (2)

For text on sugarbirds & white-eyes see pages 278

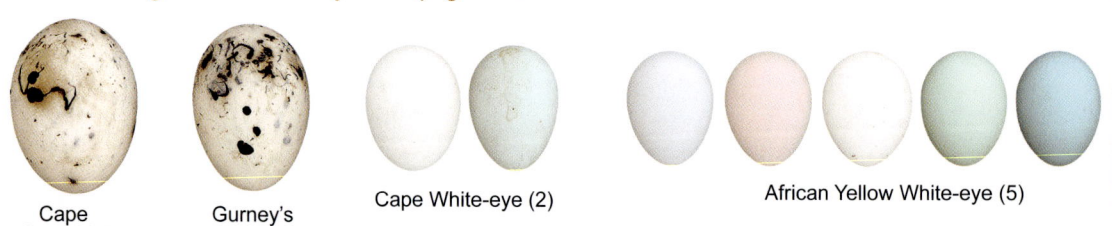

Cape Sugarbird

Gurney's Sugarbird

Cape White-eye (2)

African Yellow White-eye (5)

Starlings, Oxpeckers, Thrushes

For text on starlings & oxpeckers see pages 280-284

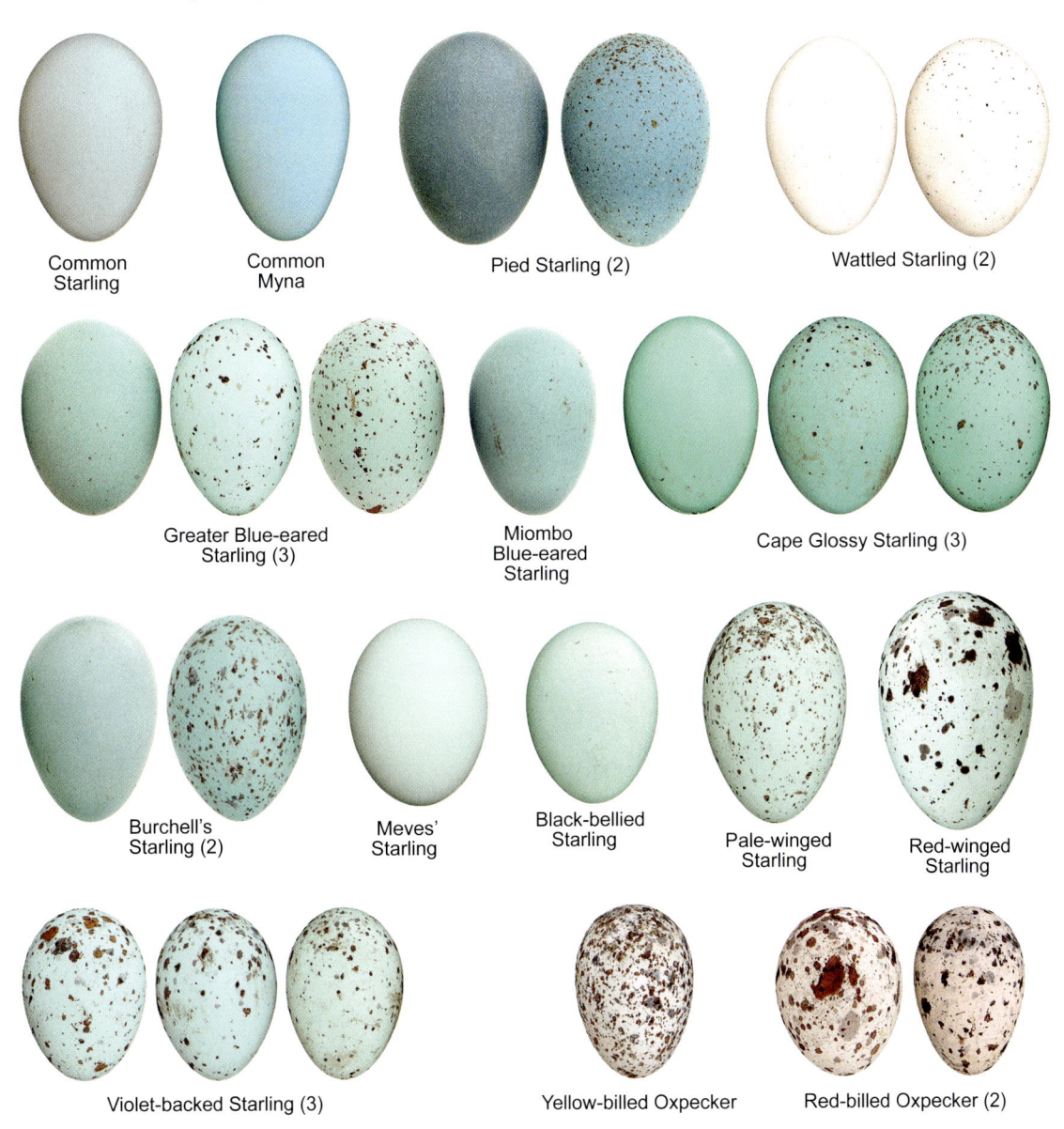

Common Starling

Common Myna

Pied Starling (2)

Wattled Starling (2)

Greater Blue-eared Starling (3)

Miombo Blue-eared Starling

Cape Glossy Starling (3)

Burchell's Starling (2)

Meves' Starling

Black-bellied Starling

Pale-winged Starling

Red-winged Starling

Violet-backed Starling (3)

Yellow-billed Oxpecker

Red-billed Oxpecker (2)

For text on these thrushes see pages 286

Spotted Ground Thrush

Orange Ground Thrush

Groundscraper Thrush (2)

Kurrichane Thrush (3)

394 Thrushes, Robins, Robin-Chats, Scrub Robins, Palm Thrushes, Chats

For text on these thrushes, alethe, robins, robin-chats, scrub robins, palm thrushes, wheatears, stonechat & chats see pages 288-294

Olive Thrush

Karoo Thrush

White-chested Alethe

White-starred Robin (2)

Swynnerton's Robin (3)

Cape Robin-Chat (2)

White-throated Robin-Chat (3)

Heuglin's Robin-Chat (3)

Chorister Robin-Chat (2)

Red-capped Robin-Chat (3)

Bearded Scrub Robin (3)

Brown Scrub Robin

White-browed Scrub Robin (3)

Kalahari Scrub Robin (2)

Karoo Scrub Robin (2)

Rufous-tailed Palm Thrush

Collared Palm Thrush (2)

Capped Wheatear (2)

Ant-eating Chat

African Stonechat (4)

Mountain Wheatear (3)

Chats, Rock Thrushes, Flycatchers

For text on chats & rock thrushes see pages 296-300

| Buff-streaked Chat (2) | Sickle-winged Chat (2) | Karoo Chat | Tractrac Chat | Familiar Chat (2) |

| Herero Chat (2) | Arnot's Chat (2) | Mocking Cliff Chat (3) |

| Boulder Chat (2) | Sentinel Rock Thrush | Cape Rock Thrush | Short-toed Rock Thrush | Miombo Rock Thrush |

For text on flycatchers see pages 302-304

| Marico Flycatcher (2) | Pale Flycatcher (3) | Chat Flycatcher (2) | Fiscal Flycatcher |

| African Dusky Flycatcher (2) | Ashy Flycatcher (2) | Grey Tit-Flycatcher | Southern Black Flycatcher (2) |

Sunbirds

For text on sunbirds see pages 306-314

Malachite Sunbird (3)

Orange-breasted Sunbird (3)

Bronzy Sunbird (2)

Copper Sunbird (2)

Olive Sunbird (4)

Grey Sunbird (3)

Amethyst Sunbird (4)

Scarlet-chested Sunbird (4)

Marico Sunbird (2)

White-bellied Sunbird (4)

Shelley's Sunbird

Purple-banded Sunbird (3)

Neergaard's Sunbird

Miombo Double-collared Sunbird (3)

Southern Double-collared Sunbird (2)

Greater Double-collared Sunbird (2)

Plain-backed Sunbird

Variable Sunbird (2)

Dusky Sunbird

Collared Sunbird (5)

Western Violet-backed Sunbird (3)

Sparrows, Sparrow-Weavers & allies, Weavers

For text on sparrow-weavers, sparrows & allies see pages 316-318

Red-billed Buffalo Weaver

Sociable Weaver (3)

White-browed Sparrow-Weaver (4)

Scaly-feathered Finch (3)

Cape Sparrow (5)

House Sparrow (2)

Southern Grey-headed Sparrow (4)

Great Sparrow (2)

Yellow-throated Petronia (3)

For text on these weavers see page 320

Southern Masked Weaver (14)

Village Weaver (7)

Lesser Masked Weaver

Weavers, Quelea, Bishops, Widowbirds

For text on these weavers see pages 322-324

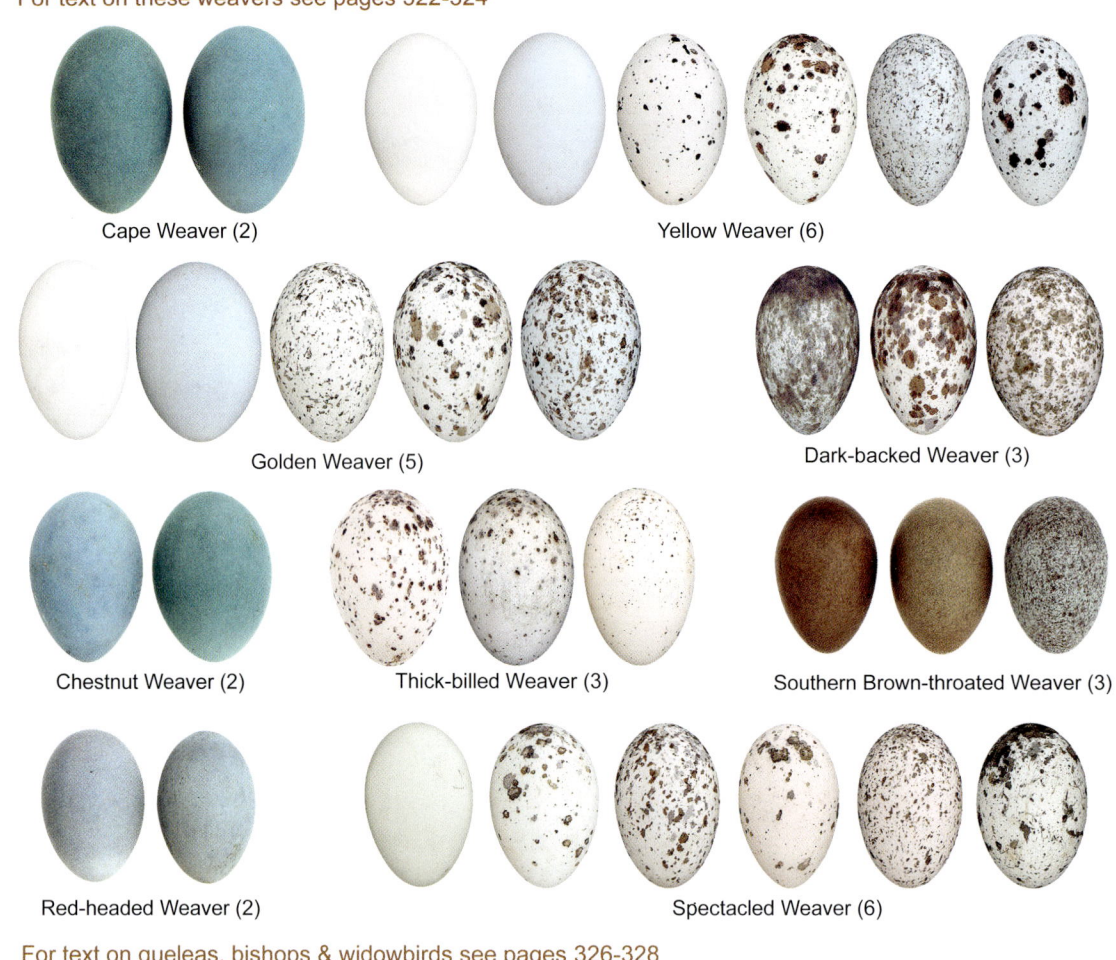

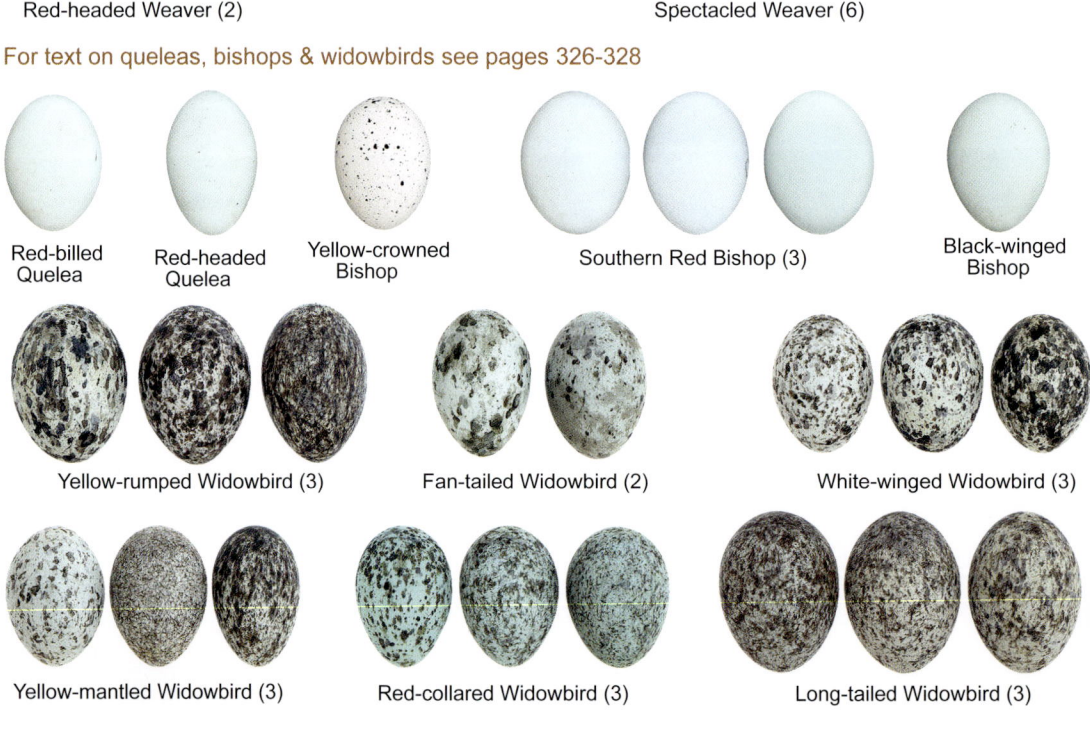

Cape Weaver (2)

Yellow Weaver (6)

Golden Weaver (5)

Dark-backed Weaver (3)

Chestnut Weaver (2)

Thick-billed Weaver (3)

Southern Brown-throated Weaver (3)

Red-headed Weaver (2)

Spectacled Weaver (6)

For text on queleas, bishops & widowbirds see pages 326-328

Red-billed Quelea

Red-headed Quelea

Yellow-crowned Bishop

Southern Red Bishop (3)

Black-winged Bishop

Yellow-rumped Widowbird (3)

Fan-tailed Widowbird (2)

White-winged Widowbird (3)

Yellow-mantled Widowbird (3)

Red-collared Widowbird (3)

Long-tailed Widowbird (3)

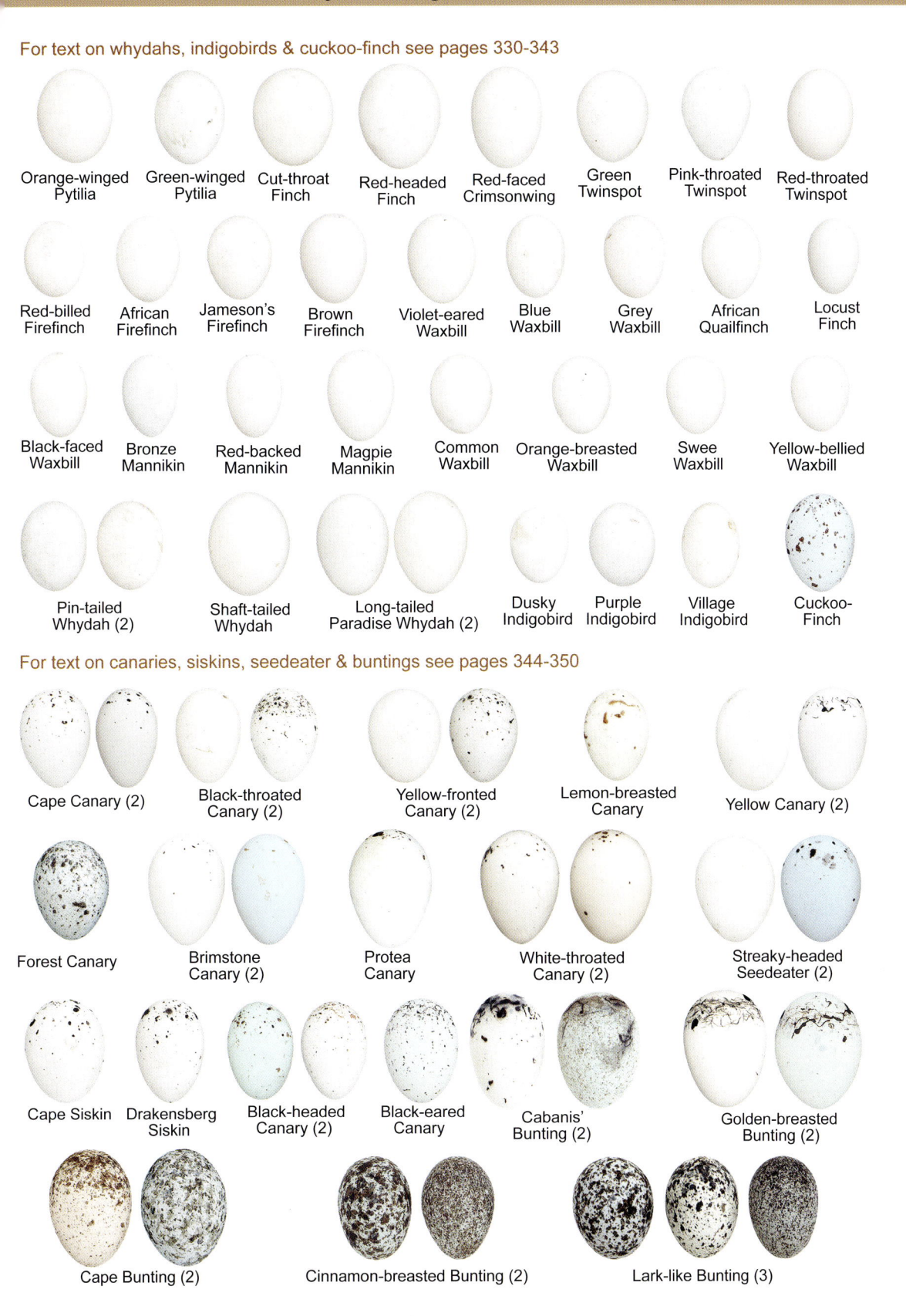

Waxbills, Whydahs, Indigobirds, Canaries, Buntings

For text on whydahs, indigobirds & cuckoo-finch see pages 330-343

Orange-winged Pytilia | Green-winged Pytilia | Cut-throat Finch | Red-headed Finch | Red-faced Crimsonwing | Green Twinspot | Pink-throated Twinspot | Red-throated Twinspot

Red-billed Firefinch | African Firefinch | Jameson's Firefinch | Brown Firefinch | Violet-eared Waxbill | Blue Waxbill | Grey Waxbill | African Quailfinch | Locust Finch

Black-faced Waxbill | Bronze Mannikin | Red-backed Mannikin | Magpie Mannikin | Common Waxbill | Orange-breasted Waxbill | Swee Waxbill | Yellow-bellied Waxbill

Pin-tailed Whydah (2) | Shaft-tailed Whydah | Long-tailed Paradise Whydah (2) | Dusky Indigobird | Purple Indigobird | Village Indigobird | Cuckoo-Finch

For text on canaries, siskins, seedeater & buntings see pages 344-350

Cape Canary (2) | Black-throated Canary (2) | Yellow-fronted Canary (2) | Lemon-breasted Canary | Yellow Canary (2)

Forest Canary | Brimstone Canary (2) | Protea Canary | White-throated Canary (2) | Streaky-headed Seedeater (2)

Cape Siskin | Drakensberg Siskin | Black-headed Canary (2) | Black-eared Canary | Cabanis' Bunting (2) | Golden-breasted Bunting (2)

Cape Bunting (2) | Cinnamon-breasted Bunting (2) | Lark-like Bunting (3)

Species index

Common names are in English (black) and Afrikaans (blue); scientific names are in *brown italics;* the numbers refer to text/nest pages (either the first number or, sometimes, the first two numbers) and egg pages (the last number)

A

Aasvoël, Baard-, 60, 361
Aasvoël, Egiptiese, 60, 361
Aasvoël, Krans-, 62, 362
Aasvoël, Monnik-, 62, 363
Aasvoël, Rüppell-, 62
Aasvoël, Wit-, 60, 361
Aasvoël, Witkop-, 62, 363
Aasvoël, Witrug-, 62, 362
Accipiter badius, 76, 367
Accipiter melanoleucus, 78, 367
Accipiter minullus, 76, 367
Accipiter ovampensis, 76, 367
Accipiter rufiventris, 76, 367
Accipiter tachiro, 74, 367
Achaetops pycnopygius, 272, 392
Acridotheres tristis, 280, 393
Acrocephalus baeticatus, 248, 390
Acrocephalus gracilirostris, 248, 390
Acrocephalus rufescens, 248, 390
Actophilornis africanus, 110, 374
Aenigmatolimnas marginalis, 94, 371
Afrotis afra, 90, 370
Afrotis afraoides, 90, 370
Agapornis lilianae, 128, 377
Agapornis roseicollis, 128, 377
Akalat, East Coast, 288
Alcedo cristata, 160, 382
Alcedo semitorquata, 160, 382
Alectoris chukar, 22, 352
Alethe, White-chested, 286, 394
Alopochen aegyptiaca, 30, 354
Amadina erythrocephala, 330, 399
Amadina fasciata, 330, 399
Amandava subflava, 340, 399
Amaurornis flavirostris, 94, 371
Amblyospiza albifrons, 324, 398
Ammomanopsis grayi, 222, 387
Anaplectes melanotis, 324, 398
Anas capensis, 32, 355
Anas erythrorhyncha, 34, 355
Anas hottentota, 34, 355
Anas platyrhynchos, 32
Anas smithii, 34, 355
Anas sparsa, 32, 355
Anas undulata, 32, 355
Anastomus lamelligerus, 40, 356
Andropadus importunus, 238, 389

Andropadus milanjensis, 238, 389
Anhinga rufa, 54, 359
Anomalospiza imberbis, 343
Anthobaphes violacea, 306, 396
Anthoscopus caroli, 212, 386
Anthoscopus minutus, 212, 386
Anthreptes longuemarei, 314, 396
Anthreptes reichenowi, 312, 396
Anthropoides paradiseus, 98, 372
Anthus brachyurus, 236, 388
Anthus caffer, 236, 388
Anthus cinnamomeus, 232, 388
Anthus crenatus, 234, 388
Anthus hoeschi, 232, 388
Anthus leucophrys, 234, 388
Anthus lineiventris, 236, 388
Anthus longicaudatus, 234
Anthus nyassae, 232, 388
Anthus pseudosimilis, 232
Anthus similis, 232, 388
Anthus vaalensis, 234, 388
Apalis chirindensis, 266
Apalis flavida, 266, 390
Apalis melanocephala, 266
Apalis ruddi, 266, 390
Apalis thoracica, 266, 390
Apalis, Bar-throated, 266, 379, 390
Apalis, Black-headed, 266
Apalis, Chirinda, 266
Apalis, Rudd's, 266, 390
Apalis, Yellow-breasted, 266, 390
Apaloderma narina, 154, 381
Aplopelia larvata, 124, 377
Apus affinis, 152, 381
Apus barbatus, 150, 381
Apus bradfieldi, 150
Apus caffer, 152, 381
Apus horus, 152, 381
Aquila rapax, 66, 364
Aquila spilogaster, 70, 366
Aquila verreauxii, 68, 365
Ardea alba, 48, 358
Ardea cinerea, 46, 358
Ardea goliath, 46, 358
Ardea melanocephala, 46, 358
Ardea purpurea, 46, 358
Ardeola ralloides, 50, 359
Ardeola rufiventris, 50, 359

Ardeotis kori, 86, 369
Arend, Bruin-, 70, 365
Arend, Dwerg-, 70, 366
Arend, Langkuif-, 66, 363
Arend, Roof-, 66, 364
Arend, Vis-, 66, 363
Asio capensis, 140, 380
Aviceda cuculoides, 58, 360
Avocet, Pied, 102, 373

B

Baardmannetjie, 316, 397
Babbler, Arrow-marked, 137, 274, 378, 392
Babbler, Bare-cheeked, 274
Babbler, Black-faced, 274, 392
Babbler, Hartlaub's, 274, 392
Babbler, Southern Pied, 274, 392
Balearica regulorum, 98, 373
Barbet, Acacia Pied, 174, 382
Barbet, Black-collared, 174, 179, 382
Barbet, Crested, 176, 382
Barbet, Green, 176
Barbet, White-eared, 174, 382
Barbet, Whyte's, 174, 382
Bateleur, 66, 364
Batis capensis, 139, 186, 384
Batis fratrum, 188, 384
Batis molitor, 186, 384
Batis pririt, 186, 384
Batis soror, 186, 384
Batis, Cape, 139, 186, 384
Batis, Chinspot, 186, 384
Batis, Pale, 186, 384
Batis, Pririt, 186, 384
Batis, Woodward's, 188, 384
Bee-eater, Böhm's, 162
Bee-eater, European, 164, 382
Bee-eater, Little, 162, 179, 382
Bee-eater, Olive, 164, 382
Bee-eater, Southern Carmine, 164, 382
Bee-eater, Swallow-tailed, 162, 382
Bee-eater, White-fronted, 162, 382
Berghaan, 66, 364
Berglyster, Kaapse, 272, 392
Berglyster, Oranjebors-, 272, 392
Berglyster, Swart-, 135, 298, 378, 395
Bergwagter, 294, 394
Bias musicus, 188, 384

Species index

Common names are in English (black) and Afrikaans (blue); scientific names are in brown italics; the numbers refer to text/nest pages (either the first number or, sometimes, the first two numbers) and egg pages (the last number)

B

Bishop, Black-winged, 326, 398
Bishop, Golden, 326, 398
Bishop, Southern Red, 326, 379, 398
Bishop, Yellow-crowned, 326, 398
Bishop, Yellow, 328, 398
Bittern, Dwarf, 52, 359
Bittern, Eurasian, 52, 359
Bittern, Little, 52, 359
Blackcap, Bush, 274, 392
Bleshoender, 96, 372
Blouvinkie, Gewone, 343, 399
Blouvinkie, Groen-, 343
Blouvinkie, Staal-, 343, 399
Blouvinkie, Witpoot-, 343, 399
Bocagia minuta, 194, 385
Bokmakierie, 196, 384
Bontpiek, 298, 395
Bontrokkie, Gewone, 294, 394
Boomkruiper, 276, 392
Boomvalk, Afrikaanse, 82, 368
Bosbontrokkie, Beloog-, 188, 384
Bosbontrokkie, Kaapse, 139, 186, 384
Bosbontrokkie, Mosambiek-, 186, 384
Bosbontrokkie, Pririt-, 186, 384
Bosbontrokkie, Woodwardse, 188, 384
Bosbontrokkie, Witlies-, 186, 384
Boskraai, Gewone, 172, 383
Boskraai, Kuifkop-, 172, 383
Boskrapper, 240, 389
Boskruiper, Geelstreep-, 240, 389
Boskruiper, Klein-, 240, 388
Boslaksman, Olyf-, 192, 384
Boslaksman, Oranjebors-, 192, 384
Boslaksman, Swartoog-, 192, 384
Bosloerie, 154, 381
Bosmusikant, 324, 398
Bossanger, Bruinkeel-, 270, 390
Bossanger, Donkerwang-, 270, 390
Bossanger, Geelpens-, 270, 390
Bossanger, Groen-, 270, 390
Bostrychia hagedash, 44, 358
Botaurus stellaris, 52, 359
Boubou, Southern, 198, 379, 385
Boubou, Swamp, 198, 385
Boubou, Tropical, 198, 385
Bradornis infuscatus, 302, 395
Bradornis mariquensis, 302, 395

Bradornis pallidus, 302, 395
Bradypterus baboecala, 252, 390
Bradypterus barratti, 252, 390
Bradypterus sylvaticus, 252, 390
Breëbek, 184, 383
Breëkoparend, 68, 365
Broadbill, African, 184, 383
Bromvoël, 72, 383
Brownbul, Terrestrial, 240, 389
Brubru, 196, 384
Bubalornis niger, 316, 397
Bubo africanus, 142, 380
Bubo capensis, 142, 380
Bubo lacteus, 142, 380
Bubulcus ibis, 48, 358
Bucorvus leadbeateri, 172, 383
Buffalo Weaver, Red-billed, 316, 397
Bugeranus carunculatus, 98, 372
Bulbul, African Red-eyed, 238, 388
Bulbul, Cape, 238, 388
Bulbul, Dark-capped, 137, 238, 378, 388
Bunting, Cabanis', 350, 399
Bunting, Cape, 350, 399
Bunting, Cinnamon-breasted, 350, 399
Bunting, Golden-breasted, 350, 378, 399
Bunting, Lark-like, 350, 399
Buphagus africanus, 284, 393
Buphagus erythrorhynchus, 284, 393
Burhinus capensis, 102, 373
Burhinus vermiculatus, 102, 373
Bushshrike, Black-fronted, 192, 384
Bushshrike, Gorgeous, 196, 384
Bushshrike, Grey-headed, 192, 384
Bushshrike, Olive, 192, 384
Bushshrike, Orange-breasted, 192, 384
Bustard, Black-bellied, 86, 370
Bustard, Denham's, 86, 369
Bustard, Kori, 86, 369
Bustard, Ludwig's, 86, 369
Buteo augur, 78, 366
Buteo rufofuscus, 78, 366
Buteo trizonatus, 78, 366
Butorides striata, 50, 359
Buttonquail, Black-rumped, 100, 373
Buttonquail, Hottentot, 100
Buttonquail, Kurrichane, 100, 373
Buzzard, Augur, 78, 366
Buzzard, Forest, 78, 366

Buzzard, Jackal, 78, 366
Buzzard, Lizard, 72, 366
Bycanistes brevis, 172, 383
Bycanistes bucinator, 172, 383
Byvanger, Klein-, 204, 386
Byvanger, Mikstert-, 135, 204, 378, 386
Byvreter, Europese, 164, 382
Byvreter, Klein-, 162, 179, 382
Byvreter, Olyf-, 164, 382
Byvreter, Roeskop-, 162
Byvreter, Rooibors-, 164, 382
Byvreter, Rooikeel-, 162, 382
Byvreter, Swaelstert-, 162, 382

C

Calamonastes fasciolatus, 268, 392
Calamonastes stierlingi, 268, 392
Calandrella cinerea, 222, 387
Calendulauda africanoides, 216, 387
Calendulauda albescens, 218, 387
Calendulauda barlowi, 218, 387
Calendulauda burra, 218, 387
Calendulauda erythrochlamys, 218, 387
Calendulauda sabota, 216, 387
Camaroptera brachyura, 139, 268, 392
Camaroptera brevicaudata, 268, 392
Camaroptera, Green-backed, 139, 268, 379, 392
Camaroptera, Grey-backed, 268, 392
Campephaga flava, 202, 385
Campethera abingoni, 182, 383
Campethera bennettii, 182, 383
Campethera cailliautii, 180, 383
Campethera notata, 182, 383
Campethera scriptoricauda, 182, 383
Campicoloides bifasciata, 296, 395
Canary, Black-eared, 348, 399
Canary, Black-headed, 348, 399
Canary, Black-throated, 344, 399
Canary, Brimstone, 346, 399
Canary, Cape, 344, 399
Canary, Forest, 346, 399
Canary, Lemon-breasted, 344, 399
Canary, White-throated, 346, 399
Canary, Yellow-fronted, 344, 399
Canary, Yellow, 346, 399
Caprimulgus fossii, 148, 381
Caprimulgus natalensis, 146, 381

Species index

Common names are in English (black) and Afrikaans (blue); scientific names are in *brown italics;* the numbers refer to text/nest pages (either the first number or, sometimes, the first two numbers) and egg pages (the last number)

C

Caprimulgus pectoralis, 146, 381
Caprimulgus rufigena, 146, 381
Caprimulgus tristigma, 148, 381
Cecropis abyssinica, 246, 389
Cecropis cucullata, 246, 389
Cecropis semirufa, 246, 389
Cecropis senegalensis, 246, 389
Centropus burchellii, 132, 378
Centropus cupreicaudus, 132, 378
Centropus grillii, 132, 378
Centropus senegalensis, 132, 378
Centropus superciliosus, 132, 378
Cercococcyx montanus, 134
Cercomela familiaris, 296, 395
Cercomela schlegelii, 296, 395
Cercomela sinuata, 296, 395
Cercomela tractrac, 296, 395
Certhilauda benguelensis, 220
Certhilauda brevirostris, 220
Certhilauda chuana, 220, 387
Certhilauda curvirostris, 220, 387
Certhilauda semitorquata, 220, 387
Certhilauda subcoronata, 220
Ceryle rudis, 160, 382
Ceuthmochares aereus, 132, 378
Chaetops aurantius, 272, 392
Chaetops frenatus, 272, 392
Chaffinch, Common, 344
Chalcomitra amethystina, 308, 396
Chalcomitra senegalensis, 308, 396
Charadrius marginatus, 108, 374
Charadrius pallidus, 108, 374
Charadrius pecuarius, 108, 374
Charadrius tricollaris, 108, 374
Chat, Ant-eating, 298, 394
Chat, Arnot's, 298, 395
Chat, Boulder, 135, 298, 378, 395
Chat, Buff-streaked, 296, 395
Chat, Familiar, 296, 395
Chat, Herero, 298, 395
Chat, Karoo, 296, 395
Chat, Mocking Cliff, 298, 395
Chat, Sickle-winged, 296, 395
Chat, Tractrac, 296, 395
Chersomanes albofasciata, 222, 387
Chlidonias hybrida, 118, 376
Chlorocichla flaviventris, 240, 389

Chrysococcyx caprius, 138, 379
Chrysococcyx cupreus, 138, 379
Chrysococcyx klaas, 138, 379
Cichladusa arquata, 294, 394
Cichladusa ruficauda, 294, 394
Ciconia ciconia, 42, 357
Ciconia episcopus, 42, 357
Ciconia nigra, 42, 357
Cinnyricinclus leucogaster, 284, 393
Cinnyris afer, 312, 396
Cinnyris bifasciatus, 310, 396
Cinnyris chalybeus, 312, 396
Cinnyris cupreus, 306, 396
Cinnyris fuscus, 314, 396
Cinnyris manoensis, 312, 396
Cinnyris mariquensis, 310, 396
Cinnyris neergaardi, 312, 396
Cinnyris shelleyi, 310, 396
Cinnyris talatala, 310, 396
Cinnyris venustus, 314, 396
Circaetus cinerascens, 64, 364
Circaetus cinereus, 64, 364
Circaetus fasciolatus, 64
Circaetus pectoralis, 64, 364
Circus maurus, 72, 367
Circus ranivorus, 72, 367
Cisticola aberrans, 254, 391
Cisticola aridula, 260, 391
Cisticola ayresii, 260, 391
Cisticola brachyptera, 256, 391
Cisticola cantans, 254, 391
Cisticola chiniana, 254, 391
Cisticola cinnamomeus, 260, 391
Cisticola erythrops, 254, 391
Cisticola fulvicapilla, 258, 391
Cisticola galactotes, 258, 391
Cisticola juncidis, 260, 391
Cisticola lais, 256, 391
Cisticola luapula, 258
Cisticola natalensis, 256, 391
Cisticola pipiens, 258, 391
Cisticola rufilata, 256, 391
Cisticola subruficapilla, 256, 391
Cisticola textrix, 260, 391
Cisticola tinniens, 258, 391
Cisticola, Ayres', 260, 391
Cisticola, Chirping, 258, 391
Cisticola, Cloud, 260, 391

Cisticola, Croaking, 256, 391
Cisticola, Desert, 260, 391
Cisticola, Grey-backed, 256, 391
Cisticola, Lazy, 254, 391
Cisticola, Levaillant's, 258, 391
Cisticola, Luapula, 258
Cisticola, Pale-crowned, 260, 391
Cisticola, Rattling, 254, 391
Cisticola, Red-faced, 254, 391
Cisticola, Rufous-winged, 258, 391
Cisticola, Short-winged, 256, 391
Cisticola, Singing, 254, 391
Cisticola, Tinkling, 256, 391
Cisticola, Wailing, 256, 391
Cisticola, Wing-snapping, 260, 391
Cisticola, Zitting, 260, 391
Clamator glandarius, 136, 379
Clamator jacobinus, 136, 378
Clamator levaillantii, 136, 378
Colius colius, 154, 381
Colius striatus, 154, 381
Columba arquatrix, 122, 377
Columba delegorguei, 122, 377
Columba guinea, 122, 377
Columba livia, 122
Coot, Red-knobbed, 96, 372
Coracias caudatus, 156, 381
Coracias naevius, 156, 381
Coracias spatulatus, 156, 381
Coracina caesia, 202, 385
Coracina pectoralis, 202, 385
Cormorant, Bank, 56, 360
Cormorant, Cape, 56, 360
Cormorant, Crowned, 56, 360
Cormorant, Reed, 56, 360
Cormorant, White-breasted, 56, 360
Corvus albicollis, 208, 386
Corvus albus, 208, 386
Corvus capensis, 208, 386
Corvus splendens, 208, 386
Corythaixoides concolor, 130, 377
Cossypha caffra, 290, 394
Cossypha dichroa, 290, 394
Cossypha heuglini, 290, 394
Cossypha humeralis, 290, 394
Cossypha natalensis, 290, 394
Coturnix coturnix, 26, 353
Coturnix delegorguei, 26, 353

Species index

Common names are in English (black) and Afrikaans (blue); scientific names are in *brown italics;* the numbers refer to text/nest pages (either the first number or, sometimes, the first two numbers) and egg pages (the last number)

C

Coucal, Black, 132, 378
Coucal, Burchell's, 132, 378
Coucal, Coppery-tailed, 132, 378
Coucal, Senegal, 132, 378
Coucal, White-browed, 132, 378
Courser, Bronze-winged, 114, 375
Courser, Burchell's, 112, 375
Courser, Double-banded, 110, 375
Courser, Temminck's, 110, 375
Courser, Three-banded, 114, 375
Crake, African, 94, 371
Crake, Baillon's, 94, 371
Crake, Black, 94, 371
Crake, Striped, 94, 371
Crane, Blue, 98, 372
Crane, Grey Crowned, 98, 373
Crane, Wattled, 98, 372
Creatophora cinerea, 280, 393
Creeper, Spotted, 276, 392
Crex egregia, 94, 371
Crimsonwing, Red-faced, 332, 399
Crithagra alario, 348, 399
Crithagra albogularis, 346, 399
Crithagra atrogularis, 344, 399
Crithagra citrinipectus, 344, 399
Crithagra flaviventris, 346, 399
Crithagra gularis, 346, 399
Crithagra leucoptera, 348, 399
Crithagra mennelli, 348, 399
Crithagra mozambica, 344, 399
Crithagra scotops, 346, 399
Crithagra sulphurata, 346, 399
Crithagra symonsi, 348, 399
Crithagra totta, 348, 399
Crombec, Long-billed, 250, 379, 390
Crombec, Red-faced, 250, 390
Crow, Cape, 208, 386
Crow, Pied, 208, 379, 386
Cryptillas victorini, 252, 390
Cryptospiza reichenovii, 332, 399
Cuckoo-Finch, 343
Cuckoo-Hawk, African, 58, 360
Cuckoo, African Emerald, 138, 379
Cuckoo, African, 134, 378
Cuckoo, Barred Long-tailed, 134
Cuckoo, Black, 134, 379
Cuckoo, Diederik, 138, 379

Cuckoo, Great Spotted, 136, 379
Cuckoo, Jacobin, 136, 378
Cuckoo, Klaas's, 138, 379
Cuckoo, Levaillant's, 136, 378
Cuckoo, Red-chested, 134, 378
Cuckoo, Thick-billed, 136, 378
Cuckooshrike, Black, 202, 385
Cuckooshrike, Grey, 202, 385
Cuckooshrike, White-breasted, 202, 385
Cuculus clamosus, 134, 379
Cuculus gularis, 134, 378
Cuculus solitarius, 134, 378
Cursorius rufus, 110, 375
Cursorius temminckii, 110, 375
Cyanomitra olivacea, 139, 308, 396
Cyanomitra veroxii, 308, 396
Cypsiurus parvus, 152, 381

D

Darter, African, 54, 359
Dassievoël, 298, 395
Delichon urbica, 246, 389
Dendrocygna bicolor, 28, 354
Dendrocygna viduata, 28, 354
Dendroperdix sephaena, 26, 352
Dendropicos fuscescens, 180, 383
Dendropicos griseocephalus, 180, 383
Dendropicos namaquus, 180, 383
Dicrurus adsimilis, 204, 386
Dicrurus ludwigii, 204, 386
Diederikkie, 138, 379
Dikkop, Gewone, 102, 373
Dikkop, Spotted, 102, 373
Dikkop, Water-, 102, 373
Dikkop, Water, 102, 373
Dobbertjie, Klein-, 38, 356
Dobbertjie, Kuifkop-, 38, 356
Dobbertjie, Swartnek-, 38, 356
Dove, African Mourning, 124, 377
Dove, Blue-spotted Wood, 126, 377
Dove, Cape Turtle, 124, 377
Dove, Cinnamon, 124, 377
Dove, Emerald-spotted Wood, 126, 377
Dove, Laughing, 126, 377
Dove, Lemon, 124, 377
Dove, Namaqua, 126, 377
Dove, Red-eyed, 124, 377
Dove, Ring-necked, 124, 377

Dove, Tambourine, 126, 377
Draaihals, 184, 383
Drawwertjie, Bloukop-, 110, 375
Drawwertjie, Bronsvlerk-, 114, 375
Drawwertjie, Drieband-, 114, 375
Drawwertjie, Dubbelband-, 110, 375
Drawwertjie, Trek-, 110, 375
Drongo, Fork-tailed, 135, 204, 378, 386
Drongo, Square-tailed, 204, 386
Dryoscopus cubla, 196, 384
Duck, African Black, 32, 355
Duck, Fulvous, 28, 354
Duck, Knob-billed, 30, 354
Duck, Maccoa, 34, 355
Duck, White-backed, 28, 354
Duck, White-faced, 28, 354
Duck, Yellow-billed, 32, 355
Duif, Geelbekbos-, 122, 377
Duif, Gewone Tortel-, 124, 377
Duif, Grootring-, 124, 377
Duif, Krans-, 122, 377
Duif, Papegaai-, 122, 377
Duif, Rooioogtortel-, 124, 377
Duif, Tuin-, 122
Duif, Withalsbos-, 122, 377
Duifie, Blouvlek-, 126, 377
Duifie, Groenvlek-, 126, 377
Duifie, Kaneel-, 124, 377
Duifie, Namakwa-, 126, 377
Duifie, Rooibors-, 126, 377
Duifie, Witbors-, 126, 377
Duiker, Bank-, 56, 360
Duiker, Kuifkop-, 56, 360
Duiker, Riet-, 56, 360
Duiker, Trek-, 56, 360
Duiker, Witbors-, 56, 360

E

Eagle-Owl, Cape, 142, 380
Eagle-Owl, Spotted, 142, 380
Eagle-Owl, Verreaux's, 142, 380
Eagle, African Fish, 66, 363
Eagle, Ayres', 70, 365
Eagle, Black-chested Snake, 64, 364
Eagle, Booted, 70, 366
Eagle, Brown Snake, 64, 364
Eagle, Crowned, 68, 365
Eagle, Long-crested, 66, 363

Species index

Common names are in English (black) and Afrikaans (blue); scientific names are in brown italics; the numbers refer to text/nest pages (either the first number or, sometimes, the first two numbers) and egg pages (the last number)

E

Eagle, Martial, 68, 365
Eagle, Southern Banded Snake, 64
Eagle, Tawny, 66, 364
Eagle, Verreaux's, 68, 365
Eagle, Wahlberg's, 70, 365
Eagle, Western Banded Snake, 64, 364
Eend, Bloubek-, 34, 355
Eend, Bruin-, 34, 355
Eend, Fluit-, 28, 354
Eend, Geelbek-, 32, 355
Eend, Gevlekte, 34, 355
Eend, Groenkop-, 32
Eend, Knobbel-, 30, 354
Eend, Koper-, 30, 354
Eend, Nonnetjie-, 28, 354
Eend, Rooibek-, 34, 355
Eend, Swart-, 32, 355
Eend, Teel-, 32, 355
Eend, Witrug-, 28, 354
Egret, Great, 48, 358
Egret, Intermediate, 48, 358
Egret, Little, 48, 358
Egret, Slaty, 50
Egret, Western Cattle, 48, 358
Egret, Yellow-billed, 48, 358
Egretta ardesiaca, 50, 359
Egretta garzetta, 48, 358
Egretta intermedia, 48, 358
Egretta vinaceigula, 50
Elanus caeruleus, 58, 360
Elminia albonotata, 206, 386
Elsie, Bont-, 102, 373
Elsie, Rooipoot-, 102, 373
Emberiza cabanisi, 350, 399
Emberiza capensis, 350, 399
Emberiza flaviventris, 350, 399
Emberiza impetuani, 350, 399
Emberiza tahapisi, 350, 399
Ephippiorhynchus senegalensis, 42, 357
Eremomela gregalis, 270, 390
Eremomela icteropygialis, 270, 390
Eremomela scotops, 270, 390
Eremomela usticollis, 270, 390
Eremomela, Burnt-necked, 270, 390
Eremomela, Green-capped, 270, 390
Eremomela, Karoo, 270, 390
Eremomela, Yellow-bellied, 270, 390

Eremopterix australis, 226, 387
Eremopterix leucotis, 226, 387
Eremopterix verticalis, 226, 387
Erythrocercus livingstonei, 250, 390
Erythropygia coryphaeus, 292, 394
Erythropygia leucophrys, 292, 394
Erythropygia paena, 292, 394
Erythropygia quadrivirgata, 292, 394
Erythropygia signata, 292, 394
Estrilda astrild, 340, 399
Estrilda erythronotos, 340, 399
Estrilda melanotis, 340, 399
Estrilda perreini, 336, 399
Estrilda quartinia, 340, 399
Estrilda thomensis, 336
Euplectes afer, 326, 398
Euplectes albonotatus, 328, 398
Euplectes ardens, 328, 398
Euplectes axillaris, 328, 398
Euplectes capensis, 328, 398
Euplectes hordeaceus, 326, 398
Euplectes macrourus, 328, 398
Euplectes orix, 326, 398
Euplectes progne, 328, 398
Eupodotis caerulescens, 88, 370
Eupodotis rueppellii, 88, 370
Eupodotis senegalensis, 90, 370
Eupodotis vigorsii, 88, 370
Eurocephalus anguitimens, 200, 385
Euryptila subcinnamomea, 268, 392
Eurystomus glaucurus, 156, 381
Excalfactoria adansonii, 26, 353

F

Falco ardosiaceus, 84
Falco biarmicus, 80, 368
Falco chicquera, 82, 368
Falco cuvierii, 82, 368
Falco dickinsoni, 84, 368
Falco fasciinucha, 80, 368
Falco peregrinus, 80, 368
Falco rupicoloides, 82, 368
Falco rupicolus, 82, 368
Falcon, Lanner, 80, 368
Falcon, Peregrine, 80, 368
Falcon, Pygmy, 84, 369
Falcon, Red-necked, 82, 368
Falcon, Taita, 80, 368

Finch, Cut-throat, 330, 399
Finch, Locust, 338, 399
Finch, Red-headed, 330, 399
Finch, Scaly-feathered, 316, 397
Finfoot, African, 110, 372
Firefinch, African, 334, 399
Firefinch, Brown, 334, 399
Firefinch, Jameson's, 334, 399
Firefinch, Red-billed, 334, 399
Fisant, Bosveld-, 24, 353
Fisant, Kaapse, 24, 353
Fisant, Klip-, 26, 353
Fisant, Natalse, 24, 353
Fisant, Rooibek-, 24, 353
Fisant, Rooikeel-, 24, 353
Fiscal, Common, 200, 378, 385
Flamingo, Greater, 40, 356
Flamingo, Lesser, 40, 356
Flamink, Groot-, 40, 356
Flamink, Klein-, 40, 356
Flap, Geelrug-, 328, 398
Flap, Kaapse, 328, 398
Flap, Kortstert-, 328, 398
Flap, Langstert-, 328, 398
Flap, Rooikeel-, 328, 398
Flap, Witvlerk-, 328, 398
Flufftail, Buff-spotted, 92, 371
Flufftail, Red-chested, 92, 371
Flufftail, Streaky-breasted, 92, 371
Flufftail, Striped, 92, 371
Flufftail, White-winged, 92, 371
Flycatcher, African Dusky, 304, 395
Flycatcher, African Paradise, 206, 386
Flycatcher, Ashy, 304, 395
Flycatcher, Blue-mantled, 206, 386
Flycatcher, Chat, 302, 395
Flycatcher, Fairy, 206, 386
Flycatcher, Fiscal, 302, 395
Flycatcher, Livingstone's, 250, 390
Flycatcher, Marico, 302, 395
Flycatcher, Pale, 302, 395
Flycatcher, Southern Black, 304, 395
Flycatcher, Vanga, 188, 384
Flycatcher, White-tailed, 206, 386
Francolin, Cape, 24, 353
Francolin, Coqui, 26, 352
Francolin, Crested, 26, 352
Francolin, Grey-winged, 22, 353

Species index

Common names are in English (black) and Afrikaans (blue); scientific names are in *brown italics;* the numbers refer to text/nest pages (either the first number or, sometimes, the first two numbers) and egg pages (the last number)

F

Francolin, Hartlaub's, 26, 353
Francolin, Natal, 24, 353
Francolin, Orange River, 22, 353
Francolin, Red-billed, 24, 353
Francolin, Red-necked, 24, 353
Francolin, Red-winged, 22, 353
Francolin, Shelley's, 22, 353
Francolin, Swainson's, 24, 353
Fret, Dikbek-, 338, 399
Fret, Gewone, 338, 399
Fret, Rooirug-, 338, 399
Fringilla coelebs, 344
Fulica cristata, 96, 372

G

Galerida magnirostris, 222, 387
Gallinago nigripennis, 110, 374
Gallinula angulata, 96, 371
Gallinula chloropus, 96, 371
Gallinule, Allen's, 96, 371
Gannet, Cape, 36, 355
Gans, Kol-, 30, 354
Gans, Dwerg-, 30, 354
Geelvink, Klein-, 320, 397
Geelvink, Swartkeel-, 320, 379, 397
Geocolaptes olivaceus, 182, 383
Geronticus calvus, 44, 358
Glansspreeu, Groot-, 282, 393
Glansspreeu, Groot-blouoor-, 282, 393
Glansspreeu, Klein-, 179, 282, 393
Glansspreeu, Klein-blouoor-, 282, 393
Glansspreeu, Langstert-, 282, 393
Glansspreeu, Spitsstert-, 284
Glansspreeu, Swartpens-, 282, 393
Glareola nuchalis, 114, 375
Glareola pratincola, 114, 375
Glasogie, Gariep-, 278, 392
Glasogie, Geel-, 179, 278, 392
Glasogie, Kaapse, 278, 392
Glaucidium capense, 144, 380
Glaucidium perlatum, 144, 380
Go-away-bird, Grey, 130, 377
Goose, African Pygmy, 30, 354
Goose, Egyptian, 30, 354
Goose, Spur-winged, 28, 354
Gorsachius leuconotus, 52, 359
Goshawk, African, 74, 367

Goshawk, Dark Chanting, 74, 367
Goshawk, Gabar, 74, 367
Goshawk, Pale Chanting, 74, 367
Goudsnip, 110, 374
Grassbird, Cape, 272, 392
Grasvoël, Breëstert-, 272, 392
Grebe, Black-necked, 38, 356
Grebe, Great Crested, 38, 356
Grebe, Little, 38, 356
Greenbul, Sombre, 238, 389
Greenbul, Stripe-cheeked, 238, 389
Greenbul, Tiny, 240, 388
Greenbul, Yellow-bellied, 240, 389
Greenbul, Yellow-streaked, 240, 389
Grootheuningwyser, 178, 179
Gryskoppie, 344
Gryskopspeg, 180, 383
Grysvalk, Dickinsonse, 84, 368
Guineafowl, Crested, 20, 352
Guineafowl, Helmeted, 20, 352
Gull, Grey-headed, 116, 375
Gull, Hartlaub's, 116, 375
Gull, Kelp, 116, 375
Guttera pucherani, 20, 352
Gymnoris superciliaris, 318, 397
Gypaetus barbatus, 60, 361
Gypohierax angolensis, 60, 361
Gyps africanus, 62, 362
Gyps coprotheres, 62, 362
Gyps rueppellii, 62

H

Haematopus moquini, 104, 373
Halcyon albiventris, 158, 382
Halcyon chelicuti, 158, 382
Halcyon leucocephala, 158, 382
Halcyon senegalensis, 158, 382
Halcyon senegaloides, 158
Haliaeetus vocifer, 66, 363
Hamerkop, 54, 356
Harrier-Hawk, African, 72, 369
Harrier, African Marsh, 72, 367
Harrier, Black, 72, 367
Hawk-Eagle, African, 70, 366
Hawk, Bat, 58, 360
Hedydipna collaris, 314, 396
Heliolais erythroptera, 264, 390
Helmetshrike, Chestnut-fronted, 190

Helmetshrike, Retz's, 137, 190, 378, 384
Helmetshrike, White, 190, 384
Helmlaksman, Stekelkop-, 190
Helmlaksman, Swart-, 137, 190, 378, 384
Helmlaksman, Wit-, 190, 384
Hemimacronyx chloris, 236, 388
Heron, Black-crowned Night, 52, 359
Heron, Black-headed, 46, 358
Heron, Black, 50, 359
Heron, Goliath, 46, 358
Heron, Green-backed, 50, 359
Heron, Grey, 46, 358
Heron, Purple, 46, 358
Heron, Rufous-bellied, 50, 359
Heron, Squacco, 50, 359
Heron, Striated, 50, 359
Heron, White-backed Night, 52, 359
Heuningvoël, Dunbek-, 178, 179
Heuningwyser, Gevlekte, 178, 179
Heuningwyser, Klein-, 178, 179
Heuningwyser, Oostelike, 178
Hieraaetus ayresii, 70, 365
Hieraaetus pennatus, 70, 366
Hieraaetus wahlbergi, 70, 365
Himantopus himantopus, 102, 373
Hirundo albigularis, 244, 389
Hirundo atrocaerulea, 244, 389
Hirundo dimidiata, 244, 389
Hirundo fuligula, 244, 389
Hirundo smithii, 244, 389
Hobby, African, 82, 368
Hoephoep, 166, 382
Honeybird, Brown-backed, 178
Honeybird, Green-backed, 178, 179
Honeyguide, Greater, 178, 179
Honeyguide, Lesser, 178, 179
Honeyguide, Pallid, 178
Honeyguide, Scaly-throated, 178, 179
Hoopoe, African, 166, 382
Hornbill, African Grey, 170, 383
Hornbill, Bradfield's, 168, 383
Hornbill, Crowned, 168, 383
Hornbill, Damara, 170
Hornbill, Monteiro's, 168, 383
Hornbill, Red-billed, 170, 383
Hornbill, Silvery-cheeked, 172, 383
Hornbill, Southern Ground, 172, 383
Hornbill, Sthn Yellow-billed, 170, 383

Species index

Common names are in English (black) and Afrikaans (blue); scientific names are in *brown italics;* the numbers refer to text/nest pages (either the first number or, sometimes, the first two numbers) and egg pages (the last number)

H

Hornbill, Trumpeter, 172, 383
Houtkapper, Bont-, 174, 382
Houtkapper, Geelbles-, 174, 382
Houtkapper, Groen-, 176
Houtkapper, Kuifkop-, 176, 382
Houtkapper, Rooikop-, 174, 179, 382
Houtkapper, Witoor-, 174, 382
Hyliota australis, 276, 392
Hyliota flavigaster, 276
Hyliota, Geelbors-, 276
Hyliota, Mashona-, 276, 392
Hyliota, Southern, 276, 392
Hyliota, Yellow-bellied, 276
Hypargos margaritatus, 332, 399
Hypargos niveoguttatus, 332, 399

I

Ibis, African Sacred, 44, 357
Ibis, Glans-, 44, 358
Ibis, Glossy, 44, 358
Ibis, Hadeda, 44, 358
Ibis, Kalkoen-, 44, 358
Ibis, Southern Bald, 44, 358
Iduna natalensis, 248, 390
Indicator indicator, 178, 179
Indicator meliphilus, 178
Indicator minor, 178, 179
Indicator variegatus, 178, 179
Indigobird, Dusky, 343, 399
Indigobird, Purple, 343, 399
Indigobird, Village, 343, 399
Indigobird, Zambezi, 343
Ispidina picta, 160, 382
Ixobrychus minutus, 52, 359
Ixobrychus sturmii, 52, 359

J

Jacana, African, 110, 374
Jacana, Lesser, 110, 374
Jagarend, Groot-, 70, 366
Jagarend, Klein-, 70, 365
Jakkalsvoël, Bos-, 78, 366
Jakkalsvoël, Rooibors-, 78, 366
Jakkalsvoël, Witbors-, 78, 366
Janfrederik, Bandkeel-, 288, 394
Janfrederik, Gewone, 290, 394
Janfrederik, Gunningse, 288

Janfrederik, Heuglinse, 290, 394
Janfrederik, Lawaaimaker-, 290, 394
Janfrederik, Natal-, 290, 394
Janfrederik, Witkeel-, 290, 378, 394
Janfrederik, Witkol-, 288, 394
Jangroentjie, 306, 396
Jynx ruficollis, 184, 383

K

Kakelaar, Pers-, 166
Kakelaar, Rooibek-, 166, 382
Kakelaar, Swartbek-, 166, 382
Kalkoentjie, Geelkeel-, 230, 388
Kalkoentjie, Oranjekeel-, 230, 388
Kalkoentjie, Rooskeel-, 230, 388
Kanarie, Berg-, 344, 399
Kanarie, Dikbek-, 346, 399
Kanarie, Geel-, 346, 399
Kanarie, Geelbors-, 344, 399
Kanarie, Geeloog-, 344, 399
Kanarie, Gestreepte, 346, 399
Kanarie, Kaapse, 344, 399
Kanarie, Streepkop-, 346, 399
Kanarie, Swartkop-, 348, 399
Kanarie, Swartoor-, 348, 399
Kanarie, Witkeel-, 346, 399
Kanarie, Witvlerk-, 348, 399
Kapokvoël, Grys-, 212, 386
Kapokvoël, Kaapse, 212, 386
Katakoeroe, Blou-, 202, 385
Katakoeroe, Swart-, 202, 385
Katakoeroe, Witbors-, 202, 385
Katlagter, Kaalwang-, 274
Katlagter, Pylvlek-, 137, 274, 378, 392
Katlagter, Swartwang-, 274, 392
Katlagter, Wit-, 274, 392
Katlagter, Witkruis-, 274, 392
Kaupifalco monogrammicus, 72, 366
Kelkiewyn, 120, 376
Kestrel, Dickinson's, 84, 368
Kestrel, Greater, 82, 368
Kestrel, Grey, 84
Kestrel, Rock, 82, 368
Kiewiet, Bont-, 106, 374
Kiewiet, Grootswartvlerk, 104, 374
Kiewiet, Kleinswartvlerk-, 104, 374
Kiewiet, Kroon-, 104, 374
Kiewiet, Lel-, 106, 374

Kiewiet, Witkop-, 106, 374
Kiewiet, Witvlerk-, 106, 374
Kingfisher, African Pygmy, 160, 382
Kingfisher, Brown-hooded, 158, 382
Kingfisher, Giant, 160, 382
Kingfisher, Grey-headed, 158, 382
Kingfisher, Half-collared, 160, 382
Kingfisher, Malachite, 160, 382
Kingfisher, Mangrove, 158
Kingfisher, Pied, 160, 382
Kingfisher, Striped, 158, 179, 382
Kingfisher, Woodland, 158, 382
Kite, Black-shouldered, 58, 360
Kite, Yellow-billed, 58, 360
Klappertjie, Hoëveld-, 216, 387
Klappertjie, Kaapse, 216
Klappertjie, Laeveld-, 214, 387
Kleinjantjie, Bandkeel-, 266, 379, 390
Kleinjantjie, Geelbors-, 266, 390
Kleinjantjie, Grys-, 266
Kleinjantjie, Ruddse, 266, 390
Kleinjantjie, Swartkop-, 266
Kliplyster, Angola-, 300, 395
Kliplyster, Kaapse, 300, 395
Kliplyster, Korttoon-, 300, 395
Kliplyster, Langtoon-, 300, 395
Kliplyster, Pretoria-, 300
Klipwagter, Berg-, 296, 395
Klopkloppie, Bleekkop-, 260, 391
Klopkloppie, Gevlekte, 260, 391
Klopkloppie, Kleinste, 260, 391
Klopkloppie, Landery-, 260, 391
Klopkloppie, Woestyn-, 260, 391
Knysnaloerie, 130, 377
Koekoek, Afrikaanse, 134, 378
Koekoek, Dikbek-, 136, 378
Koekoek, Gevlekte, 136, 379
Koekoek, Langstert-, 134
Koekoek, Swart-, 134, 379
Koekoekvalk, 58, 360
Koester, Berg-, 232, 388
Koester, Bos-, 232, 388
Koester, Bosveld-, 236, 388
Koester, Donker-, 234, 388
Koester, Geelbors-, 236, 388
Koester, Gestreepte, 236, 388
Koester, Gewone, 232, 388
Koester, Kimberley-, 232

Species index

Common names are in English (black) and Afrikaans (blue); scientific names are in *brown italics;* the numbers refer to text/nest pages (either the first number or, sometimes, the first two numbers) and egg pages (the last number)

K

Koester, Klip-, 234, 388
Koester, Kortstert-, 236, 388
Koester, Langstert-, 234
Koester, Nicholsonse, 232, 388
Koester, Vaal-, 234, 388
Kolpensie, Groen-, 332, 399
Kolpensie, Rooikeel-, 332, 399
Kolpensie, Rooskeel-, 332, 399
Koningriethaan, Groot-, 96, 372
Koningriethaan, Klein-, 96, 371
Konkoit, 196, 384
Korhaan, Blou-, 88, 370
Korhaan, Blue, 88, 370
Korhaan, Bos-, 90, 370
Korhaan, Karoo, 88, 370
Korhaan, Langbeen-, 86, 370
Korhaan, Northern Black, 90, 370
Korhaan, Red-crested, 90, 370
Korhaan, Rüppell's, 88, 370
Korhaan, Southern Black, 90, 370
Korhaan, Swartvlerk-, 90, 370
Korhaan, Vaal-, 88, 370
Korhaan, White-bellied, 90, 370
Korhaan, Witpens-, 90, 370
Korhaan, Witvlerk-, 90, 370
Korhaan, Woestyn-, 88, 370
Koringvoël, 316, 397
Kraai, Huis-, 208, 386
Kraai, Swart-, 208, 386
Kraai, Witbors-, 208, 379, 386
Kraai, Withals-, 208, 386
Kraanvoël, Blou-, 98, 372
Kraanvoël, Lel-, 98, 372
Kroonarend, 68, 365
Kwartel, Afrikaanse, 26, 353
Kwartel, Blou-, 26, 353
Kwartel, Bont-, 26, 353
Kwarteltjie, Bosveld-, 100, 373
Kwarteltjie, Kaapse, 100
Kwarteltjie, Swartrug-, 100, 373
Kwartelvinkie, Gewone, 338, 399
Kwartelvinkie, Rooivlerk-, 338, 399
Kwêkwêvoël, Groenrug-, 268, 379, 392
Kwêkwêvoël, Grysrug-, 268, 392
Kwelea, Rooibek-, 326, 398
Kwelea, Rooikop-, 326, 398
Kwêvoël, 130, 377

Kwikkie, Berg-, 228, 388
Kwikkie, Bont-, 228, 388
Kwikkie, Gewone, 228, 388

L

Lagonosticta nitidula, 334, 399
Lagonosticta rhodopareia, 334, 399
Lagonosticta rubricata, 334, 399
Lagonosticta senegala, 334, 399
Laksman, Bontrok-, 196, 384
Laksman, Fiskaal-, 200, 378, 385
Laksman, Kortstert-, 188, 384
Laksman, Kremetart-, 200, 385
Laksman, Langstert-, 200, 385
Laksman, Rooibors-, 135, 198, 379, 385
Laksman, Souzase, 200, 385
Lamprotornis acuticaudus, 284
Lamprotornis australis, 282, 393
Lamprotornis bicolor, 280, 393
Lamprotornis chalybaeus, 282, 393
Lamprotornis elisabeth, 282, 393
Lamprotornis mevesii, 282, 393
Lamprotornis nitens, 282, 393
Langstertjie, Bruinsy-, 262, 390
Langstertjie, Drakensberg-, 264, 390
Langstertjie, Karoo-, 264, 390
Langstertjie, Namakwa-, 262, 390
Langstertjie, Rooioor-, 262, 390
Langstertjie, Swartband-, 262, 390
Langstertjie, Woud-, 264, 390
Langtoon, Dwerg-, 110, 374
Langtoon, Groot-, 110, 374
Laniarius atrococcineus, 135, 198, 385
Laniarius bicolor, 198, 385
Laniarius ferrugineus, 198, 385
Laniarius major, 198, 385
Lanioturdus torquatus, 188, 384
Lanius collaris, 200, 385
Lanius souzae, 200, 385
Lapwing, African Wattled, 106, 374
Lapwing, Black-winged, 104, 374
Lapwing, Blacksmith, 106, 374
Lapwing, Crowned, 104, 374
Lapwing, Long-toed, 106, 374
Lapwing, Senegal, 104, 374
Lapwing, White-crowned, 106, 374
Lark, Agulhas Long-billed, 220
Lark, Barlow's, 218, 387

Lark, Benguela Long-billed, 220
Lark, Botha's, 224, 387
Lark, Cape Clapper, 216
Lark, Cape Long-billed, 220, 387
Lark, Dune, 218, 387
Lark, Dusky, 222
Lark, Eastern Clapper, 216, 387
Lark, Eastern Long-billed, 220, 387
Lark, Fawn-coloured, 216, 387
Lark, Flappet, 214, 387
Lark, Gray's, 222, 387
Lark, Karoo Long-billed, 220
Lark, Karoo, 218, 387
Lark, Large-billed, 222, 387
Lark, Melodious, 214, 387
Lark, Monotonous, 214, 387
Lark, Pink-billed, 224, 387
Lark, Red-capped, 222, 387
Lark, Red, 218, 387
Lark, Rudd's, 216, 387
Lark, Rufous-naped, 214, 387
Lark, Sabota, 216, 387
Lark, Sclater's, 224, 387
Lark, Short-clawed, 220, 387
Lark, Spike-heeled, 222, 387
Lark, Stark's, 224, 387
Larus cirrocephalus, 116, 375
Larus dominicanus, 116, 375
Larus hartlaubii, 116, 375
Lepelaar, 44, 357
Leptoptilos crumeniferus, 42, 357
Lewerik, Barlowse, 218, 387
Lewerik, Bosveld-, 214, 387
Lewerik, Dikbek-, 222, 387
Lewerik, Donker-, 222
Lewerik, Drakensberg-, 216, 387
Lewerik, Grasveldlangbek-, 220, 387
Lewerik, Grysrug-, 226, 387
Lewerik, Kaokolangbek-, 220
Lewerik, Karoo-, 218, 387
Lewerik, Karoolangbek-, 220
Lewerik, Kortklou-, 220, 387
Lewerik, Namakwa-, 224, 387
Lewerik, Namib-, 222, 387
Lewerik, Overberglangbek-, 220
Lewerik, Pienkbek-, 224, 387
Lewerik, Rooi-, 218, 387
Lewerik, Rooikop-, 222, 387

Species index

Common names are in English (black) and Afrikaans (blue); scientific names are in *brown italics;* the numbers refer to text/nest pages (either the first number or, sometimes, the first two numbers) and egg pages (the last number)

L

Lewerik, Rooinek-, 214, 387
Lewerik, Rooirug-, 226, 387
Lewerik, Sabota-, 216, 387
Lewerik, Spot-, 214, 387
Lewerik, Swartoor-, 226, 387
Lewerik, Vaalbruin-, 216, 387
Lewerik, Vaalrivier-, 224, 387
Lewerik, Vlakte-, 222, 387
Lewerik, Weskuslangbek-, 220, 387
Lewerik, Woestyn-, 224, 387
Lewerik, Duin-, 218, 387
Lioptilus nigricapillus, 274, 392
Lissotis melanogaster, 86, 370
Loerie, Bloukuif-, 130, 377
Loerie, Langkuif-, 130, 377
Loerie, Mosambiek-, 130
Lonchura bicolor, 338, 399
Lonchura cucullata, 338, 399
Lonchura fringilloides, 338, 399
Longclaw, Cape, 230, 388
Longclaw, Rosy-throated, 230, 388
Longclaw, Yellow-throated, 230, 388
Lophaetus occipitalis, 66, 363
Lophotis ruficrista, 90, 370
Lourie, Grey, 130, 377
Lovebird, Lilian's, 128, 377
Lovebird, Rosy-faced, 128, 377
Lybius torquatus, 174, 382
Lyster, Geelbek-, 288, 394
Lyster, Gevlekte, 286, 393
Lyster, Natal-, 286, 393
Lyster, Olyf-, 288, 394
Lyster, Oranje-, 286, 393
Lyster, Rooibek-, 286, 393
Lyster, Witborswoud-, 286, 393

M

Macheiramphus alcinus, 58, 360
Macrodipteryx vexillarius, 148, 381
Macronyx ameliae, 230, 388
Macronyx capensis, 230, 388
Macronyx croceus, 230, 388
Mahem, 98, 373
Makou, Wilde-, 28, 354
Malaconotus blanchoti, 192, 384
Malcorus pectoralis, 262, 390
Malgas, Wit-, 36, 355

Malkoha, Green, 132, 378
Mallard, 32
Mandingoa nitidula, 332, 399
Mannikin, Bronze, 338, 399
Mannikin, Magpie, 338, 399
Mannikin, Red-backed, 338, 399
Maraboe, 42, 357
Martin, Banded, 242, 389
Martin, Brown-throated, 242, 389
Martin, Common House, 246, 389
Martin, Rock, 244, 389
Mees, Akasiagrys-, 210, 386
Mees, Gewone Swart-, 210, 386
Mees, Miombogrys-, 210, 386
Mees, Ovamboswart-, 210, 386
Mees, Piet-tjou-tjou-Grys-, 210, 386
Mees, Rooipens-, 212, 386
Mees, Vaalpens-, 212
Meeu, Gryskop-, 116, 375
Meeu, Hartlaubse, 116, 375
Meeu, Swartrug-, 116, 375
Megaceryle maxima, 160, 382
Meitjie, 138, 379
Melaenornis pammelaina, 304, 395
Melba, Gewone, 330, 399
Melba, Oranjevlerk-, 330, 399
Melierax canorus, 74, 367
Melierax metabates, 74, 367
Melocichla mentalis, 272, 392
Merops apiaster, 164, 382
Merops boehmi, 162
Merops bullockoides, 162, 382
Merops hirundineus, 162, 382
Merops nubicoides, 164, 382
Merops pusillus, 162, 382
Merops superciliosus, 164, 382
Micronisus gabar, 74, 367
Microparra capensis, 110, 374
Milvus parasitus, 58, 360
Mirafra africana, 214, 387
Mirafra apiata, 216
Mirafra cheniana, 214, 387
Mirafra fasciolata, 216, 387
Mirafra passerina, 214, 387
Mirafra ruddi, 216, 387
Mirafra rufocinnamomea, 214, 387
Monticola angolensis, 300, 395
Monticola brevipes, 300, 395

Monticola explorator, 300, 395
Monticola pretoriae, 300
Monticola rupestris, 300, 395
Mooimeisie, 138, 379
Moorhen, Common, 96, 371
Moorhen, Lesser, 96, 371
Môrelyster, Palm-, 294, 394
Môrelyster, Rooistert-, 294, 394
Morus capensis, 36, 355
Mossie, Geelvlek-, 318, 397
Mossie, Gewone, 318, 379, 397
Mossie, Groot-, 318, 397
Mossie, Gryskop-, 318, 397
Mossie, Huis-, 318, 397
Mossie, Witkeel-, 318
Motacilla aguimp, 228, 388
Motacilla capensis, 228, 388
Motacilla clara, 228, 388
Mousebird, Red-faced, 154, 381
Mousebird, Speckled, 154, 381
Mousebird, White-backed, 154, 381
Muisvoël, Gevlekte, 154, 381
Muisvoël, Rooiwang-, 54, 381
Muisvoël, Witkruis-, 154, 381
Muscicapa adusta, 304, 395
Muscicapa caerulescens, 304, 395
Mycteria ibis, 40, 356
Myioparus plumbeus, 304, 395
Myna, Common, 280, 393
Myrmecocichla formicivora, 298, 394

N

Nagreier, Gewone, 52, 359
Nagreier, Witrug-, 52, 359
Naguil, Afrikaanse, 146, 381
Naguil, Donker-, 148, 381
Naguil, Laeveld-, 148, 381
Naguil, Natalse, 146, 381
Naguil, Rooiwang-, 146, 381
Naguil, Wimpelvlerk-, 148, 381
Namibornis herero, 298, 395
Neafrapus boehmi, 150
Necrosyrtes monachus, 62, 363
Nectarinia famosa, 306, 396
Nectarinia kilimensis, 306, 396
Neddicky, 258, 391
Neddikkie, 258, 391
Neophron percnopterus, 60, 361

Species index

Common names are in English (black) and Afrikaans (blue); scientific names are in *brown italics*; the numbers refer to text/nest pages (either the first number or, sometimes, the first two numbers) and egg pages (the last number)

N

Neotis denhami, 86, 369
Neotis ludwigii, 86, 369
Netta erythrophthalma, 34, 355
Nettapus auritus, 30, 354
Neushoringvoël, Bradfieldse, 168, 383
Neushoringvoël, Damara-, 170
Neushoringvoël, Geelbek-, 170, 383
Neushoringvoël, Gekroonde, 168, 383
Neushoringvoël, Grys-, 170, 383
Neushoringvoël, Monteirose, 168, 383
Neushoringvoël, Rooibek-, 170, 383
Nicator gularis, 240, 389
Nicator, Eastern, 240, 389
Nightjar, Fiery-necked, 146, 381
Nightjar, Freckled, 148, 381
Nightjar, Pennant-winged, 148, 381
Nightjar, Rufous-cheeked, 146, 381
Nightjar, Square-tailed, 148, 381
Nightjar, Swamp, 146, 381
Nikator, Geelvlek-, 240, 389
Nilaus afer, 196, 384
Nimmersat, 40, 356
Notopholia corruscus, 282, 393
Numida meleagris, 20, 352
Nuwejaarsvoël, Bont-, 136, 378
Nuwejaarsvoël, Gestreepte, 136, 378
Nycticorax nycticorax, 52, 359

O

Oceanodroma leucorhoa, 36, 355
Oena capensis, 126, 377
Oenanthe monticola, 294, 394
Oenanthe pileata, 294, 394
Oewerswael, Afrikaanse, 242, 389
Oewerswael, Gebande, 242, 389
Onychognathus morio, 284, 393
Onychognathus nabouroup, 284, 393
Ooievaar, Grootswart-, 42, 357
Ooievaar, Oopbek-, 40, 356
Ooievaar, Saalbek-, 42, 357
Ooievaar, Wit-, 42, 357
Ooievaar, Wolnek-, 42, 357
Ooruil, Gevlekte, 142, 380
Ooruil, Kaapse, 142, 380
Ooruil, Reuse-, 142, 380
Openbill, African, 40, 356
Oreophilais robertsi, 264, 390

Oriole, African Golden, 204, 386
Oriole, Black-headed, 204, 386
Oriole, Green-headed, 204, 386
Oriolus auratus, 204, 386
Oriolus chlorocephalus, 204, 386
Oriolus larvatus, 204, 386
Ortygospiza atricollis, 338, 399
Ortygospiza locustella, 338, 399
Osprey, Western, 60, 368
Ostrich, Common, 20, 352
Otus senegalensis, 144, 380
Owl, African Grass, 140, 380
Owl, African Scops, 144, 380
Owl, African Wood, 140, 380
Owl, Marsh, 140, 380
Owl, Pel's Fishing, 142, 380
Owl, Southern White-faced, 144, 380
Owl, Western Barn, 140, 380
Owlet, African Barred, 144, 380
Owlet, Pearl-spotted, 144, 380
Oxpecker, Red-billed, 284, 393
Oxpecker, Yellow-billed, 284, 393
Oxyura maccoa, 34, 355
Oystercatcher, African, 104, 373

P

Pachycoccyx audeberti, 136, 378
Painted Snipe, Greater, 110, 374
Palm Thrush, Collared, 294, 394
Palm Thrush, Rufous-tailed, 294, 394
Pandion haliaetus, 60, 368
Papegaai, Bloupens-, 128, 377
Papegaai, Bosveld-, 128, 377
Papegaai, Bruinkop-, 128, 377
Papegaai, Savanne-, 128, 377
Papegaai, Woud-, 128, 377
Paradysvink, Breëstert-, 343
Paradysvink, Gewone, 342, 399
Parakeet, Rose-ringed, 128
Parisoma layardi, 276, 392
Parisoma subcaeruleum, 276, 392
Parkiet, Njassa-, 128, 377
Parkiet, Ringnek-, 128
Parkiet, Rooiwang-, 128, 377
Parrot, Rüppell's, 128, 377
Parrot, Brown-headed, 128, 377
Parrot, Cape, 128, 377
Parrot, Grey-headed, 128, 377

Parrot, Meyer's, 128, 377
Partridge, Chukar, 22, 352
Parus afer, 210, 386
Parus carpi, 210, 386
Parus cinerascens, 210, 386
Parus griseiventris, 210, 386
Parus niger, 210, 386
Parus rufiventris, 212, 386
Parus rufiventris, 212
Passer diffusus, 318, 397
Passer domesticus, 318, 397
Passer griseus, 318
Passer melanurus, 318, 397
Passer motitensis, 318, 397
Patrys, Asiatiese, 22, 352
Patrys, Berg-, 22, 353
Patrys, Bos-, 26, 352
Patrys, Kalahari-, 22, 353
Patrys, Rooivlerk-, 22, 353
Patrys, Laeveld-, 22, 353
Pavo cristatus, 20, 352
Peafowl, Indian, 20, 352
Pelecanus onocrotalus, 54, 359
Pelecanus rufescens, 54, 359
Pelican, Great White, 54, 359
Pelican, Pink-backed, 54, 359
Pelikaan, Klein-, 54, 359
Pelikaan, Wit-, 54, 359
Peliperdix coqui, 26, 352
Penduline Tit, Cape, 212, 386
Penduline Tit, Grey, 212, 386
Penguin, African, 36, 355
Petrel, Leach's Storm, 36, 355
Petrochelidon spilodera, 246, 389
Petronia, Yellow-throated, 318, 397
Phalacrocorax africanus, 56, 360
Phalacrocorax capensis, 56, 360
Phalacrocorax coronatus, 56, 360
Phalacrocorax lucidus, 56, 360
Phalacrocorax neglectus, 56, 360
Philetairus socius, 316, 397
Phoeniconaias minor, 40, 356
Phoenicopterus roseus, 40, 356
Phoeniculus damarensis, 166
Phoeniculus purpureus, 166, 382
Phragmacia substriata, 262, 390
Phyllastrephus debilis, 240, 388
Phyllastrephus flavostriatus, 240, 389

Species index

Common names are in English (black) and Afrikaans (blue); scientific names are in *brown italics*; the numbers refer to text/nest pages (either the first number or, sometimes, the first two numbers) and egg pages (the last number)

P

Phyllastrephus terrestris, 240, 389
Phylloscopus ruficapillus, 250, 390
Piet-my-vrou, 134, 378
Pietjiekanarie, Berg-, 348, 399
Pietjiekanarie, Kaapse, 348, 399
Pigeon, African Green, 122, 377
Pigeon, African Olive, 122, 377
Pigeon, Common, 122
Pigeon, Delegorgue's, 122, 377
Pigeon, Eastern Bronze-naped, 122, 377
Pigeon, Feral, 122
Pikkewyn, Bril-, 36, 355
Pinarocorus nigricans, 222
Pinarornis plumosus, 135, 298, 395
Pipit, African Rock, 234, 388
Pipit, African, 232, 388
Pipit, Buffy, 234, 388
Pipit, Bushveld, 236, 388
Pipit, Kimberley, 232
Pipit, Long-billed, 232, 388
Pipit, Long-tailed, 234
Pipit, Mountain, 232, 388
Pipit, Plain-backed, 234, 388
Pipit, Short-tailed, 236, 388
Pipit, Striped, 236, 388
Pipit, Wood, 232, 388
Pipit, Yellow-breasted, 236, 388
Pitta angolensis, 184, 383
Pitta, African, 184, 383
Pitta, Angola-, 184, 383
Platalea alba, 44, 357
Platysteira peltata, 188, 384
Plectropterus gambensis, 28, 354
Plegadis falcinellus, 44, 358
Plocepasser mahali, 316, 397
Ploceus bicolor, 324, 398
Ploceus capensis, 322, 398
Ploceus cucullatus, 320, 397
Ploceus intermedius, 320, 397
Ploceus ocularis, 324, 398
Ploceus olivaceiceps, 324
Ploceus rubiginosus, 322, 398
Ploceus subaureus, 322, 398
Ploceus velatus, 320, 397
Ploceus xanthops, 322, 398
Ploceus xanthopterus, 322, 398
Plover, Chestnut-banded, 108, 374

Plover, Kittlitz's, 108, 374
Plover, Three-banded, 108, 374
Plover, White-fronted, 108, 374
Pochard, Southern, 34, 355
Podica senegalensis, 110, 372
Podiceps cristatus, 38, 356
Podiceps nigricollis, 38, 356
Pogoniulus bilineatus, 176, 382
Pogoniulus chrysoconus, 176, 382
Pogoniulus pusillus, 176, 382
Pogonocichla stellata, 288, 394
Poicephalus cryptoxanthus, 128, 377
Poicephalus fuscicollis, 128, 377
Poicephalus meyeri, 128, 377
Poicephalus robustus, 128, 377
Poicephalus rueppellii, 128, 377
Polemaetus bellicosus, 68, 365
Polihierax semitorquatus, 84, 369
Polyboroides typus, 72, 369
Porphyrio alleni, 96, 371
Porphyrio madagascariensis, 96, 372
Porzana pusilla, 94, 371
Pou, Gom-, 86, 369
Pou, Ludwigse, 86, 369
Pou, Mak-, 20, 352
Pou, Veld-, 86, 369
Pratincole, Collared, 114, 375
Pratincole, Rock, 114, 375
Prinia flavicans, 262, 390
Prinia hypoxantha, 264, 390
Prinia maculosa, 264, 390
Prinia subflava, 262, 390
Prinia, Black-chested, 262, 390
Prinia, Drakensberg, 264, 390
Prinia, Karoo, 264, 390
Prinia, Tawny-flanked, 262, 390
Prionops plumatus, 190, 384
Prionops retzii, 190, 384
Prionops scopifrons, 190
Prodotiscus regulus, 178
Prodotiscus zambesiae, 178, 179
Promerops cafer, 278, 392
Promerops gurneyi, 278, 392
Psalidoprocne holomelaena, 242, 389
Psalidoprocne orientalis, 242, 389
Pseudalethe fuelleborni, 286, 393
Pseudhirundo griseopyga, 242, 389
Psittacula krameri, 128

Pternistis adspersus, 24, 353
Pternistis afer, 24, 353
Pternistis capensis, 24, 353
Pternistis hartlaubi, 26, 353
Pternistis natalensis, 24, 353
Pternistis swainsonii, 24, 353
Pterocles bicinctus, 120, 376
Pterocles burchelli, 120, 376
Pterocles gutturalis, 120, 376
Pterocles namaqua, 120, 376
Ptilopsis granti, 144, 380
Puffback, Black-backed, 196, 384
Pycnonotus capensis, 238, 388
Pycnonotus nigricans, 137, 238, 388
Pycnonotus tricolor, 238, 388
Pyrenestes minor, 332
Pytilia afra, 330, 399
Pytilia melba, 330, 399
Pytilia, Green-winged, 330, 399
Pytilia, Orange-winged, 330, 399

Q

Quail, Blue, 26, 353
Quail, Common, 26, 353
Quail, Harlequin, 26, 353
Quailfinch, African, 338, 399
Quelea erythrops, 326, 398
Quelea quelea, 326, 398
Quelea, Red-billed, 326, 398
Quelea, Red-headed, 326, 398

R

Rail, African, 94, 371
Rallus caerulescens, 94, 371
Raven, White-necked, 208, 386
Recurvirostra avosetta, 102, 373
Reier, Blou-, 46, 358
Reier, Geelbekwit-, 48, 358
Reier, Groenrug-, 50, 359
Reier, Grootwit-, 48, 358
Reier, Kleinwit-, 48, 358
Reier, Ral-, 50, 359
Reier, Reuse-, 46, 358
Reier, Rooi-, 46, 358
Reier, Rooikeel-, 50
Reier, Rooipens-, 50, 359
Reier, Swart-, 50, 359
Reier, Swartkop-, 46, 358

Species index

Common names are in English (black) and Afrikaans (blue); scientific names are in *brown italics;* the numbers refer to text/nest pages (either the first number or, sometimes, the first two numbers) and egg pages (the last number)

R

Reier, Vee-, 48, 358
Renostervoël, Geelbek-, 284, 393
Renostervoël, Rooibek-, 284, 393
Rhinopomastus cyanomelas, 166, 382
Rhinoptilus africanus, 110, 375
Rhinoptilus chalcopterus, 114, 375
Rhinoptilus cinctus, 114, 375
Riethaan, Afrikaanse, 94, 371
Riethaan, Gestreepte, 94, 371
Riethaan, Groot-, 94, 371
Riethaan, Klein-, 94, 371
Riethaan, Swart-, 94, 371
Rietreier, Dwerg-, 52, 359
Rietreier, Groot-, 52, 359
Rietreier, Klein-, 52, 359
Rietsanger, Kaapse, 248, 390
Rietsanger, Klein-, 248, 390
Rietsanger, Rooibruin-, 248, 390
Riparia cincta, 242, 389
Riparia paludicola, 242, 389
Robin-Chat, Cape, 290, 394
Robin-Chat, Chorister, 290, 394
Robin-Chat, Heuglin's, 290, 394
Robin-Chat, Red-capped, 290, 394
Robin-Chat, White-browed, 290, 394
Robin-Chat, White-throated, 290, 378, 394
Robin, Swynnerton's, 288, 394
Robin, White-starred, 288, 394
Rock Thrush, Cape, 300, 395
Rock Thrush, Miombo, 300, 395
Rock Thrush, Pretoria, 300
Rock Thrush, Sentinel, 300, 395
Rock Thrush, Short-toed, 300, 395
Rockjumper, Cape, 272, 392
Rockjumper, Drakensberg, 272, 392
Rockrunner, 272, 392
Roller, Broad-billed, 156, 381
Roller, Lilac-breasted, 156, 381
Roller, Purple, 156, 381
Roller, Racket-tailed, 156, 381
Rooiassie, 340, 399
Rooibekkie, Koning-, 342, 399
Rooibekkie, Pylstert-, 342, 399
Sterretjie, Rooibors, 118, 376
Rostratula benghalensis, 110, 374
Rotsvoël, 72, 392
Rynchops flavirostris, 116, 376

S

Saadbrekertjie, Oostelike, 332
Saagvlerkswael, Swart-, 242, 389
Saagvlerkswael, Tropiese, 242, 389
Sagittarius serpentarius, 60, 361
Salpornis spilonotus, 276, 392
Sandgrouse, Burchell's, 120, 376
Sandgrouse, Double-banded, 120, 376
Sandgrouse, Namaqua, 120, 376
Sandgrouse, Yellow-throated, 120, 376
Sandpatrys, Dubbelband-, 120, 376
Sandpatrys, Geelkeel-, 120, 376
Sandpatrys, Gevlekte, 120, 376
Sanger, Breëstert-, 252, 390
Sanger, Gebande, 268, 392
Sanger, Geel-, 248, 390
Sanger, Geelkeel-, 250, 390
Sanger, Kaapse Vlei-, 252, 390
Sanger, Kaneelbors-, 268, 392
Sanger, Knysnaruigte-, 252, 390
Sanger, Rooiborsruigte-, 252, 390
Sanger, Rooivlerk-, 264, 390
Sanger, Ruigte-, 252, 390
Sanger, Stierlingse, 268, 392
Sarkidiornis melanotos, 30, 354
Sarothrura affinis, 92, 371
Sarothrura ayresi, 92, 371
Sarothrura boehmi, 92, 371
Sarothrura elegans, 92, 371
Sarothrura rufa, 92, 371
Saw-wing, Black, 242, 389
Saw-wing, Eastern, 242, 389
Saxicola torquatus, 294, 394
Schoenicola brevirostris, 252, 390
Schoutedenapus myoptilus, 150
Scimitarbill, Common, 166, 382
Scleroptila africanus, 22, 353
Scleroptila levaillantii, 22, 353
Scleroptila levaillantoides, 22, 353
Scleroptila shelleyi, 22, 353
Scopus umbretta, 54, 356
Scotopelia peli, 142, 380
Scrub Robin, Bearded, 292, 394
Scrub Robin, Brown, 292, 394
Scrub Robin, Kalahari, 292, 394
Scrub Robin, Karoo, 292, 394
Scrub Robin, White-browed, 292, 394
Secretarybird, 60, 361

Seedcracker, Lesser, 332
Seedeater, Protea, 348, 399
Seedeater, Streaky-headed, 346, 399
Sekretarisvoël, 60, 361
Serinus canicollis, 344, 399
Shelduck, South African, 30, 354
Sheppardia gunningi, 288
Shikra, 76, 367
Shoveler, Cape, 34, 355
Shrike-Flycatcher, Black-and-White, 188, 384
Shrike, Crimson-breasted, 135, 198, 378, 385
Shrike, Magpie, 200, 385
Shrike, Southern White-crowned, 200, 385
Shrike, Souza's, 200, 385
Shrike, White-tailed, 188, 384
Sigelus silens, 302, 395
Singvalk, Bleek-, 74, 367
Singvalk, Donker-, 74, 367
Siskin, Cape, 348, 399
Siskin, Drakensberg, 348, 399
Skaapwagter, Hoëveld-, 294, 394
Skerpbekheuningvoël, 178
Skimmer, African, 116, 376
Skoorsteenveër, 44, 357
Slangarend, Bruin, 64, 364
Slangarend, Dubbelband-, 64
Slangarend, Enkelband-, 64, 364
Slangarend, Swartbors-, 64, 364
Slanghalsvoël, 54, 359
Slangverklikker, 292, 394
Slopeend, Kaapse, 34, 355
Smithornis capensis, 184, 383
Sneeubal, 196, 384
Snip, Afrikaanse, 110, 374
Snipe, African, 110, 374
Sparrow-Weaver, White-browed, 316, 397
Sparrow, Cape, 318, 379, 397
Sparrow, Great, 318, 397
Sparrow, House, 318, 397
Sparrow, Northern Grey-headed, 318
Sparrow, Southern Grey-headed, 318, 397
Sparrowhawk, Black, 78, 367
Sparrowhawk, Little, 76, 367
Sparrowhawk, Ovambo, 76, 367
Sparrowhawk, Rufous-breasted, 76, 367
Sparrowlark, Black-eared, 226, 387
Sparrowlark, Chestnut-backed, 226, 387
Sparrowlark, Grey-backed, 226, 387

411

Species index

Common names are in English (black) and Afrikaans (blue); scientific names are in *brown italics;* the numbers refer to text/nest pages (either the first number or, sometimes, the first two numbers) and egg pages (the last number)

S

Speckled Pigeon, 122, 377
Speg, Baard-, 180, 383
Speg, Bennettse, 182, 383
Speg, Gevlekte, 180, 383
Speg, Goudstert-, 179, 182, 383
Speg, Grond-, 182, 383
Speg, Kardinaal-, 180, 383
Speg, Knysna-, 182, 383
Speg, Tanzaniese, 182, 383
Spekvreter, Gewone, 296, 395
Spekvreter, Herero-, 298, 395
Spekvreter, Karoo-, 296, 395
Spekvreter, Vlakte-, 296, 395
Spekvreter, Woestyn-, 296, 395
Sperwer, Afrikaanse, 74, 367
Sperwer, Gebande, 76, 367
Sperwer, Klein-, 76, 367
Sperwer, Ovambo-, 76, 367
Sperwer, Rooibors, 76, 367
Sperwer, Swart-, 78, 367
Sperwer, Witkruis-, 74, 367
Spheniscus demersus, 36, 355
Sphenoeacus afer, 272, 392
Spilopelia senegalensis, 126, 377
Spinetail, Böhm's, 150
Spinetail, Mottled, 150, 381
Spizocorys conirostris, 224, 387
Spizocorys fringillaris, 224, 387
Spizocorys sclateri, 224, 387
Spizocorys starki, 224, 387
Spookvoël, 192, 384
Spoonbill, African, 44, 357
Sporopipes squamifrons, 316, 397
Spreeu, Bleekvlerk-, 284, 393
Spreeu, Europese, 280, 393
Spreeu, Indiese, 280, 393
Spreeu, Lel-, 280, 393
Spreeu, Rooivlerk-, 284, 379, 393
Spreeu, Witbors-, 179, 284, 393
Spreeu, Witgat-, 280, 393
Sprinkaanvoël, Rooivlerk-, 114, 375
Sprinkaanvoël, Withals-, 114, 375
Stactolaema leucotis, 174, 382
Stactolaema olivacea, 176
Stactolaema whytii, 174, 382
Starling, Black-bellied, 282, 393
Starling, Burchell's, 282, 393

Starling, Cape Glossy, 179, 282, 393
Starling, Common, 280, 393
Starling, Greater Blue-eared, 282, 393
Starling, Meves', 282, 393
Starling, Miombo Blue-eared, 282, 393
Starling, Pale-winged, 284, 393
Starling, Pied, 280, 393
Starling, Red-winged, 284, 379, 393
Starling, Sharp-tailed, 284
Starling, Violet-backed, 179, 284, 393
Starling, Wattled, 280, 393
Stekelstert, Gevlekte, 150, 381
Stekelstert, Witpens-, 150
Stenostira scita, 206, 386
Stephanoaetus coronatus, 68, 365
Sterna balaenarum, 118, 376
Sterna bergii, 118, 376
Sterna caspia, 118, 375
Sterna dougallii, 118, 376
Sterretjie, Damara-, 118, 376
Sterretjie, Geelbek-, 118, 376
Sterretjie, Reuse-, 118, 375
Sterretjie, Witbaard-, 118, 376
Stilt, Black-winged, 102, 373
Stompstert, Bosveld-, 250, 379, 390
Stompstert, Rooiwang-, 250, 390
Stonechat, African, 294, 394
Stork, Black, 42, 357
Stork, Marabou, 42, 357
Stork, Saddle-billed, 42, 357
Stork, White, 42, 357
Stork, Woolly-necked, 42, 357
Stork, Yellow-billed, 40, 356
Stormswael, Swaelstert-, 36, 355
Strandkiewiet, Drieband-, 108, 374
Strandkiewiet, Geelbors-, 108, 374
Strandkiewiet, Rooiband-, 108, 374
Strandkiewiet, Vaal-, 108, 374
Streepkoppie, Geel-, 350, 399
Streepkoppie, Klip-, 350, 399
Streepkoppie, Rooirug-, 350, 378, 399
Streepkoppie, Rooivlerk-, 350, 399
Streepkoppie, Vaal-, 350, 399
Streptopelia capicola, 124, 377
Streptopelia decipiens, 124, 377
Streptopelia semitorquata, 124, 377
Strix woodfordii, 140, 380
Struthio camelus, 20, 352

Sturnus vulgaris, 280, 393
Sugarbird, Cape, 278, 392
Sugarbird, Gurney's, 278, 392
Suikerbekkie, Blou-, 314, 396
Suikerbekkie, Bloukeel-, 312, 396
Suikerbekkie, Bloukruis-, 312, 396
Suikerbekkie, Brons-, 306, 396
Suikerbekkie, Geelpens-, 314, 396
Suikerbekkie, Groot-rooiband-, 312, 396
Suikerbekkie, Grys-, 308, 379, 396
Suikerbekkie, Klein-rooiband-, 312, 396
Suikerbekkie, Koper-, 306, 396
Suikerbekkie, Kortbek-, 314, 379, 396
Suikerbekkie, Marico-, 310, 396
Suikerbekkie, Miombo-rooiband-, 312, 396
Suikerbekkie, Namakwa-, 314, 396
Suikerbekkie, Olyf-, 139, 308, 396
Suikerbekkie, Oranjebors-, 306, 396
Suikerbekkie, Purperband-, 310, 396
Suikerbekkie, Rooibors-, 308, 396
Suikerbekkie, Swart-, 308, 396
Suikerbekkie, Swartpens-, 310, 396
Suikerbekkie, Witpens-, 310, 396
Suikervoël, Kaapse, 278, 392
Suikervoël, Rooibors-, 278, 392
Sunbird, Bronzy, 306, 396
Sunbird, Amethyst, 308, 396
Sunbird, Collared, 314, 379, 396
Sunbird, Copper, 306, 396
Sunbird, Dusky, 314, 396
Sunbird, Greater Double-collared, 312, 396
Sunbird, Grey, 308, 379, 396
Sunbird, Malachite, 306, 396
Sunbird, Marico, 310, 396
Sunbird, Miombo Double-collared, 312, 396
Sunbird, Neergaard's, 312, 396
Sunbird, Olive, 139, 308, 396
Sunbird, Orange-breasted, 306, 396
Sunbird, Plain-backed, 312, 396
Sunbird, Purple-banded, 310, 396
Sunbird, Scarlet-chested, 308, 396
Sunbird, Shelley's, 310, 396
Sunbird, Southern Double-collared, 312, 396
Sunbird, Variable, 314, 396
Sunbird, Western Violet-backed, 314, 396
Sunbird, White-bellied, 310, 396
Swael, Blou-, 244, 389
Swael, Draadstert-, 244, 389

Species index

Common names are in English (black) and Afrikaans (blue); scientific names are in brown italics; the numbers refer to text/nest pages (either the first number or, sometimes, the first two numbers) and egg pages (the last number)

S

Swael, Familie-, 246, 389
Swael, Grootstreep-, 246, 389
Swael, Gryskruis-, 242, 389
Swael, Huis-, 246, 389
Swael, Kleinstreep-, 246, 389
Swael, Krans-, 244, 389
Swael, Moskee-, 246, 389
Swael, Pêrelbors-, 244, 389
Swael, Rooibors-, 246, 389
Swael, Witkeel-, 244, 389
Swallow, Blue, 244, 389
Swallow, Greater Striped, 246, 389
Swallow, Grey-rumped, 242, 389
Swallow, Lesser Striped, 246, 389
Swallow, Mosque, 246, 389
Swallow, Pearl-breasted, 244, 389
Swallow, Red-breasted, 246, 389
Swallow, South African Cliff, 246, 389
Swallow, White-throated, 244, 389
Swallow, Wire-tailed, 244, 389
Swamphen, African, 96, 372
Swartaasvoël, 62, 362
Swartpiek, 298, 394
Swempie, 26, 352
Swie, Suidelike, 340, 399
Swie, Tropiese, 340, 399
Swift, African Black, 150, 381
Swift, African Palm, 152, 381
Swift, Alpine, 152, 381
Swift, Bradfield's, 150
Swift, Horus, 152, 381
Swift, Little, 152, 381
Swift, Mottled, 150, 381
Swift, Scarce, 150
Swift, White-rumped, 152, 381
Swynnertonia swynnertoni, 288, 394
Sylvietta rufescens, 250, 390
Sylvietta whytii, 250, 390
Sysie, Angola-, 336
Sysie, Gewone Blou-, 336, 399
Sysie, Koningblou-, 336, 399
Sysie, Rooibek-, 340, 399
Sysie, Rooiwangwoud-, 332, 399
Sysie, Swartwang-, 340, 399
Sysie, Grys-, 336, 399

T

Tachybaptus ruficollis, 38, 356
Tachymarptis aequatorialis, 150, 381
Tachymarptis melba, 152, 381
Tadorna cana, 30, 354
Tarentaal, Gewone, 20, 352
Tarentaal, Kuifkop-, 20, 352
Tauraco corythaix, 130, 377
Tauraco livingstonii, 130, 377
Tauraco porphyreolophus, 130, 377
Tauraco schalowi, 130
Tchagra australis, 137, 194, 385
Tchagra senegalus, 194, 385
Tchagra tchagra, 194, 385
Tchagra, Black-crowned, 194, 385
Tchagra, Brown-crowned, 137, 194, 385
Tchagra, Marsh, 194, 385
Tchagra, Southern, 194, 385
Teal, Cape, 32, 355
Teal, Hottentot, 34, 355
Teal, Red-billed, 34, 355
Telacanthura ussheri, 150, 381
Telophorus nigrifrons, 192, 384
Telophorus olivaceus, 192, 384
Telophorus sulfureopectus, 192, 384
Telophorus viridis, 196, 384
Telophorus zeylonus, 196, 384
Terathopius ecaudatus, 66, 364
Tern, Caspian, 118, 375
Tern, Damara, 118, 376
Tern, Roseate, 118, 376
Tern, Swift, 118, 376
Tern, Whiskered, 118, 376
Terpsiphone viridis, 206, 386
Thalassornis leuconotus, 28, 354
Thamnolaea arnoti, 298, 395
Thamnolaea cinnamomeiventris, 298, 395
Thick-knee, Spotted, 102, 373
Thick-knee, Water, 102, 373
Threskiornis aethiopicus, 44, 357
Thrush, Groundscraper, 286, 393
Thrush, Karoo, 288, 394
Thrush, Kurrichane, 286, 393
Thrush, Olive, 288, 394
Thrush, Orange Ground, 286, 393
Thrush, Spotted Ground, 286, 393
Tinker, Geelbles-, 176, 382
Tinker, Rooibles-, 176, 382

Tinker, Swartbles-, 176, 382
Tinkerbird, Red-fronted, 176, 382
Tinkerbird, Yellow-fronted, 176, 382
Tinkerbird, Yellow-rumped, 176, 382
Tinktinkie, Bosveld-, 254, 391
Tinktinkie, Groot-, 256, 391
Tinktinkie, Grysrug-, 256, 391
Tinktinkie, Huil-, 256, 391
Tinktinkie, Kortvlerk-, 256, 391
Tinktinkie, Luapula-, 258
Tinktinkie, Lui-, 254, 391
Tinktinkie, Piepende, 258, 391
Tinktinkie, Rooi-, 256, 391
Tinktinkie, Rooiwang-, 254, 391
Tinktinkie, Singende, 254, 391
Tinktinkie, Swartrug-, 258, 391
Tinktinkie, Vlei-, 258, 391
Tiptol, Kaapse, 238, 388
Tiptol, Rooibek-, 274, 392
Tiptol, Rooioog-, 238, 388
Tiptol, Swartoog-, 137, 238, 378, 388
Tit-Flycatcher, Grey, 304, 395
Tit, Ashy, 210, 386
Tit, Carp's, 210, 386
Tit, Cinnamon-breasted, 212
Tit, Grey, 210, 386
Tit, Miombo, 210, 386
Tit, Rufous-bellied, 212, 386
Tit, Southern Black, 210, 386
Titbabbler, Chestnut-vented, 276, 392
Titbabbler, Layard's, 276, 392
Tjagra, Grysbors-, 194, 385
Tjagra, Rooivlerk-, 137, 194, 385
Tjagra, Swartkroon-, 194, 385
Tjagra, Vlei-, 194, 385
Tjeriktik, Bosveld-, 276, 392
Tjeriktik, Grys-, 276, 392
Tobie, Swart-, 104, 373
Tockus alboterminatus, 168, 383
Tockus bradfieldi, 168, 383
Tockus damarensis, 170
Tockus erythrorhynchus, 170, 383
Tockus leucomelas, 170, 383
Tockus monteiri, 168, 383
Tockus nasutus, 170, 383
Torgos tracheliotus, 62, 362
Trachyphonus vaillantii, 176, 382
Treron calvus, 122, 377

Species index

Common names are in English (black) and Afrikaans (blue); scientific names are in *brown italics;* the numbers refer to text/nest pages (either the first number or, sometimes, the first two numbers) and egg pages (the last number)

T

Tricholaema leucomelas, 174, 382
Trigonoceps occipitalis, 62, 363
Trochocercus cyanomelas, 206, 386
Trogon, Narina, 154, 381
Troupant, Geelbek-, 156, 381
Troupant, Gewone, 156, 381
Troupant, Groot-, 156, 381
Troupant, Knopstert-, 156, 381
Turaco, Knysna, 130, 377
Turaco, Livingstone's, 130, 377
Turaco, Purple-crested, 130, 377
Turaco, Schalow's, 130
Turdoides bicolor, 274, 392
Turdoides gymnogenys, 274
Turdoides hartlaubii, 274, 392
Turdoides jardineii, 137, 274, 392
Turdoides melanops, 274, 392
Turdus libonyana, 286, 393
Turdus litsitsirupa, 286, 393
Turdus olivaceus, 288, 394
Turdus smithi, 288, 394
Turnix hottentottus, 100
Turnix nanus, 100, 373
Turnix sylvaticus, 100, 373
Turtur afer, 126, 377
Turtur chalcospilos, 126, 377
Turtur tympanistria, 126, 377
Twinspot, Green, 332, 399
Twinspot, Pink-throated, 332, 399
Twinspot, Red-throated, 332, 399
Tyto alba, 140, 380
Tyto capensis, 140, 380

U

Uil, Bos-, 140, 380
Uil, Gebande, 144, 380
Uil, Gras-, 140, 380
Uil, Nonnetjie-, 140, 380
Uil, Skops-, 144, 380
Uil, Vis-, 142, 380
Uil, Vlei-, 140, 380
Uil, Witkol-, 144, 380
Uil, Witwang-, 144, 380
Upupa africana, 166, 382
Uraeginthus angolensis, 336, 399
Uraeginthus granatina, 336, 399
Urocolius indicus, 154, 381
Urolestes melanoleucus, 200, 385

V

Valk, Akkedis-, 72, 366
Valk, Blou-, 58, 360
Valk, Donkergrys-, 84
Valk, Dwerg-, 84, 369
Valk, Edel-, 80, 368
Valk, Grootrooi-, 82, 368
Valk, Kaalwang-, 72, 369
Valk, Krans-, 82, 368
Valk, Rooinek-, 82, 368
Valk, Swerf-, 80, 368
Valk, Taita-, 80, 368
Valk, Vlermuis-, 58, 360
Vanellus albiceps, 106, 374
Vanellus armatus, 106, 374
Vanellus coronatus, 104, 374
Vanellus crassirostris, 106, 374
Vanellus lugubris, 104, 374
Vanellus melanopterus, 104, 374
Vanellus senegallus, 106, 374
Versamelvoël, 316, 397
Vidua chalybeata, 343, 399
Vidua codringtoni, 343
Vidua funerea, 343, 399
Vidua macroura, 342, 399
Vidua obtusa, 343
Vidua paradisaea, 342, 399
Vidua purpurascens, 343, 399
Vidua regia, 342, 399
Vink, Bandkeel-, 330, 399
Vink, Goudgeel-, 326, 398
Vink, Koekoek-, 343
Vink, Rooi-, 326, 379, 398
Vink, Rooikop-, 330, 399
Vink, Vuurkop-, 326, 398
Visvalk, 60, 368
Visvanger, Blou-, 160, 382
Visvanger, Bont-, 160, 382
Visvanger, Bosveld-, 158, 382
Visvanger, Bruinkop-, 158, 382
Visvanger, Dwerg-, 160, 382
Visvanger, Gestreepte, 158, 179, 382
Visvanger, Gryskop-, 158, 382
Visvanger, Kuifkop-, 160, 382
Visvanger, Mangliet-, 158
Visvanger, Reuse-, 160, 382
Vleikuiken, Gestreepte, 92, 371
Vleikuiken, Gevlekte, 92, 371
Vleikuiken, Rooibors-, 92, 371
Vleikuiken, Streepbors-, 92, 371
Vleikuiken, Witvlerk-, 92, 371
Vleiloerie, Gestreepte, 132, 378
Vleiloerie, Gewone, 132, 378
Vleiloerie, Groen-, 132, 378
Vleiloerie, Groot-, 132, 378
Vleiloerie, Senegal-, 132, 378
Vleiloerie, Swart-, 132, 378
Vleivalk, Afrikaanse, 72, 367
Vleivalk, Witkruis-, 72, 367
Vlieëvanger, Blougrys-, 304, 395
Vlieëvanger, Bloukuif-, 206, 386
Vlieëvanger, Donker-, 304, 395
Vlieëvanger, Fee-, 206, 386
Vlieëvanger, Fiskaal-, 302, 395
Vlieëvanger, Groot-, 302, 395
Vlieëvanger, Marico-, 302, 395
Vlieëvanger, Muiskleur-, 302, 395
Vlieëvanger, Paradys-, 206, 386
Vlieëvanger, Rooistert-, 250, 390
Vlieëvanger, Swart-, 304, 395
Vlieëvanger, Waaierstert-, 304, 395
Vlieëvanger, Witpens-, 188, 384
Vlieëvanger, Witstert-, 206, 386
Volstruis, 20, 352
Vulture, Bearded, 60, 361
Vulture, Cape, 62, 362
Vulture, Egyptian, 60, 361
Vulture, Hooded, 62, 363
Vulture, Lappet-faced, 62, 362
Vulture, Palm-nut, 60, 361
Vulture, Rüppell's, 62
Vulture, White-backed, 62, 362
Vulture, White-headed, 62, 363
Vuurvinkie, Bruin-, 334, 399
Vuurvinkie, Jamesonse, 334, 399
Vuurvinkie, Kaapse, 334, 399
Vuurvinkie, Rooibek-, 334, 399

W

Wagtail, African Pied, 228, 388
Wagtail, Cape, 228, 388
Wagtail, Mountain, 228, 388
Warbler, African Reed, 248, 390
Warbler, Barratt's, 252, 390
Warbler, Broad-tailed, 252, 390
Warbler, Cinnamon-breasted, 268, 392

Species index

Common names are in English (black) and Afrikaans (blue); scientific names are in *brown italics*; the numbers refer to text/nest pages (either the first number or, sometimes, the first two numbers) and egg pages (the last number)

W

Warbler, Dark-capped Yellow, 248, 390
Warbler, Greater Swamp, 248, 390
Warbler, Knysna, 252, 390
Warbler, Lesser Swamp, 248, 390
Warbler, Little Rush, 252, 390
Warbler, Moustached, 272, 392
Warbler, Namaqua, 262, 390
Warbler, Red-winged, 264, 390
Warbler, Roberts', 264, 390
Warbler, Rufous-eared, 262, 390
Warbler, Victorin's, 252, 390
Warbler, Yellow-throated Woodland, 250, 390
Waterfiskaal, Moeras-, 198, 385
Waterfiskaal, Suidelike, 198, 379, 385
Waterfiskaal, Tropiese, 198, 385
Waterhoender, Groot-, 96, 371
Waterhoender, Klein-, 96, 371
Waterploeër, 116, 376
Watertrapper, 110, 372
Wattle-eye, Black-throated, 188, 384
Waxbill, Black-faced, 340, 399
Waxbill, Blue, 336, 399
Waxbill, Cinderella, 336
Waxbill, Common, 340, 399
Waxbill, Grey, 336, 399
Waxbill, Orange-breasted, 340, 399
Waxbill, Swee, 340, 399
Waxbill, Violet-eared, 336, 399
Waxbill, Yellow-bellied, 340, 399
Weaver, Cape, 322, 398
Weaver, Chestnut, 322, 398
Weaver, Dark-backed, 324, 398
Weaver, Eastern Golden, 322, 398
Weaver, Golden, 322, 398
Weaver, Holub's Golden, 322, 398
Weaver, Lesser Masked, 320, 397
Weaver, Olive-headed, 324
Weaver, Red-headed, 324, 398
Weaver, Scaly-feathered, 316, 397
Weaver, Sociable, 316, 397
Weaver, Southern Brown-throated, 322, 398
Weaver, Southern Masked, 320, 379, 397
Weaver, Spectacled, 324, 379, 398
Weaver, Thick-billed, 324, 398
Weaver, Village, 320, 397
Weaver, Yellow, 322, 398
Wewer, Bontrug-, 320, 397
Wewer, Bril-, 324, 379, 398
Wewer, Bruin-, 322, 398
Wewer, Bruinkeel-, 322, 398
Wewer, Buffel-, 316, 397
Wewer, Dikbek-, 324, 398
Wewer, Geel-, 322, 398
Wewer, Goud-, 322, 398
Wewer, Kaapse, 322, 398
Wewer, Olyfkop-, 324
Wewer, Rooikop-, 324, 398
Wheatear, Capped, 294, 394
Wheatear, Mountain, 294, 394
White-eye, African Yellow, 179, 278, 392
White-eye, Cape, 278, 392
White-eye, Orange River, 278, 392
Whydah, Broad-tailed Paradise, 343
Whydah, Long-tailed Paradise, 342, 399
Whydah, Pin-tailed, 342, 399
Whydah, Shaft-tailed, 342, 399
Widowbird, Fan-tailed, 328, 398
Widowbird, Long-tailed, 328, 398
Widowbird, Red-collared, 328, 398
Widowbird, White-winged, 328, 398
Widowbird, Yellow-mantled, 328, 398
Widowbird, Yellow-rumped, 328, 398
Wielewaal, Afrikaanse, 204, 386
Wielewaal, Groenkop-, 204, 386
Wielewaal, Swartkop-, 204, 386
Willie, Geelbors-, 240, 389
Willie, Gewone, 238, 389
Willie, Streepwang-, 238, 389
Windswael, Bont-, 150, 381
Windswael, Horus-, 152, 381
Windswael, Klein-, 152, 381
Windswael, Muiskleur-, 150
Windswael, Palm-, 152, 381
Windswael, Skaars-, 150
Windswael, Swart-, 150, 381
Windswael, Witkruis-, 152, 381
Windswael, Witpens-, 152, 381
Wipstert, Baard-, 292, 394
Wipstert, Bruin-, 292, 394
Wipstert, Gestreepte, 292, 394
Wipstert, Kalahari-, 292, 394
Witkruisarend, 68, 365
Woodhoopoe, Green, 166, 382
Woodhoopoe, Violet, 166
Woodpecker, Bearded, 180, 383
Woodpecker, Bennett's, 182, 383
Woodpecker, Cardinal, 180, 383
Woodpecker, Golden-tailed, 182, 179, 383
Woodpecker, Green-backed, 180, 383
Woodpecker, Ground, 182, 383
Woodpecker, Knysna, 182, 383
Woodpecker, Olive, 180, 383
Woodpecker, Speckle-throated, 182, 383
Wou, Geelbek-, 58, 360
Wren-Warbler, Barred, 268, 392
Wren-Warbler, Stierling's, 268, 392
Wryneck, Red-throated, 184, 383

Z

Zoothera gurneyi, 286, 393
Zoothera guttata, 286, 393
Zosterops pallidus, 278, 392
Zosterops senegalensis, 278, 392
Zosterops virens, 278, 392

African Broadbill, see page 185

Derek Engelbrecht

Notes

Notes

Naming egg shapes

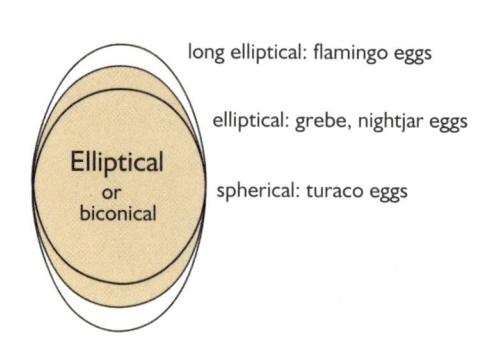

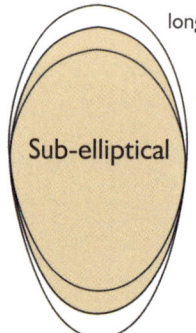

Elliptical or biconical
- long elliptical: flamingo eggs
- elliptical: grebe, nightjar eggs
- spherical: turaco eggs

Sub-elliptical
- long sub-elliptical: pelican, darter, cormorant eggs
- sub-elliptical: swift eggs
- short sub-elliptical: coot egg

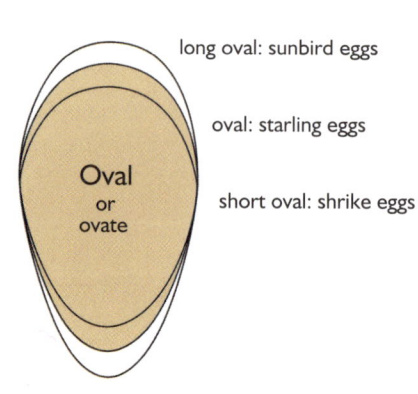

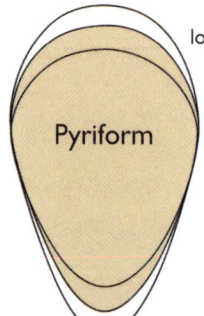

Oval or ovate
- long oval: sunbird eggs
- oval: starling eggs
- short oval: shrike eggs

Pyriform
- long pyriform: stilt eggs
- pyriform: jacana eggs
- short pyriform: secretarybird eggs